# Beginning Databases with PostgreSQL

## From Novice to Professional, Second Edition

NEIL MATTHEW AND RICHARD STONES

**Beginning Databases with PostgreSQL: From Novice to Professional, Second Edition**

**Copyright © 2005 by Neil Matthew and Richard Stones**

ISBN (pbk): 1-59059-478-9

Printed and bound in the United States of America 9 8 7 6 5 4 3 2 1

Lead Editor: Jason Gilmore
Contributing Author: Jon Parise
Technical Reviewer: Robert Treat
Editorial Board: Steve Anglin, Dan Appleman, Ewan Buckingham, Gary Cornell, Tony Davis, Jason Gilmore, Jonathan Hassell, Chris Mills, Dominic Shakeshaft, Jim Sumser
Assistant Publisher: Grace Wong
Project Manager: Sofia Marchant
Copy Manager: Nicole LeClerc
Copy Editor: Marilyn Smith
Production Manager: Kari Brooks-Copony
Production Editor: Katie Stence
Compositor: Susan Glinert
Proofreader: Elizabeth Berry
Indexer: John Collin
Artist: Kinetic Publishing Services, LLC
Cover Designer: Kurt Krames
Manufacturing Manager: Tom Debolski

Distributed to the book trade in the United States by Springer-Verlag New York, Inc., 233 Spring Street, 6th Floor, New York, NY 10013, and outside the United States by Springer-Verlag GmbH & Co. KG, Tiergartenstr. 17, 69112 Heidelberg, Germany.

In the United States: phone 1-800-SPRINGER, fax 201-348-4505, e-mail orders@springer-ny.com, or visit http://www.springer-ny.com. Outside the United States: fax +49 6221 345229, e-mail orders@springer.de, or visit http://www.springer.de.

For information on translations, please contact Apress directly at 2560 Ninth Street, Suite 219, Berkeley, CA 94710. Phone 510-549-5930, fax 510-549-5939, e-mail info@apress.com, or visit http://www.apress.com.

The source code for this book is available to readers at http://www.apress.com in the Downloads section.

# Contents at a Glance

# Contents

## ▪CHAPTER 13  Accessing PostgreSQL from C Using libpq

# About the Authors

**NEIL MATTHEW** has been interested in and has programmed computers since 1974. A mathematics graduate from the University of Nottingham, Neil is just plain keen on programming languages and likes to explore new ways of solving computing problems. He has written systems to program in BCPL, FP (Functional Programming), Lisp, Prolog, and a structured BASIC. He even wrote a 6502 microprocessor emulator to run BBC microcomputer programs on UNIX systems.

In terms of UNIX experience, Neil has used almost every flavor since the late 1970s, including BSD UNIX, AT&T System V, Sun Solaris, IBM AIX, and many others. Neil has been using Linux since August 1993, when he acquired a floppy disk distribution of Soft Landing (SLS) from Canada, with kernel version 0.99.11. He has used Linux-based computers for hacking C, C++, Icon, Prolog, Tcl, and Java, at home and at work. Most of Neil's home projects were originally developed using SCO UNIX, but they've all ported to Linux with little or no trouble. He says Linux is mush easier because it supports quite a lot of features from other systems, so that both BSD- and System V-targeted programs will generally compile with little or no change.

As the head of software and principal engineer at Camtec Electronics in the 1980s, Neil programmed in C and C++ for real-time embedded systems. Since then, he has worked on software development techniques and quality assurance. After a spell as a consultant with Scientific Generics, he is currently working as a systems architect with Celesio AG.

Neil is married to Christine and has two children, Alexandra and Adrian. He lives in a converted barn in Northamptonshire, England. His interests include solving puzzles by computer, music, science fiction, squash, mountain biking, and not doing it yourself.

**RICK STONES** started programming at school, more years ago than he cares to remember, on a 6502-powered BBC micro, which with the help of a few spare parts, continued to function for the next 15 years. He graduated from the University of Nottingham with a degree in Electronic Engineering, but decided software was more fun.

Over the years, he has worked for a variety of companies, from the very small, with just a dozen employees, to the very large, including the IT services giant EDS. Along the way, he has worked on a range of projects, from real-time communications to accounting systems, very large help desk systems, and more recently, as the technical authority on a large EPoS and retail central systems program.

A bit of a programming linguist, Rick has programmed in various assemblers, a rather neat proprietary telecommunications language called SL-1, some FORTRAN, Pascal, Perl, SQL, and smidgeons of Python and C++, as well as C. (Under duress, he even admits that he was once reasonably proficient in Visual Basic, but tries not to advertise this aberration.)

Rick lives in a village in Leicestershire, England, with his wife Ann, children Jennifer and Andrew, and two cats. Outside work, his main interest is classical music, especially early religious music, and he even does his best to find time for some piano practice. He is currently trying to learn to speak German.

# About the Technical Reviewer

 **ROBERT TREAT** is a long-time open-source user, developer, and advocate. He has worked with a number of projects, but his favorite is certainly PostgreSQL. His current involvement includes helping maintain the postgresql.org web sites, working on phpPgAdmin, and contributing to the PostgreSQL core whenever he can. He has contributed several articles to the PostgreSQL "techdocs" site, was a presenter at OSCon 2004, worked as the PHP Foundry Admin on sourceforge.net, and has been recognized as a Major Developer for his work within the PostgreSQL community. Outside the free software world, Robert enjoys spending time with his three children, Robert, Dylan, and Emma, and with his high school sweetheart-turned-wife, Amber.

# Acknowledgments

**W**e would like to thank the many people who helped to make this book possible.

Neil would like to thank his wife, Christine, for her understanding, and children Alex and Adrian for not complaining too loudly at dad spending so long in The Den writing.

Rick would like to thank his wife, Ann, and children, Jennifer and Andrew, for their very considerable patience during the evenings and weekends while dad was yet again "doing book work."

Special thanks must go to Robert Treat, our technical reviewer. We are indebted to him for his excellent, detailed reviewing of our work and the many helpful comments and suggestions he made.

We would also like to thank Jon Parise for writing the PHP chapter for us, and Meeraj and Gavin for their kind permission to reuse some earlier material.

We are grateful to the entire Apress team for providing a smooth road from writing to production. To Gary Cornell and Jason Gilmore for getting the project off the ground, Sofia Marchant for coping admirably with a project schedule that initially appeared to require time travel, Nancy Wright for the transfer of material from the first edition, Marilyn Smith for first-class copy editing, Katie Stence for production editing, and Jason (again) for his editor role. We've learned a lot more about how books get made, and this one is certainly a better book than it would have been without this team's efforts.

Thanks are also due to the PostgreSQL development team for creating such a strong database system, allowing us to cover a great deal of SQL with an open-source product.

We would also like to thank our employer, Celesio, for support during the production of both editions of this book.

# Introduction

**W**elcome to *Beginning Databases with PostgreSQL*.

Early in our careers, we came to recognize the qualities of open-source software. Not only is it often completely free to use, but it can also be of extremely high quality. If you have a problem, you can examine the source code to see how it works. If you find a bug, you can fix it yourself or pass it on to someone else to fix it for you. We have been working with open-source software since 1978 or so, including using the wonderful GNU tools, including GNU Emacs and GCC. We started using Linux in 1993 and have been delighted to be able to create a complete, free computing environment using a Linux kernel and the GNU tools, together with the X Window System, to provide a graphical user interface. PostgreSQL fits beautifully with this, providing an exceptional database system that adheres to the same open-source principles. (For more on open source and the freedom it can bring, please visit http://www.opensource.org.)

Databases are remarkably useful things. Many people find a "desktop database" useful for small applications in the office and around the home. Many web sites are data-driven, with content being extracted from databases behind the web server. As databases are becoming ubiquitous, we feel that there is a need for a book that includes some database theory and teaches good practice.

We have written this book to be a general introduction to databases, with broad coverage of the range of capabilities that modern, relational database systems have and how to use them effectively. With PostgreSQL as their database system, no one has an excuse for not doing things "properly." It supports good database design, is resilient and scalable, and runs on just about every type of computer you can think of, including Linux, UNIX, Windows, Mac OS X, AIX, Solaris, and HP-UX.

Oh, in case you were wondering, PostgreSQL is pronounced "post-gres-cue-el" (not "post-gray-ess-cue-el").

The book is roughly divided into thirds. The first part covers getting started, both with databases in general (what they are and what they are useful for) and with PostgreSQL in particular (how to obtain it, install it, start it, and use it). If you follow along with the examples, by the end of Chapter 5, you will have built your first working database and be able to use several tools to do useful things with it, such as entering data and executing queries.

The second part of the book explores in some depth the heart of relational databases: the query language SQL. Through sample programs and "Try It Out" sections, you will learn many aspects of database programming, ranging from simple data insertions and updates, through powerful types of queries, to extending the database server functionality with stored procedures and triggers. A great deal of the material in this section is database-independent, so knowledge gained here will stand you in good stead if you need to develop with another type of database. Of course, all of the material is illustrated with examples using PostgreSQL and a sample database. Chapters on PostgreSQL system administration and good practice in database design complete this section.

The third part of the book concentrates on harnessing the power of PostgreSQL in your own programs. These chapters cover connecting to a database, executing queries, and dealing with the results using a wide range of programming languages. Whether you are developing a dynamic web site with PHP or Perl, an enterprise application in Java or C#, or a client program in C, you will find a chapter to help you.

This is the second edition of *Beginning Databases with PostgreSQL*; the first edition was published by Wrox Press in 2001. Since then, every chapter has been updated with material to cover the latest version of PostgreSQL, version 8. We have taken the opportunity in this edition to add a new chapter on accessing PostgreSQL from the C# language to complement revised chapters covering C, Perl, PHP, and Java.

# CHAPTER 1

■■■

# Introduction to PostgreSQL

This book is all about one of the most successful open-source software products of recent times, a relational database called PostgreSQL. PostgreSQL is finding an eager audience among database aficionados and open-source developers alike. Anyone who is creating an application with nontrivial amounts of data can benefit from using a database. PostgreSQL is an excellent implementation of a relational database, fully featured, open source, and free to use.

PostgreSQL can be used from just about any major programming language you care to name, including C, C++, Perl, Python, Java, Tcl, and PHP. It very closely follows the industry standard for query languages, SQL92, and is currently implementing features to increase compliance with the latest version of this standard, SQL:2003. PostgreSQL has also won several awards, including the Linux Journal Editor's Choice Award for Best Database three times (for the years 2000, 2003, and 2004) and the 2004 Linux New Media Award for Best Database System.

We are perhaps getting a little ahead of ourselves here. You may be wondering what exactly PostgreSQL is, and why you might want to use it.

In this chapter, we will set the scene for the rest of the book and provide some background information about databases in general, the different types of databases, why they are useful, and where PostgreSQL fits into this picture.

## Programming with Data

Nearly all nontrivial computer applications manipulate large amounts of data, and a lot of applications are written primarily to deal with data rather than perform calculations. Some writers estimate that 80% of all application development in the world today is connected in some way to complex data stored in a database, so databases are a very important foundation to many applications.

Resources for programming with data abound. Most good programming books will contain chapters on creating, storing, and manipulating data. Three of our previous books (published by Wrox Press) contain information about programming with data:

- *Beginning Linux Programming, Third Edition* (ISBN 0-7645-4497-7) covers the DBM library and the MySQL database system.

- *Professional Linux Programming* (ISBN 1-861003-01-3) contains chapters on the PostgreSQL and MySQL database systems.

- *Beginning Databases with MySQL* (ISBN 1-861006-92-6) covers the MySQL database system.

# Constant Data

Data comes in all shapes and sizes, and the ways that we deal with it will vary according to the nature of the data. In some cases, the data is simple—perhaps a single number such as the value of $\pi$ that might be built into a program that draws circles. The application itself may have this as a hard-coded value for the ratio of the circumference of a circle to its diameter. We call this kind of data *constant*, as it will never need to change.

Another example of constant data is the exchange rates used for the currencies of some European countries. In so-called "Euro Land," the countries that are participating in the single European currency (euro) fixed the exchange rates between their national currencies to six decimal places. Suppose we developed a Euro Land currency converter application. It could have a hard-coded table of currency names and base exchange rates, the numbers of national units to the euro. These rates will never change. We are not quite finished though, as it is possible for this table of currencies to grow. As countries sign up for the euro, their national currency exchange rate is fixed, and they will need to be added to the table. When that happens, the currency converter needs to be changed, its built-in table changed, and the application rebuilt. This will need to be done every time the currency table changes.

A better method would be to have the application read a file containing some simple currency data, perhaps including the name of the currency, its international symbol, and exchange rate. Then we can just alter the file when the table needs to change, and leave the application alone.

The data file that we use has no special structure; it's just some lines of text that mean something to the particular application that reads it. It has no inherent structure. Therefore we call it a *flat file*. Here's what our currency file might look like:

```
France     FRF    6.559570
Germany    DEM    1.955830
Italy      ITL    1936.270020
Belgium    BEF    40.339901
```

# Flat Files for Data Storage

Flat files are extremely useful for many application types. As long as the size of the file remains manageable, so that we can easily make changes, a flat file scheme may be sufficient for our needs.

Many systems and applications, particularly on UNIX platforms, use flat files for their data storage or data interchange. An example is the UNIX password file, which typically has lines that look like this:

```
neil:*:500:100:Neil Matthew:/home/neil:/bin/bash
nick:*:501:100:Rick Stones:/home/rick:/bin/bash
```

These examples consist of a number of elements of information, or *attributes*, together making up a *record*. The file is arranged so that each line represents a single record, and the whole file acts to keep the related records together. Sometimes this scheme is not quite good enough, however, and we need to add extra features to support the job the application must do.

# Repeating Groups and Other Problems

Suppose that we decide to extend the currency exchange rate application (introduced earlier in the chapter) to record the language spoken in each country, together with its population and area. In a flat file, we essentially have one record per line, each record made up of several attributes. Each individual attribute in a record is always in the same place; for example, the currency symbol is always the second attribute. So, we could think of looking at the data by columns, where a column is always the same type of information.

To add the language spoken in a particular country, we might think that we just need to add a new column to each of our lines. We hit a snag with this as soon as we realize that some countries have more than one official language. So, in our record for Belgium, we would need to include both Flemish and French. For Switzerland, we would need to add four languages. The flat file would now look something like this:

```
France      FRF  6.559570     French   60424213  547030
Germany     DEM  1.955830     German   82424609  357021
Italy       ITL  1936.270020  Italian  58057477  301230
Belgium     BEF  40.339901    Flemish  French    10348276  30528
Switzerland CHF  1.5255       German   French    Italian   Romansch  7450867  41290
```

This problem is known as *repeating groups*. We have the situation where a perfectly valid item (language) can be repeated in a record, so not only does the record (row) repeat, but the data in that row repeats as well. Flat files do not cope with this, as it is impossible to determine where the languages stop and the rest of the record starts. The only way around this is to add some structure to the file, and then it would not be a flat file anymore.

The repeating groups problem is very common and is the issue that really started the drive toward more sophisticated database management systems. We can attempt to resolve this problem by using ordinary text files with a little more structure. These are still often referred to as flat files, but they are probably better described as structured text files.

Here's another example. An application that stores the details of DVDs might need to record the year of production, director, genre, and cast list. We could design a file that looks a little like a Windows .ini file to store this information, like this:

```
[2001: A Space Odyssey]
year=1968
director=Stanley Kubrick
genre=science fiction
starring=Keir Dullea
starring=Leonard Rossiter
...

[Toy Story]
...
```

We have solved the repeating groups problem by introducing some tags to indicate the type of each element in the record. However, now our application must read and interpret a more complex file just to get its data. Updating a record and searching in this kind of structure can be quite difficult. How can we make sure that the descriptions for genre or classification are chosen from a specific subset? How can we easily produce a sorted list of Kubrick-directed films?

As data requirements become increasingly complex, we are forced to write more and more application code for reading and storing our data. If we extend our DVD application to include information useful to a DVD rental store owner—such as membership details, rentals, returns, and reservations—the prospect of maintaining all of that information in flat files becomes very unappealing.

Another common problem is simply that of size. Although the structured text file could be scanned by brute force to answer complex queries such as, "Tell me the addresses of all my members who have rented more than one comedy movie in the last three months," not only will it be very difficult to code, but the performance will be dire. This is because the application has no choice but to process the whole file to look for any piece of information, even if the question relates to just a single entry, such as "Who starred in *2001: A Space Odyssey*?"

What we need is a general-purpose way of storing and retrieving data, not a solution invented many times to fit slightly different, but very similar, problems as in a generic data-handling system.

What we need is a database and a database management system.

# What Is a Database Management System?

The Merriam-Webster online dictionary (http://www.merriam-webster.com) defines a *database* as a usually large collection of data organized especially for rapid search and retrieval (as by a computer).

A *database management system* (DBMS) is usually a suite of libraries, applications, and utilities that relieve an application developer from the burden of worrying about the details of storing and managing data. It also provides facilities for searching and updating records. DBMSs come in a number of flavors developed over the years to solve particular kinds of data-storage problems.

## Database Models

During the 1960s and 1970s, developers created databases that solved the repeating groups problem in several different ways. These methods result in what are termed *models* for database systems. Research performed at IBM provided much of the basis for these models, which are still in use today.

A main driver in early database system designs was efficiency. One of the common ways to make systems more efficient was to enforce a fixed length for database records, or at least have a fixed number of elements per record (columns per row). This essentially avoids the repeating group problem. If you are a programmer in just about any procedural language, you will readily see that in this case, you can read each record of a database into a simple C structure. Real life is rarely that accommodating, so we need to find ways to deal with inconveniently structured data. Database systems designers did this by introducing different database types.

## Hierarchical Database Model

The IMS database system from IBM in the late 1960s introduced the hierarchical model for databases. In this model, considering data records to be composed of collections of others solves the repeating groups problem.

The model can be compared to a bill of materials used to describe how a complex manufactured product is composed. For example, let's say a car is composed of a chassis, a body, an engine, and four wheels. Each of these major components is broken down further. An engine comprises some cylinders, a cylinder head, and a crankshaft. These components are broken down further until we get to the nuts and bolts that make up every part in an automobile.

Hierarchical model databases are still in use today, including Software AG's ADABAS. A hierarchical database system is able to optimize the data storage to make it more efficient for particular questions; for example, to determine which automobile uses a particular part.

## Network Database Model

The network model introduces the idea of pointers within the database. Records can contain references to other records. So, for example, you could keep a record for each of your company's customers. Each customer has placed many orders with you over time (a repeating group). The data is arranged so that the customer record contains a pointer to just one order record. Each order record contains both the order data for that specific order and a pointer to another order record.

Returning to our currency application, we might end up with record structures that look a little like those shown in Figure 1-1.

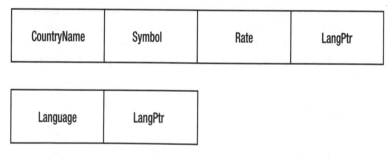

**Figure 1-1.** *Currency application record types*

Once the data is loaded, we end up with a linked (hence, the name *network* model) list used for the languages, as shown in Figure 1-2. The two different record types shown here would be stored separately, each in its own table.

Of course, to be more efficient in terms of storage, the actual database would not repeat the language names over and over again, but would probably contain a third table of language names, together with an identifier (often a small integer) that would be used to refer to the language name table entry in the other record types. This is called a *key*.

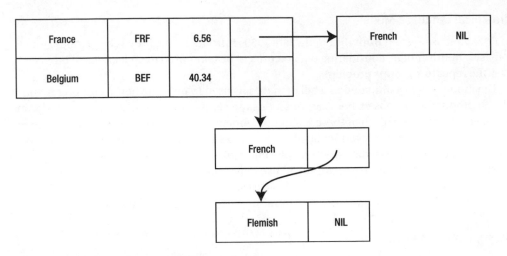

**Figure 1-2.** *Currency application data structure*

A network model database has some strong advantages. If you need to discover all of the records of one type that are related to a specific record of another type (in this example, the languages spoken in a country), you can find them extremely quickly by following the pointers from the starting record.

There are, however, some disadvantages, too. If you want to list the countries that speak French, you need to follow the links from all of the country records, which for large databases will be extremely slow. This can be fixed by having other linked lists of pointers specifically for languages, but it rapidly becomes very complex and is clearly not a general-purpose solution, since you need to decide in advance how the pointers will be designed. Writing applications that use a network model database can also be very tiresome, as the application typically must take responsibility for setting up and maintaining the pointers as records are updated and deleted.

## Relational Database Model

The theory of DBMSs took a gigantic leap forward in 1970 with the publication of "A Relational Model of Data for Large Shared Data Banks," a paper by E. F. Codd (see http://www.acm.org/classics/nov95/toc.html). This revolutionary paper introduced the idea of relations and showed how tables could be used to represent facts that relate to real-world objects, and therefore, hold data about them.

By this time, it had also become clear that the initial driving force behind database design, efficiency, was often less important than another concern: data integrity. The relational model emphasizes data integrity much more than either of the earlier models. *Referential integrity* refers to making sure that data in the database makes sense at all times, so that, for example, all orders have customers. (We will have much more to say about integrity in Chapter 12, when we cover database design.)

Records in a table in a relational database are known as *tuples*, and this is the terminology you will see used in some parts of the PostgreSQL documentation. A tuple is an ordered group of components, or attributes, each of which has a defined type.

Several important rules define a relational database management system (RDBMS). All tuples must follow the same pattern, in that they all have the same number and types of components. Here is an example of a set of tuples:

```
{"France", "FRF", 6.56}
{"Belgium", "BEF", 40.34}
```

Each of these tuples has three attributes: a country name (string), a currency (string), and an exchange rate (a floating-point number). In a relational database, all records that are added to this set, or table, must follow the same form, so the following are disallowed:

```
{"Germany", "DEM"}
```

This has too few attributes.

```
{"Switzerland", "CHF", "French", "German", "Italian", "Romansch"}
```

This has too many attributes.

```
{1936.27, "ITL", "Italy"}
```

This has incorrect attribute types (wrong order).

Furthermore, in any table of tuples, there should be no duplicates. This means that in any table in a properly designed relational database, there cannot be any identical rows or records. This might seem to be a rather draconian restriction. For example, in a system that records orders placed by customers, it would appear to disallow the same customer from ordering the same product twice. In the next chapter, we will see that there is an easy way to work around this requirement, by adding an attribute.

Each attribute in a record must be *atomic*; that is, it must be a single piece of data, not another record or a list of other attributes. Also, the type of corresponding attributes in every record in the table must be the same. Technically, this means that they must be drawn from the same set of values or domain. In practical terms, it means they will all be a string, an integer, a floating-point value, or some other type supported by the database system.

The attribute (or attributes) used to distinguish a particular record in a table from all the other records in a table is called a *primary key*. In a relational database, each relation, or table, must have a primary key for each record to make it unique—different from all the others in that table.

One last rule that determines the structure of a relational database is referential integrity. As we noted earlier, this is a desire that all of the records in the database make sense at all times. Database application programmers must be careful to make sure that their code does not break the integrity of the database. Consider what happens when we delete a customer. If we try to remove the customer from the customer relation, we also need to delete all of his orders from the orders table. Otherwise, we will be left with records about orders that have no valid customer.

We will see much more on the theory and practice of relational databases in later chapters. For now, it is enough to know that the relational model for databases is based on some mathematical concepts of sets and relations, and that there are some rules that need to be observed by systems that are based on this model.

# Query Languages

RDBMSs offer ways to add and update data, of course, but their real power stems from their ability to allow users to ask questions about the data stored, in the form of *queries*. Unlike many earlier database designs, which were often structured around the type of question that the data needed to answer, relational databases are much more flexible at answering questions that were not known at the time the database was designed.

Codd's proposals for the relational model use the fact that relations define sets, and sets can be manipulated mathematically. He suggested that queries might use a branch of theoretical logic called the predicate calculus, and that query languages would use this as their base. This would bring unprecedented power for searching and selecting data sets. Modern database systems, including PostgreSQL, hide all the mathematics behind an expressive and easy-to-learn *query language*.

One of the first implementations of a query language was QUEL, used in the Ingres database developed in the late 1970s. Another query language that takes a different approach is QBE (Query By Example). At around the same time a team at IBM's research center developed SQL (Structured Query Language), usually pronounced "sequel."

## SQL Standards and Variations

SQL has become very widely adopted as a standard for database query languages and is defined in a series of international standards. The most commonly used definition is ISO/IEC 9075:1992, "Database Language SQL." This is more simply referred to as SQL92. These standards replaced an earlier standard, SQL89. The latest version of the SQL standard is ISO/IEC 9075:2003, more simply referred to as SQL:2003.

At present, most RDBMSs comply with the SQL92 version of the standard, or sometimes ANSI X3.135-1992, which is an identical United States standard differing only in some cover pages. There are three levels of conformance to SQL92: Entry SQL, Intermediate SQL, and Full SQL. By far, the most common conformance level is Entry SQL.

---

■**Note**    PostgreSQL is very close to SQL92: Entry SQL conformance, with only a few slight differences. The developers keep a close eye on standards compliance, and PostgreSQL becomes more compliant with each release.

---

Today, just about every useful database system supports SQL to some extent. In theory, SQL acts as a good unifier, since database applications written to use SQL as the interface to the database can be ported to other database systems with little cost in terms of time and effort. Commercial pressures however, dictate that database manufacturers distinguish their products one from another. This has led to SQL variations, not helped by the fact that the standard for SQL does not define commands for many of the database administration tasks that are an essential part of using a database in the real world. So, there are differences between the SQL used by Oracle, SQL Server, PostgreSQL, and other database systems.

## SQL Command Types

The SQL language comprises three types of commands:

- **Data Manipulation Language (DML):** This is the part of SQL that you will use 90% of the time. It is made up of the commands for inserting, deleting, updating, and selecting data from the database.

- **Data Definition Language (DDL):** These are the commands for creating tables, defining relationships, and controlling other aspects of the database that are more structural than data related.

- **Data Control Language (DCL):** This is a set of commands that generally control permissions on the data, such as defining access rights. Many database users will never use these commands, because they work in larger company environments where one or more database administrators are employed specifically to manage the database, and usually one of their roles is to control permissions.

## A Brief Introduction to SQL

You will see a lot of SQL in this book. Here, we will take a brief look at some examples as an introduction. We will see that we do not need to worry about the formal basis of SQL to be able to use it.

Here is some SQL for creating a new table in a database. This example creates a table for customers:

```
CREATE TABLE customer
(
    customer_id    serial,
    title          char(4),
    fname          varchar(32),
    lname          varchar(32) not null,
    addressline    varchar(64),
    town           varchar(32),
    zipcode        char(10) not null,
    phone          varchar(16),
);
```

We state that the table requires an identifier, which will act as a primary key, and that this is to be generated automatically by the database system. It has type serial, which means that every time a customer is added, a new, unique customer_id will be created in sequence. The customer title is a text attribute of four characters, and zipcode has ten characters. The other attributes are variable-length strings up to a defined maximum length, some of which must be present (those marked not null).

Next, we have some SQL statements that can be used to populate the table we have just created. These are very straightforward:

```
INSERT INTO customer(title, fname, lname, addressline, town, zipcode, phone)
    VALUES('Mr','Neil','Matthew','5 Pasture Lane','Nicetown','NT3 7RT','267 1232');
INSERT INTO customer(title, fname, lname, addressline, town, zipcode, phone)
    VALUES('Mr','Richard','Stones','34 Holly Way','Bingham','BG4 2WE','342 5982');
```

The heart of SQL is the SELECT statement. It is used to create result sets that are groups of records (or attributes from records) that match a particular set of criteria. The criteria can be quite complex if required. These result sets can then be used as the targets for changes with an UPDATE statement or deleted with a DELETE statement.

Here are some examples of SELECT statements:

```
SELECT * FROM customer

SELECT * FROM customer, orderinfo
    WHERE orderinfo.customer_id = customer.customer_id GROUP BY customer_id

SELECT customer.title, customer.fname, customer.lname,
    COUNT(orderinfo.orderinfo_id) AS "Number of orders"
FROM customer, orderinfo
    WHERE customer.customer_id = orderinfo.customer_id
    GROUP BY customer.title, customer.fname, customer.lname
```

These SELECT statements list all the customers, all the customer orders, and count the orders each customer has made, respectively. We will see the results of these SQL statements in Chapter 2, and learn much more about SELECT in Chapter 4.

---

■**Note** SQL command keywords such as SELECT and INSERT are case-insensitive, so they can be written in either uppercase or lowercase. In this book, we have used uppercase to aid readability.

---

As you read through this book, we will be teaching you SQL, so by the time you get to the end, you will be comfortable with a wide range of SQL statements and how to use them.

## Database Management System Responsibilities

As we stated earlier, a DBMS is a suite of programs that allow the construction of databases and applications that use them. The responsibilities of a DBMS include the following:

- **Creating the database:** Some systems will manage one large file and create one or more databases inside it; others may use many operating system files or use a raw disk partition directly. Users need not worry about the low-level structure of these files, as the DBMS provides all of the access developers and users need.

- **Providing query and update facilities:** A DBMS will have a method of asking for data that matches certain criteria, such as all orders made by a particular customer that have not yet been delivered. Before the widespread introduction of the SQL standard, the way that queries like this were expressed varied from system to system.

- **Multitasking:** If a database is used in several applications, or is accessed concurrently by several users at the same time, the DBMS will make sure that each user's request is processed without impacting the others. This means that users need to wait in line only if someone else is writing to the precise item of data that they wish to read (or write). It is possible to have many simultaneous reads of data going on at the same time. In practice, different database systems support different degrees of multitasking, and may even have configurable levels, as we will see in Chapter 9.

- **Maintaining an audit trail:** A DBMS will keep a log of all the changes to the data for a period of time. This can be used to investigate errors, but perhaps even more important, can be used to reconstruct data in the event of a fault in the system, perhaps an unscheduled power down. A data backup and an audit trail of transactions can be used to completely restore the database in case of disk failure.

- **Managing the security of the database:** A DBMS will provide access controls so that only authorized users can manipulate the data held in the database and the structure of the database itself (the attributes, tables, and indices). Typically, there will be a hierarchy of users defined for any particular database, from a superuser who can change anything, through users with permission to add or delete data, down to users who can only read data. The DBMS will have facilities to add and delete users, and specify which features of the database system they are able to use.

- **Maintaining referential integrity:** Many database systems provide features that help to maintain referential integrity—the correctness of the data, as mentioned earlier. They will report an error when a query or update would break the relational model rules.

# What Is PostgreSQL?

Now we are in a position to say what PostgreSQL actually is. It is a DBMS that incorporates the relational model for its databases and supports the SQL standard query language.

PostgreSQL also happens to be very capable and very reliable, and it has good performance characteristics. It runs on just about any UNIX platform, including UNIX-like systems, such as FreeBSD, Linux, and Mac OS X. It can also run on Microsoft Windows NT/2000/2003 servers, or even on Windows XP for development. And, as we mentioned at the beginning of this chapter, it's free and open source.

PostgreSQL can be compared favorably to other DBMSs. It contains just about all the features that you would find in other commercial or open-source databases, and a few extras that you might not find elsewhere.

PostgreSQL features (as listed in the PostgreSQL FAQ) include the following:

- Transactions

- Subselects

- Views

- Foreign key referential integrity

- Sophisticated locking

- User-defined types

- Inheritance

- Rules

- Multiple-version concurrency control

Since release 6.5, PostgreSQL has been very stable, with a large series of regression tests performed on each release to ensure its stability. The release of the 7.*x* series brought conformance to SQL92 closer than ever, and an irksome row-size restriction was removed.

The release of PostgreSQL that we used in this book, version 8, added several new features:

- Native Microsoft Windows version

- Table spaces

- Ability to alter column types

- Point-in-time recovery

PostgreSQL has proven to be very reliable in use. Each release is very carefully controlled, and beta releases are subject to at least a month's testing. With a large user community and universal access to the source code, bugs can get fixed very quickly.

The performance of PostgreSQL has been improving with each release, and the latest benchmarks show that, in some circumstances, it compares well with commercial products. Some less fully featured database systems will outperform it at the cost of lower overall functionality. Then again, for simple enough applications, so will a flat-file database!

## A Short History of PostgreSQL

PostgreSQL can trace its family tree back to 1977 at the University of California at Berkeley (UCB). A relational database called Ingres was developed at UCB between 1977 and 1985. Ingres was a popular UCB export, making an appearance on many UNIX computers in the academic and research communities. To serve the commercial marketplace, the code for Ingres was taken by Relational Technologies/Ingres Corporation and became one of the first commercially available RDBMSs.

---

**Note** Today, Ingres has become CA-INGRES II, a product from Computer Associates. Interestingly, it has been recently released under an Open Source license.

---

Meanwhile, back at UCB, work on a relational database server called Postgres continued from 1986 to 1994. Again, this code was taken up by a commercial company and offered for sale as a product. This time it was Illustra, since swallowed up by Informix. Around 1994, SQL features were added to Postgres, and its name was changed to Postgres95.

By 1996, Postgres was becoming very popular, and the developers decided to open up its development to a mailing list, starting what has become a very successful collaboration of volunteers driving Postgres forward. At this time, Postgres underwent its final name change, ditching the dated "95" tag for a more appropriate "SQL," to reflect the support Postgres now has for the query language standard. PostgreSQL was born.

Today, a team of Internet developers develops PostgreSQL in much the same manner as other open-source software such as Perl, Apache, and PHP. Users have access to the source code and contribute fixes, enhancements, and suggestions for new features. The official PostgreSQL releases are made via http://www.postgresql.org.

Commercial support is available from several companies. See the list at http://techdocs.postgresql.org/companies.php.

## The PostgreSQL Architecture

One of PostgreSQL's strengths derives from its architecture. In common with commercial database systems, PostgreSQL can be used in a client/server environment. This has many benefits for both users and developers.

The heart of a PostgreSQL installation is the database server process. It runs on a single server. Applications that need to access the data stored in the database are required to do so via the database process. These client programs cannot access the data directly, even if they are running on the same computer as the server process.

---

■**Note** PostgreSQL does not yet have the high-availability features of a few enterprise-class commercial database systems that can spread the load across several servers, giving additional scalability and resilience. There are some PostgreSQL-sanctioned projects underway at http://gborg.postgresql.org that aim to add these features, and there are some commercial solutions available.

---

This separation into client and server allows applications to be distributed. You can use a network to separate your clients from your server and develop client applications in an environment that suits the users. For example, you might implement the database on UNIX and create client programs that run on Microsoft Windows. Figure 1-3 shows a typical distributed PostgreSQL application.

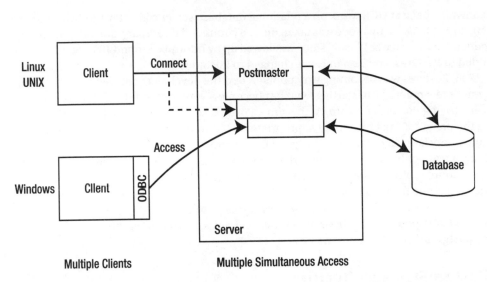

**Figure 1-3.** *PostgreSQL architecture*

In Figure 1-3, you can see several clients connecting to the server across a network. For PostgreSQL, this needs to be a TCP/IP network—a local area network (LAN) or possibly even the Internet. Each client connects to the main database server process (shown as postmaster in Figure 1-3), which creates a new server process specifically for servicing access requests for this client.

Concentrating the data handling in a server, rather than attempting to control many clients accessing the same data stored in a shared directory on a server, allows PostgreSQL to efficiently maintain the data's integrity, even with many simultaneous users.

The client programs connect using a message protocol specific to PostgreSQL. It is possible, however, to install software on the client that provides a standard interface for the application to work to, such as the Open Database Connectivity (ODBC) standard or the Java Database Connectivity (JDBC) standard used by Java programs. The availability of an ODBC driver allows many existing applications to use PostgreSQL as a database, including Microsoft Office products such as Excel and Access. You will see examples of different PostgreSQL connection methods in Chapters 3, 5, and 13 through 18.

The client/server architecture for PostgreSQL allows a division of labor. A server machine well suited to the storage and access of large amounts of data can be used as a secure data repository. Sophisticated graphical applications can be developed for the clients. Alternatively, a web-based front-end can be created to access the data and return results as web pages to a standard web browser, with no additional client software at all. We will return to these ideas in Chapters 5 and 15.

## Data Access with PostgreSQL

With PostgreSQL, you can access your data in several ways:

- Use a command-line application to execute SQL statements. We will do this throughout the book.

- Embed SQL directly into your application (using embedded SQL). We will see how to do this for C applications in Chapter 14.

- Use function calls (APIs) to prepare and execute SQL statements, scan result sets, and perform updates from a large variety of different programming languages. Chapter 13 covers C language APIs for PostgreSQL.

- Access the data in a PostgreSQL database indirectly using a driver such as ODBC (see Chapter 3) or the JDBC standard (see Chapter 17), or by using a standard library such as Perl's DBI (see Chapter 16).

# What Is Open Source?

As we start the twenty-first century, much is being made of open-source software, of which PostgreSQL is such a good example. But what does *open source* mean exactly?

The term *open source* has a very specific meaning when applied to software. It means that the software is supplied with the source code included. It does not necessarily mean that there are no conditions applied to the software's use. It is still licensed in that you are given permission to use the software in certain ways.

An Open Source license will grant you permission to use the software, modify it, and redistribute it without paying license fees. This means that you may use PostgreSQL in your organization as you see fit.

If you have problems with open-source software, because you have the source code, you can either fix them yourself or give the code to someone else to try to fix. There are now many commercial companies offering support for open-source products, so that you do not have to feel neglected if you choose to use an open-source product.

There are many different variations on Open Source licenses, some more liberal than others. All of them adhere to the principle of source code availability and allowing redistribution.

The most liberal license is the Berkeley Software Distribution (BSD) license, which says in effect, "Do what you will with this software. There is no warranty." The license for PostgreSQL (http://www.postgresql.org/about/licence) echoes the BSD license sentiments and takes the form of a copyright statement that says, "Permission to use, copy, modify, and distribute this software and its documentation for any purpose, without fee, and without a written agreement is hereby granted, provided that the above copyright notice and this paragraph and the following two paragraphs appear in all copies." The paragraphs that follow this statement disclaim liability and warranty.

# Resources

There are many printed and online sources of further information about databases in general and about PostgreSQL.

For more on the theory of databases, check out the Database Theory section of David Frick's site at `http://www.frick-cpa.com/ss7/default.htm`.

The official PostgreSQL site is `http://www.postgreSQL.org`, where you can find more on the history of PostgreSQL, download copies of PostgreSQL, browse the official documentation, and much more besides (including learning how to pronounce PostgreSQL).

PostgreSQL is also the foundation of the former Red Hat Database, now known as PostgreSQL-Red Hat Edition. You can find more on this version of PostgreSQL and tools developed for it by Red Hat at `http://sources.redhat.com/rhdb/`.

For more information about open-source software and the principle of freedom in software, take a few moments to visit these two sites: `http://www.gnu.org` and `http://www.opensource.org`.

# CHAPTER 2

### ■ ■ ■

# Relational Database Principles

**I**n this chapter, we will examine what makes a database system, particularly a relational one like PostgreSQL, so useful for real-world data. We will start by looking at spreadsheets, which have much in common with relational databases but also have significant limitations. We will learn how a relational database, such as PostgreSQL, has many advantages over spreadsheets. Along the way, we will continue our rather informal look at SQL.

In particular, this chapter will cover the following topics:

- Spreadsheets: their problems and limitations

- How databases store data

- How to access data in a database

- Basic database design, with multiple tables

- Relationships between tables

- Some basic data types

- The NULL token, used to indicate an unknown value

## Limitations of Spreadsheets

Spreadsheet applications, such as Microsoft Excel, are widely used as a way of storing and inspecting data. It's easy to sort the data in different ways, and see the features and patterns in the data just by looking at it.

Unfortunately, people often mistake a tool that is good for inspecting and manipulating data for a tool suitable for storing and sharing complex and perhaps business-critical data. The two needs are often very different.

Most people will be familiar with one or more spreadsheets and quite at home with data being arranged in a set of rows and columns. Figure 2-1 shows a typical example—an OpenOffice (http://www.openoffice.org/) spreadsheet holding data about customers.

| | A | B | C | D | E | F | G | H |
|---|---|---|---|---|---|---|---|---|
| 1 | Miss | Jenny | Stones | 27 Rowan Avenue | Hightown | NT2 1AQ | 023 9876 | |
| 2 | Mr | Andrew | Stones | 52 The Willows | Lowtown | LT5 7RA | 876 3527 | |
| 3 | Miss | Alex | Matthew | 4 The Street | Nicetown | NT2 2TX | 010 4567 | |
| 4 | Mr | Adrian | Matthew | The Barn | Yuleville | YV67 2WR | 487 3871 | |
| 5 | Mr | Simon | Cozens | 7 Shady Lane | Oakenham | OA3 6QW | 514 5926 | |
| 6 | Mr | Neil | Matthew | 5 Pasture Lane | Nicetown | NT3 7RT | 267 1232 | |
| 7 | Mr | Richard | Stones | 34 Holly Way | Bingham | BG4 2WE | 342 5982 | |
| 8 | Mrs | Ann | Stones | 34 Holly Way | Bingham | BG4 2WE | 342 5982 | |
| 9 | Mrs | Christine | Hickman | 36 Queen Street | Histon | HT3 5EM | 342 5432 | |
| 10 | Mr | Mike | Howard | 86 Dysart Street | Tibsville | TB3 7FG | 505 5482 | |
| 11 | Mr | Dave | Jones | 54 Vale Rise | Bingham | BG3 8GD | 342 8264 | |
| 12 | Mr | Richard | Neill | 42 Thatched Way | Winnersby | WB3 6GQ | 505 6482 | |
| 13 | Mrs | Laura | Hardy | 73 Margarita Way | Oxbridge | OX2 3HX | 821 2335 | |
| 14 | Mr | Bill | O'Neill | 2 Beamer Street | Welltown | WT3 8GM | 435 1234 | |
| 15 | Mr | David | Hudson | 4 The Square | Milltown | MT2 6RT | 961 4526 | |
| 16 | | | | | | | | |
| 17 | | | | | | | | |
| 18 | | | | | | | | |

**Figure 2-1.** *A simple spreadsheet*

Certainly, such information is easy to see and modify. Each customer has a separate *row*, and each piece of information about the customer is held in a separate *column*, as labeled in Figure 2-2. The intersection of a column and a row is a *cell*.

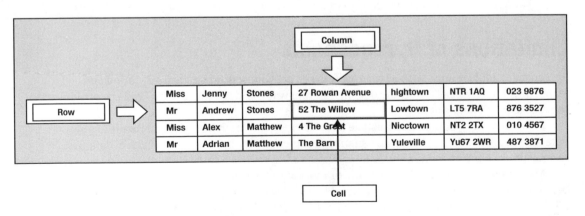

**Figure 2-2.** *Some spreadsheet terminology*

This simple spreadsheet incorporates several features that will be handy to remember when we start designing databases. For example, the first and last names are held in separate columns, which makes it easy to sort the data by last name if required.

So what is wrong with storing customer information in a spreadsheet? Spreadsheets are fine, as long as you:

- Don't have too many customers

- Don't have many complex details for each customer

- Don't need to store any other repeating information, such as the various orders each customer has placed

- Don't want several people to be able to update the information simultaneously

- Do ensure the spreadsheet gets backed up regularly if it holds important data

Spreadsheets are a fantastic idea, and they are great tools for many types of problems. However, just as you wouldn't (or at least shouldn't) try to hammer in a nail with a screwdriver, sometimes spreadsheets are not the right tool for the job.

Just imagine what it would be like if a large company, with tens of thousands of customers, kept the master copy of its customer list in a simple spreadsheet. In a big company, it's likely that several people would need to update the list. Although file locking can ensure that only one person updates the list at any one time, as the number of people trying to update the list grows, they will spend longer and longer waiting for their turn to edit the list. What we would like is to allow many people to simultaneously read, update, add, and delete rows, and let the computer ensure there are no conflicts. Clearly, simple file locking will not be adequate to efficiently handle this problem.

Another problem with spreadsheets is their strict two dimensions. Suppose we also wanted to store details of each order a customer placed. We could start putting order information next to each customer, but as the number of orders per customer grew, the spreadsheet would get more and more complex. Consider the outcome when we start trying to add some basic order information for each customer, as shown in Figure 2-3.

Unfortunately, it's not looking quite so elegant anymore. We now have rows of arbitrary length, which does not give us an easy way to calculate how much each customer has spent with us. Eventually, we will exceed the number of columns allowed in each row. It's the repeating groups problem we saw in the previous chapter. Multiple sheets inside a spreadsheet can help, but they are not an ideal solution to the problem.

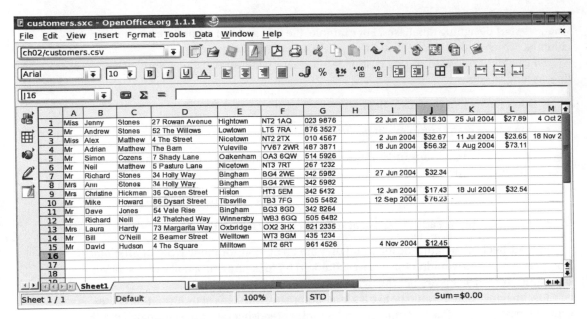

**Figure 2-3.** *Spreadsheet with repeating order information*

## A SPREADSHEET CHALLENGE

Here is an example of how easily you can exceed the capabilities of a spreadsheet. An acquaintance was trying to set up a spreadsheet as a favor for friends who run a small business. This small business makes leather items, and the price of the item depended not only on the time and effort required to make the item, but also on the unit cost of the leather used in the manufacture. The owners would buy leather in batches of different types, each of which would have a unit price that varied significantly depending on both the grade and the timing of the purchase. Then they would use their stock on a first in, first used basis as they made items for sale, normally many per batch of leather purchased. The challenge was to create a spreadsheet to do the following:

- Track the overall current stock value.

- Track how many batches of leather are in stock of each grade.

- Track how much had been paid for the batch and grade currently being used on a particular item being made.

After days of effort, they discovered that this apparently straightforward stockkeeping requirement is a surprisingly difficult problem to transfer to a spreadsheet. The variable nature of the number of stock records does not fit well with the spreadsheet philosophy.

The point we are making here is that spreadsheets are great in their place, but there are limits to their usefulness.

# Storing Data in a Database

When you look at it superficially, a relational database, such as PostgreSQL, has many similarities to a spreadsheet. However, when you know about a database's underlying structure, you can see that it is much more flexible, principally because of its ability to relate tables together in complex ways. It can efficiently store much more complex data than a spreadsheet, and it also has many other features that make it a better choice as a data store. For example, a database can manage multiple simultaneous users.

Let's first look at storing our simple, single-sheet customer list in a database, to see what benefits this might have. Later in the chapter, we will extend this and see how PostgreSQL can help us solve our customer orders problem.

As we saw in the previous chapter, databases are made up of *tables*, or in more formal terminology, *relations*. We will stick to using the term *tables* in this book. A table contains *rows* of data (more formally called *tuples*), and each data row consists of a number of *columns*, or *attributes*.

First, we need to design a table to hold our customer information. The good news is that a spreadsheet of data is often an almost ready-made solution, since it holds the data in a number of rows and columns. To get started with a basic database table, we need to decide on three things:

- How many columns do we need to store the attributes associated with each item?

- What type of data goes in each attribute (column)?

- How can we distinguish different rows containing different items?

Note that the order of rows doesn't matter in a database table. In a spreadsheet, the order of the rows is normally very important, but in a database table, there is no order. That's because when you ask to look at the data in a database table, the database is free to give you the rows of data in any order it chooses, unless you specifically ask for it ordered in a particular way. If you need to see the data in a particular order, you achieve this by the way it is *retrieved* from the database, rather than how it is stored. We will see how to retrieve ordered data in Chapter 4, when we look at the ORDER BY clause of the SELECT statement.

## Choosing Columns

If you look back at our original spreadsheet for our customer information in Figure 2-1, you can see that we have already decided on what seems a sensible set of columns for each customer: first name, last name, ZIP code, and so on. So, we've already answered the question of how many columns we should have.

An important difference between spreadsheet rows and database rows is that the number of columns in a database table must be the same for all the rows. That's not a problem in our original version of the spreadsheet.

## Choosing a Data Type for Each Column

The second criterion is to determine what type of data goes in each column. While spreadsheets allow each cell to have a different type, in a database table, each column must have the same type. Just like most programming languages, databases use *types* to classify different data values. Most of the time, the basic types are all you need to know. The main choices are integer numbers, floating-point numbers, fixed-length text, variable-length text, and dates. Often, the easiest way to decide the appropriate type is simply to look at some sample data.

In our customer data, it might be appropriate to use a text type for all the columns, even though the phone numbers are numbers. Storing the phone number as a simple number often presents some problems: it could easily result in the loss of leading zeros, prevent us from storing international dial codes (+), disallow using brackets around area codes, and so on. Obviously, a phone number can be much more than a simple string of numerals. Then again, using a character string to store the phone number might not be the best decision, since we could also accidentally store all sorts of strange characters, but it seems a better starting point than a number type. The initial design can always be refined later.

We can see that the length of the title (Mr, Mrs, Dr) is always very short—probably never longer than four characters. Similarly, ZIP codes also have a fixed maximum length. Therefore, we will make both of these columns fixed-length fields, but leave all the other columns as variable length, since there is no easy way of knowing how long a person's last name might be, for example.

We will come back to PostgreSQL data types in the "Basic Data Types" section later in this chapter and also in Chapter 8.

## Identifying Rows Uniquely

Our last problem in transforming our spreadsheet into a database table is a little more subtle, as it comes from the way databases manage relations between tables. We need to decide what makes each row of customer data different from any other customer row in the database. In other words, how do we tell our customers apart? In a spreadsheet, we tend not to worry about the exact details of what distinguishes customers. However, in a database design, this is a key question, since relational database rules require each row to be unique in some way.

The obvious solution to distinguishing customers might seem to be by name, but unfortunately, that's often not good enough. It is quite possible that two customers will have the same name. Another item you might choose is the phone number, but that fails when two customers live at the same address. At this point, you might suggest using a combination of name and phone number.

Certainly, it's unlikely that two customers will have both the same name and the same phone number, but quite apart from being inelegant, another problem is lurking. What happens if a customer changes to a new phone provider and subsequently the phone number changes? By our definition, a unique customer must then be a new customer, because it is different from the customer we had before. Of course, we know that it is the same customer, with a new phone number. In a database, it's generally bad practice to pick a unique identifying feature for a customer that might subsequently change, as it's hard to manage changes to unique identifiers.

This sort of problem, identifying uniqueness, turns up frequently in database design. What we have been doing is looking for a *primary key*—an easy way to distinguish one row of customer data from all the other rows. Unfortunately, we have not yet succeeded, but all is not lost, since the standard solution is to assign a unique number to each customer.

We simply give each customer a unique number, and bingo, we have a distinct way to tell customers apart, regardless of whether they change their phone number, move to a new residence, or even change their name. This type of addition to a row to provide a unique key when no good choice exists in the actual data is called adding a *surrogate key*. This is such a common occurrence in real-world data that there is even a special data type in most databases, the serial data type, to help solve the problem. We will discuss this type later in the chapter, in the "Basic Data Types" section.

Now that we have decided on a database design for our initial table, it's time to store our data in a database. Figure 2-4 shows our data in a PostgreSQL database being viewed using a simple command-line tool, psql, in a terminal window on a Linux machine.

```
🌀 Shell - Konsole <2>  🌀                                               _ □ X
Session  Edit  View  Bookmarks  Settings  Help

bpsimple=# select * from customer;
 customer_id | title |   fname   |  lname  |   addressline    |   town    | zipcode  |  phone
-------------+-------+-----------+---------+------------------+-----------+----------+----------
           1 | Miss  | Jenny     | Stones  | 27 Rowan Avenue  | Hightown  | NT2 1AQ  | 023 9876
           2 | Mr    | Andrew    | Stones  | 52 The Willows   | Lowtown   | LT5 7RA  | 876 3527
           3 | Miss  | Alex      | Matthew | 4 The Street     | Nicetown  | NT2 2TX  | 010 4567
           4 | Mr    | Adrian    | Matthew | The Barn         | Yuleville | YV67 2WR | 487 3871
           5 | Mr    | Simon     | Cozens  | 7 Shady Lane     | Oakenham  | OA3 6QW  | 514 5926
           6 | Mr    | Neil      | Matthew | 5 Pasture Lane   | Nicetown  | NT3 7RT  | 267 1232
           7 | Mr    | Richard   | Stones  | 34 Holly Way     | Bingham   | BG4 2WE  | 342 5982
           8 | Mrs   | Ann       | Stones  | 34 Holly Way     | Bingham   | BG4 2WE  | 342 5982
           9 | Mrs   | Christine | Hickman | 36 Queen Street  | Histon    | HT3 5EM  | 342 5432
          10 | Mr    | Mike      | Howard  | 86 Dysart Street | Tibsville | TB3 7FG  | 505 5482
          11 | Mr    | Dave      | Jones   | 54 Vale Rise     | Bingham   | BG3 8GD  | 342 8264
          12 | Mr    | Richard   | Neill   | 42 Thatched Way  | Winnersby | WB3 6GQ  | 505 6482
          13 | Mrs   | Laura     | Hardy   | 73 Margarita Way | Oxbridge  | OX2 3HX  | 821 2335
          14 | Mr    | Bill      | O'Neill | 2 Beamer Street  | Welltown  | WT3 8GM  | 435 1234
          15 | Mr    | David     | Hudson  | 4 The Square     | Milltown  | MT2 6RT  | 961 4526
(15 rows)

bpsimple=# ▊

👤 🖥 Shell
```

**Figure 2-4.** *Command-line viewing of customer data from a database*

Notice that we have added an extra column, customer_id, as our unique way of referencing a customer. It is our primary key for the table. As you can see, the data looks much as it did in a spreadsheet, laid out in rows and columns. In later chapters, we will explain the actual mechanics of defining a database table, storing, and accessing the data, but rest assured, it's not difficult.

# Accessing Data in a Database

You can easily view your PostgreSQL data using the psql tool from the command line, as you saw in Figure 2-4. However, PostgreSQL is not restricted to command-line use. Figure 2-5 shows the more user-friendly graphic approach of pgAdmin III, a free tool available from http://www.pgadmin.org/, and also bundled with the Windows distributions of PostgreSQL from version 8. We will see more about graphical interfaces in Chapter 5.

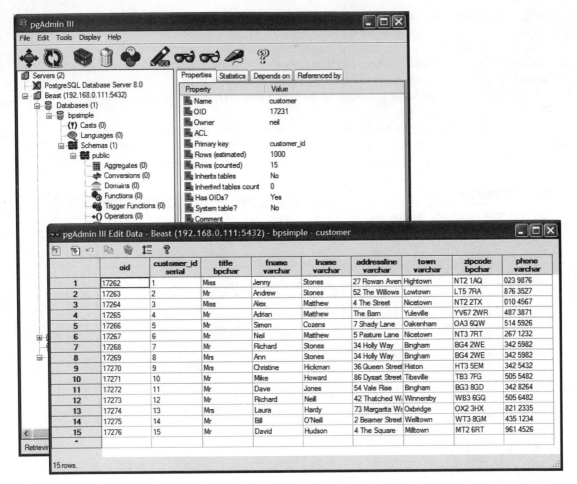

**Figure 2-5.** *Viewing customer data from a database with pgAdmin III*

## Accessing Data Across a Network

Of course, if we could only access our data on the machine on which it was physically stored, the situation really wouldn't have improved much over the single spreadsheet file being shared among different users.

PostgreSQL is a server-based database, and as described in the previous chapter, once configured, will accept requests from clients across a network. Although the client can be on the same machine as the database server, for multiuser access, this won't normally be the case. For Microsoft Windows users, an ODBC driver is available, so we can arrange to connect any Windows desktop application that supports ODBC across a network to a server holding our data. Figure 2-6 shows Microsoft Access on a Windows PC accessing a PostgreSQL database running on a Linux machine. This is done using linked external tables via an ODBC connection across the network.

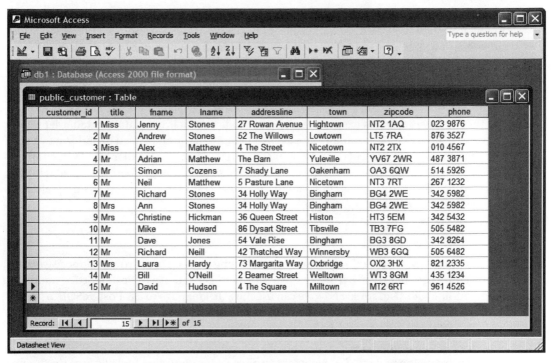

**Figure 2-6.** *Accessing the same data from Microsoft Access*

Now we can access the same data from many machines across the network at the same time. We have one copy of the data, securely held on a central server, accessible to multiple desktops running different operating systems, across a network.

We will see the technical details of configuring an ODBC connection in Chapter 5.

## Handling Multiuser Access

PostgreSQL, like all relational databases, can automatically ensure that conflicting updates to the database can never occur. It looks to the users as though they all have unrestricted access to all the information at the same time, but behind the scenes, PostgreSQL is monitoring changes and preventing conflicting updates.

This ability to allow many people to apparently have simultaneous read and write access to the same data, but ensure that it remains consistent, is a very important feature of databases. When a user changes a column, you either see it before it changes or after it changes; you never see partial updates.

A classic example is a bank database transferring money between two accounts. If, while the money was being transferred, someone were to run a report on the amount of money in all the accounts, it's very important that the total be correct. It may not matter in the report which account the money was in at the instant the report was run, but it is important that the report doesn't see the in-between point, where one account has been debited but the other not credited.

Relational databases like PostgreSQL hide any intermediate states, so they cannot be seen by other users. This is termed *isolation*. The report operation is isolated from the money-transfer operation, so it appears to happen either before or after, but never at exactly the same instant. We will come back to this concept of isolation in Chapter 9 when we look at Transactions.

## Slicing and Dicing Data

Now that we have seen how easy it is to access the data once it is in a database table, let's have a first look at how we might actually process that data. We frequently need to perform two very basic operations on big sets of data: selecting rows that match a particular set of values and selecting a subset of the columns of the data. In database terminology, these are called *selection* and *projection* respectively. That may sound somewhat complex, but accomplishing selection and projection is actually quite simple.

### Selection

Let's start by looking at selection, where we are selecting a subset of the rows. Suppose we want to see all our customers who live in the town Bingham. Let's return to PostgreSQL's standard command-line tool, psql, to see how we can use the SQL language to ask PostgreSQL to get the data we want. The SQL command we need is very simple:

```
SELECT * FROM customer WHERE town = 'Bingham'
```

If you are typing in your SQL statements (using a command-line tool like psql or a graphical tool such as pgAdmin III), you also need to add a semicolon at the end. The semicolon tells psql that this is the end of a command, because longer commands might extend over more than one line. Generally, in this book, we will show the semicolon.

PostgreSQL responds by returning all the rows in the customer table, where the town column contains Bingham, as shown in Figure 2-7.

```
bpsimple=# select * from customer where town = 'Bingham';
 customer_id | title |  fname  | lname  | addressline  |  town   | zipcode |  phone
-------------+-------+---------+--------+--------------+---------+---------+----------
           7 | Mr    | Richard | Stones | 34 Holly Way | Bingham | BG4 2WE | 342 5982
           8 | Mrs   | Ann     | Stones | 34 Holly Way | Bingham | BG4 2WE | 342 5982
          11 | Mr    | Dave    | Jones  | 54 Vale Rise | Bingham | BG3 8GD | 342 8264
(3 rows)

bpsimple=#
```

**Figure 2-7.** *Selecting a subset of the data rows*

So that was selection, where we choose particular rows from a table. As you can see, that was pretty easy. Don't worry about the details of the SQL statement yet. We will come back to that more formally in Chapter 5.

## Projection

Now let's look at projection, where we are selecting particular columns from a table. Suppose we wanted to select just the first name and last names from our customer table. You will remember that we called those columns fname and lname. The command to retrieve the names is also quite simple:

```
SELECT fname, lname FROM customer;
```

PostgreSQL responds by returning the appropriate columns, as shown in Figure 2-8.

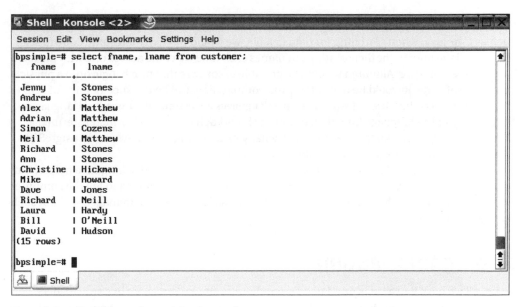

**Figure 2-8.** *Selecting a subset of the data columns*

You might reasonably suppose that sometimes we want to do both operations on the data at the same time; that is, select particular column values but only from particular rows. That's pretty easy in SQL as well. For example, suppose we wanted to know only the first names and last names of all our customers who live in Bingham. We can simply combine our two SQL statements into a single command:

```
SELECT fname, lname FROM customer WHERE town = 'Bingham';
```

PostgreSQL responds with our requested data, as shown in Figure 2-9.

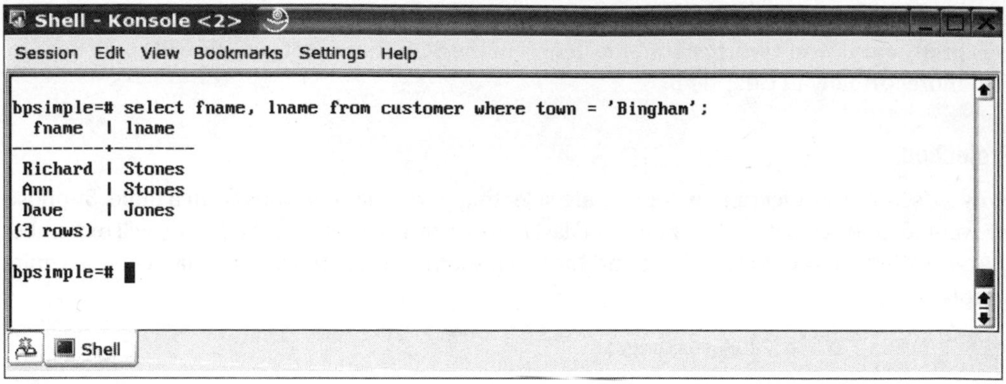

**Figure 2-9.** *Selecting a subset of both columns and rows*

There is one very important thing to notice here. In many traditional programming languages, such as C or Java, when searching for data in a file, we would have written some code to scan through all the lines in the file, printing out names each time we came across one with the town we were searching for. Although it might be possible to squeeze that much logic onto a physical single line of code, it would be a very long and complex line, unlike the succinct line of SQL shown here. This is because C, Java, and similar languages are essentially procedural languages. You specify in the language how the computer should behave. In SQL, which is termed a *declarative language*, you tell the computer what you are trying to achieve, and PostgreSQL works some internal magic to handle this task for you.

This might seem a little strange if you have never used a declarative language before, but once you get used to the idea, it seems obvious that it's a much better idea to tell the computer what you want, rather than how to do it. You will wonder how you have managed without such languages till now.

# Adding Information

So far, all we have looked at is our database emulating a single worksheet in a spreadsheet, and we've just touched the surface of SQL's features. As we will see in this book, however, relational databases such as PostgreSQL are very rich in useful features, which take them well beyond the realms of spreadsheet capabilities. One of the most important capabilities of databases is their ability to link data together across tables, and that is what we will look at now.

## Using Multiple Tables

Recall our customer order problem, where our simple customer spreadsheet suddenly became very untidy once additional order information was stored for each customer. How do we store information about orders from customers when we don't know in advance how many orders a customer might make? As you can probably guess from the title of this section, the way to solve this problem with a relational database is to add another table to store this information.

Just as we designed our `customer` table, we start by deciding what information we want to store about each order. For now, let's assume that we want to store the name of the customer who placed the order, the date the order was placed, the date it was shipped, and how much we charged for delivery. As in our `customer` table, we will also add a unique reference number for each order, rather than try to make any assumptions about what might be unique. There is obviously no need to store all the customer details again. We already know that given a `customer_id`, we can find all the details of that customer in the `customer` table.

You might be wondering why we've omitted the details of what was ordered. Certainly, that is an important aspect of orders to most customers—they like to get what they ordered. If you're thinking that it's a similar problem to not knowing in advance how many orders a customer will place, you're quite right. We have no idea how many items will be on each order. The repeating groups problem is never far away. We will leave this aside for now and deal with it in the "Creating a Simple Database Design" section later in this chapter.

Figure 2-10 shows our order information table with some sample data, again shown in the graphical tool, pgAdmin III.

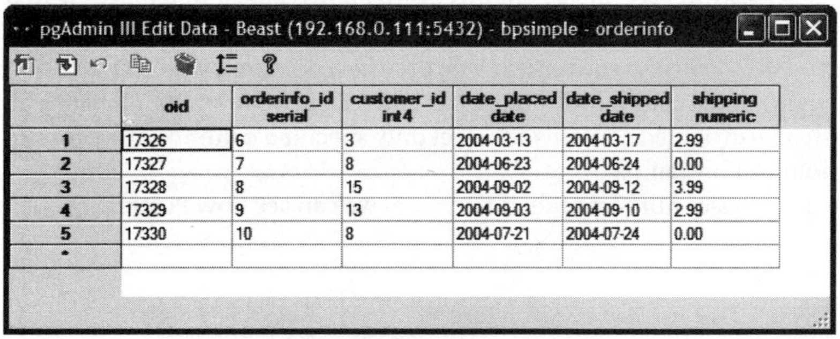


| | oid | orderinfo_id serial | customer_id int4 | date_placed date | date_shipped date | shipping numeric |
|---|---|---|---|---|---|---|
| 1 | 17326 | 6 | 3 | 2004-03-13 | 2004-03-17 | 2.99 |
| 2 | 17327 | 7 | 8 | 2004-06-23 | 2004-06-24 | 0.00 |
| 3 | 17328 | 8 | 15 | 2004-09-02 | 2004-09-12 | 3.99 |
| 4 | 17329 | 9 | 13 | 2004-09-03 | 2004-09-10 | 2.99 |
| 5 | 17330 | 10 | 8 | 2004-07-21 | 2004-07-24 | 0.00 |
| * | | | | | | |

**Figure 2-10.** *Some order information viewed in pgAdmin III*

We haven't put too much data in the table, as it is easier to experiment on smaller amounts of data. You will notice an extra column, `oid`, which isn't part of our user data. This is a special column used internally by PostgreSQL. The current version of PostgreSQL defaults to creating this column on all tables, but hides it from the `SELECT *` command. We will discuss this column in Chapter 8.

## Relating a Table with a Join Operation

Now we have details of our customers, and at least summary details of their orders, stored in our database. In many ways, this is no different from using a pair of spreadsheets: one for our customer details and one for their order details. It's time to look at what we can do using these tables in combination, and start to see the power of databases. We do this by selecting data from both tables at the same time. This is called a *join*, which, after selection and projection from a single table, is the third most common SQL data-retrieval operation.

Suppose we want to list all the orders and the customers who placed them. In a procedural language, such as C, we would need to write code to scan one of the tables, perhaps starting with the customer table, then for each customer, we look for and print out any orders they have placed. That's not difficult, but it's certainly a bit time-consuming and tedious to code. I'm sure you will be pleased to know we can find the answer much more easily with SQL, using a join operation. All we need to do is tell SQL three things:

- The columns we want

- The tables we want the data retrieved from

- How the two tables relate to each other

The command we need is the example presented in the previous chapter:

```
SELECT * FROM customer, orderinfo
    WHERE customer.customer_id = orderinfo.customer_id;
```

As you can probably guess, this asks for all columns from our two tables, and tells SQL that the column customer_id in the table customer holds the same information as the customer_id column in the orderinfo table. Note the convenient *table.column* notation, which enables us to specify both a table name and a column within that table. The * in our command means all columns. We could instead use named columns to select only specified columns, if we just wanted names and amounts, for example.

Now that we have a database with some tables and data, we can see how PostgreSQL responds in Figure 2-11.

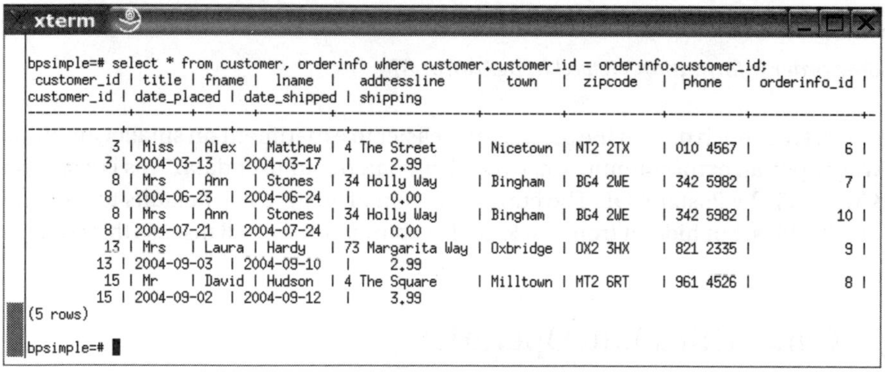

**Figure 2-11.** *Selecting data from two tables in one operation*

This is a bit untidy, since the rows wrap to fit in the window, but you can see how PostgreSQL has answered our query, without us needing to specify exactly how to solve the problem.

Let's leap ahead briefly, and see a much more complex query we could perform using SQL on these two tables. Suppose we wanted to see how frequently different customers had placed orders with us. This requires a significantly more advanced bit of SQL:

```
SELECT customer.title, customer.fname, customer.lname,
    count(orderinfo.orderinfo_id) AS "Number of orders"
FROM customer, orderinfo
WHERE customer.customer_id = orderinfo.customer_id
GROUP BY customer.title, customer.fname, customer.lname;
```

That's a complex bit of SQL, but without going into the details, you can see that we still have not told SQL how to answer the question; we've just specified the question in a very precise way using SQL. We also managed it all in a single statement. For the record, Figure 2-12 shows how PostgreSQL responds.

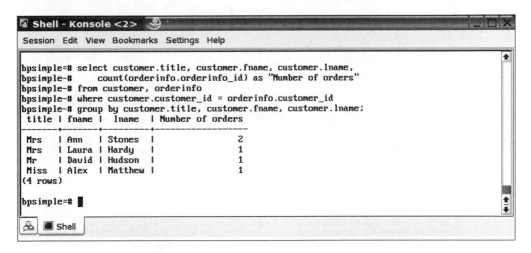

**Figure 2-12.** *Retrieving order frequency*

Some database experts may like typing SQL directly into a window using a command-line tool, and it certainly is useful sometimes, but it's not everyone's preference. If you prefer to build your queries graphically, that's not a problem. As noted earlier in this chapter, you can simply access the database via an ODBC driver and use a Windows graphical user interface (GUI), for example. Figure 2-13 shows the same query being designed and executed in Access on a Windows machine, using the PostgreSQL ODBC driver and linked external tables. We will see some other GUI tools, such as Rekall running on a Linux desktop, in Chapter 5.

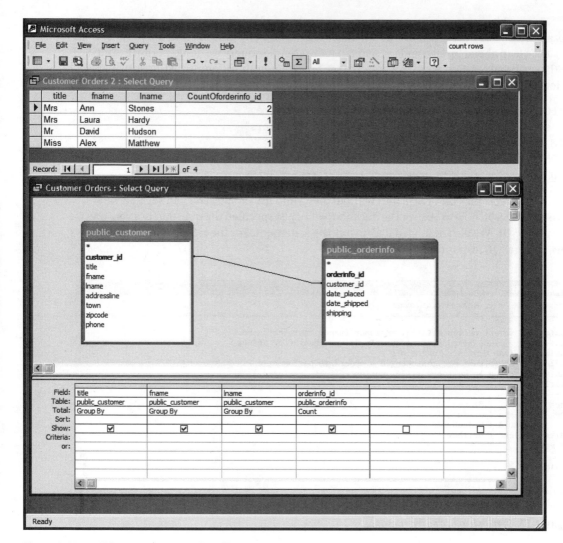

**Figure 2-13.** *Building a query graphically*

In our particular environment, the data is still stored on a Linux machine, but the user hardly needs to be aware of the technical details. Generally, in this book, we will use the command line for teaching SQL, because that way you will learn the basics before moving on to more complex SQL commands. Of course, you are welcome to use a GUI rather than a command-line tool to construct your SQL commands; it's your choice.

# Designing Tables

So far, we have only two tables in our database, and we have not really talked about how we decide what goes in each table, except in the very informal way of doing what looked reasonable. This design, which includes tables, columns, and relationships, is more correctly called a *schema*.

Designing a database schema with more than a couple of dozen tables can be quite challenging if the data is complex. Database designers earn their money by being good at this difficult task. Fortunately, for relatively simple databases, with up to perhaps ten tables, it's possible to come up with a fairly good design just by applying some basic rules of thumb, rather than needing to apply rules in a more formal way.

In this section, we are going to look at the simple sample database we are starting to build, and figure out a way to decide what tables we need.

# Understanding Some Basic Rules of Thumb

When a database is designed, it is often *normalized*; that is, a set of rules is applied to ensure that data is broken down in an appropriate fashion. In Chapter 12, we will look at database design in a formal way. To get started, all we require are some simple ground rules. These rules are just to help you understand the initial database, named bpsimple, we will be using to explore SQL and PostgreSQL in this and the following chapters. We strongly suggest that you don't just read these rules, and then dash off to design a database with 20 tables. Work your way through the book—at least until Chapter 12.

---

■**Tip** If you're interested in learning more about normal forms, we suggest Joe Celko's *SQL for Smarties* (ISBN 1-55860-576-2). It has some excellent definitions of the various rules of normalization, as well as other rules Dr. E. F. Codd defined for the relational model and many advanced examples of SQL usage.

---

## Rule One: Break Down the Data into Columns

The first rule is to put only one piece of information, or data *attribute*, in each column. This comes naturally to most people, provided they consciously think about it. In our original spreadsheet, we have already quite naturally broken down the information for each customer into different columns, so the name was separate from the ZIP code, for example.

In a spreadsheet, this rule just makes it simpler to work on the data; for example, to sort by the ZIP code. In a database, however, it is essential that the data is correctly broken down into attributes.

Why is this so important in databases? From a practical point of view, it is difficult to specify that you want the data between the twenty-ninth and thirty-fifth characters from an address column, because that happens to be where the ZIP code lives. There is bound to be some place where the rule does not hold, and you get the wrong piece of data. Another reason for the data to be correctly broken down is that all columns in a database must have the same type, unlike a spreadsheet, which is quite forgiving about the types of data in a column.

## Rule Two: Have a Unique Way of Identifying Each Row

You will remember that when we tried to decide how to identify each row in the spreadsheet example at the beginning of this chapter, we had a problem of not being sure what would be unique. As was mentioned, this was because there was no primary key. In general, it doesn't need to be a single column that is unique; it could be a pair of columns taken together, or occasionally even the combination of three columns that uniquely identifies a row. It is rare, and probably a mistake, if you find yourself requiring more than three columns to uniquely identify a row.

In any case, there must be a way of saying, with absolute certainty, if I look at the contents of a particular column, or group of columns in this row, I know it will have a value different from all other rows in this table. If you cannot find a column, or at most a combination of three columns, that uniquely identifies each row, it's time to add an extra column to fulfill that purpose. In our customer table, we added an extra column, customer_id, to identify each row.

### Rule Three: Remove Repeating Information

Recall that when we tried to store order information in the customer table, it looked rather untidy because of the repeating groups. For each customer, we repeated order information as many times as was required. This meant that we could never know how many columns were needed for orders. In a database, the number of columns in a table is effectively fixed by the design. So we must decide in advance how many columns we need, what type they are, and name each column before we can store any data. Never try to store repeating groups of data in a single row.

The way around this restriction is to do exactly what we did with our orders and customers data: split the data into separate tables. Then you can join the tables together when you need data from both tables. In our example, we used the column customer_id to join the two tables.

More formally, what we had was a *many-to-one relationship*; that is, there could be many orders received from a single customer.

### Rule Four: Get the Naming Right

This is occasionally the hardest rule to implement well. What do we call a table or column? Tables and columns should have short, meaningful names. If you cannot decide what to call something, it's often a clue that all is not well in your table and column design.

In addition to coming up with appropriate names, most database designers have their own personal rules of thumb, or *naming conventions*, that they use to ensure the naming of tables and columns in a database is consistent. Don't have some table names singular and some plural. For example, rather than naming one table office and the other departments, use office and department. If you decide on a naming rule for an id column—perhaps the table name with an appended _id—stick to that rule. If you use abbreviations, always use them consistently. If a column in one table is a key to another table (a *foreign key*, as explained in Chapter 12), try to give them the same base name. In a complex database, it can get very annoying when names are not quite consistent, such as customer_id, customer_ident, cust_id, and cust_no.

Achieving this apparently simple goal of getting the names right is often surprisingly challenging, but the rewards in simplified maintenance are considerable.

## Creating a Simple Database Design

We can draw our database design, or schema, using an entity relationship diagram. For our two-table database, such a diagram might look like Figure 2-14.

**■Note** An *entity relationship diagram* is a graphical way of representing the logical structure of our data. It helps us visualize how the different entities in our data relate to each other.

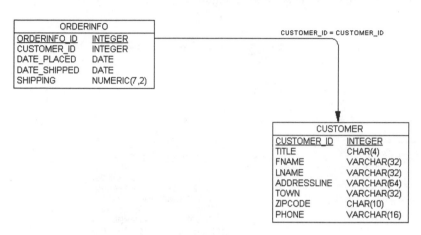

**Figure 2-14.** *A simple entity relationship diagram*

This diagram shows our two tables, the column, the data types, and the sizes in each column, and also tells us that customer_id is the column that joins the two tables together. Notice that the arrow goes from the orderinfo table to the customer table. This is a hint that for each orderinfo entry, there is at most a single entry in the customer table, but that for each customer there may be many orders. Also notice that some columns are underlined, which indicates that the column is guaranteed to be unique. These columns form the primary key for the tables.

It's important that you remember which way a one-to-many relationship goes; getting it confused can cause a lot of problems. You should also notice that we have been very careful to name the column we want to use to join the two tables the same in each table: customer_id. This is not essential. We could have called the two columns foo and bar if we had wanted to, but, as noted in the previous section, consistent naming is a great help in the long run.

The next stage is to extend our very simple two-table design into something slightly more realistic. We will design it as a simple order-management database, called bpsimple.

## Extending Beyond Two Tables

Clearly, the information we have so far is lacking, in that we don't know what items were in each order. You may remember that we deliberately omitted the actual items from each order, promising to come back to that problem. It's now time to sort out the actual items in each order.

The problem we have is that we don't know in advance how many items there will be in each order. It's almost the same as not knowing in advance how many orders a customer might place. Each order might have one, two, three, or a hundred items in it. We must separate the information that a customer placed an order from the details of what was in that order. Basically, what we might try is something like what is shown in Figure 2-15.

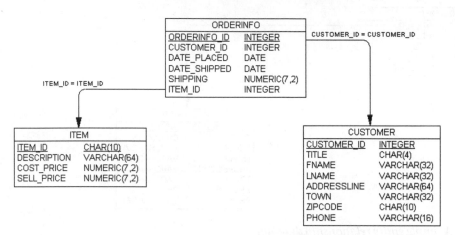

**Figure 2-15.** *An attempt at relating customers and ordered items*

Much like the customer and orderinfo tables, we separate the information into two tables, and then join them together. We have, however, created a subtle problem here.

If you think carefully about the relationship between an order and an item that may be ordered, you will realize that not only could each orderinfo entry relate to many items, but each item could also appear in many orders, if different customers order the same item.

We will consider this problem further in Chapter 12, but for now, you will be pleased to know that there is a standard solution to this difficulty. You create a third table between the two tables, which implements a *many-to-many relationship*. This is actually easier to do than it is to explain, so let's just go ahead and create a table, orderline, to link the orders with the items, as shown in Figure 2-16.

We have created a table that has rows corresponding to each line of an order. For any single line, we can determine the order it was from using the orderinfo_id column and the item referenced using the item_id column. A single item can appear in many order lines, and a single order can contain many order lines. Each order line refers to only a single item, and it can appear in only a single order.

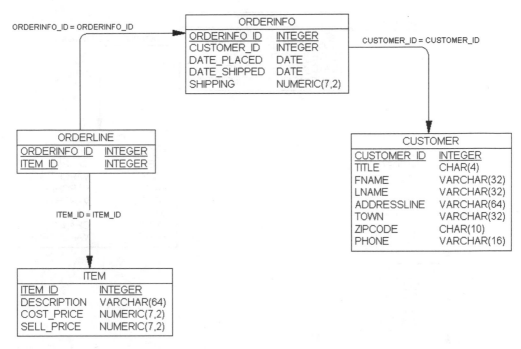

**Figure 2-16.** *Relating customers and orders*

You will also notice that we did not need to add a unique id column to identify each row. That is because the combination of orderinfo_id and item_id is always unique. There is one very subtle problem lurking, however. What happens if a customer orders two of an item in a single order? We cannot just enter another row in orderline, because we just said that the combination of orderinfo_id and item_id is always unique. Do we need to add yet another special table to cater to orders that contain more than one of any item? Fortunately, we don't need to do this. There is a much simpler approach. We just need to add a quantity column to the orderline table, and all will be well (see Figure 2-17, in the following section).

## Completing the Initial Design

We have just two more pieces of information we need to store before we have the main structure of the first cut of our database design in place. We want to store the barcode that goes with each product, and we also want to store the quantity we have in stock for each item.

It's possible that each product will have more than one barcode, because when manufacturers significantly change the packaging of a product, they often also change the barcode. For example, you have probably seen packs that offer "20% extra for free" (often referred to in the trade as *overfill packs*). Manufacturers will generally change the barcode of these promotion packs, but essentially the product is unchanged. Therefore, we may have a many barcodes-to-one item relationship. We add an additional table to hold the barcodes, as shown in Figure 2-17.

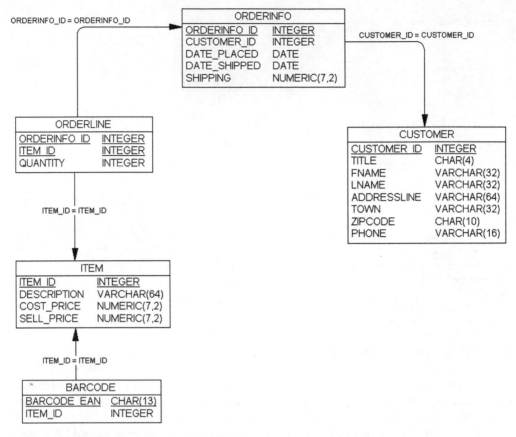

**Figure 2-17.** *Adding the barcode relationship*

Notice that the arrow points from the barcode table to the item table, because there may be many barcodes for each item. Also notice that the barcode_ean column is the primary key, since there must be a unique row for each barcode, and a single item could have several barcodes, but no barcode can ever belong to more than one item. (EAN is a European standard for product barcodes.)

The last addition we need to make to our database design is to hold the stock quantity for each item. If most items were in stock, and the stock information were fairly basic, we could simply store a stock quantity directly in the item table. However, this won't work if we offer many items, but only a few are normally in stock, and we need to store a lot of information about the stocked items. For example, in a warehouse operation, we may need to store location information, batch numbers, and expiration dates. If we had an item file with 500,000 items in it, but only held the top 1,000 items in stock, this would be very wasteful. There is a standard way of resolving this problem, using what is called a *supplementary table*. We will take this approach to store stock information for our sample database, as shown in Figure 2-18.

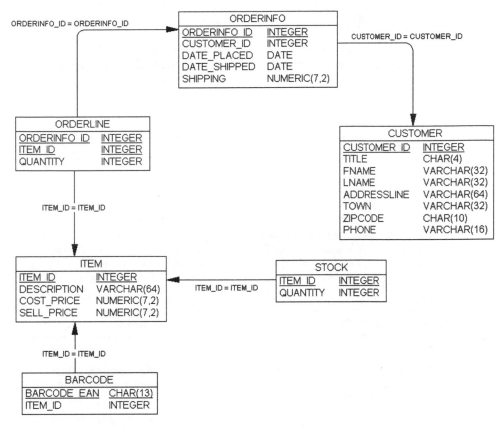

**Figure 2-18.** *The design of the* bpsimple *database*

We create a new table to store the supplementary information (stock quantity, in this example), and then create only the rows that are required for items that are in stock, linking the information back to the main table. Notice the stock table uses item_id as a unique key, and it holds information that relates directly to items, using item_id to join to the relevant row in the item table. The arrow points to the item table, because that is the master table, even though it is not a many-to-one relationship in this case. As in the other tables, the underlining indicates the table's primary key (the information guaranteed to be unique).

As it stands, the design is clearly overly complex, since the additional information we are keeping is so small. We will leave the schema design the way it is to show how it is done, and later in the book, we will demonstrate how to access data when there is additional information in supplementary tables like this one. For those who like sneaking a look ahead, we will use what's called an *outer join*.

---

■**Note** In Chapter 8, we will see how we can enforce in the database the rules about relationships between tables, and in Chapter 12 we will revisit the design of databases in more detail. When we get to Chapter 8, we will discover some more advanced techniques to better manage the consistency of our database, and we will enhance our design into a bpfinal schema.

---

# Basic Data Types

In our sample database, we've used some basic, generic data types, as summarized in Table 2-1. These can be translated into actual PostgreSQL types when we create the real tables in the next chapter.

**Table 2-1.** *Data Types in the Sample Database*

| Data Type | Description |
| --- | --- |
| integer | A whole number. |
| serial | An integer, but automatically set to a unique number for each row that is added. This is the type we would use for the _id columns. The figures in this chapter show such fields as integer, because that's the underlying type in the database. |
| char | A character array of fixed size, with the size shown in parentheses after the type. For these column types, PostgreSQL will always store exactly the specified number of characters. If we use a char(256) to store just one character, there will still be (at least) 256 bytes held in the database and returned when the data is retrieved. |
| varchar | This is also a character array, but as its name suggests, it is of variable length. Generally, the space used in the database will be much the same as the actual size of the data stored. When you ask for a varchar field to be returned, it returns just the number of characters you stored. The maximum length is given in the parentheses after the type. |
| date | This allows you to store year, month, and day information. There are other related types that allow us to store time information as well as date information. We will meet these later in Chapter 8. |
| numeric | This allows you to store numbers with a specified number of digits (the first number in the parentheses) and using a fixed number of decimal places (the second number in the parentheses). Hence, numeric(7,2) would store exactly seven digits, two of them after the decimal place. |

As noted earlier in the chapter, since the need to add a special unique column is so common in databases, there is a built-in solution in most databases: a data type known as serial. This special type is effectively an integer that automatically increments as rows are added to the table, assigning a new, unique number as each row is added. When we add a new row to a table that has a serial column, we don't specify a value for that column, but allow the database to automatically assign the next number. Most databases, when they assign serial values, don't take into account any rows that are deleted. The number assigned will just go on incrementing for each new row. We will look at how to handle out-of-sequence problems with serial data types in Chapter 6.

In Chapter 8, we will look at PostgreSQL's other data types, which will give us a chance to reexamine some of these data type choices. Appendix B provides a summary of the PostgreSQL data types.

# Dealing with the Unknown: NULLs

In the orderinfo table in our sample database design, we have a date ordered and a date shipped column, both of type date. What do we do when an order has been received but not yet shipped? What should we store in the date shipped column? We could store a special date, a *sentinel value*, that lets us know that we have not yet shipped the order. On UNIX-type systems, we might use January 1, 1970, which is traditionally the date from which UNIX systems count. That date is well before the date of any orders we expect to store in the database, so we would always know that this special date means not yet shipped.

However, having special values scattered in tables shows poor design and is rather error-prone. For example, if a new programmer starts on the project and doesn't realize there is a special date, the programmer might try calculating the average time between the order and shipping date, and come up with some very strange answers if there are a few shipped dates set before the order was placed.

Fortunately, all relational database systems support a very special value called NULL, which usually means unknown at this time. Notice that it doesn't mean zero, or empty string, or anything that can be represented by the data type of the field. An unknown value is very different from zero or a blank string. Indeed, NULL is not really a value at all.

The concept of a NULL is often confusing to novice database users. (The Romans also had trouble with things that are not there, so there is no zero in Roman numerals.) In database terminology, NULL generally means a value is unknown, but it also has one or two additional and rather subtle variations on that meaning.

It's important to take care of NULLs, because they can pop up at odd times and cause you surprises, usually unpleasant ones. So in our orderinfo table, we could set date shipped to NULL before an order is shipped, where the meaning "unknown at this time" is exactly what we require.

There is another subtly different use for NULL (not so common), which is to mean "not relevant for this row." Suppose you were doing a survey of people and one of the questions was about the color of spectacles. For people who don't wear spectacles, this is clearly a nonsensical question. This is a case where NULL might be used in the column to record that the information is not relevant for this particular row.

One feature of NULL is that if you compare two NULLs, the answer is always unknown. This sometimes confuses people, but if you think about the meaning of NULL as unknown, it's perfectly logical that testing for equality on two unknowns gives the answer unknown. SQL has a special way of checking for NULLs, by asking IS NULL. This allows you to find and test NULL values if you need to do so. IS NULL is discussed further in Chapter 4.

NULL type values do behave in a slightly different way from more conventional values. Therefore, it is possible to specify when you design a table that some columns cannot hold NULL values. It is normally a good idea to specify the columns as NOT NULL, when you are sure that NULL should never be accepted, such as for primary key columns. Some database designers advocate an almost complete ban on NULL, but they do have their uses, so we normally advocate allowing NULL values on selected columns, where there is a genuine possibility that unknown values are required. NOT NULL is discussed further in Chapter 8.

# Reviewing the Sample Database

In this chapter, we have been designing, in a rather ad-hoc manner, a simple database, named bpsimple, to look after customers, orders, and items, such as might be used in a small shop (see Figure 2-18, earlier in this chapter). As the book progresses, we will be using this database to demonstrate SQL and other PostgreSQL features. We will also be discovering the limitations of our existing design, and looking at how it can be improved in some areas.

The simplified database we are using has many elements of what a real retail database might look like; however, it also has many simplifications. For example, an item might have a full description for the stock file, a short description that appears on the till when it is sold, and yet another description that appears on shelf edge labels. The address information we are storing for customers is very simplified. We cannot cope with long addresses, where there is a village name or a state. We also cannot handle overseas orders.

It is often more feasible to start with a reasonably solid base and expand, rather than try to cater to every possible requirement in your initial design. This database is adequate for our initial needs.

In the next chapter, we will look at installing PostgreSQL, creating the tables for our sample database, and populating them with some sample data.

# Summary

In this chapter, we considered how a single database table is much like a single spreadsheet, with four important differences:

- All items in a column must have the same type.

- The number of columns must be the same for all rows in a table.

- It must be possible to uniquely identify each row.

- There is no implied row order in a database table, as there would be in a spreadsheet.

We have seen how we can extend our database to multiple tables, which lets us manage many-to-one relationships in a simple way. We gave some informal rules of thumb to help you understand how a database design needs to be structured. We will come back to the subject of database design in a much more rigorous fashion in later chapters.

We have also seen how to work around many-to-many relationships that turn up in the real world, breaking them down into a pair of one-to-many relationships by adding an extra table.

Finally, we worked on extending our initial database design so we have a demonstration database design, or schema, to work with as the book progresses.

In the next chapter, we will see how to get the PostgreSQL up and running on various platforms.

■ ■ ■

# CHAPTER 3

# Getting Started
# with PostgreSQL

In this chapter, we will look at installing and setting up PostgreSQL on various operating systems. If you need to install it on a Linux system, precompiled binary packages provide an easy route. If you are running a UNIX or UNIX-like system—such as Linux, FreeBSD, AIX, Solaris, HP-UX, or Mac OS X—it is not difficult to compile PostgreSQL from the source code.

We will also cover how to install and set up PostgreSQL on Windows platforms, using the Windows installer introduced in PostgreSQL version 8.0. Earlier versions can be installed on Windows, but this requires some additional software to create a UNIX-like environment. We therefore recommend version 8.0 or later for Windows systems.

Finally, we will prepare for the examples in the following chapters by creating the sample database discussed in Chapter 2.

In particular, this chapter will cover the following topics:

- Installing PostgreSQL from Linux binaries

- Installing PostgreSQL from the source code

- Setting up PostgreSQL on Linux and UNIX systems

- Installing and setting up PostgreSQL on Windows

- Creating a database with tables and adding data

## Installing PostgreSQL on Linux and UNIX Systems

If you are running a Linux system installed from a recent distribution, you may already have PostgreSQL installed or available to you as an installable package on the operating system installation disks. If not, you can use RPM packages to install PostgreSQL on many Linux distributions or flavors. Additionally, you can build and install PostgreSQL from the source code on just about any UNIX-compatible system.

## Installing PostgreSQL from Linux Binaries

Probably the easiest way to install PostgreSQL on Linux is by using precompiled binary packages. The binaries for PostgreSQL are available for download as RPM (RPM Package Manager, formerly Red Hat Package Manager) packages for various Linux distributions. At the time of writing this book, RPM packages are available at `http://www.postgresql.org/` for the following operating systems:

- Red Hat 9

- Red Hat Advanced Server 2.1

- Red Hat Enterprise Linux 3.0

- Fedora Core 1, 2 (including 64-bit), and 3

You can find binary packages at `http://www.rpmfind.net` for other Linux distributions, including the following:

- SuSE Linux 8.2 and 9.*x*

- Conectiva Linux

- Mandrake

- Yellow Dog PPC

---

■**Note**  Debian Linux users can install PostgreSQL using `apt-get`.

---

Table 3-1 lists the PostgreSQL binary packages. For a functional database and client installation, you need to download and install at least the base, libs, and server packages.

**Table 3-1.** *PostgreSQL Binary Packages*

| Package | Description |
| --- | --- |
| postgresql | The base package including clients and utilities |
| postgresql-libs | Shared libraries required from clients |
| postgresql-server | Programs to create and run a server |
| postgresql-contrib | Contributed extensions |

**Table 3-1.** *PostgreSQL Binary Packages (Continued)*

| Package | Description |
|---|---|
| postgresql-devel | Header files and libraries for development |
| postgresql-docs | Documentation |
| postgresql-jdbc | Java database connectivity for PostgreSQL |
| postgresql-odbc | Open database connectivity for PostgreSQL |
| postgresql-pl | PostgreSQL server support for Perl |
| postgresql-python | PostgreSQL server support for Python |
| postgresql-tcl | PostgreSQL server support for Tcl |
| postgresql-test | PostgreSQL test suite |

The exact filenames will have version numbers appended with the package. It is advisable to install a matching set of packages, all with the same revision level. In a package with the version number 8.*x.y*, the *x.y* portion determines the revision level.

## Installing the RPMs

To install the RPMs, you can use any of the following techniques:

- Use the RPM Package Manager application. Make sure that you have logged on as the superuser (root) to perform the installation.

- Use the graphical package manager of your choice, such as KPackage, to install the RPMs.

- Place all the RPM files in a single directory and, as superuser (root), execute the following command to unpack the packages and install all the files they contain into their correct places for your distribution:

```
$ rpm -i *.rpm
```

You can also install from the PostgreSQL packages that are bundled along with your Linux distribution, such as in Red Hat or SuSE Linux. For example, on SuSE Linux 9.*x*, you can install a version of PostgreSQL by running the YaST2 installation tool and selecting the packages listed in Table 3-1, as shown in Figure 3-1.

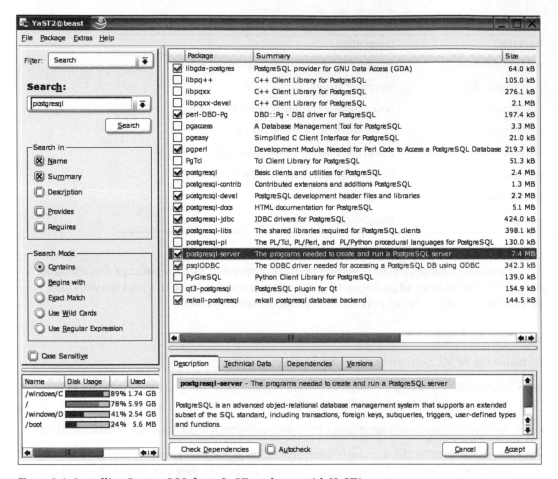

**Figure 3-1.** *Installing PostgreSQL from SuSE packages with YaST2*

## Upgrading to a New PostgreSQL Version

PostgreSQL is under continuous development, so new versions become available from time to time. Installing from RPM packages has the advantage that you can very simply upgrade to the most recent version. To do that, just let rpm know that you are performing an upgrade rather than a first-time installation by specifying the -U option instead of the -i option:

```
$ rpm -U *.rpm
```

However, before performing an upgrade, you should back up the existing data in the database. Any precautions that must be taken when performing an upgrade to the latest release will be noted at the PostgreSQL home site and in the release notes. Backing up existing databases is discussed in detail in Chapter 11 of this book.

---

■**Caution** If you are installing a new version of PostgreSQL as an upgrade to an existing installation, be sure to read the release notes for the new version before starting. In some cases, it may be necessary to back up and restore your PostgreSQL databases during an upgrade if, for example, the new version has introduced changes in the way that data is stored.

---

## Anatomy of a PostgreSQL Installation

A PostgreSQL installation consists of a number of applications, utilities, and data directories. The main PostgreSQL application (postmaster) contains the server code that services the requests to access data from clients. Utilities such as pg_ctl are used to control a master server process that needs to be running all the time the server is active.

PostgreSQL uses a data directory to store all of the files needed for a database. This directory not only stores the tables and records, but also system parameters. A typical installation would have all of the components of a PostgreSQL installation shown in Table 3-2, arranged in sub-directories of one PostgreSQL directory. One common location (and the default when you install from source code, as described in the next section) is /usr/local/pgsql.

**Table 3-2.** *PostgreSQL Installation Anatomy*

| Directory | Description |
| --- | --- |
| bin | Applications and utilities such as pg_ctl and postmaster |
| data | The database itself, initialized by initdb |
| doc | Documentation in HTML format |
| include | Header files for use in developing PostgreSQL applications |
| lib | Libraries for use in developing PostgreSQL applications |
| man | Manual pages for PostgreSQL tools |
| share | Sample configuration files |

There is a drawback with the single directory approach: both fixed program files and variable data are stored in the same place, which is often not ideal.

The files that PostgreSQL uses fall into two main categories:

- Files that are written to while the database server is running, including data files and logs. The data files are the heart of the system, storing all of the information for all of your databases. The log file that the database server produces will contain useful information about database accesses and can be a big help when troubleshooting problems. It effectively just grows as log entries are added.

- Files that are not written to while the database server is running, which are effectively read-only files. These files include the PostgreSQL applications like postmaster and pg_ctl, which are installed once and never change.

For a more efficient and easier to administer setup, you might wish to separate the different categories of files. PostgreSQL offers the flexibility to store the applications, logs, and data in different places, and some Linux distributions have made use of this flexibility to good effect. For example, in SuSE Linux 9.*x*, the PostgreSQL applications are stored with other applications in /usr/bin, the log file is in /var/log/postgresql, and the data is in /var/lib/pgsql/data. This means that it is easy to arrange backups of the critical data separately from the not-so-critical files, such as the log files.

Other distributions will have their own scheme for file locations. You can use rpm to list the files that have been installed by a particular package. To do this, use the query option, like this:

```
$ rpm -q -l postgresql-libs
/usr/lib/libecpg.so.4
/usr/lib/libecpg.so.4.1
...
/usr/share/locale/zh_TW/LC_MESSAGES/libpq.mo
$
```

To see where all the files have been installed, you will need to run rpm for all of the packages that make up the complete PostgreSQL set. Different distributions may call the packages by slightly different names. For example, SuSE Linux uses the package name pg_serv for the server package, so the query option looks like this:

```
$ rpm -q -l pg_serv
/etc/init.d/postgresql
/etc/logrotate.d/postgresql
...
/var/lib/pgsql/data/pg_options
$
```

Alternatively, you can use one of the graphical package manager tools, such as KPackage, which comes with the KDE desktop environment. Figure 3-2 shows an example of viewing a package's contents with KPackage.

The disadvantage of installing from a Linux distribution is that it is not always clear where everything lives. So, if you wish to upgrade to the most recent release, it can be tricky to ensure that you have untangled the original installation. An alternative is to install PostgreSQL from the source code, as described in the next section. If you have no intention of installing from source, you can skip the next section and continue with the PostgreSQL setup described in the "Setting Up PostgreSQL on Linux and UNIX" section.

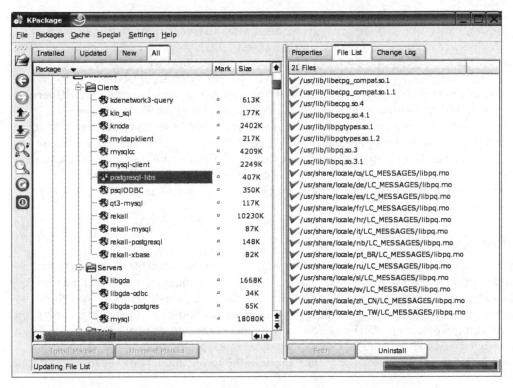

**Figure 3-2.** *Examining a package's contents with KPackage*

## Installing PostgreSQL from the Source Code

As explained in the previous section, you can use RPM packages to install PostgreSQL on many Linux distributions or flavors. Additionally, you can build and install PostgreSQL from the source code on just about any UNIX-compatible system, including Mac OS X.

The source code for PostgreSQL is available at http://www.postgresql.org. Here, you will find the code for the latest release and often the source code for beta test versions of the next release. Unless you like to live on the edge, it is probably a good idea to stick to the most recent stable release.

You can find the entire PostgreSQL source code in a single, compressed archive file, either in gzipped-tarball format, with a name something like postgresql-8.0.0.tar.gz, or in bzipped-tarball format, with a name like postgresql-8.0.0.tar.bz2. At the time of writing, the PostgreSQL tarball was around 13MB in size. To ease the download process in case of an unreliable or slow connection, the source is also available in a set of smaller files:

- postgresql-8.0.0.base.tar.gz

- postgresql-8.0.0.docs.tar.gz

- postgresql-8.0.0.opt.tar.gz

- postgresql-8.0.0.test.tar.gz

The exact filenames depend on the current version revision number at the time.

Compiling PostgreSQL is very simple. If you are familiar with compiling open-source products, there will be no surprises for you here. Even if this is your first experience in compiling and installing an open-source product, you should have no difficulty.

To perform the source-code compilation, you will need a Linux or UNIX system with a complete development environment installed. This includes a C compiler and the GNU version of the make utility (needed to build the database system). Linux distributions generally ship with a suitable development environment containing the GNU tools from the Free Software Foundation. These include the excellent GNU C compiler (gcc), which is the standard compiler for Linux. The GNU tools are available for most other UNIX platforms, too, and we recommend them for compiling PostgreSQL. You can download the latest tools from http://www.gnu.org. Once you have a development environment installed, the compilation of PostgreSQL is straightforward.

### Extracting the Code

Start the installation as a normal user. Copy your source-code tarball file to an appropriate directory for compiling. This does not need to be—in fact, it should not be—the final resting place of your PostgreSQL installation. One possible choice is a subdirectory in your home directory, since you do not need superuser permissions to compile PostgreSQL; you only need those permissions to install it once it's built. We generally prefer to unpack source code into a directory specifically created for maintaining source code products, /usr/src, but you can unpack anywhere you have sufficient disk space for the compilation. You need to allow around 90MB or so.

Unpack the tarball to extract the source code:

```
$ tar zxf postgresql-8.0.0.tar.gz
```

The extraction process will have made a new directory, related to the version of PostgreSQL you are building. Move into that directory:

```
$ cd postgresql-8.0.0
```

---

**Tip** You should find a file, INSTALL, in this directory that contains detailed manual build instructions, in the unlikely event that the automated method outlined here fails for some reason.

---

### Configuring the Compilation

The build process uses a configuration script, configure, to tailor the build parameters to your specific environment. To accept all defaults, you can simply run configure without arguments. Here is an example of running configure on a Linux system:

```
$ ./configure
checking build system type... i686-pc-linux-gnu
checking host system type... i686-pc-linux-gnu
checking which template to use... linux
checking whether to build with 64-bit integer date/time support... no
checking whether NLS is wanted... no
checking for default port number... 5432
checking for gcc... gcc
...
$
```

The configure script sets variables that control the way the PostgreSQL software is built, taking into account the type of platform on which you are compiling, the features of your C compiler, and so on. The configure script will automatically set locations for the installation. The default locations are for PostgreSQL to be compiled to use /usr/local/pgsql as the main directory for its operation, with subdirectories for applications and data.

You can use arguments to configure to change the default location settings, to set the network port the database server will use, and to include support for additional server-side programming languages for stored procedures. These options are listed in Table 3-3.

**Table 3-3.** *PostgreSQL Configure Script Options*

| Option | Description |
| --- | --- |
| --prefix=*prefix* | Install in directories under *prefix*; defaults to /usr/local/pgsql |
| --bindir=*dir* | Install application programs in *dir*; defaults to *prefix*/bin |
| --with-docdir=*dir* | Install documentation in *dir*; defaults to *prefix*/doc |
| --with-pgport=*port* | Set the default TCP port number for serving network connections |
| --with-tcl | Compile server-side support for Tcl stored procedures |
| --with-perl | Compile server-side support for Perl stored procedures |
| --with-python | Compile server-side support for Python stored procedures |

To see a full list of options to configure, you can use the --help argument:

```
$ ./configure --help
`configure' configures PostgreSQL 8.0.0 to adapt to many kinds of systems.

Usage: ./configure [OPTION]... [VAR=VALUE]...

To assign environment variables (e.g., CC, CFLAGS...), specify them as
VAR=VALUE.  See below for descriptions of some of the useful variables.
...
$
```

You do not need to settle on final locations for the database files and the log file at this stage. You can always specify these locations to the server process, when you start it after installation.

## Building the Software

Once the compilation is configured, you can build the software using make. The PostgreSQL build process uses a sophisticated set of makefiles to control the compilation process. Due to this, we recommend that you use a version of GNU make for the build. This is the default on Linux. On other UNIX platforms, you may need to install GNU make separately. Often, this will be given the name gmake to distinguish it from the version of make supplied with the operating system. In the instructions here, make refers to GNU make.

The next step is to run make to compile the software:

```
$ make
...
All of PostgreSQL successfully made. Ready to install.
```

If all goes well, you should see a large number of compilations proceeding. You will be finally rewarded with the message that everything has been made successfully.

When make has finished, you need to copy the programs to their final resting places. You use make to do this for you, too, but you need to be the superuser first:

```
$ su
# make install
...
PostgreSQL installation complete.
# exit
$
```

Once the software is built and installed, you can query the configuration of a PostgreSQL system with pg_config:

```
pg_config --bindir | --includedir | --libdir | --configure | --version
```

The pg_config command will report the directory where the PostgreSQL programs are installed (--bindir), the location of C include files (--includedir) and object code libraries (--libdir), and the version of PostgreSQL (--version):

```
$ pg_config --version
PostgreSQL 8.0.0
$
```

The build-time configuration can be reported by using pg_config --configure. This will report the command-line options passed to the configure script when the PostgreSQL server was configured for compilation.

That's just about all there is to installing PostgreSQL. You now have a set of programs that make up the PostgreSQL database server in the right place on your system.

At this point, you are in the same situation as you would have been had you installed from packages. Now it's time to turn our attention to setting up PostgreSQL now that it's installed.

# Setting Up PostgreSQL on Linux and UNIX

After you have PostgreSQL installed, whether from RPMs or compiled from the source code, you need to take a few steps to get it up and running. First, you should create a postgres user. Then you create a data directory for the database and the initial database structures. At that point, you can start PostgreSQL by starting the postmaster process.

## Creating the postgres User

The main database process for PostgreSQL, postmaster, is quite a special program. It is responsible for dealing with all data access from all users to all databases. It must allow users to access their data but not access other users' data, unless authorized. To do this, it needs to have sole control of all of the data files, so that no normal user can access any of the files directly. The postmaster process will control access to the data files by checking the permissions granted to the users that request access and performing the access on their behalf.

Strictly speaking, PostgreSQL needs to run only as a non-root user, which could be any normal user; if you install in your home directory, it could be your own user. However, a PostgreSQL installation typically uses the concept of a pseudo user to enforce data access. A user, often called postgres, is created for the sole purpose of owning the data files and has no other access rights. A postgres pseudo user provides some additional security, as no one can log in as the postgres user and gain illicit access. This user identity is used by the postmaster program to access the database files on behalf of others.

The first step in establishing a working PostgreSQL system is, therefore, to create this postgres user. The precise procedure for making new users differs from system to system. Linux users can (as root) simply use useradd:

```
# useradd postgres
```

Other UNIX systems may require you to create a home directory, edit the configuration files, or run the appropriate administration tool on your Linux distribution. Refer to your operating system documentation for details about using such administration tools.

## Creating the Database Directory

Next, you must create, as root, the directory PostgreSQL is going to use for its databases and change its owner to be postgres:

```
# mkdir /usr/local/pgsql/data
# chown postgres /usr/local/pgsql/data
```

Here, we are using the default location for the database. You might choose to store the data in a different location, as we discussed earlier, in the "Anatomy of a PostgreSQL Installation" section.

## Initializing the Database

You initialize the PostgreSQL database by using the initdb utility, specifying where in your file system you want the database files to reside. This will do several things, including creating the data structures PostgreSQL needs to run and creating an initial working database, template1.

You need to assume the identity of the postgres user to run the initdb utility. To do this, the most reliable way is to change your identity in two steps, first becoming root with su and then becoming postgres as follows. (As a normal user, you may not have permission to assume another user's identity, so you must become the superuser first.)

```
$ su
# su - postgres
pg$
```

Now the programs you run will assume the rights of the postgres user and will be able to access the PostgreSQL database files. For clarity, we have shown the shell prompt for commands executed as the postgres user as pg$.

---

■**Caution** Do not be tempted to shortcut the process of using the postgres user and run these programs as root. For security reasons, running server processes as root can be dangerous. If there were a problem with the process, it could result in an outsider gaining access to your system via the network. For this reason, postmaster will refuse to run as root.

---

Initialize the database with initdb:

```
pg$ /usr/local/pgsql/bin/initdb -D /usr/local/pgsql/data
The files belonging to this database system will be owned by user "postgres".
This user must also own the server process.

The database cluster will be initialized with locale en_GB.UTF-8.
The default database encoding has accordingly been set to UNICODE.
...
WARNING: enabling "trust" authentication for local connections
You can change this by editing pg_hba.conf or using the -A option the
next time you run initdb.

Success. You can now start the database server using:

    /usr/local/pgsql/bin/postmaster -D /usr/local/pgsql/data
or
    /usr/local/pgsql/bin/pg_ctl -D /usr/local/pgsql/data -l logfile start
pg$
```

If all goes well, you will have a new, completely empty database in the location you specified with the -D option to initdb.

## Granting Connection Permissions

By default, PostgreSQL will not allow general remote access. To grant permission to connect, you must edit a configuration file, pg_hba.conf. This file lives in the database file area (/usr/local/pgsql/data in our example), and contains entries that grant or reject permission for users to connect to the database. By default, local users may connect and remote users cannot. Its format is fairly simple, and the default file shipped with PostgreSQL contains many helpful comments for adding entries. You can grant permission for individual users, hosts, groups of computers, and individual databases, as necessary.

For example, to allow the user neil on a machine with IP address 192.168.0.3 to connect to the bpsimple database, add the following line to pg_hba.conf:

```
host        bpsimple        neil        192.168.0.3/32        md5
```

Note that in versions of PostgreSQL earlier than 8.0, the pg_hba.conf file used host address specifications using an IP address and subnet mask, so the preceding example would need to be written as follows:

```
host        bpsimple        neil        192.168.0.3        255.255.255.255        md5
```

Here, we will add an entry to allow any computer on the local network (in this case the subnet 192.168.*x.x*) to connect to any database with password authentication. (If you require a different access policy, refer to the comments in the configuration file.) We add a line to the end of pg_hba.conf that looks like this:

```
host        all        all        192.168.0.0/16        md5
```

This means that all computers with an IP address that begins 192.168 can access all databases.

Alternatively, if we trust all of the users on all of the machines in a network, we can allow unrestricted access by specifying trust as the authentication mechanism, like this:

```
host        all        all        192.168.0.0/16        trust
```

The PostgreSQL postmaster server process reads a configuration file, postgresql.conf (also in the data directory) to set a number of runtime options, including (if not otherwise specified in a -D option or the PGDATA environment variable) the location of the database data files. The configuration file is well commented, providing guidance if you need to change any settings. There is also a section on runtime configuration in the PostgreSQL documentation.

As an example, we can allow the server to listen for network connections by setting the listen_addresses variable in postgresql.conf, instead of using the now deprecated -i option to postmaster, as follows:

```
listen_addresses='*'
```

In fact, setting configuration options in postgresql.conf is the recommended approach for controlling the behavior of the postmaster process.

## Starting the postmaster Process

Now you can start the server process itself. Again, you use the -D option to tell postmaster where the database files are located. If you want to allow users on a network to access your data, you can specify the -i option to enable remote clients (if you haven't enabled listen_addresses in postgresql.conf, as in the preceding example):

```
pg$ /usr/local/pgsql/bin/postmaster -i -D /usr/local/pgsql/data >logfile 2>&1 &
```

This command starts postmaster, redirects the process output to a file (called logfile in the postgres user's home directory), and merges standard output with standard error by using the shell construction 2>&1. You can choose a different location for your log file by redirecting output to another file.

The pg_ctl utility provided with PostgreSQL offers a simple way of starting, stopping, and restarting (the equivalent of stop followed by start) the postmaster process. If PostgreSQL is fully configured using the postgresql.conf configuration file, as mentioned in the previous section, it is possible to start, stop, and restart with these commands:

```
pg_ctl start
pg_ctl stop
pg_ctl restart
```

### Connecting to the Database

Now you can check that the database is functioning by trying to connect to it. The psql utility is used to interact with the database system and perform simple administrative tasks such as creating users, creating databases, and creating tables. We will use it to create and populate the sample database later in the chapter, and it is covered in more detail in Chapter 5. For now, you can simply try to connect to a database. The response you get should show that you have postmaster running:

```
pg$ /usr/local/pgsql/bin/psql
psql: FATAL 1: Database "postgres" does not exist in the system catalog.
```

Don't be taken aback by the fatal error it displays. By default, psql connects to the database on the local machine and tries to open a database with the same name as the user running the program. We have not created a database called postgres, so the attempt fails. It does indicate, however, that postmaster is running and able to respond with details of the failure.

To specify a particular database to connect to, use the -d option to psql. A new PostgreSQL system does contain some databases that are used by the system as the base for new databases you might create. One such database is called template1. If you need to, you can connect to this database for administration purposes.

To check network connectivity, you can use psql installed on another machine on the network as a client, or any other PostgreSQL compatible application. With psql, you specify the host (either the name or IP address) with the -h option, and one of the system databases (as you haven't yet created a real database):

```
remote$ psql -h 192.168.0.111 -d template1
Welcome to psql 8.0.0, the PostgreSQL interactive terminal.

Type:  \copyright for distribution terms
       \h for help with SQL commands
       \? for help with psql commands
       \g or terminate with semicolon to execute query
       \q to quit

template1=# \q

remote$
```

## Configuring Automatic Startup

The final step you need to take is to arrange for the postmaster server process to be started automatically every time the machine is rebooted. Essentially, all you need to do is make sure that postmaster is run at startup. Again, there is little standardization between Linux and UNIX variants as to how this should be done. Refer to your installation's documentation for specific details.

If you have installed PostgreSQL from a Linux distribution, it is likely that the startup is already configured by the RPM packages you installed. On SuSE Linux, PostgreSQL is automatically started when the system enters multiuser mode, by a script in /etc/rc.d/init.d called postgresql.

If you are creating a startup script yourself, the easiest thing to do is create a simple shell script that starts postmaster with the parameters you need, and add a call to your script from one of the scripts that is run automatically at startup, such as those found in /etc/rc.d. Be sure that postmaster is run as the user postgres. Here is an example of a script that does the job for a default PostgreSQL installation built from source code:

```sh
#!/bin/sh

# Script to start and stop PostgreSQL

SERVER=/usr/local/pgsql/bin/postmaster
PGCTL=/usr/local/pgsql/bin/pg_ctl
PGDATA=/usr/local/pgsql/data
OPTIONS=-i
LOGFILE=/usr/local/pgsql/data/postmaster.log

case "$1" in
    start)
            echo -n "Starting PostgreSQL..."

            su -l postgres -c "nohup $SERVER $OPTIONS -D $PGDATA >$LOGFILE 2>&1 &"
            ;;
    stop)
            echo -n "Stopping PostgreSQL..."
            su -l postgres -c "$PGCTL -D $PGDATA stop"
            ;;
    *)
            echo "Usage: $0 {start|stop}"
            exit 1
            ;;
esac
exit 0
```

**Note** On Debian Linux, you may need to use su - in place of su -l.

Create an executable script file with this script in it. Call it, for example, MyPostgreSQL. Use the chmod command to make it executable, as follows:

```
# chmod a+rx MyPostgreSQL
```

Then you need to arrange that the script is called to start and stop PostgreSQL when the server boots and shuts down:

```
MyPostgreSQL start
MyPostgreSQL stop
```

For systems (such as many Linux distributions) that use System V type init scripting, you can place the script in the appropriate place. For SuSE Linux, for example, you would place the script in /etc/rc.d/init.d/MyPostgreSQL, and make symbolic links to it from the following places to automatically start and stop PostgreSQL as the server enters and leaves multiuser mode:

```
/etc/rc.d/rc2.d/S25MyPostgreSQL
/etc/rc.d/rc2.d/K25MyPostgreSQL
/etc/rc.d/rc3.d/S25MyPostgreSQL
/etc/rc.d/rc3.d/K25MyPostgreSQL
```

Refer to your system's documentation on startup scripts for more specific details.

## Stopping PostgreSQL

It is important that the PostgreSQL server process is shut down in an orderly fashion. This will allow it to write any outstanding data to the database and free up shared memory resources it is using.

To cleanly shut down the database, use the pg_ctl utility as postgres or root, like this:

```
# /usr/local/pgsql/bin/pg_ctl -D /usr/local/pgsql/data stop
```

If startup scripts are in place, you can use those, as in this example:

```
# /etc/rc.d/init.d/MyPostgreSQL stop
```

The scripts also make sure that the database is shut down properly when the machine is halted or rebooted.

---

### RESOURCES

To make life a little easier when dealing with PostgreSQL, it might be of some use to add the PostgreSQL applications directory to your execution path, and similarly the manual pages. To do this for the standard UNIX shell, place the following commands in your shell startup file (.profile or .bashrc):

```
PATH=$PATH:/usr/local/pgsql/bin
MANPATH=$MANPATH:/usr/local/pgsql/man
export PATH MANPATH
```

The source code for the current and latest test releases of PostgreSQL can be found at http://www.postgresql.org. More resources for PostgreSQL are listed in Appendix G of this book.

# Installing PostgreSQL on Windows

Let's begin this section with some good news for Windows users. Although PostgreSQL was developed for UNIX-like platforms, it was written to be portable. It has been possible for some time now to write PostgreSQL client applications for Windows, and from version 7.1 onwards, PostgreSQL could be compiled, installed, and run as a PostgreSQL server on Microsoft Windows NT 4, 2000, XP, and Server 2003.

With PostgreSQL version 8.0, a native Windows version is available, offering a Windows installer for both server and client software, which makes installing on Windows a breeze. Prior to version 8.0, Windows users needed to install some additional software to support some UNIX features on Windows.

---

■**Note** PostgreSQL 8.0 is supported on Windows 2000, Windows XP, and Windows Server 2003. It requires features not present in Windows 95, 98, and Me, so it will not run on those versions. It can be persuaded to run on Windows NT, but the installation must be performed by hand, as the PostgreSQL installer does not work correctly for Windows NT.

---

It may seem that an open-source platform like Linux would be the natural home of an open-source database like PostgreSQL. Indeed, we would not recommend running a production database on a desktop version of Windows, but installing on Windows can have its advantages. For example, having the PostgreSQL utilities like psql on the same machine as some client applications can be useful in testing new database installations and troubleshooting connection problems, even if you don't need to run the server on Windows. Running the database server on a development machine can avoid any potential problems with developers needing to share a server instance elsewhere.

## Using the Windows Installer

The installer for the Windows version of PostgreSQL is a separate PostgreSQL-related project with its home page at http://pgfoundry.org/projects/pginstaller. The latest version of the installer may be downloaded from the home page or one of the PostgreSQL mirror sites.

The installer is packaged as a Microsoft Windows Installer (.msi) file inside a ZIP archive. To run the installer, you will need version 2.0 or later of the Windows Installer. A suitable version is included with Windows XP and later. If necessary, the Windows Installer can be downloaded from http://www.microsoft.com (search for "Windows Installer redistributable").

The PostgreSQL MSI package has a filename similar to postgresql-8.0.0.msi. To start the installation wizard, just double-click this file to start the installer. After choosing a language to use for installation and reading the installation notes presented, you will see the installation options dialog box, as shown in Figure 3-3.

You can also use this dialog box to set the locations for the PostgreSQL applications and the PostgreSQL database files.

Click PostgreSQL, and then click Browse to set the location for the application installation (the default is C:\Program Files\PostgreSQL\8.0.0).

Click Data directory, and then click Browse to set the location of the database files (the default is C:\Program Files\PostgreSQL\8.0.0\data).

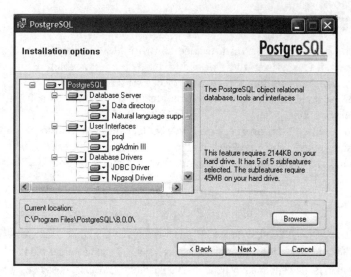

**Figure 3-3.** *PostgreSQL installation options*

The locations of other components can be similarly set if required; they will default to subfolders of the application installation folder. We recommend leaving them at their default locations.

Here, you can choose which components you need to install, depending on how you will use the machine on which PostgreSQL is being installed: as a database server, a client, a development machine, or a mixture. The installation options are summarized in Table 3-4.

**Table 3-4.** *PostgreSQL Installation Options*

| Option | Meaning |
| --- | --- |
| Database Server | The PostgreSQL database |
| Natural language support | Support for status and error messages in non-English languages |
| psql | The PostgreSQL command-line interface |
| pgAdmin III | A graphical PostgreSQL management console |
| JDBC Driver | The PostgreSQL JDBC driver for Java clients |
| Npgsql Driver | The PostgreSQL Microsoft .NET driver |
| ODBC Driver | The PostgreSQL ODBC driver |
| OLEDB Provider | The PostgreSQL OLEDB Provider |
| Documentation | HTML format documentation |
| Development | Support files and utilities for creating PostgreSQL clients |

The following are our recommendations for each type of setup:

- To set up a simple database server, it is sufficient to select the Database Server option. This will result in an installation that needs to be managed remotely from another machine. It is helpful to also include the `psql` command-line interface, even for a server-only installation.

- To set up a machine for managing a remote server, we suggest you choose the psql and pgAdmin III options. These can be installed independently of the database server.

- To set up a machine that will run applications that connect to a remote PostgreSQL database, choose the appropriate drivers. As mentioned in Chapter 2 and covered in more detail in Chapter 5, you can use the ODBC driver to connect applications such as Microsoft Access and Excel to PostgreSQL. Java and .NET applications need the JDBC and Npgsql drivers, respectively. The OLEDB Provider allows PostgreSQL to be used with OLEDB clients such as Microsoft Visual Studio.

- To set up a machine that will be used to develop client applications, such as those covered in Chapters 13 and 14, choose the Development option to install appropriate header files and libraries. You will also need a development environment such as Microsoft Visual Studio or Cygwin (`http://www.cygwin.com`) to compile your applications.

For our installation, we selected all of the available options.

The next step in the installation is to configure the database server to run as a service, as shown in Figure 3-4. This is the recommended option, as it will allow the PostgreSQL server to be automatically started when Windows is booted.

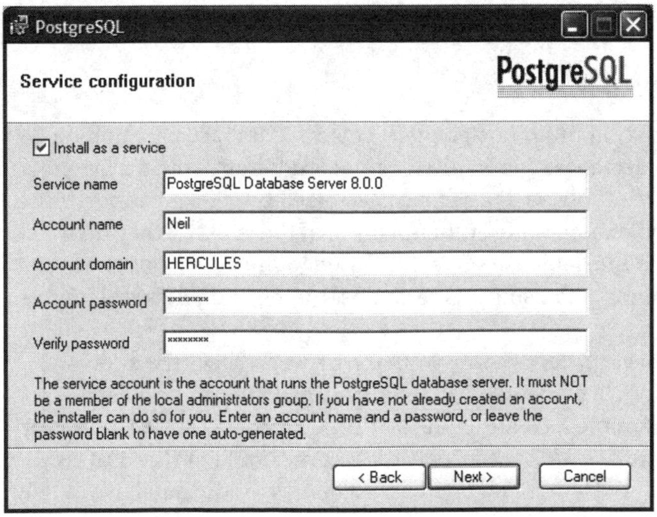

**Figure 3-4.** *PostgreSQL service configuration*

PostgreSQL must run as a non-administrator user. This avoids any potential security risk from running a service that accepts network connections as a user that has administrative privileges. In the unlikely event of security vulnerabilities in PostgreSQL being discovered and exploited, then only files and data managed by PostgreSQL would be at risk, rather than the entire server. You can either create an account on Windows for the purposes of running PostgreSQL or have the installer do it for you: just give an account name to the installer, and it will create it, if it does not already exist.

Next, initialize the PostgreSQL database, as shown in Figure 3-5. (Note that for an upgrade installation, it will not be necessary to perform the database initialization step, as you would normally want the existing database to be preserved.)

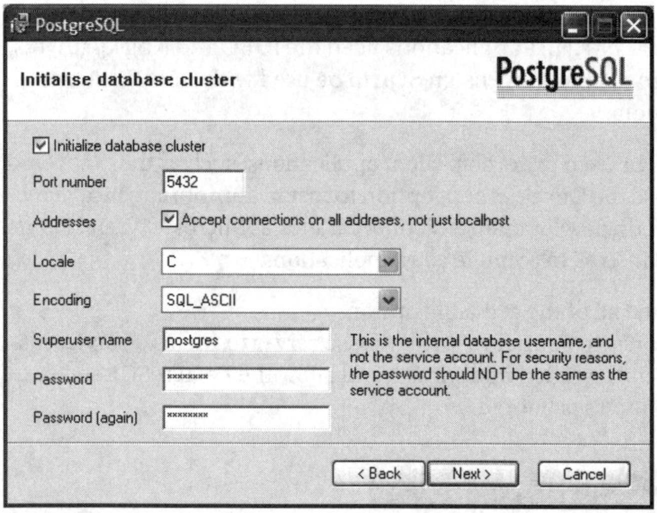

**Figure 3-5.** *PostgreSQL database initialization*

Here, you specify a superuser account for PostgreSQL. This is a database user that has permissions to create and manage databases within the server. It is different from the Windows account that is used to run the server. PostgreSQL accounts are used by clients connecting to the database, and PostgreSQL itself manages the authentication of these users; they do not need to have Windows accounts on the database server. As noted in the dialog box shown in Figure 3-5, there are security advantages to using a different username and password for the database superuser.

To allow the database server to accept connections from the network, check the Addresses check box. Without this selected, only clients running on the server machine will be able to connect. Although this option will start the server listening on the network, you still have control over who can connect and where from. We will cover client access configuration in the next section.

In our installation, we have left the locale and encoding schemes for the database at their default values. If you are installing a PostgreSQL database in an environment that requires the use of a specific character set or locale, these options can be set here. If you are not familiar with character sets and locales, then the defaults will probably work just fine.

In Chapter 9, we will cover stored procedures, which are functions that you can execute on the server to perform tasks more efficiently than in a client application. PostgreSQL supports stored procedures written in a variety of programming languages, including its own PL/pgSQL,

Perl, Python, and others. To run the examples in Chapter 9, you need to select the PL/pgSQL option in the next installation dialog box, Procedural Languages, shown in Figure 3-6.

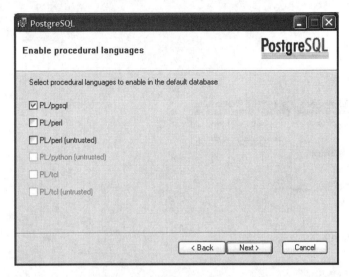

**Figure 3-6.** *PostgreSQL procedural languages*

The next installation dialog box deals with contributed modules, and its settings can safely be left at the defaults. (We do not cover these advanced topics in this book.)

The installation will now proceed and complete. The database server processes should be running. They will be visible as `postmaster.exe` and several `postgres.exe` processes in Task Manager, as shown in Figure 3-7.

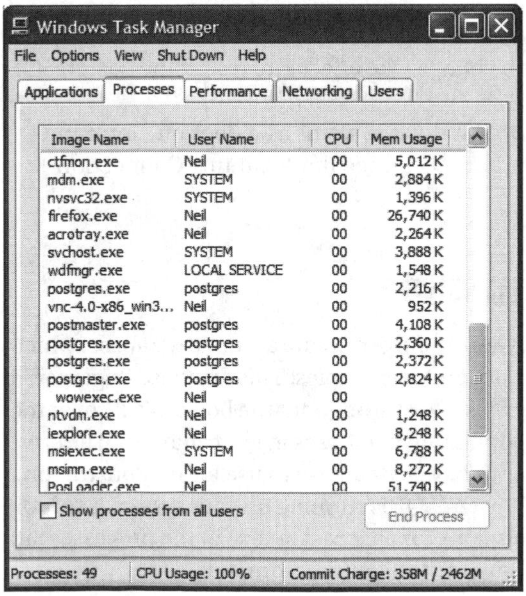

**Figure 3-7.** *PostgreSQL processes*

The PostgreSQL applications and utilities are installed in a new program group accessible from the Start menu, as shown in Figure 3-8.

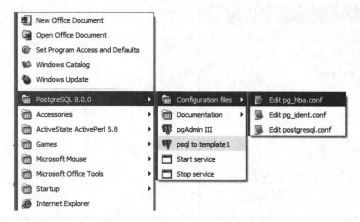

**Figure 3-8.** *PostgreSQL program menu*

## Configuring Client Access

To configure remote hosts and users that can connect to the PostgreSQL service, you need to edit the pg_hba.conf file. This file contains many comments that document the options available for remote access. In our sample installation, we want to allow users from any host on the local network to access all of the databases on our server. To do this, we add the following line at the end of the file:

```
host    all    all    192.168.0.0/16    trust
```

This means that all computers with an IP address that begins 192.168 can access all databases.

The simplest way to make this configuration change take effect is to restart the PostgreSQL server.

The pg_hba.conf file takes the same form on Windows systems as it does on Linux and UNIX systems. For other examples of configuration access, see the "Granting Connection Permissions" section earlier in this chapter.

# Creating the Sample Database

Now that we have PostgreSQL up and running, we are going to create a simple database, which we will call bpsimple, to support our customer order tables examples. This database (together with a variant called bpfinal created in Chapter 8) is used throughout the book. We'll cover the details of creating databases and creating and populating databases in later chapters. Here, we will just show the steps and SQL scripts, so that we have a database to use for demonstration.

Before we start, one simple way to check if PostgreSQL is running on your system is to look for the postmaster process. On Windows systems, look for postmaster.exe in the processes tab of Task Manager. On UNIX and Linux systems, run the following command:

```
$ ps -el | grep post
```

If there is a process running called postmaster (the name might be abbreviated in the display), then you are running a PostgreSQL server.

## Creating User Records

Before we can create a database, we need to tell PostgreSQL about the valid users by creating records for them within the system. Valid users of a PostgreSQL database system can read data, insert data, or update data; create databases of their own; and control access to the data those databases hold. To create user records, we use PostgreSQL's createuser utility.

On Linux and UNIX systems, use su (from root) to become the PostgreSQL user, postgres. Then run createuser to register the user. The user login name given is recorded as a valid PostgreSQL user. Let's give user rights to the (existing UNIX/Linux) user neil:

```
$ su
# su - postgres
pg$ /usr/local/pgsql/bin/createuser neil
Shall the new user be able to create databases? (y/n) y
Shall the new user be able to create new users (y/n) y
CREATE USER
pg$
```

On Windows systems, open a Command Prompt window and change the directory to the location of the PostgreSQL application (the default is C:\Program Files\PostgreSQL\8.0.0 in our installation). Then run the createuser.exe utility:

```
C:\Program Files\PostgreSQL\8.0.0\bin>createuser -U postgres -P neil
Enter password for new user:
Enter it again:
Shall the new user be allowed to create databases? (y/n) y
Shall the new user be allowed to create more new users? (y/n) y
Password:
CREATE USER
```

The -U option is used to specify the identity you want to use for creating the new user. It must be a PostgreSQL user with permission to create users, normally the PostgreSQL user you named when you performed the installation. The -P option causes createuser to prompt for a password for the new user.

Here, we have allowed neil to create new databases, and he is allowed to create new users. Some of the examples in the book use another user, rick, who also has permission to create databases, but does not have permission to create new users. If you would like to exactly replicate these examples, now is a good time to create this user.

Once you have created a PostgreSQL user with these rights, you will be able to create the bpsimple database.

## Creating the Database

To create the database on Linux and UNIX systems, change back to your own (non-root) login and run the following command:

```
$ /usr/local/pgsql/bin/createdb bpsimple
CREATE DATABASE
$
```

On Windows systems, run the `createdb.exe` command:

```
C:\Program Files\PostgreSQL\8.0.0\bin>createdb -U neil bpsimple
Password:
CREATE DATABASE
```

You should now be able to connect (locally) to the server, using the interactive terminal `psql`. On Linux and UNIX systems, use the following command:

```
$ /usr/local/pgsql/bin/psql -U neil -d bpsimple
Welcome to psql 8.0.0, the PostgreSQL interactive terminal.
...
bpsimple=#
```

On Windows systems, use this command:

```
C:\Program Files\PostgreSQL\8.0.0\bin>psql -U neil -d bpsimple
Password:
Welcome to psql 8.0.0, the PostgreSQL interactive terminal.

Type:  \copyright for distribution terms
       \h for help with SQL commands
       \? for help with psql commands
       \g or terminate with semicolon to execute query
       \q to quit

Warning: Console codepage (850) differs from windows codepage (1252)
         8-bit characters will not work correctly. See PostgreSQL
         documentation "Installation on Windows" for details.


bpsimple=#
```

Alternatively, you can select the Windows Start menu item `psql` to `template1`, and then change the database within `psql`:

```
template1=# \c bpsimple
You are now connected to database "bpsimple".
bpsimple=#
```

You are now logged into PostgreSQL, ready to execute some commands. To exit back to the shell, use the command \q.

Next, we will use a set of SQL statements to create and populate the sample database.

## Creating the Tables

You can create the tables in your bpsimple database by typing in the SQL commands that follow at the psql command prompt. However, it's easier to download the code bundle from the Downloads section of the Apress web site (http://www.apress.com), unpack it, and then execute the commands using \i <*filename*>. (The \i command in psql can be used to execute groups of SQL statements and other PostgreSQL commands stored in text files, called *scripts*.) The commands are just plain text, so you can always edit them with your preferred text editor if you want.

To run the create_tables-bpsimple.sql script to create the tables, enter the following:

```
bpsimple=# \i create_tables-bpsimple.sql
CREATE TABLE
...
bpsimple=#
```

It is a very good practice to script all database schema (tables, indexes, and procedures) statements. That way, if the database needs to be re-created, you can do that from the scripts. Scripts should also be used whenever the schema needs to be updated.

Here is the SQL for creating our tables (the ones we designed in Chapter 2), which you will find in create_tables-bpsimple.sql in the code bundle:

```
CREATE TABLE customer
(
    customer_id     serial                          ,
    title           char(4)                         ,
    fname           varchar(32)                     ,
    lname           varchar(32)         NOT NULL,
    addressline     varchar(64)                     ,
    town            varchar(32)                     ,
    zipcode         char(10)            NOT NULL,
    phone           varchar(16)                     ,
    CONSTRAINT      customer_pk PRIMARY KEY(customer_id)
);


CREATE TABLE item
(
    item_id         serial                          ,
    description     varchar(64)         NOT NULL,
    cost_price      numeric(7,2)                    ,
    sell_price      numeric(7,2)                    ,
    CONSTRAINT      item_pk PRIMARY KEY(item_id)
);
```

```
CREATE TABLE orderinfo
(
    orderinfo_id      serial                          ,
    customer_id       integer             NOT NULL,
    date_placed       date                NOT NULL,
    date_shipped      date                            ,
    shipping          numeric(7,2)                    ,
    CONSTRAINT        orderinfo_pk PRIMARY KEY(orderinfo_id)
);


CREATE TABLE stock
(
    item_id           integer             NOT NULL,
    quantity          integer             NOT NULL,
    CONSTRAINT        stock_pk PRIMARY KEY(item_id)
);


CREATE TABLE orderline
(
    orderinfo_id      integer             NOT NULL,
    item_id           integer             NOT NULL,
    quantity          integer             NOT NULL,
    CONSTRAINT        orderline_pk PRIMARY KEY(orderinfo_id, item_id)
);


CREATE TABLE barcode
(
    barcode_ean       char(13)            NOT NULL,
    item_id           integer             NOT NULL,
    CONSTRAINT        barcode_pk PRIMARY KEY(barcode_ean)
);
```

## Removing the Tables

If, at some later date, you wish to delete all the tables (also known as *dropping* the tables) and start again, you can. The command set is in the drop_tables.sql file, and looks like this:

```
DROP TABLE barcode;
DROP TABLE orderline;
DROP TABLE stock;
DROP TABLE orderinfo;
DROP TABLE item;
DROP TABLE customer;
```

```
DROP SEQUENCE customer_customer_id_seq;
DROP SEQUENCE item_item_id_seq;
DROP SEQUENCE orderinfo_orderinfo_id_seq;
```

Be warned, if you drop the tables, you also lose any data in them!

---

**■Note** The `drop_tables.sql` script also explicitly drops the special attributes, called *sequences*, that PostgreSQL uses to maintain the automatically incrementing `serial` columns. In PostgreSQL version 8.0 and later, these sequences will be automatically dropped when the relevant table is dropped, but we have retained the commands for compatibility with earlier versions.

---

If you run this script after creating the tables, then you should run the `create_tables-bpsimple.sql` script again before attempting to populate the tables with data.

## Populating the Tables

Last, but not least, we need to add some data to the tables, or *populate* the tables.

The sample data is in the code bundle available from the Apress web site, as `pop_tablename.sql`. If you choose to use your own data, your results will be different from the ones presented in the book. So, until you are confident, it's probably best to stick with our sample data.

The line wraps are simply a necessity of the fitting the commands on the printed page. You can type each command on a single line. You do need to include the terminating semicolon, which tells `psql` where each SQL command ends.

### Customer table

```
INSERT INTO customer(title, fname, lname, addressline, town, zipcode, phone)
VALUES('Miss','Jenny','Stones','27 Rowan Avenue','Hightown','NT2 1AQ','023 9876');
INSERT INTO customer(title, fname, lname, addressline, town, zipcode, phone)
VALUES('Mr','Andrew','Stones','52 The Willows','Lowtown','LT5 7RA','876 3527');
INSERT INTO customer(title, fname, lname, addressline, town, zipcode, phone)
VALUES('Miss','Alex','Matthew','4 The Street','Nicetown','NT2 2TX','010 4567');
INSERT INTO customer(title, fname, lname, addressline, town, zipcode, phone)
VALUES('Mr','Adrian','Matthew','The Barn','Yuleville','YV67 2WR','487 3871');
INSERT INTO customer(title, fname, lname, addressline, town, zipcode, phone)
VALUES('Mr','Simon','Cozens','7 Shady Lane','Oakenham','OA3 6QW','514 5926');
INSERT INTO customer(title, fname, lname, addressline, town, zipcode, phone)
VALUES('Mr','Neil','Matthew','5 Pasture Lane','Nicetown','NT3 7RT','267 1232');
INSERT INTO customer(title, fname, lname, addressline, town, zipcode, phone)
VALUES('Mr','Richard','Stones','34 Holly Way','Bingham','BG4 2WE','342 5982');
INSERT INTO customer(title, fname, lname, addressline, town, zipcode, phone)
VALUES('Mrs','Ann','Stones','34 Holly Way','Bingham','BG4 2WE','342 5982');
```

```
INSERT INTO customer(title, fname, lname, addressline, town, zipcode, phone)
VALUES('Mrs','Christine','Hickman','36 Queen Street','Histon','HT3 5EM','342 5432');
INSERT INTO customer(title, fname, lname, addressline, town, zipcode, phone)
VALUES('Mr','Mike','Howard','86 Dysart Street','Tibsville','TB3 7FG','505 5482');
INSERT INTO customer(title, fname, lname, addressline, town, zipcode, phone)
VALUES('Mr','Dave','Jones','54 Vale Rise','Bingham','BG3 8GD','342 8264');
INSERT INTO customer(title, fname, lname, addressline, town, zipcode, phone)
VALUES('Mr','Richard','Neill','42 Thatched Way','Winersby','WB3 6GQ','505 6482');
INSERT INTO customer(title, fname, lname, addressline, town, zipcode, phone)
VALUES('Mrs','Laura','Hardy','73 Margarita Way','Oxbridge','OX2 3HX','821 2335');
INSERT INTO customer(title, fname, lnamc, addressline, town, zipcode, phone)
VALUES('Mr','Bill','O\'Neill','2 Beamer Street','Welltown','WT3 8GM','435 1234');
INSERT INTO customer(title, fname, lname, addressline, town, zipcode, phone)
VALUES('Mr','David','Hudson','4 The Square','Milltown','MT2 6RT','961 4526');
```

### Item table

```
INSERT INTO item(description, cost_price, sell_price)
VALUES('Wood Puzzle', 15.23, 21.95);
INSERT INTO item(description, cost_price, sell_price)
VALUES('Rubik Cube', 7.45, 11.49);
INSERT INTO item(description, cost_price, sell_price)
VALUES('Linux CD', 1.99, 2.49);
INSERT INTO item(description, cost_price, sell_price)
VALUES('Tissues', 2.11, 3.99);
INSERT INTO item(description, cost_price, sell_price)
VALUES('Picture Frame', 7.54, 9.95);
INSERT INTO item(description, cost_price, sell_price)
VALUES('Fan Small', 9.23, 15.75);
INSERT INTO item(description, cost_price, sell_price)
VALUES('Fan Large', 13.36, 19.95);
INSERT INTO item(description, cost_price, sell_price)
VALUES('Toothbrush', 0.75, 1.45);
INSERT INTO itcm(description, cost_price, sell_price)
VALUES('Roman Coin', 2.34, 2.45);
INSERT INTO item(description, cost_price, sell_price)
VALUES('Carrier Bag', 0.01, 0.0);
INSERT INTO item(description, cost_price, sell_price)
VALUES('Speakers', 19.73, 25.32);
```

### Barcode table

```
INSERT INTO barcode(barcode_ean, item_id) VALUES('6241527836173', 1);
INSERT INTO barcode(barcode_ean, item_id) VALUES('6241574635234', 2);
INSERT INTO barcode(barcode_ean, item_id) VALUES('6264537836173', 3);
INSERT INTO barcode(barcode_ean, item_id) VALUES('6241527746363', 3);
INSERT INTO barcode(barcode_ean, item_id) VALUES('7465743843764', 4);
INSERT INTO barcode(barcode_ean, item_id) VALUES('3453458677628', 5);
```

```
INSERT INTO barcode(barcode_ean, item_id) VALUES('6434564564544', 6);
INSERT INTO barcode(barcode_ean, item_id) VALUES('8476736836876', 7);
INSERT INTO barcode(barcode_ean, item_id) VALUES('6241234586487', 8);
INSERT INTO barcode(barcode_ean, item_id) VALUES('9473625532534', 8);
INSERT INTO barcode(barcode_ean, item_id) VALUES('9473627464543', 8);
INSERT INTO barcode(barcode_ean, item_id) VALUES('4587263646878', 9);
INSERT INTO barcode(barcode_ean, item_id) VALUES('9879879837489', 11);
INSERT INTO barcode(barcode_ean, item_id) VALUES('2239872376872', 11);
```

### Orderinfo table

```
INSERT INTO orderinfo(customer_id, date_placed, date_shipped, shipping)
VALUES(3,'03-13-2000','03-17-2000', 2.99);
INSERT INTO orderinfo(customer_id, date_placed, date_shipped, shipping)
VALUES(8,'06-23-2000','06-24-2000', 0.00);
INSERT INTO orderinfo(customer_id, date_placed, date_shipped, shipping)
VALUES(15,'09-02-2000','09-12-2000', 3.99);
INSERT INTO orderinfo(customer_id, date_placed, date_shipped, shipping)
VALUES(13,'09-03-2000','09-10-2000', 2.99);
INSERT INTO orderinfo(customer_id, date_placed, date_shipped, shipping)
VALUES(8,'07-21-2000','07-24-2000', 0.00);
```

### Orderline table

```
INSERT INTO orderline(orderinfo_id, item_id, quantity) VALUES(1, 4, 1);
INSERT INTO orderline(orderinfo_id, item_id, quantity) VALUES(1, 7, 1);
INSERT INTO orderline(orderinfo_id, item_id, quantity) VALUES(1, 9, 1);
INSERT INTO orderline(orderinfo_id, item_id, quantity) VALUES(2, 1, 1);
INSERT INTO orderline(orderinfo_id, item_id, quantity) VALUES(2, 10, 1);
INSERT INTO orderline(orderinfo_id, item_id, quantity) VALUES(2, 7, 2);
INSERT INTO orderline(orderinfo_id, item_id, quantity) VALUES(2, 4, 2);
INSERT INTO orderline(orderinfo_id, item_id, quantity) VALUES(3, 2, 1);
INSERT INTO orderline(orderinfo_id, item_id, quantity) VALUES(3, 1, 1);
INSERT INTO orderline(orderinfo_id, item_id, quantity) VALUES(4, 5, 2);
INSERT INTO orderline(orderinfo_id, item_id, quantity) VALUES(5, 1, 1);
INSERT INTO orderline(orderinfo_id, item_id, quantity) VALUES(5, 3, 1);
```

### Stock table

```
INSERT INTO stock(item_id, quantity) VALUES(1,12);
INSERT INTO stock(item_id, quantity) VALUES(2,2);
INSERT INTO stock(item_id, quantity) VALUES(4,8);
INSERT INTO stock(item_id, quantity) VALUES(5,3);
INSERT INTO stock(item_id, quantity) VALUES(7,8);
INSERT INTO stock(item_id, quantity) VALUES(8,18);
INSERT INTO stock(item_id, quantity) VALUES(10,1);
```

With the PostgreSQL system running, the database created, and the tables made and populated, we are ready to continue our exploration of PostgreSQL features.

# Summary

In this chapter, we have taken a look at some of the options for installing PostgreSQL on Linux, UNIX-compatible systems, and Windows. The simplest way is probably to use some form of precompiled binary package. We provided step-by-step instructions for compiling, installing, and confirming a working installation on Linux systems from packages, UNIX-compatible systems from source code, and Windows systems using the Microsoft Windows installer.

Finally, we created a sample database that we will be using throughout the rest of the book to demonstrate the features of the PostgreSQL system. We'll begin in the next chapter by exploring how to access your data.

# CHAPTER 4

■ ■ ■

# Accessing Your Data

**S**o far in this book, our encounters with SQL have been rather informal. We have seen some statements that retrieve data in various ways, as well as some SQL for creating and populating tables.

In this chapter, we will take a slightly more formal look at SQL, starting with the SELECT statement. In fact, this whole chapter is devoted to the SELECT statement. Your first impression might be that a whole chapter on one part of SQL is a bit excessive, but the SELECT statement is at the heart of the SQL language. Once you understand SELECT, you really have done the hard part of learning SQL.

In the next chapter, we will talk about some of the GUI clients you can use, but for now, we will be using psql, a simple command-line tool that ships with PostgreSQL, to access the database.

In this chapter, we'll cover the following topics:

- Using the psql command to interact with the PostgreSQL database

- Using some simple SELECT statements for retrieving data

- Improving the output readability by overriding column names

- Controlling the order of rows in retrieved data

- Suppressing duplicate rows

- Performing mathematical calculations while retrieving data

- Aliasing table names for convenience

- Using pattern matching to specify what data to retrieve

- Making comparisons using various data types

- Retrieving data from multiple tables in a single SELECT statement

- Relating three or more tables in a SELECT statement

By now, you should have PostgreSQL up and running. Throughout this chapter, we will be using the sample database we designed in Chapter 2 and created and populated in Chapter 3.

# Using psql

Assuming you have followed the instructions in Chapter 3, you should now have a database called bpsimple, accessible from your normal PostgreSQL login prompt.

---

■**Caution**  You should never use the postgres user for accessing the PostgreSQL server, except in the special case of database administration.

---

## Starting Up on Linux Systems

If you are on a Linux system, and you created an ordinary user without a password, to start psql accessing the bpsimple database, you include your username in the connection command. For example, to access the database as user rick, you would enter:

```
$ psql -d bpsimple -U rick
```

You should see the following:

```
Welcome to psql, the PostgreSQL interactive terminal.

Type:  \copyright for distribution terms
       \h for help with SQL commands
       \? for help on internal slash commands
       \g or terminate with semicolon to execute query
       \q to quit

bpsimple=>
```

We are now ready to enter commands. If you created the user with a password, you may be prompted for a password, depending on the exact authentication configuration. We will explain more about authentication in Chapter 11.

## Starting Up on Windows Systems

If you are using Windows, begin by opening the Start menu and choosing the command psql to template1. You'll be prompted for the postgres user password. After successful connecting, switch to the bpsimple database and your own username (here, we show user rick) using the \c command, like this:

```
template1=# \c bpsimple rick
You are now connected to database "bpsimple" as user "rick".
bpsimple=>
```

Notice the prompt changes from =# to => to show that you no longer have permission to create databases.

Alternatively, you could create a shortcut for the menu command. For example, here we connect to a remote server (the -h option) on IP address 192.168.0.3, to database (the -d option) bpsimple, as the user rick (the -U option).

```
"C:\Program Files\PostgreSQL\8.0\bin\psql.exe" -h 192.168.0.3 -d bpsimple -U rick
```

Replace rick with postgres for a connection as the administrative user, and you can omit the -h option if the server is local.

## Resolving Startup Problems

If psql complains about pg_shadow, then you have not yet created the supplied username as a database user. If it complains about not knowing the username or lack of permissions, then you may not have granted permissions correctly. Refer to Chapter 3 for details on how to grant permissions.

If you have come unstuck, the easiest way to fix things at this stage is to delete the database and user, and then re-create them. To do so, exit the psql command using the command \q, which will return you to the command-line prompt (Linux) or close the Windows Command Prompt window.

Next, reconnect to the database server as the postgres user. In Linux, do this from the prompt like this:

```
$ psql -d template1
```

On Windows, use the Start menu command psql to template1.

Enter the password you used during the installation process, and you should see this prompt:

```
template1=#
```

Now delete the user database and the user (rick in this example) like this:

```
template1=# DROP DATABASE bpsimple;
DROP DATABASE
template1=# DROP USER rick;
DROP USER
template1=#
```

Next, re-create the user and choose a password (apress4789 in this example):

```
template1=# CREATE USER rick WITH CREATEDB PASSWORD 'apress4789';
CREATE USER
template1=#
```

The CREATEDB option allows users to create their own databases.

Now reconnect to the database, as your newly created user:

```
template1=# \c template1 rick
Password:
template1=#
```

You are now connected to database `template1` as your new user (again, `rick` in this example).

Next, create the `bpsimple` database:

```
template1=> CREATE DATABASE bpsimple;
CREATE DATABASE
template1=>
```

Reattach to the `bpsimple` database as the new user:

```
template1=> \c bpsimple rick
You are now connected to database "bpsimple" as user "rick".
bpsimple=>
```

You will then need to rerun the steps described at the end of the previous chapter, starting from the "Creating the Tables" section, in order to create the sample tables and data we will use in this chapter.

If you see an error message like this when trying to create the database:

```
ERROR:  source database "template1" is being accessed by other users
```

this means that there is some other session attached to the database `template1`—perhaps another `psql` session or a GUI tool such as pgAdmin III. Ensure your current `psql` session is the only one in use, and then try again.

To check if you have the tables created for the `bpsimple` database, enter \dt, and then press Return, and you should see output similar to this:

```
bpsimple=> \dt
            List of relations
 Schema |     Name    | Type  |  Owner
--------+-------------+-------+----------
 public | barcode     | table | rick
 public | customer    | table | rick
 public | item        | table | rick
 public | orderinfo   | table | rick
 public | orderline   | table | rick
 public | stock       | table | rick
(6 rows)

bpsimple=>
```

The Owner column will show your login name (`rick` in this example).

■**Note** You may see some tables with names such as pg_ts_dict, pg_ts_parser, pg_ts_cfg, and pg_ts_cfgmap. These are additional tables added by some optional user-contributed tools. You can safely ignore them.

You can see the same information in pgAdmin III by navigating to Databases, then bpsimple, then Schemas, then public, and then Tables, as shown in Figure 4-1.

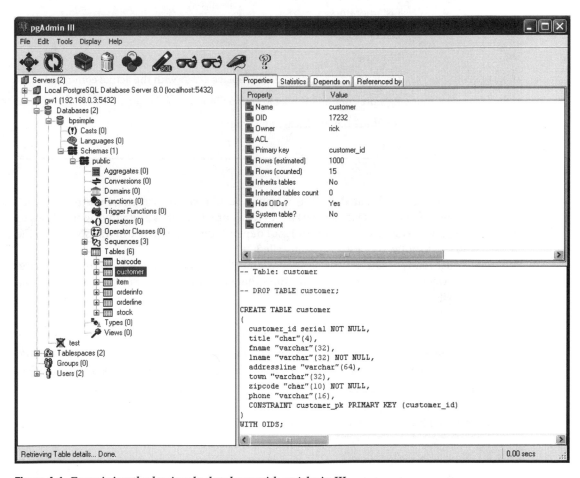

**Figure 4-1.** *Examining the bpsimple database with pgAdmin III*

We'll cover database and user management in considerable detail in Chapter 11.

## Using Some Basic psql Commands

We will use only a few basic psql commands in this chapter (we will meet the full set in Chapter 5). For now, the commands you need to know are listed in Table 4-1.

**Table 4-1.** *Basic psql Commands*

| Command | Description |
| --- | --- |
| \? | Get a help message |
| \do | List operators |
| \dt | List tables |
| \dT | List types |
| \h *<cmd>* | Get help on a SQL command; replace *<cmd>* with the actual command |
| \i *<filename>* | Execute commands read from the filename *<filename>* |
| \r | Reset the buffer (discard any typing) |
| \q | Quit psql |

Each of the commands listed in Table 4-1 must be followed by pressing Return (or Enter). You should also be able to use the arrow keys to recall previous lines and move within lines to edit them. On Linux systems, this feature of psql depends on the presence of the GNU readline facility, which is usually, but not always, installed.

Now we are ready to start accessing our PostgreSQL database using SQL commands. In the next chapter, we will meet some of the GUI tools that you can use with PostgreSQL, but in this chapter, we will use the psql tool.

---

■**Note** If you prefer to use the GUI tools, you may want to look ahead to Chapter 5 first. Then you can return to this chapter. You should be able to try all of the examples in this chapter from any GUI tool that allows you to type SQL directly to PostgreSQL, such as pgAdmin III (http://www.pgadmin.org/). However, we suggest working through at least this chapter with the command line, because it is often very handy to know the basics of accessing PostgreSQL using only a command-line tool.

---

# Using Simple SELECT Statements

As with all relational databases, we retrieve data from PostgreSQL using the SELECT statement. It's probably the most complex statement in SQL, but it really is at the heart of using relational databases effectively.

Let's start our investigation of SELECT by simply asking for all the data in a particular table. We do this by using a very basic form of the SELECT statement, specifying a list of columns and a FROM clause with a table name:

```
SELECT <comma-separated list of columns> FROM <table name>
```

If we can't remember what the exact column names are called, or want to see all the columns, we can just use an asterisk (*) in place of the column list.

---

■**Note** In this book, we show SQL keywords that structure the commands in uppercase in the text to make them stand out clearly. SQL is not case-sensitive, although a few implementations do make table names case-sensitive. Data stored in SQL databases is case-sensitive, so the character string "Newtown" is different from the character string "newtown".

---

### Try It Out: Select All Columns from a Table

We will start by fetching all the data from the item table:

```
SELECT * FROM item;
```

Remember that the semicolon (;) is for the benefit of psql, to tell it you have finished typing. Strictly speaking, it is not part of SQL. If you prefer, you can terminate SQL statements typed into psql with \g, which has the same effect as the semicolon. If you are using a different tool to send SQL to PostgreSQL, you may not need either of these terminators.

Enter the command, and you'll see PostgreSQL's response:

```
bpsimple=> SELECT * FROM item;
 item_id |  description  | cost_price | sell_price
---------+---------------+------------+------------
       1 | Wood Puzzle   |      15.23 |      21.95
       2 | Rubic Cube    |       7.45 |      11.49
       3 | Linux CD      |       1.99 |       2.49
       4 | Tissues       |       2.11 |       3.99
       5 | Picture Frame |       7.54 |       9.95
       6 | Fan Small     |       9.23 |      15.75
       7 | Fan Large     |      13.36 |      19.95
       8 | Toothbrush    |       0.75 |       1.45
       9 | Roman Coin    |       2.34 |       2.45
      10 | Carrier Bag   |       0.01 |       0.00
      11 | Speakers      |      19.73 |      25.32
(11 rows)
bpsimple=>
```

### How It Works

We simply asked PostgreSQL for all the data from all the columns in the item table, using an * for the column names. PostgreSQL gave us just that, but neatly arranged with column headings and a pipe (|) symbol to separate each column. It even told us how many rows we retrieved.

But suppose we didn't want all the columns? In general, you should ask PostgreSQL, or indeed any relational database, to retrieve only the data you actually want. Each column of each row that is retrieved adds a little extra work. There is no point in making the server do work unnecessarily; it's always nice to keep things clean and efficient.

You will also find that, once you start having SQL embedded in other languages (see Chapter 14), specifying exact columns will protect you against changes to the database schema. For example, if you use * to retrieve all columns and an additional column had been inserted in a table since the code was tested, you may find that you are processing data from a different column than the one you intended. If a column that you are using is deleted, then the SQL in your program will fail, since the column can no longer be retrieved; however, that is a much easier bug to find and correct than some application code accessing the wrong column while processing data. If you specify the columns by name, you have the option of searching all your code to see if the column names appear, before making changes to the database, and preventing bugs from ever occurring.

Let's try restricting the columns we retrieve. As we saw in the syntax earlier, we do this by specifying each column we want, separated by a comma. If we don't want the columns in the order we specified when we created the database table, that's fine—we can specify the columns in any order we like, and they will be returned in that order.

### Try It Out: Select Named Columns in a Specific Order

To retrieve the name of the town and last name of all our customers, we must specify the name of the columns for town and last name, and, of course, the table from which to retrieve them. Here is the statement we need and PostgreSQL's response:

```
bpsimple=> SELECT town, lname FROM customer;
    town    |  lname
------------+---------
 Hightown   | Stones
 Lowtown    | Stones
 Nicetown   | Matthew
 Yuleville  | Matthew
 Oakenham   | Cozens
 Nicetown   | Matthew
 Bingham    | Stones
 Bingham    | Stones
 Histon     | Hickman
 Tibsville  | Howard
 Bingham    | Jones
 Winersby   | Neill
 Oxbridge   | Hardy
 Welltown   | O'Neill
 Milltown   | Hudson
(15 rows)

bpsimple=>
```

**How It Works**

PostgreSQL returns all the data rows from the table we specified, but only from the columns we requested. It also returns the column data in the order in which we specified the columns in the SELECT statement.

# Overriding Column Names

You will notice that the output uses the database column name as the heading for the output. Sometimes, this is not very easy to read, particularly when the column in the output isn't an actual database column, so it has no name. There is a very simple syntax for specifying the display name (a column name *alias*) to use with each column, which is to add AS "*<display name>*" after each column in the SELECT statement. You can specify the names of all columns you select or just a few. Where you don't specify the name, PostgreSQL just uses the column name.

For example, to change the preceding output to add meaningful names, we would use this:

```
SELECT town, lname AS "Last Name" FROM customer;
```

We will see an example of this in use in the next section. It's worth noting that, in the SQL92 standard, the AS clause is optional; however, as of release 8.0, PostgreSQL still requires the AS keyword.

# Controlling the Order of Rows

So far, we have retrieved the data from the columns we wanted, but the data is not always in the most suitable order for viewing. The data we are seeing may look as though it is in the order we inserted it into the database, but that is probably simply because we have not been updating the data by inserting and deleting rows.

As we mentioned in Chapter 2, unlike in a spreadsheet, the order of rows in a database is unspecified. The database server is free to store rows in the most effective way, which is not usually the most natural way for viewing the data. The output you see is not sorted in any meaningful order, and the next time you ask for the same data, it could be displayed in a different order. Generally, the data will be returned in the order it is stored in the database internally. No SQL database, PostgreSQL included, is obliged to return the data in a particular order, unless you specifically request it to be ordered when you retrieve it.

We can control the order in which data is displayed from a SELECT statement by adding an ORDER BY clause to the SELECT statement, which specifies the order we would like the data to be returned. The syntax is as follows:

```
SELECT <comma-separated list of columns> FROM <table name> ORDER BY <column name>
[ASC | DESC]
```

The slightly strange-looking syntax at the end means that after the column name, we can write either ASC (short for ascending) or DESC (short for descending). By default, ascending order is used. The data is then returned to us ordered by the column we specified, sorted in the direction we requested.

**Try It Out: Order the Data**

In this example, we will sort the data by town, and we will also override the default column name for the lname column, similar to what we saw in the previous section, to make the output slightly easier to read.

Here is the command we require and PostgreSQL's response:

```
bpsimple=> SELECT town, lname AS "Last Name" FROM customer ORDER BY town;
   town     | Last Name
------------+------------
 Bingham    | Stones
 Bingham    | Stones
 Bingham    | Jones
 Hightown   | Stones
 Histon     | Hickman
 Lowtown    | Stones
 Milltown   | Hudson
 Nicetown   | Matthew
 Nicetown   | Matthew
 Oakenham   | Cozens
 Oxbridge   | Hardy
 Tibsville  | Howard
 Welltown   | O'Neill
 Winnersby  | Neill
 Yuleville  | Matthew
(15 rows)

bpsimple=>
```

Notice that since we want the data in ascending order, we can omit the ASC, as ascending is the default sort order. As you can see, the data is now sorted in ascending order by town.

**How It Works**

This time, we made two changes to our previous statement. We added an AS clause to change the name of the second column to Last Name, which makes it easier to read, and we also added an ORDER BY clause to specify the order in which PostgreSQL should return the data to us.

Sometimes, we need to go a little further and order the data by more than a single column. For example, in the previous output, although the data is ordered by town, there is not much order in the Last Name. We can see, for example, that Jones is listed after Stones under all the customers found in the town Bingham.

We can more precisely order the output by specifying more than one column in the ORDER BY clause. If we want to, we can even specify that the order is ascending for one column and descending for another column.

**Try It Out: Order the Data Using ASC and DESC**

Let's try our SELECT again, but this time, we will sort the town names into descending order, and then sort the last names into ascending order where rows share the same town name.

The statement we need and PostgreSQL's response are as follows:

```
bpsimple=> SELECT town, lname AS 'Last Name' FROM customer
ORDER BY town DESC, lname ASC;
   town       | Last Name
--------------+-----------
 Yuleville    | Matthew
 Winnersby    | Neill
 Welltown     | O'Neill
 Tibsville    | Howard
 Oxbridge     | Hardy
 Oakenham     | Cozens
 Nicetown     | Matthew
 Nicetown     | Matthew
 Milltown     | Hudson
 Lowtown      | Stones
 Histon       | Hickman
 Hightown     | Stones
 Bingham      | Jones
 Bingham      | Stones
 Bingham      | Stones
(15 rows)
bpsimple=>
```

**How It Works**

As you can see, PostgreSQL first orders the data by town in descending order, which was the first column we specified in our ORDER BY clause. It then orders those entries that have multiple last names for the same town in an ascending order. This time, although Bingham is now last in the rows retrieved, the last names of our customers in that town are ordered in an ascending fashion.

Usually, the columns by which you can order the output are restricted, not unreasonably, to columns you have requested in the output. PostgreSQL, at least in the current version, does not enforce this standard restriction, and it will accept a column in the ORDER BY clause that is not in the selected column list. However, this is nonstandard SQL, and we suggest that you avoid relying on this feature.

# Suppressing Duplicates

You may have noticed that there are several duplicate rows in the previous output. For example, the following town and last name rows appear twice:

```
Nicetown  | Matthew
Bingham   | Stones
```

What's going on here? In the original data, there are indeed two customers in Nicetown named Matthew and two customers in Bingham named Stones. For reference, here are the rows, showing the first names as well:

```
Nicetown  | Matthew | Alex
Nicetown  | Matthew | Neil
Bingham   | Stones  | Richard
Bingham   | Stones  | Ann
```

When PostgreSQL listed two rows for Nicetown and Matthew, and two rows for Bingham and Stones, it was quite correct. There are two customers in each of those towns with the same last names. They look exactly the same because we did not ask for the columns that distinguish them.

The default behavior is to list all the rows, but that is not always what we want. For example, we might want just a list of towns where we have customers, perhaps to determine where we should build distribution centers. Based on our knowledge so far, we might reasonably try this:

```
bpsimple=> SELECT town FROM customer ORDER BY town;
    town
-----------
 Bingham
 Bingham
 Bingham
 Hightown
 Histon
 Lowtown
 Milltown
 Nicetown
 Nicetown
 Oakenham
 Oxbridge
 Tibsville
 Welltown
 Winersby
 Yuleville
(15 rows)

bpsimple=>
```

PostgreSQL has listed all the towns, once for each time a town appeared in the customer table. This is correct, but it's probably not quite the listing we would like. What we actually need is a list where each town appeared just once; in other words, a list of distinct towns.

In SQL, you can suppress duplicate rows by adding the keyword DISTINCT to the SELECT statement. The syntax is as follows:

```
SELECT DISTINCT <comma-separated list of columns> FROM <table name>
```

As with pretty much all the clauses on SELECT, you can combine this with other clauses, such as renaming columns or specifying an order.

**Try It Out: Use DISTINCT**

Let's get a list of all the towns that appear in our customer table, without duplicates. We can try the following code to get the response:

```
bpsimple=> SELECT DISTINCT town FROM customer;
    town
-----------
 Bingham
 Hightown
 Histon
 Lowtown
 Milltown
 Nicetown
 Oakenham
 Oxbridge
 Tibsville
 Welltown
 Winersby
 Yuleville
(12 rows)

bpsimple=>
```

**How It Works**

The DISTINCT keyword tells PostgreSQL to remove all duplicate rows. Notice that the output is now ordered by town. This is because of the way PostgreSQL has chosen to implement the DISTINCT clause for your data. In general, you cannot assume the data will be sorted in this way. If you want the data sorted in a particular way, you must add an ORDER BY clause to specify the order.

Notice that the DISTINCT clause is not associated with a particular column. You can suppress only rows that are duplicated in all the columns you select, not suppress duplicates of a particular column. For example, suppose that we used this form:

```
SELECT DISTINCT town, fname FROM customer;
```

We would again get 15 rows, because there are 15 different town and first name combinations.

A word of warning is in order here: Although it might look like a good idea to always use DISTINCT with SELECT, in practice, this is a bad idea for two reasons. First, by using DISTINCT, you are asking PostgreSQL to do significantly more work in retrieving your data and checking for duplicates. Unless you know there will be duplicates that need to be removed, you shouldn't use the DISTINCT clause. The second reason is a bit more pragmatic. Occasionally, DISTINCT will mask errors in your data or SQL that would have been easy to spot if duplicate rows had been displayed.

---

■**Caution** Use DISTINCT only where you actually need it, because it requires more work and may mask errors.

---

# Performing Calculations

We can also perform simple calculations on data in the rows we retrieve before sending them to the output.

Suppose we wanted to display the cost price of items in our `item` table. We could just execute `SELECT` as shown here:

```
bpsimple=> SELECT description, cost_price FROM item;
  description   | cost_price
----------------+------------
 Wood Puzzle    |      15.23
 Rubic Cube     |       7.45
 Linux CD       |       1.99
 Tissues        |       2.11
 Picture Frame  |       7.54
 Fan Small      |       9.23
 Fan Large      |      13.36
 Toothbrush     |       0.75
 Roman Coin     |       2.34
 Carrier Bag    |       0.01
 Speakers       |      19.73
(11 rows)

bpsimple=>
```

Suppose we wanted to see the price in cents. We can do a simple calculation in SQL, like this:

```
bpsimple=> SELECT description, cost_price * 100 FROM item;
  description   | ?column?
----------------+----------
 Wood Puzzle    |  1523.00
 Rubic Cube     |   745.00
 Linux CD       |   199.00
 Tissues        |   211.00
 Picture Frame  |   754.00
 Fan Small      |   923.00
 Fan Large      |  1336.00
 Toothbrush     |    75.00
 Roman Coin     |   234.00
 Carrier Bag    |     1.00
 Speakers       |  1973.00
(11 rows)

bpsimple=>
```

It seems a little weird, with the decimal points and the strange column name, so let's get rid of the decimal points by using a SQL function, and also explicitly name the resulting column. We use the `cast` function to change the type of the column, which, in conjunction with an `AS` clause to name the column, gives us the better-looking output:

```
bpsimple=> SELECT description, cast((cost_price * 100) AS int AS "Cost Price"
FROM item;
description    | Cost Price
---------------+---------------
Wood Puzzle    |        1523
Rubic Cube     |         745
Linux CD       |         199
Tissues        |         211
Picture Frame  |         754
Fan Small      |         923
Fan Large      |        1336
Toothbrush     |          75
Roman Coin     |         234
Carrier Bag    |           1
Speakers       |        1973
(11 rows)

bpsimple=>
```

We'll talk more about the cast function later in this chapter, in the "Setting the Time and Date Style" section.

# Choosing the Rows

So far in this chapter, we have always worked with all the rows of data, or at least all the distinct rows. It's time to look at how we can choose the specific rows we want to see. You probably won't be surprised to learn that we do this with yet another clause on the SELECT statement: the WHERE clause.

The simplified syntax for WHERE is as follows:

```
SELECT <comma-separated list of columns> FROM <table name> WHERE <conditions>
```

There are many possible conditions, which can also be combined by the keywords AND, OR, and NOT.

The standard comparison operators used in conditions are listed in Table 4-2. The comparison operators can be used on most types, both numeric and string, although there are some special conditions when working with dates, which we will see later in this chapter.

**Table 4-2.** *Standard Comparison Operators*

| Operator | Description |
|----------|-------------|
| <        | Less than |
| <=       | Less than or equal to |
| =        | Equal to |
| >=       | Greater than or equal to |
| >        | Greater than |
| <>       | Not equal to |

We will start with a simple condition, choosing to retrieve rows for people who live in the town Bingham:

```
bpsimple=> SELECT town, lname, fname FROM customer WHERE town = 'Bingham';
town    | lname  | fname
--------+--------+----------
Bingham | Stones | Richard
Bingham | Stones | Ann
Bingham | Jones  | Dave
(3 rows)

bpsimple=>
```

That was pretty straightforward, wasn't it? Notice the single quotes round the string Bingham, which are needed to make it clear that this is a string. Also notice that because Bingham is being matched against data in the database, it is case-sensitive. If we had used ... town = 'bingham', no data would have been returned.

We can have multiple conditions, combined using AND, OR, and NOT, with parentheses to make the expression clear. We can also use conditions on columns that don't appear in the list of columns we have selected. You will remember that this generally isn't true for clauses such as ORDER BY.

### Try It Out: Use Operators

Let's try a more complicated set of conditions. Suppose we want to see the names of our customers who do not have a title of Mr., but do live in either Bingham or Nicetown. Here is the statement we need and PostgreSQL's response:

```
bpsimple=> SELECT title, fname, lname, town FROM customer WHERE title <> 'Mr'
bpsimple-> AND (town = 'Bingham' OR town = 'Nicetown');
title | fname | lname   | town
------+-------+---------+----------
 Miss | Alex  | Matthew | Nicetown
 Mrs  | Ann   | Stones  | Bingham
(2 rows)

bpsimple=>
```

### How It Works

Although it might look a little complex at first glance, this statement is actually quite simple. The first part is just our usual SELECT, listing the columns we want to see in the output. After the WHERE clause, we initially check that the title is not Mr. Then, using AND, we check that another condition is true. This second condition is that the town is either Bingham or Nicetown. Notice that we need to use parentheses to make it clear how the clauses are to be grouped.

You should be aware that PostgreSQL, or any other relational database, is not under any obligation to process the clauses in the order you write them in the SQL statement. All that is promised is that the result will be the correct answer to the SQL "question." Generally, relational databases have sophisticated optimizers, which look at the request, and then determine the optimal way to satisfy it. Optimizers are not perfect, and you will very occasionally come across statements that run better when rewritten in different ways. For reasonably simple statements like this one, we can safely assume the optimizer will do a good job.

---

■**Tip**  If you want to know how PostgreSQL will process a SQL statement, you can get it to tell you by prefixing the SQL with EXPLAIN. Rather than execute the statement, PostgreSQL will tell you how the statement would be processed.

---

## Using More Complex Conditions

One of the things that we frequently need to do when working with strings is to allow partial matching. For example, we may be looking for a person named Robert, but the name may have been shortened in the database to Rob or Bob. There are some special operations in SQL that make working with strings, either partial ones or lists of strings, easier.

The first new condition is IN, which allows us to check against a list of items, rather than using a string of OR conditions. Consider the following:

```
SELECT title, fname, lname, town FROM customer WHERE title <> 'Mr' AND
(town = 'Bingham' OR town = 'Nicetown');
```

We can rewrite this as follows:

```
SELECT title, fname, lname, town FROM customer WHERE title <> 'Mr' AND
town IN ('Bingham', 'Nicetown');
```

We will get the same result, although it's possible the output rows could be in a different order, since we did not use an ORDER BY clause. There is no particular advantage in using the IN clause in this case, except for the simplification of the expression. When we meet subqueries in Chapter 7, we will use IN again, as it offers more advantages in those situations.

The next new condition is BETWEEN, which allows us to check a range of values by specifying the endpoints. Suppose we wanted to select the rows with customer_id values between 5 and 9. Rather than write a sequence of OR conditions, or an IN with many values, we can simply write this:

```
bpsimple=> SELECT customer_id, town, lname FROM customer WHERE customer_id
BETWEEN 5 AND 9;
customer_id |   town   | lname
-------------+----------+---------
          5 | Oahenham | Cozens
          6 | Nicetown | Matthew
          7 | Bingham  | Stones
          8 | Bingham  | Stones
          9 | Histon   | Hickman
(5 rows)
bpsimple=>
```

It's also possible to use BETWEEN with strings; however, you need to be careful, because the answer may not always be exactly what you were expecting, and you must know the case, since, as mentioned earlier, string comparisons are case-sensitive.

### Try It Out: Use Complex Conditions

Let's try a BETWEEN statement, comparing strings. Suppose we wanted a distinct list of all the towns that start with letters between *B* and *N*. All of the towns in the customer table start with a capital letter, so we might write the following:

```
bpsimple=> SELECT DISTINCT town FROM customer WHERE town BETWEEN 'B' AND 'N';
   town
----------
 Bingham
 Hightown
 Histon
 Lowtown
 Milltown
(5 rows)

bpsimple=>
```

If you look at these results closely, you'll see that this SQL doesn't work as expected. Where is Newtown? It certainly starts with an *N*, but it hasn't been listed.

### Why It Didn't Work

The reason this statement didn't work is that PostgreSQL, as per the SQL standard, pads the string you give it with blanks until it is the same length as the string it is checking against. So when the comparison arrived at Newtown, PostgreSQL compared *N*     (*N* followed by six spaces) with Newtown, and because whitespace appears in the ASCII table before all the other letters, it decided the Newtown came after *N*    , so it shouldn't be included in the list.

### How to Make It Work

It's actually quite easy to make this work as expected. Either we need to prevent the behavior of adding blanks to the search string by adding some additional *z* characters after the *N* or search using the next letter in the alphabet, *O*, in the BETWEEN clause. Of course, if there were a town called *O*, we would then erroneously retrieve it, so you need to be careful using this method. It's generally better to use *z* rather than *Z*, because *z* appears after *Z* in the ASCII table. Thus, our SQL should read as follows:

```
SELECT DISTINCT town FROM customer WHERE town BETWEEN 'B' AND 'Nz';
```

Notice that we didn't add a z after the B, because the B string being padded with blanks does work to find all towns that start with a *B*, since it is the starting point, rather than the endpoint. Also if there were a town that started with the letters *Nzz*, we would again fail to find it, because we would then compare Nz against Nzz, and decide that Nzz came after Nz, because the third string location would have been padded to a space, which comes before the z in the third place of the string we are comparing against.

This type of matching has rather subtle behavior, so if you do use BETWEEN with strings, always think carefully about exactly what is being matched.

# Pattern Matching

The string-comparison operations we have seen until now are fine as far as they go, but they don't help very much with real-world string pattern matching. The SQL condition for pattern matching is LIKE.

Unfortunately, LIKE uses a different set of string-comparison rules from all other programming languages we know. However, as long as you remember the rules, it's easy enough to use. When comparing strings with LIKE, you use a percent sign (%) to mean any string of characters, and you use an underscore (_) to match a single character. For example, to match towns beginning with the letter *B*, we would write this:

```
... WHERE town LIKE  'B%'
```

To match first names that end with e, we would write this:

```
... WHERE fname LIKE '%e';
```

To match first names that are exactly four characters long, we would use four underscore characters, like this:

```
... WHERE fname LIKE '_ _ _ _';
```

We can also combine the two types in a single string.

### Try It Out: Pattern Matching

Let's find all the customers who have first names that have an *a* as the second character. Here is the SQL statement to achieve this:

```
bpsimple=> SELECT fname, lname FROM customer WHERE fname LIKE '_a%';
fname | lname
------+--------
Dave  | Jones
Laura | Hardy
David | Hudson
(3 rows)

bpsimple=>
```

### How It Works

The first part of the pattern, _a, matches strings that start with any single character, then have a lowercase *a*. The second part of the pattern, %, matches any remaining characters. If we didn't use the trailing %, only strings exactly two characters long would have been matched.

## Limiting the Results

In the examples we have been using so far, the number of result rows returned has always been quite small, because we have only a few sample rows in our sample database. In a real-world database we could easily have many thousands of rows that match the selection criteria. If we are working on our SQL, refining our statements, we almost certainly do not want to see many thousands of rows scrolling past on our screen. A few sample rows to check our logic would be quite sufficient.

PostgreSQL has an extra clause on the SELECT statement, LIMIT, which is not part of the SQL standard but is very useful when we want to restrict the number of rows returned.

If you append LIMIT and a number to your SELECT clause, only rows up to the number you specified will be returned, starting from the first row. A slightly different way to use LIMIT is in conjunction with the OFFSET clause, which specifies a starting position.

It's easier to show it in action than to describe it. Here we display only the first five matching rows:

```
bpsimple=> SELECT customer_id, town FROM customer LIMIT 5;
 customer_id |   town
-------------+-----------
           1 | Hightown
           2 | Lowtown
           3 | Nicetown
           4 | Yuleville
           5 | Oahenham
(5 rows)

bpsimple=>
```

The following skips the first two result rows, then returns the next five rows:

```
bpsimple=> SELECT customer_id, town FROM customer LIMIT 5 OFFSET 2;
 customer_id |   town
-------------+-----------
           3 | Nicetown
           4 | Yuleville
           5 | Oahenham
           6 | Nicetown
           7 | Bingham
(5 rows)

bpsimple=>
```

It's also possible to use OFFSET on its own, like this:

```
bpsimple=> SELECT customer_id, town FROM customer OFFSET 12;
 customer_id |   town
-------------+----------
          13 | Oxbridge
          14 | Welltown
          15 | Milltown
(3 rows)

bpsimple=>
```

If you want to combine LIMIT with other SELECT clauses, the LIMIT clause should always appear after the normal SELECT statement, followed only by the OFFSET clause, if you use it.

# Checking for NULL

So far, we do not know a way of checking to see if a column contains a NULL value. We can check if it equals a value or string, or if it doesn't equal a value or string, but that's not sufficient.

You will remember from Chapter 2 that NULL is a special column value that means either unknown or not relevant. We need to look at checking for NULL separately, because it requires special consideration to ensure that the results are as expected.

Suppose we have an integer column tryint in a table testtab that we know stores 0, 1, or NULL. We can check if it is 0 by writing this:

```
SELECT * FROM testtab WHERE tryint = 0;
```

We can check if it is 1 by writing this:

```
SELECT * FROM testtab WHERE tryint = 1;
```

We need another check to see if the value is NULL. PostgreSQL supports the standard SQL syntax for checking whether a value is NULL. We do this with the use of IS NULL, like this:

```
SELECT * FROM testtab WHERE tryint IS NULL;
```

Notice that we use the keyword IS rather than an = sign.

We can also test to see if the value is something other than NULL by adding a NOT to invert the test:

```
SELECT * FROM testtab WHERE tryint IS NOT NULL;
```

Why do we suddenly need this extra bit of syntax? You are probably familiar with two-valued logic, where everything is either true or false. What is happening here is that we have stumbled into *three-value logic*, with true, false, and unknown.

Unfortunately, this property of NULL, being unknown, has some other effects outside the immediate concern of checking for NULL.

Suppose we ran our statement on a table where some values of tryint were NULL:

```
SELECT * FROM testtab WHERE tryint = 1;
```

What does our tryint = 1 mean when tryint is actually NULL? We are asking the question, "Is unknown equal to 1?" This is interesting, because we can't know that the statement is false, but neither can we know it to be true. So the answer must be unknown, hence the rows where NULL appears are not matched. If we reversed the test, and compared tryint != 1, the rows with NULL would also not be found, because that condition would not be true either. This can be confusing, because we have apparently used two tests, with opposite conditions, and still not retrieved all the rows from the table.

It's important to be aware of these issues with NULL, because it's all too easy to forget about NULL values. If you start getting slightly unexpected results when using conditions on a column that can have NULL values, verify whether the rows consisting of the NULL value are the cause of your problems.

# Checking Dates and Times

PostgreSQL has two basic types for handling date and time information: timestamp, which holds both a date and a time; and date, which holds day, month, and year information. PostgreSQL has some built-in functions that help us work with dates and time, which are traditionally rather difficult units to manipulate. Here, we'll concentrate on those that are most commonly used. (You can find all of the built-in functions listed in the online documentation.)

Before we start, we need to tackle one of those apparently trivial problems that can so easily cause confusion: how do we specify a date?

When we write the date 1/2/2005, what do we mean? Europeans generally mean the first day of February 2005, but Americans usually mean the second day of January 2005. This is because Europeans generally read dates as *DD/MM/YYYY*, but Americans expect *MM/DD/YYYY*. Just to add to the confusion, the ISO standard 8601 (officially adopted in Europe as European Standard EN 28601) specifies the logical (but rarely seen in everyday use) date format *YYYY-MM-DD*.

PostgreSQL lets you change the way dates are handled to suit your local needs, so before we get into checking dates and time, it's probably sensible to look at how you control this aspect of PostgreSQL's behavior.

## Setting the Time and Date Style

Unfortunately, PostgreSQL's method of setting the way the date and time are handled is, at first sight at least, a little strange.

There are two things you can control:

- The order in which days and months are handled, United States or European style

- The display format; for example, numbers only or more textual date output

The unfortunate part of the story is that PostgreSQL uses the same variable to handle both settings, which frankly, can be a bit confusing. The good news is that PostgreSQL defaults to using the unambiguous ISO-8601 style date and time output, which is always written in the form *YYYY-MM-DD hh:mm:ss.ssTZD*. This gives you the year, month, day, hours, minutes, seconds, decimal part of a second to two places, and a time zone designator, which indicates a plus or minus number of hours difference between local time and UTC. For example, a full date and time would look like 2005-02-01 05:23:43.23+5, which equates to February 1, 2005, at 23 minutes and 43.23 seconds past five o'clock in the morning, and the time zone used is five hours ahead of UTC. If you specify the time in UTC, with no time zone, the standard says you should use a *Z* (pronounced "Zulu") to indicate this, although it seems common to omit the *Z*.

For input in the form *NN/NN/NNNN*, PostgreSQL defaults to expecting the month before the day (United States style). For example, 2/1/05 is the first of February. Alternatively, you can use a format like February 1, 2005, or the ISO style 2005-02-01. If that behavior is all you need, you are in luck—you don't need to know any more about controlling how PostgreSQL accepts and displays dates, and you can skip ahead to the next section on date and time functions.

The default style is actually controlled by the postgresql.conf file, in the data directory, which has a line of the form datestyle = 'iso, mdy'. So, you could change the default globally, if you wish.

If you need more control over how dates are handled, PostgreSQL does allow this, but it can be a little tricky. The confusing thing is that there are two independent features to control, and you set them both using datestyle. Do remember, however, that this is all to do with presentation. Internally, PostgreSQL stores dates in a way totally independent of any representation that users expect when data is input or retrieved.

The syntax as a command to psql is as follows:

```
SET datestyle TO 'value';
```

To set the order in which months and days are handled, you set the datestyle value to either US, for month-first behavior (02/01/1997, for February 1) or European for day-first behavior (01/02/1997 for February 1).

To change the display format, you also set datestyle, but to one of four different values:

- ISO for the ISO-8601 standard, using - as the field separator, as in 1997-02-01

- SQL for the traditional style, as in 02/01/1997

- Postgres for the default PostgreSQL style, as in Sat Feb 01

- German for the German style, as in 01.02.1997

---

■**Note** In the current release, the Postgres format defaults to displaying in SQL style for both date and timestamps.

---

You set the datestyle variable to the value pair by separating the values with a comma. So, for example, to specify that we want dates shown in SQL style, but using the European convention of day before month, we use this setting:

```
SET datestyle TO 'European, SQL';
```

Rather than set the date-handling style locally in session, you can set it for an entire installation, or set the default for a session. If you want to set the default style for date input for a complete installation, you can set the environment variable PGDATESTYLE before starting the `postmaster` master server process. Setting the same options using the environment variable in Linux, we would use the following:

```
PGDATESTYLE="European, SQL"
export PGDATESTYLE
```

A much better way of changing the default date handling is to edit the configuration file `postgresql.conf` (found in the `data` subdirectory of your installation), and set an option such as `datestyle='European, SQL'` or `datestyle = 'iso, mdy'`, depending on your preferences. You will need to restart the PostgreSQL server after making this change for it to become effective.

If you want to set the date style for individual users, you use the same environment variable, but set for the `local` user, before `psql` is invoked. A local setting will override any global setting you have made.

Before we demonstrate how this all works, it's very handy to remember the special PostgreSQL function `cast`, which allows you to convert one format into another. We saw it briefly earlier in this chapter, when we looked at doing calculations in the `SELECT` statement, but there is much more to it than the simple conversion to integer we saw earlier. Although PostgreSQL does a pretty good job of getting types correct, and you shouldn't need conversion functions often, they can be very useful occasionally. The conversion we need to use to investigate our date and time values is the following to get a date:

```
cast('string' AS date)
```

Alternatively, to get a value that includes a time:

```
cast('string' AS timestamp)
```

We are also going to use a little trick to demonstrate this function more easily. Almost every time you use the `SELECT` statement, you will be fetching data from a table. However, you can use `SELECT` to get data that isn't in a table at all, as in this example:

```
bpsimple=> SELECT 'Fred';
?column?
--------------
 Fred
(1 row)

bpsimple=>
```

PostgreSQL is warning us that we haven't selected any columns, but it is quite happy to accept the `SELECT` syntax without a table name, and just returns the string we specified.

We can use the same feature, in conjunction with `cast`, to see how PostgreSQL treats dates and time, without needing to create a temporary table to experiment with.

**Try It Out: Set Date Formats**

We start off with the environment variable `PGDATESTYLE` unset, so you can see the default behavior, and then set the date style, so you can see how things progress. We enter a date in ISO format, so this is always a safe option, and PostgreSQL outputs in the same format. There is no ambiguity in either of these statements:

```
bpsimple=> SELECT cast('2005-02-1' AS date);
?column?
------------
2005-02-01
(1 row)
bpsimple=>
```

Changing the style to US and SQL format, we still enter the date in ISO style, which is unambiguous; it's still the first of February, but now the output shows the more conventional, but possibly ambiguous, United States style *MM/DD/YYYY* output:

```
bpsimple=> SET datestyle TO 'US, SQL';
SET VARIABLE
bpsimple=> SELECT cast('2005-02-1' AS date);
?column?
------------
02/01/2005
(1 row)
bpsimple=>
```

Now is a good time to also ask psql what the internal variable datestyle is set to:

```
bpsimple=> SHOW datestyle;
 DateStyle
-----------
 SQL, MDY
(1 row)
bpsimple=>
```

In older versions of PostgreSQL, the output was more verbose, so you may see something slightly different, depending on which version of PostgreSQL you are using.

Now let's try some more formats:

```
bpsimple=> SET datestyle TO 'European, SQL';
SET
bpsimple=> SELECT cast('2005 02 1' AS date);
    date
------------
 01/02/2005
(1 row)

bpsimple=>
```

With the output set to European, the display changes to *DD/MM/YYYY*.

Let's go back to ISO input and output:

```
bpsimple=> SET datestyle TO 'European, ISO';
SET
bpsimple=> SELECT cast('2005-02-1' AS date);
    date
------------
 2005-02-01
(1 row)

bpsimple=>
```

The European setting has no effect, because ISO is the same for all locales.

Now let's consider times. We use the timestamp type, which displays time:

```
bpsimple=> SELECT cast('2005-02-1' AS timestamp);
        ?column?
-----------------------
 2005-02-01 00:00:00
(1 row)

bpsimple=>
```

We didn't specify any hours or minutes, so they all default to zero.

Let's try PostgreSQL-style output:

```
bpsimple=> SET datestyle TO 'European, Postgres';
SET
bpsimple=> SELECT cast('2005-02-1' AS timestamp);
        timestamp
--------------------------
 Tue 01 Feb 00:00:00 2005
(1 row)

bpsimple=>
```

This produces output that is unambiguous and rather more reader-friendly.

**How It Works**

As you can see, we can vary the way both dates and times are displayed, as well as how ambiguous input strings, such as 01/02/2005, are interpreted.

Time zones are much simpler than date formats. Providing that your local environment variable TZ or configuration option in postgresql.conf is correctly set, PostgreSQL will manage time zones without further ado.

## Using Date and Time Functions

Now that we have seen how dates work, we can look at a couple of useful functions you might need when comparing dates:

- date_part(*units required, value to use*) allows you to extract a particular component of a date, such as the month.

- now simply gets the current date and time, and is equivalent to the more standard "magic variable" current_timestamp.

Suppose we wanted to select the rows from our orderinfo table where the date the order was placed is in September. We know September is the ninth month; therefore, we just ask the following:

```
bpsimple=> SELECT * FROM orderinfo WHERE date_part('month',date_placed)=9;
 orderinfo_id | customer_id | date_placed | date_shipped | shipping
--------------+-------------+-------------+--------------+----------
            3 |          15 | 02-09-2004  | 12-09-2004   |     3.99
            4 |          13 | 03-09-2004  | 10-09-2004   |     2.99
(2 rows)

bpsimple=>
```

PostgreSQL extracts the appropriate rows for us. Note the date is being displayed in ISO format. We can extract the following parts from a date or timestamp:

- Year

- Month

- Day

- Hour

- Minute

- Second

We can also compare dates, using the same operators that we can use with numbers: <>, <=, <, >, >=, and =. Here is an example:

```
bpsimple=> SELECT * FROM orderinfo WHERE date_placed >= cast('2004 07 21' AS date);
 orderinfo_id | customer_id | date_placed | date_shipped | shipping
--------------+-------------+-------------+--------------+----------
            3 |          15 | 02-09-2004  | 12-09-2004   |     3.99
            4 |          13 | 03-09-2004  | 10-09-2004   |     2.99
            5 |           8 | 21-07-2004  | 24-07-2004   |     0.00
(3 rows)

bpsimple=>
```

Notice that we need to convert our string to a date, using the cast operation, and that we stick to the unambiguous ISO style dates.

The second function, now, simply gives us the current date and time, which would be handy if, for example, we were adding a new row for an order being placed while the customer was on the phone, or in real time over the Internet.

```
bpsimple=> SELECT now(), current_timestamp;
              now               |            timestamptz
--------------------------------+-----------------------------------
 Sat 16 Oct 13:46:05.99938 2004 BST | Sat 16 Oct 13:46:05.99938 2004 BST
(1 row)

bpsimple=>
```

We can also do simple calculations using dates. For example, to discover the number of days between an order being placed and shipped, we could use a query like this:

```
bpsimple=> SELECT date_shipped - date_placed FROM orderinfo;
 ?column?
---------
        4
        1
       10
        7
        3
(5 rows)

bpsimple=>
```

This returns the number of days between the two dates stored in the database.

---

■**Note** More extensive details on PostgreSQL's handling of dates, times, time zones, and related conversion functions can be found in the online documentation.

---

# Working with Multiple Tables

By now, you should have a good idea of how we can select data from a table, picking which columns we want, which rows we want, and how to control the order of the data. We have also seen how to perform simple calculations, make type conversions, and handle the rather special date and time formats.

It's now time to move on to one of the most important features of SQL, and indeed, relational databases in general: relating data in one table to data in another table automatically. The good news is that it's all done with the SELECT statement, and everything that you have learned so far about SELECT is just as true with many tables as it was with a single table.

## Relating Two Tables

Before we look at the SQL for using many tables at the same time, let's have a quick recap of the material we saw in Chapter 2 about relating tables.

You will remember that we have a customer table, which stores details of our customers, and an orderinfo table, which stores details of the orders they have placed. This allows us to store details of each customer only once, no matter how many orders they placed. We linked the two tables together by having a common piece of data, the customer_id, stored in both tables.

If we think about this as a picture, we could imagine a row in the customer table, which has a customer_id, being related to none, one, or many rows in the orderinfo table, where the same customer_id value appears, as illustrated in Figure 4-2.

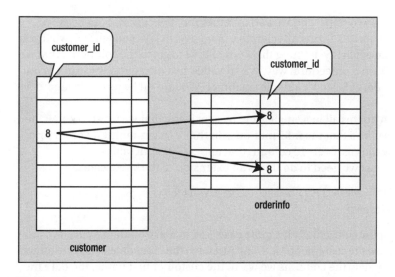

**Figure 4-2.** *The customer table and orderinfo table relationship*

We could say that the value 8 for customer_id in the row in the customer table relates to two rows in the orderinfo table, where the column customer_id also appears. Of course, we didn't need to have the two columns with the same name, but given that they both store the customer's ID, it would have been very confusing, and inconsistent, to give them different names.

Suppose we wanted to find all the orders that had been placed by our customer Ann Stones. Logically, what we do is first look in our customer table to find this customer:

```
bpsimple=> SELECT customer_id FROM customer WHERE fname = 'Ann'
AND lname = 'Stones';
customer_id
-------------
          8
(1 row)

bpsimple=>
```

Now that we know the customer_id, we can check for orders from this customer:

```
bpsimple=> SELECT * FROM orderinfo WHERE customer_id = 8;
 orderinfo_id | customer_id | date_placed | date_shipped | shipping
--------------+-------------+-------------+--------------+----------
            2 |           8 | 23-06-2004  | 24-06-2004   |     0.00
            5 |           8 | 21-07-2004  | 24-07-2004   |     0.00
(2 rows)
```

```
bpsimple=>
```

This worked, but it took two steps, and we had to remember the customer_id between steps. As we explained in Chapter 2, SQL is a declarative language; that is, you tell SQL what you want to achieve, rather than explicitly defining the steps of how to get to the solution. What we have just done is to use SQL in a procedural way. We specified two discrete steps to get to our answer and discover the orders placed by a single customer. Wouldn't it be more elegant to do it all in one step?

Indeed, in SQL we can do this all in a single step, by specifying that we want to know the orders placed by Ann Stones and that the information is in the customer table and orderinfo table, which are related by the customer_id column that appears in both tables.

The new bit of SQL syntax we need to do this is an extension to the WHERE clause:

```
SELECT <column list> FROM <table list> WHERE <join condition>
AND <row-selection conditions>
```

That looks a little complex, but actually it's quite easy. Just to make our first example a little simpler, let's assume we know the customer ID is 8, and just fetch the order date(s) and customer first name(s). We need to specify the columns we want, the customer first name, the date the order was placed, that the two tables are related by customer_id column, and that we want only rows where the customer_id is 8.

You will immediately realize we have a slight problem. How do we tell SQL which customer_id we want to use: the one in the customer table or the one in the orderinfo table? Although we are about to check that they are equal, this might not always be the case, so how do we handle columns whose name appears in more than one table? We simply specify the column name using the extended syntax: *tablename.columnname*. We can then unambiguously describe every column in our database.

In general, PostgreSQL is quite forgiving, and if a column name appears in only one table in the SELECT statement, we don't need to explicitly use the table name as well. In this case, we will use customer.fname, even though fname would have been sufficient, because it's a little easier to read, especially when you are learning SQL. The first part of our statement, therefore, needs to be:

```
SELECT customer.fname, orderinfo.date_placed FROM customer, orderinfo
```

That indicates to PostgreSQL the columns and tables we wish to use.

Now we need to specify our conditions. We have two different conditions: that the customer_id is 8 and that the two tables are related, or joined, using customer_id. Just as we saw earlier with multiple conditions, we do this by using the keyword AND to specify multiple conditions that must all be true:

```
WHERE customer.customer_id = 8 AND customer.customer_id = orderinfo.customer_id;
```

Notice that we need to tell SQL a specific `customer_id` column, using the
*tablename.columnname* syntax, even though, in practice, it would not matter which of the two
tables' `customer_id` column were checked against 8, since we also specify that they must have
the same value. Putting it all together, the statement we need is as follows:

```
bpsimple=> SELECT customer.fname, orderinfo.date_placed
 FROM customer, orderinfo
 WHERE customer.customer_id = 8
 AND customer.customer_id = orderinfo.customer_id;


 fname | date_placed
-------+-------------
 Ann   | 2004-06-23
 Ann   | 2004-07-21
(2 rows)


bpsimple=>
```

It's much more elegant than multiple steps, isn't it? Perhaps more important, by specifying the
entire problem in a single statement, we allow PostgreSQL to fully optimize the way the data
is retrieved.

**Try It Out: Relate Tables**

Now we know the principle, let's try our original question and find all the orders placed by Ann
Stones, assuming we don't know the `customer_id`.

We now only know a name, rather than a customer ID; therefore, our SQL is slightly more
complex. We must specify the customer by name:

```
bpsimple=> SELECT customer.fname, orderinfo.date_placed
FROM customer, orderinfo
WHERE customer.fname = 'Ann' AND customer.lname = 'Stones'
AND customer.customer_id = orderinfo.customer_id;
 fname | date_placed
-------+-------------
 Ann   | 2004-06-23
 Ann   | 2004-07-21
(2 rows)


bpsimple=>
```

**How It Works**

Just as we saw in our earlier example, we specify the columns we want, (`customer.fname`,
`orderinfo.date_placed`), the tables involved (`customer`, `orderinfo`), the selection conditions
(`customer.fname = 'Ann' AND customer.lname = 'Stones'`), and how the two tables are related
(`customer.customer_id = orderinfo.customer_id`).

SQL does the rest for us. It doesn't matter if the customer has placed no orders, one order, or many orders. SQL is perfectly happy to execute the SQL query, provided it's valid, even if there are no rows that match the condition.

Let's now look at another example. Suppose we want to list all the products we have, with their barcodes. You will remember that barcodes are held in the barcode table, and items are stored in the item table. The two tables are related by having an item_id column in each table. You may also remember that the reason we split this out into two tables is that many products, or items, actually have multiple barcodes.

Using our newfound expertise in joining tables, we know that we need to specify the columns we want, the tables, and how they are related, or joined together. Being confident, we also decide to order the result by the cost price of the item:

```
bpsimple=> SELECT description, cost_price, barcode_ean FROM item, barcode
  WHERE barcode.item_id = item.item_id ORDER BY cost_price;
 description   | cost_price |  barcode_ean
---------------+------------+----------------
 Toothbrush    |       0.75 | 6241234586487
 Toothbrush    |       0.75 | 9473625532534
 Toothbrush    |       0.75 | 9473627464543
 Linux CD      |       1.99 | 6264537836173
 Linux CD      |       1.99 | 6241527746363
 Tissues       |       2.11 | 7465743843764
 Roman Coin    |       2.34 | 4587263646878
 Rubic Cube    |       7.45 | 6241574635234
 Picture Frame |       7.54 | 3453458677628
 Fan Small     |       9.23 | 6434564564544
 Fan Large     |      13.36 | 8476736836876
 Wood Puzzle   |      15.23 | 6241527836173
 Speakers      |      19.73 | 9879879837489
 Speakers      |      19.73 | 2239872376872
(14 rows)

bpsimple=>
```

This looks reasonable, except several items seem to appear more than once, and we don't remember stocking two different speakers. Also, we don't remember stocking that many items. What's going on here?

Let's count the number of items we stock, using our newfound SQL skills:

```
bpsimple=> SELECT * FROM item;
```

PostgreSQL responds with the data, showing 11 rows. (More experienced SQL users would use the more efficient SELECT count(*) FROM item; this function is introduced in Chapter 7.)

We stock only 11 items, but our earlier query found 14 rows. Did we make a mistake?

No, all that's happened is that for some items, such as Toothbrush, there are many different barcodes against a single product. PostgreSQL simply repeated the information from the item table against each barcode, so that it listed all the barcodes and the item each one belonged to.

You can check this out by also selecting the item ID, by adding it to the SELECT statement, like this:

```
bpsimple=> SELECT item.item_id, description, cost_price, barcode_ean
  FROM item, barcode
  WHERE barcode.item_id = item.item_id ORDER BY cost_price;
 item_id |  description  | cost_price |  barcode_ean
---------+---------------+------------+---------------
       8 | Toothbrush    |       0.75 | 6241234586487
       8 | Toothbrush    |       0.75 | 9473625532534
       8 | Toothbrush    |       0.75 | 9473627464543
       3 | Linux CD      |       1.99 | 6264537836173
       3 | Linux CD      |       1.99 | 6241527746363
       4 | Tissues       |       2.11 | 7465743843764
       9 | Roman Coin    |       2.34 | 4587263646878
       2 | Rubic Cube    |       7.45 | 6241574635234
       5 | Picture Frame |       7.54 | 3453458677628
       6 | Fan Small     |       9.23 | 6434564564544
       7 | Fan Large     |      13.36 | 8476736836876
       1 | Wood Puzzle   |      15.23 | 6241527836173
      11 | Speakers      |      19.73 | 9879879837489
      11 | Speakers      |      19.73 | 2239872376872
(14 rows)

bpsimple=>
```

Notice that we have specified precisely which table item_id comes from, since it appears in the item table as well as the barcode table.

It is now clear what exactly is going on. If the data you get returned from a SELECT statement looks a little odd, it's often a good idea to add all the id type columns to the SELECT statement, just to see what is happening.

## Aliasing Table Names

Earlier in the chapter, we saw how we could change column names in the output using AS to give more descriptive names. It's also possible to alias table names, if you wish. This is handy in a few special cases, where you need two names for the same table, but more commonly, it is used to save on typing. You will also see it used frequently in GUI tools, where it makes SQL generation a little easier.

To alias a table name, you simply put the alias name immediately after the table name in the FROM part of the SQL clause. Once you have done this, you can use the alias name, rather than the real table name, in the rest of the SQL statement.

Suppose we had this simple SQL statement:

```
SELECT lname FROM customer;
```

As we saw earlier, you can explicitly name the column by preceding it with the table name, like this:

```
SELECT customer.lname FROM customer;
```

If we alias the `customer` table to cu, we could instead prefix the column with cu like this:

```
SELECT cu.lname FROM customer cu;
```

Notice that we have added a cu directly after the table name, as well as prefixing the column with cu.

When a single table is involved, aliasing table names is not very interesting. With multiple tables, it starts to be a bit more useful. Consider our earlier query:

```
SELECT customer.fname, orderinfo.date_placed FROM customer, orderinfo WHERE
customer.fname = 'Ann' AND customer.lname = 'Stones' AND customer.customer_id =
orderinfo.customer_id;
```

With aliases for table names, we could write this as follows:

```
SELECT cu.fname, oi.date_placed FROM customer cu, orderinfo oi
WHERE cu.fname = 'Ann'
AND cu.lname = 'Stones' AND cu.customer_id = oi.customer_id;
```

Aliases table names can be useful both to make the SQL clearer and to avoid typing long table names many times in a complex query.

## Relating Three or More Tables

Now that we know how to relate two tables together, can we extend the idea to three or even more tables? Yes, we can. SQL is a very logical language, so if we can do something with *N* items, we can almost always do it with *N*+1 items. Of course, the more tables you include, the more work PostgreSQL needs to do, so queries with many tables can be rather slow, especially if many of the tables have very large numbers of rows.

Suppose we wanted to relate customer information to actual item IDs ordered?

If you look at our schema in Figure 4-3, you will see we need to use three tables to get from the customer to the actual ordered items: `customer`, `orderinfo`, and `orderline`. Redrawing our earlier diagram with three tables, it would look like Figure 4-4.

Here, we can see that customer 123 matches several rows in the `orderinfo` table—those with `orderinfo` IDs of 579, 426, 723, and 114—and each of these, in turn, relates to one or more rows in the `orderline` table. Notice that there is no direct relationship between `customer` and `orderline`. We must use the `orderinfo` table, since that contains the information that binds the customers to their orders.

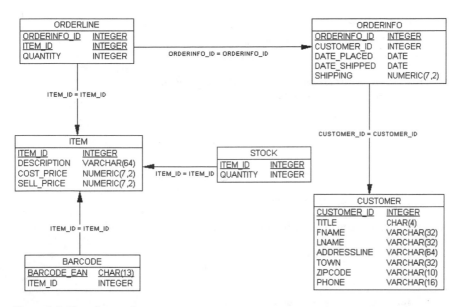

**Figure 4-3.** *Database schema*

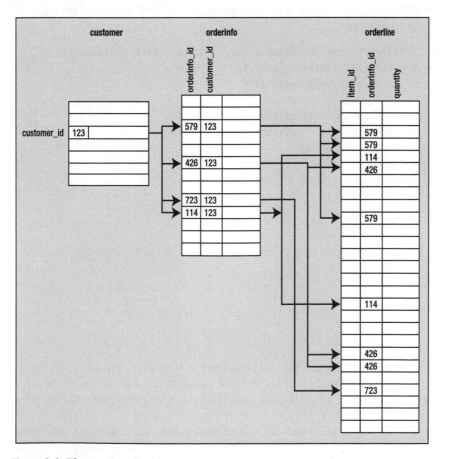

**Figure 4-4.** *Three related tables*

**Try It Out: Join Multiple Tables**

Let's first build a three-table join to discover the item_ids for
Ann Stones's orders. We start with the columns we need:

```
SELECT customer.fname, customer.lname, orderinfo.date_placed,
  orderline.item_id, orderline.quantity
```

Then we list the tables involved:

```
FROM customer, orderinfo, orderline
```

Then we specify how the customer and orderinfo tables are related:

```
WHERE customer.customer_id = orderinfo.customer_id
```

We must also specify how the orderinfo and orderline tables are related:

```
orderinfo.orderinfo_id = orderline.orderinfo_id
```

Now our conditions:

```
customer.fname = 'Ann' AND customer.lname = 'Stones';
```

Putting them all together, and spreading the typing over several lines (notice the bpsimple ->
continuation prompt), we get this:

```
bpsimple=> SELECT customer.fname, customer.lname, orderinfo.date_placed,
bpsimple-> orderline.item_id,orderline.quantity
bpsimple-> FROM customer, orderinfo, orderline
bpsimple-> WHERE
bpsimple-> customer.customer_id = orderinfo.customer_id AND
bpsimple-> orderinfo.orderinfo_id = orderline.orderinfo_id AND
bpsimple-> customer.fname = 'Ann' AND
bpsimple-> customer.lname = 'Stones';
 fname | lname  | date_placed | item_id | quantity
-------+--------+-------------+---------+----------
 Ann   | Stones | 2004-06-23  |       1 |        1
 Ann   | Stones | 2004-06-23  |       4 |        2
 Ann   | Stones | 2004-06-23  |       7 |        2
 Ann   | Stones | 2004-06-23  |      10 |        1
 Ann   | Stones | 2004-07-21  |       1 |        1
 Ann   | Stones | 2004-07-21  |       3 |        1
(6 rows)

bpsimple=>
```

Notice that whitespace outside strings is not significant to SQL, so we can add extra spaces
and line breaks to make the SQL easier to read. The psql program just issues a continuation
prompt, bpsimple->, and waits till it sees a semicolon before it tries to interpret what we have
been typing.

Having seen how easy it is to go from two tables to three tables, let's take our query a step
further and list all the items by description that our customer Ann Stones has ordered. To do this,

we need to use an extra table, the item table, to get at the item description. The rest of the query however, is pretty much as before:

```
bpsimple=> SELECT customer.fname, customer.lname, orderinfo.date_placed,
bpsimple-> item.description, orderline.quantity
bpsimple-> FROM customer, orderinfo, orderline, item
bpsimple-> WHERE
bpsimple-> customer.customer_id = orderinfo.customer_id AND
bpsimple-> orderinfo.orderinfo_id = orderline.orderinfo_id AND
bpsimple-> orderline.item_id = item.item_id AND
bpsimple-> customer.fname = 'Ann' AND
bpsimple-> customer.lname = 'Stones';
 fname | lname  | date_placed | description | quantity
-------+--------+-------------+-------------+----------
 Ann   | Stones | 2004-06-23  | Wood Puzzle |        1
 Ann   | Stones | 2004-06-23  | Tissues     |        2
 Ann   | Stones | 2004-06-23  | Fan Large   |        2
 Ann   | Stones | 2004-06-23  | Carrier Bag |        1
 Ann   | Stones | 2004-07-21  | Wood Puzzle |        1
 Ann   | Stones | 2004-07-21  | Linux CD    |        1
(6 rows)

bpsimple=>
```

**How It Works**

Once you have seen how three-table joins work, it's not difficult to extend the idea to more tables. We added the item description to the list of columns to be shown, added the item table to the list of tables to select from, and added the information about how to relate the item table to the tables we already had, orderline.item_id = item.item_id. You will notice that Wood Puzzle is listed twice, since it was purchased on two different occasions.

In this SELECT, we have displayed at least one column from each of the tables we used in our join. There is actually no need to do this. If we had just wanted the customer name and item description, we could have simply chosen not to retrieve the columns we didn't need.

A version retrieving fewer columns is just as valid, and may be marginally more efficient than our earlier attempt:

```
SELECT customer.fname, customer.lname, item.description
FROM customer, orderinfo, orderline, item
WHERE
    customer.customer_id = orderinfo.customer_id AND
    orderinfo.orderinfo_id = orderline.orderinfo_id AND
    orderline.item_id = item.item_id AND
    customer.fname = 'Ann' AND
    customer.lname = 'Stones';
```

To conclude this example, let's go back to something we learned early in the chapter: how to remove duplicate information using the DISTINCT keyword.

### Try It Out: Add Extra Conditions

Suppose we want to discover what type of items Ann Stones bought. All we want listed are the descriptions of items purchased, ordered by the description. We don't even want to list the customer name, since we know that already (we are using it to select the data). We need to select only the item.description, and we also need to use the DISTINCT keyword, to ensure that Wood Puzzle is listed only once, even though it was bought several times:

```
bpsimple=> SELECT DISTINCT  item.description
bpsimple-> FROM customer, orderinfo, orderline, item
bpsimple-> WHERE
bpsimple-> customer.customer_id = orderinfo.customer_id AND
bpsimple-> orderinfo.orderinfo_id = orderline.orderinfo_id AND
bpsimple-> orderline.item_id = item.item_id AND
bpsimple-> customer.fname = 'Ann' AND
bpsimple-> customer.lname = 'Stones'
bpsimple-> ORDER BY item.description;
 description
-------------
 Carrier Bag
 Fan Large
 Linux CD
 Tissues
 Wood Puzzle
(5 rows)

bpsimple=>
```

### How It Works

We simply take our earlier SQL, remove the columns we no longer need, add the DISTINCT keyword after SELECT to ensure each row appears only once, and add our ORDER BY condition after the WHERE clause.

That's one of the great things about SQL: once you have learned a feature, it can be applied in a general way. ORDER BY, for example, works with many tables in just the same way as it works with a single table.

# The SQL92 SELECT Syntax

You may have noticed that the WHERE clause actually has two slightly different jobs. It specifies the conditions to determine which rows we wish to retrieve (customer.fname = 'Ann') but also specifies how multiple tables relate to each other (customer.customer_id = orderinfo.customer_id).

This didn't really cause anyone any problems for many years, until the SQL standards committee tried to extend the syntax to help handle the increasingly complex jobs to which SQL was being put. When the SQL92 standard was released, a new form of the SELECT statement syntax was added to separate these two subtly different uses. This new syntax (sometimes referred to as the SQL92/99 syntax, or the ANSI syntax) was surprisingly slow to catch on with many SQL databases. Microsoft was an early adopter in SQL Server 6.5, and PostgreSQL added support in version 7.1, but it took Oracle till version 9 to support the new syntax.

The new syntax uses the JOIN … ON syntax to specify how tables relate, leaving the WHERE clause free to concentrate on which rows to select. The new syntax moves the linking of tables into the FROM section of the SELECT statement, away from the WHERE clause. So the syntax changes from this:

```
SELECT <column list> FROM <table list>
    WHERE <join condition> <row-selection conditions>
```

to this:

```
SELECT <column list> FROM <table> JOIN <table> ON <join condition>
    WHERE <row-selection conditions>
```

It's easier than it looks—really! Suppose we wanted to join the customer and orderinfo tables, which share a common key of customer_id. Instead of writing the following:

```
FROM customer, orderinfo WHERE customer.customer_id = orderinfo.customer_id
```

we would write this:

```
FROM customer JOIN orderinfo ON customer.customer_id = orderinfo.customer_id
```

This is slightly more long-winded, but it is both clearer and an easier syntax to extend, as we will see when we look at outer joins in Chapter 7.

Extensions to more than two tables are straightforward. Consider our earlier query:

```
SELECT customer.fname, customer.lname, item.description
FROM customer, orderinfo, orderline, item
WHERE
    customer.customer_id = orderinfo.customer_id AND
    orderinfo.orderinfo_id = orderline.orderinfo_id AND
    orderline.item_id = item.item_id AND
    customer.fname = 'Ann' AND
    customer.lname = 'Stones';
```

In the SQL92 syntax, this becomes:

```
SELECT customer.fname, customer.lname, item.description
FROM customer
    JOIN orderinfo ON customer.customer_id = orderinfo.customer_id
    JOIN orderline ON orderinfo.orderinfo_id = orderline.orderinfo_id
    JOIN item ON orderline.item_id = item.item_id
WHERE
    customer.fname = 'Ann' AND
    customer.lname = 'Stones';
```

Both versions of the SELECT statement produce identical results.

However, many users seem to have stuck with the earlier syntax, which is still valid and slightly more succinct for many SQL statements. We present the newer SQL92 version here, so you will be familiar with the syntax, but generally in this book, we will stick with the older-style joins, except where we meet outer joins in Chapter 7.

# Summary

This has been a fairly long chapter, but we have covered quite a lot. We have discussed the SELECT statement in some detail, discovering how to choose columns and rows, how to order the output, and how to suppress duplicate information. We also learned a bit about the date type, and how to configure PostgreSQL's behavior in interpreting and displaying dates, as well as how to use dates in condition statements.

We then moved on to the heart of SQL: the ability to relate tables together. After our first bit of SQL that joined a pair of tables, we saw how easy it was to extend this to three and even four tables. We finished off by reusing some of the knowledge we gained early in the chapter to refine our four-table selection to home in on displaying exactly the information we were searching for, and removing all the extra columns and duplicate rows.

The good news is that we have now seen all the everyday features of the SELECT statement, and once you understand the SELECT statement, much of the rest of SQL is reasonably straightforward. We will be coming back to the SELECT statement in Chapter 7 to look at some more advanced features that you will need from time to time, but you will find that much of SQL you need to use in the real world has been covered in this chapter.

■ ■ ■

# PostgreSQL Command-Line and Graphical Tools

**A** PostgreSQL database is generally created and administered with the command-line tool, `psql`, which we have used in earlier chapters to get started. Command-line tools similar to `psql` are common with commercial databases. Oracle has one such tool called SQL*Plus, for example.

While command-line tools are generally complete, in the sense that they contain ways to perform all the functions that you need, they can be a little user-unfriendly. On the other hand, they make no great demands in terms of graphics cards, memory, and so on.

In this chapter, we will begin by taking a closer look at `psql`. Next, we will cover how to set up an ODBC data source to use a PostgreSQL database, which is necessary for some of the tools described in this chapter. Then we will meet some of the graphical tools available for working with PostgreSQL databases. Some of the tools can also be used for administering databases, which is the topic of Chapter 11. In this chapter, we will concentrate on general database tasks.

In particular, we'll examine the following tools in this chapter:

- `psql`

- ODBC

- pgAdmin III

- phpPgAdmin

- Rekall

- Microsoft Access

- Microsoft Excel

## psql

The `psql` tool allows us to connect to a database, execute queries, and administer a database, including creating a database, adding new tables and entering or updating data, using SQL commands.

## Starting psql

As we have already seen, we start psql by specifying the database to which we wish to connect. We need to know the host name of the server and the port number the database is listening on (if it is not running on the default of 5432), plus a valid username and password to use for the connection. The default database will be the one on the local machine with the same name as the current user login name.

To connect to a named database on a server, we invoke psql with a database name, like this:

```
$ psql -d bpsimple
```

We can override defaults for the database name, username, server host name, and listening port by setting the environment variables PGDATABASE, PGUSER, PGHOST, and PGPORT, respectively. These defaults may also be overridden by using the -d, -U, -h, and -p command-line options to psql.

---

**■Note** We can run psql only by connecting to a database. This presents a "chicken-and-egg" problem for creating our first database. We need a user account and a database to connect to. We created a default user, postgres, when we installed PostgreSQL in Chapter 3, so we can use that to connect to create new users and databases. To create a database, we connect to a special database included with all PostgreSQL installations, template1. Once connected to template1, we can create a database, and then either quit and restart psql or use the \c internal psql command to reconnect to the new database.

---

When psql starts up, it will read a startup file, .psqlrc, if one exists and is readable in the current user's home directory. This file is similar to a shell script startup file and may contain psql commands to set the desired behavior, such as setting the format options for printing tables and other options. We can prevent the startup file from being read by starting psql with the -X option.

## Issuing Commands in psql

Once running, psql will prompt for commands with a prompt that consists of the name of the database we are connected to, followed by =>. For users with full permissions on the database, the prompt is replaced with =#.

psql commands are of two different types:

- **SQL commands:** We can issue any SQL statement that PostgreSQL supports to psql, and it will execute it.

- **Internal commands:** These are psql commands used to perform operations not directly supported in SQL, such as listing the available tables and executing scripts. All internal commands begin with a backslash and cannot be split over multiple lines.

---

■**Tip** You can ask for a list of all supported SQL commands by executing the internal command \h. For help on a specific command, use \h *<sql_command>*. The internal command \? gives a list of all internal commands.

---

SQL commands to psql may be spread over multiple lines. When this occurs, psql will change its prompt to -> or -# to indicate that more input is expected, as in this example:

```
$ psql -d bpsimple
...
bpsimple=# SELECT *
bpsimple-# FROM customer
bpsimple-# ;
...
$
```

To tell psql that we have completed a long SQL command that might spread across multiple lines, we need to end the command with a semicolon. Note that the semicolon is not a required part of the SQL command, but is just there to let psql know when we are finished. For example, in the SELECT statement shown here, we may have wanted to add a WHERE clause on the next line.

We can tell psql that we will never split our commands over more than one line by starting psql with the -S option. In that case, we do not need to add the semicolon to the end of our commands. The psql prompt will change to ^> to remind us that we are in single-line mode. This will save us a small amount of typing and may be useful for executing some SQL scripts.

## Working with the Command History

On PostgreSQL platforms that support history recording, each command that we ask psql to execute is recorded in a history, and we can recall previous commands to run again or edit. Use the arrow keys to scroll through the command history and edit commands. This feature is available unless you have turned it off with the -n command-line option (or it has not been compiled in the build for your platform).

We can view the query history with the \s command or save it to a file with \s *<file>*. The last query executed is kept in a query buffer. We can see what is in the query buffer with \p, and we can clear it with \r. We can edit the query buffer contents with an external editor with \e. The editor will default to vi (on Linux and UNIX), but you can specify your own favorite editor by setting the EDITOR environment variable before starting psql. We can send the query buffer to the server with \g, which gives a simple way to repeat a query.

## Scripting psql

We can collect a group of psql commands (both SQL and internal) in a file and use it as a simple script. The \i internal command will read a set of psql commands from a file.

This feature is especially useful for creating and populating tables. We used it in Chapter 3 to create our sample database, bpsimple. Here is part of the create_tables-bpsimple.sql script file that we used:

```
CREATE TABLE customer
(
    customer_id           serial                          ,
    title                 char(4)                         ,
    fname                 varchar(32)                     ,
    lname                 varchar(32)            NOT NULL,
    addressline           varchar(64)                     ,
    town                  varchar(64)                     ,
    zipcode               char(10)               NOT NULL,
    phone                 varchar(16)                     ,
    CONSTRAINT            customer_pk PRIMARY KEY(customer_id)
);

CREATE TABLE item
(
    item_id               serial                          ,
    description           varchar(64)            NOT NULL,
    cost_price            numeric(7,2)                    ,
    sell_price            numeric(7,2)                    ,
    CONSTRAINT            item_pk PRIMARY KEY(item_id)
);
```

We give script files a .sql extension by convention, and execute them with the \i internal command:

```
bpsimple=#\i create_tables-bpsimple.sql
CREATE TABLE
CREATE TABLE
...
bpsimple=#
```

Here, the script is located in the directory where we started psql, but we can execute a script stored elsewhere by giving the full path to it.

Another use of script files is for simple reports. If we want to keep an eye on the growth of a database, we could put a few commands in a script file and arrange to run it every once in a while. To report the number of customers and orders taken, create a script file called report.sql that contains the following lines and execute it in a psql session:

```
SELECT count(*) FROM customer;
SELECT count(*) FROM orderinfo;
```

Alternatively, we can use the -f command line option to get psql to execute the file and then exit:

```
$ psql -f report.sql bpsimple
  count
--------
     15
(1 row)
```

```
    count
   --------
        5
  (1 row)
  $
```

If a password is required to access the database, psql will prompt for one. We can specify a different database user with the -U option to psql.

We can redirect query output to a file by using the -o command-line option, or to a file or filter program with the \o internal command from within a session. For example, from within a psql session, we can create a text file called customers.txt containing all of our customers by issuing the following commands:

```
bpsimple=# \o customers.txt
bpsimple=# SELECT * FROM customer;
bpsimple=# \o
```

The final command, \o without a filename parameter, stops the redirecting of query output and closes the output file.

## Examining the Database

We can explore the structure of our database using a number of internal psql commands. The *structure* includes the names and definition of the tables that make up the database, any functions (stored procedures and triggers) that may have been defined, the users that have been created, and so on.

The \d command lists all of the relations—tables, sequences, and views, if any—in our database. Here is an example:

```
bpsimple=# \d customer
                             Table "public.customer"
    Column    |          Type          |              Modifiers
--------------+------------------------+-------------------------------------------
 customer_id  | integer                | not null default nextval(...)
 title        | character(4)           |
 fname        | character varying(32)  |
 lname        | character varying(32)  | not null
 addressline  | character varying(64)  |
 town         | character varying(32)  |
 zipcode      | character(10)          | not null
 phone        | character varying(16)  |
Indexes:
    "customer_pk" PRIMARY KEY, btree (customer_id)

bpsimple=#
```

The \dt command restricts the listing to tables only. See Table 5-2 in the "Internal Commands Quick Reference" section for more internal psql commands.

# psql Command-Line Quick Reference

The command syntax for psql is:

psql [*options*] [*dbname* [*username*]]

The psql command-line options and their meanings are shown in Table 5-1. To see the complete list of options to psql, use the following command:

$ psql --help

**Table 5-1.** *psql Command-Line Options*

| Option | Meaning |
|---|---|
| -a | Echo all input from script |
| -A | Unaligned table output mode; same as -P format=unaligned |
| -c <*query*> | Run only single query (or internal command) and exit |
| -d <*dbname*> | Specify database name to connect to (default: $PGDATABASE or current login name) |
| -e | Echo queries sent to server |
| -E | Display queries that internal commands generate |
| -f <*filename*> | Execute queries from file, then exit |
| -F <*string*> | Set field separator (default: |); same as -P fieldsep=<*string*> |
| -h <*host*> | Specify database server host (default: $PGHOST or local machine) |
| -H | Set HTML table output mode; same as -P format=html |
| --help | Show help, then exit |
| -l | List available databases, then exit |
| -n | Disable readline; prevents line editing |
| -o <*filename*> | Send query output to *filename* (use the form |pipe to send output to a filter program) |
| -p <*port*> | Specify database server port (default: $PGPORT or compiled-in default, usually 5432) |
| -P *var*[=*arg*] | Set printing option *var* to *arg* (see \pset command) |
| -q | Run quietly (no messages, only query output) |
| -R <*string*> | Set record separator (default: newline); same as -P recordsep=<*string*> |
| -s | Set single-step mode (confirm each query) |

**Table 5-1.** *psql Command-Line Options (Continued)*

| Option | Meaning |
|---|---|
| -S | Set single-line mode (end of line terminates query rather than semicolon) |
| -t | Print rows only; same as -P tuples_only |
| -T <text> | Set HTML table tag options (width, border); same as -P tableattr=<text> |
| -U <username> | Specify database username (default: $PGUSER or current login) |
| -v name=value | Set psql variable name to value |
| --version | Show version information and exit; also –V |
| -W | Prompt for password (should happen automatically, if a password is required) |
| -x | Turn on expanded table output; same as -P expanded |
| -X | Do not read startup file (~/.psqlrc) |

## psql Internal Commands Quick Reference

The supported internal psql commands are shown in Table 5-2. In many versions of PostgreSQL, some of these commands have more legible longer forms (such as \list for \l).

**Table 5-2.** *psql Internal Commands*

| Command | Meaning |
|---|---|
| \? | List all available psql internal commands |
| \a | Toggle between unaligned and aligned mode |
| \c[onnect] [dbname|- [user]] | Connect to new database; use - as the database name to connect to the default database if you need to give a username |
| \C <title> | Set table title for output; same as \pset title |
| \cd <dir> | Change the working directory |
| \copy ... | Perform SQL COPY with data stream to the client machine |
| \copyright | Show PostgreSQL usage and distribution terms |
| \d <table> | Describe table (or view, index, sequence) |
| \d{t|i|s|v} | List tables/indices/sequences/views |
| \d{p|S|l} | List permissions/system tables/lobjects |
| \da | List aggregates |

**Table 5-2.** *psql Internal Commands (Continued)*

| Command | Meaning |
|---|---|
| \db | List tablespaces |
| \dc | List conversions |
| \dC | List casts |
| \dd [*object*] | List comment for table, type, function, or operator |
| \dD | List domains |
| \df | List functions |
| \dg | List groups |
| \dl | List large objects; also \lo list |
| \dn | List schemas |
| \do | List operators |
| \dT | List data types |
| \du | List users |
| \e [*file*] | Edit the current query buffer or *file* with external editor |
| \echo <*text*> | Write text to standard output |
| \encoding <*encoding*> | Set client encoding |
| \f <*sep*> | Change field separator |
| \g [*file*] | Send query to back-end (and results in *file*, or \|pipe) |
| \h [*cmd*] | Help on syntax of SQL commands; use * for detail on all commands |
| \H | Toggle HTML mode |
| \i <*file*> | Read and execute queries from *file* |
| \l | List all databases |
| \lo_export, \lo_import, \lo_list, \lo_unlink | Perform large object operations |
| \o [*file*] | Send all query results to *file*, or \|pipe |
| \p | Show the content of the current query buffer |
| \pset <*opt*> | Set table output option, which can be one of the following: format, border, expanded, fieldsep, footer, null, recordsep, tuples_only, title, tableattr, pager |
| \q | Quit psql |
| \qecho <*txt*> | Write text to query output stream (see \o) |
| \r | Reset (clear) the query buffer |
| \s [*file*] | Print history or save it in *file* |

**Table 5-2.** *psql Internal Commands (Continued)*

| Command | Meaning |
|---|---|
| \set <var> <value> | Set internal variable |
| \t | Show only rows (toggles between modes) |
| \T <tags> | Set HTML table tags; same as \pset tableattr |
| \timing | Toggle timing of commands |
| \unset <var> | Unset (delete) internal variable |
| \w <file> | Write current query buffer to *file* |
| \x | Toggle expanded output |
| \z | List access permissions for tables, views, and sequences |
| \! [cmd] | Escape to shell or execute a shell command |

# ODBC Setup

Several of the tools discussed in this chapter, as well as some of the programming language interfaces discussed in later chapters, use the ODBC standard interface to connect to PostgreSQL. ODBC defines a common interface for databases and is based on X/Open and ISO/IEC programming interfaces. In fact, ODBC stands for Open Database Connectivity and is not (as is often believed) limited to Microsoft Windows clients. Programs written in many languages—like C, C++, Ada, PHP, Perl, and Python—can make use of ODBC. OpenOffice, Gnumeric, Microsoft Access, and Microsoft Excel are just a few examples of applications that can use ODBC.

To use ODBC on a particular client machine, we need both an application written for the ODBC interface and a driver for the particular database that we want to use. PostgreSQL has an ODBC driver called psqlodbc, which we can install on our clients. Often, clients will be running on machines that are different from the server, and possibly different from each other, requiring us to compile the ODBC driver on several client platforms. For example, we might have the database server on Linux and our client applications running on Windows and Mac OS X.

The source code and a binary installation for Windows are available from the psqlODBC project home page at http://gborg.postgresql.org/project/psqlodbc/.

---

■**Note** The standard Windows installation of PostgreSQL also contains a version of the ODBC driver that can be installed on a Windows server at the same time as the database.

---

## Installing the ODBC Driver

On Microsoft Windows, ODBC drivers are made available through the Control Panel's Administrative Tools Data Sources applet, as shown in Figure 5-1.

**Figure 5-1.** *The ODBC Data Sources applet*

The Drivers tab of this applet lists the installed ODBC drivers, as shown in Figure 5-2.

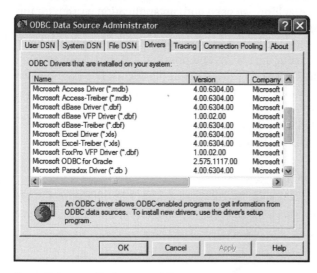

**Figure 5-2.** *Installed ODBC drivers*

To install the PostgreSQL ODBC driver, we need to perform two steps:

1. Download a suitable version of the driver from `http://gborg.postgresql.org/project/ psqlodbc`. If you have a version of Windows that includes the Microsoft Windows Installer, the MSI version of the drivers is the recommended choice, as it is much smaller; otherwise, download the full installation. At the time of writing, both versions of the driver are located in compressed archive files named `psqlodbc-07_03_0200.zip`.

2. Extract the driver installation file from the downloaded archive. It will be named either `psqlodbc.msi` or `psqlodbc.exe`. Double-click the installation file and follow the instructions to install the PostgreSQL ODBC driver.

After performing these two steps, we can confirm that we have successfully installed the driver by again selecting the Drivers tab in the ODBC applet and noting that PostgreSQL now appears in the list, as shown in Figure 5-3.

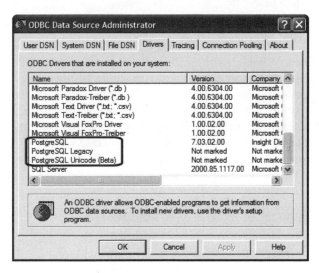

**Figure 5-3.** *PostgreSQL ODBC driver installed*

## Creating a Data Source

Now we will be able to use ODBC-aware applications to connect to PostgreSQL databases. To make a specific database available, we need to create a data source, as follows:

1. Select User DSN in the ODBC applet to create a data source that will be available to the current user. (If you select System DSN, you can create data sources that all users can see.)

2. Click Add to begin the creation process. A dialog box for selecting which driver the data source will use appears, as shown in Figure 5-4.

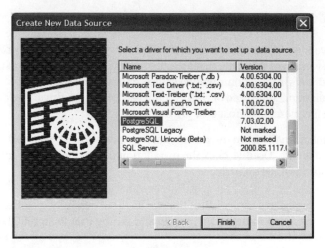

**Figure 5-4.** *Creating a PostgreSQL data source*

3. Select the PostgreSQL driver and click Finish.

4. We now have a PostgreSQL driver entry that must be configured. A Driver Setup box will appear for us to enter the details of this data source. As shown in Figure 5-5, give the data source a name and a description, and set the network configuration. Here, we are creating an ODBC connection to a copy of our bpsimple database running on a Linux server using the IP address of the server. (If you are running a fully configured naming service such as DNS or WINS, you can use a machine name for the server.) We also specify the username and password to be used at the server to access the database we have chosen.

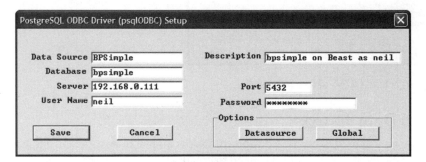

**Figure 5-5.** *Configuring a PostgreSQL data source*

---

**■Tip** Additional options are available under the Global and DataSource options in the ODBC Driver Setup dialog box. If you will be using ODBC applications to update data or insert new data into the PostgreSQL database, you may need to configure the data source to support this. To do this, click the DataSource button and make sure that the Read Only box is not checked in the dialog box that appears.

---

5. Click Save to complete the setup.

We are now ready to access our PostgreSQL database from ODBC applications such as Microsoft Access and Excel, as we will discuss later in this chapter. Next, we will look at some open-source alternatives, starting with pgAdmin III.

# pgAdmin III

pgAdmin III is a full-featured graphical interface for PostgreSQL databases. It is free software, community-maintained at http://www.pgadmin.org. According to the web site, pgAdmin is "a powerful administration and development platform for the PostgreSQL database, free for any use." It runs on Linux, FreeBSD, and Windows 2000/XP. Versions for Sun and Mac OS X are being developed.

pgAdmin III offers a variety of features. With it, we can do the following:

- Create and delete tablespaces, databases, tables, and schemas

- Execute SQL with a query window

- Export the results of SQL queries to files

- Back up and restore databases or individual tables

- Configure users, groups, and privileges

- View, edit, and insert table data

Let's look at how to get up and running with this versatile tool.

## Installing pgAdmin III

With the release of pgAdmin III, the developers have made installation of the program much simpler. Previous versions require the PostgreSQL ODBC driver to be installed to provide access to the database, but this dependency has been removed. If you have used an earlier version of pgAdmin, we recommend that you consider upgrading.

---

■**Note** The standard Windows installation of PostgreSQL includes a version of pgAdmin III that can be installed on a Windows server along with the database or on a client without a database.

---

Binary packages for Microsoft Windows 2000/XP, FreeBSD, Debian Linux, Slackware Linux, and Linux distributions that use the RPM package format (such as Red Hat and SuSE Linux) are available to download from `http://www.pgadmin.org/pgadmin3/download.php`.

Download the appropriate package for the system you want to run pgAdmin III and install it. The Windows package contains an installer to execute, packaged in a compressed archive ZIP file. After installation, you should have a new program (pgAdmin III) in the Windows Start menu.

## Using pgAdmin III

Before we can use pgAdmin III in earnest, we need to make sure that we can create objects in the database we want to maintain. This is because pgAdmin III augments the database with objects of its own that are stored on the server. To perform all of the maintenance functions with pgAdmin III, we need to log on as a user that has complete privileges for the database— a superuser, in other words. If we choose a user without superuser status, we will get an error.

---

■**Tip** We will be looking at users and permissions in Chapter 11. If your PostgreSQL database installation was performed on Windows with the default settings, you should have a user `postgres` that is used to control the database, and you can try to log on as that user. If you installed on Linux or UNIX following the steps in Chapter 3, you will have created a suitable user; we used `neil`.

---

We can manage several database servers at once with pgAdmin III, so our first task is to create a server connection. Select Add Server from the File menu to bring up a dialog box very similar to the one we used to create an ODBC connection earlier. Figure 5-6 shows a connection being made to a PostgreSQL database on a Linux server.

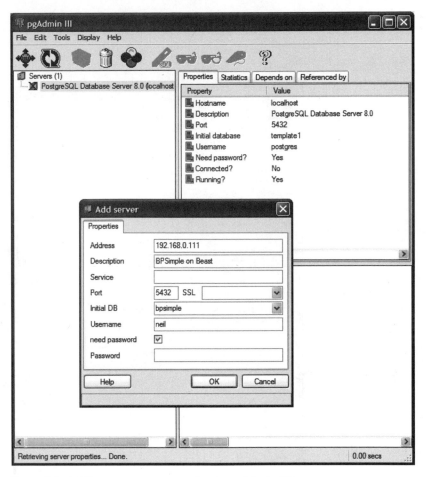

**Figure 5-6.** *Adding a server connection in pgAdmin III*

Once the server connection has been created, we can connect to the database server and browse the databases, tables, and other objects that the server is providing. Figure 5-7 shows an example of pgAdmin III exploring the tables of the bpsimple database and examining the lname attribute of the customer table.

**Figure 5-7.** *Examining table properties with pgAdmin III*

One feature of pgAdmin III that is potentially very useful is its backup and restore functionality. This provides a simple interface to the PostgreSQL pg_dump utility, which we will cover in Chapter 11. We can back up and restore individual tables or an entire database. There are options to control how and where the backup file is created and what method will be used to restore the database, if necessary (for example, by using the \copy command or SQL INSERT statements).

To open the Backup dialog box, right-click the object (database or table) to back up and select Backup. Figure 5-8 shows the Backup dialog box for the bsimple database.

**Figure 5-8.** *The pgAdmin III Backup dialog box*

We will cover more of pgAdmin III's features for managing databases in Chapter 11.

# phpPgAdmin

A web-based alternative for managing PostgreSQL databases is phpPgAdmin. This is an application (written in the PHP programming language) that is installed on a web server and provides a browser-based interface for administration of database servers. The project home page is at http://phppgadmin.sourceforge.net/.

With phpPgAdmin, we can perform many tasks with our databases, including the following:

- Manage users and groups

- Create tablespaces, databases, and schemas

- Manage tables, indexes, constraints, triggers, rules, and privileges

- Create views, sequences, and functions

- Create and run reports

- Browse table data

- Execute arbitrary SQL

- Export table data in many formats: SQL, COPY (data suitable for the SQL COPY command), XML, XHTML, comma-separated values (CSV), tab-delimited, and pg_dump

- Import SQL scripts, COPY data, XML files, CSV files, and tab-delimited files

## Installing phpPgAdmin

Installing phpPgAdmin is very straightforward. The program is available as a download package in several formats, including ZIP and compressed tarball (.tar.gz). The package needs to be extracted into a folder served by a web server that supports the PHP programming language. A popular choice for this is the Apache web server configured with the mod_php extension. More information about Apache and PHP can be found at http://www.apache.org and http://www.php.net, respectively. Many Linux distributions provide a suitably configured Apache installation.

The only configuration that phpPgAdmin requires is the setting of some variables in its configuration file, conf/conf.inc.php. The following extract shows the lines in this file that need to be configured to set up phpPgAdmin to manage a database on another server.

```
// Display name for the server on the login screen
$conf['servers'][0]['desc'] = 'Beast';

// Hostname or IP address for server.  Use '' for UNIX domain socket.
$conf['servers'][0]['host'] = '192.168.0.111';

// Database port on server (5432 is the PostgreSQL default)
$conf['servers'][0]['port'] = 5432;

// Change the default database only if you cannot connect to template1
$conf['servers'][0]['defaultdb'] = 'template1';
```

## Using phpPgAdmin

To demonstrate the cross-platform potential of phpPgAdmin, Apache, and PostgreSQL, Figures 5-9 and 5-10 show a browser running on an Apple Mac, accessing an Apache web server with phpPgAdmin installed running on Windows XP (at address 192.168.0.3), managing a database on a Linux server called Beast at address 192.168.0.111. Figure 5-11 depicts the customer table data being viewed. The URL for the browser is http://192.168.0.3/phpPgAdmin/index.php.

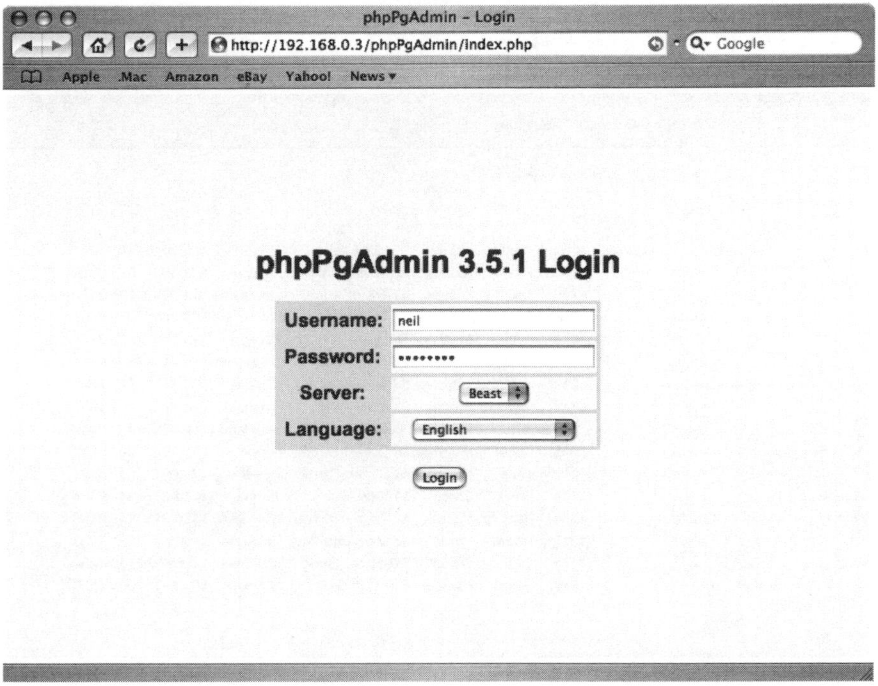

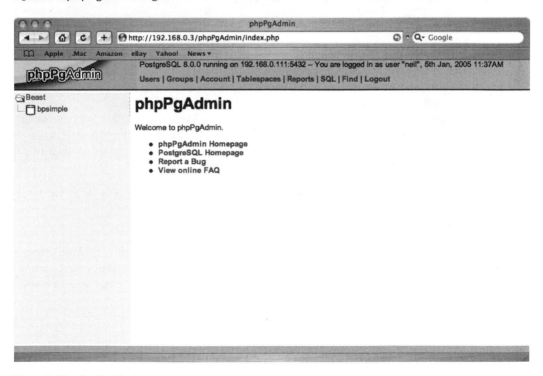

**Figure 5-9.** *phpPgAdmin login*

**Figure 5-10.** *phpPgAdmin main page*

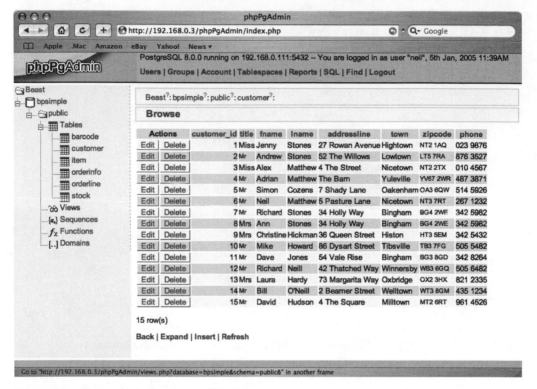

**Figure 5-11.** *phpPgAdmin browsing table data*

One feature of phpPgAdmin  that is potentially very useful is its data import functionality. If we have some data that we would like to import into a PostgreSQL table, phpPgAdmin can help. One way of importing data is to make it available as a comma-separated values (CSV) file. Applications such as Microsoft Excel are able to export data in this format.

Let's consider a simple example. Suppose that from an Excel spreadsheet, we have saved some rows for the item table in the bpsimple database, in a CSV with headings format. This means that there are column names present in the first row, followed by the data, like this:

```
description,cost_price,sell_price
Wood Puzzle,15.23,21.95
Rubik Cube,7.45,11.49
Linux CD,1.99,2.49
```

We start the import process by selecting the table we want to import into, clicking Import, and selecting the import file type (CSV in this example) and the import filename, as shown in Figure 5-12. We can then click Import, and (assuming we have permission) the new rows will be incorporated into our database table.

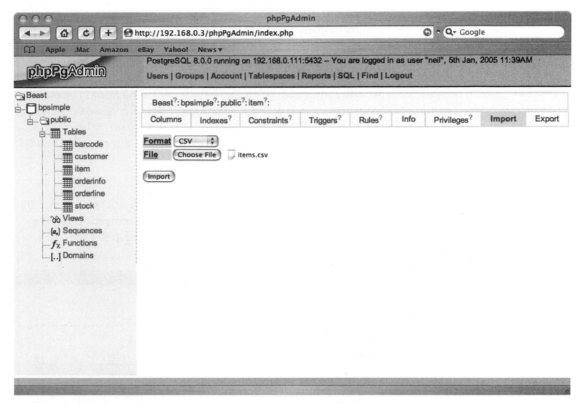

**Figure 5-12.** *Importing data with phpPgAdmin*

# Rekall

Rekall is a multiplatform database front-end originally developed by theKompany (http://
www.thekompany.com/) as a tool to extract, display, and update data from several different database types. It works with PostgreSQL, MySQL, and IBM DB2 using native drivers, and other
databases using ODBC.

While Rekall does not include the PostgreSQL-specific administration features found in
pgAdmin III and phpPgAdmin, it does add some very useful user functionality. In particular,
it contains a visual query designer and a form builder for creating data-entry applications.
Furthermore, Rekall uses the Python programming language for scripting, allowing sophisticated database applications to be constructed.

Rekall has been made available under a dual-license scheme. There is a commercial
version and also a community-developed open-source version released under the GNU Public
License (GPL). Both are available at http://www.rekallrevealed.org/. The open-source version

can be built and installed on Linux and other systems that are running the KDE desktop environment or have the appropriate KDE libraries available. Rekall is beginning to be provided as part of Linux distributions, including SuSE Linux 9.1. It connects to PostgreSQL using a native driver. The commercial version of Rekall adds a Microsoft Windows version and support for ODBC database connections.

Rekall is very easy to use and comes with an on-line handbook, called *Rekall Unbound*, which provides information on every aspect of Rekall's features. It can be accessed either from Rekall's help manual or through the KDE Konqueror web browser at the URL `help:/rekall`.

Here, we will take a quick look at the open-source version of Rekall, running on SuSE Linux 9.1.

## Connecting to a Database

Connections to databases are created using a connection wizard that prompts for a host, database name, and user credentials. Several options are available for each connection, but the defaults work just fine. Figure 5-13 shows a database connection initiated in Rekall.

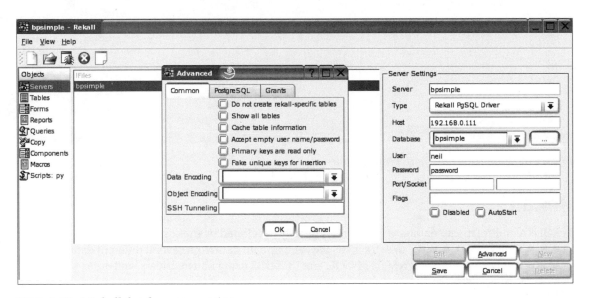

**Figure 5-13.** *A Rekall database connection*

Once we are connected to a database, we can browse the tables, view, and edit data. This process is depicted in Figure 5-14.

For many of its operations, Rekall provides a data view and a design view. Switching to the design view reveals the structure of the object. So, when browsing a table, the design view shows us the definition of the table and its columns. We can use the design view to create new objects, such as tables, forms, and queries. For forms and queries, the data view allows us to use the form to enter data or view the results of the query.

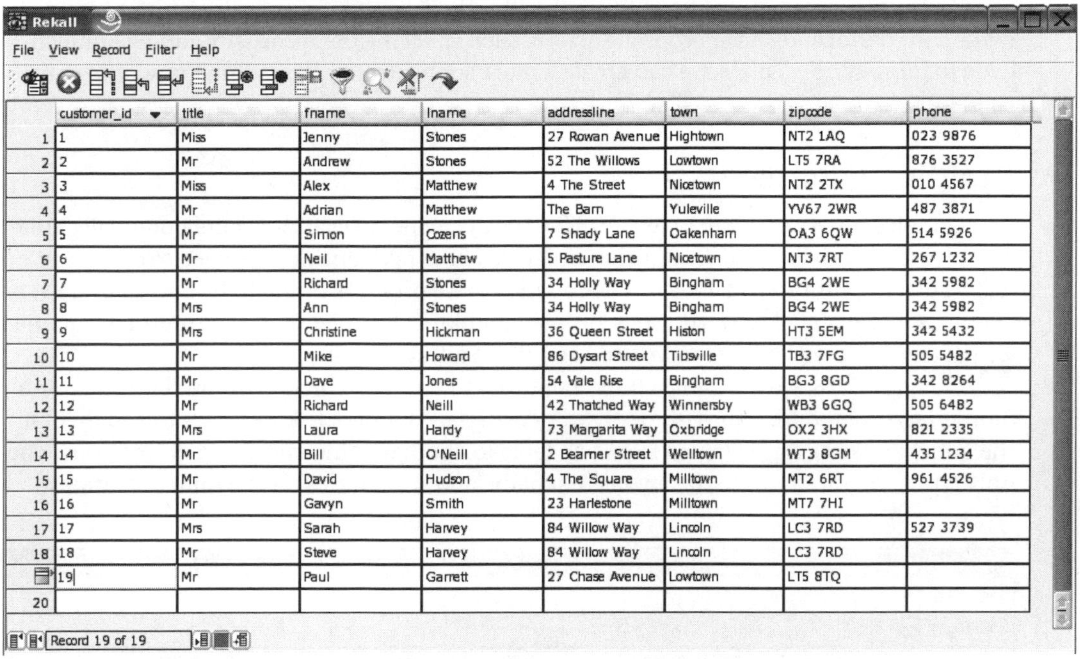

**Figure 5-14.** *Browsing a table with Rekall*

## Creating Forms

The support for forms in Rekall is extensive. We can create a new form very quickly using a form wizard, which simply asks which columns from which table should be included on the form. A graphical designer allows us to lay out the form if the default is not suitable. We can add buttons to the form to provide navigation (next record, delete records, and so on), and there is an optional navigation toolbar that can be added to forms. Figure 5-15 shows a form for the customer table. This form is nearly the default produced by Rekall; only the text labels for the data have been changed.

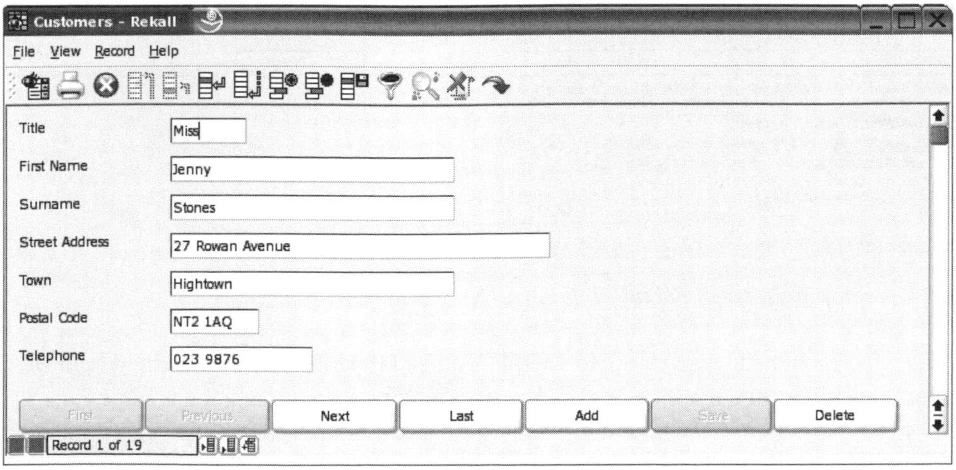

**Figure 5-15.** *A simple data-entry form in Rekall*

Each of the buttons on the form is scriptable. The default form contains actions written in Python for performing an appropriate action, such as saving the record. By adding our own code to these script actions, we can create a more sophisticated form, perhaps adding entry validation.

## Building Queries

The graphical query designer in Rekall allows us to create, save, and execute potentially quite complex queries by essentially drawing a picture of the relationships we need to express. We will be dealing with some fairly complex queries as we progress through the book. For now, to give a taste of what Rekall can do, let's look at a couple of examples that show one of the queries we used in Chapter 4 being constructed and the results being displayed.

In Figure 5-16, we are using a three-table join to find out which items our customer Ann Stones has ordered from us. This query was created by double-clicking tables to add them to the query and dragging columns from one table to another to indicate the required joins. The only typing required was to specify the first name and surname of the customer of interest.

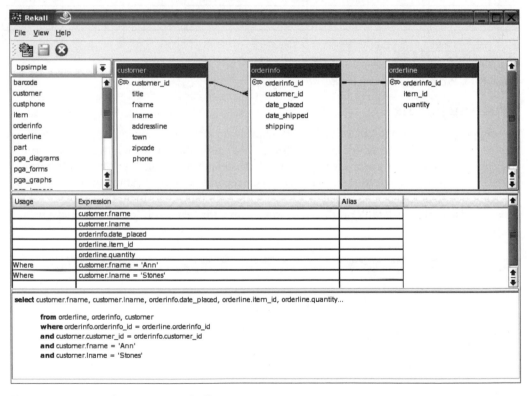

**Figure 5-16.** *A complex query in Rekall*

When we switch to the data view, we see the results of the query being executed, and we get the same results as in Chapter 4. This task is shown in Figure 5-17.

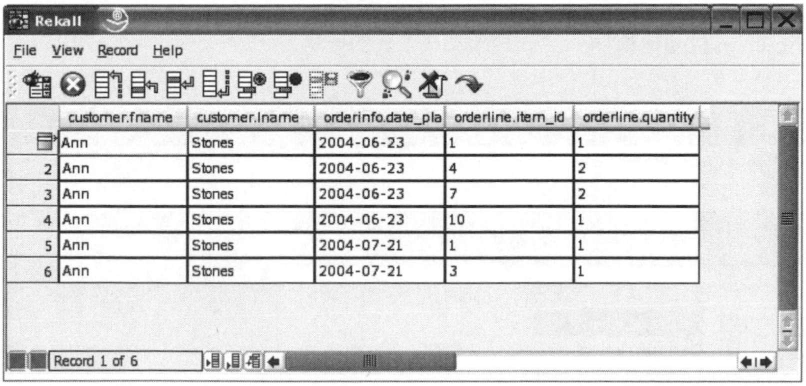

**Figure 5-17.** *Query results in Rekall*

# Microsoft Access

Although it may seem an odd idea at first sight, we can use Microsoft Access with PostgreSQL. If Access is already a database system, why would we want to use PostgreSQL to store data? And, as there are a number of tools available that work with PostgreSQL, why do we need to use Microsoft Access?

First, when developing a database system, we need to consider requirements for matters such as data volumes, the possibility of multiple concurrent users, security, robustness, and reliability. You may decide on PostgreSQL because it fits better with your security model, your server platforms, and your data-growth predictions.

Second, although PostgreSQL running on a UNIX or Linux server may be the ideal environment for your data, it might not be the best, or most familiar, environment for your users and their applications. There is a case for allowing users to use tools such as Access or other third-party applications to create reports or data-entry forms for PostgreSQL databases. Since PostgreSQL has an ODBC interface, this is not only possible but remarkably easy.

Once you have established the link from Access to PostgreSQL, you can use all of the features of Access to create easy-to-use PostgreSQL applications. In this section, we will look at creating an Access database that uses data stored on a remote PostgreSQL server, and writing a simple report based on that data. (We assume that you are reasonably familiar with creating Access databases and applications.)

## Using Linked Tables

Access allows us to import a table into a database in a number of different ways, one of which is by means of a *linked table*. This is a table that is represented in Access as a query. The data is retrieved from another source when it is needed, rather than being copied into the database. This means that when the data changes in the external database, the change is also reflected in Access.

In the `bpsimple` database, we have a table called `item` that records a unique identifier for each product we sell, a description of that product, a cost price, and a selling price. As an example, let's go through the steps to create a simple Access database to update and report on the product information stored in our sample database system.

1. In Access, create a new blank database. Click Tables in the list on the left side of the window, as shown in Figure 5-18.

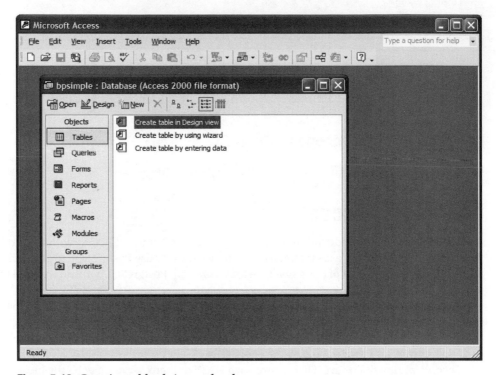

**Figure 5-18.** *Creating a blank Access database*

2. Click New to bring up the New Table dialog box and select the Link Table option, as shown in Figure 5-19.

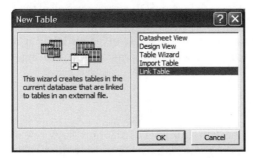

**Figure 5-19.** *Adding a link table*

3. In the Link dialog box that appears, choose files of type ODBC Databases to bring up the ODBC data source selection dialog box. Select Machine Data Source and the appropriate PostgreSQL database connection, as shown in Figure 5-20. We created a suitable database connection in the "ODBC Setup" section earlier in this chapter,

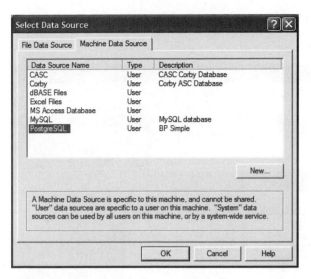

**Figure 5-20.** *Selecting an ODBC data source*

4. When the connection is made, you are presented with a list of available tables in the remote database. You can choose to link one or more tables from this list. For our example, we will select public.item to link the item table to our Access database, as shown in Figure 5-21.

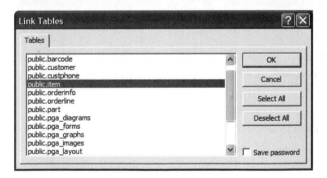

**Figure 5-21.** *Selecting the tables to link*

---

■**Note** Before Access can link a table, it needs to know which of the fields in the table it can use to uniquely identify each record. In other words, it needs to know which columns form the primary key. For this table, the item_id column is the primary key, so Access will select that. For tables that do not have a defined primary key, Access will prompt you to select a column to use. If a table has a composite key, you can select more than one column.

---

Now we will see that the Access database has a new table, also called item, that we can browse and edit, just as if the data were held in Access. This is depicted in Figure 5-22.

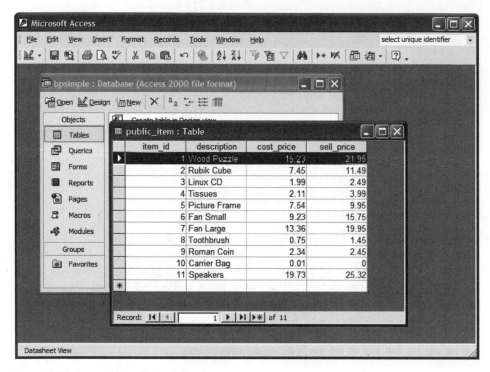

**Figure 5-22.** *Browsing a link table*

That's just about all there is to linking a PostgreSQL database table to Access.

---

■**Note** You might see slightly different screens than the ones in the figures shown here, depending on your version of Windows and Access. If you see an additional column in your table called oid, this is the internal PostgreSQL object Identifier and can be ignored. To prevent the object_id column being shown, be sure to uncheck the OID column options in the ODBC data source configuration.

---

## Entering Data and Creating Reports

We can use the table browser in Access to examine data in the PostgreSQL table and to add more rows. Figure 5-23 shows an Access data-entry form being used to add items to the item table. We can use the programming features of Access to create more sophisticated data-entry applications that perform validation on entries or prevent the modification of existing data.

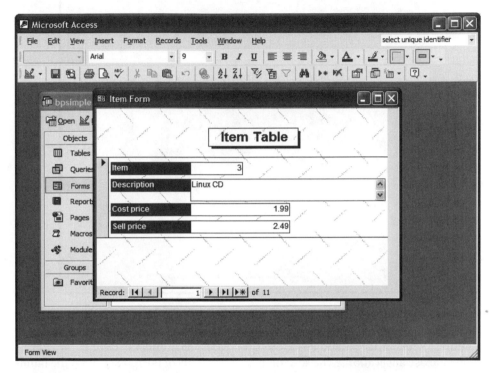

**Figure 5-23.** *A simple Access data-entry form*

Creating reports is just as easy. Use the Access report designer to generate reports based on the data stored in PostgreSQL tables, just as you would any other Access table. We can include derived columns in the report to answer questions about the data in the table. For example, Figure 5-24 shows an Access report that displays the markup (that is, the difference between the sell_price and the cost_price) that we are applying to the products in the item table.

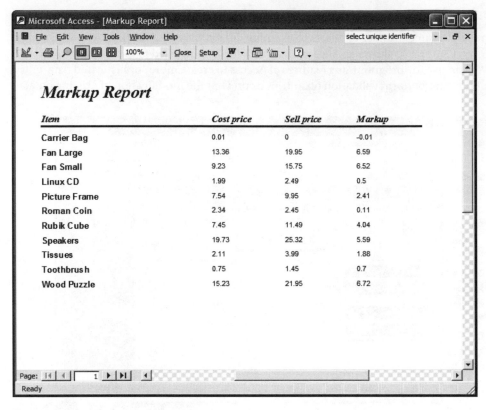

**Figure 5-24.** *A simple Access report*

Combining Microsoft Access and PostgreSQL increases the number of options you have for creating database applications. The scalability and reliability of PostgreSQL with the familiarity and ease of use of Microsoft Access may be just what you need.

# Microsoft Excel

As with Microsoft Access, you can employ Microsoft Excel to add functionality to your PostgreSQL installation. This is similar to the way you can work with Access; you include data in your spreadsheets that is taken from (or rather, linked to) a remote data source. When the data changes, you can refresh the spreadsheet and have the spreadsheet reflect the new data. Once you have made a spreadsheet based on PostgreSQL data, you can use Excel's features, such as charting, to create graphical representations of your data.

Let's extend our report example from Access to make a chart showing the markup we have applied to the products in the item table.

1. We need to tell Excel that some portion of a spreadsheet needs to be linked to an external database table. Starting from a blank spreadsheet, choose the menu option to import external data with a new database query, as shown in Figure 5-25.

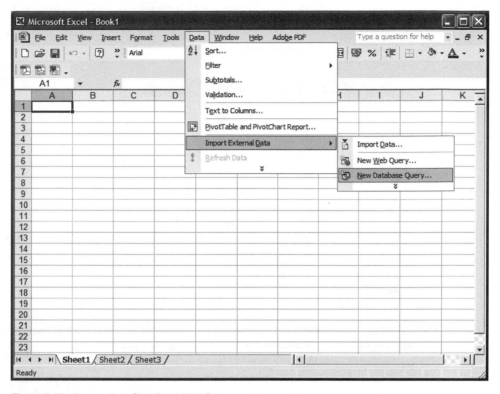

**Figure 5-25.** *Importing data into Excel*

2. We are presented with an ODBC data source selection dialog box to select our data source, as with Access (see Figure 5-20). Select the appropriate PostgreSQL database connection.

3. When the connection to the database is made, you can choose which table you want to use, and which columns you want to appear in the spreadsheet. For this example, we select the item identifier, the description, and both prices from the item table, as shown in Figure 5-26.

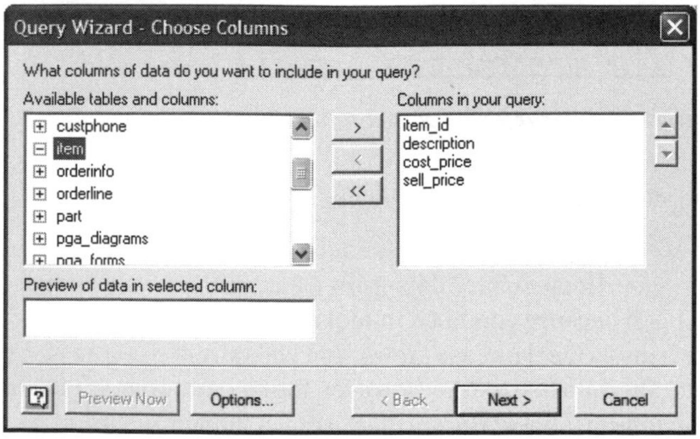

**Figure 5-26.** *Choosing columns to import into Excel*

4. If you want to restrict the number of rows that appear in your spreadsheet, you can do this by specifying selection criteria at the next dialog box. In Figure 5-27, we select those products with a selling price greater than $2.

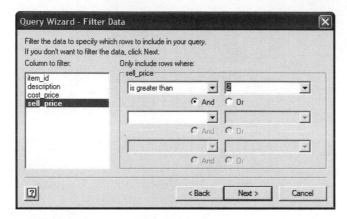

**Figure 5-27.** *Restricting rows to import*

5. Finally, you can choose to have the data sorted by a particular column or group of columns, in either sort direction. For this example, we choose to sort by the selling price, in ascending order, as shown in Figure 5-28.

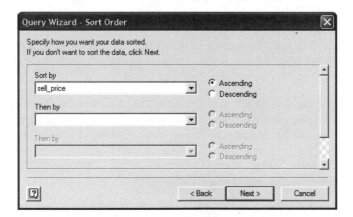

**Figure 5-28.** *Defining the sort criteria for imported data*

6. Choose to return the data to Excel in the next dialog box.

7. Now, you get the chance to specify where in your spreadsheet you want the data to appear. It is probably a good idea to have data from a PostgreSQL table appear on a worksheet by itself. This is because you need to make sure that you provide for the number of rows increasing as the database grows. You will refresh the spreadsheet data and will need space for the data to expand. However, for this example, we simply allow the data to occupy the top-left area of the sheet, as shown in Figure 5-29.

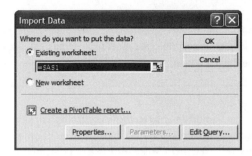

**Figure 5-29.** *Choosing an import location*

Now we can see the data present in our worksheet, as shown in Figure 5-30.

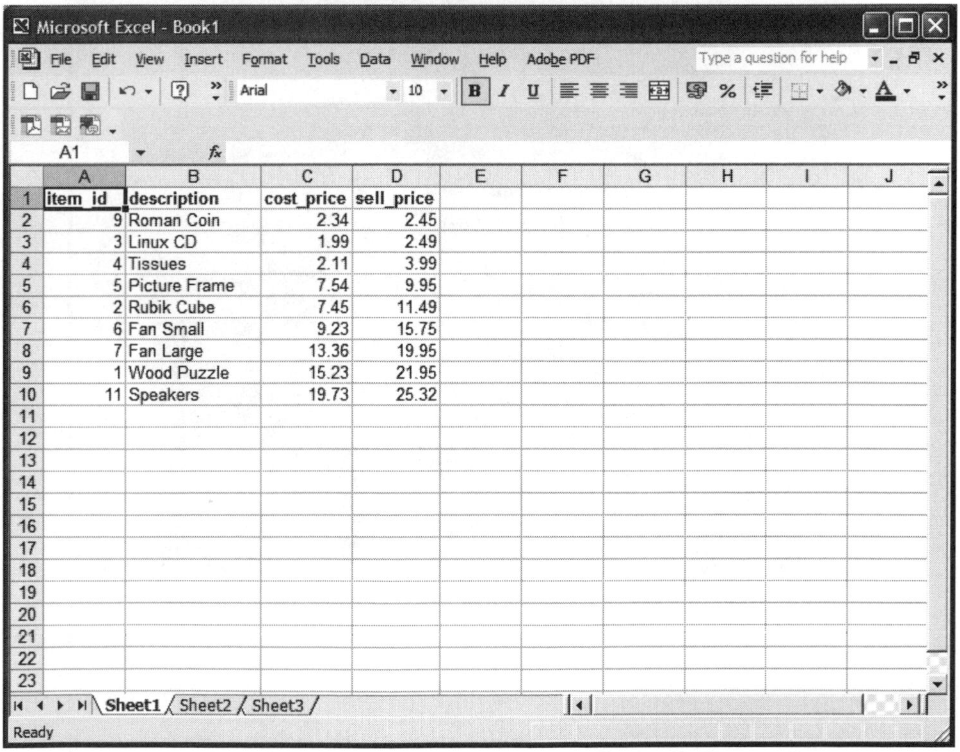

| | A | B | C | D |
|---|---|---|---|---|
| 1 | item_id | description | cost_price | sell_price |
| 2 | 9 | Roman Coin | 2.34 | 2.45 |
| 3 | 3 | Linux CD | 1.99 | 2.49 |
| 4 | 4 | Tissues | 2.11 | 3.99 |
| 5 | 5 | Picture Frame | 7.54 | 9.95 |
| 6 | 2 | Rubik Cube | 7.45 | 11.49 |
| 7 | 6 | Fan Small | 9.23 | 15.75 |
| 8 | 7 | Fan Large | 13.36 | 19.95 |
| 9 | 1 | Wood Puzzle | 15.23 | 21.95 |
| 10 | 11 | Speakers | 19.73 | 25.32 |

**Figure 5-30.** *Viewing imported data in Excel*

We could use this spreadsheet to perform calculations on the data. For example, we might calculate the sales margin being earned from each product by setting up an additional column with an appropriate formula.

■**Caution** When the data changes in the database, Excel will not automatically update its version of the rows. To make sure that the data you are viewing in Excel is accurate, you must refresh the data. This is simply done by selecting the Refresh Data option on the Data menu.

We can also employ some of Excel's features to add value to our PostgreSQL application. In the example shown in Figure 5-31, we have added a chart showing the markup on each product. It is simply built by using the Excel Chart Wizard and selecting the PostgreSQL data area of the sheet as the source data for the chart. When the data in the PostgreSQL database changes and we refresh the spreadsheet, the chart will automatically update.

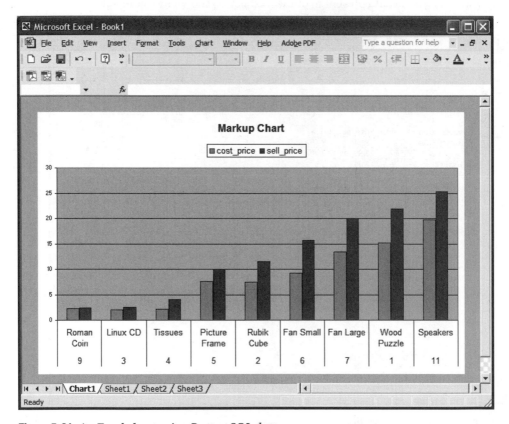

**Figure 5-31.** *An Excel chart using PostgreSQL data*

# Resources for PostgreSQL Tools

A good place to start to look for tools to use with PostgreSQL is pgFoundry, the PostgreSQL project's web site at http://pgfoundry.org. The GBorg site at http://gborg.postgresql.org/ also currently hosts many PostgreSQL-related projects. It is probable that these PostgreSQL project web sites will become merged and be accessible at http://projects.postgresql.org.

You can find a list of graphical tools that support PostgreSQL at `http://techdocs.postgresql.org/guides/GUITools`.

A session monitor for PostgreSQL, called `pgmonitor`, is in development and can be found at `http://gborg.postgresql.org/project/pgmonitor`. This is a Tcl/Tk program that allows you to monitor activity on your database. It needs to run on the database server, but it can display on a client machine if you are running the X Window System on UNIX or a UNIX-like operating system.

# Summary

In this chapter, we looked at some of the tools we have at our disposal for getting the most out of PostgreSQL. The standard distribution comes with the command-line tool, `psql`, which is capable of carrying out most of the operations we need for creating and maintaining databases.

Database administration can be carried out on a client machine using the very capable pgAdmin III tool or over a network using the browser-based phpPgAdmin tool.

We can view data, design queries graphically, and create data-entry forms using Rekall, for free on Linux, and through a commercial product on Windows.

We can use Microsoft Office products, including Excel and Access, to manipulate and report on data held in a PostgreSQL database. This allows us to combine the scalability and reliability of the PostgreSQL system running on a UNIX or Linux platform with the easy use of familiar tools.

Now that we've reviewed some of the PostgreSQL tools, in the next chapter, we will return to the topic of using SQL to handle the data in a PostgreSQL database, focusing on inserting, updating, and deleting data.

# Data Interfacing

So far, we have looked at why a relational database, and PostgreSQL in particular, is a powerful tool for organizing and retrieving data. In the previous chapter, we examined some of the graphical tools, such as pgAdmin III, that can also be used for administering PostgreSQL. We have even looked at how to use Microsoft Access with PostgreSQL and add more functionality to it by using Microsoft Excel. Of course, none of these tools would be much use to us without any data in the database. In Chapter 3, we populated our bpsimple database using some SQL scripts.

In this chapter, we will move beyond the basics and learn more about handling data. We are going to look in detail at how to insert data into a PostgreSQL database, update data already in the database, and delete data from a database.

As we progress through this chapter, we will cover the following topics:

- Adding data to the database with INSERT

- Inserting data into serial columns

- Inserting NULL values

- Loading data from text files using the \copy command

- Loading data directly from another application

- Updating data in the database with UPDATE

- Deleting data from the database with DELETE

## Adding Data to the Database

Surprisingly perhaps, after the complexities of the SELECT statement that we saw in Chapter 4, adding data into a PostgreSQL database is quite straightforward. We add data to PostgreSQL using the INSERT statement. We can add data to only a single table at any one time, and generally we do that one row at a time.

### Using Basic INSERT Statements

The basic SQL INSERT statement has a very simple syntax:

```
INSERT INTO tablename VALUES (list of column values);
```

We specify a list of comma-separated column values, which must be in the same order as the columns in the table.

---

■**Caution** Although this syntax is very appealing because of its simplicity, it is also rather dangerous as it relies on knowledge of the table structure—specifically, the order of the columns—which might change if the database is modified to support additional data. Therefore, we urge you to avoid this syntax, and instead use the safer syntax shown later, in the "Using Safer INSERT Statements" section. In the safer syntax, the column names are specified as well as the data values. We present the simple syntax here, because you will see it in common use, but we recommend that you avoid using it.

---

### Try It Out: Use INSERT Statements

Let's add some new rows to the `customer` table. The first thing we must do is to discover the correct column order. This is the same order in which they were listed in the original `CREATE TABLE` command. If we don't have access to that table-creation SQL, which is unfortunately all too common, then we can use the `psql` command-line tool to describe the table, using the `\d` command. Suppose we wanted to look at the definition of the `customer` table in our database (as presented in Chapter 3). We would use the `\d` command to ask for its description to be shown. Let's do that now:

```
bpsimple=# \d customer
                            Table "public.customer"
   Column    |          Type          |                   Modifiers

-------------+------------------------+-------------------------------------------
-------------------------
 customer_id | integer                | not null default nextval('public.customer
_customer_id_seq'::text)
 title       | character(4)           |
 fname       | character varying(32)  |
 lname       | character varying(32)  | not null
 addressline | character varying(64)  |
 town        | character varying(32)  |
 zipcode     | character(10)          | not null
 phone       | character varying(16)  |
Indexes:
    "customer_pk" primary key, btree (customer_id)

bpsimple=#
```

The display is slightly confused by the wrapping introduced to get it on the page, but it does show us the column order for our `customer` table. You will notice that the `customer_id` column isn't described exactly as we specified in the `CREATE TABLE` statement we saw in Chapter 3. This is because of the way PostgreSQL implements our serial definition of customer_id. For now, we just need to remember that it is an integer field. We will explain how PostgreSQL implements serial columns in Chapter 8.

To insert character data, we must enclose it in single quotes ('). Numbers do not need any special treatment. For NULLs, we just write NULL, or, as we will see later in a more complex form of the INSERT statement, simply provide no data for that column.

Now that we know the column order, we can write our INSERT statement like this:

```
bpsimple=# INSERT INTO customer VALUES(16, 'Mr', 'Gavyn', 'Smith',
bpsimple-# '23 Harlestone', 'Milltown', 'MT7 7HI', '746 3725');
INSERT 17331 1

bpsimple=#
```

The exact number you see after the INSERT will almost certainly be different in your case. The important thing is that PostgreSQL has inserted the new data. The first number is actually an internal PostgreSQL identification number, called an *OID*, which is normally hidden.

---

■**Note** The OID (Object IDentification) number is a unique, normally invisible number assigned to every row in PostgreSQL. When you initialize the database, a counter is created. This counter is used to uniquely number every row. Here, the INSERT command has been executed, 17331 is the OID assigned to the new row, and 1 is the number of rows inserted. This OID number is not part of standard SQL, and it will not normally be sequential within a table, so we urge you to be aware of its existence but never to use it in applications. Starting in release 8.0, PostgreSQL has the option to avoid creating OIDs on tables, so even their very existence is not reliable.

---

We can easily check that the data has been inserted correctly by using a SELECT statement to retrieve it, like this:

```
bpsimple=# SELECT * FROM customer WHERE customer_id > 15;
customer_id | title | fname | lname |  addressline  |   town   | zipcode | phone
------------+-------+-------+-------+---------------+----------+---------+---------
         16 | Mr    | Gavyn | Smith | 23 Harlestone | Milltown | MT7 7HI | 746 3725
(1 row)

bpsimple=#
```

Depending on the size of your terminal window, the display may be wrapped, but you should be able to see that the data was correctly inserted.

Suppose that we want to insert another row, where the last name is O'Rourke. What do we do with the single quote that is already in the data? If a single quote must appear in a character string, we precede it with a backslash (\). The backslash is called an *escape* character, and it indicates that the following character has no special meaning and is part of the data. So, to insert Mr. O'Rourke's data, we escape the quote in his name using a single backslash (\), like this:

```
INSERT INTO customer VALUES(17, 'Mr', 'Shaun', 'O\'Rourke',
    '32 Sheepy Lane', 'Milltown', 'MT9 8NQ', '746 3956');
```

Check that the data has been inserted:

```
bpsimple=# SELECT * FROM customer WHERE customer_id > 15;
customer_id | ti | fname |  lname  |   addressline   |   town   | zipcode |  phone
------------+----+-------+---------+-----------------+----------+---------+---------
         16 | Mr | Gavyn | Smith   | 23 Harlestone   | Milltown | MT7 7HI | 746 3725
         17 | Mr | Shaun | O'Rourke | 32 Sheepy Lane | Milltown | MT9 8NQ | 746 3956
(2 rows)

bpsimple=#
```

---

**Note** In some cases, to fit the output on the page, we've needed to make some slight changes. For example, here, we've abbreviated `title` to `ti`. These adjustments are just for legibility, and we've made sure that the point of each example is clear.

---

**How It Works**

We used the INSERT statement to add data to the customer table, specifying column values in the same order as they were created in the table. To add a number to a column, just write the number. To add a string, enclose it in single quotes. To insert a single quote into the string, we must precede the single quote with a backslash character (\). If we ever need to insert a backslash character, then we would write a pair, like this \\.

Suppose we want to insert another row, where the address is something strange, such as Midtown Street A\33. What do we do with the single backslash that is already in the data? We would escape the single backslash by using two backslashes, like this:

```
INSERT INTO customer VALUES(18, 'Mr', 'Jeff', 'Baggott',
    'Midtown Street A\\33', 'Milltown', 'MT9 8NQ', '746 3956');
```

This is how it looks:

```
bpsimple=# SELECT * FROM customer WHERE addressline='Midtown Street A\\33';
c_id | ti | fname | lname  |    addressline     |   town   | zipcode |  phone
-----+----+-------+--------+--------------------+----------+---------+----------
  18 | Mr | Jeff  | Baggott | Midtown Street A\33 | Milltown | MT9 8NQ | 746 3956
(1 row)

bpsimple=#
```

# Using Safer INSERT Statements

While INSERT statements like the ones we just tried out work, it is not always convenient to specify every single column or to get the data order exactly the same as the table column order. This adds an element of risk in that we may accidentally write an INSERT statement with the column data in the wrong order. This would result in the addition of incorrect data to our database.

In the previous example, suppose we had erroneously exchanged the position of the fname and lname columns. The data would have been inserted successfully, because both columns are text columns, and PostgreSQL would have been unable to detect our mistake. If we had later asked for a list of the last names of our customers, Gavyn would have appeared as a valid customer last name, rather than Smith, as we intended.

Poor-quality data, or just plain incorrect data, is a major problem in databases, and we generally take as many precautions as we can to ensure that only correct data gets in. Simple mistakes might be easy to spot in our sample database with just tens of rows, but in a database with tens of thousands of customers, spotting mistakes—particularly within data with unusual names—would be very difficult indeed.

Fortunately, there is a slight variation of the INSERT statement that is both easier to use and much safer as well:

```
INSERT INTO tablename(list of column names)
VALUES (list of column values corresponding to the column names);
```

In this variant of the INSERT statement, we must list the column names and data values for those columns in the same order, which can be different from the order we used when we created the table. Using this variant, we no longer need to know the order in which the columns were defined in the database. We also have a nice, clear, almost side-by-side list of column names and the data we are about to insert into them.

### Try It Out: Insert Values Corresponding to Column Names

Let's add another row to the database, this time explicitly naming the columns, like this:

```
INSERT INTO customer(customer_id, title, fname, lname, addressline, ...)
VALUES(19, 'Mrs', 'Sarah', 'Harvey', '84 Willow Way', ...)
```

We can enter an INSERT statement over several lines, making it easier to read, and check that we have the column names and data values in the same order.

Let's execute an example, typing it in over several lines so it is easier to read:

```
bpsimple=# INSERT INTO
bpsimple-# customer(customer_id, title, lname, fname, addressline, town,
bpsimple-#          zipcode, phone)
bpsimple-# VALUES(19, 'Mrs', 'Harvey', 'Sarah',  '84 Willow Way', 'Lincoln',
bpsimple-#           'LC3 7RD', '527 3739');
INSERT 22592 1

bpsimple=#
```

Notice how much easier it is to compare the names of the fields with the values being inserted into them. We deliberately swapped the fname and lname column positions, just to show it could be done. You can use any column order you like; all that matters is that the values match the order in which you list the columns.

You will also notice the psql prompt changes on subsequent lines, and it remains changed until we terminate the command with a semicolon.

■**Tip** We strongly recommend that you always use the named column form of the INSERT statement, because the explicit naming of columns makes it much safer to use.

## Inserting Data into Serial Columns

At this point, it is time to confess to a minor sin we have been committing with the customer_id column. Up to this point in the chapter, we have not covered how to insert data into some columns of a table while leaving others alone. With the second form of the INSERT statement, using named columns, we can do this and see how it is particularly important when inserting data into tables with serial type columns.

You will remember from Chapter 2 that we met the rather special data type serial, which is effectively an integer, but automatically increments to give us an easy way of creating unique ID numbers for each row. So far in this chapter, we have been inserting data into rows, providing a value for the customer_id column, which is a serial type data field.

Let's take a look at the data in our customer table so far:

```
bpsimple=# SELECT customer_id, fname, lname, addressline FROM customer;
 customer_id |   fname   |   lname   |      addressline
-------------+-----------+-----------+----------------------
           1 | Jenny     | Stones    | 27 Rowan Avenue
           2 | Andrew    | Stones    | 52 The Willows
           3 | Alex      | Matthew   | 4 The Street
           4 | Adrian    | Matthew   | The Barn
           5 | Simon     | Cozens    | 7 Shady Lane
           6 | Neil      | Matthew   | 5 Pasture Lane
           7 | Richard   | Stones    | 34 Holly Way
           8 | Ann       | Stones    | 34 Holly Way
           9 | Christine | Hickman   | 36 Queen Street
          10 | Mike      | Howard    | 86 Dysart Street
          11 | Dave      | Jones     | 54 Vale Rise
          12 | Richard   | Neill     | 42 Thatched Way
          13 | Laura     | Hardy     | 73 Margarita Way
          14 | Bill      | O'Neill   | 2 Beamer Street
          15 | David     | Hudson    | 4 The Square
          16 | Gavyn     | Smith     | 23 Harlestone
          17 | Shaun     | O'Rourke  | 32 Sheepy Lane
          18 | Jeff      | Baggott   | Midtown Street A\33
          19 | Sarah     | Harvey    | 84 Willow Way
(19 rows)

bpsimple=#
```

Certainly, all looks well. However, there is a slight problem because, by forcing values into the customer_id column, we have inadvertently confused PostgreSQL's internal serial counter.

Suppose we try inserting another row, this time allowing the serial type to provide our automatically incrementing customer_id value:

```
bpsimple=# INSERT INTO customer(title, fname, lname, addressline, town,
bpsimple-# zipcode, phone)
bpsimple-# VALUES('Mr', 'Steve', 'Clarke',  '14 Satview way', 'Lincoln',
bpsimple-# 'LC4 3ED', '527 7254');
ERROR:  duplicate key violates unique constraint "customer_pk"

bpsimple=#
```

Clearly, something has gone wrong, since we did not provide any duplicate values. What has happened is that earlier in the chapter, when we were providing values for customer_id, we bypassed PostgreSQL's automatic allocation of IDs in the serial column and caused the automatic allocation system to get out of step with the actual data in the table.

---

■**Caution** Avoid providing values for serial data columns when inserting data.

---

The out-of-step sequence problem is reasonably rare, but most commonly occurs as a result of one of the following:

- You have dropped and re-created the table, but did not drop and re-create the sequence (PostgreSQL version 8.0 and later does this automatically).

- You mixed styles of adding data—allowing PostgreSQL to pick values for some serial columns and explicitly specifying values for some serial columns yourself.

In this case, the latter occurred. Having gotten ourselves into a bit of a mess, how do we recover? The answer is that we need to give PostgreSQL a helping hand, and put its internal sequence number back in step with the actual data.

## Accessing Sequence Numbers

When the customer table was created, the customer_id column was defined as having type serial. You may have noticed that PostgreSQL then gave us some informational messages, saying that it was creating a customer_customer_id_seq sequence. Also, when we ask PostgreSQL to describe the table using \d, we see the column is specially defined:

```
customer_id integer not null default nextval('customer_customer_id_seq'::text)
```

PostgreSQL has created a special counter for the column, a *sequence*, which it can use to generate unique IDs. Notice that the sequence is always named <*tablename*>_<*columnname*>_seq. The default behavior for the column has been automatically specified by PostgreSQL to be the result of the function nextval('customer_customer_id_seq'). When we failed to provide data for the column in our INSERT statement, this is the function that was being automatically executed by PostgreSQL for us. By inserting or providing data to this column, we have upset this automatic mechanism, since the function will not get called if data is provided. Fortunately, we are not reduced to deleting all the data from the table and starting again, because PostgreSQL allows us to directly manipulate the sequence number.

When inserting data like this, you can usually find the value of a sequence number using the `currval` function:

```
currval('sequence name');
```

PostgreSQL will tell you the current value of the sequence number:

```
bpsimple=# SELECT currval('customer_customer_id_seq');
 currval
---------
      16
(1 row)

bpsimple=#
```

---

■**Note** Strictly speaking, `currval` tells you the value from the last call to `nextval`, so for this to work, either a new row will need to have been inserted or `nextval` called explicitly in this `psql` session.

---

As you can see, PostgreSQL thinks that the current number for the last row in the table is 16, but, in fact, the last row is 19. When we try to insert data into the `customer` table, leaving the `customer_id` column to PostgreSQL, it attempts to provide a value for the column by calling the `nextval` function:

```
nextval('sequence number');
```

This function first increments the provided sequence number, and then returns the result. We can try this directly:

```
bpsimple=# SELECT nextval('customer_customer_id_seq');
 nextval
---------
      17
(1 row)

bpsimple=#
```

Of course, we could get to the correct value for the sequence by repeatedly calling `nextval`, but that would not be much use if the value were too large or too small. Instead, we can use the `setval` function:

```
setval('sequence number', new value);
```

First, we need to discover what the sequence value should be. This is accomplished by selecting the maximum value of the column that is already in the database. To do this, we will use the `max(column name)` function, which simply tells us the maximum value stored in a column:

```
bpsimple=# SELECT max(customer_id) FROM customer;
 max
-----
  19
(1 row)

bpsimple=#
```

PostgreSQL will respond with the largest number that it found in the customer_id column in the customer table. (We will discuss the max(*column name*) function in more detail in the next chapter.) Now we set the sequence, using the function setval(*sequence, value*), which allows us to set a sequence to any value we choose. The current largest value in the table is 19, and the sequence number is always incremented before its value is used. Therefore, the sequence should normally have the same number as the current biggest value in the table:

```
bpsimple=# SELECT setval('customer_customer_id_seq', 19);
 setval
--------
     19
(1 row)

bpsimple=#
```

Now that the sequence number is correct, we can insert our data, allowing PostgreSQL to provide the value for the serial column customer_id:

```
bpsimple=# INSERT INTO customer(title, fname, lname, addressline, town,
bpsimple-# zipcode, phone) VALUES('Mr', 'Steve', 'Clarke',  '14 Satview
bpsimple-# way', 'Lincoln', 'LC4 3ED', '527 7254');
INSERT 21459 1
bpsimple=#
```

Success! PostgreSQL is now back in step, and it will continue to create serial values correctly.

PostgreSQL versions 7.3 and later allow you to use the DEFAULT keyword in INSERT statements to indicate that a column's declared default value should be inserted, which is especially useful in keeping sequence values in line. Where we have been adding rows using explicit customer_id values, we can write statements like this instead:

```
INSERT INTO customer(customer_id, title, fname, lname,
    addressline, town, zipcode, phone)
VALUES(DEFAULT, 'Mrs', 'Sarah', 'Harvey',
    '84 Willow Way', 'Lincoln', 'LC3 7RD', '527 3739');
```

Here, the default value of the customer_id is the next value in the sequence, as customer_id is a serial column.

We will return to the topic of default column values in Chapter 8.

## Inserting NULL Values

We briefly mentioned in Chapter 2 that NULL values could be inserted into columns using the INSERT statement. Let's look at this in a little more detail.

If you are using the first form of the INSERT statement, where you insert data into the columns in the order they were defined when the table was created, you simply write NULL in the column value. Note that you must not use quotes, as this is not a string. You should also remember that NULL is a special undefined value in SQL, not the same as an empty string.

Consider our previous example:

```
INSERT INTO customer VALUES(16, 'Mr', 'Gavyn', 'Smith',
    '23 Harlestone', 'Milltown', 'MT7 7HI', '746 3725');
```

Suppose that we did not know the first name. The table definition allows NULL in the fname column, so adding data without knowing the first name is perfectly valid. If we had written this:

```
INSERT INTO customer VALUES(16, 'Mr', '', 'Smith',
    '23 Harlestone', 'Milltown', 'MT7 7HI', '746 3725');
```

it would not be what we intended, because we would have added an empty string as the first name, perhaps implying that Mr. Smith has no first name. What we intended was to use a NULL, because we do not know the first name.

The correct INSERT statement would have been as follows:

```
INSERT INTO customer VALUES(16, 'Mr', NULL, 'Smith',
    '23 Harlestone', 'Milltown', 'MT7 7HI', '746 3725');
```

Notice the lack of quotes around NULL. If quotes had been used, fname would have been set to the string 'NULL', rather than the *value* NULL.

Using the second (safer) form of the INSERT statement, where columns are explicitly named, it is much easier to insert NULL values where we neither list the column nor provide a value for it, like this:

```
INSERT INTO customer(title, lname, addressline, town, zipcode, phone)
VALUES('Mr', 'Smith', '23 Harlestone', 'Milltown', 'MT7 7HI', '746 3725');
```

Notice that the fname column is neither listed nor is a value defined for it. Alternatively, we could have listed the column, and then written NULL in the value list.

This will not work if we try to add a NULL value in a column that is defined as not allowing NULL values. Suppose we try to add a customer with no last name (lname) column:

```
bpsimple=# INSERT INTO customer(title, fname, addressline, town, zipcode,
bpsimple-# phone) VALUES('Ms', 'Gill', '27 Chase Avenue', 'Lowtown',
bpsimple-# 'LT5 8TQ', '876 1962');
ERROR:  null value in column "lname" violates not-null constraint
bpsimple=#
```

Notice that we did not provide a value for lname, so the INSERT was rejected, because the customer table is defined to not allow NULL in that column:

```
bpsimple=# \d customer
                              Table "public.customer"
    Column     |         Type          |                  Modifiers

---------------+-----------------------+-------------------------------------------
-----------------------------
 customer_id   | integer               | not null default nextval('public.customer
_customer_id_seq'::text)
 title         | character(4)          |
 fname         | character varying(32) |
 lname         | character varying(32) | not null
 addressline   | character varying(64) |
 town          | character varying(32) |
 zipcode       | character(10)         | not null
 phone         | character varying(16) |
Indexes:
    "customer_pk" primary key, btree (customer_id)

bpsimple=#
```

We will see in Chapter 8 how we can more generally define explicit default values to be used in columns when data is inserted with no value, by specifying a default value for a column.

## Using the \copy Command

Although INSERT is the standard SQL way of adding data to a database, it is not always the most convenient. Suppose we had a large number of rows to add to the database, but already had the actual data available, perhaps in a spreadsheet. One way to get started on inserting data into the database would be to use a spreadsheet export, so we would probably export the spreadsheet as a comma-separated values (CSV) file. We can then use a text editor like Emacs, or at least one with a macro facility, to convert all our data into INSERT statements.

Consider the following data:

```
Miss,Jenny,Stones,27 Rowan Avenue,Hightown,NT2 1AQ,023 9876
Mr,Andrew,Stones,52 The Willows,Lowtown,LT5 7RA,876 3527
Miss,Alex,Matthew,4 The Street,Nicetown,NT2 2TX,010 4567
```

We might transform it into a series of INSERT statements, so it looks like this:

```
INSERT INTO customer(title, fname, lname, addressline, town, zipcode, phone)
VALUES('Miss','Jenny','Stones','27 Rowan Avenue','Hightown',
     'NT2 1AQ','023 9876');
INSERT INTO customer(title, fname, lname, addressline, town, zipcode, phone)
 VALUES('Mr','Andrew','Stones','52 The Willows','Lowtown',
     'LT5 7RA','876 3527');
INSERT INTO customer(title, fname, lname, addressline, town, zipcode, phone)
 VALUES('Miss','Alex','Matthew','4 The Street','Nicetown',
     'NT2 2TX','010 4567');
```

Then save it in a text file with a .sql extension.

We could then use the \i command in psql to execute the statements in the file. This is how the pop_customer.sql file works (we used this in Chapter 3 to initially populate our database). Notice here that we allowed PostgreSQL to generate the unique customer_id value.

This isn't very convenient, however. It would be much nicer if data could be moved between flat files and the database in a more general way. There are a couple of ways of doing this in PostgreSQL. Rather confusingly, both are called the copy command. There is a PostgreSQL SQL command called COPY, which can save and restore data to flat files, but its use is limited to the database administrator, as files are read and written on the server to which normal users would not necessarily have access. More useful is the general-purpose \copy command, which implements almost all the functionality of COPY, but can be used by everyone, and data is read and written on the client machine. The SQL-based COPY command is, therefore, almost totally redundant.

---

■**Note** The COPY command does have one advantage: it is significantly quicker than \copy, because it executes directly in the server process. The \copy command executes in the client process, potentially having to pass all the data across a network. COPY can also be slightly more reliable when errors occur. Unless you have very large amounts of data, however, the difference will not be that noticeable.

---

The \copy command has this basic syntax for importing data:

```
\copy tablename FROM 'filename'
    [USING DELIMITERS 'a single character to use as a delimiter']
    [WITH NULL AS 'a string that means NULL']
```

It looks a little imposing, but it is quite simple to use. The sections in square braces, [ ], are optional, so you only need to use them if required. Do notice, however, that the filename needs to be enclosed in single quotes.

The option USING DELIMITERS 'a single character to use as a delimiter' allows you to specify how each column is separated in the input file. By default, a tab character is assumed to separate columns in the input data. In our case, we will assume that we have started with a CSV file that we have exported from a spreadsheet. In practice, the CSV format is often not a good choice because the comma character can appear in the data, and address data is particularly prone to containing comma characters. Unfortunately, spreadsheets often do not offer sensible alternatives to CSV file exports, so you may need to work with what you've got. Given the choice, a pipe character, |, is often useful as a delimiter, as it very rarely appears in user data.

The option WITH NULL AS 'a string that means NULL' allows you to specify a string that should be interpreted as NULL. By default, \N is assumed. Notice that in the \copy command, you must include single quotes around the string, because that tells PostgreSQL that it is a string, although quotes will not be expected in the actual data. So, if you want the string NOTHING to be loaded as a NULL value in the database, you would specify the option WITH NULL AS 'NOTHING'. Then if we did not know Mr. Hudson's first name, for example, the data should look like this:

```
15,Mr,NOTHING,Hudson,4 The Square, Milltown,MT2 6RT,961 4526
```

When inserting data directly, it is very important to watch out that the data is "clean." You need to ensure that no columns are missing, all quote characters have been correctly escaped with a backslash, there are no binary characters present, and so on. PostgreSQL will catch most of these mistakes for you, and load only valid data, but untangling several thousand rows of data that have almost been completely loaded is a slow, unreliable, and unrewarding job. It is well worth going to the effort to clean the data as much as possible *before* attempting to "bulk load" it with the \copy command.

**Try It Out: Load Data Using \copy**

Let's create some additional customer data in a cust.txt file that looks like this:

```
21,Miss,Emma,Neill,21 Sheepy Lane,Hightown,NT2 1YQ,023 4245
22,Mr,Gavin,Neill,21 Sheepy Lane,Hightown,NT2 1YQ,023 4245
23,Mr,Duncan,Neill,21 Sheepy Lane,Hightown,NT2 1YQ,023 4245
```

You can create the simple cust.txt file using any text editor, or use the file included with this book's downloadable code (available from the Downloads section of the Apress web site, at http://www.apress.com). Conveniently, there are no NULLs to worry about, so we just need to specify the comma as the column separator. To load this data, execute this command:

```
\copy customer from 'cust.txt' using delimiters ','
```

Notice there is no semicolon (;) at the end of this command, since it is a \ command directly to psql, not SQL. psql responds with the rather brief \., which tells us that all is well.

Then execute the following:

```
SELECT * FROM customer;
```

We will see that the additional rows have been added.

There is, however, a slight problem lurking. Remember the sequence number that can get out of step? Unfortunately, using \copy to load data is one way this can happen. Let's check what has happened to our sequence number:

```
bpsimple=# SELECT max(customer_id) FROM customer;
 max
-----
  23
(1 row)

bpsimple=# SELECT currval('customer_customer_id_seq');
 currval
---------
      21
(1 row)

bpsimple=#
```

Oops! The maximum value stored in customer_id is currently 23, so the next ID allocated should be 24, but the sequence is going to try to allocate 22 as the next value. Never mind— it's easy to correct:

```
bpsimple=# SELECT setval('customer_customer_id_seq', 23);
 setval
--------
     23
(1 row)

bpsimple=#
```

**How It Works**

We used the \copy command to directly load data that had been exported from a spreadsheet in CSV format into our customer table. We subsequently had to correct the sequence number that generates customer_id numbers for the serial column customer_id in the table, which takes significantly less effort than that we would have needed to expend to convert our CSV format data into a series of INSERT statements.

# Loading Data Directly from Another Application

If the data already resides in a desktop database, such as Microsoft Access, there is an even easier way to load the data into PostgreSQL. We can simply attach the PostgreSQL table to the Access database via ODBC and insert data into a PostgreSQL table.

Often, when you are doing this, you will find that your existing data is not quite what you need, or that it needs some reworking before being inserted into its final destination table. Even if the data is in the correct format, it is often a good idea not to attempt to insert it directly into the database, but rather to first move it to a loading table, and then transfer it from this loading table to the real table. Using an intermediate loading table is a common method in real-world applications for inserting data into a database, particularly when the quality of the original data is uncertain. The data is first loaded into the database in a holding table, checked, corrected if necessary, and then moved into the final table.

Usually, you will write a custom application or stored procedure to check and correct the data, a topic covered in detail in Chapter 10. Once the data is ready to load into the final table though, there is a useful variant of the INSERT command that allows us to move data between tables, transferring multiple rows in one command. It is the only time an INSERT statement affects multiple rows with a single statement. This is the INSERT INTO statement.

The syntax for inserting data from one table into another is as follows:

```
INSERT INTO tablename(list of column names) SELECT normal select statement
```

**Try It Out: Load Data Between Tables**

Suppose we have a holding table, tcust, that has some additional customer data to be loaded into our master customer table. We will make our holding table definition look like this:

```
CREATE TABLE tcust
(
    title                   char(4)                         ,
    fname                   varchar(32)                     ,
    lname                   varchar(32)                     ,
    addressline             varchar(64)                     ,
    town                    varchar(32)                     ,
    zipcode                 char(10)                        ,
    phone                   varchar(16)
);
```

Notice that there are no primary keys or constraints of any kind. It is normal when cross-loading data into a loading table to make it as easy as possible to get the data into that table. Removing the constraints makes this easier. Also notice that all the required columns are there, except the customer_id sequence number, which PostgreSQL can create for us as we load the data.

Suppose we have loaded some data into tcust (via ODBC, \copy, or some other method), validated, and corrected it. (A suitable script for creating and populating the tcust table is included in this book's downloadable code, available from the Apress web site.) Then a SELECT output looks like this:

```
bpsimple=# SELECT * FROM tcust;
 title | fname  | lname   | addressline    | town    | zipcode    | phone
-------+--------+---------+----------------+---------+------------+----------
 Mr    | Peter  | Bradley | 72 Milton Rise | Keynes  | MK41 2HQ   |
 Mr    | Kevin  | Carney  | 43 Glen Way    | Lincoln | LI2 7RD    | 786 3454
 Mr    | Brian  | Waters  | 21 Troon Rise  | Lincoln | LI7 6GT    | 786 7243
(3 rows)

bpsimple=#
```

The first thing to notice is that we have not yet managed to find a phone number for Mr. Bradley. This may or may not be a problem. Let's decide that, for now, we don't wish to load this row, but we do wish to load all the other customers. In a real-world scenario, we may be trying to load hundreds of new customers, and it is quite probable that we will want to load groups of them as the data for each group is validated or cleaned.

The first part of the INSERT is quite easy to write. We will use the full syntax of INSERT, specifying precisely the columns we wish to load. This is normally the sensible choice:

```
INSERT INTO customer(title, fname, lname, addressline, town, zipcode, phone)
```

Notice that we do not specify that we are loading the customer_id. You will remember that by leaving this blank, we allow PostgreSQL to automatically create values for us, which is always the safer way to allow serial values to be created.

We now need to write the SELECT part of the statement, which will feed this INSERT statement. Remember that we do not wish to insert the information for Mr. Bradley yet, because his phone number is set to NULL, as we are still trying to find it. We could, if we wanted to, load Mr. Bradley's data, since the phone column *will* accept NULL values. What we are doing here is applying a slightly more stringent real-world usage rule to the data than is required by the low-level database rules. We write a SELECT statement like this:

```
SELECT title, fname, lname, addressline, town, zipcode, phone FROM tcust
WHERE phone IS NOT NULL;
```

Of course, this is a perfectly valid statement on its own. Let's test it:

```
bpsimple=# SELECT title, fname, lname, addressline, town, zipcode, phone
bpsimple-# FROM tcust WHERE phone IS NOT NULL;
 title | fname | lname  |  addressline   |  town   | zipcode  |  phone
-------+-------+--------+----------------+---------+----------+----------
 Mr    | Kevin | Carney | 43 Glen Way    | Lincoln | LI2 7RD  | 786 3454
 Mr    | Brian | Waters | 21 Troon Rise  | Lincoln | LI7 6GT  | 786 7243
(2 rows)

bpsimple=#
```

That looks correct. It finds the rows we need, and the columns are in the same order as the INSERT statement. So, we can now put the two statements together and execute them, like this:

```
bpsimple=# INSERT INTO customer(title, fname, lname, addressline, town,
bpsimple-# zipcode, phone) SELECT title, fname, lname, addressline, town,
bpsimple-# zipcode, phone FROM tcust WHERE phone IS NOT NULL;
INSERT 0 2
bpsimple=#
```

Notice that psql tells us that two rows have been inserted. Now, being extra cautious, let's fetch those rows from the customer table, just to be absolutely sure they were loaded correctly:

```
bpsimple=# SELECT customer_id, fname, lname, addressline FROM customer WHERE
bpsimple-# town = 'Lincoln';
 customer_id  fname | lname  |  addressline
-------------+-------+--------+----------------
          19 | Sarah | Harvey | 84 Willow Way
          20 | Steve | Clarke | 14 Satview way
          24 | Brian | Waters | 21 Troon Rise
          25 | Kevin | Carney | 43 Glen Way
(4 rows)

bpsimple=#
```

We actually get more than two rows, because we already had customers from Lincoln. We can see, however, that our data has been inserted correctly, and customer_id values were created for us.

Now that some of the data from tcust has been loaded into the live customer table, we would normally delete those rows from tcust. For the purposes of the example, we are going to leave that data alone for now and delete it in a later example.

**How It Works**

We specified the columns we wanted to load in the customer table, and then selected the same set of data, in the same order from the tcust table. We did not specify that we would load the customer_id column, so PostgreSQL used its sequence numbers to generate unique IDs for us.

An alternative method, which you may find easier, particularly if there is a lot of data to load, is to add an additional column to the temporary table, perhaps a column isvalid of type boolean. You then load all the data into the temporary table, and set all the isvalid values to false, using the UPDATE statement that we will meet more formally in the next section of this chapter:

```
UPDATE tcust SET isvalid = 'false';
```

We have not specified a WHERE clause; therefore, all rows have the isvalid column set to false. We can then continue work on the data, modifying it where necessary. When we are happy that a row is correct and complete, we set the isvalid column to true. We can then load the corrected data, selecting only the rows where isvalid is true:

```
bpsimple=# INSERT INTO customer(title, fname, lname, addressline, town,
bpsimple-#  zipcode, phone)
bpsimple-# SELECT title, fname, lname, addressline, town, zipcode, phone
bpsimple-#  FROM tcust WHERE isvalid = true;
```

Once these rows are loaded, we can remove them from the tcust table, like this:

```
DELETE FROM tcust WHERE isvalid = true;
```

Then continue to work on the remaining data in the tcust table. (We will discuss the DELETE statement near the end of this chapter.)

# Updating Data in the Database

Now we know how to get data into the database by using INSERT, and how to retrieve it again, using SELECT. Unfortunately, data does not tend to stay static for very long. People move to different addresses, change phone numbers, and so on. We need a way of updating the data in the database. In PostgreSQL, as in all SQL-based databases, this is done with the UPDATE statement.

## Using the UPDATE Statement

The UPDATE statement is remarkably simple. Its syntax is as follows:

```
UPDATE tablename SET columnname = value  WHERE condition
```

If we want to set several columns at the same time, we simply specify them as a comma-separated list, like this:

```
UPDATE customer SET town = 'Leicester', zipcode = 'LE4 2WQ' WHERE some condition
```

We can update as many columns simultaneously as we like, provided that each column appears only once. You will notice that you can use only a single table name. This is due to the syntax of SQL. In the rare event that you need to update two separate, but related, tables, you must write two separate UPDATE statements. You can put those UPDATE statements into a *transaction* to ensure that either both updates are performed or no updates are performed. We will look at transactions more closely in Chapter 9.

### Try It Out: Use the UPDATE Statement

Suppose we have now tracked down the phone number of Mr. Bradley (missing from our tcust table), and want to update the data into our live customer table. The first part of the UPDATE statement is easy:

```
UPDATE tcust SET phone = '352 3442'
```

Now we need to specify the row to update, which is simply:

```
WHERE fname = 'Peter' and lname = 'Bradley';
```

With UPDATE statements, it is always a good idea to check the WHERE clause. Let's do that now:

```
bpsimple=# SELECT fname, lname, phone FROM tcust
bpsimple-# WHERE fname = 'Peter' AND lname = 'Bradley';
 fname | lname   | phone
-------+---------+-------
 Peter | Bradley |
(1 row)

bpsimple=#
```

We can see that the single row we want to update is being selected, so we can go ahead and put the two halves of the statement together and execute it:

```
bpsimple=# UPDATE tcust SET phone = '352 3442'
bpsimple-# WHERE fname = 'Peter' AND lname = 'Bradley';
UPDATE 1
bpsimple=#
```

PostgreSQL tells us that one row has been updated. We could, if we wanted, reexecute our SELECT statement to check that all is well.

### How It Works

We built our UPDATE statement in two stages. First, we wrote the UPDATE command part that would actually change the column value, and then we wrote the WHERE clause to specify which rows to update. After testing the WHERE clause, we executed the UPDATE statement, which changed the row as required.

Why were we so careful to test the WHERE clause and warn about not executing the first part of the UPDATE statement? The answer is because it is perfectly valid to have an UPDATE statement with no WHERE clause. By default, UPDATE will then update *all* the rows in the table, which is almost never what was intended. It can also be quite hard to correct.

tcust is just temporary experimental data, so let's use it to test an UPDATE with no WHERE clause:

```
bpsimple=# UPDATE tcust SET phone = '999 9999';
UPDATE 3
bpsimple=#
```

Notice that psql has told us that three rows have been updated. Now look at what we have:

```
bpsimple=# SELECT fname, lname, phone FROM tcust;
 fname |  lname   |  phone
-------+----------+----------
 Kevin | Carney   | 999 9999
 Brian | Waters   | 999 9999
 Peter | Bradley  | 999 9999
(3 rows)

bpsimple=#
```

This is almost certainly not what we wanted!

---

■**Caution** Always test the WHERE clause of UPDATE statements before executing them. A simple error in a WHERE clause can result in many, or even all, of the rows in the table being updated with the same values.

---

If you do intend to update many rows, rather than retrieve all the data, you can simply check how many rows you are matching using the count(*) syntax, which we will meet in more detail in the next chapter. For now, all you need to know is that replacing the column names in a SELECT statement with count(*) will tell you how many rows were matched, rather than returning the data in the rows. In fact, that's about all there is to the count(*) statement, but it does turn out to be quite useful in practice. Here is an example of our SELECT statement to check how many rows are matched by the WHERE clause:

```
bpsimple=# SELECT count(*) from tcust
bpsimple-# WHERE fname = 'Peter' AND lname = 'Bradley';
 count
-------
     1
(1 row)

bpsimple=#
```

This tells us that the WHERE clause is sufficiently restrictive to specify a single row. Of course, with different data, even specifying both fname and lname may not be sufficient to uniquely identify a row.

# Updating from Another Table

PostgreSQL has an extension that allows updates from another table, using the syntax:

```
UPDATE tablename FROM tablename WHERE condition
```

This is an extension to the SQL standard.

### Try It Out: Update with FROM

For the purpose of checking out the UPDATE with FROM option, let's create a table named cust-phone that contains the customer names and their phone numbers. The table looks like this:

```
CREATE TABLE custphone
(
    customer_id                 serial,
    fname                       varchar(32),
    lname                       varchar(32) NOT NULL,
    phone_num                   varchar(16)

);
```

Let's also insert some data into the newly created custphone table that holds the customers and their phone numbers:

```
bpsimple=# INSERT INTO custphone(fname, lname, phone_num)
bpsimple=# VALUES('Peter', 'Bradley', '352 3442');
INSERT 22593 1
bpsimple=#
```

Now we need to specify the row to be updated in the tcust table:

```
bpsimple=# UPDATE tcust SET phone = custphone.phone_num FROM custphone
bpsimple=# WHERE tcust.fname = 'Peter' AND tcust.lname = 'Bradley';
UPDATE 1

bpsimple=#
```

### How It Works

We created a new table that contains the phone numbers of the customers. Then we inserted data into the new table. Finally, we executed the UPDATE statement, which changed the row as required.

While UPDATE uses subqueries to control the rows that are updated, the FROM clause allows the inclusion of columns from other tables in the SET clause. In fact, the FROM clause isn't even required. This is because PostgreSQL creates a reference to any table used in a query by default.

# Deleting Data from the Database

The last thing we need to learn about in this chapter is deleting data from tables. Prospective customers may never actually place an order, orders get canceled, and so on, so we often need to delete data from the database.

## Using the DELETE Statement

The normal way of deleting data is to use the DELETE statement. This has syntax similar to the UPDATE statement:

```
DELETE FROM tablename WHERE condition
```

Notice that there are no columns listed, since DELETE works on rows. If you want to remove data from a column, you must use the UPDATE statement to set the value of the column to NULL or some other appropriate value.

Now that we have copied our data for our two new customers from tcust to our live customer table, we can go ahead and delete those rows from our tcust table.

### Try It Out: Delete Data

We know just how dangerous omitting the WHERE clause in statements that change data can be. We can appreciate that accidentally deleting data is even more serious, so we will start by writing and checking our WHERE clause using a SELECT statement:

```
bpsimple=# SELECT fname, lname FROM tcust WHERE town = 'Lincoln';
 fname | lname
-------+--------
 Kevin | Carney
 Brian | Waters
(2 rows)

bpsimple=#
```

That's good—it retrieves the two rows we were expecting.

Now we can prepend the DELETE statement on the front and, after a last visual check that it looks correct, execute it:

```
bpsimple=# DELETE FROM tcust WHERE town = 'Lincoln';
DELETE 2
bpsimple=#
```

---

■**CAUTION** Deleting from the database is that easy, so be very careful!

---

### How It Works

We wrote and tested a WHERE clause to choose the rows that we wanted to delete from the database. We then executed a DELETE statement that deleted them.

Just like UPDATE, DELETE can work on only a single table at any one time. If we ever need to delete related rows from more than one table, we will use a *transaction*, which we will meet in Chapter 9.

## Using the TRUNCATE Statement

There is one other way of deleting data from a table. It deletes *all* of the data from a table, and unless it is contained within a PostgreSQL version 7.4 or later transaction, it will give you no way of recovering the data. The command is TRUNCATE, and its syntax is as follows:

```
TRUNCATE TABLE tablename
```

This is a command to be used with caution, and only when you are very sure that you want to permanently delete all the data in a table. In some ways, it is similar to dropping and re-creating the table, except it is much easier to use and doesn't reset the sequence number.

### Try It Out: Use The TRUNCATE Statement

Suppose we have now finished with our tcust table, and want to delete all the data in it. We could DROP the table, but then if we needed it again, we would need to re-create it. Instead, we can TRUNCATE it, to delete all the rows in the table:

```
bpsimple=# TRUNCATE TABLE tcust;
TRUNCATE TABLE
bpsimple=# SELECT count(*) FROM tcust;
 count
-------
     0
(1 row)

bpsimple=#
```

All the rows are now deleted.

### How It Works

TRUNCATE simply deletes all the rows from the specified table.

If you have a large table, perhaps with many thousands of rows, and want to delete all the rows from it, by default, PostgreSQL does not physically remove the rows, but scans through them all, marking each one as deleted. This helps in restoring the data in case the transaction is rolled back. Even though on the command line we might not have explicitly asked for a transaction, all commands automatically get executed inside a transaction. The action of scanning and marking many thousands of rows of a table slows down execution. The TRUNCATE statement deletes the contents of the table very efficiently without scanning the data. So, on very large tables, it executes much more efficiently than DELETE.

---

**■Tip** There are two ways to delete all the rows from a table: DELETE without a WHERE clause and TRUNCATE. TRUNCATE, although not in SQL92, is a very common SQL statement for efficiently deleting all rows from a table.

---

You should stick to using DELETE almost all of the time, as it is a much safer way of deleting data. Also DELETE works in some cases where TRUNCATE does not, such as on tables with foreign keys. However, in special cases where you want to efficiently and irrevocably delete all rows from a table, TRUNCATE is the solution.

# Summary

In this chapter, we looked at the three other parts of data manipulation along with SELECT: the ability to add data with the INSERT command, modify data with the UPDATE command, and remove data with the DELETE command.

We learned about the two forms of the INSERT command, with data explicitly included in the INSERT statement or INSERT from data SELECTed from another table. We saw how it is safer to use the longer form of the INSERT statement, where all columns are listed, so there is less chance of mistakes. We also met INSERT's cousin command, the rather useful PostgreSQL extension \copy, which allows data to be inserted into a table directly from a local file.

We looked at how you need to be careful with the sequence counters for serial fields, and how to check the value of a sequence, and if necessary, change it. We saw that, in general, it is better to allow PostgreSQL to generate sequence numbers for you, by not providing data for serial type columns.

We saw how the very simple UPDATE and DELETE statements work, and how to use them with WHERE clauses, just as with the SELECT statement. We also mentioned that you should always test UPDATE and DELETE statements with WHERE clauses using a SELECT statement, as mistakes here can cause problems that are difficult to rectify.

Finally, we looked at the TRUNCATE statement, a very efficient way of deleting all rows from a table. Since this is an irrevocable deletion, unless managed by transactions, it should be used with caution.

# CHAPTER 7

■ ■ ■

# Advanced Data Selection

In Chapter 4, we looked in some detail at the SELECT statement and how we can use it to retrieve data. This included selecting columns, selecting rows, and joining tables together. In the previous chapter, we looked at ways of adding, updating, and removing data. In this chapter, we return to the SELECT statement, examining its more advanced features. You may rarely need to use some of these features, but it's useful to know them so that you have a good understanding of what is possible in SQL.

In this chapter, we will meet some special functions called *aggregates*, which allow us to get results based on a group of rows. We will then describe some more advanced joins that provide more control over our query results than the simple joins discussed in Chapter 4. We will also meet a whole new group of queries called *subqueries*, where we use multiple SELECT statements in a single query. Finally, we will discuss the very important *outer join*, which allows us to join tables together in a more flexible way than we have seen so far.

As we progress through this chapter, we will cover the following topics:

- Aggregate functions

- Subqueries

- UNION joins

- Self joins

- Outer joins

## Aggregate Functions

In previous chapters, we used a couple of special functions for producing statistics from selections: the max(*column name*) function, to tell us the largest value in a column, and the count(*) function to tell us the number of rows in a table. These functions belong to a small group of SQL functions called *aggregates*. The functions in this group include those listed in Table 4-1.

**Table 4-1.** *Aggregate Functions*

| Aggregate | Description |
|---|---|
| count(*) | Provides a row count for a table |
| count(*column name*) | Counts the number of rows in the table where the value in the specified column is not NULL |
| min(*column name*) | Returns the minimum value found in the specified column |
| max(*column name*) | Returns the maximum value found in the specified column |
| sum(*column name*) | Returns the total sum of the entries in the specified numeric column |
| avg(*column name*) | Returns the average of the entries in the specified column |

Aggregates are often quite useful and generally easy to use. In this section, we'll introduce each of the functions listed in Table 4-1. PostgreSQL supports other aggregates, including functions for variance and standard deviation. Details can be found the PostgreSQL documentation.

---

■**Tip**   psql's \da command lists all of the aggregates used by PostgreSQL.

---

SELECT statements using any of these aggregate functions can include two optional clauses: GROUP BY and HAVING. The syntax is as follows (shown here with the count(*) function):

```
SELECT count(*) column list FROM table name
WHERE condition [GROUP BY column name [HAVING aggregate condition]]
```

The optional GROUP BY clause is an additional condition that can be applied to SELECT statements. It is normally useful only when an aggregate function is being used. It can also be used to provide a function similar to ORDER BY, which we met in Chapter 4, but by working on the aggregate column. The optional HAVING clause allows us to pick out particular rows where the function result meets some condition, and we have already used a GROUP BY clause. This all sounds a bit complicated, but it's actually quite easy in practice, as we'll see in this chapter.

## The Count Function

We will start by looking at the count function, which, as you can see from Table 4-1, has two forms: count(*) and count(*column name*).

### Count(*)

The count(*) function provides a row count for a table. It acts as a special column name in a SELECT statement. Let's try out a very simple count(*) just to get the basic idea.

---

**■Note** In the examples in this chapter, as with others, we start with clean base data in the sample data-base, so readers can dip into chapters as they choose. This does mean that some of the output will be slightly different if you continue to use sample data from a previous chapter. The downloadable code for this book (available from the Downloads section of the Apress web site at http://www.apress.com) provides scripts to make it easy to drop the tables, re-create them, and repopulate them with clean data, if you wish to do so.

---

### Try It Out: Use Count(*)

Suppose we wanted to know how many customers in the customer table live in the town of Bingham. We could simply write a SQL query like this:

```
SELECT * FROM customer WHERE town = 'Bingham';
```

Or, for a more efficient version that returns less data, we could write a SQL query like this:

```
SELECT customer_id FROM customer WHERE town = 'Bingham';
```

This works, but in a rather indirect way. Suppose the customer table contained many thousands of customers, with perhaps over a thousand of them living in Bingham. In that case, we would be retrieving a great deal of data that we don't need. The count(*) function solves this for us, by allowing us to retrieve just a single row with the count of the number of selected rows in it.

We write our SELECT statement as we normally do, but instead of selecting real columns, we use count(*), like this:

```
bpsimple=# SELECT count(*) FROM customer WHERE town = 'Bingham';
 count
-------
     3
(1 row)

bpsimple=#
```

If we want to count all the customers, we can just omit the WHERE clause:

```
bpsimple=# SELECT count(*) FROM customer;
 count
-------
    15
(1 row)

bpsimple=#
```

You can see we get just a single row, with the count in it. If you want to check the answer, just replace count(*) with customer_id to show the real data.

**How It Works**

The count(*) function allows us to retrieve a count of objects, rather than the objects themselves. It is vastly more efficient than getting the data itself, because all of the data that we don't need to see does not need to be retrieved from the database, or worse still, sent across a network.

---

■**Tip** You should never retrieve data when all you need is a count of the number of rows.

---

## GROUP BY and Count(*)

Suppose we wanted to know how many customers live in each town. We could find out by selecting all the distinct towns, and then counting how many customers were in each town. This is a rather procedural and tedious way of solving the problem. Wouldn't it be better to have a declarative way of simply expressing the question directly in SQL? You might be tempted to try something like this:

```
SELECT count(*), town FROM customer;
```

It's a reasonable guess based on what we know so far, but PostgreSQL will produce an error message, as it is not valid SQL syntax. The additional bit of syntax you need to know to solve this problem is the GROUP BY clause.

The GROUP BY clause tells PostgreSQL that we want an aggregate function to output a result and reset each time a specified column, or columns, change value. It's very easy to use. You simply add a GROUP BY *column name* to the SELECT with a count(*) function. PostgreSQL will tell you how many of each value of your column exists in the table.

**Try It Out: Use GROUP BY**

Let's try to answer the question, "How many customers live in each town?"

Stage one is to write the SELECT statement to retrieve the count and column name:

```
SELECT count(*), town FROM customer;
```

We then add the GROUP BY clause, to tell PostgreSQL to produce a result and reset the count each time the town changes by issuing a SQL query like this:

```
SELECT count(*), town FROM customer GROUP BY town;
```

Here it is in action:

```
bpsimple=# SELECT count(*), town FROM customer GROUP BY town;
 count |    town
-------+-----------
     1 | Milltown
     2 | Nicetown
     1 | Welltown
     1 | Yuleville
     3 | Bingham
```

```
     1 | Histon
     1 | Hightown
     1 | Lowtown
     1 | Tibsville
     1 | Oxbridge
     1 | Winnersby
     1 | Oakenham
(12 rows)
```

bpsimple=#

As you can see, we get a listing of towns and the number of customers in each town.

**How It Works**

PostgreSQL orders the result by the column listed in the GROUP BY clause. It then keeps a running total of rows, and each time the town name changes, it writes a result row and resets its counter to zero. You will agree that this is much easier than writing procedural code to loop through each town.

We can extend this idea to more than one column if we want to, provided all the columns we select are also listed in the GROUP BY clause. Suppose we wanted to know two pieces of information: how many customers are in each town and how many different last names they have. We would simply add lname to both the SELECT and GROUP BY parts of the statement:

```
bpsimple=# SELECT count(*), lname, town FROM customer GROUP BY town, lname;
 count |  lname   |    town
-------+----------+-----------
     1 | Hardy    | Oxbridge
     1 | Cozens   | Oakenham
     1 | Matthew  | Yuleville
     1 | Jones    | Bingham
     2 | Matthew  | Nicetown
     1 | O'Neill  | Welltown
     1 | Stones   | Hightown
     2 | Stones   | Bingham
     1 | Hudson   | Milltown
     1 | Hickman  | Histon
     1 | Neill    | Winnersby
     1 | Howard   | Tibsville
     1 | Stones   | Lowtown
(13 rows)
```

bpsimple=#

Notice that Bingham is now listed twice, because there are customers with two different last names, Jones and Stones, who live in Bingham.

Also notice that this output is unsorted. Versions of PostgreSQL prior to 8.0 would have sorted first by town, then lname, since that is the order they are listed in the GROUP BY clause. In PostgreSQL 8.0 and later, we need to be more explicit about sorting by using an ORDER BY clause. We can get sorted output like this:

```
bpsimple=# SELECT count(*), lname, town FROM customer GROUP BY town, lname
bpsimple=# ORDER BY town, lname;
 count |  lname   |    town
-------+----------+-----------
     1 | Jones    | Bingham
     2 | Stones   | Bingham
     1 | Stones   | Hightown
     1 | Hickman  | Histon
     1 | Stones   | Lowtown
     1 | Hudson   | Milltown
     2 | Matthew  | Nicetown
     1 | Cozens   | Oakenham
     1 | Hardy    | Oxbridge
     1 | Howard   | Tibsville
     1 | O'Neill  | Welltown
     1 | Neill    | Winnersby
     1 | Matthew  | Yuleville
(13 rows)

bpsimple=#
```

## HAVING and Count(*)

The last optional part of a SELECT statement is the HAVING clause. This clause may be a bit
confusing to people new to SQL, but it's not difficult to use. You just need to remember that
HAVING is a kind of WHERE clause for aggregate functions. We use HAVING to restrict the results
returned to rows where a particular aggregate condition is true, such as count(*) > 1. We use it
in the same way as WHERE to restrict the rows based on the value of a column.

---

■**Caution** Aggregates cannot be used in a WHERE clause. They are valid only inside a HAVING clause.

---

Let's look at an example. Suppose we want to know all the towns where we have more than
a single customer. We could do it using count(*), and then visually look for the relevant towns.
However, that's not a sensible solution in a situation where there may be thousands of towns.
Instead, we use a HAVING clause to restrict the answers to rows where count(*) was greater than
one, like this:

```
bpsimple=# SELECT count(*), town FROM customer
bpsimple=# GROUP BY town HAVING count(*) > 1;
 count |   town
-------+----------
     3 | Bingham
     2 | Nicetown
(2 rows)

bpsimple=#
```

Notice that we still must have our GROUP BY clause, and it appears before the HAVING clause. Now that we have all the basics of count(*), GROUP BY, and HAVING, let's put them together in a bigger example.

**Try It Out: Use HAVING**

Suppose we are thinking of setting up a delivery schedule. We want to know the last names and towns of all our customers, except we want to exclude Lincoln (maybe it's our local town), and we are interested only in the names and towns with more than one customer.

This is not as difficult as it might sound. We just need to build up our solution bit by bit, which is often a good approach with SQL. If it looks too difficult, start by solving a simpler, but similar problem, and then extend the initial solution until you solve the more complex problem. Effectively, take a problem, break it down into smaller parts, and then solve each of the smaller parts.

Let's start with simply returning the data, rather than counting it. We sort by town to make it a little easier to see what is going on:

```
bpsimple=# SELECT lname, town FROM customer
bpsimple=#  WHERE town <> 'Lincoln' ORDER BY town;
  lname   |    town
----------+-----------
 Stones   | Bingham
 Stones   | Bingham
 Jones    | Bingham
 Stones   | Hightown
 Hickman  | Histon
 Stones   | Lowtown
 Hudson   | Milltown
 Matthew  | Nicetown
 Matthew  | Nicetown
 Cozens   | Oakenham
 Hardy    | Oxbridge
 Howard   | Tibsville
 O'Neill  | Welltown
 Neill    | Winnersby
 Matthew  | Yuleville
(15 rows)

bpsimple=#
```

Looks good so far, doesn't it?

Now if we use count(*) to do the counting for us, we also need to GROUP BY the lname and town:

```
bpsimple=# SELECT count(*), lname, town FROM customer
bpsimple-#  WHERE town <> 'Lincoln' GROUP BY lname, town ORDER BY town;
 count |  lname   |    town
-------+----------+-----------
     2 | Stones   | Bingham
     1 | Jones    | Bingham
     1 | Stones   | Hightown
     1 | Hickman  | Histon
     1 | Stones   | Lowtown
     1 | Hudson   | Milltown
     2 | Matthew  | Nicetown
     1 | Cozens   | Oakenham
     1 | Hardy    | Oxbridge
     1 | Howard   | Tibsville
     1 | O'Neill  | Welltown
     1 | Neill    | Winnersby
     1 | Matthew  | Yuleville
(13 rows)

bpsimple=#
```

We can actually see the answer now by visual inspection, but we are almost at the full solution, which is simply to add a HAVING clause to pick out those rows with a count(*) greater than one:

```
bpsimple=# SELECT count(*), lname, town FROM customer
bpsimple-#  WHERE town <> 'Lincoln' GROUP BY lname, town HAVING count(*) > 1;
 count |  lname   |   town
-------+----------+----------
     2 | Matthew  | Nicetown
     2 | Stones   | Bingham
(2 rows)

bpsimple=#
```

As you can see, the solution is straightforward when you break down the problem into parts.

### How It Works

We solved the problem in three stages:

- We wrote a simple SELECT statement to retrieve all the rows we were interested in.

- Next, we added a count(*) function and a GROUP BY clause, to count the unique lname and town combination.

- Finally, we added a HAVING clause to extract only those rows where the count(*) was greater than one.

There is one slight problem with this approach, which isn't noticeable on our small sample database. On a big database, this iterative development approach has some drawbacks. If we were working with a customer database containing thousands of rows, we would have customer lists scrolling past for a very long time while we developed our query. Fortunately, there is often an easy way to develop your queries on a sample of the data, by using the primary key. If we add the condition WHERE customer_id < 50 to all our queries, we could work on a sample of the first 50 customer_ids in the database. Once we were happy with our SQL, we could simply remove the WHERE clause to execute our solution on the whole table. Of course, we need to be careful that the sample data we used to test our SQL is representative of the full data set and be wary that smaller samples may not have fully exercised our SQL.

## Count(*column name*)

A slight variant of the count(*) function is to replace the * with a column name. The difference is that COUNT(*column name*) counts occurrences in the table where the provided column name is not NULL.

### Try It Out: Use Count(*column name*)

Suppose we add some more data to our customer table, with some new customers having NULL phone numbers:

```
INSERT INTO customer(title, fname, lname, addressline, town, zipcode)
VALUES('Mr','Gavyn','Smith','23 Harlestone','Milltown','MT7 7HI');
INSERT INTO customer(title, fname, lname, addressline, town, zipcode, phone)
VALUES('Mrs','Sarah','Harvey','84 Willow Way','Lincoln','LC3 7RD','527 3739');
INSERT INTO customer(title, fname, lname, addressline, town, zipcode)
VALUES('Mr','Steve','Harvey','84 Willow Way','Lincoln','LC3 7RD');
INSERT INTO customer(title, fname, lname, addressline, town, zipcode)
VALUES('Mr','Paul','Garrett','27 Chase Avenue','Lowtown','LT5 8TQ');
```

Let's check how many customers we have whose phone numbers we don't know:

```
bpsimple=# SELECT customer_id FROM customer WHERE phone IS NULL;
 customer_id
-------------
          16
          18
          19
(3 rows)

bpsimple=#
```

We see that there are three customers for whom we don't have a phone number. Let's see how many customers there are in total:

```
bpsimple=# SELECT count(*) FROM customer;
 count
-------
    19
(1 row)

bpsimple=#
```

There are 19 customers in total. Now if we count the number of customers where the phone column is not NULL, there should be 16 of them:

```
bpsimple=# SELECT count(phone) FROM customer;
 count
-------
    16
(1 row)

bpsimple=#
```

**How It Works**

The only difference between count(*) and count(*column name*) is that the form with an explicit column name counts only rows where the named column is not NULL, and the * form counts all rows. In all other respects, such as using GROUP BY and HAVING, count(*column name*) works in the same way as count(*).

### Count(DISTINCT *column name*)

The count aggregate function supports the DISTINCT keyword, which restricts the function to considering only those values that are unique in a column, not counting duplicates. We can illustrate its behavior by counting the number of distinct towns that occur in our customer table, like this:

```
bpsimple=# SELECT count(DISTINCT town) AS "distinct", count(town) AS "all"
bpsimple=# FROM customer;
 distinct | all
----------+-----
       12 |  15
(1 row)

bpsimple=#
```

Here, we see that there are 15 towns, but only 12 distinct ones (Bingham and Nicetown) appear more than once.

Now that we understand count(*) and have learned the principles of aggregate functions, we can apply the same logic to all the other aggregate functions.

## The Min Function

As you might expect, the min function takes a column name parameter and returns the minimum value found in that column. For numeric type columns, the result would be as expected. For temporal types, such as date values, it returns the largest date, which might be either in the past or future. For variable-length strings (varchar type), the result is slightly unexpected: it compares the strings after they have been right-padded with blanks.

---

■**Caution** Be wary of using min or max on varchar type columns, because the results may not be what you expect.

---

For example, suppose we want to find the smallest shipping charge we levied on an order. We could use min, like this:

```
bpsimple=# SELECT min(shipping) FROM orderinfo;
 min
------
 0.00
(1 row)

bpsimple=#
```

This shows the smallest charge was zero.

Notice what happens when we try the same function on our phone column, where we know there are NULL values:

```
bpsimple=# SELECT min(phone) FROM customer;
   min
----------
 010 4567
(1 row)

bpsimple=#
```

Now you might have expected the answer to be NULL, or an empty string. Given that NULL generally means unknown, however, the min function ignores NULL values. Ignoring NULL values is a feature of all the aggregate functions, except count(*). (Whether there is any value in knowing the smallest phone number is, of course, a different question.)

## The Max Function

It's not going to be a surprise that the max function is similar to min, but in reverse. As you would expect, max takes a column name parameter and returns the maximum value found in that column.

For example, we could find the largest shipping charge we levied on an order like this:

```
bpsimple=# SELECT max(shipping) FROM orderinfo;
 max
------
 3.99
(1 row)

bpsimple=#
```

Just as with min, NULL values are ignored with max, as in this example:

```
bpsimple=# SELECT max(phone) FROM customer;
   max
----------
 961 4526
(1 row)

bpsimple=#
```

That is pretty much all you need to know about max.

## The Sum Function

The sum function takes the name of a numeric column and provides the total. Just as with min and max, NULL values are ignored.

For example, we could get the total shipping charges for all orders like this:

```
bpsimple=# SELECT sum(shipping) FROM orderinfo;
 sum
------
 9.97
(1 row)

bpsimple=#
```

Like count, the sum function supports a DISTINCT variant. You can ask it to add up only the unique values, so that multiple rows with the same value are counted only once:

```
bpsimple=# SELECT sum(DISTINCT shipping) FROM orderinfo;
 sum
------
 6.98
(1 row)

bpsimple=#
```

Note that in practice, there are few real-world uses for this variant.

## The Avg Function

The last aggregate function we will look at is avg, which also takes a column name and returns the average of the entries. Like sum, it ignores NULL values. Here is an example:

```
bpsimple=# SELECT avg(shipping) FROM orderinfo;
      avg
--------------
 1.9940000000000000
(1 row)

bpsimple=#
```

The avg function can also take a DISTINCT keyword to work on only distinct values:

```
bpsimple=# SELECT avg(DISTINCT shipping) FROM orderinfo;
      avg
--------------
 2.3266666666666667
(1 row)

bpsimple=#
```

**■Note** In standard SQL and in PostgreSQL's implementation, there are no mode or median functions. However, a few commercial vendors do support them as extensions.

# The Subquery

Now that we have met various SQL statements that have a single SELECT in them, we can look at a whole class of data-retrieval statements that combine two or more SELECT statements in several ways.

A *subquery* is where one or more of the WHERE conditions of a SELECT are other SELECT statements. Subqueries are somewhat more difficult to understand than single SELECT statement queries, but they are very useful and open up a whole new area of data-selection criteria.

Suppose we want to find the items that have a cost price that is higher than the average cost price. We can do this in two steps: find the average price using a SELECT statement with an aggregate function, and then use the answer in a second SELECT statement to find the rows we want (using the cast function, which was introduced in Chapter 4), like this:

```
bpsimple=# SELECT avg(cost_price) FROM item;
      avg
--------------
 7.2490909090909091
(1 row)

bpsimple=# SELECT * FROM item
bpsimple-#     WHERE cost_price > cast(7.249 AS numeric(7,2));
 item_id |   description   | cost_price | sell_price
---------+-----------------+------------+------------
       1 | Wood Puzzle     |      15.23 |      21.95
       2 | Rubik Cube      |       7.45 |      11.49
       5 | Picture Frame   |       7.54 |       9.95
       6 | Fan Small       |       9.23 |      15.75
       7 | Fan Large       |      13.36 |      19.95
      11 | Speakers        |      19.73 |      25.32
(6 rows)

bpsimple=#
```

This does seem rather inelegant. What we really want to do is pass the result of the first query straight into the second query, without needing to remember it and type it back in for a second query.

The solution is to use a subquery. We put the first query in brackets and use it as part of a WHERE clause to the second query, like this:

```
bpsimple=# SELECT * from ITEM
bpsimple-#   WHERE cost_price > (SELECT avg(cost_price) FROM item);
 item_id |  description  | cost_price | sell_price
---------+---------------+------------+------------
       1 | Wood Puzzle   |      15.23 |      21.95
       2 | Rubik Cube    |       7.45 |      11.49
       5 | Picture Frame |       7.54 |       9.95
       6 | Fan Small     |       9.23 |      15.75
       7 | Fan Large     |      13.36 |      19.95
      11 | Speakers      |      19.73 |      25.32
(6 rows)

bpsimple=#
```

As you can see, we get the same result, but without needing the intermediate step or the cast function, since the result is already of the right type. PostgreSQL runs the query in brackets first. After getting the answer, it then runs the outer query, substituting the answer from the inner query.

We can have many subqueries using various WHERE clauses if we want. We are not restricted to just one, although needing multiple, nested SELECT statements is rare.

**Try It Out: Use a Subquery**

Let's try a more complex example. Suppose we want to know all the items where the cost price is above the average cost price, but the selling price is below the average selling price. (Such an indicator suggests our margin is not very good, so we hope there are not too many items that fit those criteria.) The general query is going to be of this form:

```
SELECT * FROM item
WHERE cost_price > average cost price
AND sell_price < average selling price
```

We already know the average cost price can be determined with the query SELECT avg(cost_price) FROM item. Finding the average selling price is accomplished in a similar fashion, using the query SELECT avg(sell_price) FROM item.

If we put these three queries together, we get this:

```
bpsimple=# SELECT * FROM item
bpsimple-#   WHERE cost_price > (SELECT avg(cost_price) FROM item) AND
bpsimple-#         sell_price < (SELECT avg(sell_price) FROM item);
 item_id |  description  | cost_price | sell_price
---------+---------------+------------+------------
       5 | Picture Frame |       7.54 |       9.95
(1 row)

bpsimple=#
```

Perhaps someone needs to look at the price of picture frames and see if it is correct!

**How It Works**

PostgreSQL first scans the query and finds that there are two queries in brackets, which are the subqueries. It evaluates each of those subqueries independently, and then puts the answers back into the appropriate part of the main query of the WHERE clause before executing it.

We could also have applied additional WHERE clauses or ORDER BY clauses. It is perfectly valid to mix WHERE conditions that come from subqueries with more conventional conditions.

## Subqueries That Return Multiple Rows

So far, we have seen only subqueries that return a single result, because an aggregate function was used in the subquery. Subqueries can also return zero or more rows.

Suppose we want to know which items we have in stock where the cost price is greater than 10.0. We could use a single SELECT statement, like this:

```
bpsimple=# SELECT s.item_id, s.quantity FROM stock s, item i
bpsimple-# WHERE i.cost_price > cast(10.0 AS numeric(7,2))
bpsimple-# AND s.item_id = i.item_id;
 item_id | quantity
---------+----------
       1 |       12
       7 |        8
(2 rows)

bpsimple=#
```

Notice that we give the tables alias names (stock becomes s; item becomes i) to keep the query shorter. All we are doing is joining the two tables (s.item_id = i.item_id), while also adding a condition about the cost price in the item table (i.cost_price > cast(10.0 AS NUMERIC(7,2))).

We can also write this as a subquery, using the keyword IN to test against a list of values. To use IN in this context, we first need to write a query that gives a list of item_ids where the item has a cost price less than 10.0:

```
SELECT item_id FROM item WHERE cost_price > cast(10.0 AS NUMERIC(7,2));
```

We also need a query to select items from the stock table:

```
SELECT * FROM stock WHERE item_id IN list of values
```

We can then put the two queries together, like this:

```
bpsimple=# SELECT * FROM stock WHERE item_id IN
bpsimple-#  (SELECT item_id FROM item
bpsimple(#   WHERE cost_price > cast(10.0 AS numeric(7,2)));
 item_id | quantity
---------+----------
       1 |       12
       7 |        8
(2 rows)

bpsimple=#
```

This shows the same result.

Just as with more conventional queries, we could negate the condition by writing NOT IN, and we could also add WHERE clauses and ORDER BY conditions.

It is quite common to be able to use either a subquery or an equivalent join to retrieve the same information. However, this is not always the case; not all subqueries can be rewritten as joins, so it is important to understand them.

If you do have a subquery that can also be written as a join, which one should you use? There are two matters to consider: readability and performance. If the query is one that you use occasionally on small tables and it executes quickly, use whichever form you find most readable. If it is a heavily used query on large tables, it may be worth writing it in different ways and experimenting to discover which performs best. You may find that the query optimizer is able to optimize both styles, so their performance is identical; in that case, readability automatically wins. You may also find that performance is critically dependent on the exact data in your database, or that it varies dramatically as the number of rows in different tables changes.

---

■**Caution** Be careful in testing the performance of SQL statements. There are a lot of variables beyond your control, such as the caching of data by the operating system.

---

## Correlated Subqueries

The subquery types we have seen so far are those where we executed a query to get an answer, which we then "plug in" to a second query. The two queries are otherwise unrelated and are called *uncorrelated subqueries*. This is because there are no linked tables between the inner and outer queries. We may be using the same column from the same table in both parts of the SELECT statement, but they are related only by the result of the subquery being fed back into the main query's WHERE clause.

There is another group of subqueries, called *correlated subqueries*, where the relationship between the two parts of the query is somewhat more complex. In a correlated subquery, a table in the inner SELECT will be joined to a table in the outer SELECT, thereby defining a relationship between these two queries. This is a powerful group of subqueries, which quite often cannot be rewritten as simple SELECT statements with joins. A correlated query has the general form:

```
SELECT columnA from table1 T1
WHERE T1.columnB =
  (SELECT T2.columnB FROM table2 T2 WHERE T2.columnC = T1.columnC)
```

We have written this as some pseudo SQL to make it a little easier to understand. The important thing to notice is that the table in the outer SELECT, T1, also appears in the inner SELECT. The inner and outer queries are, therefore, deemed to be correlated. You will notice we have aliased the table names. This is important, as the rules for table names in correlated subqueries are rather complex, and a slight mistake can give strange results.

---

■**Tip** We strongly suggest that you always alias all tables in a correlated subquery, as this is the safest option.

---

When this correlated subquery is executed, something quite complex happens. First, a row from table T1 is retrieved for the outer SELECT, then the column T1.columnB is passed to the inner query, which then executes, selecting from table T2 but using the information that is passed in. The result of this is then passed back to the outer query, which completes evaluation of the WHERE clause, before moving on to the next row. This is illustrated in Figure 7-1.

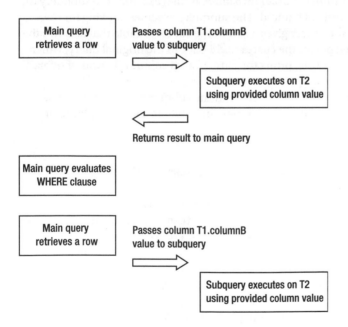

**Figure 7-1.** *The execution of a correlated subquery*

If this sounds a little long-winded, that is because it is. Correlated subqueries often execute quite inefficiently. However, they do occasionally solve some particularly complex problems. So, it's well worth knowing they exist, even though you may use them only infrequently.

### Try It Out: Execute a Correlated Subquery

On a simple database, such as the one we are using, there is little need for correlated subqueries, but we can still use our sample database to demonstrate their use.

Suppose we want to know the date when orders were placed for customers in Bingham. Although we could write this more conventionally, we will use a correlated subquery, like this:

```
bpsimple=# SELECT oi.date_placed FROM orderinfo oi
bpsimple-#  WHERE oi.customer_id =
bpsimple-#  (SELECT c.customer_id from customer c
bpsimple(#   WHERE c.customer_id = oi.customer_id and town = 'Bingham');
 date_placed
-------------
 2000-06-23
 2000-07-21
(2 rows)

bpsimple=#
```

### How It Works

The query starts by selecting a row from the orderinfo table. It then executes the subquery on the customer table, using the customer_id it found. The subquery executes, looking for rows where the customer_id from the outer query gives a row in the customer table that also has the town Bingham. If it finds one, it then passes the customer_id back to the original query, which completes the WHERE clause, and if it is true, prints the date_placed column. The outer query then proceeds to the next row, and the sequence repeats.

It is also possible to create a correlated subquery with the subquery in the FROM clause. Here is an example that finds all of the data for customers in Bingham that have placed an order with us.

```
bpsimple=# SELECT * FROM orderinfo o,
bpsimple=#                (SELECT * FROM customer c WHERE town = 'Bingham') c
bpsimple=# WHERE c.customer_id = o.customer_id;
 orderinfo_id | customer_id | date_placed | date_shipped | shipping |
 customer_id | title | fname | lname | addressline | town    | zipcode  | phone
--------------+-------------+-------------+--------------+----------+-----------+-----------
--+-------+-------+--------+--------------+---------+------------+----------
            2 |           8 | 2004-06-23  | 2004-06-24   |    0.00  |
 8 | Mrs  | Ann   | Stones | 34 Holly Way | Bingham | BG4 2WE    | 342 5982
            5 |           8 | 2004-07-21  | 2004-07-24   |    0.00  |
 8 | Mrs  | Ann   | Stones | 34 Holly Way | Bingham | BG4 2WE    | 342 5982
(2 rows)

bpsimple=#
```

The subquery result takes the place of a table in the main query, in the sense that the subquery produces a set of rows containing just those customers in Bingham.

Now you have an idea of how correlated subqueries can be written. When you come across a problem that you cannot seem to solve in SQL with more common queries, you may find that the correlated subquery is the answer to your difficulties.

## Existence Subqueries

Another form of subquery tests for existence using the EXISTS keyword in the WHERE clause, without needing to know what data is present.

Suppose we want to list all the customers who have placed orders. In our sample database, there are not many. The first part of the query is easy:

```
SELECT fname, lname FROM customer c;
```

Notice that we have aliased the table name customer to c, ready for the subquery. The next part of the query needs to discover if the customer_id also exists in the orderinfo table:

```
SELECT 1 FROM orderinfo oi WHERE oi.customer_id = c.customer_id;
```

There are two very important aspects to notice here. First, we have used a common trick. Where we need to execute a query but don't need the results, we simply place 1 where a column name would be. This means that if any data is found, a 1 will be returned, which is an easy and efficient way of saying true. This is a weird idea, so let's just try it:

```
bpsimple=# SELECT 1 FROM customer WHERE town = 'Bingham';
 ?column?
----------
        1
        1
        1
(3 rows)

bpsimple=#
```

It may look a little odd, but it does work. It is important not to use count(*) here, because we need a result from each row where the town is Bingham, not just to know how many customers are from Bingham.

The second important thing to notice is that we use the table customer in this subquery, which was actually in the main query. This is what makes it correlated. As before, we alias all the table names. Now we need to put the two halves together.

For our query, using EXISTS is a good way of combining the two SELECT statements together, because we only want to know if the subquery returns a row:

```
bpsimple=# SELECT fname, lname FROM customer c
bpsimple-# WHERE EXISTS (SELECT 1 FROM orderinfo oi
bpsimple(#                WHERE oi.customer_id = c.customer_id);
 fname |  lname
-------+---------
 Alex  | Matthew
 Ann   | Stones
 Laura | Hardy
 David | Hudson
(4 rows)

bpsimple=#
```

An EXISTS clause will normally execute more efficiently than other types of joins or IN conditions. Therefore, it's often worth using it in preference to other types of joins in cases where you have a choice of how to write the subquery.

# The UNION Join

We are now going to look at another way multiple SELECT statements can be combined to give us more advanced selection capabilities. Let's start with an example of a problem that we need to solve.

In the previous chapter, we used the tcust table as a loading table, while adding data into our main customer table. Now suppose that in the period between loading our tcust table with new customer data and being able to clean it and load it into our main customer table, we were asked for a list of all the towns where we had customers, including the new data. We might reasonably have pointed out that since we hadn't cleaned and loaded the customer data into the main table yet, we could not be sure of the accuracy of the new data, so any list of towns combining the two lists might not be accurate either. However, it may be that verified accuracy wasn't important. Perhaps all that was needed was a general indication of the geographical spread of customers, not exact data.

We could solve this problem by selecting the town from the customer table, saving it, and then selecting the town from the tcust table, saving it again, and then combining the two lists. This does seem rather inelegant, as we would need to query two tables, both containing a list of towns, save the results, and merge them somehow.

Isn't there some way we could combine the town lists automatically? As you might gather from the title of this section, there is a way, and it's called a UNION join. These joins are not very common, but in a few circumstances, they are exactly what is needed to solve a problem, and they are also very easy to use.

**Try It Out: Use a UNION Join**

Let's begin by putting some data back in our tcust table, so it looks like this:

```
bpsimple=# SELECT * FROM tcust;
title| fname  | lname   | addressline    | town     | zipcode    | phone
-----+---------+----------+-----------------+----------+------------+---------
 Mr  | Peter   | Bradley  | 72 Milton Rise  | Keynes   | MK41 2HQ   |
 Mr  | Kevin   | Carney   | 43 Glen Way     | Lincoln  | LI2 7RD    | 786 3454
 Mr  | Brian   | Waters   | 21 Troon Rise   | Lincoln  | LI7 6GT    | 786 7245
 Mr  | Malcolm | Whalley  | 3 Craddock Way  | Welltown | WT3 4GQ    | 435 6543
(4 rows)

bpsimple=#
```

We already know how to select the town from each table. We use a simple pair of SELECT statements, like this:

```
SELECT town FROM tcust;
SELECT town FROM customer;
```

Each gives us a list of towns. In order to combine them, we use the UNION keyword to stitch the two SELECT statements together:

```
SELECT town FROM tcust UNION SELECT town FROM customer;
```

We input our SQL statement, splitting it across multiple lines to make it easier to read. Notice the psql prompt changes from =# to -# to show it's a continuation line, and that there is only a single semicolon, right at the end, because this is all a single SQL statement:

```
bpsimple=# SELECT town FROM tcust
bpsimple-# UNION
bpsimple-# SELECT town FROM customer;
   town
-----------
 Bingham
 Hightown
 Histon
 Keynes
 Lincoln
 Lowtown
 Milltown
 Nicetown
 Oahenham
 Oxbridge
 Tibsville
 Welltown
 Winersby
 Yuleville
(14 rows)

bpsimple=#
```

### How It Works

PostgreSQL has taken the list of towns from both tables and combined them into a single list. Notice, however, that it has removed all duplicates. If we wanted a list of all the towns, including duplicates, we could have written UNION ALL, rather than just UNION.

This ability to combine SELECT statements is not limited to a single column; we could have combined both the towns and ZIP codes:

```
SELECT town, zipcode FROM tcust UNION SELECT town, zipcode FROM customer;
```

This would have produced a list with both columns present. It would have been a longer list, because zipcode is included, and hence there are more unique rows to be retrieved.

There are limits to what the UNION join can achieve. The two lists of columns you ask to be combined from the two tables must each have the same number of columns, and the chosen corresponding columns must also have compatible types.

Let's see another example of a UNION join using the different, but compatible columns, title and town:

```
bpsimple=# SELECT title FROM customer
bpsimple-# UNION
bpsimple-# SELECT town FROM tcust;
  title
----------
 Keynes
 Lincoln
 Miss
 Mr
 Mrs
 Welltown
(6 rows)

bpsimple=#
```

The query, although rather nonsensical, is valid, because PostgreSQL can combine the columns, even though title is a fixed-length column and town is a variable-length column, because they are both strings of characters. If we tried to combine customer_id and town, for example, PostgreSQL would tell us that it could not be done, because the column types are different.

Generally, this is all you need to know about UNION joins. Occasionally, they are a handy way to combine data from two or more tables.

# Self Joins

One very special type of join is called a *self join*, and it is used where we want to use a join between columns that are in the same table. It's quite rare to need to do this, but occasionally, it can be useful.

Suppose we sell items that can be sold as a set or individually. For the sake of example, say we sell a set of chairs and a table as a single item, but we also sell the table and chairs separately. What we would like to do is store not only the individual items, but also the relationship between them when they are sold as a single item. This is frequently called *parts explosion*, and we will meet it again in Chapter 12.

Let's start by creating a table that can hold not only an item ID and its description, but also a second item ID, like this:

```
CREATE TABLE part (part_id int, description varchar(32), parent_part_id INT);
```

We will use the parent_part_id to store the component ID of which this is a component. For this example, our table and chairs set has an item_id of 1, which is composed of chairs, item_id 2, and a table, item_id 3. The INSERT statements would look like this:

```
bpsimple=# INSERT INTO part(part_id, description, parent_part_id)
bpsimple-# VALUES(1, 'table and chairs', NULL);
INSERT 21579 1

bpsimple=# INSERT INTO part(part_id, description, parent_part_id)
bpsimple-# VALUES(2, 'chair', 1);
INSERT 21580 1

bpsimple=# INSERT INTO part(part_id, description, parent_part_id)
bpsimple-# VALUES(3, 'table', 1);
INSERT 21581 1

bpsimple=#
```

Now we have stored the data, but how do we retrieve the information about the individual parts that make up a particular component? We need to join the part table to itself. This turns out to be quite easy. We alias the table names, and then we can write a WHERE clause referring to the same table, but using different names:

```
bpsimple=# SELECT p1.description, p2.description FROM part p1, part p2
bpsimple-# WHERE p1.part_id = p2.parent_part_id;
   description     | description
------------------+-------------
 table and chairs | chair
 table and chairs | table
(2 rows)

bpsimple=#
```

This works, but it is a little confusing, because we have two output columns with the same name. We can easily rectify this by naming them using AS:

```
bpsimple=# SELECT p1.description AS "Combined", p2.description AS "Parts"
bpsimple-# FROM part p1, part p2 WHERE p1.part_id = p2.parent_part_id;
    Combined      | Parts
------------------+-------
 table and chairs | chair
 table and chairs | table
(2 rows)

bpsimple=#
```

We will see self joins again in Chapter 12, when we look at how a manager/subordinate relationship can be stored in a single table.

# Outer Joins

Another class of joins is known as the *outer join*. This type of join is similar to more conventional joins, but it uses a slightly different syntax, which is why we have postponed meeting them until now.

Suppose we want to have a list of all items we sell, indicating the quantity we have in stock. This apparently simple request turns out to be surprisingly difficult in the SQL we know so far, although it can be done. This example uses the item and stock tables in our sample database. As you will remember, all the items that we might sell are held in the item table, and only items we actually stock are held in the stock table, as illustrated in Figure 7-2.

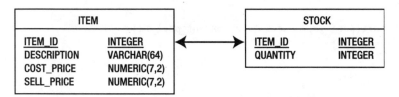

**Figure 7-2.** *Schema for the item and stock tables*

Let's work through a solution, beginning with using only the SQL we know so far. Let's try a simple SELECT, joining the two tables:

```
bpsimple=# SELECT i.item_id, s.quantity FROM item i, stock s
bpsimple-# WHERE i.item_id = s.item_id;
 item_id | quantity
---------+----------
       1 |       12
       2 |        2
       4 |        8
       5 |        3
       7 |        8
       8 |       18
      10 |        1
(7 rows)

bpsimple=#
```

It's easy to see (since we happen to know that our item_ids in the item table are sequential, with no gaps), that some item_ids are missing. The rows that are missing are those relating to items that we do not stock, since the join between the item and stock tables fails for these rows, as the stock table has no entry for that item_id. We can find the missing rows, using a subquery and an IN clause:

```
bpsimple=# SELECT i.item_id FROM item i
bpsimple-# WHERE i.item_id NOT IN
bpsimple-#   (SELECT i.item_id FROM item i, stock s
bpsimple(#    WHERE i.item_id = s.item_id);
 item_id
---------
       3
       6
       9
      11
(4 rows)

bpsimple=#
```

We might translate this as, "Tell me all the item_ids in the item table, excluding those that also appear in the stock table."

The inner SELECT statement is simply the one we used earlier, but this time, we use the list of item_ids it returns as part of another SELECT statement. The main SELECT statement lists all the known item_ids, except that the WHERE NOT IN clause removes those item_ids found in the subquery.

So now we have a list of item_ids for which we have no stock, and a list of item_ids for which we do have stock, but retrieved using different queries. What we need to do now is glue the two lists together, which is the job of the UNION join. However, there is a slight problem. Our first statement returns two columns, item_id and quantity, but our second SELECT returns only item_ids, as there is no stock for these items. We need to add a dummy column to the second SELECT, so it has the same number and types of columns as the first SELECT. We will use NULL. Here is our complete query:

```
SELECT i.item_id, s.quantity FROM item i, stock s WHERE i.item_id = s.item_id
UNION
SELECT i.item_id, NULL FROM item i WHERE i.item_id NOT IN
    (SELECT i.item_id FROM item i, stock s WHERE i.item_id = s.item_id);
```

This looks a bit complicated, but let's give it a try:

```
bpsimple=# SELECT i.item_id, s.quantity FROM item i, stock s
bpsimple-# WHERE i.item_id = s.item_id
bpsimple-# UNION
bpsimple-# SELECT i.item_id, NULL FROM item i
bpsimple-# WHERE i.item_id NOT IN
bpsimple-#   (SELECT i.item_id FROM item i, stock s WHERE i.item_id = s.item_id);
 item_id | quantity
---------+----------
       1 |       12
       2 |        2
       3 |
       4 |        8
       5 |        3
       6 |
```

```
 7 |        8
 8 |       18
 9 |
10 |        1
11 |
(11 rows)
```

```
bpsimple=#
```

In the early days of SQL, this was pretty much the only way of solving this type of problem, except that SQL89 did not allow the NULL we used in the second SELECT statement as a column. Fortunately, most vendors allowed the NULL, or life would have been even more difficult. If we had not been allowed to use NULL, we would have used 0 (zero) as the next best alternative. NULL is better because 0 is potentially misleading; NULL will always be blank.

To get around this rather complex solution for what is a fairly common problem, vendors invented outer joins. Unfortunately, because this type of join did not appear in the standard, all the vendors invented their own solutions, with similar ideas but different syntax.

Oracle and DB2 used a syntax with a + sign in the WHERE clause to indicate that all values of a table must appear (the preserved table), even if the join failed. Sybase used *= in the WHERE clause to indicate the preserved table. Both of these syntaxes are reasonably straightforward, but unfortunately different, which is not good for the portability of your SQL.

When the SQL92 standard appeared, it specified a very general-purpose way of implementing joins, resulting in a much more logical system for outer joins. Vendors have, however, been slow to implement the new standard. (Sybase 11 and Oracle 8, which both came out after the SQL92 standard, did not support it, for example.) PostgreSQL implemented the SQL92 standard method starting in version 7.1.

---

■**Note** If you are running a version of PostgreSQL prior to version 7.1, you will need to upgrade to try the last examples in this chapter. It's probably worth upgrading if you are running a version older than 7.x anyway, as version 8 has significant improvements over older versions.

---

The SQL92 syntax for outer joins replaces the WHERE clause we are familiar with, using an ON clause for joining tables, and adds the LEFT OUTER JOIN keywords. The syntax looks like this:

```
SELECT columns FROM table1
  LEFT OUTER JOIN table2 ON table1.column = table2.column
```

The table name to the left of LEFT OUTER JOIN is always the preserved table, the one from which all rows are shown.

So, now we can rewrite our query, using this new syntax:

```
SELECT i.item_id, s.quantity FROM item i
  LEFT OUTER JOIN stock s ON i.item_id = s.item_id;
```

Does this look almost too simple to be true? Let's give it a go:

```
bpsimple=# SELECT i.item_id, s.quantity FROM item i
bpsimple-# LEFT OUTER JOIN stock s ON i.item_id = s.item_id;
 item_id | quantity
---------+----------
       1 |       12
       2 |        2
       3 |
       4 |        8
       5 |        3
       6 |
       7 |        8
       8 |       18
       9 |
      10 |        1
      11 |
(11 rows)

bpsimple=#
```

As you can see, the answer is identical to the one we got from our original version.

You can see why most vendors felt they needed to implement an outer join, even though it wasn't in the original SQL89 standard.

There is also the equivalent RIGHT OUTER JOIN, but the LEFT OUTER JOIN is used more often (at least for Westerners, it makes more sense to list the known items down the left side of the output rather than the right).

### Try It Out: Use a More Complex Condition

The simple LEFT OUTER JOIN we have used is great as far as it goes, but how do we add more complex conditions?

Suppose we want only rows from the stock table where we have more than two items in stock, and overall, we are interested only in rows where the cost price is greater than 5.0. This is quite a complex problem, because we want to apply one rule to the item table (that cost_price > 5.0) and a different rule to the stock table (quantity > 2), but we still want to list all rows from the item table where the condition on the item table is true, even if there is no stock at all.

What we do is combine ON conditions that work on left-outer-joined tables only, with WHERE conditions that limit all the rows returned after the table join has been performed.

The condition on the stock table is part of the outer join. We don't want to restrict rows where there is no quantity, so we write this as part of the ON condition:

```
ON i.item_id = s.item_id AND s.quantity > 2
```

For the item condition, which applies to all rows, we use a WHERE clause:

```
WHERE i.cost_price > cast(5.0 AS numeric(7,2));
```

Putting them both together, we get this:

```
bpsimple=# SELECT i.item_id, i.cost_price, s.quantity FROM item i
bpsimple-# LEFT OUTER JOIN stock s
```

```
bpsimple-# ON i.item_id = s.item_id AND s.quantity > 2
bpsimple-# WHERE i.cost_price > cast(5.0 AS numeric(7,2));
 item_id | cost_price | quantity
---------+------------+----------
       1 |      15.23 |       12
       2 |       7.45 |
       5 |       7.54 |        3
       6 |       9.23 |
       7 |      13.36 |        8
      11 |      19.73 |
(6 rows)


bpsimple=#
```

**How It Works**

We use a LEFT OUTER JOIN to get all the values from the item table, optionally joining to the stock table where both a row exists and the quantity is greater than 2. This gives us a set of rows where all the rows from the item table appear, but the quantity column (from the stock table) will contain NULL unless it both has an entry for that item and the quantity value is greater than 2. The WHERE clause is then applied, which allows through rows only where the cost price (from the item table) is greater than 5.0.

# Summary

We started the chapter looking at aggregate functions that we can use in SQL to select single values from a number of rows. In particular, we met the count(*) function, which you will find widely used to determine the number of rows in a table. We then met the GROUP BY clause, which allows us to select groups of rows to apply the aggregate function to, followed by the HAVING clause, which allows us to restrict the output of rows containing particular aggregate values.

Next, we took a look at subqueries, where we use the results from one query in another query. We saw some simple examples and touched on a much more difficult kind of query, the correlated subquery, where the same column appears in both parts of a subquery.

Then we looked briefly at the UNION join, which allows us to combine the output of two queries in a single result set. Although this is not widely used, it can occasionally be very useful.

Finally we met outer joins, a very important feature that allows us to perform joins between two tables, retrieving rows from the first table, even when the join to the second table fails.

In this chapter, we have covered some difficult aspects of SQL. You have now seen a wide range of SQL syntax, so if you see some advanced SQL in existing systems, you will at least have a reasonable understanding of what is being done. Don't worry if some parts still seem a little unclear. One of the best ways of truly understanding SQL is to use it, and use it extensively. Get PostgreSQL installed, install the test database and some sample data, and experiment.

In the next chapter, we will look in more detail at data types, creating tables, and other information that you need to know to build your own database.

■ ■ ■

# Data Definition
# and Manipulation

**U**p until now, we have concentrated on the PostgreSQL tools and data manipulation. Although we created a database early in the book, we looked only superficially at table creation and the data types available in PostgreSQL. We kept our table definitions simple by just using primary keys and defining a few columns that do not accept NULL values.

In a database, the quality of the data should always be one of our primary concerns. Having very strict rules about the data, enforced at the lowest level by the database, is one of the most effective measures we can use to maintain the data in a consistent state. This is also one of the features that distinguish true databases from simple indexed files, spreadsheets, and the like.

In this chapter, we will look in more detail at the data types available in PostgreSQL and how to manipulate them. Then we will look at how tables are managed, including how to use constraints, which allow us to significantly tighten the rules applied when data is added to or removed from the tables in the database. Next, we will take a brief look at views. Finally, we will explore foreign key constraints in depth and use them in the creation of an updated version of our sample database. We will create the bpfinal database, which we will use in the examples in the following chapters.

In this chapter, we will cover the following topics:

- Data types

- Data manipulation

- Table management

- Views

- Foreign key constraints

# Data Types

At the most basic level, PostgreSQL supports the following types of data:

- Boolean

- Character

- Number

- Temporal (time-based)

- PostgreSQL extension types

- Binary Large Object (BLOB)

Here, we will look at each of these types, except BLOB, which is less commonly used. If you're interested in BLOB types, see Appendix F for details on how to use them.

## The Boolean Data Type

The Boolean type is probably the simplest possible type. It can store only two possible values, true and false, and NULL, for when the value is unknown. The type declaration for a Boolean column is officially boolean, but it is almost always shortened to simply bool.

When data is inserted into a Boolean column in a table, PostgreSQL is quite flexible about what it will interpret as true and false. Table 8-1 offers a list of acceptable values and their interpretation. Anything else will be rejected, apart from NULL. Like SQL keywords, these are also case-insensitive; for example, 'TRUE' will also be interpreted as a Boolean true.

**Table 8-1.** *Ways of Specifying Boolean Values*

| Interpreted As True | Interpreted As False |
| --- | --- |
| '1' | '0' |
| 'yes' | 'no' |
| 'y' | 'n' |
| 'true' | 'false' |
| 't' | 'f' |

---

■**Note** When PostgreSQL displays the contents of a boolean column, it will show only t, f, and a space character for a true, false, and NULL, respectively, regardless of how you set the column value ('true', 'y', 't', and so on). Since PostgreSQL stores only one of the three possible states, the exact phrase you used to set the column value is never stored, only the interpreted value.

---

**Try It Out: Use Boolean Values**

Let's create a simple table with a bool column, and then experiment with some values. Rather than experiment in our bpsimple database with our "real" data, we will create a test database to use for these purposes. If you worked with the examples in Chapter 3, you may already have created this database, and just need to connect to it. If not, create it and then connect to it, as follows:

```
bpsimple=> CREATE DATABASE test;
CREATE DATABASE
bpsimple=> \c test
You are now connected to database "test".
test=>
```

Now we will create a table, testtype, with a variable-length string and a Boolean column, insert some data, and see what PostgreSQL stores. Here is our short psql session:

```
test=> CREATE TABLE testtype (
test(> valused varchar(10),
test(> boolres bool
test(> );
CREATE TABLE
test=>
test=> INSERT INTO testtype VALUES('TRUE', TRUE);
INSERT 17862 1
test=> INSERT INTO testtype VALUES('1', '1');
INSERT 17863 1
test=> INSERT INTO testtype VALUES('t', 't');
INSERT 17864 1
test=> INSERT INTO testtype VALUES('no', 'no');
INSERT 17865 1
test=> INSERT INTO testtype VALUES('f', 'f');
INSERT 17866 1
test=> INSERT INTO testtype VALUES('Null', NULL);
INSERT 17867 1
test=> INSERT INTO testtype VALUES('FALSE', FALSE);
INSERT 17868 1
test=>
```

Let's check that the data has been inserted:

```
test=> SELECT * FROM testtype;
 valused | boolres
---------+---------
 TRUE    | t
 1       | t
 t       | t
 no      | f
 f       | f
 Null    |
 FALSE   | f
(7 rows)

test=>
```

**How It Works**

We created a table testtype with two columns. The first column holds a string, and the second holds a Boolean value. We then inserted data into the table, each time making the first value a string, to remind us what we inserted, and the second the same value, but to be stored as a Boolean value. We also inserted a NULL, to show that PostgreSQL (unlike at least one commercial database) does allow NULL to be stored in a boolean type. We then extracted the data again, which showed us how PostgreSQL had interpreted each value we passed to it as one of true, false, or NULL.

## Character Data Types

The character data types are probably the most widely used in any database. There are three character type variants, used to represent the following string variations:

- A single character

- Fixed-length character strings

- Variable-length character strings

These are standard SQL character types, but PostgreSQL also supports a text type, which is similar to the variable-length type, except that we do not need to declare any upper limit to the length. This is not a standard SQL type, however, so it should be used with caution. The standard types are defined using char, char(*n*), and varchar(*n*). Table 8-2 shows the PostgreSQL character types.

**Table 8-2.** *PostgreSQL Character Types*

| Definition | Meaning |
| --- | --- |
| char | A single character. |
| char(*n*) | A set of characters exactly *n* characters in length, padded with spaces. If you attempt to store a string that is too long, an error will be generated. |
| varchar(*n*) | A set of characters up to *n* characters in length, with no padding. PostgreSQL has an extension to the SQL standard that allows specifying varchar without a length, which makes the length effectively unlimited. |
| text | Effectively, an unlimited length character string, like varchar but without the need to define a maximum. This is a PostgreSQL extension to the SQL standard. |

Given a choice of three standard types to use for character strings, which should you pick? As always, there is no definitive answer. If you know that your database is going to run only on PostgreSQL, you could use text, since it is easy to use and doesn't force you to decide on the maximum length. Its length is limited only by the maximum row size that PostgreSQL can support. If you are using a version of PostgreSQL earlier than 7.1, the row limit is around 8KB (unless you recompiled from source and changed it). From PostgreSQL 7.1 onwards, that limit is gone. The actual limit for any single field in a table for PostgreSQL versions 7.1 and later is 1GB; in practice, you should never need a character string that long.

The major downside is that text is not a standard type. So, if there is even a slight chance that you will one day need to port your database to something other than PostgreSQL, you should avoid text. Generally, we have not used the text type in this book, preferring the more standard SQL type definitions, varchar and char.

Conventionally char(*n*) is used where the length of the string to be stored is fixed or varies only slightly between rows, and varchar(n) is used for strings where the length may vary significantly. This is because in some databases, the internal storage of a fixed-length string is more efficient than a variable-length one, even though some additional, unnecessary characters may be stored. However, internally, PostgreSQL will use the same representation for both char and varchar types. So, for PostgreSQL, which type you use is more a personal preference. Where the length varies significantly between different rows of data, choose the varchar(*n*) type. Also, if you're not sure about the length, use varchar(*n*).

Just as with the boolean type, all character types can also contain NULL, unless you specifically define the column to not permit NULL values.

**Try It Out: Use Character Types**

Let's see how the PostgreSQL character types work. First, we need to drop our testtype table, and then we can re-create it with some different column types:

```
test=> DROP TABLE testtype;
DROP TABLE
test=>
test=> CREATE TABLE testtype (
test(>     singlechar      char,
test(>     fixedchar       char(13),
test(>     variablechar    varchar(128)
test(> );
CREATE TABLE
test=>
test=> INSERT INTO testtype VALUES('F', '0-349-10177-9', 'The Wasp Factory');
INSERT 17871 1
test=> INSERT INTO testtype VALUES('S', '1-85723-457-X', 'Excession');
INSERT 17872 1
test=> INSERT INTO testtype VALUES('F', '0-349-10768-8', 'Whit');
INSERT 17873 1
test=> INSERT INTO testtype VALUES(NULL, '', 'T.B.D.');
INSERT 17874 1
test=> INSERT INTO testtype VALUES('L', 'A String that is too long', 'L');
ERROR:  value too long for type character(13)
test=>
test=> SELECT * FROM testtype;
 singlechar |   fixedchar   |   variablechar
------------+---------------+------------------
 F          | 0-349-10177-9 | The Wasp Factory
 S          | 1-85723-457-X | Excession
 F          | 0-349-10768-8 | Whit
            |               | T.B.D.
(4 rows)
```

```
test=>
test=> SELECT fixedchar, length(fixedchar), variablechar FROM testtype
test-> WHERE singlechar = 'S';
   fixedchar   | length | variablechar
---------------+--------+--------------
 1-85723-457-X |     13 | Excession
(1 row)

test=> SELECT fixedchar, length(fixedchar), variablechar FROM testtype
test-> WHERE singlechar IS NULL;
   fixedchar   | length | variablechar
---------------+--------+--------------
               |      0 | T.B.D.
(1 row)

test=>
```

**How It Works**

We created a table with three columns, one for each of the different standard SQL types. The singlechar column holds a single character, the fixedchar column holds exactly 13 characters, and the variablechar column holds up to 128 characters. We then stored different data in the columns, and retrieved them again to show that PostgreSQL has stored the data correctly, although in the psql output, you can't actually see the padding.

We also tried to store a string that is too long in our fixedchar column. This generated an error, and no data was inserted.

We retrieved rows where the length of the string fixedchar is different, and used the built-in function length() to determine its size. We will look at some other functions that are useful for manipulating data in the "Functions Useful for Data Manipulation" section later in this chapter.

---

■**Note** In versions of PostgreSQL before 8.0, the length() function in this example would always have been 13, since the storage type char(n) is fixed-length and data is always padded with spaces, but now the length() function ignores those spaces and returns a more useful result.

---

# Number Data Types

The number types in PostgreSQL are slightly more complex than those we have met so far, but they are not particularly difficult to understand. There are two distinct types of numbers that we can store in the database: integers and floating-point numbers. These subdivide again, with a special subtype of integer, the serial type (which we have already used to create unique values in a table) and different sizes of integers, as shown in Table 8-3.

**Table 8-3.** *PostgreSQL Integer Number Types*

| Subtype | Standard Name | Description |
|---|---|---|
| small integer | smallint | A 2-byte signed integer, capable of storing numbers from –32768 to 32767 |
| integer | int | A 4-byte integer, capable of storing numbers from –2147483648 to 2147483647 |
| serial | | Same as integer, except that its value is normally automatically entered by PostgreSQL |

Floating-point numbers also subdivide, into those offering general-purpose floating-point values and fixed-precision numbers, as shown in Table 8-4.

**Table 8-4.** *PostgreSQL Floating-Point Number Types*

| Subtype | Standard Name | Description |
|---|---|---|
| float | float($n$) | A floating-point number with at least the precision $n$, up to a maximum of 8 bytes of storage. |
| float8 | real | A double-precision (8-byte) floating-point number. |
| numeric | numeric($p,s$) | A real number with $p$ digits, $s$ of them after the decimal point. Unlike float, this is always an exact number, but less efficient to work with than ordinary floating-point numbers. |
| money | numeric(9,2) | A PostgreSQL-specific type, though common in other databases. The money type became deprecated in version 8.0 of PostgreSQL, and may be removed in later releases. You should use numeric instead. |

The split of the two types into integer and floating-point numbers is easy enough to understand, but what might be less obvious is the purpose of the numeric type.

Floating-point numbers are stored in scientific notation, with a mantissa and exponent. With the numeric type, you can specify both the precision and the exact number of digits stored when performing calculations. You can also specify the number of digits held after the decimal point. The actual decimal-point location comes for free!

---

■**Caution** A common mistake is to think that numeric(5,2) can store a number, such as 12345.12. This is not correct. The total number of digits stored is only five, so a declaration of numeric(5,2) can store only up to 999.99 before overflowing.

---

PostgreSQL will generally catch attempts to insert values into fields that cannot store them, so attempting to insert overly large numbers into any number column will fail.

### Try It Out: Use Number Types

Now we can experiment with the number data types. First, we need to drop our testtype table, and then re-create it with some different column types:

```
test=> DROP TABLE testtype;
DROP TABLE

test=> CREATE TABLE testtype (
test(>     asmallint    smallint,
test(>     anint        int,
test(>     afloat       float(2),
test(>     areal        real,
test(>     anumeric     numeric(5,2)
test(> );
CREATE TABLE

test=> INSERT INTO testtype VALUES(2, 2, 2.0, 2.0, 2.0);
INSERT 17883 1
test=> INSERT INTO testtype VALUES(-100, -100, 123.456789, 123.456789, 123.456789);
INSERT 17884 1
test=> INSERT INTO testtype VALUES(-32768, -123456789, 1.23456789,
test-> 1.23456789, 1.23456789);
INSERT 17885 1
test=> INSERT INTO testtype VALUES(-32768, -123456789, 123456789.123456789,
test-> 23456789.123456789, 123456789.123456789);
ERROR:  numeric field overflow
DETAIL:  The absolute value is greater than or equal to 10^8 for field with
precision 5, scale 2.
test=>
test=> INSERT INTO testtype VALUES(-32768, -123456789, 123456789.123456789,
test-> 123456789.123456789, 123.123456789);
INSERT 17886 1
test=>
test=> SELECT * FROM testtype;
 asmallint |   anint    |    afloat     |     areal      | anumeric
-----------+------------+---------------+----------------+----------
         2 |          2 |             2 |              2 |     2.00
      -100 |       -100 |       123.457 |        123.457 |   123.46
    -32768 | -123456789 |       1.23457 |        1.23457 |     1.23
    -32768 | -123456789 | 1.23457e+008 |   1.23457e+008 |   123.12
(4 rows)

test=>
```

**How It Works**

We created a table with a small integer column, a normal integer column, a floating-point number, a real number, and a numeric with a precision of 5 and a scale of 2.

You can see that float and real behave in a very similar fashion, but the numeric column behaves somewhat differently. Rather than storing approximate numbers, numeric rounds the number to store a fixed number of digits after the decimal place. The INSERT fails if we try to store a number in it that is too large. Also notice that both float and real have rounded numbers; for example, 123.456789 has been rounded to 123.457.

## Temporal Data Types

We looked at temporal data types, which store time-related information, in Chapter 4, when we saw how to control data formats. PostgreSQL has a range of types relating to date and time, as shown in Table 8-5, but we will generally confine ourselves to the standard SQL92 types in this book.

**Table 8-5.** *PostgreSQL Temporal Data Types*

| Definition | Meaning |
| --- | --- |
| date | Stores date information |
| time | Stores time information |
| timestamp | Stores a date and time |
| interval | Stores information about a difference in timestamps |
| timestamptz | A PostgreSQL extension that stores a timestamp and time zone information |

## Special Data Types

From its origins as a research database system, PostgreSQL has acquired some unusual data types to store geometric and network data types, as shown in Table 8-6. The use of any of these PostgreSQL special features will make portability of a PostgreSQL database quite poor, so generally, we tend to avoid these extensions. For further information about these types, consult the PostgreSQL documentation, under "Data Types."

**Table 8-6.** *PostgreSQL Special Data Types*

| Definition | Meaning |
| --- | --- |
| box | A rectangular box |
| line | A set of points |
| point | A geometric pair of numbers |
| lseg | A line segment |
| polygon | A closed geometric line |
| cidr or inet | An IP version 4 address, such as 196.192.12.45 |
| macaddr | A MAC (Ethernet physical) address |

---

■**Note** PostgreSQL also allows you to create your own types for use in the database, using the SQL CREATE
TYPE command. This is not commonly needed, and it is performed in a manner unique to PostgreSQL. Further
details can be found in the documentation. Be aware that creating your own types is likely to result in a database schema that is very specific to PostgreSQL, as user-created types tend not to be portable.

---

# Arrays

PostgreSQL has another unusual feature: the ability to store arrays in tables. This was not a
standard SQL feature until SQL99, so it is not common in database implementations. Normally,
an array would be implemented using an additional table. However, the array facility can
sometimes be useful, particularly when you need to store a fixed number of repeating elements,
and it is very easy to use.

There are two syntaxes for creating arrays: the original PostgreSQL way and the more standard SQL99 way. We will look briefly at both methods here.

## PostgreSQL-Style Arrays

To declare a column in a table as an array, you simply add [ ] after the type; there is no need to
declare the number of elements. If you do declare a size, PostgreSQL accepts the definition, but
it doesn't enforce the number of elements.

### Try It Out: Use the PostgreSQL Syntax for Arrays

As an example, suppose we decided to have a table of employees, with an indicator to show
which days of the week they worked. Normally, this would require a column for each day or a
separate table to hold the workdays. In PostgreSQL, we can simplify this and hold an array of
working days directly, as follows:

```
test=> CREATE TABLE empworkday (
test(>      refcode char(5),
test(>      workdays int[]
test(> );
CREATE TABLE
test=>
```

This creates a table named empworkday with two columns: a character reference code and
an array of integers called workdays. To insert values into the array column, we need to enclose
a comma-separated list of values in a pair of {} delimiters, like this:

```
test=> INSERT INTO empworkday VALUES('val01', '{0,1,0,1,1,1,1}');
INSERT 17892 1
test=> INSERT INTO empworkday VALUES('val02', '{0,1,1,1,1,0,1}');
INSERT 17893 1
test=>
```

We can now select all the values of the array elements at once, like this:

```
test=> SELECT * FROM empworkday;
 refcode |    workdays
---------+-----------------
 val01   | {0,1,0,1,1,1,1}
 val02   | {0,1,1,1,1,0,1}
(2 rows)

test=>
```

We can also select individual elements by giving an array index:

```
test=> SELECT workdays[2] FROM empworkday WHERE refcode = 'val02';
 workdays
----------
        1
(1 row)
test=>
```

### How It Works

PostgreSQL behaves much like a conventional programming language, storing an array of values, with the added benefit that you don't need to specify the size of the array. If you select the whole of an array, PostgreSQL displays all the values, separated by commas, between curly braces.

One thing to notice is that PostgreSQL's first array element is at offset 1, rather than 0, as is common with many programming languages. If you try to select a nonexistent array element, a NULL will be returned.

---

■**Note** PostgreSQL also allows multidimensional arrays. For more information about PostgreSQL arrays, see the documentation.

---

## SQL99-Style Arrays

In the SQL99 standard, a new array declaration syntax was introduced. This is more explicit than the PostgreSQL style in that the number of elements must be declared, which is not enforced in the PostgreSQL implementation of the standard.

### Try It Out: Use the SQL99 Syntax for Arrays

Let's delete our earlier table and repeat the experiment using SQL99-style array declarations:

```
test=> DROP TABLE empworkday;
DROP TABLE
test=> CREATE TABLE empworkday (
test(>      refcode char(5),
test(>      workdays int array[7]
test(> );
CREATE TABLE
test=> INSERT INTO empworkday VALUES('val01', '{0,1,0,1,1,1,1}');
INSERT 17899 1
test=> INSERT INTO empworkday VALUES('val02', '{0,1,1,1,1,0,1}');
INSERT 17900 1
test=>
test=> SELECT * FROM empworkday;
 refcode |     workdays
---------+-----------------
 val01   | {0,1,0,1,1,1,1}
 val02   | {0,1,1,1,1,0,1}
(2 rows)

test=>
test=> SELECT workdays[2] FROM empworkday WHERE refcode = 'val02';
 workdays
----------
        1
(1 row)
test=>
```

**How It Works**

As you can see, the behavior of SQL99-style arrays is identical to that of PostgreSQL-style arrays. Only the declaration syntax is different.

# Data Manipulation

PostgreSQL offers some facilities for manipulating table data. Here, we will look at some built-in functions and "magic" variables. We will also take a closer look at the oid column that PostgreSQL adds to tables.

## Converting Between Data Types

From time to time, we need to convert between data types in a database. Type conversions may be useful, and are sometimes necessary, such as when working with dates and times. For example, we may be processing date values that have come from another system and been loaded into the database as strings. Converting these strings to date data types will enable us to query by date, something that could not be done if we left them as simple strings.

---

■**Note** Generally, you should be concerned at seeing type conversions, since too many type conversions in an application may indicate a design flaw in the database.

---

There is quite a degree of variation in how relational databases do type conversions. PostgreSQL uses a cast notation:

```
cast(column-name AS type-definition-to-convert-to)
```

An alternative, more succinct, double-colon syntax can be used in place of a simple column name in a SELECT statement:

```
column-name::type-definition-to-convert-to
```

Suppose we wanted to grab the date from the orderinfo table in our original bpsimple database as a char(10). We would write the following:

```
SELECT cast(date_placed AS char(10)) FROM orderinfo;
```

Executing this in our bpsimple database, we see this:

```
bpsimple=> SELECT cast(date_placed AS char(10)) FROM orderinfo;
 date_placed
-------------
 2004-03-13
 2004-06-23
 2004-09-02
 2004-09-03
 2004-07-21
(5 rows)

bpsimple=>
```

We can use cast (or ::) on values as well as columns, and we can name the result to provide a column heading, as we will do in the next example.

**Try It Out: Cast Types**

Suppose we want to produce a list of items, showing the price to the nearest dollar. We can do this easily by simply casting the price to an integer. We will select the "raw" price as well, to show that PostgreSQL is rounding the price.

```
bpsimple=> SELECT sell_price, sell_price::int AS "Guide Price" FROM item
WHERE sell_price > 5.0;
 sell_price | Guide Price
------------+-------------
      21.95 |          22
       9.95 |          10
      15.75 |          16
      19.95 |          20
      25.32 |          25
      11.49 |          11
(6 rows)

bpsimple=>
```

**How It Works**

We cast the sell_price column to an integer (sell_price::int) and also named it (AS "Guide Price"). We could just as well have written this using the cast notation; the two casting forms are interchangeable.

Comparing the two columns, we can see how PostgreSQL makes sensible decisions about rounding. In older versions of PostgreSQL, it was more frequently necessary to perform explicit casting between data types. Generally, the current version makes reasonable conversions automatically.

Note that it is not possible to universally convert between types. For example, you cannot cast a date as an integer.

## Functions for Data Manipulation

PostgreSQL provides some general-purpose functions that you can use for manipulating columns, which are listed in Table 8-7. See Chapter 10 for more information about PostgreSQL's built-in functions.

**Table 8-7.** *Useful Data Manipulation Functions*

| Function | Description |
|---|---|
| length(*column-name*) | Returns the length of a string. |
| trim(*column-name*) | Removes leading and trailing spaces. |
| strpos(*column-name*, *string*) | Returns the position of a string in the column. |
| substr(*column-name*, *position*, *length*) | Returns the length characters from the string, starting the search from the given character position. The first character is counted as position 1. |
| round(*column-name*, *length*) | Rounds a number to a given number of decimal places. |
| abs(*number*) | Gets the absolute value of a number. |

These functions are used in the same way as the cast function, as described in the previous section. Here's an example of using the substr and round functions:

```
bpsimple=> SELECT substr(description, 3, 5), round(sell_price, 1) FROM item;
 substr | round
--------+-------
 od Pu  |  22.0
 nux C  |   2.5
 ssues  |   4.0
 cture  |  10.0
 n Sma  |  15.8
 n Lar  |  20.0
 othbr  |   1.5
 man C  |   2.5
 rrier  |   0.0
 eaker  |  25.3
 bik C  |  11.5
(11 rows)

bpsimple=>
```

## Magic Variables

Occasionally, we want to store some information in the database that relates to the current user or time in some way, perhaps to implement an audit trail. PostgreSQL provides several "magic" variables for doing this. The following are the most useful of these variables:

- CURRENT_DATE

- CURRENT_TIME

- CURRENT_TIMESTAMP

- CURRENT_USER

You can use these just like column names, or you can SELECT them without including a table name at all:

```
bpsimple=> SELECT item_id, quantity, CURRENT_TIMESTAMP FROM stock;
 item_id | quantity |           timestamptz
---------+----------+---------------------------------
       1 |       12 | 2004-10-19 18:03:14.500694+01
       2 |        2 | 2004-10-19 18:03:14.500694+01
       4 |        8 | 2004-10-19 18:03:14.500694+01
       5 |        3 | 2004-10-19 18:03:14.500694+01
       7 |        8 | 2004-10-19 18:03:14.500694+01
       8 |       18 | 2004-10-19 18:03:14.500694+01
      10 |        1 | 2004-10-19 18:03:14.500694+01
(7 rows)
```

```
bpsimple=> SELECT CURRENT_USER, CURRENT_TIME;
 current_user  |       timetz
--------------+--------------------
 rick         | 18:03:40.862712+01
(1 row)

bpsimple=>
```

These magic variables can also be used in INSERT and UPDATE statements, as in this example:

```
INSERT INTO orderinfo(orderinfo_id, customer_id, date_placed, date_shipped,
  shipping) VALUES (5, 8, CURRENT_DATE, NULL, 0.0);
```

## The OID Column

You will have noticed that each time we insert data, PostgreSQL responds with an almost arbitrary looking number, as well as the number of rows inserted. As we mentioned briefly in Chapter 6, this number is an internal reference number, an object ID, that PostgreSQL stores against each row—a normally hidden column named oid.

Most relational databases do not have such a column, or if they do, it is not accessible to the users. With PostgreSQL, we can see this number by explicitly naming it when we SELECT from a table, like this:

```
bpsimple=> SELECT oid, fname, lname FROM customer;
  oid  |   fname   |  lname
-------+-----------+---------
 19888 | Jenny     | Stones
 19889 | Andrew    | Stones
 19890 | Alex      | Matthew
 19891 | Adrian    | Matthew
 19892 | Simon     | Cozens
 19893 | Neil      | Matthew
 19894 | Richard   | Stones
 19895 | Ann       | Stones
 19896 | Christine | Hickman
 19897 | Mike      | Howard
 19898 | Dave      | Jones
 19899 | Richard   | Neill
 19900 | Laura     | Hardy
 19901 | Bill      | O'Neill
 19902 | David     | Hudson
(15 rows)

bpsimple=>
```

Your database will almost certainly have different values for the oid column. You will also see OID appear in an ODBC driver configuration. You can choose to display it or hide it.

It is possible to prevent the oid column from being added to user tables in the database by setting the default_with_oids flag to false in the postgresql.conf configuration file or explicitly specifying WITHOUT OIDS when you create the table. The default in version 8.0 of PostgreSQL is to create oid columns on user tables. However, in future releases of PostgreSQL, the default will probably change to not create oid columns. Consequently, you should never rely on an oid column being present in your database, and we suggest you avoid using either the WITH OIDS or WITHOUT OIDS option in table-creation statements.

# Table Management

Now that we know about PostgreSQL data types, we can use them when we create tables. We have already seen the CREATE TABLE SQL command, which we used to create tables in our sample database, but we will cover it more formally here. We will also explore some additional features, such as temporary tables, altering tables after creation, and deleting tables when they are no longer required.

## Creating Tables

The basic syntax for creating tables is as follows:

```
CREATE [TEMPORARY] TABLE table-name (
    { column-name type [ column-constraint ] [,...] }
    [ CONSTRAINT table-constraint ]
) [ INHERITS (existing-table-name) ]
```

This may look a little complex, but it is actually quite straightforward. The first line simply says that you create tables by using CREATE TABLE, followed by the name of the table and an opening parenthesis. TEMPORARY allows you to create a temporary table, as described in the "Using Temporary Tables" section later in this chapter.

Next, you list the column name, its type, and an optional column constraint. You can essentially have an unlimited number of columns in your table, each one separated by a comma. The optional column constraint allows you to specify additional rules for the column, and you have already seen the most common example, NOT NULL.

After the list of columns comes an optional table-level constraint, which allows you to write additional table-level rules that must be obeyed by the data in the table, such as a column value must always be smaller than a number. For example, a day-of-the-week column might be constrained to be less than 7. We'll discuss both column and table constraints in the following sections.

Last comes a PostgreSQL extension, INHERITS, which allows a new table being created to inherit the columns from an existing table. The new table contains all the columns that are in the tables listed after the INHERITS keyword, in addition to those specified directly. See the PostgreSQL documentation for more information about using INHERITS.

> **■Tip** We strongly advise you to always store the commands you use for creating your database in a script, and always use that script for creating your database. If you need to change the database design, it is much easier and more reliable to modify the script than to re-create the database. Then you won't need to try to recall the commands you used initially to create the database all those months (or was it just days…) ago. You will find that the effort of initially creating a script, and keeping it up-to-date, pays you back many, many times over.

## Using Column Constraints

It is common to have columns in a table where certain rules apply. We have seen some simple ones already, such as ensuring that a customer's last name is NOT NULL. Sometimes, we want to impose rules that govern the data when it is known, such as ensuring that a pay rate column will accept values only above a minimum or ensuring that columns are unique. Applying constraints to columns allows us to perform these checks at the lowest level of our complete application—in the database.

For hard-and-fast basic rules, enforcing them at the database level is a good technique, since it is independent of the application, so any application bugs that might allow illegal values to slip through will be caught by the database. It is also often easier to apply the rule by writing a definition when a table is created, rather than by writing application logic code to support the rule.

Table 8-8 shows the principal constraints that you will find useful. (There are also more advanced constraints, which are defined in the PostgreSQL documentation.) We won't discuss the REFERENCES constraints here, but will cover it later in the chapter, in the "Foreign Key Constraints" section.

**Table 8-8.** *Principal Column Constraints*

| Definition | Meaning |
| --- | --- |
| NOT NULL | The column cannot have a NULL value stored in it. |
| UNIQUE | The value stored in the column must be different for each row in the database. PostgreSQL allows you to have as many rows as you like with NULL in a column declared UNIQUE. |
| PRIMARY KEY | Effectively, a combination of NOT NULL and UNIQUE. Each table may have only a single column marked PRIMARY KEY. (You can have multiple columns marked both NOT NULL and UNIQUE, however.) If you need to create a composite primary key (a primary key that comprises more than one column), you must use a table-level constraint, rather than the column-level constraint. |
| DEFAULT *default-value* | Allows you to provide a default value when inserting data. (Strictly speaking, this is not a constraint option, but it's easier to consider it along with the true constraints.) |
| CHECK (*condition*) | Allows you to check a condition when inserting or updating data. |
| REFERENCES | Constrains the value to be one that appears in a column in a separate table. |

With the exception of PRIMARY KEY, you can have as many columns with as many constraints as you need. It is possible, but not common, to name column-level constraints.

One particular point to note is what happens when a NULL value is added to a column with a UNIQUE constraint. PostgreSQL considers each NULL to be unique, so it allows you to have as many rows as you like with NULL in a column declared UNIQUE. According to the SQL standard, only a single NULL should be allowed, so this is a slight deviation from the standard. Arguably, the SQL standard is more logical, since if NULL is unknown, there is no way of knowing that two of them are different, but the PostgreSQL implementation is probably more intuitive.

### Try It Out: Apply Column Constraints

The easiest way to understand column constraints is to see them in action. Let's create a new table in the test database we created earlier, and then use it to experiment with some constraints:

```
bpsimple=> \c test
You are now connected to database "test".
test=> CREATE TABLE testcolcons (
test(>     colnotnull INT NOT NULL,
test(>     colunique INT UNIQUE,
test(>     colprikey INT PRIMARY KEY,
test(>     coldefault INT DEFAULT 42,
test(>     colcheck INT CHECK( colcheck < 42)
test(> );
NOTICE:  CREATE TABLE / PRIMARY KEY will create implicit index
"testcolcons_pkey" for table "testcolcons"
NOTICE:  CREATE TABLE / UNIQUE will create implicit index
"testcolcons_colunique_key" for table "testcolcons"
CREATE TABLE
test=>
```

You can see that PostgreSQL warns us that it has created indexes to enforce the PRIMARY KEY and UNIQUE constraints. It has also picked meaningful names for us.

Now that we have created a table with a variety of constraints on the columns, we can try inserting some data and see how the constraints work in practice:

```
test=> INSERT INTO testcolcons(colnotnull, colunique, colprikey, coldefault,
test(> colcheck) VALUES(1,1,1,1,1);
INSERT 17497 1
test=> INSERT INTO testcolcons(colnotnull, colunique, colprikey,
test(> oldefault, colcheck) VALUES(2,2,2,2,2);
INSERT 17498 1
test=> INSERT INTO testcolcons(colnotnull, colunique, colprikey,
test(> coldefault, colcheck) VALUES(2,2,2,2,2);
ERROR:  duplicate key violates unique constraint "testcolcons_pkey"
test=>
```

This INSERT has failed, because the index testcolcons_pkey found a duplicate value. We need to use a little common sense here, and realize that an index called testcolcons_pkey is referring to a primary key index on the testcolcons table (hardly a great leap of intuition).

Each table can have only one primary key; therefore, there is no ambiguity in the index being called `tablename_pkey`.

However, PostgreSQL does allow us to insert two rows where the colunique column contains NULL (which could be considered a little dangerous):

```
test=> INSERT INTO testcolcons(colnotnull, colunique, colprikey,
coldefault, colcheck) VALUES(1,NULL,98,1,1);
INSERT 17503 1
test=> INSERT INTO testcolcons(colnotnull, colunique, colprikey,
coldefault, colcheck) VALUES(1,NULL,99,1,1);
INSERT 17504 1
test=>
```

If we use actual values, PostgreSQL rejects the INSERT:

```
test=> INSERT INTO testcolcons(colnotnull, colunique, colprikey,
test(> coldefault, colcheck) VALUES(2,2,9,2,2);
ERROR:  Cannot insert a duplicate key into unique index testcolcons_colunique_key
test=>
```

This time, the INSERT fails because the index `testcolcons_colunique_key` found a duplicate. We can have many columns declared UNIQUE, so PostgreSQL names the index `tablename_columnname_key`, making it clear which column is causing the problem:

```
test=> INSERT INTO testcolcons(colnotnull, colunique, colprikey,
test(> coldefault, colcheck) VALUES(3,3,3,3,100);
ERROR:  new row for relation "testcolcons" violates check constraint
"testcolcons_colcheck_check"
test=>
```

This time, the problem is that the CHECK constraint on the column colcheck failed, because we tried to insert a value larger than 42. Notice the constraint is named `tablename_columnname_check`, so the source of the problem is easy to locate:

```
test=> UPDATE testcolcons SET colunique = 1 WHERE colnotnull = 2;
ERROR:  duplicate key violates unique constraint
"testcolcons_colunique_key"testcolcons_colunique_key
test=>
```

We cannot update the value of colunique, because there is already a row in the table where the column has that value:

```
test=> INSERT INTO testcolcons(colnotnull, colunique, colprikey, colcheck)
test-> VALUES(3,3,3,41);
INSERT 17505 1
test=> SELECT * FROM testcolcons;
 colnotnull | colunique | colprikey | coldefault | colcheck
------------+-----------+-----------+------------+----------
          1 |         1 |         1 |          1 |        1
          2 |         2 |         2 |          2 |        2
          1 |           |        98 |          1 |        1
          1 |           |        99 |          1 |        1
          3 |         3 |         3 |         42 |       41
(5 rows)

test=>
```

Finally, we fail to provide a value for the coldefault column (notice it is not listed in the column list), and see that the default value is used.

If we want to check the constraints on a table, we can ask psql to list them, using the \d *tablename* command, like this:

```
test=> \d testcolcons
    Table "public.testcolcons"
  Column     |  Type   | Modifiers
------------+---------+------------
 colnotnull | integer | not null
 colunique  | integer |
 colprikey  | integer | not null
 coldefault | integer | default 42
 colcheck   | integer |
Indexes:
    "testcolcons_pkey" PRIMARY KEY, btree (colprikey)
    "testcolcons_colunique_key" UNIQUE, btree (colunique)
Check constraints:
    "testcolcons_colcheck_check" CHECK (colcheck < 42)

test=>
```

**How It Works**

PostgreSQL uses a variety of methods to implement constraints. It is not possible to control the order in which constraints are checked, however. The exact error you get will depend on PostgreSQL internal implementation. What you can know for sure is that all constraints will be checked before the data is stored in the database. You can also use transactions, which are introduced in Chapter 9, to ensure that all or none of a set of requested changes are made to the database.

# Using Table Constraints

Table constraints are very similar to column constraints, but as the name suggests, apply to the entire table, rather than to an individual column. Sometimes, we need to specify constraints, such as a primary key, at a table level rather than a column level. For example, we saw in our orderline table we needed to use two columns, orderinfo_id and item_id, together as a composite key to identify a row, since only the combination of columns must be unique. This type of constraint is expressed at the table level.

The four table-level constraints are listed in Table 8-9.

**Table 8-9.** *Principal Table Constraints*

| Name | Description |
| --- | --- |
| UNIQUE(*column-list*) | The value stored in the columns listed must be different from that stored in all other rows of this column. |
| PRIMARY KEY(*column-list*) | Effectively a combination of NOT NULL and UNIQUE. Each table may have only a single PRIMARY KEY constraint, either as a table constraint or as a column constraint. |
| CHECK (*condition*) | Allows you to check a condition when inserting or updating data. |
| REFERENCES | Constrains the value to be one that appears in a column in a separate table. |

As you can see, the table-level constraints bear more than a passing resemblance to the column-level constraints. The differences are as follows:

- Table-level constraints can refer to more than one column.

- Table-level constraints are listed after all the columns.

**Try It Out: Use Table-Level Constraints**

Let's see how table-level constraints work. First, create a table with some constraints:

```
test=> CREATE TABLE ttconst (
test(>     mykey1 int,
test(>     mykey2 int,
test(>     mystring varchar(15),
test(>     CONSTRAINT cs1 CHECK (mystring <> ''),
test(>     CONSTRAINT cs2 PRIMARY KEY(mykey1, mykey2)
test(> );
NOTICE:  CREATE TABLE / PRIMARY KEY will create implicit index "cs2"
for table "ttconst"
CREATE TABLE
test=>
```

Notice that, as with the column-level constraint, PostgreSQL has created an index to enforce the primary key constraint. Let's insert some rows to get started:

```
test=> INSERT INTO ttconst VALUES(1,1,'Hello');
INSERT 19381 1
test=> INSERT INTO ttconst VALUES(1,2,'Bye');
INSERT 19382 1
test=>
```

Now try to insert a row that violates the rule that mystring cannot be an empty string:

```
test=> INSERT INTO ttconst VALUES(1,2,'');
ERROR:  new row for relation "ttconst" violates check constraint "cs1"
test=>
```

The table-level CHECK constraint works almost identically to the column-level one, rejecting the row because the string was empty.

Now if we try inserting a row that violates the rule that the combination of mykey1 and mykey2 must be unique, we can see the second constraint, cs2, being enforced:

```
test=> INSERT INTO ttconst VALUES(2,2,'Chow');
INSERT 19383 1
test=> INSERT INTO ttconst VALUES(2,2,'Chow');
ERROR:  duplicate key violates unique constraint "cs2"
test=>
```

When both mykey values are the same, the row is rejected, because the primary key constraint has now been violated.

**How It Works**

As you can see, table-level constraints are very similar to their column-level equivalents. In general, it is better to use a column-level constraint if that is all that is required. However, where we need a mix of column-level and table-level constraints in the same table, such as in our bpsimple database, we prefer to use a table-level primary key constraint on all the tables, for the sake of consistency.

# Altering Table Structures

Unfortunately, life is complicated, and no matter how carefully you gather requirements and implement your database, the day will come when you need to alter the design of a table.

We saw one way we might solve this in Chapter 6, using INSERT INTO where the data is gathered by selecting data from an existing table. We could follow this procedure:

- Create a new working table with an identical structure to the existing table.

- Use INSERT INTO to populate the working table with data identical to the original table.

- Drop (delete) the existing table.

- Re-create the table with the same name, but with the changes we need.

- Use INSERT INTO again to populate the altered table from the working table.

- Delete the working table.

That is clearly a great deal of work, however, especially if the table contains a lot of data or is referenced by triggers or views and all we want to do is add a column to a table. PostgreSQL, in line with the SQL standard, allows us to add, delete, and rename columns on the fly; that is, while the table contains data. You can even rename the table itself.

It is also possible to add and remove constraints from a table and change default values; however, there are some restrictions on these changes for practical reasons. For example, you cannot add a constraint to a table that already contains data that would violate the new constraint.

---

■**Note** In older versions of PostgreSQL there is an additional restriction, in that you can't create a new column that has a NOT NULL or a DEFAULT setting, since data in the table already exists. If necessary, it's not hard to work around this: simply add the column without any constraints, update the data in the table, and then add the required column constraint. From PostgreSQL 8.0 onwards, you can add a column with a default value and with a NOT NULL constraint, provided you also supply a default value.

---

To make these changes, we use the ALTER TABLE command. The syntax of ALTER TABLE is simple, but has several variants:

```
ALTER TABLE table-name ADD COLUMN column-name column-type
ALTER TABLE table-name DROP COLUMN column-name
ALTER TABLE table-name RENAME COLUMN old-column-name TO new-column-name
ALTER TABLE table-name column-name TYPE new-type [ USING expression ]
ALTER TABLE table-name ALTER COLUMN [SET DEFAULT value | DROP DEFAULT]
ALTER TABLE table-name ALTER COLUMN [SET NOT NULL | DROP NOT NULL]
ALTER TABLE table-name ADD CHECK check-expression
ALTER TABLE table-name ADD CONSTRAINT name constraint-definition
ALTER TABLE old-table-name RENAME TO new-table-name
```

Columns that are added to a table with existing data will have NULL stored as their value for the existing rows.

### Try it Out: Alter a Table

Before we see some ALTER TABLE statements in action, let's check the existing structure of our ttconst table:

```
test=> \d ttconst
           Table "public.ttconst"
  Column  |         Type          | Modifiers
----------+-----------------------+-----------
 mykey1   | integer               | not null
 mykey2   | integer               | not null
 mystring | character varying(15) |
Indexes:
    "cs2" PRIMARY KEY, btree (mykey1, mykey2)
Check constraints:
    "cs1" CHECK (mystring::text <> ''::text)

test=>
```

First, we add a new column:

```
test=> ALTER TABLE ttconst ADD COLUMN mydate DATE;
```

Now we rename the newly added column:

```
test=> ALTER TABLE ttconst RENAME COLUMN mydate TO birthdate;
ALTER TABLE
test=> \d ttconst
           Table "public.ttconst"
  Column   |         Type          | Modifiers
-----------+-----------------------+-----------
 mykey1    | integer               | not null
 mykey2    | integer               | not null
 mystring  | character varying(15) |
 birthdate | date                  |
Indexes:
    "cs2" PRIMARY KEY, btree (mykey1, mykey2)
Check constraints:
    "cs1" CHECK (mystring::text <> ''::text)

test=>
```

Now let's try changing some constraints and other rules:

```
test=> ALTER TABLE ttconst DROP CONSTRAINT cs1;
ALTER TABLE
test=> ALTER TABLE ttconst ADD CONSTRAINT cs3 UNIQUE(birthdate);
NOTICE:  ALTER TABLE / ADD UNIQUE will create implicit index "cs3" for table "tt
const"
ALTER TABLE
test=> ALTER TABLE ttconst ALTER COLUMN mystring SET DEFAULT 'Hello';
ALTER TABLE
```

Next, let's look at the new table definition:

```
test=> \d ttconst
                    Table "public.ttconst"
  Column   |         Type          |            Modifiers
-----------+-----------------------+------------------------------------
 mykey1    | integer               | not null
 mykey2    | integer               | not null
 mystring  | character varying(15) | default 'Hello'::character varying
 birthdate | date                  |
Indexes:
    "cs2" PRIMARY KEY, btree (mykey1, mykey2)
    "cs3" UNIQUE, btree (birthdate)

test=>
```

As you can see, the new rules are in place, just as though we had set them up when we created the table.

It's also possible to change the type of a column, providing the conversion is logical. Here, we change a date to a varchar:

```
test=> ALTER TABLE ttconst ALTER birthdate TYPE varchar(32);
ALTER TABLE
test=>
```

It's more common to just need to alter a column size; for example, increasing the size of a varchar type column:

```
test=> ALTER TABLE ttconst ALTER mystring TYPE varchar(32);
ALTER TABLE
test=>
```

Finally, we rename the whole table:

```
test=> ALTER TABLE ttconst RENAME TO ttconst2;
ALTER TABLE
test=>
```

### How It Works

As you can see, ALTER TABLE is a powerful command that allows you to modify existing table structures, both columns and constraints, even if they already contain data.

---

■**NOTE** Prior to PostgreSQL 8.0, the ALTER TABLE command was more limited, so if you are running an older version, you may find that some options are not available to you.

---

The ability to alter table structures should never be used as an excuse for lack of attention to detail in the initial table design. ALTER TABLE should mostly be needed when requirements change. Using it at other times is generally a hint that your original design could have been improved before you started the work of actually creating tables in your database.

One thing you should be very wary of is constantly changing a table structure by adding new columns. New columns are always added at the end of the table, and so may not reflect the logical purpose of the table very well. Suppose we had forgotten a title column when we created our customer table, and then used ALTER TABLE to add it later. The column would have been added at the end, which would have made the design of the customer table look a little strange, with a person's title coming after the phone number. Instead, you may prefer to use the following procedure to add columns:

- Create a new table with a temporary name, but the correct columns in the most logical order.

- Use INSERT INTO ... SELECT ... to populate it as a duplicate of the table being changed.

- Delete the old table.

- Rename the new table with the same name as the old table.

You do need to be careful that sequences and triggers, which we will discuss in Chapter 10, may also need to be dropped and re-created when tables are dropped and renamed.

## Deleting Tables

Deleting a table is very simple:

```
DROP TABLE table-name
```

Presto! Your table has disappeared, along with any data that was in it. Of course, you should use this command with caution.

## Using Temporary Tables

All the SQL examples we have seen so far have managed to achieve our desired result in a single, albeit occasionally complex, SELECT statement. Usually, this is a good practice, because as we've said, SQL is a declarative language. If you define what you want to achieve, SQL finds the best way of getting the result for you. However, sometimes it is just not possible, or convenient, to do everything in a single SELECT statement. In some cases, you need temporary results to be held.

Often, the temporary storage you need is a table, so you can store many rows. Of course, you could always create a table, do your processing, and then delete the table again, but that entails a risk that the intermediate tables will occasionally not get deleted, either because your application has a bug or due to simple forgetfulness of an interactive user working directly on the database. The net result is stray tables, usually with strange names, left around in your database. Unfortunately, it is not always clear which tables are intended to be just intermediate work tables, and can be deleted, and which are for long-term use.

SQL offers a very simple solution to this problem: temporary tables. When you create the table, rather than use CREATE TABLE, you use CREATE TEMPORARY TABLE (you can also use CREATE TEMP TABLE, which is just a synonym). The table is created for you in the usual way, except that when your session ends and your connection to the database is terminated, the temporary table is automatically deleted for you.

# Views

When you have a complex database, or sometimes when you have various users with different permissions, you need to create the illusion of a table, or a *view*. Let's look at an example to clarify this concept.

Suppose we want to allow people in the warehouse to look at the items and barcodes in our database. Currently, these are split across two tables, item and barcode. While correct from a design point of view, we might wish to present a simpler view to people accessing the data, perhaps allowing them to use some of the GUI tools we saw in Chapter 5. Rather than change our design, we can do this with a view.

## Creating Views

The syntax for creating a view is very simple:

```
CREATE VIEW name-of-view AS select-statement;
```

You can then query this view as though it were a table. (At the time of writing, in PostgreSQL, by default, views are read-only.) You SELECT data from a view just as you would a table, and can join it to other tables, as well as use WHERE clauses. Each time you execute a SELECT using the view, the data is rebuilt, so the data is always up-to-date. It is not a frozen copy stored at the time the view was created.

---

■**Note** In some other databases, views, and hence the underlying data in the tables, can be updated, just like tables.

---

Suppose we want to create a view that provides a simplified display of the item table. We just want to see the item_id, description and the sell_price. The SELECT statement would be as follows:

```
SELECT item_id, description, sell_price FROM item;
```

For example, to create this as a view called item_price, we would write:

```
CREATE VIEW item_price AS SELECT item_id, description, sell_price FROM item;
```

This could then be used in a SELECT statement as though item_price were a table.

**Try It Out: Create a View**

Recall from Chapter 5 that we had a minor difficulty with the price definition in the item table. Assuming that we consider our definition of price as numeric(7,2) to be correct, we can still keep this definition, but present a different view of the type, using a view with a cast in the SELECT statement.

Let's create a view of the item table that alters what users see in three ways:

- We want to hide the cost_price.

- We want to present only a short item description.

- We want to hide all expensive items, which for this example, we will declare to be anything over $20.

We can do this by creating a view, like this:

```
bpsimple=> CREATE VIEW item_price AS SELECT item_id, description::varchar(10),
bpsimple-> sell_price AS price FROM item WHERE sell_price <= 20.0;
CREATE VIEW
bpsimple=>
```

Now when we SELECT data from the view, it behaves like a subset of the columns in the original table:

```
bpsimple=> SELECT * FROM item_price;
 item_id | description | price
---------+-------------+-------
       3 | Linux CD    |  2.49
       4 | Tissues     |  3.99
       5 | Picture Fr  |  9.95
       6 | Fan Small   | 15.75
       7 | Fan Large   | 19.95
       8 | Toothbrush  |  1.45
       9 | Roman Coin  |  2.45
      10 | Carrier Ba  |  0.00
       2 | Rubik Cube  | 11.49
(9 rows)

bpsimple=>
```

**How It Works**

We did several things in our example. First, we truncated the description column to 10 characters, by casting it as description::varchar(10). Next, we hid the cost price, by not including it in the list of columns, and even being a little sneaky by renaming the sell price sell_price AS price so there is no clue there might also be cost price held in the table. Finally, we restricted the rows that are returned by the view WHERE sell_price <= 20.0. (In Chapter 11, we will cover how to use permissions to not allow ordinary users to access the original item table.)

We are not restricted to using only one table in a view. We can use a complex SQL statement to access as many tables as we like.

**Try It Out: Create a View from Multiple Tables**

Let's create a view that will solve our problem of presenting a simplified display of the item and barcode tables, hiding the price information and the split of data into two tables. We will call the view all_items:

```
bpsimple=> CREATE VIEW all_items AS SELECT i.item_id, i.description, b.barcode_ean
bpsimple-> FROM item i, barcode b WHERE i.item_id = b.item_id;
CREATE VIEW
bpsimple=>
```

This creates a new view, which we can now use just like a table:

```
bpsimple-> SELECT * FROM all_items;
 item_id |   description  |   barcode_ean
---------+----------------+----------------
       1 | Wood Puzzle    | 6241527836173
       2 | Rubik Cube     | 6241574635234
       3 | Linux CD       | 6264537836173
       3 | Linux CD       | 6241527746363
       4 | Tissues        | 7465743843764
       5 | Picture Frame  | 3453458677628
       6 | Fan Small      | 6434564564544
       7 | Fan Large      | 8476736836876
       8 | Toothbrush     | 6241234586487
       8 | Toothbrush     | 9473625532534
       8 | Toothbrush     | 9473627464543
       9 | Roman Coin     | 4587263646878
      11 | Speakers       | 9879879837489
      11 | Speakers       | 2239872376872
(14 rows)

bpsimple=>
```

Notice that this is exactly the same as if we had typed the following:

```
SELECT i.item_id, i.description, b.barcode_ean FROM item i, barcode b
WHERE i.item_id = b.item_id;
```

As you can see, however, it hides the complexity from the end users.

If we want to list the views in our database, we can use the \dv command. The \d *name-of-view* command will describe the view, allowing us to see the SQL being used:

```
bpsimple=> \dv
          List of relations
 Schema |    Name    | Type | Owner
--------+------------+------+-------
 public | all_items  | view | rick
 public | item_price | view | rick
(2 rows)

bpsimple=> \d all_items
            View "public.all_items"
   Column    |         Type          | Modifiers
-------------+-----------------------+-----------
 item_id     | integer               |
 description | character varying(64)  |
 barcode_ean | character(13)         |
View definition:
 SELECT i.item_id, i.description, b.barcode_ean
   FROM item i, barcode b
  WHERE i.item_id = b.item_id;

bpsimple=>
```

**How It Works**

We created a view called all_items, which behaves like a table, except that it builds its data from some hidden SQL.

Some people are tempted to think that views are such a good idea that all tables should be hidden behind views. While some level of data hiding is often good, using a view is not as efficient as using the actual tables, particularly if the SQL that defines the view is complex and uses more than a single table. Databases that have all their data hidden behind views can suffer from poor performance, and users will not be able to optimize their SQL performance, perhaps because the column they need is in a view that does a big table join. Even though users want only one column, if you have forced them to use the view, they will be executing the complex SQL behind the view, decreasing performance. While views can be good for you, too much of a good thing can be harmful!

# Deleting and Replacing Views

To delete a view, drop it, as follows:

```
DROP VIEW name-of-view
```

Unlike dropping a table, however, dropping a view does not affect the underlying data.

If you want to replace an existing view with a view with the same name and returning the same set of columns, you can use a special version of the syntax to do this in a single statement:

```
CREATE OR REPLACE VIEW name-of-view AS select-statement
```

# Foreign Key Constraints

We now come to one of the most important kinds of constraints, called foreign key constraints.

In Chapter 2, when we drew our diagram of a sample bpsimple database, we had tables with data that joined, or were related, to other tables. Figure 8-1 shows that database schema design.

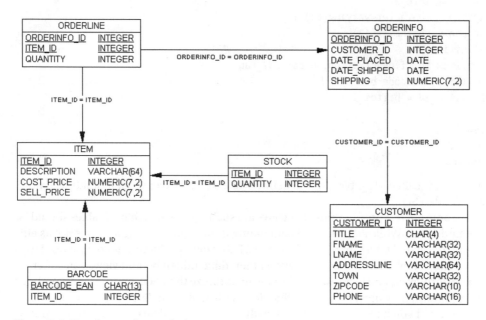

**Figure 8-1.** *Database schema design*

You can see how columns in one table relate to columns in another. For example, the customer_id in the orderinfo table relates to the customer_id in the customer table. So, given an orderinfo_id, we can use the customer_id from the same row to discover the name and address of the customer to which the order relates. We learned that the customer_id is a primary key in the customer table; that it uniquely identifies a single row in the customer table.

Here is another important piece of terminology: the customer_id in the orderinfo table is a *foreign key*. This means that although customer_id in the orderinfo table is not a primary key in that table, the column it joins to in the customer table is a unique key in the customer table. Notice that there is no reverse relationship—no column in the customer table is a unique key of any other table. Hence, we say that the customer table has no foreign keys.

Part of the intrinsic structure of our database design is our goal that each and every `customer_id` in the `orderinfo` table also appears in the `customer` table. The `customer_id` in `orderinfo` is called a foreign key. We would like to enforce the rule about the relationship between these two tables in the database, as it's a much more reliable place to enforce data-integrity rules than in an application, and this is called a *foreign key constraint*.

When we create a foreign key constraint, PostgreSQL will check that the column in the particular table is declared such that it must be unique. It is very common for the column referenced by a foreign key to be the primary key in the other table. Using foreign key constraints is an excellent way to ensure that inter-table relationships are not corrupted due to the deletion of a particular primary key (foreign to another table) in a given table.

It is possible for a table to have more than one foreign key. For example, in the `orderline` table, `orderinfo_id` is a foreign key, since it joins with the `orderinfo_id`, which is a primary key in the `orderinfo` table, and `item_id` is also a foreign key, because it joins with `item_id` in the `item` table that is a primary key in the `item` table.

In the `item` table, `item_id` is a primary key in the `item` table, since it uniquely identifies a row, and it is also a foreign key in the `stock` table. It is perfectly acceptable for a single column to be both a primary and foreign key, and this implies a (usually optional) one-to-one relationship between rows in the two tables.

Although we don't have any examples in our sample database, it is also possible for a pair of columns combined to be a foreign key, just as the `orderinfo_id` and `item_id` combined are a primary key in the `orderline` table.

These relationships are absolutely crucial to our database. If we have a row in our `orderinfo` table where the `customer_id` doesn't match a `customer_id` in the `customer` table, we have a major data-integrity problem. We have an order and no idea of the customer who placed the order. Although we can use application logic to enforce our relationship rules, as we said earlier, it is much safer, and often easier, to declare them as database rules.

You will not be surprised to learn that it is possible to declare such foreign key relationships as constraints on columns and tables, much like the constraints we have already met. This is usually done when tables are created, as part of the `CREATE TABLE` command, using the `REFERENCES` type of constraint. It is also possible to add foreign key constraints later, using the `ALTER TABLE` *table-name* `ADD CONSTRAINT` *name constraint-definition* syntax.

We are now going to move on from our `bpsimple` database, and create a `bpfinal` database, that implements foreign key constraints, to enforce data integrity.

## Foreign Key As a Column Constraint

Here is the basic syntax for declaring a column to be a foreign key in another table:

```
[CONSTRAINT arbitrary-name] existing-column-name type REFERENCES
foreign-table-name(column-in-foreign-table)
```

Naming the constraint is optional, but as we will see later, it is a considerable help in understanding error messages.

To define a foreign key constraint on the `customer_id` column in the `orderinfo` table, relating it to the `customer` table, we use the `REFERENCES` keyword along with the name of the foreign table and column, like this:

```
CREATE TABLE orderinfo
(
    orderinfo_id        serial ,
    customer_id         integer NOT NULL REFERENCES customer(customer_id),
    date_placed         date NOT NULL,
    date_shipped        date ,
    shipping            numeric(7,2) ,
    CONSTRAINT          orderinfo_pk PRIMARY KEY(orderinfo_id)
);
```

We will see the effect of the REFERENCES constraint shortly.

## Foreign Key As a Table Constraint

Although you can declare foreign key constraints at the column level, we prefer to declare them at the table level, along with primary key constraints. You cannot use a column constraint when multiple columns in the current table are involved in the relationship, so in these cases, you must write it as a table-level constraint.

---

■**Tip** Rather than mixing column and table-level foreign key constraints, it is better to always use the table form.

---

The table form is very similar to the column form, but comes after all columns have been listed:

CONSTRAINT [*arbitrary-name*] FOREIGN KEY (*column-list*) REFERENCES
*foreign-table-name*(*column-list-in-foreign-table*)

We can update our definition of the orderinfo table to declare a constraint that the column customer_id is a foreign key, because it relates to the primary key column customer_id in the customer table.

```
CREATE TABLE orderinfo
(
    orderinfo_id                serial ,
    customer_id                 integer NOT NULL,
    date_placed                 date NOT NULL,
    date_shipped                date ,
    shipping                    numeric(7,2) ,
    CONSTRAINT                  orderinfo_pk PRIMARY KEY(orderinfo_id),
    CONSTRAINT orderinfo_customer_id_fk FOREIGN KEY(customer_id) REFERENCES
        customer(customer_id)
);
```

## Adding a Foreign Key Constraint to an Existing Table

Before creating the table from scratch, let's briefly revisit the ALTER TABLE command, and see how we could use this to retrospectively add a foreign key constraint.

First let's look at the existing table:

```
bpsimple=> \d orderinfo
                               Table "public.orderinfo"
    Column     |    Type     |                                  Modifiers


--------------+-------------+-------------------------------------------------
 orderinfo_id | integer     | not null default nextval
    ('public.orderinfo_orderinfo_id_seq'::text)
 customer_id  | integer     | not null
 date_placed  | date        | not null
 date_shipped | date        |
 shipping     | numeric(7,2) |
Indexes:
    "orderinfo_pk" PRIMARY KEY, btree (orderinfo_id)
bpsimple=>
```

Now we alter the table to add a new foreign key constraint:

```
bpsimple=> ALTER TABLE orderinfo ADD CONSTRAINT
    orderinfo_customer_id_fk FOREIGN KEY(customer_id)
    REFERENCES customer(customer_id);
ALTER TABLE
bpsimple=>
```

Let's check that the table has been correctly updated:

```
bpsimple=> \d orderinfo
                              Table "public.orderinfo"
    Column     |    Type     |                                  Modifiers


--------------+-------------+-------------------------------------------------
 orderinfo_id | integer     | not null default nextval
    ('public.orderinfo_orderinfo_id_seq'::text)
 customer_id  | integer     | not null
 date_placed  | date        | not null
 date_shipped | date        |
 shipping     | numeric(7,2) |
Indexes:
    "orderinfo_pk" PRIMARY KEY, btree (orderinfo_id)
Foreign-key constraints:
    "orderinfo_customer_id_fk" FOREIGN KEY (customer_id) REFERENCES
        customer(customer_id)

bpsimple=>
```

It's a little complex, but we can clearly see our new foreign key constraint listed at the end.

### Creating Tables with Foreign Key Constraints

It's time to take a leap forward from our initial `bpsimple` database and work on our final version of the design, `bpfinal`:

```
bpsimple=> CREATE DATABASE bpfinal;
CREATE DATABASE
bpsimple=> \c bpfinal
You are now connected to database "bpfinal".
bpfinal=>
```

Now we are ready to start re-creating our tables using our newfound knowledge of foreign key constraints to enforce referential integrity at the database level.

We must start with our `customer` table (the definition is unchanged from our previous design), since we cannot reference it in our `orderinfo` table until it exists.

```
bpfinal=> CREATE TABLE customer
bpfinal-> (
bpfinal(>     customer_id                 serial,
bpfinal(>     title                       char(4),
bpfinal(>     fname                       varchar(32),
bpfinal(>     lname                       varchar(32) NOT NULL,
bpfinal(>     addressline                 varchar(64),
bpfinal(>     town                        varchar(32),
bpfinal(>     zipcode                     char(10) NOT NULL,
bpfinal(>     phone                       varchar(16),
bpfinal(>     CONSTRAINT                  customer_pk PRIMARY KEY
    (customer_id)
bpfinal(> );
NOTICE:  CREATE TABLE will create implicit sequence "customer_customer_id_seq"
for serial column "customer.customer_id"
NOTICE:  CREATE TABLE / PRIMARY KEY will create implicit index "customer_pk"
for table "customer"
CREATE TABLE
bpfinal=>
```

Now that we have our `customer` table, we can populate it as before, using the `\i` command:

```
bpfinal=> \i pop_customer.sql
```

Next, we create our `orderinfo` table:

```
bpfinal=> CREATE TABLE orderinfo
bpfinal-> (
bpfinal(>     orderinfo_id                serial,
bpfinal(>     customer_id                 integer NOT NULL,
bpfinal(>     date_placed                 date NOT NULL,
bpfinal(>     date_shipped                date,
```

```
bpfinal(>      shipping                          numeric(7,2) ,
bpfinal(>      CONSTRAINT                        orderinfo_pk PRIMARY KEY
   (orderinfo_id),
bpfinal(>      CONSTRAINT orderinfo_customer_id_fk FOREIGN KEY(customer_id)
   REFERENCES customer(customer_id)
bpfinal(> );
NOTICE:  CREATE TABLE will create implicit sequence "orderinfo_orderinfo_id_seq"
 for serial column "orderinfo.orderinfo_id"
NOTICE:  CREATE TABLE / PRIMARY KEY will create implicit index "orderinfo_pk"
 for table "orderinfo"
CREATE TABLE
bpfinal=>
```

Let's take a quick look at the definition:

```
bpfinal=> \d orderinfo
                              Table "public.orderinfo"
    Column    |    Type     |                   Modifiers

--------------+-------------+--------------------------------------------------
 orderinfo_id | integer     | not null default nextval('public.orderinfo_orderi
nfo_id_seq'::text)
 customer_id  | integer     | not null
 date_placed  | date        | not null
 date_shipped | date        |
 shipping     | numeric(7,2) |
Indexes:
    "orderinfo_pk" PRIMARY KEY, btree (orderinfo_id)
Foreign-key constraints:
    "orderinfo_customer_id_fk" FOREIGN KEY (customer_id) REFERENCES customer(cus
tomer_id)

bpfinal=>
```

Now we can repopulate the orderinfo table from our SQL script:

```
bpfinal=> \i pop_orderinfo.sql
```

So, now we are almost back to where we started, with one very important difference: the orderinfo table has a foreign key constraint, which says that rows in the orderinfo table have the customer_id column referring to the customer_id column in the customer table. This means that we cannot delete rows from the customer table if the row is being referenced by a column in the orderinfo table.

**Try It Out: Use Foreign Key Constraints**

We will start by checking to see what customer_id values we have in the orderinfo table:

```
bpfinal=> select orderinfo_id, customer_id from orderinfo;
 orderinfo_id | customer_id
--------------+-------------
            1 |           3
            2 |           8
            3 |          15
            4 |          13
            5 |           8
(5 rows)

bpfinal=>
```

We now know that there are five rows in orderinfo that have customer_id values that refer to customers in the customer table, and that the customers referred to have IDs 3, 8, 13, and 15. There are only four customers referred to, because the rows with orderinfo_id 2 and 5 both refer to the same customer.

Let's try to delete the row from the customer table with customer_id 3:

```
bpfinal=> DELETE FROM customer WHERE customer_id = 3;
ERROR:  update or delete on "customer" violates foreign key constraint
"orderinfo_customer_id_fk" on "orderinfo"
DETAIL:  Key (customer_id)=(3) is still referenced from table "orderinfo".
bpfinal=>
```

PostgreSQL prevents us from deleting the row. Also, notice that naming the constraint orderinfo_customer_id_fk allows us to more easily identify the source of the complaint. PostgreSQL is even kind enough to tell us exactly which customer_id key value had the problem, which although obvious in this example, may not be in more complex cases. PostgreSQL will allow us to delete rows from the customer table where there is no related orderinfo entry:

```
bpfinal=> DELETE FROM customer WHERE customer_id = 4;
DELETE 1

bpfinal=>
```

### How It Works

Behind the scenes, PostgreSQL adds some additional checking. For each row we try to delete from the customer table, it checks that the row is not being referred to by a row in a different table—in this case, the orderinfo table.

Any attempts to violate the rule result in the command being rejected and the data left unchanged. We can still delete a customer, but we must make sure the customer does not have any orders first.

PostgreSQL also checks that we don't try to insert rows into the orderinfo table that refer to nonexistent customers, as in this example:

```
bpfinal=> INSERT INTO orderinfo(customer_id, date_placed, shipping)
bpfinal-> VALUES(250,'07-25-2000', 0.00);
ERROR:  insert or update on table "orderinfo" violates foreign key constraint
"orderinfo_customer_id_fk"
DETAIL:  Key (customer_id)=(250) is not present in table "customer".
bpfinal=>
```

It is important to realize what a big step forward we have made here. We have taken very effective steps to ensure that the relationships between tables are enforced by the database. No longer is it possible to have rows in orderinfo referring to nonexistent customers.

We can now update our original table creation script to add foreign key constraints to all the tables that refer to other tables: orderinfo, orderline, stock, and barcode. The only slightly complex constraint is orderline, where the orderinfo_id column refers to the orderinfo table, and the item_id column refers to the item table. This is not a problem; we simply specify two constraints, one for each column:

```
CREATE TABLE orderline
(
    orderinfo_id                    integer            NOT NULL,
    item_id                         integer            NOT NULL,
    quantity                        integer            NOT NULL,
    CONSTRAINT                      orderline_pk PRIMARY KEY(orderinfo_id,
        item_id),
    CONSTRAINT orderline_orderinfo_id_fk FOREIGN KEY(orderinfo_id) REFERENCES
        orderinfo(orderinfo_id),
    CONSTRAINT orderline_item_id_fk FOREIGN KEY(item_id) REFERENCES item(item_id)
);
```

The final version of the database creation script can be found in Appendix E. We will be using this database, bpfinal, for the rest of the book. You can download it, along with the other code samples, from the Downloads section of the Apress web site (http://www.apress.com).

When you use this database, you will also find that you must populate the tables in an order that fulfills the foreign key constraints; you can no longer populate the orderinfo table before populating the customer table for the orders to reference. We suggest this order:

- customer

- item

- orderinfo

- orderline

- stock

- barcode

# Foreign Key Constraint Options

It might be that we get into a situation where we have entries in the orderinfo table referring to the customer table, but we need to update the customer_id. As it stands, we can't easily do this, because if we attempt to change the customer_id (actually a very bad idea, since it is a serial column!), the foreign key constraint in orderinfo will prevent it, since the rule says that the customer_id stored in each orderinfo row must always refer to a customer_id entry in the customer table.

We can't change the customer_id in the orderinfo table, because the entry in the customer table doesn't exist yet, and we can't change the entry in the customer table, because it is being referred to by the orderinfo table.

The SQL standard allows two ways to resolve the situation where you briefly need to make a data change that violates a foreign key constraint, but you will restore the correct integrity to the data before the transaction completes:

- Make the constraint deferrable.

- Specify rules in the foreign key constraint about how to handle violations.

## Deferrable Constraints

The first way to allow the foreign key constraint to be violated in certain circumstances is to add the keywords INITIALLY DEFERRED at the end of the foreign key constraint:

```
CREATE TABLE orderinfo
(
    orderinfo_id                serial ,
    customer_id                 integer NOT NULL,
    date_placed                 date NOT NULL,
    date_shipped                date ,
    shipping                    numeric(7,2) ,
    CONSTRAINT                  orderinfo_pk PRIMARY KEY(orderinfo_id),
    CONSTRAINT orderinfo_customer_id_fk FOREIGN KEY(customer_id)
        REFERENCES customer(customer_id) INITIALLY DEFERRED
);
```

This changes the way foreign key constraints are enforced. Normally, PostgreSQL will check that foreign key constraints are met before any change is allowed to the database. If you use transactions (which we will meet in the next chapter) and INITIALLY DEFERRED, PostgreSQL will allow foreign key constraints to be violated, providing the constraint is violated only during a transaction, and the violation has been corrected before the transaction ends. In practice, what happens is that PostgreSQL suspends checking of the constraint until it is about to complete the current transaction.

As we will see in Chapter 9, a transaction is a group of SQL commands that must either all be completely executed or none executed. Hence, we could start a transaction, update the customer_id in the customer table, update the related customer_id values in the orderinfo table, commit the transaction, and then PostgreSQL would permit this. All it will check is that the constraints are met when the transaction ends.

## ON UPDATE and ON DELETE

An alternative solution is to specify rules in the foreign key constraint about how to handle violation in two circumstances: UPDATE and DELETE operations. Two actions are possible:

- We could CASCADE the change from the table with the primary key.

- We could SET NULL to make the column NULL, since it no longer references the primary table.

Here is an example:

```
CREATE TABLE orderinfo
(
    orderinfo_id                serial ,
    customer_id                 integer NOT NULL,
    date_placed                 date NOT NULL,
    date_shipped                date ,
    shipping                    numeric(7,2) ,
    CONSTRAINT                  orderinfo_pk PRIMARY KEY(orderinfo_id),
    CONSTRAINT orderinfo_customer_id_fk FOREIGN KEY(customer_id)
        REFERENCES customer(customer_id) ON DELETE CASCADE
);
```

This example tells PostgreSQL that if we delete a row in customer with a customer_id that is being used in the orderinfo table, it should automatically delete the related rows in orderinfo. This might be what we intended, but it is normally a dangerous choice. It is usually much better to ensure applications delete rows in the correct order, so we make sure there are no orders for a customer before deleting the customer entry.

The SET NULL option is usually used with UPDATE or DELETE statements. It looks like this:

```
CREATE TABLE orderinfo
(
    orderinfo_id                serial ,
    customer_id                 integer NOT NULL,
    date_placed                 date NOT NULL,
    date_shipped                date ,
    shipping                    numeric(7,2) ,
    CONSTRAINT                  orderinfo_pk PRIMARY KEY(orderinfo_id),
    CONSTRAINT orderinfo_customer_id_fk FOREIGN KEY(customer_id)
        REFERENCES customer(customer_id) ON UPDATE SET NULL
);
```

This says that if the row being referred to by `customer_id` is deleted from the `customer` table, set the column in the `orderinfo` table to `NULL`.

You may have noticed that for our table, this isn't going to work. We declared `customer_id` as `NOT NULL`, so it cannot be updated to a `NULL` value. We did this because we did not want to allow the possibility of rows in the `orderinfo` table having `NULL` `customer_id` values. After all, what does an order with an unknown customer mean? It's probably a mistake.

These options can be combined, so you can write the following:

```
ON UPDATE SET NULL ON DELETE CASCADE
```

---

■**Caution** Use `ON UPDATE` and `ON DELETE` with considerable caution. It is much safer to force application programmers to code `UPDATE` and `DELETE` statements in the right order and use transactions than it is to `CASCADE DELETE` rows and suddenly store `NULL` values in columns because a different table was changed.

---

In Chapter 10, we will see how to use triggers and stored procedures to give much the same effect, but in a way that gives us more control over the changes in other tables.

## Summary

We covered a lot of material in this chapter. We started by looking more formally at the data types supported by PostgreSQL, especially the common SQL standard types, but also mentioning some of PostgreSQL's more unusual extension types, such as arrays. We then looked at how you can manipulate column data—converting between types, using substrings of the data, and accessing information with PostgreSQL's "magic" variables.

We then moved on to look at table management, focusing on a very important topic: constraints. We saw that there are effectively two ways of defining constraints: against a single column and at a table level. Even simple constraints can help us to enforce the integrity of data at the database level.

Next, we saw how to use a view to create an "illusion" of a table. Views can provide a simpler way for users to access data, as well as hide some data we may not want to be accessible to everyone.

Our final topic was one of the most important types of constraints: foreign keys. These allow us to define formally in the database how different tables relate to each other. Most important, they allow us to enforce these rules, such as to ensure that we can never delete a customer that has order information relating to that customer in a different table.

Having learned how to enforce referential integrity in our database, we created an updated database design, `bpfinal`, which we will be using for the remainder of this book.

In the next chapter, we will cover transactions and locking, which are very important when considering more than one user needing to simultaneously access a database.

# CHAPTER 9

■■■

# Transactions and Locking

**S**o far in this book, we have avoided any in-depth discussion of the multiuser aspects of PostgreSQL, simply stating the idealized view that, like any good relational database, PostgreSQL hides the details of supporting multiple concurrent users. It simply provides a fast and efficient database server that delivers a service to its clients as if all the simultaneous users had exclusive access. Particularly with small and lightly loaded databases, this idealized view is generally achieved in practice. However, the reality is that PostgreSQL, although very capable, cannot perform magic, and the isolation of each user from all the others requires work behind the scenes.

In this chapter, we will look at two important aspects of database support for multiple users: transactions and locking. Transactions allow you to collect a number of discrete changes to the database into a single work unit. Locking prevents conflicts when different users make changes to the database at the same time.

In this chapter, we will cover the following topics:

- What constitutes a transaction

- Benefits of transactions in a single-user database

- Transaction with multiple users

- Row and table locking

## What Are Transactions?

As we've said in previous chapters, ideally, you should write database changes as a single declarative statement. However, in real-world applications, there soon comes a point at which you need to make several changes to a database that cannot be expressed in a single SQL statement. Although they are not made in just one statement, you still need *all* of the changes to occur to update the database correctly. If a problem occurs with any part of the group of changes, then *none* of the database changes should be made. In other words, you need to perform a single, indivisible unit of work, which will require several SQL statements to be executed, with either all of the SQL statements executing successfully or none of them executing.

The classic example is that of transferring money between two accounts in a bank, perhaps represented in different tables in a database, so that one account is debited and the other is credited. If you debit one account and fail to credit the second for some reason, you must return the money to the first account, or behave as though it was never debited in the first place.

No bank could remain in business if money occasionally disappeared when transferring it between accounts.

In databases based on ANSI SQL, as PostgreSQL is, performing this all-or-nothing task is achieved with *transactions*. A transaction is a logical unit of work that must not be subdivided.

## Grouping Data Changes into Logical Units

What do we mean by a *logical unit of work*? It is simply a set of logical changes to the database, which must either all occur or all must fail, just like the previous example of the transfer of money between accounts. In PostgreSQL, these changes are controlled by four key phrases:

- BEGIN starts a transaction.

- SAVEPOINT *savepointname* asks the server to remember the current state of the transaction. This statement can be used only after a BEGIN and before a COMMIT or ROLLBACK; that is, while a transaction is being performed.

- COMMIT says that all the elements of the transaction are complete and should now be made persistent and accessible to all concurrent and subsequent transactions.

- ROLLBACK [TO *savepointname*] says that the transaction is to be abandoned, and all changes made to data by that SQL transaction are cancelled. The database should appear to all users as if none of the changes had ever occurred since the previous BEGIN, and the transaction is closed. The alternative version, with the addition of the TO clause, allows rollback to a named savepoint, and does not complete a transaction.

---

**Note** The ANSI SQL92 standard did not define the BEGIN SQL phrase. It defines transactions as starting automatically (hence the phrase would be redundant), but it is a very common extension present, and required, in many relational databases. SQL99 added the statement START TRANSACTION, which has the same effect as BEGIN. PostgreSQL from 7.3 onwards accepts the newer syntax as well as the BEGIN syntax, but we stick to the BEGIN syntax, as it is currently more common.

---

## Concurrent Multiuser Access to Data

A second aspect of transactions is that any transaction in the database is isolated from other transactions occurring in the database at the same time. In an ideal world, each transaction would behave as though it had exclusive access to the database. Unfortunately, as we will see later in this chapter when we look at transactions with multiple users, the practicalities of achieving good performance mean that some compromises often must be made.

Let's look at a different example of where a transaction is needed. Suppose you are trying to book an airline ticket online. You check the flight you want and discover a ticket is available. Although unknown to you, it is the very last ticket on that flight. While you are typing in your credit card details, another customer with an account at the airline makes the same check for tickets. You have not yet purchased your ticket, so the other person sees a free seat and books it while you are still typing in your credit card details. You now submit to buy the ticket, and because the system knew there was a seat available when you started the transaction, it incorrectly assumes a seat is still available, and debits your card. (Of course, airlines have more sophisticated systems that prevent such basic ticket-booking errors, but this example does illustrate the principle.)

You disconnect, confident your seat has been booked, and perhaps even check that your credit card has been debited. The reality is, however, that you purchased a nonexistent seat. At the instant your transaction was processed, there were no free seats.

The code executed by the booking application may have looked a little like this:

```
Check if seats available.
If yes, offer seat to customer.
If customer accepts offer, ask for credit card number.
Authorize credit card transaction with bank.
Debit card.
Assign seat.
Reduce the number of free seats available by the number purchased.
```

Such a sequence of events is perfectly valid, if only a single customer ever uses the system at any one time. The trouble occurred because there were two customers. What actually happened is depicted in Table 9-1.

**Table 9-1.** *Overlapping Events*

| Customer 1 | Customer 2 | Free Seats on Plane |
|---|---|---|
| Check if seats available | | 1 |
| | Check if seats available | 1 |
| If yes, offer seat to customer | | 1 |
| | If yes, offer seat to customer | 1 |
| If customer accepts offer, ask for credit card or account number | | 1 |
| | If customer accepts offer, ask for credit card or account number | 1 |
| Get credit card number | Get account number | 1 |
| Authorize credit card transaction with bank | | 1 |
| | Check account is valid | 1 |
| | Update account with new transaction | 1 |
| Debit card | Assign seat | 1 |
| Assign seat | Reduce number of free seats available by number purchased | 0 |
| Reduce number of free seats available by number purchased | | −1 |

How could we solve the problem with this ticket-booking application? We could improve things considerably by rechecking that a seat was available closer to the point at which we take the money, but however close we do the check, it's inevitable that the "check a seat is available" step is separated from the "take money" step, even if only by a tiny amount of time.

We could go to the opposite extreme to solve the problem, allowing only one person to access the ticket-booking system at any one time, but the performance would be terrible and customers would go elsewhere.

In application terms, what we have is a critical section of code—a small section of code that needs exclusive access to some data. We could write our application using a semaphore, or similar technique, to manage access to the critical section of code. This would require every application that accessed the database to use the semaphore. However, rather than writing application logic, it is often easier to use a database to solve the problem.

In database terms, what we have here is a transaction—the set of data manipulations from checking the seat availability through to debiting the account or card and assigning the seat, all of which must happen as a single unit of work.

## ACID Rules

ACID is a frequently used acronym to describe the four properties a transaction must have:

**Atomic:** A transaction, even though it is a group of individual actions on the database, must happen as a single unit. A transaction must happen exactly once, with no subsets and no unintended repetition of the action. In our banking example, the money movement must be atomic. The debit of one account and the credit of the other must both happen as though they were a single action, even if several consecutive SQL statements are required.

**Consistent:** At the end of a transaction, the system must be left in a consistent state. We touched on this in Chapter 8, when we saw that we could declare a constraint as deferrable; in other words, the constraint should be checked only at the end of a transaction. In our banking example, at the end of a transaction, all accounts must accurately reflect the intended credits and debits.

**Isolated:** This means that each transaction, no matter how many transactions are currently in progress in a database, must appear to be independent of all the other transactions. In our airline ticket-booking example, transactions processing two concurrent customers must behave as though they each have exclusive use of the database. In practice, we know this cannot be true if we are to have sensible performance on multiuser databases, and indeed this turns out to be one of the places where the practicalities of the real world can impinge most significantly on our ideal database behavior. We will discuss isolating transactions later in the chapter, in the "Transactions with Multiple Users" section.

**Durable:** Once a transaction has completed, it must stay completed. Once money has been successfully transferred between accounts, it must stay transferred, even if the power fails and the machine running the database has an uncontrolled power down. In PostgreSQL, as with most relational databases, this is achieved using a transaction log file, as described in the following section. Transaction durability happens without user intervention.

## Transaction Logs

As mentioned in the previous section, transaction log files are used internally by the database to make sure that a transaction endures. The way the transaction log file works is simple. As a transaction executes, not only are the changes written to the database, but also to a log. Once a transaction completes, a marker is written to say the transaction has finished, and the log file data is forced to permanent storage, so it is secure, even if the database server crashes. Should the database server die for some reason in the middle of a transaction, then as the server restarts, it is able to automatically ensure that completed transactions are correctly reflected in the database (by rolling forward transactions in the transaction log, but not in the database). No changes from transactions that were still in progress when the server went down appear in the database.

The transaction log that PostgreSQL maintains not only records all the changes that are being made to the database, but also records how to reverse them. Obviously, this file could get very large very quickly. Once a COMMIT statement is issued for a transaction, PostgreSQL then knows that it is no longer required to store the "undo" information, since the database change is now irrevocable, at least by the database (the application could execute additional code to reverse changes).

PostgreSQL actually uses a technique where data is written to the transaction log ahead of it being written to disk for the tables, because it knows that once the data is written to the log file, it can recover the intended state of the table data from the log, even if the system should fail before the real data files have been updated. This is called Write Ahead Logging (WAL), and interested readers can find more details in the PostgreSQL documentation.

# Transactions with a Single User

Before we look at the more complex aspects of transactions and how they behave with multiple, concurrent users of the database, we need to see how they behave with a single user. Even in this rather simplistic way of working, there are real advantages to using transactions.

The big benefit of transactions is that they allow you to execute several SQL statements, and then at a later stage, allow you to undo the work you have done, if you so decide. Alternatively, if one of your SQL statements fails, you can undo the work you have done back to a predetermined point.

Using a transaction, the application does not need to worry about storing what changes have been made to the database and how to undo them. It can simply ask the database engine to undo a whole batch of changes at once. Logically, the sequence is depicted in Figure 9-1.

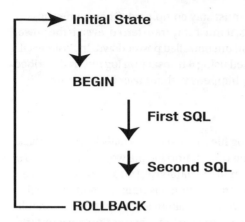

**Figure 9-1.** *Rolling back a set of changes*

If you decide all your changes to the database are valid after the "Second SQL" step shown in Figure 9-1, however, and you wish to apply them to the database so they become permanent, then all you do is replace the ROLLBACK statement with a COMMIT statement, as depicted in Figure 9-2.

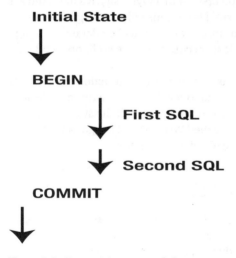

**Figure 9-2.** *Commiting a set of changes*

After the COMMIT, all changes to the database are committed and can be considered permanently written to the data files, so they will not be lost due to power failures or application errors.

**Try It Out: Perform a Simple Transaction**

Let's try a very simple transaction, where we change a single row in a table, and then use the ROLLBACK statement to cancel the change. We will use the test database for these experiments.

First, connect to the test database (if it does not exist, just use a CREATE DATABASE test command), and then create a pair of simple tables to experiment with:

```
bpfinal=> \c test
You are now connected to database "test".
test=> CREATE TABLE ttest1 (
test(>  ival1 integer,
test(>  sval1 varchar(64)
test(> );
CREATE TABLE
test=> CREATE TABLE ttest2 (
test(>  ival2 integer,
test(>  sval2 varchar(64)
test(> );
CREATE TABLE
test=>
```

Now we can try a simple transaction:

```
test=> INSERT INTO ttest1 (ival1, sval1) VALUES (1, 'David');
INSERT 17784 1
test=> BEGIN;
BEGIN
test=> UPDATE ttest1 SET sval1 = 'Dave' WHERE ival1 = 1;
UPDATE 1
test=> SELECT sval1 FROM ttest1 WHERE ival1 = 1;
 sval1
-------
 Dave
(1 row)

test=> ROLLBACK;
ROLLBACK
test=> SELECT sval1 FROM ttest1 WHERE ival1 = 1;
 sval1
-------
 David
(1 row)

test=>
```

**How It Works**

We initially inserted a single row and stored the name 'David'. We then started the transaction by using the BEGIN command. Next, we updated the sval1 column of the row to set the name to 'Dave'. When we did a SELECT on this row, it showed the data had changed. We then called ROLLBACK. PostgreSQL used its internal transaction log to undo the changes since BEGIN was executed, so the next time we SELECT the row, our change had been rolled back.

Interestingly, if we used a second psql session and queried the database immediately after the update of David to Dave, but before executing the ROLLBACK, we would still see David in the database. This is because PostgreSQL is isolating users, other than the user currently making the change, from uncommitted database data updates. We will discuss this further in the "Transactions with Multiple Users" section later in this chapter.

## Transactions Involving Multiple Tables

Transactions are not limited to a single table or simple updates to data. Let's look at a more complex example involving multiple tables and using both an UPDATE statement and an INSERT statement.

### Try It Out: Perform Transactions with Multiple Tables

Let's experiment with transactions that affect multiple tables. First, ensure both tables are empty, and then insert a row into the first table:

```
test=> DELETE FROM ttest1;
DELETE 1
test=> DELETE FROM ttest2;
DELETE 0
test=> INSERT INTO ttest1 (ival1, sval1) VALUES (1, 'David');
INSERT 17793 1
```

Now start a transaction and make some changes:

```
test=> BEGIN;
BEGIN
test=> INSERT INTO ttest2 (ival2, sval2) VALUES (42, 'Arthur');
INSERT 17794 1
test=> UPDATE ttest1 SET sval1 = 'Robert' WHERE ival1 = 1;
UPDATE 1
test=> SELECT * FROM ttest1;
 ival1 | sval1
-------+--------
     1 | Robert
(1 row)

test=> SELECT * FROM ttest2;
 ival2 | sval2
-------+--------
    42 | Arthur
(1 row)
```

Now perform a ROLLBACK and check the effect:

```
test=> ROLLBACK;
ROLLBACK
test=> SELECT * FROM ttest1;
 ival1 | sval1
-------+-------
     1 | David
(1 row)

test=> SELECT * FROM ttest2;
 ival2 | sval2
-------+-------
(0 rows)

test=>
```

**How It Works**

The ROLLBACK caused the data added as a result of the INSERT statement to be removed and the UPDATE to the item table to be reversed. This demonstrates how a transaction grouping a set of changes together can work across multiple tables..

## Transactions and Savepoints

The previous examples use the basic transaction syntax, which is all that many applications need. However, savepoints can be useful for situations where you want to be able to roll back to a specified point in the transaction. This requires the extended version of the transaction syntax, with a named savepoint and the ROLLBACK TO command.

If we might need to undo just some of the operations in a transaction, we can create a named savepoint, which we can then roll back to, rather than rolling back all the way to the BEGIN statement. Figure 9-3 illustrates the sequence.

In the example in Figure 9-3, we start by executing a BEGIN statement, which starts our transaction, and then execute two SQL statements. We then create a savepoint called parta, and execute a third SQL statement. We then execute a ROLLBACK TO parta statement, which effectively undoes the effect of the third SQL statement. We can then issue some more SQL, before finally executing a COMMIT to make our database changes permanent.

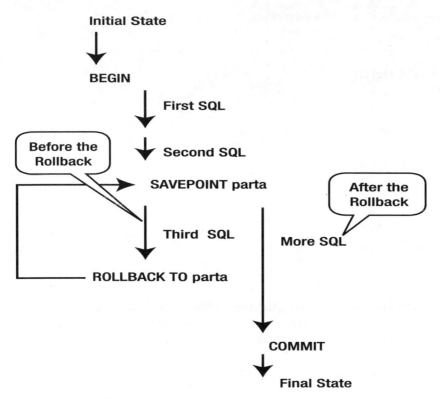

**Figure 9-3.** *Using a savepoint*

**Try It Out: Use Savepoints**

Let's see a savepoint in action. The name of the savepoint is arbitrary; we use first here, but we could have called it Tux, Getreidegasse, or just about any other name.

```
test=> DELETE FROM ttest1;
DELETE 1
test=> DELETE FROM ttest2;
DELETE 0
test=> INSERT INTO ttest1 (ival1, sval1) VALUES (1, 'David');
INSERT 17795 1
test=> BEGIN;
BEGIN
test=> INSERT INTO ttest2 (ival2, sval2) VALUES (42, 'Arthur');
INSERT 17796 1
test=> SAVEPOINT first;
SAVEPOINT
test=> UPDATE ttest1 SET sval1 = 'Robert' WHERE ival1 = 1;
UPDATE 1
test=> SELECT * FROM ttest1;
```

```
 ival1 | sval1
-------+--------
     1 | Robert
(1 row)
test=> ROLLBACK TO first;
ROLLBACK
test=> SELECT * FROM ttest1;
 ival1 | sval1
-------+-------
     1 | David
(1 row)

test=> SELECT * FROM ttest2;
 ival2 | sval2
-------+--------
    42 | Arthur
(1 row)
test=>
```

We are still in transaction at this point and can still roll back to the initial BEGIN state:

```
test=>
test=> ROLLBACK;
ROLLBACK
test=> SELECT * FROM ttest1;
 ival1 | sval1
-------+-------
     1 | David
(1 row)

test=> SELECT * FROM ttest2;
 ival2 | sval2
-------+-------
(0 rows)

test=>
```

Now that a ROLLBACK has been issued to the initial BEGIN statement, the transaction is considered complete, and we cannot issue another ROLLBACK or COMMIT, until after a new BEGIN statement:

```
test=> INSERT INTO ttest2 (ival2, sval2) VALUES (99, 'Chris');
INSERT 17797 1
test=> COMMIT;
WARNING:  there is no transaction in progress
COMMIT
test=>
```

Also, once we have issued a COMMIT to say the transaction is complete, it has been written to the database permanently, and there is no going back:

```
test=> SELECT * FROM ttest2;
 ival2 | sval2
-------+-------
    99 | Chris
(1 row)

test=> BEGIN;
BEGIN
test=> UPDATE ttest2 SET sval2 = 'Gill' WHERE ival2 = 99;
UPDATE 1
test=> COMMIT;
COMMIT
test=> ROLLBACK;
WARNING:  there is no transaction in progress
ROLLBACK
test=> SELECT * FROM ttest2;
 ival2 | sval2
-------+-------
    99 | Gill
(1 row)
test=>x
```

**How It Works**

As this example demonstrated, savepoints allow us to both roll back to an intermediate point in a transaction or all of the way back to the start of the transaction. Once a ROLLBACK has been executed, the database looks exactly as though the rolled-back changes never happened. Once a transaction has been committed, it can no longer be undone by a ROLLBACK.

## Transaction Limitations

Although transactions work very well, they do have some limitations. These involve nesting, size, and duration.

### Nesting

You cannot nest transactions in PostgreSQL (or most other relational databases, for that matter). In PostgreSQL, if you try to execute a BEGIN statement while it's already in a transaction, PostgreSQL will produce a warning message, telling you a transaction is already in progress.

Some databases silently accept several BEGIN statements. A COMMIT or ROLLBACK command always works against the first BEGIN statement, however, so although it looked as though the transactions were nested, in reality, subsequent BEGIN commands were being ignored.

### Transaction Size

It is advisable to keep transactions small. As we will see later in this chapter, PostgreSQL (and other relational databases) must do a lot of work to ensure that transactions from different users are kept separate. A consequence of this is that the parts of a database involved in a transaction frequently need to become locked, to ensure that transactions are kept separate. Therefore, you should try to make sure that each transaction is no larger than it needs to be. Including large amounts of unnecessary changes in each transaction will result in excessive amounts of locking taking place in the database, impacting both performance and other users' ability to access data. We'll discuss locking in more detail in the "Locking" section later in this chapter.

### Transaction Duration

Transactions should not be kept open over extended time periods. Although PostgreSQL locks the database automatically for you, a long-running transaction usually prevents other users from accessing data involved in the transaction until the transaction is committed or rolled back. Therefore, you should also avoid having a transaction in progress when any user dialogue is required. It is advisable to collect all the information required from the user first, and then process the information in a transaction, unhindered by unpredictable user-response times.

Consider a poorly behaved application that started a transaction when a person sat down to work at a terminal in the morning, and left the transaction running all day while the user made various changes to the database. As the user did work on the database, more and more of it would become locked, waiting for those changes to be committed. If the user committed the data only at the end of the day, the ability for other users to access the data would be severely impacted, and the overall application would probably be considered unusable for any situation that requires multiple users.

You should also be aware that although a COMMIT statement usually executes quite rapidly, since it generally has very little work to perform, rolling back transactions typically involves at least as much work for the database as performing them initially, and consequently can take some time to execute. Therefore, if you start a transaction, and it takes two minutes to execute all the SQL, then decide to do a ROLLBACK to cancel it all, don't expect the rollback to be instantaneous. It could easily take longer than two minutes to undo all the changes.

# Transactions with Multiple Users

As we saw earlier in the chapter, transactions that need to work for multiple, concurrent users must be isolated from each other (the *I* part of ACID). Although PostgreSQL's default behavior for handling isolation will suffice in most cases, there are circumstances where it is useful to understand it in more detail.

## Implementing Isolation

One of the most difficult aspects of relational databases is isolation between different users for updates to the database. Of course, achieving isolation is not difficult if we don't care about performance. Simply allowing a single connection to the database, with only a single transaction in progress at any one time, will ensure complete isolation between different transactions.

Unfortunately, the multiuser performance would be terrible. The difficult part of transaction isolation is in achieving practical isolation without significantly damaging performance or preventing multiuser access to the database.

To lessen the impact of isolation on performance, the ANSI SQL standard defines different levels of isolation that databases can implement. This allows the database administrator to trade between performance and the degree of isolation individual database users receive. Usually, a relational database will implement at least one of these levels by default, and also allow users to specify at least one other isolation level to use.

The ANSI SQL standard defines isolation levels in terms of *undesirable phenomena* that can happen in multiuser databases when transactions interact. These phenomena are called dirty reads, unrepeatable reads, phantom reads, and lost updates. Let's see what each of these terms means, and then how the ANSI isolation levels are defined.

## Dirty Reads

A *dirty read* occurs when some SQL in a transaction reads data that has been changed by another transaction, but the transaction changing the data has not yet committed its block of work.

As we discussed earlier, a transaction is a logical unit or block of work that must be atomic. Either all the elements of a transaction occur or none of them occur. Until a transaction has been committed, there is always the possibility that it will fail or be abandoned with a ROLLBACK command. Therefore, no other users of the database should see this changed data before a COMMIT.

Table 9-2 illustrates what different transactions might see as the fname of the customer with customer_id 15 when dirty reads are allowed and when they are not allowed.

**Table 9-2.** *Dirty Reads*

| Transaction 1 | Data Seen by Transaction 1 | Data Seen by Other Transactions with Dirty Reads Allowed | Data Seen by Other Transactions with Dirty Reads Prohibited |
|---|---|---|---|
| BEGIN | | | |
| | David | David | David |
| UPDATE customer SET fname='Dave' WHERE customer_id - 15; | | | |
| | Dave | Dave | David |
| COMMIT | | | |
| | Dave | Dave | Dave |
| BEGIN | | | |
| UPDATE customer SET fname = 'David' WHERE customer_id = 15; | | | Dave |
| | David | David | Dave |
| ROLLBACK | | | |
| | Dave | Dave | Dave |

Notice how a dirty read has permitted other transactions to see data that has not yet been committed to the database. This means they can see changes that are later discarded, because of the ROLLBACK command.

---

■**Note** PostgreSQL never permits dirty reads.

---

## Unrepeatable Reads

An *unrepeatable read* is very similar to a dirty read, but is more restrictively defined. An unrepeatable read occurs where a transaction reads a set of data, then later rereads the data and discovers it has changed. This is much less serious than a dirty read, but not quite ideal. An illustration of the unrepeatable read process is shown in Table 9-3.

**Table 9-3.** *Unrepeatable Reads*

| Transaction 1 | Data Seen by Transaction 1 | Data Seen by Other Transactions with Unrepeatable Reads Allowed | Data Seen by Other Transactions with Unrepeatable Reads Prohibited |
|---|---|---|---|
| BEGIN | | BEGIN | BEGIN |
| | David | David | David |
| UPDATE customer SET fname = 'Dave' WHERE customer_id = 15; | | | |
| | Dave | David | David |
| COMMIT | | | |
| | Dave | Dave | David |
| | | COMMIT | COMMIT |
| | | BEGIN | BEGIN |
| SELECT fname FROM customer WHERE customer_id = 15; | | Dave | Dave |

Notice the unrepeatable read means that a transaction can see changes committed by other transactions, even though the reading transaction has not itself committed. If unrepeatable reads are prevented, other transactions do not see changes made to the database until they themselves have committed changes.

By default, PostgreSQL permits unrepeatable reads, although as we will see later, we can change this default behavior.

## Phantom Reads

*Phantom reads* are quite similar to unrepeatable reads, but occur when a new row appears in a table while a different transaction is updating the table, and the new row should have been updated but was not.

Suppose we had two transactions updating the item table. The first is adding one dollar to the selling price of all items, and the second is adding a new item. This process is depicted in Table 9-4.

**Table 9-4.** *Phantom Reads*

| Transaction 1 | Transaction 2 |
|---|---|
| BEGIN | BEGIN |
| UPDATE item SET sell_price = sell_price + 1; | |
| | INSERT INTO item(….) VALUES(…); |
| COMMIT | |
| | COMMIT |

What should the sell_price of the item added by Transaction 2 be? The INSERT statement started before the UPDATE statement was committed; therefore, we might reasonably expect it to be greater by one than the price we inserted. If a phantom read occurs, however, the new record that appears after Transaction 1 determines which rows to UPDATE, and the price of the new item does not get incremented.

Phantom reads are extremely rare, and almost impossible to demonstrate, so generally you do not need to worry about them. By default, PostgreSQL will allow phantom reads.

## Lost Updates

*Lost updates* are slightly different from the previous three cases, which are generally an application-level problem and not related to the way the relational database works. A lost update, on the other hand, occurs when two different changes are written to the database, and the second update causes the first to be lost.

Suppose two users are using a screen-based application, which updates the item table. This process is shown in Table 9-5.

**Table 9-5.** *Lost Updates*

| User 1 | Data Seen by User 1 | User 2 | Data Seen by User 2 |
|---|---|---|---|
| Attempting to change the selling price from 21.95 to 22.55 | | Attempting to change the cost price from 15.23 to 16.00 | |
| BEGIN | | BEGIN | |
| SELECT cost_price, sell_price FROM item WHERE item_id = 1; | 15.23, 21.95 | SELECT cost_price, sell_price FROM item WHERE item_id = 1; | 15.23, 21.95 |
| UPDATE item SET cost_price = 15.23, sell_price = 22.55 WHERE item_id = 1; | | | |
| | 15.23, 22.55 | | |
| COMMIT | | | |
| | | | 15.23, 22.55 |
| | | UPDATE item SET cost_price = 16.00, sell_price = 21.95 WHERE item_id = 1; | |
| | 15.23, 22.55 | | 16.00, 21.95 |
| | | COMMIT | |
| | 16.00, 21.95 | | 16.00, 21.95 |

The sell_price change made by User 1 has been lost, not because there was a database error, but because User 2 read the sell_price, "kept it" for a while, and then wrote it back to the database, destroying the change that User 1 had made. The database has quite correctly isolated the two sets of changes, but the application has still lost data.

There are several ways around this problem; which is the most appropriate depends on individual applications. As a first step, applications should keep transactions as short as possible, never holding them in progress for longer than is absolutely necessary. As a second step, applications should write back only data that they have changed. These two steps will prevent many occurrences of lost updates, including the mistake demonstrated in Table 9-5.

Of course, it is possible for both users to have been trying to update the sell_price; in which case, a change would still have been lost. A more comprehensive way to prevent lost updates is to encode the value you are trying to change in the UPDATE statement, as illustrated in Table 9-6.

**Table 9-6.** *An Application Work-Around to Lost Updates*

| User 1 | Data Seen by User 1 | User 2 | Data Seen by User 2 |
|---|---|---|---|
| Attempting to change the selling price from 21.95 to 22.55 | | Attempting to change the selling price from 21.95 to 22.99 | |
| BEGIN | | BEGIN | |
| Read sell_price WHERE item_id = 1 | 21.95 | Read sell_price WHERE item_id = 1 | 21.95 |
| UPDATE item SET cost_price = 15.23, sell_price = 22.55 WHERE item_id = 1 AND sell_price = 21.95; | | | |
| | 22.55 | | 21.95 |
| COMMIT | | | |
| | | | 22.55 |
| | | UPDATE item SET cost_price = 16.00, sell_price = 21.95 WHERE item_id = 1 AND sell_price = 21.95; | |
| | | Update fails with row not found, since the sell_price has been changed | |

Although this is not a perfect cure, since it works only if the first transaction commits before the second UPDATE statement is run, it does significantly reduce the risks of losing updates.

## ANSI Isolation Levels

The ANSI standard defines different isolation levels a database may use as combinations of the first three types of undesirable phenomena: dirty reads, unrepeatable reads, and phantom reads. These levels are listed in Table 9-7.

**Table 9-7.** *ANSI Isolation Level vs. Undesirable Behavior*

| Isolation Level Definition | Dirty Read | Unrepeatable Read | Phantom Read |
|---|---|---|---|
| Read Uncommitted | Possible | Possible | Possible |
| Read Committed | Not Possible | Possible | Possible |
| Repeatable Read | Not Possible | Not Possible | Possible |
| Serializable | Not Possible | Not Possible | Not Possible |

You can see that as the isolation level moves from Read Uncommitted to the ultimate Serializable level, the types of undesirable behavior that might occur are reduced.

## Changing the Isolation level

By default, PostgreSQL's isolation mode is set to READ COMMITTED, for the Read Committed level, as listed in Table 9-7. The other mode available is SERIALIZABLE, for the Serializable level.

At the time of writing, PostgreSQL does not implement the intermediate level Repeatable Read or the entry level Read Uncommitted. Generally, Read Uncommitted is such poor behavior that few databases offer it as an option, and it would be a rare application that was brave (or foolhardy!) enough to choose to use it. The intermediate level Repeatable Read provides added protection only against phantom reads, which are extremely rare, so the lack of this level is of no real consequence. It is common for databases to offer less than the full set of possibilities, and providing Read Committed and Serializable is a good compromise solution.

You can change the isolation level by using the SET TRANSACTION ISOLATION LEVEL command, which has the following syntax:

```
SET TRANSACTION ISOLATION LEVEL { READ COMMITTED | SERIALIZABLE }
```

Unless you have a very good reason to change it, we suggest you don't adjust the default isolation level of your PostgreSQL database.

## Using Explicit and Implicit Transactions

Throughout this chapter, we have been explicitly using BEGIN and COMMIT (or ROLLBACK) to delimit our transactions. Earlier in the book, before we knew about transactions, however, we were happily making changes to our database without a BEGIN command to be seen.

By default, PostgreSQL operates in an auto-commit mode, sometimes referred to as *chained mode* or *implicit transaction mode*, where each SQL statement that can modify data acts as though it was a complete transaction in its own right. This is great for experimentation on the command line, and for allowing new users to experiment without needing to learn too much SQL. However, it's not so good for real applications, where we want to have access to transactions with explicit COMMIT or ROLLBACK statements.

In other relational database management systems that implement different modes, you normally must issue an explicit command to change the mode; for example, SET CHAINED in Sybase or SET IMPLICIT_TRANSACTIONS for Microsoft SQL Server.

In PostgreSQL, all you need to do is issue the command BEGIN, and PostgreSQL automatically switches into a mode where the following commands are in a transaction, until you issue a COMMIT or ROLLBACK statement.

The SQL standard considers all SQL statements to occur in a transaction, with the transaction starting automatically on the first SQL statement and continuing until a COMMIT or ROLLBACK is encountered. Thus, standard SQL does not define a BEGIN command. However, the PostgreSQL way of performing transactions, with an explicit BEGIN, is quite common.

# Locking

Most databases implement transactions, particularly when isolating different user transactions from each other, using locks to restrict access to the data from other users. Simplistically, there are two types of locks:

- A *shared* lock, which allows other users to read, but not update the data

- An *exclusive* lock, which prevents other transactions from even reading the data

For example, the server will lock rows that are being changed by a transaction until the transaction is complete, and then the locks are released. This is all done automatically, usually without users of the database even being aware that locking is happening.

The actual mechanics and strategies required for locking are highly complex, with many different types of locks being used, depending on circumstances. The documentation for PostgreSQL describes eight different types of lock permutations. PostgreSQL also implements an unusual mechanism for isolating transactions using a multiversion model, which reduces conflicts between locks and significantly improves its performance compared with other schemes.

Fortunately, users of the database generally need to worry about locking only in two circumstances: avoiding deadlocks (and recovering from them) and explicit locking by an application.

## Avoiding Deadlocks

What happens when two different applications both try to change the same data at the same time? It's easy to see—just start up two psql sessions and attempt to change the same row in both of them. This process is depicted in Table 9-8.

**Table 9-8.** *Deadlock*

| Session 1 | Session 2 |
|---|---|
| UPDATE row 14 | |
| | UPDATE row 15 |
| UPDATE row 15 | |
| | UPDATE row 14 |

At this point, both sessions are blocked, since each is waiting for the other to release.

This behavior is a clue as to why PostgreSQL defaults to a Read Committed mode of transaction isolation. There is a trade-off between concurrency, performance, and minimizing the number of locks held on one side, and consistency and ideal behavior on the other. As you increase the isolation level, the multiuser performance of your database will degrade, as indicated in Figure 9-4.

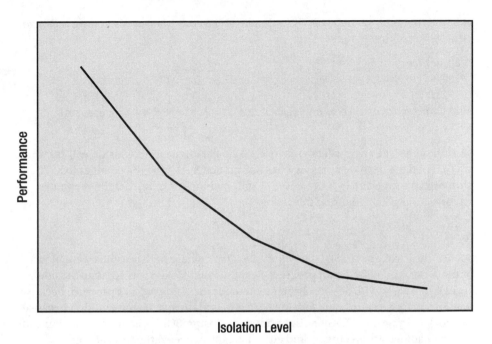

**Figure 9-4.** *Performance traded against isolation level*

As the behavior of the database becomes more ideal, the number of locks required increases, the concurrency between different users decreases, and so overall performance falls. It's an unfortunate but inevitable trade-off.

In general, if two user sessions try to access the same row, there is no real impact on the users, except the second user must wait for the first user's access to complete. A much more serious occurrence is when two sessions block each other.

### Try It Out: Experiment with Deadlocks

Let's experiment using the `bpfinal` database schema we designed at the end of Chapter 8. Start two `psql` sessions, connected to `bpfinal`, and try the following sequence of commands:

| Session 1 | Session 2 |
|---|---|
| `BEGIN` | |
| | `BEGIN` |
| `UPDATE customer SET fname = 'D' WHERE customer_id = 15;` | |
| | `UPDATE customer SET fname = 'B' WHERE customer_id = 14;` |
| `UPDATE customer SET fname = 'Bill' WHERE customer_id = 14;` | |
| | `UPDATE customer SET fname = 'Dave' WHERE customer_id = 15;` |

You will find that both sessions block, and then after a short pause, you'll see a message similar to this in one of the sessions:

```
ERROR:  deadlock detected
DETAIL:  Process 2018 waits for ShareLock on transaction 2788; blocked by
    process 2017.
Process 2017 waits for ShareLock on transaction 2789; blocked by process 2018.
bpfinal=>
```

The session seeing the error will have its update canceled; the other session will continue. The session that had the deadlock message has been rolled back, and the changes lost. The other session can continue and execute a COMMIT statement to make the database changes permanent (or a ROLLBACK to abandon the changes).

**How It Works**

What happened here was PostgreSQL detected a deadlock where both sessions were blocked waiting for the other, and neither can progress. Session 1 first locked row 15, then Session 2 came along and locked row 14. Session 1 then tried to lock 14, but couldn't proceed, because that row was locked by Session 2, and Session 2 tried to update row 15, but couldn't because that row was locked by Session 1. After a short interval, PostgreSQL's deadlock detection code detected that a deadlock was occurring and automatically canceled the transaction.

There is no way to be sure which session PostgreSQL will choose to terminate in advance. It will try to pick the one that it considers to have done the least work, but this is far from a perfect science.

Applications can, and should, take steps to prevent deadlocks from occurring. The simplest technique is the one we suggested earlier: keep your transactions as short as possible. The fewer the rows and the tables involved in a transaction, and shorter the time the locks must be held, the less chance there is for a conflict to occur.

The other technique is almost as simple: try to make application code always process tables and rows in the same order. In our example, if both sessions had tried to update the rows in the same order, there would not have been a problem. Session 1 would have been able to update both its rows and complete, while Session 2 briefly paused, before continuing after Session 1's transaction completed. It's also possible to write code that retries when a deadlock occurs, but it is always better to design your application to avoid the problem, rather than code a retry after a failure.

# Explicit Locking

Occasionally, you may find the automatic locking that PostgreSQL provides is not sufficient for your needs. In that case, you may need to explicitly lock some rows or perhaps an entire table. You should avoid explicit locking if at all possible. The SQL standard does not even define a way of locking a complete table. This option is a PostgreSQL extension (a very common extension you will see in many databases).

It is possible to lock rows or tables only inside a transaction. Once the transaction completes, either with a COMMIT or ROLLBACK, all locks acquired during the transaction will be automatically released. There is also no way of explicitly releasing locks during a transaction, for the very simple reason that releasing the lock on a row that is changed during a transaction might allow another application to change it, which would prevent a ROLLBACK undoing the initial change.

## Locking Rows

The most common need is to lock a number of rows prior to making changes to them. This can be a way of avoiding deadlocks as well. By locking in advance all the rows that you know you will need to change, you can ensure other applications will not create a conflict part of the way through your changes.

To lock a set of rows, we simply issue a SELECT statement, appending FOR UPDATE, as in this example:

```
SELECT 1 FROM item WHERE sell_price > 5.0 FOR UPDATE;
```

Provided that we are in a transaction, this will lock all the rows in item where the sell_price is greater than 5. In this case, we didn't need any rows returned, so we simply selected 1, as a convenient way of minimizing the data returned.

### Try It Out: Lock Rows

Suppose we wanted to lock all the rows in the customer table where the customer lived in Nicetown, because we need to change the telephone code (perhaps because the area code is being split into several new ones). We need to ensure we can access all the rows, but require some procedural code to then process each row in turn, calculating what the new telephone code should be. Again, we will try this with the bpfinal database we created in Chapter 8.

```
bpfinal=> BEGIN
BEGIN
bpfinal => SELECT customer_id FROM customer WHERE town = 'Nicetown' FOR
    UPDATE;
 customer_id
-------------
           3
           6
(2 rows)

bpfinal =>
```

At this point, the two rows with customer_id values 3 and 6 have been locked, and we can test this by trying to UPDATE them in a different psql session:

```
bpfinal 1=> BEGIN;
BEGIN
bpfinal => UPDATE customer SET phone = '023 3376' WHERE customer_id = 2;
UPDATE 1
 bpfinal => UPDATE customer SET phone = '023 3267' WHERE customer_id = 3;
```

At this point, the second session blocks, until we press Ctrl+C to interrupt it, or the first session commits or rolls back.

**How It Works**

The first session, using SELECT … FOR UPDATE, causes the rows with customer_ id values 3 and 6 to be locked. Other sessions are able to update different rows in the customer table, but not rows 3 and 6 until the transaction that locked them completes.

## Locking Tables

In PostgreSQL, it is possible to lock tables, though we strongly recommend you avoid this if at all possible, and stick to the SQL standard mechanisms for ensuring client isolation.

The syntax for locking tables is as follows:

```
LOCK [ TABLE ] table-name
LOCK [ TABLE ] table-name IN [ ROW | ACCESS ] { SHARE | EXCLUSIVE } MODE
LOCK [ TABLE ] table-name IN SHARE ROW EXCLUSIVE MODE
```

Generally, applications that require a table to be locked use the simplest syntax:

```
LOCK TABLE table-name
```

This is the same as the following:

```
LOCK TABLE table-name ACCESS EXCLUSIVE MODE
```

This prevents any application from accessing the table in any way. Although rather draconian, this is probably the behavior you want in the rare circumstances when a table-level lock is required. For more details about the different types of locks, see the PostgreSQL documentation.

# Summary

In this chapter, we looked at transactions and locking. We saw how transactions are useful even in single-user databases, because they allow us to group SQL commands together in a single atomic unit, which either happens or is abandoned. We next covered how transactions work in a multiuser environment.

We then moved on to look at what the ANSI SQL standard terms *undesirable phenomena*, and how different levels of transaction consistency are defined by eliminating different types of undesirable behavior. We also discussed how eliminating undesirable features may cause performance degradation, so it's necessary to strike a balance between ideal behavior and acceptable performance.

Finally, we looked at locking. We saw how simple techniques can reduce the risk of deadlocks, where two or more applications can become stuck waiting for each other to complete. We also discussed explicit locking, which allows us to lock specific rows in a table, or indeed a whole table, within a transaction.

Although transaction and locking are not always the most interesting of topics, a general understanding of how they work is very important to writing well-behaved applications. We want to build applications that not only perform correctly, but also interact in the database in a way that minimizes the performance implications, to get the most out of PostgreSQL's multiuser capabilities.

In the next chapter, we will explore other ways to get the most out of PostgreSQL, extending its behavior by using stored procedures and triggers.

■ ■ ■

# Functions, Stored Procedures, and Triggers

In this chapter, we are going to examine a few ways in which we can extend and enhance the features of PostgreSQL introduced thus far. Much of the material in this chapter is specific to PostgreSQL, although most commercial relational database management systems, such as Oracle, include similar features.

To begin, we will look at more of the operators that PostgreSQL supports within SELECT statements, including advanced matching and mathematical operators that allow us to construct sophisticated tests in WHERE clauses. Next, we will see how operators are implemented as functions in PostgreSQL and look at a few additional functions that add to the expressive power of our SELECT statements.

PostgreSQL allows a developer to extend the database server functionality by creating new features using the C programming language and loading them into the server when the database starts up. An extension can be as simple as a single extra function or as complex as a complete programming language in its own right. Several such extensions, known as *loadable procedural languages*, are included with the standard PostgreSQL distribution. These languages allow us to create our own functions, known as *stored procedures*, quickly and more easily than writing in C. We will take a brief look at one of the loadable languages, PL/pgSQL, in this chapter. PL/pgSQL is PostgreSQL-specific, but similar languages are available in other databases. For example, Oracle has PL/SQL, and Sybase has Transact-SQL.

Stored procedures can also be executed automatically by the PostgreSQL server when particular conditions arise within the database. For example, when a row deletion from a table is attempted, a stored procedure can be executed to enforce referential integrity by deleting related rows in other tables, or perhaps preventing the deletion from occurring. These autonomous actions are known as *triggers*, and we will see them in action here as well.

In this chapter, we will cover the following topics:

- PostgreSQL operators
- PostgreSQL built-in functions
- Procedural languages, specifically PL/pgSQL
- Stored procedures
- SQL functions
- Triggers

# Operators

We have already seen and used some simple operators in SELECT statements, beginning in Chapter 4. For example, we can use a numerical comparison operator to limit a selection to rows that obey a condition, such as items that have a cost price greater than $4:

```
bpfinal=# SELECT * FROM item WHERE cost_price > 4;
 item_id |   description  | cost_price | sell_price
---------+----------------+------------+------------
       1 | Wood Puzzle    |      15.23 |      21.95
       2 | Rubik Cube     |       7.45 |      11.49
       5 | Picture Frame  |       7.54 |       9.95
       6 | Fan Small      |       9.23 |      15.75
       7 | Fan Large      |      13.36 |      19.95
      11 | Speakers       |      19.73 |      25.32
(6 rows)

bpfinal=#
```

Here, the operator > is applied between the cost_price attribute and a given number.

We can go further and include other attributes and operators to create more complex conditions:

```
bpfinal=# SELECT * FROM item WHERE (sell_price*100)%100 = 99;
 item_id | description | cost_price | sell_price
---------+-------------+------------+------------
       4 | Tissues     |       2.11 |       3.99
(1 row)

bpfinal=#
```

Here, we have used the multiplication operator in conjunction with a remainder to list the items that have a selling price that ends in .99.

We can also use operators to perform regular expression matches:

```
bpfinal=# SELECT * FROM item WHERE description ~* '^[PR].*E$';
 item_id |   description  | cost_price | sell_price
---------+----------------+------------+------------
       2 | Rubik Cube     |       7.45 |      11.49
       5 | Picture Frame  |       7.54 |       9.95
(2 rows)

bpfinal=#
```

Here, the operator performs a case-insensitive regular expression match to discover which items have descriptions that start with a lowercase or uppercase *p* or *r* and end with *e*.

As you can see, there are many operators supported by PostgreSQL. In fact, if you count the different variations of the same operator (that is, consider comparing integers as being distinct from comparing floating-point numbers or comparing strings), there are around 600 operators available.

## Operator Precedence and Associativity

Many of the PostgreSQL operators look and act very much like the normal arithmetic operators that you will find in many programming languages. The operators have a precedence hard-coded into the parser that determines the order in which operators are executed in compound expressions. As usual, the precedence can be overridden using parentheses.

PostgreSQL allows the use of operators and functions outside WHERE clauses of SELECT statements:

```
bpfinal=# SELECT 1+2*3;
 ?column?
----------
        7
(1 row)
bpfinal=# SELECT (1+2)*3 AS answer;
 answer
--------
      9
(1 row)

bpfinal=#
```

Here, we can see that the result of the expression 1+2*3 is reported as 7, displayed as an unknown column and given the name ?column? by default. In the second example, the operator precedence is overridden and the result is named as answer.

Although most of the operators behave exactly as you might expect if you have programmed in C or any other programming language, some of the operator precedence rules may be surprising. As in C, the Boolean operators have a lower precedence than arithmetic operators, so parentheses are often required to get the desired operator execution order. If in doubt, make the order explicit with parentheses.

PostgreSQL operators also display associativity, either right or left, which determines the order in which operators of the same precedence are evaluated. Arithmetic operators such as addition and subtraction are left associative, so that 1+2-3 evaluates as if it had been written (1+2)-3. Others, such as the Boolean equality operator, are right associative, so that x = y = z is evaluated as x = (y = z).

Table 10-1 lists the lexical precedence (in descending order) of the most common PostgreSQL operators.

**Table 10-1.** *PostgreSQL Operator Precedence*

| Operator | Associativity | Meaning |
|---|---|---|
| `::` | | Typecast (synonym for CAST) |
| `[]` | Left | Array selection |
| `.` | Left | Object (schema, table, column) selection |
| `-` | Right | Unary minus (integer negation) |
| `^` | Left | Exponentiation |
| `* / %` | Left | Multiplicative operators |
| `+ -` | Left | Additive operators |
| `IS` | | Test (for `TRUE`, `FALSE`, `UNKNOWN`, and `NULL`) |
| `ISNULL` | | Test (for `NULL`) |
| `NOTNULL` | | Test (for non-`NULL`) |
| `OR` | Left | Logical disjunction |
| `IN` | | Test for membership of a set |
| `BETWEEN` | | Test for inclusion in a range |
| `LIKE ILIKE SIMILAR` | | Test for a string match |
| `<>` | | Test for inequality |
| `=` | Right | Test for equality |
| `NOT` | Right | Logical negation |
| `AND` | Left | Logical conjunction |
| All other operators | | User-defined and built-in operators not listed here all have the same precedence |

**Note** Older versions of PostgreSQL supported operators for calculating natural logarithms and anti-logarithms (`:` and `;`), but these are deprecated and have been removed from recent releases of PostgreSQL, including 8.0. Use the `ln` and `exp` functions instead.

## Arithmetic Operators

PostgreSQL provides a range of arithmetic operators. The most common arithmetic operators are listed in Table 10-2. All of these have the same precedence and are left associative.

**Table 10-2.** *Common PostgreSQL Arithmetic Operators*

| Operator | Example | Meaning |
|---|---|---|
| + | 2+3 is 5 | Addition |
| - | 3-2 is 1 | Subtraction |
| * | 2*3 is 6 | Multiplication |
| / | 3/2 is 1<br>3/2.0 is 1.5<br>3/2::float8 is 1.5 | Division |
| % | 22 % 7 is 1 | Remainder (modulo) |
| ^ | 4^3 is 64 | Raise to power (exponentiation) |
| & | 14 & 23 is 6 | Binary AND |
| \| | 14 \| 23 is 31 | Binary OR |
| # | 14 # 23 is 25 | Binary XOR |
| >> | 128 >> 4 is 8 | Shift right |
| << | 1 << 4 is 16 | Shift left |

There are also a number of unary arithmetic operators, shown in Table 10-3.

**Table 10-3.** *PostgreSQL Unary Operators*

| Operator | Example | Meaning |
|---|---|---|
| % | %2.3 is 2 | Truncate |
| ! | 4! is 24 | Factorial |
| !! | !!4 is 24 | Factorial as a left operator |
| @ | @(-2) is 2 | Absolute value |
| \|/ | \|/64 is 8 | Square Root |
| \|\|/ | \|\|/64 is 4 | Cube root |
| ~ | ~15 is −16 | Binary NOT |

In general, the arithmetic operators work as they should. PostgreSQL will use the version of the operator that matches the argument used. So, when you divide one whole number by another, you will get a whole number result. When you divide a floating-point number by another, you will get a floating-point result. As shown in Table 10-2, to force a floating-point result, one of the arguments should be cast as a floating-point number.

## Comparison and String Operators

PostgreSQL provides the usual array of comparison operators, such as less-than and greater-than. These operators work on many of the types that PostgreSQL supports, so for example, you can use the greater-than operator to test for alphabetical ordering of strings as well as relative sizes of numeric values.

The result of a comparison operator is either true or false, which psql will display as t or f. A listing of available comparison operators is presented in Table 10-4.

**Table 10-4.** *PostgreSQL Comparison Operators*

| Operator | Example | Meaning |
|----------|---------|---------|
| < | 2 < 3<br>'axy' < 'azz' | Less than |
| <= | 2 <= 3 | Less than or equal to |
| <><br>!= | 2 <> 3<br>2 != 3 | Not equal to |
| = | 3 = 1+2 | Equal to |
| > | 3 > 2 | Greater than |
| >= | 3 >= 2 | Greater than or equal to |

Strings have their own set of operators in PostgreSQL. There are operators for concatenating strings and for matching strings according to various rules. They are summarized in Table 10-5.

**Table 10-5.** *PostgreSQL String Operators*

| Operator | Example | Meaning |
|----------|---------|---------|
| \|\| | 'abc' \|\| 'def' is 'abcdef' | String concatenation |
| ~~ | 'xyzzy' ~~ '%zz%' | Synonym for LIKE |
| !~~ | 'xyzzy' !~~ '%aa%' | Synonym for NOT LIKE |
| ~ | 'xyzzy' ~ 'y.*y' | Regular expression substring match; use leading ^ and trailing $ to anchor the match to the beginning, end, or both |
| ~* | 'xyzzy' ~* '^X.*Y$' | Regular expression match, case-insensitive |
| !~ | 'xyzzy' !~ 'aa' | Does not match (inverse of ~) |
| !~* | 'xyzzy' !~* 'AA' | Does not match, case-insensitive (inverse of ~*) |

In a regular expression match, a string is compared to an expression similar to that used in the UNIX grep utility or the Perl match operators.

## Other Operators

PostgreSQL supports a whole host of additional operators for comparing and manipulating the PostgreSQL-specific data types such as points, circles, time intervals, and IP addresses. For more information, refer to Section II of the PostgreSQL documentation.

---

**Tip** The PostgreSQL documentation can be installed as a set of HTML pages that can be viewed locally with any web browser. Select `file://usr/local/pgsql/doc/html/index.html` or go online to `http://www.postgresql.org`.

---

All of the operators are listed in the pg_operator table of the database, and psql can list all of the operators and functions with the \do and \df internal commands.

# Built-in Functions

PostgreSQL boasts a very long list of built-in functions that we can use in SELECT expressions. A categorized summary of available functions follows:

- Functional equivalents to the operators presented in the preceding section

- Other mathematical functions

- Other functions for handling strings of characters

- Functions for handling dates and times

- Text-formatting functions

- Functions for the PostgreSQL geometric types such as point and circle

- IP address functions

The built-in functions (and user-defined ones) are recorded in a system table of the PostgreSQL database, pg_proc. As at PostgreSQL version 8.0 and later, this table has more than 1,700 entries.

In psql, you can list all functions and their arguments using the \df command. Also, comments about any specific functions or group of functions can be displayed using the \dd command.

Many built-in functions provide an equivalent function for each mathematical and logical operator. Examples include `int4shl` and `float8mul` as the equivalent of the shift left operator (`<<`) for integers and the multiplication operator (`*`) for floating-point values. Additional mathematical functions are listed in Table 10-6, all of which operate on floating-point numbers and return a floating-point number, unless otherwise stated.

**Table 10-6.** *Common PostgreSQL Mathematical Functions*

| Function | Meaning |
| --- | --- |
| `abs(x)` | Absolute value |
| `degrees(r)` | Converts angular measures from radians to degrees |
| `radians(d)` | Converts angular measures from degrees to radians |
| `exp(x)` | Natural antilogarithm, raise *e* to a power |
| `ln(x)` | Natural logarithm |
| `log(x)` | Natural logarithm to base 10 |
| `log(b,x)` | Logarithm to a given base, b |
| `mod(x,y)` | Remainder after dividing x by y (also has an integer version) |
| `pi()` | Returns $\pi$ |
| `pow(x,y)` | Raises x to the power of y |
| `random()` | Returns a random number between `0.0` and `1.0` |
| `round(x)` | Rounds to nearest whole number |
| `round(x,d)` | Rounds to specified number of decimal places, d |
| `trunc(x)` | Truncates to whole number (towards zero) |
| `trunc(x,d)` | Truncates to specified number of decimal places, d |
| `ceil(x)` | Returns smallest integer not less than given argument |
| `floor(x)` | Returns largest integer not greater than given argument |
| `sqrt(x)` | Square root |
| `cbrt(x)` | Cube root |
| `float8(i)` | Takes an integer argument and returns an equivalent `float8` |
| `float4(i)` | Takes an integer argument and returns an equivalent `float4` |
| `int4(x)` | Returns an integer, rounding if necessary |

Trigonometric functions are supported, as listed in Table 10-7. All angular arguments and results are in radians.

**Table 10-7.** *PostgreSQL Trigonometric Functions*

| Function | Meaning |
|----------|---------|
| sin | Sine |
| cos | Cosine |
| tan | Tangent |
| cot | Cotangent |
| asin | Inverse sine |
| acos | Inverse cosine |
| atan | Inverse tangent |
| atan2 | Two-argument arctangent, given a, b computes atan(a/b) |

PostgreSQL includes the standard SQL string functions, with their own syntax. These functions are presented in Table 10-8. For these functions, a string can be of type char, varchar, or text. PostgreSQL extends string-manipulation features with additional functions of its own. Refer to the PostgreSQL documentation for more information.

**Table 10-8.** *Common PostgreSQL String Functions*

| Function | Meaning |
|----------|---------|
| char_length(s)<br>character_length(s) | Length of a string |
| octet_length(s) | Amount of storage consumed by a string |
| lower(s) | Converts a string to lowercase |
| upper(s) | Converts a string to uppercase |
| position(s1 in s2) | Position at which s1 appears in s2 |
| substring(s from n for m) | Extracts a substring from s of length m starting at position n |
| trim([leading \| trailing \| both] [s1] from s2) | Removes characters s1 from string s2, either from the start, the end, or both; removes spaces by default if s1 not given |

An important formatting function worth mentioning here is the to_char function. It plays the same role in PostgreSQL that printf does in C, handling all manner of formatting values for printing or display. It will format a date and time value according to a date template, and can format numeric values in many different ways (including roman numerals).

> **■Note** For more information on all PostgreSQL functions, see the PostgreSQL documentation or browse the regression tests distributed with the PostgreSQL source code.

# Procedural Languages

As was mentioned in the chapter introduction, it is possible to define our own functions for use within a PostgreSQL database. This is useful when we want to capture a particular calculation or query and reuse it in a number of places.

The SQL needed to create a new function is CREATE FUNCTION, which has the following basic syntax:

```
CREATE FUNCTION name ( [ ftype [, ...] ] )
    RETURNS rtype
    AS definition
    LANGUAGE 'langname'
```

The parts of the function definition do not need to be in this order, and a popular choice is to state the language being used before the definition, like this:

```
CREATE FUNCTION name ( [ ftype [, ...] ] )
    RETURNS rtype
    LANGUAGE 'langname'
    AS definition
```

> **■Note** There is another form of CREATE FUNCTION that allows compiled object code to be incorporated into the PostgreSQL server, typically created from C source code.

A very simple function that increments its single argument might be written like this:

```
CREATE FUNCTION add_one(int4) RETURNS int4 AS '
    BEGIN
        RETURN $1 + 1;
    END;
' LANGUAGE 'plpgsql';
```

The definition of the function is given as a single string that may span several lines and may be written in any language supported by PostgreSQL as a loadable procedural language. In this case, PL/pgSQL is used, as indicated by the LANGUAGE clause specifying plpgsql. PL/pgSQL is a programming language developed specifically for programming stored procedures for PostgreSQL.

---

■**Note** The loadable procedural languages PL/Tcl, PL/Perl, and PL/Python allow you to create PostgreSQL extensions in the Tcl, Perl, and Python programming languages, respectively.

---

To handle a procedural language, PostgreSQL must first be extended by including a handler function typically written in C. For PL/pgSQL, a handler is included in the distribution as a shared library.

When a function is created, its definition is stored within the database. When the function is called for the first time, the definition is compiled by the handler into an executable form and then executed. This means that we may not be advised of an error in our function until we try to use it.

Before writing our own functions in our loadable language of choice, we first must arrange for PostgreSQL to support the language. This is what we will do next for PL/pgSQL.

## Getting Started with PL/pgSQL

We will use PL/pgSQL as the loadable procedural language for the sample stored procedures in this chapter. In a standard PostgreSQL installation, the handler function for PL/pgSQL is included in the shared library `plpgsql.so` in the directory `/usr/local/pgsql/lib` for UNIX and Linux, or `plpgsql.dll` in the `\lib` folder of an installation on Microsoft Windows.

Each PostgreSQL database on a server has its own list of procedural languages. When we install a procedural language, we can choose which of the databases will run stored procedures in that language. This is partly for security, as it is possible to create functions that will either accidentally or maliciously consume CPU resources by, for example, looping indefinitely. This could form the basis of a denial-of-service (DoS) attack by making the server so busy it cannot respond to new requests. Therefore, by default, PostgreSQL databases do not have procedural languages installed. To use PL/pgSQL, we need to install the handler ourselves.

---

■**Note** The database administrator can add languages to the `template1` database, in which case, all new databases will have those languages by default.

---

To install PL/pgSQL for our `bpfinal` database, we could use the CREATE LANGUAGE command within `psql` and load the shared library, creating the handler function explicitly. This is complex enough to warrant a helper script, and one is provided in the PostgreSQL installation. The command we need is `createlang`:

```
createlang [options] langname dbname
```

The options are listed in Table 10-9.

**Table 10-9.** *createlang Script Options*

| Option | Meaning |
|---|---|
| -h, --host=*hostname* | Specifies the database server host |
| -p, --port=*port* | Specifies the database server port |
| -U, --username=*username* | Specifies username to connect as |
| -W, --password | Prompts for password |
| -d, --dbname=*dbname* | Sets the database to install language in |
| -L, --pglib=*directory* | Finds language interpreter file in *directory* |
| -e, --echo | Shows commands being sent to the server |
| -l, --list | Shows a list of currently installed languages |

Normal users cannot add languages to databases, so we will usually connect as the postgres superuser:

```
$ createlang -U postgres plpgsql bpfinal
```

We can check that the language is present by listing languages with createlang, or by querying the system table pg_language with psql or pgAdmin:

```
$ createlang -l bpfinal
Procedural Languages
  Name   | Trusted?
---------+----------
 plpgsql | yes

$ psql -d bpfinal

bpfinal=# SELECT * FROM pg_language;
 lanname  | lanispl | lanpltrusted | lanplcallfoid | lanvalidator |     lanacl
----------+---------+--------------+---------------+--------------+---------------
 internal | f       | f            |             0 |         2246 |
 c        | f       | f            |             0 |         2247 |
 plpgsql  | t       | t            |         17601 |        17602 |
 sql      | f       | t            |             0 |         2248 | {=U/postgres}
(4 rows)

bpfinal=#
```

■**Note** createlang can be used to install other procedural languages. The command to install Pl/Tcl, for example, is createlang pltcl.

Superusers can remove support for languages from databases by executing DROP LANGUAGE from within psql:

```
bpfinal=# DROP LANGUAGE 'plpgsql';
DROP LANGUAGE

bpfinal=#
```

**Try It Out: Create a First Stored Procedure**

We are now ready to begin working with PL/pgSQL stored procedures by writing our own functions. Let's start by checking that everything works by implementing the add_one function shown earlier:

```
bpfinal=# CREATE FUNCTION add_one (int4) RETURNS int4 as '
bpfinal'# BEGIN return $1 + 1; end;' language 'plpgsql';
CREATE FUNCTION
bpfinal=# SELECT add_one(2) AS answer;
 answer
--------
      3
(1 row)

bpfinal=#
```

**How It Works**

The CREATE FUNCTION command stores the definition of the function add_one written in PL/pgSQL to the database. It is executed when the SELECT expression is evaluated. Note that PL/pgSQL keywords such as BEGIN and LANGUAGE are not case-sensitive and the layout of the command does not matter. We could have defined the function like this:

```
bpfinal=# CREATE function
bpfinal-# add_one(int4) RETURNS int4
bpfinal-# AS '
bpfinal'# BEGIN
bpfinal'#   RETURN $1 + 1;
bpfinal'# END;
bpfinal'# '
bpfinal-# LANGUAGE 'plpgsql';
CREATE FUNCTION

bpfinal=#
```

# Function Overloading

PostgreSQL considers functions to be distinct if they have different names, if they have a different number of parameters, or if their parameters have different types. We can create further add_one functions that deal with different types if we wish. Consider what happens when we use our add_one function on a floating-point value:

```
bpfinal=# SELECT add_one(3.1);
ERROR:  function add_one(numeric) does not exist
HINT:  No function matches the given name and argument types. You may need to add
explicit type casts.

bpfinal=#
```

PostgreSQL returns an error, because it could not locate a version of the add_one function that takes a floating-point value as its parameter.

---

**Note** Earlier versions of PostgreSQL would have executed this add_one function by automatically converting the floating-point value to an integer. The value 3.1 would have been rounded down to 3, and the function would have returned 4.

---

If we wish to have an increment function for floating-point numbers, we just need to create another definition of add_one:

```
bpfinal=# CREATE FUNCTION
bpfinal-# add_one(float8) RETURNS float8
bpfinal-# AS '
bpfinal'# BEGIN
bpfinal'#   RETURN $1 + 1;
bpfinal'# END;
bpfinal'# '
bpfinal-# LANGUAGE 'plpgsql';
CREATE FUNCTION
bpfinal=# SELECT add_one(3.1);
 add_one
---------
     4.1
(1 row)

bpfinal=#
```

This time, we get the result we want because PostgreSQL can find and execute an appropriate version of the add_one function. This behavior, known as *function overloading*, can be quite useful, but also fairly confusing. To keep the functions distinct, we must refer to them in a way that indicates their parameters. In this case, we have two functions that we can refer to as add_one(int4) and add_one(float8).

---

**Tip** A more convenient way to create functions is to edit script files containing function definitions and to use the psql \i command to read them.

---

## Listing Functions

If we need to see the source code for our functions once they have been loaded into the database, we can use the `psql \df+` internal command or query the table used for storing procedures, which is the `pg_proc` table:

```
bpfinal=# SELECT prosrc FROM pg_proc WHERE proname = 'add_one';
 prosrc
--------

begin
        return $1 + 1;
end;


begin
        return $1 + 1;
end;

(2 rows)

bpfinal=#
```

## Deleting Functions

Functions can be dropped from a database with `DROP FUNCTION`. We must be sure to specify the correct version of a function for overloaded functions, and to drop all versions of a function if we want to remove the function completely:

```
bpfinal=# DROP FUNCTION add_one(int4);
DROP FUNCTION
bpfinal=# DROP FUNCTION add_one(float8);
DROP FUNCTION

bpfinal=#
```

## Quoting

One slight complication that arises when using PL/pgSQL for stored procedures concerns quoting. The entire function definition is given to the `CREATE FUNCTION` command as a single quoted string. This means that if we have single quotes within our function definition, they must be escaped. We do this by using two quotes together to stand for a quote within a string. If our procedure uses a quoted string with quotes embedded and already escaped, we must escape those as well. It is possible to end up needing a row of four consecutive quotes (or more). Here is an example:

```
create function ... as ' ... return ''string with a single '''' in it ''; ...' ...
```

Thankfully, in PostgreSQL version 8.0 and later, the feature called *dollar quoting* is available. Similar to the way that Perl and the UNIX/Linux shells work, dollar quoting allows us to choose a string to use in place of an opening and closing quote. By choosing a suitable string that does not occur in our procedure, we do not need to use any escapes. A dollar quote is a string of zero or more characters between $ characters. So, the previous example looks like this:

```
create function ... as $$ ... return 'string with a single '' in it '; ... $$ ...
```

If we have the string $$ in our procedure, we can choose a different dollar quote:

```
create function ... as $WHAT$ ... return 'string with a $$ in it '; ... $WHAT$ ...
```

The examples in this chapter from now on will use dollar quoting. If you are using a version of PostgreSQL before 8.0, we suggest that you upgrade to the latest version. Otherwise, you will need to use traditional quoting.

# Anatomy of a Stored Procedure

Now that we have seen how to create, execute, and drop a sample stored procedure, it is time to move on to consider the construction of PL/pgSQL stored procedures in more detail.

PL/pgSQL is a block-structured language, like Pascal or C, with variables having declarations and block scope. Each block has an optional label; it may have some variable declarations, and encloses statements that make up the block between BEGIN and END keywords. The syntax for a block is as follows:

```
[<<label>>]
[DECLARE declarations]
BEGIN
    statements
END;
```

---

■**Note** PL/pgSQL is case-insensitive. All keywords and variable names may be written in either case.

---

A PL/pgSQL function is defined with a CREATE FUNCTION statement with a block as the definition part, enclosed in quotes (either single quotes or dollar quotes).

```
-- For all PostgreSQL versions
CREATE FUNCTION name ( [ ftype [, ...] ] )
    RETURNS rtype
    AS 'block definition'
    LANGUAGE 'plpgsql';
```

```
-- For PostgreSQL 8.0 and later
CREATE FUNCTION name ( [ [arg] ftype [, ...] ] )
    RETURNS rtype
    AS $$
        block definition
    $$ LANGUAGE plpgsql;
```

Within the definition, as shown in our examples, a double dash (--) introduces a comment that extends to the end of the line and will be ignored. We'll look at using comments shortly.

## Function Arguments

A PL/pgSQL function can take zero or more parameters, and the types of the parameters are given in parentheses after the function name. The types are built-in PostgreSQL types, such as int4 or float8. All stored procedures must return a value, and the return type is specified in the RETURNS clause of the function definition.

Within a function body, the parameters of the function are referred to as $1, $2, and so on, in the order they are defined. We will see later that it is possible to give the parameters names using an ALIAS declaration. In PostgreSQL 8.0, it became possible to give names to parameters where they are declared.

Consider this simple stored procedure that provides a floating-point geometric average of two integers:

```
-- geom_avg
-- get a geometric average of two integers
create function geom_avg(int4, int4) returns float8 as $$
begin
        return sqrt($1 * $2::float8);
end;
$$ language plpgsql;
```

Using parameter naming in PostgreSQL 8.0, we can declare the same function like this:

```
-- geom_avg
-- get a geometric average of two integers
create function geom_avg(a int4, b int4) returns float8 as $$
begin
        return sqrt(a * b::float8);
end;
$$ language plpgsql;
```

Notice that we have cast one of the integer values to a floating-point value so that we are certain to pass a floating-point result of the multiplication to the sqrt function. If we do not do this, we will run the risk of getting an error saying that the function sqrt(int4) does not exist, as was the case before version 8.0 of PostgreSQL. Where functions are overloaded, the use of a cast will ensure that we call the desired version of the function.

# Comments

As you can see from the examples so far, PL/pgSQL allows comments to be included in function definitions. In fact there are two types of comments: single-line comments and block comments.

A standard SQL single-line comment is introduced by two dashes (--). Everything following the two dashes up to the end of the line is ignored:

```
-- This is a single line comment
create    -- comments can
function -- come anywhere, and extend to the end of the line
```

Block comments are used to introduce larger blocks of text as comments or for temporarily removing sections of code not required. The syntax is the same as C and C++, with blocks of comments being surrounded by /* and */:

```
/*
        This is a block comment used to describe
        the use and behavior of the following function
*/
create function blah() returns integer as $$
begin
        /* comment out call to func
        func();
        */
        return 1;
end;
$$ language plpgsql;
```

Block comments cannot be nested, but you can use single-line comments to prevent the block comment delimiters from being interpreted as a block comment.

# Declarations

PL/pgSQL functions can declare local variables for use within the function. Each variable has a type that can be one of the PostgreSQL built-in types, a user-defined type, or a type that corresponds to a row in a table.

Variable declarations for a function are written in the DECLARE section of a function definition or a block within a function. As is usual with block-structured languages such as C and C++, variables declared for a block are visible only within that block or blocks within that block. Variables declared in an inner block with the same name as a variable outside that block hide the outer block's variable:

```
DECLARE
        n1 integer;
        n2 integer;
BEGIN
        -- can use n1 and n2 in here
        n2 := 1;
        DECLARE
                n2 integer; -- hides the earlier n2
                n3 integer;
```

```
        BEGIN
                -- can use n1, n2 and n3 in here
                n2 := 2;
        END;
        -- n3 no longer available here
        -- n2 still has value 1 here
END;
```

All variables used in a function must be declared before they can be used, except for loop control variables that we will meet later. A variable may not have the same name as a PL/pgSQL keyword, which are reserved. Table 10-10 lists the PostgreSQL PL/pgSQL keywords.

**Table 10-10.** *PostgreSQL PL/pgSQL Keywords*

| | | |
|---|---|---|
| alias | assign | begin |
| close | constant | cursor |
| debug | declare | default |
| diagnostics | dotdot | else |
| elsif | end | exception |
| execute | exit | fetch |
| for | from | get |
| if | in | info |
| into | is | log |
| loop | next | not |
| notice | null | open |
| or | perform | raise |
| rename | result_oid | return |
| return_next | reverse | row_count |
| select | then | to |
| type | when | warning |
| while | | |

There are several ways to declare a variable, depending on its intended use. These declaration variations are discussed next.

## ALIAS

The simplest declaration is an ALIAS declaration that gives a name to a positional parameter to a function. This helps us to write slightly more meaningful code, and code that is more robust against changes in parameter numbers and ordering. The ALIAS declaration has this syntax:

*name* ALIAS FOR $n;

A new variable called name is made available, which acts as another name for the specified positional parameter. For example, we might have written the geom_avg function as follows:

```
create function geom_avg(integer, integer) returns float8 as '
declare
    first alias for $1;
    second alias for $2;
begin
    return sqrt(first * second::float8);
end;
' language 'plpgsql';
```

As noted earlier, in PostgreSQL 8.0 we can create aliases for the positional parameters automatically by naming them in the functional declaration. The following definition is equivalent to the previous one:

```
create function geom_avg(first integer, second integer) returns float8 as $$
begin
        return sqrt(first * second::float8);
end;
$$ language plpgsql;
```

## RENAME

It is also possible to rename variables with a RENAME declaration. This can be useful inside trigger functions that we will see later, but is generally not recommended, as it can make code difficult to read. The syntax of a RENAME declaration is as follows:

RENAME *original* TO *new*;

### A Simple Variable Declaration

A simple variable is declared by giving it a name, a type, and optionally an initial value. Here is the syntax:

*name* [CONSTANT] *type* [NOT NULL] [{ DEFAULT | := } *value*];

The CONSTANT modifier declares that the variable may not be changed. It must, therefore, include an initial value in its declaration.

The NOT NULL clause instructs PostgreSQL to raise a runtime error if the variable is ever given a NULL value.

The initial value does not need to be a constant, and it is evaluated and assigned each time the function is called or when the block in which the variable is declared is entered. For example, giving an initial value of now for a timestamp variable would result in the variable taking the current time when it is executed, not when it was compiled.

The type may be a PostgreSQL built-in type; that is, you can declare variables with the same data type or structure of another database item. The advantage of specifying the variable's type in this indirect fashion is that the stored procedure code remains correct, even when changes are made in the database. The syntax is as follows:

*builtintype*
*variable*%TYPE
*table.column*%TYPE

Here are some examples of variable declarations:

```
n integer := 1;
mypi constant float8 := pi();
pizza_pi mypi%TYPE;
mydesc item.description%type := 'extra large size pizza';
```

In the example, the declaration of `mydesc` will result in a variable suitable for handling the `description` column in the `item` table of our sample database. If that column were defined as `char(64)` when we declared the variable, but later changed to a `char(80)`, the code using `mydesc` would still work, and PostgreSQL would create the correct type of variable.

---

■**Note** We have assumed dollar quoting for the examples here. Using single quoting instead, we would need to have double-quoted the string we initialize `mydesc` with, as this declaration will be appearing inside a single-quoted string as part of a function definition.

---

## A Composite Variable Declaration

A *composite variable* is one that corresponds to a complete row in a particular table. It has fields that correspond to each column in the table. We can declare and use composite variables in our stored procedures, either as `rowtype` or `record`.

To declare a composite variable, we use the `rowtype` declaration syntax as follows:

*name table*%rowtype;

The result of this declaration will be a variable that itself has fields, one for each column in the table on which it is based. Consider the following:

```
contact customer%rowtype;
```

This will create a variable called `contact` with fields corresponding to columns in the `customer` table. To use the fields, we use the syntax *variable.field*. Here is an example code fragment:

```
DECLARE
        contact customer%rowtype;
        address text;
BEGIN
        contact.zipcode := 'XY1 6ZZ';
        contact.fname := NULL;
        address := contact.addressline || contact.town;
...
END;
```

A second kind of composite type is the record type. This is a type that acts much like a rowtype, but is not based on a particular table when it is defined. The record will have fields that match whatever is assigned to the record at runtime. Records are useful in code that must work as triggers that are called from different tables, such as in a general-purpose procedure used to log row deletions. They can also be used to store the results of SELECT statements in a general way. A record declaration is very simple:

```
name record;
```

We will see more of records when we cover assignment via selections and in triggers.

## Assignments

PL/pgSQL variables are assigned new values in assignment statements. The syntax for an assignment is as follows:

```
reference := expression;
```

*reference* is a variable name or field in a composite type, such as a rowtype or record. The expression may be a constant; another variable; or a field reference of a complex expression constructed with operators, casts, and function calls. Here are some examples of assignments:

```
n1: = 23;
long_variable_names_are_OK := (n1 + 45)/2;
f2 := add_one(n1)::float8 * sqrt(2.0);

/* Composite types may be assigned one field at a time
   by referring to individual fields: */

contact.zipcode := 'AB12 3CD';
```

### SELECT INTO Statement

An alternative assignment mechanism is an extension to SELECT. We can assign a variable, a list of variables, an entire row type variable, or a record with a SELECT INTO statement. The syntax is an extension of the normal SQL SELECT:

```
SELECT expressions INTO target [FROM ...];
```

Some simple examples of using SELECT in place of an assignment operator follow:

```
SELECT sqrt(2.0) INTO sqrt2;
SELECT add_one(n1) INTO n1;
SELECT 1,2,3,4 INTO n1, n2, n3, n4;
SELECT 'Mole', 'Adrian' INTO contact.lname, contact.fname;
```

We can assign an entire rowtype at once, if we specify values for each column in the correct order:

```
DECLARE
        product item%rowtype;
BEGIN
        select NULL, 'Widget', '1.45', '1.99' into product;
END;
```

Where assigned values and variables are of different types, PostgreSQL will apply appropriate casts where it can. In the preceding example, the cost and sell prices are of type numeric(7,2), but they are successfully assigned from string values.

Assignments are executed by the PostgreSQL server as SELECT statements, even when the := operator form is used. We can use the power of SELECT to assign variables based on the content of the database by including a FROM clause and optional WHERE conditions:

```
SELECT * INTO product FROM item WHERE item_id = 9;
```

We must take care that the SELECT returns only one row, because additional rows will be silently discarded; only the first returned row is assigned to variables listed. We will see a little later that we can arrange for code to be executed for each row in a SELECT that returns multiple rows.

It is possible that a SELECT will return no rows; in that case, the assignment will not be performed. To detect this case, we can use the PostgreSQL special Boolean variable, called FOUND, set during an assignment using SELECT INTO:

```
SELECT * INTO product FROM item WHERE description ~~ '%Cube%';
IF NOT FOUND THEN
-- take some recovery action
END IF;
```

## PERFORM

In some cases, we may not wish to capture the result of a SELECT, possibly if it is used to call a function with side effects. In this case, we can evaluate the expression or query and discard the result with PERFORM:

```
PERFORM query;
```

The PERFORM statement essentially executes the SELECT query and ignores the result.

# Execution Control Structures

PL/pgSQL provides structures for controlling the flow of execution within a function. These are the return, conditional branch, and loop statements.

## Returning from Functions

Returning a value from a function is accomplished by using a RETURN statement:

RETURN *expression*;

Processing for the function stops after the expression has been evaluated. The value of the expression is made available to the caller of the function as the function result. The value must be compatible with the return type declared for the function, and it will be cast if necessary.

In PL/pgSQL, a function must return a value, and a runtime error will occur if the end of the outermost block of a function is reached without executing a RETURN.

## Exceptions and Messages

A function's execution can also be stopped if some condition arises that makes it impossible to continue. Rather than return a value, the function may raise an exception. An exception causes PostgreSQL to write an entry in the log, and it can cause a stored procedure to terminate immediately. The RAISE statement logs the exception, which can be one of several levels of seriousness.

RAISE *level* '*format*' [, *variable* ...];

PostgreSQL defines several levels for exceptions, as listed in Table 10-11.

**Table 10-11.** *PostgreSQL Exception Levels*

| Level | Behavior |
|---|---|
| DEBUG, LOG, INFO | Writes a message in the log (usually suppressed) |
| NOTICE, WARNING | Writes a message in the log and sends it to the application |
| EXCEPTION | Writes a message in the log and terminates the stored procedure |

The DEBUG level is useful for capturing additional information during development. The NOTICE level provides warnings for nonfatal errors. The warnings are made available to client applications, if required, by the NOTIFY mechanisms. The EXCEPTION level is used for fatal errors, where the stored procedure is unable to continue. For more information on configuring the behavior of exceptions, refer to the PostgreSQL documentation.

The *format* string is used to lay out an error message. Within this string, each % character is replaced in turn by the values of the variables. Unlike printf in C, you may not use expressions in a RAISE statement, only identifiers.

Consider the following:

RAISE DEBUG 'The value of n is %', n;

This results in a log entry in the PostgreSQL log file (on Linux this is often /usr/local/pgsql/data/postmaster.log) that reads something like this:

DEBUG: The value of n is 4

Here is a sample procedure:

```
create function scope() returns integer AS $$
DECLARE
    n integer := 4;
BEGIN
    RAISE DEBUG 'n is %', n;
    return n;
END;
$$ language plpgsql;
```

If we execute this stored procedure within psql, no message is displayed:

```
bpfinal=# SELECT scope();
 scope
-------
    4
(1 row)

bpfinal=#
```

When we increase the seriousness level in the RAISE statement to NOTICE, we do see a message from psql, as well as in the log file:

```
bpfinal=# SELECT scope();
NOTICE:  n is 4
 scope
-------
    4
(1 row)

bpfinal=#
```

Finally, at level EXCEPTION, the stored procedure terminates prematurely with an error:

```
bpfinal=# SELECT scope();
ERROR:  n is 4

bpfinal=#
```

## Conditionals

PL/pgSQL supports several types of *conditionals*, which are constructs that execute one of two or more sets of statements, or return one of two or more results, depending on a test. These are probably the most useful parts of PL/pgSQL.

### IF-THEN-ELSE

The most common conditional is the IF statement, similar to many other programming languages. It has the following syntax:

```
IF expression
THEN
    statements
[ELSE
    statements]
END IF;
```

If the *expression* evaluates to true, the statements in the THEN part of the IF are executed. Otherwise, if there is an (optional) ELSE part, the statements therein are executed.

As in other programming languages, IF statements can be nested by including another IF statement inside the THEN or ELSE parts.

**NULLIF and CASE**

There are also two SQL conditional functions that return values depending on a test. These are NULLIF and CASE, and they can be used in stored procedures and regular SQL in PostgreSQL.

The NULLIF function returns NULL if an input matches a specified value, and returns the input unchanged if not. It has the following syntax:

```
NULLIF(input, value)
```

This returns NULL if the test *input* = *value* is true; otherwise, it returns *input*.

The CASE function chooses one of a number of values, depending on an input value. The syntax is as follows:

```
CASE
    WHEN expression
    THEN expression
    ...
ELSE expression
END;
```

There may be as many WHEN/THEN pairs as needed. The expression as a whole returns the result of evaluating the expression in the THEN part corresponding to the first WHEN expression to yield true. If no WHEN parts match, the ELSE expression is evaluated. For example, the following will set res to 5, 6, or 7, depending on whether n2 is 1, 2, or some other value:

```
res := CASE
        WHEN n2 = 1
            THEN 5
        WHEN n2 = 2
            THEN 6
        ELSE 7
END;
```

## Loops

PL/pgSQL has a particularly rich set of *looping* mechanisms, also known as *iterative control structures*, which provide ways to execute statements a number of times.

The simplest loop is one that is uncontrolled, and unless terminated with an EXIT statement, will run indefinitely:

```
[<<label>>]
LOOP
    statements
END LOOP;
```

All of PL/pgSQL LOOP constructs may be labeled, as can BEGIN ... END blocks. This label is used as a target for an EXIT statement that causes the specified loop to be terminated (for readers familiar with C, this would be equivalent to a multilevel version break—something that C lacks):

```
EXIT [label] [WHEN expression];
```

This causes the LOOP labeled with *label* to be terminated, while execution continues at the next statement after the end of the loop. The label must refer to the current LOOP or a containing LOOP. If no label is given, the current loop is terminated. If a WHEN clause is given, the EXIT is not performed unless *expression* evaluates to true.

Here is an example of an indefinite loop:

```
<<indefinite>>
LOOP
        n := n + 1;
        EXIT indefinite WHEN n >= 10;
END LOOP;
```

## WHILE Loop

The WHILE loop is a structure that provides an alternative to the indefinite loop. It executes a set of statements for as long as a condition remains true. The syntax is as follows:

```
[<<label>>]
WHILE expression
LOOP
    statements
END LOOP;
```

## FOR Loop

We can arrange to execute a loop a fixed number of times with a FOR loop:

```
FOR name IN [REVERSE] from .. to
LOOP
    statements
END LOOP;
```

This type of loop executes its body once for each value in the range given by the integer expressions *from* and *to*. A new variable is created for the loop and is called *name*. It takes each of the values in the range in turn, incrementing by one each time the loop body is executed.

If REVERSE is specified, the loop runs in the opposite direction, with the variable name being decremented.

Here is a simple example of a FOR loop in action:

```
FOR cid IN 1 .. 15
LOOP
        SELECT * INTO row FROM customer
        WHERE customer_id = cid;
        -- process a customer
END LOOP;
```

This loop executes 15 times, with the variable cid taking the values 1 through 15, selecting the customers one at a time into a row variable. The lower and upper bounds on the loop variable may be expressions, so we might try to scan the entire customer table, rather than just the first 15, as follows:

```
SELECT COUNT(*) INTO ncustomers FROM customer;
FOR cid IN 1 .. ncustomers
...
```

A neater solution is an alternative form of the FOR loop that allows us to execute a loop once for each row returned by an arbitrary SELECT:

```
FOR row IN SELECT ...
LOOP
    statements
END LOOP;
```

For each of the rows returned by the SELECT, the row variable is assigned and the statements executed. The variable used to store the row must have been previously declared, either as a record or a rowtype. The last row processed will still be available when the loop ends or is terminated with an EXIT.

As an example, the following code fragment prints the family names of all our customers when run in psql:

```
DECLARE
    row record;
BEGIN
    FOR row IN SELECT * FROM customer
    LOOP
        RAISE NOTICE 'Family Name is %', row.lname;
    END LOOP;
...
END
```

Now that we have met all of the programming structures in PL/pgSQL, it is time to consider putting some of them to use.

**Try It Out: Create a Stored Procedure**

Suppose that we would like to think about using the sample database to help with ordering more products from our suppliers as we run low on stock. We already have a stock table that keeps track of the number of available items we have to sell. We would like to be able to use this information to automatically raise orders on our suppliers.

The following is a stored procedure that takes the first step toward the goal of automated reordering. The reorders function looks in the stock table for items that have a stock holding of less than a given value. For each of these items, it writes a record in a new table, reorders.

```
-- Drop if necessary and create a temporary table for raising orders
drop table reorders;
create table reorders
(
  item_id integer,
  message text
);

-- reorders
-- scan the stock table to raise reorders of item low on stock
create function reorders(min_stock int4) returns integer as $$
declare

    reorder_item integer;
    reorder_count integer;
    stock_row stock%rowtype;
    msg text;
begin
    select count(*) into reorder_count from stock
            where quantity <= min_stock;
    for stock_row in select * from stock
                    where quantity <= min_stock
    loop
        declare
            item_row item%rowtype;
        begin
            select * into item_row from item
                where item_id = stock_row.item_id;
            msg = 'order more ' ||
                    item_row.description || 's at ' ||
                    to_char(item_row.cost_price,'99.99');
            insert into reorders
                values (stock_row.item_id, msg);
        end;
    end loop;
    return reorder_count;
end;
$$ language plpgsql;
```

Save the above code in sproc.sql (or download it from the Apress web site at http://www.apress.com).

When we create the function and execute it specifying a minimum stock level of 3, we get a return result of 3, indicating that there are three items with a current stock level less than or equal to 3:

```
bpfinal=# \i sproc.sql
DROP TABLE
CREATE TABLE
CREATE FUNCTION
bpfinal=# SELECT reorders(3);
 reorders
----------
        3
(1 row)
bpfinal=#
```

The reorders table has been populated with the item identifiers of the three items we are running low on:

```
bpfinal=# SELECT * FROM reorders;
 item_id |              message
---------+-------------------------------------
       2 | order more Rubik Cubes at    7.45
       5 | order more Picture Frames at   7.54
      10 | order more Carrier Bags at     .01
(3 rows)

bpfinal=#
```

We can verify the result by querying the stock table:

```
bpfinal=# SELECT * FROM stock;
 item_id | quantity
---------+----------
       1 |       12
       2 |        2
       4 |        8
       5 |        3
       7 |        8
       8 |       18
      10 |        1
(7 rows)

bpfinal=#
```

### How It Works

The reorders function uses a SELECT statement to retrieve all of the rows in the stock table that have a low quantity level. A LOOP is used to iterate over the results of the SELECT. The body of the loop, which uses an INSERT to add to the reorders table, is executed for each row in the result set. The return result from reorders is provided by another SELECT that counts the matching rows in the stock table.

We could have used CREATE TEMPORARY TABLE to create the reorders table. In that case, the table would automatically be dropped when we quit our database session. We used a CREATE TABLE here so that the reorders table persists, which we might need if our reordering application is separate from the stock check.

To complete the automated ordering system, we would need to extract the items and place orders on the suppliers. We would also probably need to set minimum stock levels for each product and add that to the item table. Similarly, the number of products to order may need to be varied, perhaps on the basis of previous sales history or seasonal factors.

## Dynamic Queries

Normally, database queries in a stored procedure are either fixed or simply parameterized. We usually query a table for rows that have a specific column that matches a given value or insert or update a row with new column values. This can be achieved with SELECT, INSERT, and UPDATE statements using PL/pgSQL variables for the values to match or to use for column values:

```
INSERT INTO reorders VALUES (stock_row.item_id, msg);
```

There are some rare instances where we might like to be able to use the value of a variable to specify a table or column name for an operation. PostgreSQL does not allow this, as it needs to be able to optimize the query only once, rather than every time the query is executed.

However, PL/pgSQL supports a generic EXECUTE statement that allows us to execute an arbitrary SQL statement, specified as a string:

```
EXECUTE query-string
```

The string for the query can be dynamically created within a stored procedure, using the string-manipulation operators that we met earlier.

Special care needs to be taken to ensure that quoting of names and literal values is correct within the string. To help with this, two functions are available. All table and column names should be processed with quote_ident, which generates a string suitable for forming part of a query. Values should be processed with quote_value.

Here is an example that creates a general-purpose update using variables for names and values:

```
EXECUTE 'UPDATE '
|| quote_ident(tablename)
|| ' SET '
    || quote_ident(columnname)
    || ' = '
    || quote_literal(columnvalue)
    || ' WHERE '
...;
```

Note that this can be an inefficient way of accessing the database, as any queries that you make must be interpreted and planned each time they need to be run.

Dynamic queries may also be used in FOR loops in place of the SELECT statement for iterating across records. The syntax for this variant is as follows:

```
FOR row IN EXECUTE query-string
LOOP
    statements
END LOOP;
```

# SQL Functions

Although in this chapter we have concentrated on PL/pgSQL as a method of creating stored procedures, it is also possible to use SQL to create functions. To do this, you specify the procedure language as 'sql' and use PostgreSQL SQL statements instead of PL/pgSQL.

As with PL/pgSQL, SQL functions take parameters, which can be referred to as $1, $2, and so on. In the function definition, $1 is automatically replaced by the first argument of the function call, $2 by the second argument, and so on. There are no control structures; you are restricted to PostgreSQL SQL statements. While PL/pgSQL includes features such as variables, conditional evaluation, and looping, SQL functions allow only argument substitution. The value returned by a SQL function is the data returned by the last SQL statement executed, usually a SELECT.

The advantage of using SQL for stored procedures is that you do not need to load the PL/pgSQL language handler into the database.

Although we have no looping, the following SQL function allows us to return more than one row of data from our function.

```
CREATE FUNCTION sqlf(text) RETURNS setof
```

If we declare the function return type as setof type, and then use an appropriate SELECT, we can arrange to return multiple rows. Here's a function that returns all customers in a given town:

```
CREATE FUNCTION sqlf(text) RETURNS setof customer AS $$
        SELECT * FROM customer WHERE town = $1;
$$ language sql;
```

When we run the function in psql, three rows are returned:

```
bpfinal=# SELECT sqlf('Bingham');
                                sqlf
-----------------------------------------------------------------------
 (7,"Mr  ",Richard,Stones,"34 Holly Way",Bingham,"BG4 2WE   ","342 5982")
 (8,"Mrs ",Ann,Stones,"34 Holly Way",Bingham,"BG4 2WE   ","342 5982")
 (11,"Mr  ",Dave,Jones,"54 Vale Rise",Bingham,"BG3 8GD   ","342 8264")
(3 rows)

bpfinal=#
```

Versions of PostgreSQL earlier than 8.0 could not handle entire rows at once in psql, and would either give an error or return an OID referring to each row. All versions allow us to select a column at a time. To do this, we use the syntax *column(function())* to extract the required column. Here, we list the last names of customers in Bingham and give the results column a name:

```
bpfinal=# SELECT lname(sqlf('Bingham')) AS customer;
 customer
----------
 Stones
 Stones
 Jones
(3 rows)

bpfinal=#
```

# Triggers

In our stored procedure example, we developed a function that would allow us to discover which products required restocking. The function wrote reminder messages into a `reorders` table. For this to be useful, we would need to ensure that this procedure is executed on a regular basis, perhaps once a day during an overnight batch process. It might be an advantage to find a way of automatically making sure the `reorders` table is always up-to-date, without needing to program our client applications to keep updating the entries.

In Chapter 8, we mentioned the concept of *referential integrity*—ensuring that the data in our database makes sense at all times. For example, if we delete a customer, we need to ensure that all of the order history relating to that customer is deleted at the same time. We have seen constraints used to ensure that PostgreSQL enforces this kind of integrity.

For some applications, constraints are not quite enough. Suppose we want to prevent the deletion of a customer when there are still outstanding orders for that customer, but allow the deletion if all orders have been shipped.

We saw in Chapter 8 how column-level and table-level constraints could be used to enforce more complex rules of data integrity, but these rules were essentially static. We could specify that a related row must exist, or enforce a rule that you cannot delete while related rows exist. However, we had no way of specifying complex conditions, such as that a row must not exist unless some other condition is also true. Nor could we carry out more complex user-defined actions when rows were added or deleted.

One solution to these problems is the use of *triggers*. With a trigger, we can arrange for PostgreSQL to execute a stored procedure when certain actions are taken, like an `INSERT`, `DELETE`, or `UPDATE` in a table.

The combination of stored procedures and triggers gives us the power to enforce quite sophisticated business rules directly in the database. As we said in Chapter 8, the best place for enforcing business rules about the data is in the database.

To use a trigger, we need to first define a trigger procedure. Then we create the trigger itself, which defines when the trigger procedure will be executed.

## Defining a Trigger Procedure

A trigger fires when a condition is met, and it executes a special type of stored procedure called a *trigger procedure*. A trigger procedure is very similar to a stored procedure, but it is slightly more restricted due to the manner in which it is called.

A trigger procedure is created as a function with no parameters and a special return type of trigger.

---

■**Note** Versions of PostgreSQL before 7.3 used a return type of opaque in place of trigger. The opaque return type is used for functions that return values which cannot be manipulated by PostgreSQL directly.

---

PostgreSQL will call a trigger procedure when changes are being made to a particular table. The procedure must either return NULL or a row that matches the structure of the table for which the trigger procedure has been called.

For AFTER triggers that are called following an UPDATE, it is generally recommended that a trigger procedure return NULL. For BEFORE triggers, the return result is used to direct the update about to be performed. If the trigger procedure returns NULL, the UPDATE is not performed. If a data row is returned, it is used as the source for the UPDATE, giving the trigger procedure the opportunity to change the data before it is committed to the database.

## Creating Triggers

Triggers are created with the CREATE TRIGGER command, which has the following syntax:

```
CREATE TRIGGER name { BEFORE | AFTER }
    { event [OR ...] }
    ON table FOR EACH { ROW | STATEMENT }
    EXECUTE PROCEDURE func ( arguments )
```

Here, *event* is one of INSERT, DELETE, or UPDATE.

The trigger effectively says, "Run this stored procedure every time this event occurs on this table."

The trigger is given a name that is used to delete the trigger when it is no longer required, by executing this statement:

```
DROP TRIGGER name ON table;
```

The trigger fires when the specified event occurs—a DELETE, INSERT, or UPDATE. We can request that the trigger fires after the event occurs; in which case, the called procedure will have access to both the original data (for updates and deletes) and the new data (for inserts and updates). We can also request that the trigger fire before the event occurs. In this case, we can prevent the update from occurring, or change the data to be inserted or updated. We can specify more than one event by listing them separated by OR.

As we know, some SQL statements can affect multiple rows of data. Where a multiple-row update causes a trigger to fire, we can choose whether the trigger fires for each row that is updated or just once for the whole update. We specify ROW if we wish the trigger to fire multiple times; otherwise, we specify STATEMENT.

The arguments passed to the function can be used to distinguish similar triggers, so that one function can be used for more than one trigger.

To automate the updates on our reorders table, we might create a stored procedure called reorder_trigger and create a trigger to call it whenever the stock table changes:

```
CREATE TRIGGER trig_reorder
AFTER INSERT OR UPDATE ON stock
FOR EACH ROW EXECUTE PROCEDURE reorder_trigger(3);
```

Note that the trigger procedure (reorder_trigger in this case) must have been defined before we create the trigger itself.

We use the trigger procedure argument to pass a minimum stock quantity, which is 3 in this case.

### Try It Out: Create a Trigger

Here is a simple trigger procedure that updates the reorders table after the stock table has been adjusted:

```
create function reorder_trigger() returns trigger AS $$
declare
    mq integer;
    item_record record;
begin
    mq := tg_argv[0];
    raise notice 'in trigger, mq is %', mq;
    if new.quantity <= mq
    then
        select * into item_record from item
        where item_id = new.item_id;
        insert into reorders
          values (new.item_id, item_record.description);
    end if;
    return NULL;
end;
$$ language plpgsql;
```

Now that we have a trigger procedure, we can define a trigger as follows:

```
CREATE TRIGGER trig_reorder
AFTER INSERT OR UPDATE ON stock
FOR EACH ROW EXECUTE PROCEDURE reorder_trigger(3);
```

Load the function and trigger definition from a script file:

```
bpfinal=# \i sproc.sql
...
CREATE FUNCTION
CREATE FUNCTION1;
CREATE TRIGGER

bpfinal=#
```

Then try adjusting the stock of an item so that it drops to 3 or below:

```
bpfinal=# UPDATE stock SET quantity = 3 WHERE item_id = 1;
NOTICE:  in trigger, mq is 3
UPDATE 1

bpfinal=#
```

We can see that the trigger has fired and raised a notice to tell us. The update to the stock proceeds, but the trigger also updates the reorders table, adding a new row:

```
bpfinal=# SELECT * FROM reorders;
 item_id |   message
---------+-------------
       1 | Wood Puzzle
(1 row)

bpfinal=#
```

### How It Works

The trigger procedure is called whenever an INSERT or UPDATE takes place on the stock table. It checks the stock quantity as it appears after the UPDATE has taken place, and if it is less than the minimum quantity, adds a record to the reorders table.

You may have noticed that we have used a couple of new features in the trigger procedure. First, the trigger procedure arguments are not referred to as $1, $2, and so on. The arguments are made available via one of a number of special variables for automatically triggering procedures. The arguments are passed in an array named TG_ARGV, starting at TG_ARGV[0]. The special variables made available to trigger procedures are listed in Table 10-12.

Second, inside the trigger procedures, two very special records are made available: OLD and NEW. These contain (for ROW triggers) the data from the row being affected by the UPDATE that fired the trigger. As you may guess, OLD contains data from before the UPDATE, and NEW contains data from after the update (or proposed UPDATE for a BEFORE trigger).

**Table 10-12.** *PostgreSQL Trigger Procedure Variables*

| Variable | Description |
| --- | --- |
| NEW | A record containing the new database row |
| OLD | A record containing the old database row |
| TG_NAME | A variable containing the name of the trigger that fired and caused the trigger procedure to run |
| TG_WHEN | A text variable containing the text 'BEFORE' or 'AFTER', depending on the type of the trigger |
| TG_LEVEL | A text variable containing 'ROW' or 'STATEMENT', depending on the trigger definition |
| TG_OP | A text variable containing 'INSERT', 'DELETE', or 'UPDATE', depending on the event that occurred resulting in this trigger being fired |
| TG_RELID | An object identifier representing the table the trigger has been activated upon |
| TG_RELNAME | The name of the table that the trigger has been fired upon |
| TG_NARGS | An integer variable containing the number of arguments specified in the trigger definition |
| TG_ARGV | An array of strings containing the procedure parameters, starting at zero; invalid indexes return NULL values |

### Try It Out: Create Another Trigger

As a final example, we can create another trigger function, which prevents a customer from being deleted if there are any orders outstanding for that customer. We check whether the date_shipped column in the orderinfo table is NULL for any orders placed by the customer about to be deleted, and disallow the deletion. If there are no outstanding orders, we can allow the deletion to go ahead, but we need to tidy up by deleting orders placed by this customer in the past, as well as the information about the items in those orders.

```
create function customer_trigger() returns trigger AS $$
declare order_record record;
beginx
    -- about to delete a customer
    -- disallow if orders pending
    select * into order_record from orderinfo
    where customer_id = old.customer_id
          and date_shipped is NULL;
    if not found
    then
        -- all OK, delete of customer can proceed
        raise notice 'deletion allowed: no outstanding orders';
```

```
-- for referential integrity we have to tidy up
-- we will need to delete all completed orders
-- but first delete the information about the orders
for order_record in select * from orderinfo
    where customer_id = old.customer_id
loop
    delete from orderline
        where orderinfo_id = order_record.orderinfo_id;
end loop;

-- now delete the order records
delete from orderinfo
        where customer_id = old.customer_id;

-- return the old record to allow customer to be deleted
return old;
else
    -- orders present return NULL to prevent deletion
    raise notice 'deletion aborted: outstanding orders present';
    return NULL;
end if;
end;
$$ language plpgsql;

create trigger trig_customer before delete on customer
for each row execute procedure customer_trigger();
```

To verify the behavior of this trigger, let's check it out. First, make one of the orders have a NULL shipped date to indicate that it is still pending:

```
bpfinal=# UPDATE orderinfo SET date_shipped = NULL WHERE orderinfo_id = 3;
UPDATE 1
bpfinal=# SELECT * FROM orderinfo;
 orderinfo_id | customer_id | date_placed | date_shipped | shipping
--------------+-------------+-------------+--------------+----------
            1 |           3 | 2004-03-13  | 2004-03-17   |     2.99
            2 |           8 | 2004-06-23  | 2004-06-24   |     0.00
            4 |          13 | 2004-09-03  | 2004-09-10   |     2.99
            5 |           8 | 2004-07-21  | 2004-07-24   |     0.00
            3 |          15 | 2004-09-02  |              |     3.99
(5 rows)

bpfinal=#
```

Now try to delete customer number 15 whose order number 3 is outstanding:

```
bpfinal=# DELETE FROM customer WHERE customer_id = 15;
NOTICE:  deletion aborted: outstanding orders present
DELETE 0

bpfinal=#
```

A notification is returned regarding outstanding orders. We see the delete affected no rows, as it was not allowed to proceed.

Deleting customers with no outstanding orders presents no problem, as long as we delete the entries in the orderinfo table first. This is because we are using a constraint on this table to prevent just this sort of maverick deletion. The trigger takes care of this and, therefore, provides us with another way to approach the referential integrity issue.

Customer number 3 has no outstanding orders, so we can delete that customer and let the trigger do all the work:

```
bpfinal=# DELETE FROM customer WHERE customer_id = 3;
NOTICE:  deletion allowed: no outstanding orders
DELETE 1

bpfinal=#
```

Checking the tables show no lingering sign of our deleted customer:

```
bpfinal=# SELECT * FROM orderinfo;
 orderinfo_id | customer_id | date_placed | date_shipped | shipping
--------------+-------------+-------------+--------------+----------
            2 |           8 | 2004-06-23  | 2004-06-24   |     0.00
            4 |          13 | 2004-09-03  | 2004-09-10   |     2.99
            5 |           8 | 2004-07-21  | 2004-07-24   |     0.00
            3 |          15 | 2004-09-02  |              |     3.99
(4 rows)

bpfinal=# SELECT * FROM orderline;
 orderinfo_id | item_id | quantity
--------------+---------+----------
            2 |       1 |        1
            2 |      10 |        1
            2 |       7 |        2
            2 |       4 |        2
            3 |       2 |        1
            3 |       1 |        1
            4 |       5 |        2
            5 |       1 |        1
            5 |       3 |        1
(9 rows)
```

```
bpfinal=#
bpfinal=# SELECT customer_id, fname, lname FROM customer;
 customer_id |   fname   |  lname
-------------+-----------+---------
           1 | Jenny     | Stones
           2 | Andrew    | Stones
           4 | Adrian    | Matthew
           5 | Simon     | Cozens
           6 | Neil      | Matthew
           7 | Richard   | Stones
           8 | Ann       | Stones
           9 | Christine | Hickman
          10 | Mike      | Howard
          11 | Dave      | Jones
          12 | Richard   | Neill
          13 | Laura     | Hardy
          14 | Bill      | O'Neill
          15 | David     | Hudson
(14 rows)
bpfinal=#
```

# Why Use Stored Procedures and Triggers?

There are numerous reasons for using stored procedures and triggers. Here are some of them:

- **Provide central validation:** We can enforce conditions on table updates in one place, independent of our client applications. If the conditions need to change, they change in one place only.

- **Track changes:** We can use a trigger to create an audit trail, writing to another table when rows in a table are updated. This could record the user who made the change, the time, the date, and perhaps even the data that changed.

- **Enhance security:** By using the PostgreSQL current_user variable, we can enforce our own security.

- **Defer deletions:** We could use a trigger to mark rows for deletion at a later date, rather than deleting them when an application tries to.

- **Provide a mapping for clients:** We can use triggers and stored procedures to create a simpler, single-table version of some of our data that can be updated more easily by our users. For example, we could create a table and link it to Microsoft Excel. As rows in this table are updated, we can update rows in the "real" tables, which might have a more complex structure.

# Summary

In this chapter, we looked at ways in which we can extend the functionality of PostgreSQL queries. We have seen that PostgreSQL provides many operators and functions that we can use to refine queries and extract information.

The procedural languages supported by PostgreSQL allow us to develop quite sophisticated server-side processing by writing procedures in PL/pgSQL, SQL, and other languages. This provides the opportunity for the database server to implement complex application functionality independently of the client.

Stored procedures are stored in the database itself and may be called by the application or, in the form of triggers, called automatically when changes are made to database tables. This gives us another means of enforcing referential integrity.

For simple referential integrity, it's generally best to stick to constraints, as they are more straightforward, efficient, and less error-prone. The power of triggers and stored procedures comes when your declarative constraints become very complex, or you wish to implement a constraint that is too complex for the declarative form.

Now that we have covered some advanced PostgreSQL techniques, in the next chapter, we will move on to the topic of how to care for a PostgreSQL database.

# CHAPTER 11

■ ■ ■

# PostgreSQL Administration

In this chapter, we will look at how to care for a PostgreSQL database. This covers items ranging from configuring access to the system through managing the placement of database files, maintaining performance, and, crucially, backing up your system.

As we progress through this chapter, we will cover the following topics:

- System-level configuration of a PostgreSQL installation

- Database initialization

- Server startup and shutdown

- User and group management

- Tablespace management

- Database and schema management

- Backup and recovery

- Ongoing maintenance of a PostgreSQL server

While learning and experimenting with these administrative tasks, you will want to use a test PostgreSQL system that doesn't contain any information you particularly care about. Making experimental system-wide changes or testing backup and restore procedures on a PostgreSQL database that contains live data is not a good idea.

## System Configuration

We saw in Chapter 3 how to install PostgreSQL, but we didn't really look in any depth at the resulting directory structure and files. Now we will explore the PostgreSQL file system and main system configuration options.

The PostgreSQL file system layout is essentially the same on Windows and Linux platforms. On a Linux system, the base directory of the installation will vary slightly, depending on which installation method you used: installing from prepackaged executables, such as binary RPMs, or compiling it yourself from source code. There may also be fewer or more directories, depending on which options you installed.

On a Windows system, by default, your installation base directory will be something like C:\Program Files\PostgreSQL\8.0.0, under which you will find several subdirectories. On Linux, the base directory for a source code installation will generally be /usr/local/pgsql. For a prebuilt binary installation, the location will vary. A common location is /var/lib/pgsql, but you may find that some of the binary files have been put in directories already in the search path, such as /usr/bin, to make accessing them more convenient.

Under the PostgreSQL base installation directory, you will normally find around seven subdirectories, depending on your options and operating system:

- bin

- data

- doc

- include

- lib

- man

- share

On Windows, the man subdirectory will be omitted, but probably at least one additional subdirectory, pgAdmin III, will be present. You will find additional directories, such and jdbc and odbc, if you installed some of the optional components.

In this section, we will take a brief tour of the seven subdirectories, and along the way look at the more important configuration files and the significant options in them that we might wish to change.

## The bin Directory

The bin directory contains a large number of executable files. Table 11-1 lists the principal files in this directory.

**Table 11-1.** *Principal Files in the bin Directory*

| Program | Description |
| --- | --- |
| postgres | Database back-end server |
| postmaster | Database listener process (the same executable as postgres) |
| psql | Command-line tool for PostgreSQL |
| initdb | Utility to initialize the database system |
| pg_ctl | PostgreSQL control—start, stop, and restart the server |
| createuser | Utility to create a database user |
| dropuser | Utility to delete a database user |
| createdb | Utility to create a database |
| dropdb | Utility to delete a database |

**Table 11-1.** *Principal Files in the bin Directory (Continued)*

| Program | Description |
|---------|-------------|
| pg_dump | Utility to back up a database |
| pg_dumpall | Utility to back up all databases in an installation |
| pg_restore | Utility to restore a database from backup data |
| vacuumdb | Utility to help optimize the database |
| ipcclean | Utility to delete shared memory segments after a crash (Linux only) |
| pg_config | Utility to report PostgreSQL configuration |
| createlang | Utility to add support for language extensions (see Chapter 10) |
| droplang | Utility to delete language support |
| ecpg | Embedded SQL compiler (optional, see Chapter 14) |

## The data Directory

The data directory contains subdirectories with data files for the base installation, and also the log files that PostgreSQL uses internally. Normally, you never need to know about the subdirectories of the data directory.

Also in this directory are several configuration files, which contain important configuration settings you may wish, or need, to change. Table 11-2 lists the user-accessible files in the data subdirectory.

**Table 11-2.** *User-Accessible Files in the data Subdirectory*

| Program | Description |
|---------|-------------|
| pg_hba.conf | Configures client authentication options |
| pg_ident.conf | Configures operating system to PostgreSQL authentication name mapping when using ident-based authentication |
| PG_VERSION | Contains the version number of the installation, for example 8.0 |
| postgresql.conf | Main configuration file for the PostgreSQL installation |
| postmaster.opts | Gives the default command-line options to the postmaster program |
| postmaster.pid | Contains the process ID of the postmaster process and an identification of the main data directory (this file is generally present only when the database is running) |

### The pg_hba.conf File

The hba (host based authentication) file tells the PostgreSQL server how to authenticate users, based on a combination of their location, type of authentication, and the database they wish to access.

A common requirement is to add configuration lines to allow access to some, or all, databases from remote machines. At the time of writing, the default configuration is quite secure, preventing access to any database from any remote machine. (See the "Client Authentication" section in the PostgreSQL documentation for full details.)

Each line in the pg_hba.conf file corresponds to a single allow or deny rule. Rules are processed in the order in which they appear in the file, so deny rules should generally precede allow rules. In PostgreSQL release 8.0, each line has the following five items:

- TYPE: This column is usually local or host for local machines or remote hosts over TCP/IP, respectively.

- DATABASE: This column provides a comma-separated list of the databases for which this rule applies, or the special name all, if the rule applies for all databases.

- USER: This column provides a comma-separated list of users for which the rule applies: all for all users or +groupname for users belonging to a specific group. (Groups are covered in the "Group Configuration" section later in this chapter.)

- CIDR-ADDRESS: CIDR stands for Classless Inter-Domain Routing. This column lists the addresses for which the rule applies, often with a bit mask. For example, the entry 192.168.0.0/8 means the rule applies for all hosts in the 192 subnetwork.

- METHOD: This column specifies how users matching the previous conditions are to be authenticated. There is a wide range of choices. Table 11-3 lists the common options.

**Table 11-3.** *Common Authentication Methods*

| Method | Description |
| --- | --- |
| trust | The user is allowed, with no need to enter any further passwords. Generally, you will not want to use this option except on experimental PostgreSQL systems, although it is a reasonable choice where security isn't an issue. |
| reject | The user is rejected. This can be useful for preventing access from a range of machines, because the rules in the file are processed in order. For example, you could reject all users from 192.168.0.4, but later in the file, accept connection from other machines in the 192.168.0.0/8 subnet. |
| md5 | The user must provide an MD5-encrypted password. This is a good choice for many situations. |
| crypt | This method is similar to the md5 method for pre-7.2 installations. All new installations should use md5 in preference. |
| password | The user must provide a plain-text password. This is not very secure, but useful when you are trying to identify login problems. |
| ident | The user is authenticated using the client name from the user's host operating system. This works with the pg_ident.conf file. |

A standard default configuration line would be something similar to this:

```
TYPE    DATABASE    USER    CIDR-ADDRESS        METHOD
local   all         all     127.0.0.1/32        md5
```

This allows all local users to access all databases, but the client system must provide the password in an MD5-encoded form. Normally, this is transparent to the user, as the client will determine that the password the client enters needs to be MD5-encoded before being sent to the PostgreSQL server. An alternative would be to replace md5 with trust, which would say that any user who had been able to log in to the local machine was also able to log in to the database, without requiring further authentication.

---

**■Note** If you use MD5 authentication, you must ensure that your PostgreSQL users have passwords, or the MD5-authenticated login will fail.

---

Generally, this minimal configuration is fine for local users, but it doesn't allow any access for users across the network. To do that, we need to add lines to the pg_hba.conf file. Suppose we wanted to allow all users on the subnetwork 192.168.0.* access to all databases, providing they had the appropriate MD5-encoded password. This is probably the most common type of addition needed to the standard configuration file. We would add the following extra line to the pg_hba.conf file:

```
host    all         all         192.168.0.0/16          md5
```

Now suppose some additional administrators require access from outside this subnet, but we don't want to permit ordinary users access. We would add a line to allow members of the PostgreSQL admins group access from anywhere on the 192 subnetwork, like this:

```
host    all         +admins     192.0.0.0/8             md5
```

Note that there is additional configuration required to allow remote connections, which must be set in the postmaster.opts file, as explained in the description of that file a bit later in this chapter.

### The pg_ident.conf File

This pg_ident.conf file is used in conjunction with the ident option of pg_hba.conf. This works by determining the username on the machine the client logged in to, and maps that name to a PostgreSQL username. It relies on the Identification Protocol, defined in RFC 1413. We would not generally consider this a very secure method of access control.

### The postgresql.conf File

postgresql.conf is the main configuration file that determines how PostgreSQL operates. The file consists of a large number of lines, each of the form:

```
option_name = value
```

This sets the required behavior for each option. Where the option is a string, the value should be enclosed in single quotes. Numbers do not need to be quoted. Boolean options should be set to either true or false.

Table 11-4 lists the main options in the postgresql.conf file.

**Table 11-4.** *Principal postgresql.conf Options*

| Option | Value and Meaning |
|---|---|
| listen_addresses | Sets the address on which PostgreSQL accepts connections. This will normally be localhost, but for machines with multiple IP addresses, you may wish to specify a specific IP address. |
| port | Sets the port on which PostgreSQL is listening. By default, this is 5432. |
| max_connections | Sets the number of concurrent connections allowed. On most operating systems, this will be 100. Increasing this number will increase the system resource overhead; in particular, the amount of shared memory in use will be increased. |
| superuser_reserved_connections | Sets the number of connections from the maximum which are reserved for superusers. By default, this is 2. You may wish to increase it to ensure superusers are never prevented from connecting to the database because too many ordinary users are connected. |
| authentication_timeout | Defines how long a client has to complete authentication before it is automatically disconnected. By default, this is 60 seconds. You may wish to decrease it if you see many unauthorized people attempting to connect to the database. |
| shared_buffers | Sets the number of buffers being used by PostgreSQL. A typical value would be 1000. Decreasing this value saves system resources on a lightly loaded system. Increasing it may improve performance on a heavily used production system. |
| work_mem | Tells PostgreSQL how much memory it can use before creating temporary files for processing intermediate results. The default is 1MB. If you have very large tables and plenty of memory, increasing this value may improve performance. |
| log_destination | Determines where PostgreSQL logs server messages by providing a comma-separated list of filenames. |
| log_min_messages | Sets the level of message that is logged. The options, from most logging down to least logging, are debug5, debug4, debug3, debug2, debug1, info, notice, warning, error, log, fatal, and panic. By default, notice will be used. |
| log_error_verbosity | Sets the amount of detail written to the logs. The default is default. Setting this option to terse reduces the amount written. Setting it to verbose writes more information. |

**Table 11-4.** *Principal postgresql.conf Options (Continued)*

| Option | Value and Meaning |
| --- | --- |
| log_connections | Logs connections to the database. This is false by default, but if you are running a secure database, you almost certainly need to change this to true. |
| log_disconnections | Logs disconnections from the database. |
| search_path | Controls the order in which schemas are searched. The default is $user,public. (See the "Schema Management" section later in this chapter.) |
| default_transaction_isolation | Sets the default transaction isolation level, which was discussed in Chapter 9. The default is read committed, which is generally a good choice. |
| deadlock_timeout | Sets the length of time before the system checks for deadlocks when waiting for a lock on a database table. By default, this is set to 1000 milliseconds. You may want to increase it on a heavily loaded production system. |
| statement_timeout | Sets a maximum time, in milliseconds, that any statement is allowed to execute. By default, this is set to 0, which disables this feature. |
| stats_start_collector | If set to true, PostgreSQL collects internal statistics, usable by the pg_stat_activity and other statistics views. |
| stats_command_string | If set to true, enables the collection of statistics on commands that are currently being executed. |
| datestyle | Sets the default date style, which was discussed in Chapter 4. The default is iso, mdy. |
| timezone | Sets the default time zone. By default, this is set to unknown, which means PostgreSQL should use the system time zone. |
| default_with_oids | Controls whether the CREATE TABLE command defaults to creating tables with OIDs. By default, this is set to true at the time of writing. This option may be required in the future should PostgreSQL default to not creating OIDs but you have an older application which relies on them being present. However, we strongly suggest that you do not assume OIDs are present. |

## The postmaster.opts File

This postmaster.opts file sets the default invocation options for the postmaster program, which is the main PostgreSQL program. Typically, it will contain the full path to the postmaster program, a -D option to set the full path to the principal data directory, and optionally, a -i flag to enable network connections. The postmaster.opts options are listed in Table 11-5.

**Table 11-5.** *postmaster Options*

| Option | Description |
| --- | --- |
| -B *nbufs* | Sets the number of shared memory buffers to *nbufs*. |
| -d *level* | Sets the level of debug information (level should be a number 1 through 5) written to the server log. |
| -D *dir* | Sets the database directory (/data) to *dir*. There is no default value. If no -D option is set, the value of the environment variable PGDATA is used. |
| -i | Allows remote TCP/IP connections to the database. |
| -l | Allows secure database connections using the Secure Sockets Layer (SSL) protocol. This requires the -i option (network access) and support for SSL to have been compiled in to the server. |
| -N cons | Sets the maximum number of simultaneous connections the server will accept. |
| -p port | Sets the TCP port number that the server should use to listen on. |
| --help | Gets a helpful list of options. |

Here is an example of a postmaster.opts file from Linux, allowing network connections:

```
/usr/local/pgsql/bin/postmaster '-i' '-D' '/usr/local/pgsql/data'
```

And here is a typical Windows file (which would all be on a single line), disallowing remote connections:

```
C:/Program Files/PostgreSQL/8.0.0/bin/postmaster.exe "-D"
    "C:/Program Files/PostgreSQL/8.0.0/data"
```

Notice the different quoting required on Windows systems.

## Other PostgreSQL Subdirectories

The following are the other subdirectories normally found under the PostgreSQL base installation directory:

- **The doc directory:** This contains the online documentation, and may contain additional documentation for user-contributed additions, depending on your installation choices.

- **The include and lib directories:** These contain the header and library files needed to create and run client applications for PostgreSQL. See Chapters 13 and 14 for details of libpq and ecpg, which use these directories.

- **The man directory:** On Linux (and UNIX) only, these contain the manual pages. Adding this to your MANPATH, (for example, $ export MANPATH=$MANPATH:/usr/local/pgsql/man) will allow you to view the PostgreSQL manual pages using the man command.

- **The share directory:** This contains a mix of configuration sample files, user-contributed material, and time zone files. There is also a list of standard SQL features supported by the current version of PostgreSQL.

# Database Initialization

When PostgreSQL is first installed, we must arrange for a database to be created. We did this back in Chapter 3 by using `initdb`.

---

**■Note** Almost all PostgreSQL installations, with the exception of those built from source, arrange for `initdb` to be called automatically if there is no database when the machine starts up.

---

It is important to initialize the PostgreSQL database correctly, as database security is enforced by user permissions on the data directories. We need to stick to the following steps to ensure that our database will be secure:

- Create a user to own the database. We recommend a user called `postgres`.

- Create a directory (`data`) to store the database files.

- Ensure that the `postgres` user owns that directory.

- Run `initdb`, as the `postgres` (never `root`) user to initialize the database.

Often, an installation script for a PostgreSQL package will perform these steps for you automatically. On Windows, this is always done automatically. However, if you need to change the defaults, or if you are manually installing the program, you need to perform these steps.

The `initdb` utility supports a few options. The most commonly used ones are listed in Table 11-6.

**Table 11-6.** *Common initdb Options*

| Option | Description |
| --- | --- |
| `-D dir, --pgdata=`*dir* | Specify the location of the data directory for this database. |
| `-W, --pwprompt` | Cause `initdb` to prompt for a database superuser password. A password will be required to enable password authentication. |

The default database installation created by `initdb` contains information about the database superuser account (we have been using `postgres`), a template database called `template1`, and other database items. This initial template database is very important, as it is used as a default template for all subsequent database creations.

To create additional databases, we must connect to the database system and request that a new database be created. We can use the command-line `createdb` utility, or, more commonly, we will do it from inside the database itself once we have logged in. We will meet both these options a little later in this chapter, in the "Database Management" section. A connection requires a username (probably with password) and a database name. In the initial installation, we have only one user, usually `postgres`, we can connect with and only one database.

Before we can connect to the database system, the server process must be running, as described in the next section.

# Server Control

The PostgreSQL database server runs as a listener process on UNIX and Linux systems, and as a system service on Windows systems. As we saw in Chapter 3, the server process is called `postmaster` and must be running for client applications to be able to connect to and use the database.

If you wish to, you can start the `postmaster` process manually on Linux. On Windows, you should always use the Control Panel's Services applet, as shown in Figure 11-1.

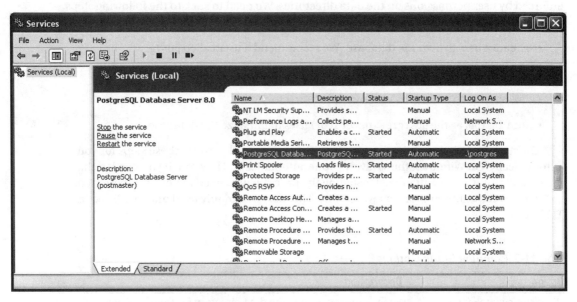

**Figure 11-1.** *Controlling the PostgreSQL service on Windows*

The rest of this section applies only to Linux (or UNIX) users.

## Running Processes on Linux and UNIX

Without any command-line arguments, the server will run in the foreground, log messages to the standard output, and use a database stored at the location given by the environment variable `$PGDATA`, if no `-D` option is specified.

Normally though, we will want to start the process in the background and log messages to a file. When a connection attempt is made to the database, the `postmaster` process starts another process called `postgres` to handle the database access for the connecting client.

It is the back-end server that reads the data and makes changes on behalf of one client application. There can be multiple `postgres` processes supporting many clients at once, but the total number of `postgres` processes is limited to a maximum, maintained by `postmaster`. The `postmaster` program has a number of parameters that allow us to control its behavior, as we saw when we examined the `postmaster.opts` file earlier in this chapter.

When it has successfully started, the postmaster process creates a file that contains its process ID and the data directory for the database. By default for source-code built systems, the file is /usr/local/pgsql/data/postmaster.pid.

The server log file should be redirected using a normal shell redirect for the standard output and standard error:

```
postmaster >postmaster.log 2>&1
```

As mentioned earlier, the postmaster process needs to be run as a non-root user created to be the owner of the database. We created such a user (postgres) in Chapter 3.

## Starting and Stopping the Server on Linux and UNIX

The standard PostgreSQL distribution contains a utility, pg_ctl, for controlling the postmaster process. We saw this briefly in Chapter 3, but we revisit it here for a more detailed exploration of its features.

The pg_ctl utility is able to start, stop, and restart the server; force PostgreSQL to reload the configuration options file; and report on the server's status. The principal options are as follows:

```
pg_ctl  start  [-w] [-s] [-D datadir] [-p path ][-o options]

pg_ctl stop [-w] [-D datadir] [-m [s[mart]] [f[ast]] [i[mmediate]]]

pg_ctl restart [-w] [-s] [-D datadir] [-m [s[mart]] [f[ast]] [i[mmediate]]]
[-o options]

pg_ctl reload [-D datadir]

pg_ctl status [ -D datadir ]
```

To use pg_ctl, you need to have permission to read the database directories, so you will need to be using the postgres user identity.

The options to pg_ctl are described in Table 11-7.

**Table 11-7.** *pg_ctl Options*

| Option | Description |
| --- | --- |
| -D datadir | Specifies the location of the database. This defaults to $PGDATA. |
| -l, --log filename | Appends server log messages to the specified file. |
| -w | Waits for the server to come up, instead of returning immediately. This waits for the server pid (process ID) file to be created. It times out after 60 seconds. |
| -W | Does not wait for the operation to complete; returns immediately. |
| -s | Sets silent mode. Prints only errors, not information messages. |
| -o "options" | Sets options to be passed to the postmaster process when it is started. |
| -m mode | Sets the shutdown mode (smart, fast, or immediate). |

When stopping or restarting the server, we have a number of choices for how we handle connected clients. Using pg_ctl stop (or restart) with smart (or s) is the default. This waits for all clients to disconnect before shutting down. fast (f) shuts down the database without waiting for clients to disconnect. In this case, client transactions that are in progress are rolled back and clients forcibly disconnected. immediate (i) shuts down immediately, without giving the database server a chance to save data, requiring a recovery the next time the server is started. This mode should be used only in an emergency when serious problems are occurring.

We can check that PostgreSQL is running using pg_ctl status. This will tell us the process ID of the listener postmaster and the command line used to start it:

```
# pg_ctl status
pg_ctl: postmaster is running (pid: 486)
Command line was:
/usr/local/pgsql/bin/postmaster '-i' '-D' '/usr/local/pgsql/data'

#
```

If you have built PostgreSQL from source code, you will normally want to create a script for inclusion in /etc/init.d. A basic version of such a script was shown in Chapter 3. Most package-based installations will provide a standard script for you. Do ensure that the PostgreSQL server gets the opportunity for a clean shutdown whenever the operating system shuts down.

# PostgreSQL Internal Configuration

We have now seen how to configure our PostgreSQL server, able to accept the remote connections as required. It's now time to look at the configuration elements of PostgreSQL that are set internally to the server. We will be looking at the following topics:

- Users and groups

- Tablespaces

- Databases and schemas

- Permissions

## Configuration Methods

Generally, there are (at least) three ways of configuring items internal to PostgreSQL:

- **SQL Commands:** We can use SQL, which has a large number of statements dedicated to maintaining configuration information internal to the database. Many of these are standard SQL statements (termed DDL, for Data Definition Language), usable on a wide range of databases, but it is an area where most databases have proprietary SQL elements. Learning how to use SQL to configure databases is important, as it helps you understand what is actually happening. Also, it is essential to know in case the graphical tools you might prefer are not available, or the bandwidth or connection available to the database is very poor.

- **Graphical tools:** We can use a graphical tool. At the time of writing, the premier graphical tool for PostgreSQL is pgAdmin III (http://www.pgadmin.org), which was introduced in Chapter 5. This tool, shown in Figure 11-2, is free for all uses; runs on Linux, FreeBSD, and Windows 2000/XP; and is very easy to use.

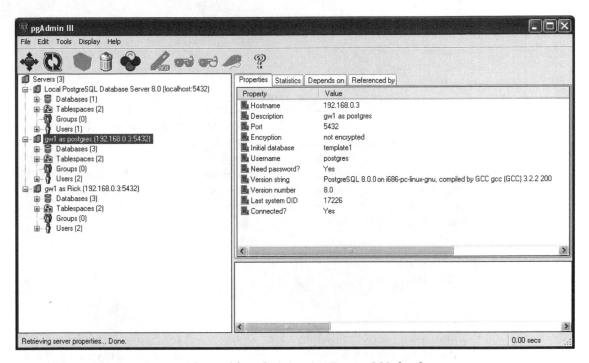

**Figure 11-2.** *pgAdmin III is a popular tool for administering PostgreSQL databases.*

- **Command-line versions:** Some configuration options, notably those for creating users and databases, have a command-line version available. Although these can be handy, particularly for getting started, they are not generally the preferred way of configuring PostgreSQL. If you wish to use them, you can simply invoke the command-line version with a parameter of --help to see usage information. It's then easy to see how the options map onto the underlying SQL syntax.

Generally, configuration must be done as an administrative user, which is postgres by default, as we saw in Chapter 3. For the rest of this chapter, we will assume you are connected to the database server as postgres, an administrative user.

## User Configuration

It's a good idea to give your users their own accounts, because then it is possible to more easily manage changes in personnel, such as employees moving to different roles where they no longer should have access to the database. Users are managed with the CREATE USER, ALTER USER, and DROP USER commands.

## Creating Users

The CREATE USER command has the following syntax:

```
CREATE USER username
    [ WITH
    | [ ENCRYPTED | UNENCRYPTED ] PASSWORD 'password'
    | CREATEDB | NOCREATEDB
    | CREATEUSER | NOCREATEUSER
    | IN GROUP groupname [, ...]
    | VALID UNTIL 'abstime' ]
```

Generally, you will always give each user a password. If you specify the option CREATEUSER, then the user will be an administrative user, able to create other users. Those administrative users' psql login will also have a # prompt, rather than the > prompt.

The CREATEDB option allows the user to create databases. If you have groups (see the next section), you can assign the user to one or more groups with the IN GROUP option. The VALID UNTIL option allows you to express a time at which the user account will expire.

For example, the following creates a user, neil, who can create other users and databases, but whose account will expire on December 31, 2006:

```
CREATE USER neil PASSWORD 'secret'
    CREATEDB CREATEUSER
    VALID UNTIL '2006-12-31';
```

## Using the createuser Utility

PostgreSQL also has a utility, createuser, which we saw briefly in Chapter 3, to help with the creation of PostgreSQL users if you wish to do this from the operating system command line. This utility has the following form:

```
createuser [options...] username
```

Options to createuser allow you to specify the database server for which you want to create a user and to set some of the user privileges, such as database creation. Table 11-8 lists the createuser options.

**Table 11-8.** *Command-Line createuser Options*

| Option | Description |
|---|---|
| -h host, --host host | Specifies the database server host. This defaults to the local machine. |
| -p port, --port port | Specifies the port. This defaults to the standard PostgreSQL listener port, 5432. |
| -U user, --username=user | Specifies the user as whom you wish to connect to the server. |
| -q, --quiet | Does not print a response. |

**Table 11-8.** *Command-Line createuser Options (Continued)*

| Option | Description |
|---|---|
| -d, --createdb | Allows this user to create databases. |
| -a, --adduser | Allows this user to create new users. |
| -P, --pwprompt | Prompts for a password to assign to the new user. A user password is required for authentication when the newly created user attempts to connect. |
| -i, --sysid=*ID number* | Specifies the user's ID number. Generally, you should not use this option but allow a default value to be used. |
| -e, --echo | Prints the command sent to the server to create the user. |
| --help | Prints a usage message. |

The createuser utility is simply a wrapper that is used to execute some PostgreSQL commands to create the user.

## Modifying Users

We modify users with the ALTER USER command. This command uses almost exactly the same options as the CREATE USER command, but can be used only with an existing username.

```
ALTER USER username
    [ WITH
    | [ ENCRYPTED | UNENCRYPTED ] PASSWORD 'password'
    | CREATEDB | NOCREATEDB
    | CREATEUSER | NOCREATEUSER
    | VALID UNTIL 'abstime' ]
```

There is also a special variant for renaming a user:

```
ALTER USER username RENAME TO new-username
```

So, if we wanted to prevent the user neil we created earlier from creating databases, we would use the following:

```
ALTER USER neil NOCREATEDB;
```

## Listing Users

We can have a quick look at the users configured on our database using the system view pg_user. Here, we just select a small number of columns, to keep the output easier to read:

```
bpsimple=# SELECT usesysid, usename, usecreatedb, usesuper, valuntil
FROM pg_user;
 usesysid | usename  | usecreatedb | usesuper |        valuntil
----------+----------+-------------+----------+------------------------
      100 | rick     | t           | f        |
        1 | postgres | t           | t        |
      101 | neil     | f           | f        | 2006-12-31 00:00:00+00
(3 rows)

bpsimple=#
```

You can see the same information by using the \du command in psql, or visually in pgAdmin III.

## Removing Users

We can remove users with the DROP USER command, which is very simple:

```
DROP USER username;
```

A command-line alternative named dropuser is also available. Its syntax is as follows:

```
dropuser [options...] username
```

The options to dropuser include the same server connection options as createuser (see Table 11-8), plus the -i option to ask the system to prompt for confirmation before deleting the user.

## Managing Users Through pgAdmin III

All these user management tasks can be done through pgAdmin III. To create a new user, right-click the Users part of the tree and select New User. This brings up the New User dialog box, as shown in Figure 11-3. To modify a user, click a username and select Properties.

If you click the SQL tab in the dialog box, you can even see the SQL that will be executed. This is helpful for checking how you do something in SQL, if you know how to do it graphically, but are not quite sure of the exact SQL syntax.

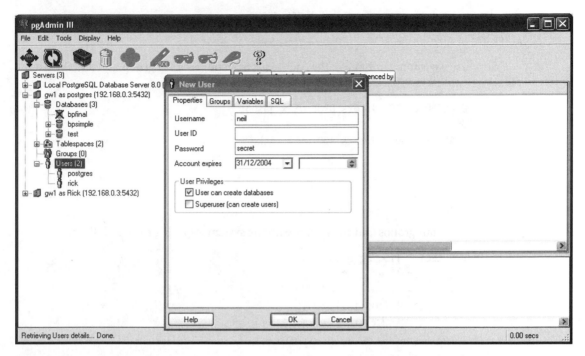

**Figure 11-3.** *Creating a user in pgAdmin III*

# Group Configuration

Groups are a configuration convenience—a useful way of grouping users together for administrative purposes. Later in the chapter, in the "Privilege Management" section, we will see how having groups makes it easier to give and remove privileges from a group of users in a single command. As with user configuration tasks, we can perform the group configuration tasks described here through pgAdmin III as well.

## Creating Groups

The syntax for the CREATE GROUP command is as follows:

```
CREATE GROUP groupname [ WITH USER comma-separated-list-of-users ]
```

For example, to add a new group, editors, and make the existing users jason and sofia members, we would use the following statement:

```
CREATE GROUP editors WITH USER jason, sofia
```

## Altering Groups

We can add and remove users from a group using ALTER GROUP, which has the following syntax:

```
ALTER GROUP groupname ADD USER username
ALTER GROUP groupname DROP USER username
```

As with CREATE GROUP, the name can be a comma-separated list of usernames.

We can also rename a group with ALTER GROUP:

```
ALTER GROUP groupname RENAME TO new-groupname
```

Suppose we wanted to remove the user jason from our editors group and add the user rick. We would use ALTER GROUP commands like this:

```
bpsimple=# ALTER GROUP editors DROP USER jason;
ALTER GROUP
bpsimple=# ALTER GROUP editors ADD USER rick;
ALTER GROUP
bpsimple=#
```

### Listing Groups

We can display our groups and their users with the system view pg_group, as follows:

```
bpsimple=# SELECT * from pg_group;
 groname | grosysid |  grolist
---------+----------+-----------
 usr     |      100 | {100,101}
(1 row)

bpsimple=#
```

The grolist column is a list of the usesysid columns we saw when we looked at the pg_user view, from which we can determine the usernames. The \dg command in psql gives similar information.

### Dropping Groups

We can remove groups with the DROP GROUP command, which is very simple:

```
DROP GROUP groupname
```

Note that dropping a group does not delete the users in that group.

## Tablespace Management

One of the key manageability features introduced in PostgreSQL release 8.0 was the concept of tablespaces. This makes it much easier for administrators to control how PostgreSQL's data tables are stored in the file system, which is useful for tasks such as managing large tables and improving performance by distributing the load across different disk drives. Prior to version 8.0, it was possible to control how PostgreSQL placed its files, but it was not easy.

A *tablespace* is actually quite a simple concept. It's a named PostgreSQL object, which corresponds to a physical location on the host operating system. Later, in the "Database Management" section, we will see how to create databases inside a tablespace, which means that the data files for that database go in the physical location associated with the tablespace. Tablespaces can be created only by administrative users possessing CREATE USER privileges.

Before creating a tablespace, we must first create a physical disk location to which to map the tablespace.

## Creating Tablespaces

Suppose we want to create a new location for storing PostgreSQL files on our Linux server in /opt/pgdata. We need to do this from the operating system command line, not from within psql. First, we must create the directory:

```
# mkdir /opt/pgdata
```

We must then change the ownership and group of the directory to be that of the operating system user we used when we installed PostgreSQL, usually postgres, using the chown command.

```
# ls -ld /opt/pgdata
drwxr-xr-x    2 root      root          4096 Nov 21 14:07 /opt/pgdata
# chown postgres.postgres /opt/pgdata
# ls -ld /opt/pgdata
drwxr-xr-x    2 postgres postgres       4096 Nov 21 14:07 /opt/pgdata
#
```

Now we are ready to create a PostgreSQL tablespace associated with our new directory. We must do this from within the psql program. Directories you wish to associate with a tablespace must always be empty before they can be associated. The command for creating tablespaces is very simple:

```
CREATE TABLESPACE tablespacename [ OWNER ownername ] LOCATION 'directory'
```

If no owner is specified, then it defaults to the person executing the command. So, here is the command to add a new tablespace to our installation:

```
bpsimple=# CREATE TABLESPACE datainopt LOCATION '/opt/pgdata';
```

We can see our tablespace by examining the pg_tablespace view, as follows:

```
bpsimple=# SELECT * FROM pg_tablespace;
  spcname   | spcowner | spclocation | spcacl
------------+----------+-------------+--------
 pg_default |        1 |             |
 pg_global  |        1 |             |
 datainopt  |        1 | /opt/pgdata |
(3 rows)

bpsimple=#
```

We can see the file system locations in the spclocation column. The spcowner column is the ID of the user who owns the tablespace, and spcacl is ownership information. The other two tablespaces, pg_default and pg_global, are the system default tablespaces, which are always present. We can see similar information using the \db command in psql.

## Altering Tablespaces

At the time of writing, it is not possible to move a tablespace's physical location. We can only change its owner and name, as follows:

```
ALTER TABLESPACE tablespacename OWNER TO newowner
ALTER TABLESPACE oldname RENAME TO newname
```

### Dropping Tablespaces

We can also drop a tablespace, but we must delete all the objects in the tablespace first, or the command will fail. Here is the command syntax:

```
DROP TABLESPACE tablespacename
```

That's all there is to creating, altering, and deleting tablespaces. This may all have seemed a bit pointless, especially since we've been working with only a small sample database. But next, we move on to creating databases, and it will become clearer how useful tablespaces can be for controlling the physical placement of database files, providing a big benefit in larger or more demanding PostgreSQL installations.

## Database Management

The key elements to any database installation are the actual databases—the objects in which all the tables and data are stored. Different database systems manage the internal databases in a variety of ways, but PostgreSQL is very straightforward. Each installation of the PostgreSQL server (sometimes referred to as a *database cluster*) can manage and serve many individual databases. Tablespaces, usernames, and groups are common across the whole PostgreSQL installation. This can be seen clearly in the way pgAdmin III lays out its tree structure, as shown in Figure 11-4.

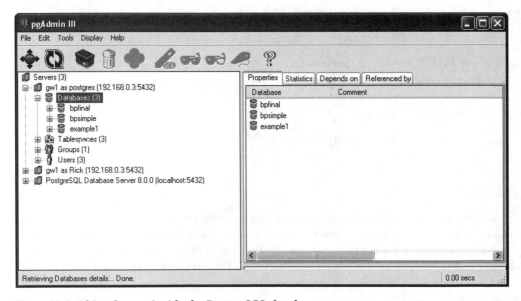

**Figure 11-4.** *Object layout inside the PostgreSQL database server*

## Creating Databases

PostgreSQL databases are created within `psql` with the `CREATE DATABASE` command, which has the following syntax:

```
CREATE DATABASE dbname
    [ [ WITH ] [ OWNER [=]owner ]
            [ TEMPLATE [=] template ]
            [ ENCODING [=] encoding ]
            [ TABLESPACE [=] tablespace ] ]
```

The database name must be unique within the PostgreSQL installation. The `OWNER` option allows the administrator to create a database owned by someone else, which is handy for users who cannot create their own databases.

The `TABLESPACE` option allows us to specify in which of the tablespaces we created earlier to place the underlying operating systems files for storing our data. This allows us to more easily control our disk usage. If no tablespace is specified, the files go in a tablespace named `pg_default`, which is automatically created when PostgreSQL is installed.

The `TEMPLATE` and `ENCODING` options specify the database layout and the multibyte encoding required. These are safely omitted in normal use. Refer to the PostgreSQL documentation for more details.

---

**Note** To use `psql`, we must be connected to a database, so to create our first database, we must connect to template1 (the default database) usually as the default user, `postgres`. We did this in Chapter 3 to create our first database.

---

## Altering and Listing Databases

We can change the name and owner of a database with the `ALTER DATABASE` command, as follows:

```
ALTER DATABASE dbname RENAME TO newname
ALTER DATABASE dbname OWNER TO newowner
```

---

**Note** There is also a variant of the `ALTER DATABASE` command for setting database options. For more information, see the PostgreSQL online documentation.

---

To list our databases, we can use the \l command in `psql`.

## Deleting Databases

To delete a database, we use the `DROP DATABASE` command, which has the following syntax:

```
DROP DATABASE dbname
```

We cannot drop a database that has any open connections, including our own connection from psql or pgAdmin III. We must switch to another database or template1 if we want to delete the database we are currently connected to.

## Creating and Deleting Databases from the Command Line

PostgreSQL provides two wrapper utilities, createdb and dropdb, to allow database creation and deletion, respectively, from the operating system command line. These utilities have the following forms:

```
createdb [ options... ]  dbname [ description ]
dropdb [ options... ]  dbname
```

The options for these utilities are very similar to the createuser and dropuser utilities described earlier. They are listed in Table 11-9.

**Table 11-9.** *Command-Line createdb and dropdb Options*

| Option | Description |
| --- | --- |
| -h, --host=*hostname* | Specifies the database server host or socket directory |
| -p, --port=*port* | Specifies the database server port |
| -U, --username=*username* | Specifies the username to connect as |
| -W, --password | Prompts for password |
| -D, --tablespace=*tablespace* | Sets the default tablespace for the new database |
| -E, --encoding=*encoding* | Sets the encoding for the new database |
| -O, --owner=*owner* | Specifies the database user to own the new database |
| -T, --template=*template* | Specifies the template database to copy for the new database |
| -e, --echo | Shows the commands being sent to the server |
| -q, --quiet | Specifies not to write any messages |
| --help | Shows this help, then exits |
| --version | Outputs version information, then exits |

If we create a new database in the tablespace datainopt we created earlier, we can see the layout of the underlying database files. We connect to the database server as the administrative user to the default database template1, and then we use psql to check the tablespace. Finally, we create the new database:

```
# psql -U postgres template1
Welcome to psql 8.0.0, the PostgreSQL interactive terminal.

Type:  \copyright for distribution terms
       \h for help with SQL commands
       \? for help with psql commands
       \g or terminate with semicolon to execute query
       \q to quit

template1=#
template1=# SELECT * FROM pg_tablespace;
  spcname   | spcowner | spclocation | spcacl
------------+----------+-------------+--------
 pg_default |        1 |             |
 pg_global  |        1 |             |
 datainopt  |        1 | /opt/pgdata |
(3 rows)

template1=# CREATE DATABASE example1 OWNER rick TABLESPACE datainopt;
CREATE DATABASE
template1=#
```

We can then look at the underlying operating system files from the command line:

```
# cd /opt/pgdata
# ls -l
total 8
drwx------   2 postgres postgres    4096 Nov 27 13:35 17864
-rw-------   1 postgres postgres       4 Nov 21 14:19 PG_VERSION
#
```

The rather strange number, 17864, is simply a name that PostgreSQL has chosen to use as a directory to store the files. The PG_VERSION file is used by PostgreSQL internally to track which version of software was used to create the database.

## Schema Management

Inside each database, there is one more level before the actual tables: a *schema*, which is a grouping of closely related database objects. Up to now, we have ignored the existence of schemas, because PostgreSQL's default behavior is to create a schema called public and place all the tables in that schema. By default, PostgreSQL assumes that it should look for any table your SQL accesses in the public schema. This means that users who have no need of schemas can pretty much ignore them.

Now that we have created a database, we can consider the use of schemas inside that database to control the grouping of tables. Schemas have two purposes:

- To help manage the access of many different users to a single database

- To allow extra tables to be associated with a standard database, but kept separate

Suppose we had an application using PostgreSQL, but we had built our own reporting on top of that application, and in the process needed to add some additional tables to the database. Without schemas, we would need to manage the names of the tables (and other database objects), so our additional tables never clashed with names that might appear in future versions of the application. Worse, if we had an upgrade that required the application database to be re-created, we may need to discard our tables and re-create them. With schemas, we can add a new schema to store our additional tables away from the application tables, but our reporting application can access both sets of tables, by simply prefixing the table names with the schema name in which the required table resides.

We will start by looking at how schemas are created and managed, and how tables are created inside named schemas. Then we will look at how this can help manage our database.

## Creating Schemas

We create a new schema using the CREATE SCHEMA command, which has the following syntax:

```
CREATE SCHEMA schemaname [ AUTHORIZATION owner-of-schema ]
```

We must be connected to the database in which we wish to create the new schema before running this command.

We can also add a helpful comment to our schema, using the COMMENT syntax:

```
COMMENT ON SCHEMA schemaname IS 'some helpful text'
```

Let's connect to our example1 database, and create a new schema owned by the user rick:

```
template1=# \c example1 postgres
You are now connected to database "example1" as user "postgres".
example1=# CREATE SCHEMA schema1 AUTHORIZATION rick;
CREATE SCHEMA
example1=#example1=# COMMENT ON SCHEMA schema1 IS 'An example schema';
COMMENT
example1=#
```

## Listing Schemas

We can list our schemas with the \dn command in psql, although the pgAdmin III graphical version is somewhat clearer, as shown in Figure 11-5.

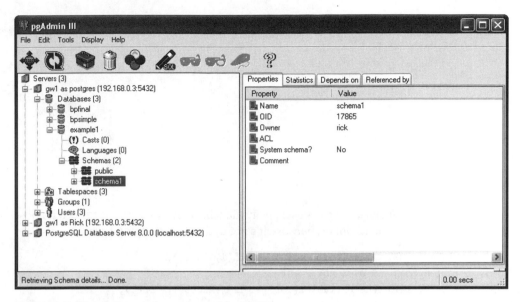

**Figure 11-5.** *Viewing our schema in pgAdmin III*

If you use the \dn command in pgsql to list the schemas, you will see some additional schemas, such as pg_catalogue and pg_toast. PostgreSQL uses these internally, and we can ignore them. The pgAdmin III program hides them, since users usually do not need to know they exist.

## Dropping Schemas

Schemas are dropped with the DROP SCHEMA command, which has the following syntax:

```
DROP SCHEMA schemaname [CASCADE]
```

The CASCADE option tells PostgreSQL to drop all objects in the schema. In general, it's probably safer to delete the tables first, then delete the schema once it is empty, as that way you are less likely to accidentally delete some tables you wanted to keep.

## Creating Tables in a Schema

If we want to create a table in our new schema, we simply prefix the table name with the name of the schema, using this syntax:

```
CREATE TABLE schemaname.tablename
(
    column definitions
);
```

Let's connect to our example1 database as the user rick and create a table:

```
example1=# \c example1 rick
Password:
You are now connected to database "example1" as user "rick".
example1=> CREATE TABLE schema1.table1
example1-> (
example1(>     col1 int,
example1(>     col2 varchar(32)
example1(> );
CREATE TABLE
example1=>
```

Now we can use our table, but we must specify the table name as schema1.table1, not just table1, or the table is hidden from us, because it's not in the schema named public:

```
example1=> INSERT INTO table1(col1, col2) VALUES(1, 'one');
ERROR:  relation "table1" does not exist
example1=> INSERT INTO schema1.table1(col1, col2) VALUES(1, 'one');
INSERT 17869 1
example1=>
```

## Setting the Schema Search Path

We can control the way in which PostgreSQL searches different schema names by setting the schema search_path, as follows:

```
example1=> SHOW search_path;

 search_path
--------------
 $user,public
(1 row)

example1=> SET search_path TO schema1, public;
SET
example1=>
```

Now it's possible to access our table without the prefix of the schema1 name:

```
example1=> INSERT INTO table1(col1, col2) VALUES(2, 'two');
INSERT 17870 1
example1=>
```

You will have noticed that when we showed the search path, as well as the default schema public, there was also a value $user. This means that if you created a schema with the same name as the user, by default, that would have been searched first for the table name. We can see this behavior in practice by experimenting with a different user, neil:

```
example1=> \c example1 neil
Password:
You are now connected to database "example1" as user "neil".
example1=# CREATE SCHEMA neil AUTHORIZATION neil;
CREATE SCHEMA
example1=# CREATE TABLE neil.table1 (
example1(# col1 int,
example1(# col2 varchar(32)
example1(# );
CREATE TABLE
example1=# INSERT INTO neil.table1(col1, col2) VALUES(42, 'this is neil');
INSERT 17482 1
example1=# SELECT * FROM table1;
 col1 |     col2
------+--------------
   42 | this is neil
(1 row)

example1=#
```

But if we go back to being the user rick in the example1 database, reset the schema search path to include schema1, and select again, we see our old table, not the table the user neil created in the neil schema:

```
example1=# \c example1 rick
Password:
You are now connected to database "example1" as user "rick".
example1=> SET search_path TO schema1;
SET
example1=> SELECT * FROM table1;
 col1 | col2
------+------
    1 | one
    2 | two
(2 rows)

example1=>
```

By default, rick does not see the schema neil, because only schemas called rick and public are searched, but when rick's search path is set to search schema1, it finds the original table table1 rather than the table of the same name owned by neil.

This is easy to see in pgAdmin III, as shown in Figure 11-6. Notice that both the schemas schema1 and neil have a table called table11.

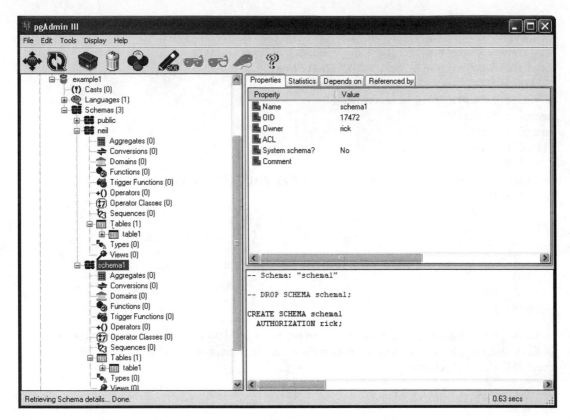

**Figure 11-6.** *Two tables with the same name, in the same database*

This ability to subdivide schemas in a database, both by explicit name by using the `schemaname.tablename` syntax and by automatically searching through a defined list of schemas, is a powerful technique if you need to use it. If, on the other hand, you have no need to use schemas, you can just accept the default `public` schema, and more or less ignore the existence of schemas.

### Listing Tables in a Schema

Currently, there is no shortcut command from the `psql` prompt to list the tables in a schema, though it is possible to access the information by using the `pg_tables` system catalog, for example:

```
example1=> SELECT schemaname, tablename, tableowner FROM pg_tables
WHERE schemaname = 'schema1';
 schemaname | tablename | tableowner
------------+-----------+------------
 schema1    | table1    | rick
 schema1    | table2    | rick
(2 rows)

example1=>
```

If you use `SELECT * FROM pg_tables`, you can see all the tables and schemas, but the format isn't particularly user-friendly.

## Privilege Management

PostgreSQL controls access to the database by using system privileges that may be granted and revoked using the `GRANT` command. By default, users may not write data to tables that they did not create. Privileges may be removed with the `REVOKE` command. Permissions can also be managed via pgAdmin III.

### Granting Privileges

The `GRANT` command has the several versions, all based around the same syntax:

```
GRANT privilege [, ...] ON object [, ...]
TO { PUBLIC | GROUP group | username } [ WITH GRANT OPTION ]
```

The basic `GRANT` command gives a list of privileges to an object or list of objects. The `WITH GRANT OPTION` allows the user or group granted the privilege to subsequently `GRANT` those privileges to others. In general, this is not a good idea, because you want to give as few users as possible administration-type privileges. The supported privileges are shown in Table 11-10.

**Table 11-10.** *Grant Privileges*

| Privilege | Description |
|---|---|
| SELECT | Allows rows to be read |
| INSERT | Allows new rows to be created |
| DELETE | Allows rows to be deleted |
| UPDATE | Allows existing rows to be changed |
| RULE | Allows creation of rules for a table or view |
| REFERENCES | Allows creation of foreign key constraints (as mentioned in Chapter 8; permission must be granted on both tables involved in the relationship) |
| TRIGGER | Allows creation of triggers on a table |
| EXECUTE | Allows execution of stored procedures |
| ALL | Grants all privileges |

The *object* may be the name of a table, a view, a tablespace or a group. The keyword `PUBLIC` is an abbreviation, meaning all users.

For instance, to allow the `authors` group to read the `customer` table and to add new customers, we could do the following, assuming we already have sufficient privileges to perform this:

```
bpfinal=# GRANT SELECT,INSERT ON customer TO GROUP editors;
GRANT
bpfinal=#
```

### Revoking Privileges

Privileges are revoked (taken away), by the REVOKE command, which is very similar to GRANT:

```
REVOKE privilege [, ...]
ON object [, ...]
FROM { PUBLIC | GROUP groupname | username }
```

For example, we can deny the user rick any access to the customer table with the following command:

```
bpfinal=# REVOKE ALL ON customer FROM rick;
REVOKE
bpfinal=#
```

A user group permission will still allow access, even if a particular user doesn't have the permission specifically. If, for example, the group authors has permission to access the customer table, and rick is a member of that group, he will still be allowed access. To complete the permission change, we would need to delete rick from all groups that can access the table.

---

■**Caution** You need to be careful that your permissions are consistent. For example, if you have a table with a serial column, which uses a sequence to create the values, then you must grant permissions on both the table and the sequence for a user to successfully insert rows. PostgreSQL will not warn you if you create combinations of permissions on different objects that are not logically consistent.

---

# Database Backup and Recovery

Backup and recovery is an area all too often overlooked, with disastrous consequences. A database system depends on its data, and data can be lost in a number of ways—from a bolt of lightning frying the hard drive, to finger trouble deleting the wrong files, to bad programming corrupting the contents of the database. All PostgreSQL databases should be backed up on a regular basis. Keeping a copy of your data elsewhere will protect you should a problem arise.

A well-thought-out backup and recovery plan is one that has been tested and shown to work, preferably with an automated backup process. It will help reduce the impact of any data loss to a minor inconvenience, rather than an enterprise-terminating experience.

Even though PostgreSQL uses ordinary files in the file system to store its data, it is not advisable to rely on normal file backup procedures for PostgreSQL databases. If the database is active when copies of the PostgreSQL files are taken, we cannot be sure that the internal state of the database will be consistent when it is restored. In theory, we could shut down the database server before copying the files, but there is a better way. PostgreSQL provides its own backup and restore mechanisms: pg_dump, pg_dumpall, and pg_restore. In addition, it is possible to do backups directly from pgAdmin III.

In what circumstances might PostgreSQL lose data? Fortunately it's not very many. These circumstances and the corresponding action are listed in Table 11-11.

**Table 11-11.** *PostgreSQL's Handling of Hazardous Events*

| Event | PostgreSQL Action |
|---|---|
| Client crash | PostgreSQL will roll back any transactions (see Chapter 9) in progress for that client. |
| Client network failure | PostgreSQL will roll back any transactions in progress for that client. |
| Server crash | PostgreSQL will roll back incomplete transactions when the server restarts. |
| Operating system crash with no data loss | PostgreSQL will roll back incomplete transactions when the server restarts. |
| Accidental deletion of database data or table | Manual recovery from a backup is required. |
| Accidental deletion from the operating system of PostgreSQL's files | Manual recovery from a backup is required. |
| Disk failure or other crash corrupting PostgreSQL's files | Manual recovery from a backup is required. |

## Creating a Backup

The easiest way to back up a database is to run `pg_dump` and redirect its output to a file. The `pg_dump` command syntax is very simple.

```
pg_dump [dbname] [options…]
```

We will discuss the full set of options that `pg_dump` offers shortly. For now, we just need to know that `-U` specifies a username.

Here is a very simple command to back up our `bpfinal` database:

```
$ pg_dump -U postgres bpfinal > bpfinal.backup
```

In essence, the backup scheme is to produce a large SQL (and PostgreSQL internal commands) script that, if executed, will re-create the database in its entirety. By default, the `pg_dump` output is a human-readable text script, which contains statements for creating users and privileges, creating tables, and adding data. Here is a small sample:

```
--
-- Name: stock; Type: TABLE; Schema: public; Owner: rick
--

CREATE TABLE stock (
    item_id integer NOT NULL,
    quantity integer NOT NULL
);
```

```
ALTER TABLE public.stock OWNER TO rick;
--
-- Data for Name: stock; Type: TABLE DATA; Schema: public; Owner: rick
--

COPY stock (item_id, quantity) FROM stdin;
1    12
2    2
4    8
5    3
7    8
8    18
10   1
\.
```

To restore the database from a backup, we need to execute the script. The script will contain commands for creating and populating tables, but does not contain the database creation. We must first create a database to restore into, and then run the script. As a side effect, this gives us a way of copying a database within an installation, or renaming it. Assuming we have an empty database created, say newbpfinal, we can restore the data from the original by using psql to execute the backup script:

```
$ createdb newbpfinal
$ psql -f bpfinal.backup newbpfinal
```

Here, the -f option to psql causes it to read commands from a file instead of from the user.

We can back up all of the databases in our installation (including internal system tables used by PostgreSQL) in one go by using pg_dumpall as the database superuser (postgres):

```
$ su - postgres
$ pg_dumpall > all.backup
```

This has the advantage of also backing up items that are common across all of the databases, such as user information. We lose the opportunity, however, to rename databases.

There are many options to pg_dump that allow us to select a single table to back up, to compress the backup file as it is produced, to include table definitions, and to specify the format of the dump output. The most useful options are listed in Table 11-12.

**Table 11-12.** *Common pg_dump Options*

| Option | Description |
|---|---|
| -f, --file=*filename* | Specifies a filename (default is standard output) |
| -F, --format=c\|t\|p | Specifies an output file format (custom, tar, or plain text) |
| -v, --verbose | Uses verbose mode |
| -Z, --compress=0-9 | Specifies the compression level for compressed formats |
| --help | Shows some help text |

**Table 11-12.** *Common pg_dump Options (Continued)*

| Option | Description |
|---|---|
| -a, --data-only | Dumps only the data, not the schema |
| -C, --create | Includes commands to create database in dump |
| -c, --clean | Drops objects prior to creation |
| --disable-triggers | Disables triggers during a data-only restore |
| -d, --inserts | Dumps data as INSERT commands, rather than COPY commands |
| -s, --schema-only | Dumps only the schema, no data |
| -S, --superuser=name | Specifies the superuser username |
| -t, --table=table | Dumps the named table only |
| -h, --host=hostname | Specifies the database server host or socket directory |
| -p, --port=port | Specifies the database server port number |
| -U, --username=name | Connects as the specified database user |

The -s option is often useful to create a copy of the database structure, without the data. Often, it's useful to have one or more copies of the live database, but with small amounts of test data for developers to work on. In countries with tight data protection laws, such as the United States and countries in the European Union, it is often a legal necessity to tightly restrict access to personal data, so live data cannot be used for test purposes.

---

■**Caution** From time to time, new versions of PostgreSQL are released, containing new features or enhancements that you will want to take advantage of. Before attempting to upgrade to a new version of PostgreSQL, *back up your data.* Unless you are sure that your data can be re-created, or it is not important, it is best to be safe. Sometimes, a database backup and restore operation is required when upgrading to a new version of PostgreSQL. Refer to the release notes for your new version of PostgreSQL to discover if a backup and restore procedure is recommended.

---

## Restoring from a Backup

To restore using an archive, we have several choices. If we did our backup into a plain-text file (we didn't specify any -F options to pg_dump), then we can simply feed the script into psql from the command line. This is a good option for small databases, because a plain-text file that can be viewed, or even edited if required, is very useful to have.

```
$ pg_dump -U postgres bpsimple > bpsimple.bak
$ createdb -U rick bpsimple2
$ psql -U rick -d bpsimple2 < bpsimple.bak
```

Notice we used the command-line `createdb` utility to create the database, ready to be loaded into. We could have connected to the database with `psql` and used the normal `CREATE DATABASE` command just as easily.

To restore a backup that contains an entire installation, we need only connect to a PostgreSQL installation that contains the default database, `template1`. A full backup created by `pg_dumpall` contains SQL statements to create each database in the backup. We need to run the backup and restore as the database superuser to have sufficient permissions to read and write all of the data, as follows:

```
$ psql -f all.backup template1
```

If we did our backup into a custom or tar format file (using the `-F` option to `pg_dump`, rather than allowing `pg_dump` to use its default format), then we must use the `pg_restore` utility to recover the database. A backup created using `pg_dump` with custom or tar formatting cannot be restored by reading the backup into `psql` as though it were an SQL script. The `pg_restore` utility has the following form:

```
pg_restore [archive] [options...]
```

The most common options to `pg_restore` are listed in Table 11-13.

**Table 11-13.** *Common pg_restore Options*

| Option | Description |
| --- | --- |
| -d, --dbname=*dbname* | Connects to database *dbname* |
| -f, --file=*filename* | Specifies a filename (by default, standard input is used) |
| -F, --format=c\|t | Specifies the backup file format (custom or tar) |
| -l, --list | Prints a summarized listing of the archive's contents |
| -v, --verbose | Uses verbose mode |
| --help | Shows some help text |
| -a, --data-only | Restores only the data, not the schema |
| -c, --clean | Cleans (drops) the schema prior to creation |
| -C, --create | Creates the target database |
| -s, --schema-only | Restores only the schema, not the data |
| -t, --table=*tablename* | Restores the named table |
| -h, --host=*hostname* | Specifies the database server host or socket directory |
| -p, --port=*port* | Specifies the database server port number |
| -U, --username=*username* | Connects as the specified database user |
| -e, --exit-on-error | Exits on error (the default is to continue) |

To back up our `bpfinal` database, compressing the backup as it's created, we use this command:

```
$ pg_dump -U postgres -F c bpfinal --compress=9 > bpf.zb
```

In real life, we would then archive this backup, perhaps after testing it on a different database installation to ensure it was a valid backup.

---

■**Caution** Do not test backup and restore procedures on a live database while you are learning. Practice
on a database installation from which you can afford to lose the data!

---

Suppose the database dbfinal has been lost, perhaps because of a disk failure. Using psql,
we create a new bpfinal database:

```
example1=> \c template1 postgres
You are now connected to database "template1" as user "postgres".
template1=#  CREATE DATABASE bpfinal OWNER rick;
CREATE DATABASE
template1=#
```

Now we can use pg_restore to get our database back:

```
$ pg_restore -U postgres -d bpfinal  bpf.zb
```

The pg_dump format using -F c will create a smaller backup file than can usually be achieved
with a plain-text format, even if you then compress the file, which gives the pg_dump with -F c
option followed by pg_restore an advantage for larger databases.

However, the flexibility of a script that can be viewed and easily restored into a database of
a different name is very useful. In general, we suggest that you stick to plain-text formats of
pg_dump, which can be restored only by using psql.

On Linux, it's easy to compress and decompress the backup file on the fly. For example,
here we back up our bpfinal database, compressing the backup as it's created, and then restore it
to a database called bpx, decompressing the archive as it's read:

```
$ pg_dump -U postgres bpfinal | gzip -9 > bpf.bc
$ createdb -U rick bpx
$ zcat bpf.bc | psql -U postgres bpx
```

This avoids the need for the additional disk space to store the uncompressed file during
either backup or recovery.

## Backing Up and Restoring from pgAdmin III

In this chapter, we have seen how pgAdmin III often provides a user-friendly mechanism for
many of the administrative tasks we must perform. You will not be surprised to discover that
pgAdmin III can also provide a GUI for backup and restore operations. Of course, it's more
difficult to automate backups using a GUI tool, but it does offer an easy way to make them.

To make a backup in pgAdmin III, right-click the database to back up and select Backup
from the context menu that appears. In the dialog box that appears, select a file to back up into,
as shown in Figure 11-7.

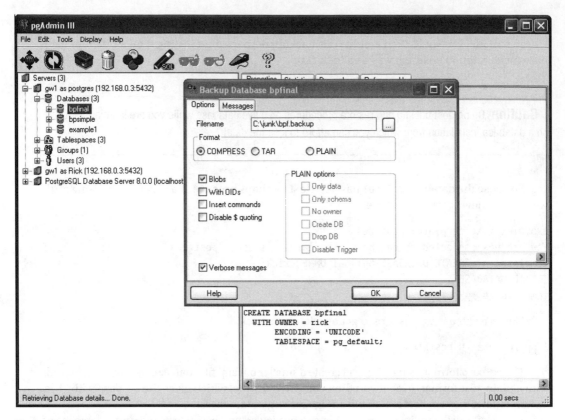

**Figure 11-7.** *Using pgAdmin III to perform a backup*

Once the backup has finished, click the Databases object of the database connection (the group object that can be expanded to show all the databases in a server) and create a new database to restore your data into. Then right-click the database to restore into, and you should see a Restore option, as shown in Figure 11-8.

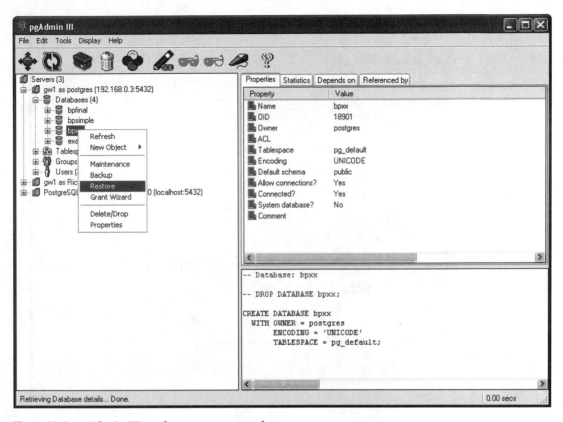

**Figure 11-8.** *pgAdmin III ready to restore some data*

In the Restore Database dialog box, shown in Figure 11-9, select the file you used to back up to earlier. This dialog box also contains a list of options, allowing partial restores, as shown in Figure 11-9. Select options as applicable, and then click OK to restore the data to a different database.

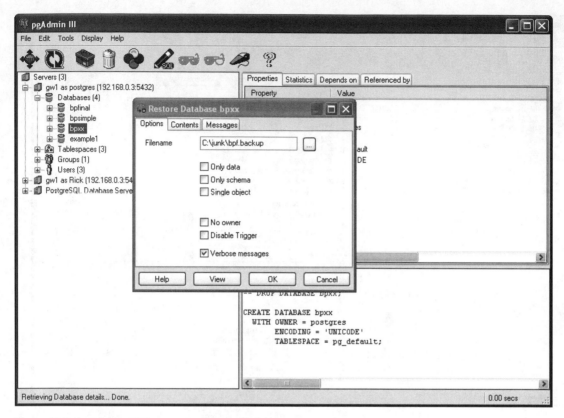

**Figure 11-9.** *pgAdmin III Restore Database dialog box*

## POINT-IN-TIME RECOVERY

A common problem with backups is that they were often taken some time before the event that caused the backed up data to need to be restored, so all the intervening work is lost. If you did a backup at 2 A.M., but the disk drive in your server failed at 5 P.M., then even after restoring from backup, you have lost many hours' work.

Starting with version 8.0 of PostgreSQL, a new feature is available, called *point-in-time recovery*, or often just PITR, which is based on the new Write Ahead Logging (WAL) features of PostgreSQL 8. PITR helps to mitigate the problem of lost work by storing additional log files of transactions away from the main database. Provided that the event that caused the main database to be corrupted didn't also corrupt the log files, then, after restoring the main database files, it is possible to "replay" events in the additional log files to recover events between the backup and the crash. Indeed, it is possible to replay the commands to an arbitrary point in time, hence the naming of this feature.

Interested readers should consult the section in the manual on online backups and PITR, but be warned this topic is reasonably complex. You should experiment with PITR on a test server before considering it for production use.

# Database Performance

Performance is frequently an issue with larger databases. No matter how quickly the database runs, there is almost always someone who will ask if it can be made to go quicker, or run at the same speed on a lower-specification machine.

In this book, we have been working with a small database with relatively few tables, each containing a handful of rows. We have not been concerned with the speed at which PostgreSQL responds to queries or the physical size of the database, because with such a small database, PostgreSQL is very quick, even on quite lowly specified hardware.

Optimizing databases is an advanced skill, requiring database design techniques and detailed knowledge of the internal workings of a database system. PostgreSQL includes a sophisticated optimizer that attempts to execute database queries as efficiently as possible, but, in some cases, it requires a helping hand.

Here, we will look at a few relatively simple ways to help maintain and perhaps improve PostgreSQL database performance, beginning with discovering how the database is currently performing.

## Monitoring Behavior

There are two ways you can look at what PostgreSQL is doing:

- Monitoring the operating system activity

- Looking at some of the statistics PostgreSQL collects internally

### Monitoring Operating System Activity

A standard way to get a quick look at the PostgreSQL user processes on Linux is to use the ps command to look for processes owned by postgres. Here is an example on a database with several remote connections:

```
$ ps -ef | grep postgres
postgres  2006     1  0 13:32 tty1     00:00:00 /usr/local/pgsql/bin/postmaster
-i -D /usr/local/pgsql/data
postgres  2009  2006  0 13:32 tty1     00:00:00 postgres: writer process
postgres  2010  2006  0 13:32 tty1     00:00:00 postgres: stats buffer
postgres  2011  2010  0 13:32 tty1     00:00:00 postgres: stats collector
postgres 13180  2006  0 19:51 tty1     00:00:00 postgres: rick bpsimple
 192.168.0.2(3170) idle
postgres 13181  2006  0 19:51 tty1     00:00:00 postgres: rick example1
 192.168.0.2(3171) idle
postgres 13195  2006  0 20:13 tty1     00:00:00 postgres: postgres template1
 192.168.0.2(3217) idle
root     13218  2032  0 20:19 tty2     00:00:00 psql -U postgres template1
postgres 13219  2006  0 20:19 tty1     00:00:00 postgres: postgres template1
$
```

The operating system command top is also useful to see what a Linux system is doing.

### Viewing PostgreSQL Statistics

The PostgreSQL statistics collector has a number of views that show internal statistics.

As an example, here is the information available in pg_stat_activity, which provides a list of the current processes and users (some columns are omitted in this example):

```
template1=# SELECT * FROM pg_stat_activity;
datid |  datname  | procpid | usesysid | usename
------+-----------+---------+----------+----------+
    1 | template1 |  13219  |        1 | postgres |
18414 | bpfinal   |  13230  |      101 | neil     |
18182 | bpsimple  |  13180  |      100 | rick     |
17864 | example1  |  13181  |      100 | rick     |
    1 | template1 |  13195  |        1 | postgres |

template1=#
```

It's also useful to check for locking. This can be done by reading the pg_locks view:

```
template1=# SELECT * FROM pg_locks;
 relation | database | transaction | pid  |      mode      | granted
----------+----------+-------------+------+----------------+---------
          |          |        7595 | 2249 | ExclusiveLock  | t
    16837 |        1 |             | 2249 | AccessShareLock | t
(2 rows)

template1=#
```

See the PostgreSQL online documentation for more details about the pg_stat_activity and pg_locks views.

## Using VACUUM

The PostgreSQL SQL VACUUM command has two uses:

- Reclaiming database storage space

- Updating optimizer statistics

The VACUUM command has the following syntax:

```
VACUUM [FULL] [FREEZE] [VERBOSE] ANALYZE
    [table [ (column [, ... ] ) ] ]
```

### Reclaiming Space

Over a period of time, a PostgreSQL data table will accumulate defunct rows—rows that occupy space in the database, but that can no longer be accessed.

Recall from Chapter 9 that during a transaction that is updating rows in a table, users must still be able to query the table and get consistent results. PostgreSQL creates new rows for the data in the transaction and makes them available once the transaction is committed. Meanwhile, queries see the old rows. When the transaction is completed, we have a table that contains both the old and new rows, but one set is no longer accessible. It is the space consumed by these inaccessible rows that VACUUM reclaims.

The command VACUUM by itself runs across the tables in a database, and marks unused rows as suitable for reuse when data is inserted. It doesn't shrink the database, but it does run very efficiently, with little effect on other users. The following is an example of VACUUM output. We add the VERBOSE option to see some statistics, and select the customer table for vacuuming. By default, VACUUM will reclaim storage in all tables in the active database.

```
bpfinal=> VACUUM VERBOSE customer;
INFO:  vacuuming "public.customer"
INFO:  index "customer_pk" now contains 15 row versions in 2 pages
DETAIL:  0 index pages have been deleted, 0 are currently reusable.
CPU 0.00s/0.00u sec elapsed 0.00 sec.
INFO:  "customer": found 0 removable, 15 nonremovable row versions in 1 pages
DETAIL:  0 dead row versions cannot be removed yet.
There were 0 unused item pointers.
0 pages are entirely empty.
CPU 0.00s/0.00u sec elapsed 0.00 sec.
VACUUM
bpfinal=>
```

With the FULL option, VACUUM reclaims all spare space and returns it to the operating system. Unfortunately this requires extensive locking on the database and much disk activity to reorganize file layouts, so it can affect the performance of other users. The FREEZE option is required only by people preparing a template database; you should not use it on normal databases. In all cases, VERBOSE provides additional output (usually a lot of it!).

The ANALYZE option recomputes various statistics that PostgreSQL uses to plan its database queries, as explained next.

## Updating Optimizer Statistics

As we have seen in earlier chapters, SQL is a declarative language. We tell PostgreSQL the result we want, and it is up to the database to work out the best way of getting that result. For example, we might say that we want to find all the customers who ordered Linux CDs between two specific dates and live in Newtown. The database may choose to scan the customer table for each customer and look for their order information, or it may decide to scan the item table for the Linux CD item, pick each order, and see which customer placed it and when.

Depending on the structure of the database, the primary keys, and the number of rows in the tables, one way may be much faster than another. PostgreSQL tries to work out which way to perform the query will be the fastest. This is what the query optimizer does: it creates a *query plan* for a query before executing it. The plan is normally based on both the structure of the database and the size of the tables involved in the query, and as described in the next section, the availability of indexes on queried columns.

We can view the query plan for any particular query by using the EXPLAIN SQL statement:

```
EXPLAIN [VERBOSE] query
```

Here it is in action:

```
bpfinal=> EXPLAIN SELECT customer_id FROM customer WHERE zipcode='BG3 8GD';
                         QUERY PLAN
----------------------------------------------------------
 Seq Scan on customer  (cost=0.00..1.19 rows=1 width=4)
   Filter: (zipcode = 'BG3 8GD'::bpchar)
(2 rows)

bpfinal=>
```

In our sample database, most queries will be performed using sequential scans of the tables, as the tables are very small. PostgreSQL estimates a cost associated with each part of the query that it is planning and tries to minimize the total.

As we can see in the results of the EXPLAIN statement, PostgreSQL is estimating a cost of between 0 and 1.19 for a scan of the customer table. It is also estimating that two rows will be found. PostgreSQL has no choice in this case but to look at each customer record in turn, comparing the zipcode.

If we look at a more complicated query, we see that the output can get quite complex:

```
bpfinal=> EXPLAIN SELECT * FROM customer, orderinfo
bpfinal->       WHERE customer.customer_id = orderinfo.customer_id;
                             QUERY PLAN
----------------------------------------------------------------------
 Hash Join  (cost=1.06..2.34 rows=5 width=436)
   Hash Cond: ("outer".customer_id = "inner".customer_id)
   ->  Seq Scan on customer  (cost=0.00..1.15 rows=15 width=408)
   ->  Hash  (cost=1.05..1.05 rows=5 width=28)
         ->  Seq Scan on orderinfo  (cost=0.00..1.05 rows=5 width=28)
(5 rows)

bpfinal=>
```

You can get more detailed information, including the total runtime required, by adding the ANALYZE option to EXPLAIN:

```
bpfinal=> EXPLAIN ANALYZE SELECT * FROM customer, orderinfo
bpfinal->       WHERE customer.customer_id = orderinfo.customer_id;
                                          QUERY PLAN

-----------------------------------------------------------------------------
 Hash Join  (cost=1.06..2.41 rows=5 width=111) (actual time=26.668..26.827 rows=
5 loops=1)
   Hash Cond: ("outer".customer_id = "inner".customer_id)
   ->  Seq Scan on customer  (cost=0.00..1.15 rows=15 width=85) (actual time=0.0
13..0.083 rows=15 loops=1)
   ->  Hash  (cost=1.05..1.05 rows=5 width=26) (actual time=5.300..5.300 rows=0
loops=1)
```

```
        -> Seq Scan on orderinfo  (cost=0.00..1.05 rows=5 width=26) (actual ti
me=5.257..5.273 rows=5 loops=1)
 Total runtime: 27.099 ms
(6 rows)

bpfinal=>
```

The cost estimates that are used by PostgreSQL are based on the tables' vital statistics, such as the number of rows that are present. These statistics are not kept precisely up-to-date as the server runs, but must be recomputed from time to time. This is what VACUUM ANALYZE does. Here's an example:

```
bpfinal=# VACUUM ANALYZE;
VACUUM
bpfinal=#
```

## Vacuuming from the Command Line

PostgreSQL provides a utility, vacuumdb, for performing the database vacuum from the command line. Its syntax is as follows:

```
vacuumdb [options] database
```

The main options to vacuumdb are listed in Table 11-14.

**Table 11-14.** *Common vacuumdb Options*

| Option | Description |
|---|---|
| -a, --all | Vacuums all databases |
| -d, --dbname=*dbname* | Specifies the database to vacuum |
| -t, --table='*table*' | Vacuums the specified table only |
| -f, --full | Does full vacuuming |
| -z, --analyze | Updates optimizer statistics |
| -v, --verbose | Uses verbose mode |
| --help | Shows some help text |
| -h, --host=*hostname* | Specifies the database server |
| -p, --port=*port* | Specifies the database server port |
| -U, --username=*username* | Specifies the username to use |

---

**Tip** For a PostgreSQL database of any size in regular use, run VACUUM ANALYZE or vacuumdb --analyze daily, perhaps as part of an overnight routine. This will ensure that the space occupied by the data remains at a minimum, and the statistics used by the query optimizer remain up-to-date, keeping performance at its best.

---

### Vacuuming from pgAdmin III

It's also possible to run a VACUUM operation from pgAdmin III. Right-click the database and select Maintenance from the context menu. As shown in Figure 11-10, the Maintain Database dialog box includes a choice for a VACUUM operation, as well as VACUUM options.

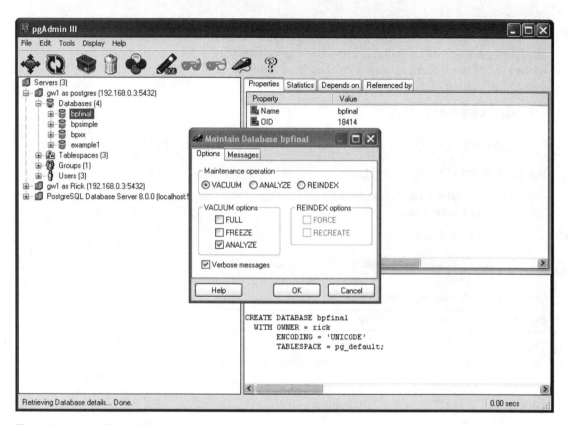

**Figure 11-10.** *pgAdmin III maintenance options*

## Creating Indexes

As we saw in the previous section, PostgreSQL creates a query plan for a query based on costs of selecting and scanning data. A sequential scan of all the rows in a table will become very expensive as the number of rows in the table increases. Databases use *indexes* to speed up searches for rows that contain specific data, as the cost of an index scan is typically much less than a sequential scan.

In fact, PostgreSQL will automatically create an index for a column defined as a primary key for a table. This means that, for example, locating a customer given their customer_id will be very quick, but locating a customer by ZIP code will still require a sequential scan.

We can create additional indexes for a table by using the SQL CREATE INDEX command, which has the following syntax:

```
CREATE [UNIQUE] INDEX indexname ON table(column)
```

The UNIQUE option specifies that the column we are indexing does not contain duplicate entries; each row has a unique value for this column. Once a unique index has been created, any attempt to add or alter data so that this condition is broken will result in an error. Use this option only if you are sure that your data will never have duplicate data for the index column.

Our sample database has too little data to really benefit from indexes, so let's create a new table to demonstrate the effect of an index.

We can create a large table by reading in a long list of words (such as /usr/share/dict/words on most Linux systems) into a table. The example we use here contains more than 100,000 words. We can use the \copy command in psql to read data directly from a file. We use the example1 database we created earlier in the chapter as a location for our new table:

```
example1=> CREATE TABLE words (word varchar(100));
CREATE TABLE
example1=> \copy words from 'file-with-many-words'
\.
example1=> SELECT COUNT(*) FROM words;
 count
--------
 106172
(1 row)

example1=>
```

Now that we have a large table, we can ask PostgreSQL how it would go about finding the word *Zulu*, which we know is near the end of the word list:

```
example1=> EXPLAIN ANALYZE SELECT word FROM words WHERE word = 'Zulu';
                                   QUERY PLAN

--------------------------------------------------------------------------------
 Seq Scan on words  (cost=0.00..22.50 rows=5 width=168) (actual time=315.460..31
 5.728 rows=1 loops=1)
     Filter: ((word)::text = 'Zulu'::text)
 Total runtime: 315.869 ms
(3 rows)

example1=>
```

Despite the fact that there arc more than 100,000 rows, PostgreSQL estimates a maximum cost of 22.5 for a scan of the table. This is just a guess, and we know that it is wildly inaccurate, since PostgreSQL will need to search almost to the end of the table to find the right row. To help PostgreSQL make a better estimate, we need to use VACUUM ANALYZE to update the table statistics after our insertion:

```
example1=> VACUUM ANALYZE words;
VACUUM
example1=> EXPLAIN ANALYZE SELECT word FROM words WHERE word = 'Zulu';
                                                 QUERY PLAN

--------------------------------------------------------------------------------
Seq Scan on words  (cost=0.00..1960.15 rows=3 width=11) (actual time=280.491..2
80.726 rows=1 loops=1)
   Filter: ((word)::text = 'Zulu'::text)
 Total runtime: 280.874 ms
(3 rows)

example1=>
```

Now PostgreSQL is estimating a cost of up to 1960 for a scan on this table. This demonstrates why it is important to run VACUUM regularly to keep the statistics up-to-date, especially after significant data updates, insertions, or deletions.

When we perform the query to retrieve Zulu, we see a very slight pause (though on today's computers, even searching 100,000 rows is only a very slight pause):

```
example1=> SELECT * FROM words WHERE word='Zulu';
word
------
Zulu
(1 row)

example1=>
```

If we turn on the timing option in psql, we can see the actual time:

```
example1=> \timing
Timing is on.
example1=> SELECT word FROM words WHERE word = 'Zulu';
 word
------
 Zulu
(1 row)

Time: 141.000 ms
example1=> \timing
Timing is off.
example1=>
```

We can speed up access to the words table by creating an index, like this:

```
example1=> CREATE INDEX words_idx ON words(word);
CREATE INDEX
example1=>
```

We can see the predicted benefit by looking at the query plan again:

```
example1=> EXPLAIN ANALYZE SELECT word FROM words WHERE word = 'Zulu';
                                               QUERY PLAN

-----------------------------------------------------------------------------
Index Scan using words_idx on words  (cost=0.00..5.62 rows=3 width=11) (actual
time=0.681..0.695 rows=1 loops=1)
   Index Cond: ((word)::text = 'Zulu'::text)
 Total runtime: 0.837 ms
(3 rows)

example1=>

example1=> SELECT * FROM words WHERE word='Zulu';
word
------
Zulu
(1 row)

example1=>
```

PostgreSQL will now use the index, and the estimated cost has dropped dramatically. If you are on a slow enough machine, or used enough words, you may even be able to notice the increase in performance.

If we look at the actual time required now that we have an index, we can see the improvement:

```
example1=> \timing
Timing is on.
example1=> SELECT word FROM words WHERE word = 'Zulu';
 word
------
 Zulu
(1 row)

Time: 6.000 ms
example1=> \timing
Timing is off.
example1=>
```

While indexes can dramatically speed up a database, and they are the key to maximizing performance, they do not come without a cost. An index will speed up access where selections are being made on matches with the indexed column, but they will make data insertions and updates slower, because the index must be updated as well as the actual data. Indexes also consume space within the database.

We need to take care in selecting which database tables and columns to index, balancing the improved selection performance against increased database size and decreased update speed. So which tables and columns should we index? Think about what each table is used for and what kinds of queries are likely to be made. Consider creating an index for the following:

- Tables that have many rows and are updated infrequently

- Columns that are not primary or foreign keys, but may be used in complex joins

- Columns that will be searched for an exact or prefix match

There are no hard-and-fast rules, and sometimes experimentation is needed.

# Summary

In this chapter, we first looked at the layout of a PostgreSQL installation, in particular it's configuration files and the key options in those files we might want to adjust. Then we looked at database initialization and server control.

Next, we discussed how we can manage the internals of a PostgreSQL server: creating databases, adding users, and managing how PostgreSQL places the physical files underlying the internal databases.

Then we looked at performing backups. Finally, we saw some simple measures we might take to maintain, or even improve, database performance.

The most important topic in this chapter was backups. However reliable PostgreSQL is—and it is very reliable—we cannot stress how important it is that you not only back up your data regularly, but also that you have tested how you would restore that data *before* you suffer a data loss. However, please don't experiment with restoring data on a production server; mistakes can be serious.

In the next chapter, we will return to the topic of database design, which we looked at briefly in Chapter 2. It presents more formal guidelines for how to design a database, and how to enforce data integrity using constraints, which we met in Chapter 8.

# Database Design

So far in this book, we have been working with a database for our simple customer/orders/products data, but we have taken the design of the tables and columns mostly for granted. Now that we understand more about the capabilities of relational databases, we are in a position to backtrack a little and look at a very important aspect of databases: designing the database structure, more formally known as a database *schema*.

When researching this chapter, we asked a friend with excellent database design skills, honed over several years, what he thought was the most important aspect of database design. His simple answer was, "Practice." Unfortunately, we can't provide a substitute for practice, but we can provide a foundation for understanding database design as you gain experience. We will explain the basics in this chapter. Also, we'll work through how we arrived at the design in our sample database.

In this chapter, we'll be looking at the following aspects of database design:

- What constitutes good database design

- Stages in database design

- Logical design

- Physical database model development

- Normal forms

- Common design patterns

## What Is a Good Database Design?

The very first step in designing a database is to understand the problem. Just as when you are designing applications, it is important to understand the problem area well, before getting immersed in any detailed design. With an understanding of the problem, you can determine what you are trying to achieve with your database design.

### Understanding the Problem

Is your planned system going to replace an existing system? If so, you have a head start, because whatever its failings or shortcomings, an existing system will have captured many important features required of the replacement system. Even if there is an existing system, it's important that you talk to the potential users of the system. If it's a database for your personal use, you still need to ask questions, but ask them of yourself.

When interviewing, particularly if you are interviewing more than one person at a time, there are some steps you can take to make the interview as productive as possible:

- Don't try to interview too many people at the same time. Two or three is about the most you should talk to at any one time.

- Inform people in advance about what you are trying to discover and send them your main questions a couple of days prior to the interview.

- See if you can get a helper to jot down notes for you, so you can concentrate on understanding what the users are saying.

- Keep the interview session short and make sure you cover the major issues, even if you need to leave some minor details undecided during the actual meeting. If some items are left unresolved, request answers by a specified date, say in a week.

- Always circulate detailed minutes after the meeting, certainly within two working days, with an explicit request to return comments within a week if any points are disputed.

The actual questions you ask will depend on your particular application. At initial interviews, start out by asking users to describe the purpose of the system and its principal functions. Try to avoid the "how" and focus on the "what." People will often try to tell you how things are done in the current system. However, you need to know *why* they are done, so you can understand the purpose better.

Potential users hold the key to a good design, even if they don't know it. If you are creating a system for your personal use, it is worthwhile to take the time to consider precisely what you need to do, and to try to anticipate how this may change over the time.

## Taking Design Aspects into Account

It's important to understand what you are trying to achieve with a database design. Different features will be important in different systems. For example, you may be building a database to collect some survey data, where once the results have been extracted, there will be no further use for the database. In this case, designing in flexibility for future expansion is usually not the most effective use of your time and energy.

Let's look at the aspects of design that may need to be taken into account when designing a database.

### Ability to Hold the Required Data

The ability to hold the required data is a fairly crucial requirement of all databases, since storing data is the very reason for having a database. However, even this apparently universal requirement can have degrees of necessity. If you are designing a reasonably complex database that you expect to evolve over time, you should seriously consider what are the "must-have" requirements and implement those first, putting to one side the "nice-to-have" requests.

Database design usually evolves through a number of design iterations, just as in the spiral model of application design, where the design iterates through a number of design-code-implement loops as the system evolves, or the Rational Unified Process, where a number of iterations occur, always working on the key requirements first. With database design, getting the fundamentals correct the first time tends to be even more important than with application design. Once the first iteration of the database is in use and storing real data, significant design changes to the core structure will generally prove difficult and time-consuming, and may require design changes in applications accessing the database.

In most database designs, even very complex ones, only about 25% of the tables (at most) in the final database implementation are fundamental to the design. Identifying and designing these core tables must be the first goal. The remaining tables are important, but they are usually peripheral to the core of the design.

## Ability to Support the Required Relationships

The design of the database should support the relationships among the data entities. It is all too easy to become so focused on the details of the data to be stored that you overlook relationships between the data items, yet this is the key breakthrough of relational databases. An application using a database design that captures all the data, but neglects these relationships, will almost always eventually suffer from data-integrity problems and excessive complexity, as other parts of the system attempt to make up for the design failings in the underlying database.

## Ability to Solve the Problem

The best-designed databases are worthless if they don't solve the problem that they were created to tackle. Throughout the design process, you must stay in touch with the problem area. If possible, communicate with the intended users of the database and explain the design to them as the major design decisions are being made.

Simply mailing the users copies of your database schema will almost certainly not do. You need to sit with them and talk through the design, explaining in business terms what the design achieves, and more important, what assumptions you have made and any limitations the design imposes. When you do this, remember to explain carefully how each major data entity can relate to other entities. If your design allows only a local IT support person to support a single department, you must mention such limitations.

It's also important, where practical, to carefully select the users you consult. The most valuable people to talk to are usually those with the broadest experience of the problem. Unfortunately, these also tend to be most senior personnel, and therefore often the busiest and most difficult to get time with.

## Ability to Impose Data Integrity

The data-integrity aspect is closely related to the earlier point about relationships. The whole purpose of a database is to store data, and the quality of that data must be very important to database designers. A lot of real-world data inevitably has deficiencies: uncertainties, hand-written forms that have illegible entries, or missing information. These are never excuses for allowing any further deterioration in data quality in the database.

Choose data types with care, impose column constraints, and if necessary, write trigger functions to maintain the data in the database with as much rigor as is reasonably practical. Of course, some common sense and pragmatism is called for sometimes, but never invent data if something is missing. If you are entering a survey into the database, for example, and some users were unable to answer some questions, it is better to store the fact that the answer was unknown than to enter a best guess.

### Ability to Impose Data Efficiency

Data efficiency is a difficult aspect of database design, because, as Donald Knuth (Professor Emeritus of The Art of Computer Programming at Stanford University) is widely quoted as saying, "Premature optimization is the root of all evil." Although he was referring to application design, this is just as true, perhaps even more so, with database design.

Unfortunately, in a large, heavily used database, it is sometimes necessary to do things that spoil the purity of the design in order to achieve more practical performance goals. You should always get the design right first, before you even consider any optimizations. Often, there are quite simple things, such as adding an index or rewriting a query, that can provide dramatic performance improvements, without compromising the core design.

What you should avoid is the temptation to arbitrarily make many small changes, such as changing a varchar type to a char type, or experimenting with indexes on different attributes. Generally, these are a waste of time and can result in a poor and inconsistent database schema, which will be difficult to maintain. You need to invest time in profiling the application first, to determine where any bottlenecks lie, and only then consider what may need changing. Even then, changing the database design itself (as opposed to less-structural changes such as adding an index or rewriting a query) should be very much a last resort.

### Ability to Accommodate Future Change

People in the software business are often surprised at just how long software remains in use, usually well beyond its design lifetime. With databases, this is even more noticeable, because migrating data from an old design to a new one is often a significant problem in its own right. There will always be pressure to enhance the existing database design, rather than start from scratch and then migrate the data at a later date.

Often, you will find that any changes you have made to your design in the supposed interests of efficiency make your design harder to evolve. As Alan Perlis said in one of his programming epigrams, "Optimization hinders evolution" (http://www.cs.yale.edu/homes/perlis-alan/quotes.html).

# Stages in Database Design

Once you know what you are trying to achieve with the database design, you're ready to begin the design process. As we hinted earlier when discussing the need to understand the problem, database design is rarely a purely technical problem. A significant aspect is to understand the needs and expectations of users before converting those requirements into a technical design. After gathering information, you can proceed to logical design, and then determining relationships.

# Gathering Information

The first stage in designing a database is to gather information about what it is for. Why are you designing a database in the first place? It is important to have a clear objective before you attempt to collect more detailed requirements. You should be able to define, in a small number of sentences—perhaps just a single sentence—your aim with the database. If you can't come up with a simple way of describing your objective, then perhaps the objective is not yet well understood or defined.

Bear this initial simple definition in mind, and if further down the track, it all seems to be getting overcomplicated and suffering from "feature-bloat," then go back to basics, focusing again on the key objectives. Once you have a clear idea of what you are trying to achieve, you can start to expand on this initial requirement.

If your new database will be replacing an existing database, your first task should be to understand the structure of the original database—whether it's relational, flat file, or perhaps just a spreadsheet. Even if the existing system is badly flawed, you can still learn from it, both good things and bad. It's likely that many of the items it currently stores will also be required in the new system, and seeing some existing data can often give you a good feel for what real-world data looks like. Ask what the existing system does well and what it does badly, or not at all. This will give you clues as to how the existing design needs to be amended.

You should write down what the system needs to do, because writing things down focuses the mind. If reports will be generated, try creating a mock-up for users to comment on. If it will take data that comes from existing paper-based forms, get hold of a copy, preferably with some real data already filled in.

At this stage, you should also be thinking about relationships and business rules, and noting any specific features and requirements that are mentioned. You need to be careful to determine which are simply rather arbitrary "this is the way we do things" type rules and prone to change, and which are factual rules about the nature of things and much less likely to change. The former are rules you will probably choose to enforce only with triggers or at the application level, so they are easy to modify. The latter are rules you should probably build into the design of the database, enforcing data integrity at a low level, since they are fundamental and unlikely to change.

# Developing a Logical Design

The first stage of actual design is to develop a logical design. This has several steps. This stage concentrates on the logical database structure, rather than focusing on implementation detail.

## Determining Entities

Once you have gathered information about the initial objectives and business requirements, you should be in a position to identify the *principal entities* (the key objects that will need to appear in the database). At this point, you shouldn't worry too much about minor entities. You just need to stay focused on the big picture and pick out the key objects that define the problem area.

In our sample database, we would identify customers, orders, and products as the key objects that we need to work with. Additional details, such as the need to track stock or how entities relate, are not important at this stage.

Once you believe you have identified the major components of your database, you need to identify the attributes of those components, in an informal way. For example, for our sample database, we would probably draw up a list of our main components, with the attributes written in plain language, like this:

### Customers and Potential Customers
Name

Address

Phone number

### Orders
Products ordered

Date placed

Date delivered

Shipping information

### Product Information
Description

Buy price

Sell price

Barcodes

Stock on hand

---

**Note** *Name* is currently not a reserved keyword in the SQL standard, but it may become a reserved word in the future. Currently, PostgreSQL will accept this as a column identifier, but at some point in the future, it may become illegal, so it is best avoided. At this stage, we are just working with plain language, so for initial design purposes, we will continue to use Name as an attribute of customers.

---

Notice that we have not yet worried about how we might store an address, nor about minor complexities, such as the possibility that each product might have several different barcodes. We have also kept the attributes names quite general, for example "Address" and "Shipping information." This helps to keep the list of attributes reasonably short and general, so we avoid focusing on the finer details too early and losing sight of the core of the design.

At this stage, some people find it helpful to write a brief description of each entity. In our small database, this is a little superfluous, as the components are so simple, but in larger databases, particularly those dealing with more abstract ideas, this can be helpful. If we were writing descriptions for the "Product information" attribute, we might have the following:

| Product Information | Description |
|---|---|
| Description | Up to 75 characters that describe the product |
| Buy price | The price paid to the supplier per item of product, excluding any delivery costs or tax |
| Sell price | The price to be paid for the item, excluding sales tax and shipping costs |
| Barcodes | The EAN13 barcode |
| Stock on hand | The quantity in stock, including any corrections applied during an inventory check |

Once you have finished this stage, take the time to check the information you gathered initially, and make sure nothing important has been overlooked.

## Converting Entities to Tables

Now you are ready to take a more technical step, and start converting components and attribute lists into something that will begin to look like a database. First, pick some sensible names for the tables.

We always name our tables in the singular form, and try to stick to a 250 single word, even if that is slightly artificial. In our sample database, it's easy to convert our names to more succinct versions such as customer or order. So rather than Product Information, we use item. Some designers prefer to use the plural for table names, but the key is to be consistent.

Next, convert the attributes into more meaningful names, and also break down some of the more general descriptions into the columns you would like to see in a database. When breaking down descriptions into column names, it's very important to ensure that each column holds just a single attribute. As we will see later in the chapter, this is essential to ensuring the database is in first normal form, a key design requirement for relational databases.

Again consistency is important, so be consistent in the way you pick attribute names. The more consistent you are in your choice of names, column types, sizes, and so on, the easier your database will be to maintain in the long term.

Starting with our customer table, we have three main attributes: Name, Address, and Phone number. Name is reasonably easy to break down. People normally have a title of some form, such as Mr., Mrs., or Dr., so we need to have a column for this. Names are quite complex. People are often tempted to use a single column for names, assuming that they can always break down the names later if required. The clue is in the word *assume*. Never assume—making assumptions is always risky, even more so in the early stages of a database design.

Suppose you have a customer with a double-barrelled last name, such as Rose Martin, or a Germanic last name, such as von Neumann. Some people might choose to enter two first names, as well as a last name, such as Jennifer Ann Stones. We may have a table of data like this:

| Title | Name |
|-------|------|
| Miss | Jennifer Ann Stones |
| Dr | John von Neumann |
| Mr | Andrew Stones |
| Mr | Adrian Alan Matthew |
| Mr | Robert Rose Martin |

With this structure, it would be impossible to reliably extract the first and last names at a later date. If you need to separate the components of the name, it is much better to capture the separation of names at the point of entry, and store them separately in the database, like this:

| Title | Fname | Lname |
|-------|-------|-------|
| Miss | Jennifer | Stones |
| Dr | John | von Neumann |
| Mr | Andrew | Stones |
| Mr | Adrian | Matthew |
| Mr | Robert | Rose Martin |

Notice that we have also decided that we are not interested in middle names, and we decide as a point of principle to store only a single first name.

Now it's possible at some point in the future to handle the components of the name separately, so we can write to Dr. von Neumann, and start the letter "Dear John," rather than "Dear John von." That sort of carelessness does not impress customers.

Our next item is Address. Addresses are always hard to handle in a database, because the form of address varies widely even in a single country. For example, in the United Kingdom, addresses are written in the form:

20 James Road,
Great Barr,
Birmingham
M11 2BA

Another address might have no house number at all:

Arden House,
Warwick Road,
Acocks Green,
Birmingham
B27 6BH

United States addresses are similar, although the ZIP code is slightly different from the British postcode style:

2560 Ninth Street,
Suite 219,
Berkeley,
California
94710

In Germany and Austria, addresses are written very differently:

Getreidegasse 9
A-5020 Salzburg

(Which just happens to be a very attractive street where Mozart was born.)

Designing a standard address structure is not easy, and often there is no perfect solution. Usually, a minimum design would be to separate out a postal town and ZIP code or equivalent, which is what we have done in our sample database. In real use, it is probably better to have at least three lines for an address, a town, a ZIP code, a state (if applicable), and a country if that might be required.

---

**■Note** If you live outside the United States, a fault you sometimes see on web forms is assuming that everyone has a state part of the address and providing a handy drop-down box to select the state, or making it a mandatory field, but forgetting to allow the "not relevant" option for the rest of the world. It is very annoying for people outside the United States trying to enter an address and discovering that state entry is mandatory, when it has no meaning for most of the world's population!

---

It is usually best to avoid insisting on a house number, as you will cause problems for people in office buildings with a name, or people who live in apartments in condominiums and have an apartment number as well as a street address number.

Another possibility is to accept an undefined number of address lines, by splitting the address lines out into a separate table. If you do this, you must remember to impose an order on the lines, so you get the address details in the correct order. Generally, most designers consider this overkill, and splitting the address into a fixed number of lines is sufficient. In general, we would recommend ensuring that the town and ZIP code are separately identified, just leaving additional lines for the remainder of the address. Occasionally, too much subdivision is a bad thing.

Assuming a simplified design for our address columns, we get the following for the customer table columns:

**Customer**

Title

Fname

Lname

Addressline

Town

Zipcode

Phone

Our item (Product Information) table is already very close to having columns described:

**Item**

Description

Buy price

Sell price

Barcodes (may be several)

Stock quantity

Notice that we have postponed the problem of multiple barcodes per item for now. We will return to this later.

Our order table is similar:

**Order**

Items ordered

Quantity of each item

Date placed

Date delivered

Shipping information

We have again postponed the details of some issues, such as multiple products being put on the same order. It's clear we will need to further break down this table before we can implement it in a real database.

# Determining Relationships and Cardinality

At this point, you should have a list of the main entities, and although it might not be a complete list, it should be at least a reasonable first pass at the main attributes for each entity. Now comes an important phase in designing a database: breaking out those attributes that can occur several times for each entity and deciding how the different entities relate to each other. This is often referred to as *cardinality*.

Some people like to consider the relationships even before generating an attribute list. We find that listing the main attributes helps in understanding the entities, so we perform that step first. There is no definitive right and wrong way; use whichever works best for you.

## Drawing Relationship Diagrams

With databases, a graphical representation of the structure of the data can be extremely helpful in understanding the design. At this stage, you are working on what is termed a *conceptual model*. You are not yet concerned about the finer implementation detail, but more about the logical structure of our data. In a conceptual data model, tables are shown as boxes, with relationships between the tables shown using lines, with symbols at the end of the line indicating the type of relationship, or the cardinality. Relationships between tables are always in two directions; therefore, there will always be a symbol at each end, and you read the diagram toward the table of interest. The symbols we will be using here are shown in Table 12-1.

---

■**Note**  There are many different diagramming techniques and styles in use in database circles. We will use a common notation; you will find other notation styles in use.

---

**Table 12-1.** *Cardinality Symbols*

| Relationship | Symbol |
|---|---|
| Zero or one | <br>Table |
| Exactly one | <br>Table |
| Zero or many | <br>Table |
| One or many | <br>Table |

Suppose we had a relationship between two tables, A and B, as shown in Figure 12-1.

**Figure 12-1.** *Simple relationship between two tables*

This means that the tables have the following relationship:

- For each row in table A, there must be exactly one row in table B.

- For each row in table B, there can be zero, one, or many rows in table A.

For example, if table A is order and table B is customer, this would say, "For each order, there must be exactly one customer. For each customer there can be zero, one, or many orders."

Now that we have the basics of the diagram elements for drawing table relationships, we can look at our example with customers, orders, and products. Our customer table has no multiple attributes, so we can leave it alone for now. Let's tackle our item table next, as this is reasonably straightforward.

Our only difficulty with the item table is that each item could have more than one barcode. As we discussed earlier in the book, having an unknown number of repeating columns in a database table is not generally possible. (PostgreSQL does have an array data type, but that is quite unusual and should be used with caution; we prefer to stick to standard column types.) Suppose most items have two barcodes, but some have three, so we decide that an easy solution is to add three columns to the item table: barcode1, barcode2, and barcode3. This seems like a nice solution to the problem, but it doesn't stand up to closer scrutiny. What happens when a product comes along that has four barcodes? Do we redesign our database structure to add a fourth barcode column? How many columns are "enough"? As we saw in Chapter 2, having repeated columns is very inflexible, and is almost always the wrong solution.

Another solution we might think of is to have a variable-length string, and "hide" barcodes in that string, perhaps separated by a character we know doesn't typically appear in barcodes, such as a semicolon. Again, this is a very bad solution, because we have stored many pieces of information in the same location. As with a good spreadsheet, it's very important to ensure that each entity is stored separately, so entities can be processed independently.

We need to separate the repeating information—the barcodes—into a new table. That way, we can arrange to store an arbitrary number of barcodes for each item. While we are breaking out the barcode, we also need to consider the relationship between an item and a barcode. Thinking from the item side first, we know that each item could have no barcodes, one barcode, or many barcodes. Thinking from the barcode end, we know that each barcode must be associated with exactly one item. A barcode on a product is always the lowest level of identifier, identifying different versions of products, such as promotional packs or overfill packs, while the core product remains the same. We can draw this relationship as shown in Figure 12-2.

**Figure 12-2.** *The relationship between item and barcode entities*

This shows that each item can have zero, one, or many barcodes, but a barcode belongs to exactly one item. Notice that we have not identified any columns to join the two tables. This will come later. The important thing at this point is to determine relationships, not how we will enforce them in the database.

Now we can move on to the order table, which is slightly harder to analyze. The first problem is how to represent the products that have been ordered. Often, orders will consist of more than one product, so we know that we have a repeating set of information relating to orders. As before, this means that we must separate the products being ordered into another table. We will call our main order table orderinfo, and call the table we split out to hold the products ordered `orderline`, since we can imagine each row of this table corresponding to a line on a paper order.

Now we need to think about the relationship between the `orderinfo` and `orderline` tables. It makes no sense to have an order for nothing, or to prevent a single order from having multiple items, so we know that `orderinfo` to `orderline` must have a one-to-many relationship. Thinking about an `orderline`, we realize that each `orderline` must relate to exactly one actual order, so the relationship between the two is that for each `orderline` entry, there must be exactly one `orderinfo` entry. Figure 12-3 illustrates this relationship.

**Figure 12-3.** *The initial design for the orderline to orderinfo relationship*

If you think about this a little more carefully, you can see a possible snag. When people go into a shop, they do not generally order things one at a time:

- I'd like a coffee please.
- I'd like a coffee please.
- I'd like a donut please.
- I'd like a milkshake please.
- I'd like a coffee please.
- I'd like a donut please.

They are much more likely to express their order as follows:

I'd like three coffees and two donuts and a milkshake please.

Currently, our design copes perfectly with the first situation, but it can cope with the second situation only by converting it to the many single lines situation.

Now we might decide this is okay, but if we are going to print out an order for a large round of coffees, milkshakes, and donuts, it's going to look a bit silly to the customer if each item has a separate line. We are also making life difficult for ourselves if we do a discount on multiple items ordered at the same time. For these reasons, we decide it would be better to store a quantity against each line, as shown in Figure 12-4. This way, we can store each type of product in an order only once, and store the quantity of the product required in a separate column.

**Figure 12-4.** *The corrected design for the orderline to orderinfo relationship*

Now we have a basic conceptual design for all our entities, as shown in Figure 12-5. It's time to relate them to each other.

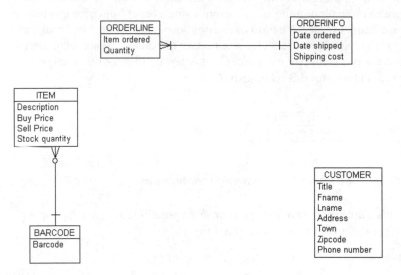

**Figure 12-5.** *First full set of entities*

We can see that we have three core groups of entities, and look at how the three groups relate to each other. In this simple database, it's immediately obvious that customer rows must relate to orderinfo rows. Looking at the relationship between items and orders, we can see that the relationship is not between the orderinfo and the item, it is between the orderline and the item.

How exactly do customers relate to orders? Clearly, each order must relate to a single customer, and each customer could have many orders, but could a customer have no orders? Although not very likely, it could happen, perhaps while a customer account is being set up, so we will allow the possibility of a customer with no orders.

Similarly, we must define the exact relationship between item and orderline. Each orderline is for an item, so this relationship is exactly one. In the opposite direction, item to orderline, any individual item could have never been ordered, or could appear on many different order lines, so the relationship is zero or many. Adding these relationships gives us Figure 12-6.

We now have what we believe to be a complete map of all the major entities and their most important attributes, broken down where we think we need to store them in individual columns, and a diagram showing the relationship between them. We have our first conceptual database design.

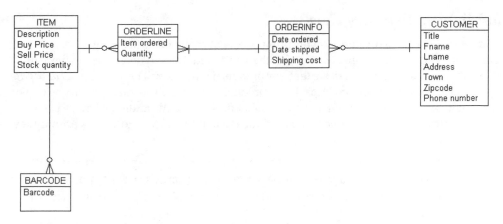

**Figure 12-6.** *The full conceptual data model*

### Validating the Conceptual Design

At this point, it's vital that you stop and validate your initial conceptual design. A mistake at this stage will be much harder to correct later. It is a well-known tenet of software engineering that the earlier you find an error, the less it costs to fix. Some studies have suggested that the cost of correcting an error increases by a factor of ten for each stage in the development process. Invest in getting the requirements capture correct and the initial design right.

This doesn't mean you can't take an iterative approach if you prefer, but it is a little harder with database design. This is because after the first iteration, you may have significant volumes of live data in your database. Migrating this data to a later design can be challenging in its own right, never mind the application developers not being impressed with needing changes in their code to handle an "improvement" in the underlying database design!

If you have access to the future users of the system, this is the point at which you should go back and talk to them. Show them the diagram, and explain to them what it means, step by step, to check that what you have designed conforms to their expectations of the system. If your design is partially based on an existing database, go back and revisit the original, to check that you have not missed anything vital. Most users will understand a basic entity relationship diagram such as this, provided that you sit with them and talk them through it. Not only does it help you validate the design, but it also makes users feel involved and consulted in the development.

# Converting to a Physical Model

Once you have a logical model of the data, which has been checked for logical correctness, you can start to move toward a physical representation of this design. This stage also has several steps.

## Establishing Primary Keys

The first step is usually to decide what the primary keys of each table will be. Here, we will work through our tables one at a time, considering them individually, and decide which piece of data (attribute) in each row will make that row unique, if any. We will be generating *candidate keys*—possible data items that make each row uniquely identifiable—and then picking one of the candidate keys to be the *primary key*. If we can't find any good candidate keys, we may resort to a logical primary key, which is an attribute created specifically to act as a primary key.

---

■**Tip** If you do find that you need to create a special key to act as a primary key, this may be an indication that your attribute list is not complete. It's always worth revisiting your attribute list if you find there is no obvious primary key.

---

We will first check for a single column that will be unique, and then look for combinations that will be unique. We must also check that none of the columns in our candidate key could ever be NULL. It would make no sense to have a primary key whose value, or part of whose value, could be unknown. Indeed, SQL databases, including PostgreSQL, will automatically enforce the restriction that you may not store a NULL value in a column being used as a primary key.

When looking for columns to use as a primary key, be aware that the shorter the field length, the more efficient searching for particular values will be and the smaller the overhead in the database will be. When you make a column a primary key, an index is constructed for that column, both to enforce the requirement that its values are unique and also to enable the database to find values in the column efficiently.

Generally, tables are searched using their primary key columns far more often than any other column, so it is important that this can be done efficiently. You can imagine that searching a column for a description that is 1,000 characters long will be much slower than searching for a particular integer value. Having a primary key column that has many characters also makes the index tree that must be built very large, adding to the overhead. For these reasons, it is important that you try to choose columns with small fields as primary keys; integer values are ideal, short strings, particularly fixed-length strings, are tolerable. Using other data types as primary key columns is usually best avoided.

Now let's identify primary keys for the tables in our sample database:

**barcode table:** This is straightforward. We have only one column, and there is only one candidate key: barcode. Barcodes are unique, and generally short; therefore, this candidate key makes a good primary key.

**customer table:** It's reasonably easy to see that no single column will give us a unique key for each row, so we move on to look at combinations of columns we might use. Let's consider some possibilities:

- First names and last name combined. This might be unique, but we can't be certain we will never have two customers with the same name.

- Last name and ZIP code. This is better, but still not guaranteed to be unique, since there could be a husband and wife who are both customers.

- First name, last name, and ZIP code. This is probably unique, but again not a certainty. It's also rather messy and inefficient to need to use three columns to get to a unique key. One is much preferable, though we will accept two.

There is no clear candidate key for the customer table, so we will need to generate a logical key that is unique for each customer. To be consistent, we will always name logical keys `<table name>_id`, which gives us customer_id.

**orderinfo table:** This table has exactly the same problem as the customer table. There is no clear way of uniquely identifying each row, so again, we will create a key: orderinfo_id.

**item table:** We could use the description here, but descriptions could be quite a large text string, and long text strings do not make good keys, since they are slow to search. There is also a small risk that descriptions might not always be unique, even though they probably should be. Again, we will create a key: item_id.

**orderline table:** This table sits between the orderinfo table and the item table. If we decide that any particular item will appear on an order only once, because we handle multiple items on the same order using a quantity column, we could consider the item to be a candidate key. In practice, this won't work, because if two different customers order the same item, it will appear in two different orderline rows. We know that we will need to find some way of relating each orderline row to its parent order in orderinfo, and since there is no column present yet that can do this, we know we will need to add one. We can postpone briefly the problem of candidate keys in the orderline table, and come back to it in a moment.

## Establishing Foreign Keys

After establishing primary keys, you can work on the mechanism to use to relate the tables together. The conceptual model shows the way the tables relate to each other, and you have also established what uniquely identifies each row in a table. When you establish foreign keys, often all you need to do is ensure that the column you have in one table identified as a primary key also appears in all the other tables that are directly related to that table.

After adjusting some column names in our tables to make them a little more meaningful, and changing the relationship lines to a physical model version, where we simply draw an arrow that points at the "must exist" table, we have a diagram that looks like Figure 12-7.

Notice how the diagram has changed from the conceptual model as we move to the physical model. Now we are showing information about how tables could be physically related, not about the cardinality of those relationships. We have shown the primary key columns underlined.

Don't worry about the data types or sizes for columns yet; that will be a later step. We have deliberately left all the column types as char(10). We will revisit the type and sizes of all the columns shortly.

For now, we need to work out how to relate tables. Usually, this simply entails checking that the primary key in the "must exist" table also exists in the table that is related to it. In this case, we needed to add customer_id to orderinfo, orderinfo_id to orderline, and item_id to barcode.

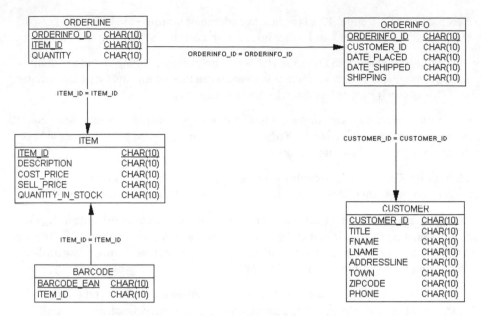

**Figure 12-7.** *Initial conversion to a physical data model*

Notice the orderline table in Figure 12-7. We can see that the combination of item_id and orderinfo_id will always be unique. Adding in the extra column we need has solved our missing primary key problem.

We have one last optimization to make to our schema. We know that, for our particular business, we have a very large number of items, but wish to keep only a few of them in stock. This means that for our item table, quantity_in_stock will almost always be zero. For just a single column, this is unimportant, but consider the problem if we wanted to store a large amount of information for a stocked item, such as the date it arrived at the warehouse, a warehouse location, expiry dates, and batch numbers. These columns would always be empty for unstocked items. For the purposes of demonstration, we will separate the stock information from the item information, and hold it in its own table. This is sometimes referred to as a *subsidiary* table.

Our physical design, with relationships added, primary keys defined (shown as underlined), and the stock information broken out, looks like Figure 12-8.

Notice we have been careful to ensure that all related columns have the same name. We didn't need to do this. We could have had a customer_ident in the orderinfo table that matched customer_id in the customer table. However, as we stressed earlier, database designs that emphasize consistency are much easier to work with. So, unless there are very good reasons to do otherwise, we strongly urge you to keep column names identical for columns that are related to each other.

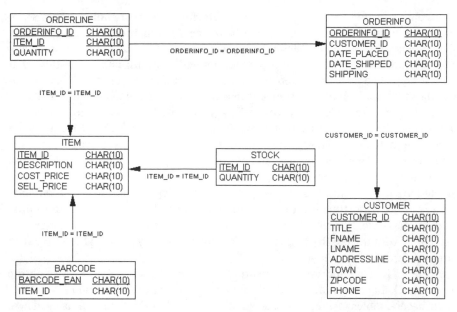

**Figure 12-8.** *Conversion to physical data model with stock as a subsidiary table*

It's also a good idea to be consistent in your naming. If you need an ident column as a primary key for a table, then stick to a naming rule, preferably one that is `<table name>_<something>`. It doesn't matter if you use id, ident, key, or pk as the suffix. What is important is that the naming is consistent across the database.

## Establishing Data Types

Once you have the tables, columns, and relationships, you can work through each table in turn, adding data types to each column. At this stage, you also need to identify any columns that will need to accept NULL values, and declare the remaining columns as NOT NULL. Notice that we start from the assumption that columns should be declared NOT NULL, and look for exceptions. This is a better approach than assuming NULL is allowed, because, as explained in Chapter 2, NULL values in columns are often hard to handle, so you should minimize their occurrence where you can.

Generally, columns to be used as primary keys or foreign keys should be set to a native data type that can be efficiently stored and processed, such as integer. PostgreSQL will automatically enforce a constraint to prevent primary keys from storing NULL values.

Assigning a data type for currency is often a difficult choice. Some people prefer a money type, if the database supports it. PostgreSQL does have a money type, but the documentation urges people to use numeric instead, which is what we have chosen to do in our sample database. You should generally avoid using a type with undefined rounding characteristics, such as a floating-point type like float(P). Fixed-precision types, such as numeric(P,S), are much safer for working with financial information, because the rounding behavior is defined.

For text strings, there are a wide choice of options. When you know the length of a field exactly, and it is a fixed length, such as barcode, you will generally choose a char(N) type, where N is the required length. For other short text strings, we also prefer to us fixed-length strings, such as char(4) for a title. This is largely a matter of preference, however, and it would be just as valid to use a variable-length type for these strings.

For variable-length text columns, PostgreSQL has the text type, which supports variable-length character strings. Unfortunately, this is not standard and, although similar extensions do appear in other databases, the ISO/ANSI definition defines only a varchar(N) text type, where N specifies a maximum length of the string. We value portability quite highly, so we stick with the more standard varchar(N) type.

Again consistency is very important. Make sure all your numeric type fields have exactly the same precision. Check that commonly used columns such as description and name, which might appear in several tables in your database, aren't defined differently (and thus used in different ways) in each. The fewer unique types and character lengths that you need to use, the easier your database will be to manage.

Let's work through the customer table, seeing how we assign types. The first thing to do is give a type to customer_id. It's a column we added specially to be a primary key, so we can make it efficient by using an integer type. Titles will be things like Mr, Mrs, or Dr. This is always a short string of characters; therefore, we make it a char(4) type. Some designers prefer to always use varchar to reduce the number of types being used, and that would also be a perfectly valid choice. It's possible not to know someone's title, so we will allow this field to store NULL values.

We then come to fname and lname, for first and last names. It's unlikely these ever need to exceed 32 characters, but we know the length will be quite variable, so we make them both varchar(32). We also decide that we could accept fname being a NULL, but not lname. Not knowing a customer's last name seems unreasonable.

In this database, we have chosen to keep all the address parts together, in a single long field. As was discussed earlier, this is probably oversimplified for the real world, but addresses are always a design challenge; there is no fixed right answer. You need to do what is appropriate for each particular design.

Notice that we store phone as a character string. It is almost always a mistake to store phone numbers as numbers in a database, because that approach does not allow international dialing codes to be stored. For example, +44 (0)116 … would be a common way of representing a United Kingdom dialing code, where the country code is 44, but if you are already in the United Kingdom, you need to add a 0 before the area code, rather than dialing the +44. Also, storing a number with leading zeros will not work in a numeric field, and in phone numbers, leading zeros are very important.

We continue assigning types to columns in this way. The final type allocation for our physical database design is shown in Figure 12-9.

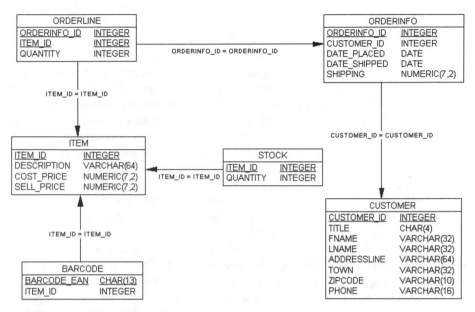

**Figure 12-9.** *Final conversion to physical data model*

## Completing the Table Definitions

At this point, you should go back and double-check that all the information you wish to store in the database is present. All the entities should be represented, and all the attributes listed with appropriate types.

You may also decide to add some *lookup*, or *static data*, tables. For example, in our sample database, we might have a lookup table of cities or titles. Generally, these lookup tables are unrelated to any other tables, and they are simply used by the application as a convenient way of soft-coding values to offer the user. You could hard-code these options into an application, but in general, storing them in a database, from which they can be loaded into an application at runtime, makes it much easier to modify the options. Then the application doesn't need to be changed to add new options. You just need to insert additional rows in the database lookup table.

## Implementing Business Rules

After the table definitions are complete, you would write, or generate from a tool, the SQL to create the database schema. If all is well, you can implement any additional business rules.

For each rule, you must consider if it is best implemented as a constraint, as discussed in Chapter 8, or as a trigger, as shown in Chapter 10. In general, you use constraints if possible, as these are much easier to work with. Some examples of constraints that we might wish to use in our simple database were shown in Chapter 10.

## Checking the Design

By now, you should have a database implemented, complete with constraints and possibly triggers to enforce business rules. Before handing over your completed work, and celebrating a job well done, it's time to test your database again. Just because a database isn't code in the conventional sense doesn't mean you can't test it. Testing is a necessity, not an optional extra!

Get some sample data, if possible part of the live data that will go into the database. Insert some of these sample rows. Check that attempting to insert NULL values into columns you don't think should ever be NULL results in an error. Attempt to delete data that is referenced by other data. Try to manipulate data to break the business rules you have implemented as triggers or constraints. Write some SQL to join tables together to generate the kind of data you would expect to find on reports.

Once your database has gone into production, it is difficult to update your design. Anything other than a minor change probably means stopping the system, unloading live data into text files, updating the database design, and reloading the data. This is not something you want to undertake any more than absolutely necessary. Similarly, once faulty data has been loaded into a table, you will often find it is referenced by other data and difficult to correct or remove from the database. Time spent testing the design before it goes live is time well spent.

If possible, go back to your intended users and show them the sample data being extracted from the database, and how you can manipulate it. Even at this belated stage, there is much to be gained by discovering an error, even a minor one, before the system goes live.

# Normal Forms

No chapter on database design would be complete without a mention of *normal forms* and *database normalization*. We have left these toward the end of the chapter, since they are rather dry when presented on their own. Now that we have walked through the design stages, you should see how the final design has conformed to these rules.

What is commonly considered the origins of database normalization is a paper written by E.F. Codd in 1969, published in *Communications of the ACM*, Vol. 13, No. 6, June 1970. In later work, various normal forms were defined. Each normal form builds on previous rules and applies more stringent requirements to the design.

In classic normalization theory, there are five normal forms, although others have been defined, such as Boyce-Codd normal form. You will be pleased to learn that only the first three forms are commonly used, and those are the ones we will look at here.

The advantage of structuring your data so that it conforms to at least the first three normal forms is that you will find it much easier to manage. Databases that are not well normalized are almost always significantly harder to maintain and more prone to storing invalid data.

## First Normal Form

First normal form requires that each attribute in a table cannot be further subdivided and that there are no repeating groups. For example, in our database design, we separate the customer name into a title, first name, and last name. We know we may wish to use them separately, so we must consider them as individual attributes and store them separately.

The second part—no repeating groups—we saw in Chapter 2 when we looked at what happened when we tried to use a simple spreadsheet to store customers and their orders. Once a customer had more than one order, we had repeating information for that customer, and our spreadsheet no longer had the same number of rows in all columns.

If we had decided earlier to hold both first names in the fname column of our customer table, this would have violated first normal form, because the column fname would actually be holding *first names*, which are clearly divisible entities. Sometimes, you need to take a pragmatic approach and argue that, provided that you are confident you will never need to consider different first names separately, they are, for the purposes of a particular database design, a single entity. Alternatively, you could decide to store only a single first name, which is an equally valid approach and the one we took for our sample database.

Another example of violating first normal form—one that is seen with worrying frequency—is to store in a single column a character string where different character positions have different meanings. For example, characters 1 through 3 tell you the warehouse, 4 through 11 the bay, and 12 the shelf. This is a clear violation of first normal form, since you do need to consider subdivisions of the column separately. In practice, this turns out to be very hard to manage. Information being stored in this way should always be considered a design mistake, not a judicious stretching of the first normal form rule.

## Second Normal Form

Second normal form says that no information in a row must depend on only part of the primary key. Suppose in our orderline table we had stored the date that the order was placed in this table, as shown in Figure 12-10.

```
        ORDERLINE
ORDERINFO ID   INTEGER
ITEM ID        INTEGER
QUANTITY       INTEGER
DATEORDERED    DATE
```

**Figure 12-10.** *Example of breaking second normal form*

Recall that our primary key for orderline is a composite of orderinfo_id and item_id. The date the order was placed depends on only the orderinfo information, not on the item ordered, so this would have violated second normal form. Sometimes, you may find you are storing data that looks as though it may violate second normal form, but in practice it does not.

Suppose we changed our prices frequently. Customers would rightly expect to pay the price shown on the day they ordered, not on the day it was shipped. In order to do this, we would need to store the selling price in the orderline table to record the price in effect on the day the order was placed. This would not violate second normal form, because the price stored in the orderline table would depend on both the item and the actual order.

## Third Normal Form

Third normal form is very similar to second normal form, but more general. It says that no information in a column that is not the primary key can depend on anything except the primary key. This is often stated as, "Non-key values must depend on the key, the whole key, and nothing but the key."

Suppose in our `customer` table we had stored a customer's age and date of birth, as shown in Figure 12-11. This would violate third normal form, because the customer's age depends on the date of birth, a non-key column, as well as the actual customer, which is given by `customer_id`, the primary key.

```
          CUSTOMER
 CUSTOMER ID   INTEGER
 TITLE         CHAR(4)
 FNAME         VARCHAR(32)
 LNAME         VARCHAR(32)
 ADDRESSLINE   VARCHAR(64)
 TOWN          VARCHAR(32)
 ZIPCODE       CHAR(10)
 PHONE         VARCHAR(16)
 AGE           INTEGER
 DATEOFBIRTH   DATE
```

**Figure 12-11.** *Example of breaking third normal form*

Although putting your database into third normal form (making its structure conform to all of the first three normalization rules) is almost always the preferred solution, there are occasions when it's necessary to break the rules. This is called *denormalizing* the database, and is occasionally necessary to improve performance. You should always design a fully normalized database first, however, and denormalize it only if you know that you have a serious problem with performance.

# Common Patterns

In database design, there are a number of common patterns that occur over and over again. It's useful to recognize these patterns, because they generally can be solved in the same way. Here, we will look briefly at three standard problems that have standard solutions.

## Many-to-Many

You have two entities, which seem to have a many-to-many relationship between them. It is never correct to implement a many-to-many table relationship in the physical database, so you need to break the relationship down further.

The solution is almost always to insert an additional table, a link table, between the two tables that apparently have a many-to-many relationship. Suppose we had two tables, `author` and `book`. Each author could have written many books, and each book, like this one, could have had contributions from more than one author. How do we represent this in a physical database?

The solution is to insert a table in between the other two tables. This link table normally contains the primary key of each of the other tables. For the author and book example, we would create a new table, `bookauthor`. As shown in Figure 12-12, this new table has a composite primary key, where each component is the primary key of one of the other tables.

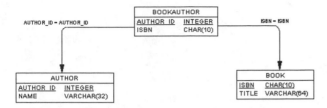

**Figure 12-12.** *Many-to-many relationship*

Now each author can appear in the author table exactly once, but have many entries in the bookauthor table, one for each book the author has written. Each book appears exactly once in the book table, but can appear in the bookauthor table more than once, if the book has more than one author. However, each individual entry in the bookauthor table is unique—the combination of book and author occurs only once.

## Hierarchy

Another frequent pattern is a hierarchy. This can appear in many different guises. Suppose we have many shops, each shop is in a geographic area, and these areas are grouped into larger areas known as regions. It might be tempting to use the design shown in Figure 12-13, where each shop stores the area and region in which it resides.

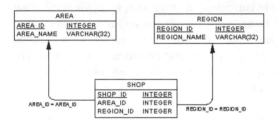

**Figure 12-13.** *Flawed hierarchy*

Although this might work, it's not ideal. Once we know the area, we also know the region, so storing both the area and region in the shop table is violating third normal form. The region stored in the shop table depends on the area, which is not the primary key for the shop table. A much better design is shown in Figure 12-14. This design correctly shows the hierarchy of shop in an area, which is itself in a region.

It may still be that you need to denormalize this ideal design for performance reasons, storing the region_id in the shop table. In this case, you should write a trigger to ensure that the region_id stored in the shop table is always correctly aligned with that found by looking for the region via the area table. This approach would add cost to the design, and increase the complexity of insertions and updates, in order to reduce the database query costs.

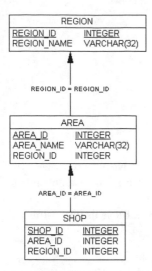

**Figure 12-14.** *Better hierarchy*

## Recursive Relationships

The recursive relationship pattern is not quite as common as the other two, but occurs frequently in a couple of situations: representing the hierarchy of staff in a company and *parts explosion*, where parts in an item-type table are themselves composed of other parts from the same table.

Let's consider the staff example. All staff, from the most junior to senior managers, have many attributes in common, such as name, phone number, employee number, salary, grades, and address. Therefore, it seems logical to have a single table that is common to all members of staff to store those details. How do we then store the hierarchy of management, particularly as different areas of the company may have a different number of levels of management to be represented?

One answer is a recursive relationship, where each entry for a staff member in the person table stores a manager_id, to record the person who is their manager. The clever bit is that the managers' information is stored in the same person table, generating a recursive relationship. So, to find a person's manager, we pick up their manager_id, and look back in the same table for that to appear as an emp_id. We have stored a complex relationship, with an arbitrary number of levels, in a simple one-table structure, as illustrated in Figure 12-15.

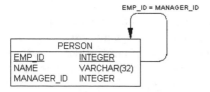

**Figure 12-15.** *Recursive relationship*

Suppose we wanted to represent a slightly more complex hierarchy, such as shown in Figure 12-16.

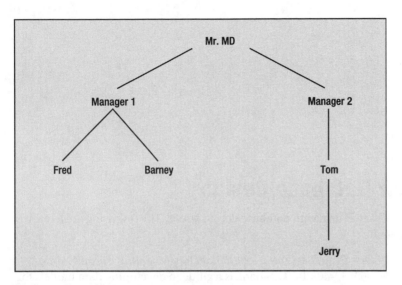

**Figure 12-16.** *Simple office hierarchy*

We would insert rows like this:

```
test=> INSERT INTO person(emp_id, name, manager_id) VALUES(1, 'Mr MD', NULL);
test=> INSERT INTO person(emp_id, name, manager_id) VALUES(2, 'Manager1', 1);
test=> INSERT INTO person(emp_id, name, manager_id) VALUES(3, 'Manager2', 1);
test=> INSERT INTO person(emp_id, name, manager_id) VALUES(4, 'Fred', 2);
test=> INSERT INTO person(emp_id, name, manager_id) VALUES(5, 'Barney', 2);
test=> INSERT INTO person(emp_id, name, manager_id) VALUES(6, 'Tom', 3);
test=> INSERT INTO person(emp_id, name, manager_id) VALUES(7, 'Jerry', 6);
```

Notice that the first number, emp_id, is unique, but the second number is the emp_id of the manager next up the hierarchy. For example, Tom has an emp_id of 6, but a manager_id of 3, the emp_id of Manager2, since this is his manager. Mr. MD doesn't have a manager, so the link to his manager is NULL.

This is fine, until we need to extract data from this hierarchy; that is, when we need to join the person table to itself, a *self join*. To do this, we need to alias the table names, as explained in Chapter 7. We can write the SQL like this:

```
test=> SELECT n1.name AS "Manager", n2.name AS "Subordinate" FROM person n1,
test-> person n2 WHERE n1.emp_id = n2.manager_id;
```

We are creating two alternative names for the person table, n1 and n2, and then we can join the emp_id column to the manager_id column. We also name our columns, using AS, to make the output more meaningful. This gives us a complete list of the hierarchy in our person table:

```
Manager     | Subordinate
------------+-------------
Mr MD       | Manager1
Mr MD       | Manager2
Manager1    | Fred
Manager1    | Barney
Manager2    | Tom
Tom         | Jerry
(6 rows)
```

# Resources for Database Design

There are many good books that deal with database design issues. The following are a few we consider particularly helpful:

- Allen, Sharon, and Terry, Evan, *Beginning Relational Data Modeling, Second Edition* (Apress, 2005; ISBN 1-59059-463-0). This book is a guide to developing data models for relational databases.

- Hernandez, Michael J., *Database Design for Mere Mortals: A Hands-On Guide to Relational Database Design, Second Edition* (Addison-Wesley, 2003; ISBN 0-20175-284-0). This book covers obtaining design information, documenting it, and designing databases in detail.

- Bowman, Judith S.; Emerson, Sandra L.; and Darnovsky, Marcy, *The Practical SQL Handbook: Using Structured Query Language* (Addison-Wesley, 1996; ISBN 0-20144-787-8). This book has a short, but very well-written, section on database design. It is also a good general-purpose book on how to write SQL.

- Pascal, Fabian, *Practical Issues in Database Management: A Reference for the Thinking Practitioner* (Addison-Wesley, 2000; ISBN: 0-20148-555-9). This book is aimed at the more experienced user. It tackles some of the more difficult issues that arise in relational database design.

# Summary

In this chapter, we took a brief look at database design, from capturing requirements, through generating a conceptual design, and finally converting the conceptual design into a physical database design or schema. Along the way, we covered selecting candidate keys, primary keys, and foreign keys. We also looked at choosing data types for our columns, and talked about the importance of consistency in database design.

We briefly mentioned normal forms, an important foundation of good design with relational databases. Finally, we looked at three common problem patterns that appear in database design, and how they are conventionally solved.

In the next chapter, we will begin to look at ways to build client applications using PostgreSQL, starting with the libpq library, which allows access to PostgreSQL from C.

# CHAPTER 13

■ ■ ■

# Accessing PostgreSQL from C Using libpq

In this chapter, we are going to begin examining ways to create client applications for PostgreSQL. Up until now in this book, we have mostly used either command-line applications such as psql that are part of the PostgreSQL distribution, or graphical tools such as pgAdmin III that have been developed specifically for PostgreSQL. In Chapter 5, we learned how general-purpose tools such as Microsoft Access and Excel can also be used to view and update data via ODBC links, and to create applications. If we want complete control over our client applications, we can consider creating custom interfaces. That's where libpq comes in.

Recall that a PostgreSQL system is built around a client/server model. Client programs, such as psql and pgAdmin III, could run on one machine, maybe a desktop PC running Windows, and the PostgreSQL server itself could run on a UNIX or Linux server. The client programs send requests across a network to the server. These messages are effectively the same as the SELECT or other SQL statements that we have used in psql. The server sends back result sets, which the client then displays.

Messages that are conveyed between PostgreSQL clients and the server are formatted and transported according to a particular protocol. The client/server protocol (which has no official name, but is sometimes referred to as the Frontend/Backend protocol) makes sure that appropriate action is taken if messages get lost, and it ensures that results are always fully delivered. It can also cope, to a degree, with client and server version mismatches. Clients developed with PostgreSQL release 6.4 or later should interoperate with future versions without too many problems.

Routines for sending and receiving these messages are included in the libpq library. To write a client application, all we need to do is use these routines and link our application with the library. For the purposes of this chapter, we are going to assume some knowledge of the C programming language.

The functions provided by the libpq library fall into three categories:

- Database connection and connection management

- SQL statement execution

- Retrieval of query result sets

As with many products that have grown and evolved over many releases, there is often more than one way of doing the same thing in libpq. In this chapter, we will concentrate on the most common methods and provide hints concerning any alternatives and instances where they might be particularly applicable.

# Using the libpq Library

All PostgreSQL client applications that use the libpq library must be written so that the source code includes the appropriate header file that defines the functions libpq provides, and the application must be linked with the correct library, which contains the code for those functions.

Client applications are known as *front-end* programs to PostgreSQL and must include the header file libpq-fc.h (the fe is for front-end). This header file provides definitions of the libpq functions and hides the internal workings of PostgreSQL that may change between releases. Sticking with libpq-fe.h will ensure that programs will compile with future releases of libpq. The header files are installed in the include subdirectory of the PostgreSQL installation (on UNIX and Linux, the default is /usr/local/pgsql/include). We need to direct the C compiler to this directory so that it can find the header files using the -I option.

---

■**Note** The header file libpq-int.h that is also provided with the PostgreSQL distribution includes definitions of the internal structures that libpq uses, but it is not recommended that it be used in normal client applications.

---

The libpq library will be installed in the lib directory of the PostgreSQL installation (the default is /usr/local/pgsql/lib). To incorporate the libpq functions in an application, we need to link against that library. The simplest way to do this is to tell the compiler to link with -lpq and specify the PostgreSQL library directory as a place to look for libraries by using the -L option.

A typical libpq program has this structure:

```
#include <libpq-fe.h>

main()
{
  /* Connect to a PostgreSQL database */

  LOOP:
  /* Execute SQL statement */
    /* Read query results */

  /* Disconnect from database */
}
```

The program would be compiled and linked into an executable program by using a command line similar to this:

```
gcc -o program program.c -I/usr/local/pgsql/include -L/usr/local/pgsql/lib -lpq
```

If you are using a PostgreSQL installation that is part of a Linux distribution, such as Red Hat Linux, you may find that the libpq library is installed in a location that the compiler searches by default, so you need to specify only the include directory option, like this:

```
$ gcc -o program program.c -I/usr/local/pgsql/include -lpq
```

Other Linux distributions and other platform installations may place the include files and libraries in different places. Generally, they will be in the include and lib directories of the base PostgreSQL install directory.

Later in this chapter, we'll see how using a makefile can make building PostgreSQL applications a little easier.

# Making Database Connections

In general, a PostgreSQL client application may connect to one or more databases as it runs. In fact, we can even connect to many databases managed by many different servers, all at the same time. The libpq library provides functions to create and maintain these connections.

When we connect to a PostgreSQL database on a server, libpq returns a handle to that database connection. This is represented by an internal structure defined in the header file as PGconn, and we can think of it as analogous to a file handle. Many of the libpq functions require a PGconn pointer argument to identify the target database connection, in much the same way that the standard I/O library in C uses a FILE pointer.

## Creating a New Database Connection

We create a new database connection using PQconnectdb, as follows:

```
PGconn *PQconnectdb(const char *conninfo);
```

The PQconnnectdb function returns a pointer to the new connection descriptor. The return result will be NULL if a new descriptor could not be allocated, perhaps because there was a lack of memory to allocate the new descriptor. A non-NULL pointer returned from PQconnectdb does not mean that the connection succeeded, however. We need to check the state of the connection, as described shortly.

The single argument to PQconnectdb is a string that specifies to which database to connect. Embedded in it are various options we can use to modify the way the connection is made. The conninfo string argument consists of space-separated options of the form *option=value*. The most commonly used options and their meanings are listed in Table 13-1. The table also shows the environment variable used by default when a connection option is not specified. We will return to the use of environment variables a little later in the chapter.

**Table 13-1.** *Common PQconnectdb Connection Options*

| Option | Meaning | Environment Variable Default |
|--------|---------|------------------------------|
| dbname | Database to connect to | $PGDATABASE or name of user if not set |
| user | Username to use when connecting | $PGUSER or name of user if not set |
| password | Password for the specified user | $PGPASSWORD or none if not set |
| host | Name of the server to connect to | $PGHOST or localhost if not set |
| hostaddr | IP address of the server to connect to | $PGHOSTADDR |
| port | TCP/IP port to connect to on the server | $PGPORT or 5432 if not set |

For example, to connect to the bpfinal database on the local machine, we would use a conninfo string like this:

```
"dbname=bpfinal"
```

To include spaces in option values, or to enter an empty value, the value must be quoted with single quotes, like this:

```
"host=beast password='' user=neil"
```

The host option names the server we want to connect to. The PQconnectdb call will result in a name lookup to determine the IP address of the server, so that the connection can be made. Usually, this is done by using the Domain Name Service (DNS) and can take a short while to complete. If you already know the IP address of the server, you can use the hostaddr option to specify the address and avoid any delay while a name lookup takes place. The format of the hostaddr value is a *dotted quad*, the normal way of writing an IP address as four byte values separated by dots:

```
"hostaddr=192.168.0.111 dbname=neil"
```

If no host or hostaddr option is specified, PQconnectdb will try to connect to the local machine.

By default, a PostgreSQL server will listen for client connections on TCP port 5432. If you need to connect to a server listening on a nondefault port number, you can specify this with the port option.

### Connecting Using Environment Variables

The options can also be specified by using environment variables, as listed in Table 13-1. For example, if no host option is set in the conninfo argument, then PQconnectdb will interrogate the environment to see if the variable PGHOST is set. If it is, the value $PGHOST will be used as the host name to connect to. We could code a client program to call PQconnectdb with an empty string and provide all the options by environment variables:

```
#include <libpq-fe.h>

int main()
{
  PGconn *conn = PQconnectdb("");
  ...
}
```

We could then assign a few environment variables and execute the program like so:

```
$ PGHOST=beast PGUSER=neil ./program
```

## Checking the State of the Connection

As mentioned earlier, the fact that PQconnectdb returns a non-NULL connection handle does not mean that the connection was made without error.

We need to use another function, PQstatus, to check the state of our connection:

```
ConnStatusType PQstatus(const PGconn *conn);
```

ConnStatusType is an enumerated type that includes (among others) the constants CONNECTION_OK and CONNECTION_BAD. PQconnectdb will return one of these two values, depending on whether or not the connection succeeded. The other status values in ConnStatusType are used for alternative connection methods, such as connecting asynchronously using PQconnectStart, as discussed in the "Working Asynchronously" section later in this chapter.

## Closing a Connection

When we have finished with a database connection, we must close it, just as we would with open file descriptors. We do this by passing the connection descriptor pointer to PQfinish:

```
void PQfinish(PGconn *conn);
```

A call to PQfinish allows the libpq library to release resources being consumed by the connection.

## Resetting a Connection

If problems arise with a connection, it may be useful to attempt to reset it. The PQreset function is provided for this purpose. It will close the connection to the back-end server and try to make a new connection with the same parameters that were used in the original connection setup:

```
void PQreset(PGconn *conn);
```

## Writing a Connection Program

We can now write possibly the shortest useful PostgreSQL program (connect.c), which can be used to check whether a connection can be made to a particular database. We will use environment variables to pass options in to PQconnectdb, but we could consider using command-line arguments or even hard-coding if it were appropriate for our application.

```
#include <stdlib.h>
#include <libpq-fe.h>

int main()
{
  PGconn *myconnection = PQconnectdb("");
  if(PQstatus(myconnection) == CONNECTION_OK)
    printf("connection made\n");
  else
    printf("connection failed\n");
  PQfinish(myconnection);
  return EXIT_SUCCESS;
}
```

Let's execute the program, first without the required options, and then after assigning the PGDATABASE and PGUSER environment variables:

```
$ gcc -o connect –I/usr/local/pgsql/include connect.c –L/usr/local/pgsql/lib -lpq
$ ./connect
connection failed
$ PGDATABASE=bpfinal PGUSER=neil ./connect
connection made
$
```

## Using a Makefile

In the preceding example, we used suitable -L and -I options to the compiler. These are always required to compile programs using libpq. If we use a makefile to control the compilation, we can add these options to the CFLAGS and LDLIBS variables, respectively. This simplifies compilation.

Here is an extremely simple makefile that can be used to compile all of the sample programs in this chapter. You can download it and the source code to the examples from the Downloads area of the Apress web site (http://www.apress.com).

```
# Makefile for sample programs
# in Beginning PostgreSQL

# Edit the base directories for your
# PostgreSQL installation

INC=/usr/local/pgsql/include
LIB=/usr/local/pgsql/lib

CFLAGS=-I$(INC)
LDLIBS=-L$(LIB) -lpq

ALL=async1 async2 connect create cursor cursor2 print select1 select2 import
```

```
all: $(ALL)

clean  :
    @rm -f  *.o *~  $(ALL)
```

Now we can build all of the programs at once by simply running make (as all of the programs are specified as dependencies of the first target in the makefile: all). We can build a single program with the command make *program* (where *program* is the name of the program we wish to build).

## Retrieving Information About Connection Errors

Note that both PQstatus and PQfinish can cope with a NULL pointer for the connection descriptor, so in our example, we did not check that the return result from PQconnectdb was valid before calling PQstatus and PQfinish. We can retrieve a readable string that describes the state of the connection or an error that has occurred by calling PQerrorMessage:

```
char *PQerrorMessage(const PGconn *conn);
```

This function returns a pointer to a descriptive string. This string will be overwritten by other libpq functions, so it should be used or copied immediately after the call to PQerrorMessage and before any call to other libpq functions.

For example, we could have made our connection failure message more helpful, like this:

```
printf("connection failed: %s", PQerrorMessage(myconnection));
```

Then we would see the following, more informative error message:

```
connection failed: FATAL:  database "neil" does not exist
```

## Learning About Connection Parameters

If we need more information about a connection after it has been made, we might consider using the members of the PGconn structure directly (defined in libpq-fe.h), but that would be a bad idea. This is because the code would probably break in some future release of libpq if the internal structure of PGconn changed. Nonetheless, we may have a genuine need to know more about the connection, so libpq provides a number of access functions that return the values of attributes of the connection:

- char *PQdb(const PGconn *conn): Returns the database name.

- char *PQuser(const PGconn *conn): Returns the username.

- char *PQpass(const PGconn *conn): Returns the user password.

- char *PQhost(const PGconn *conn): Returns the server name.

- char *PQport(const PGconn *conn): Returns the server port number.

- char *PQoptions(const PGconn *conn): Returns the options associated with a connection.

All of these values will not change during the lifetime of a connection.

# Executing SQL with libpq

Now that we can connect to a PostgreSQL database from within a C program, the next step is to execute SQL statements. The query process is initiated with the PQexec function:

```
PGresult *PQexec(PGconn *conn, const char *sql_string);
```

We pass a SQL statement to PQexec, and the server we are connected to via the non-NULL connection conn executes it. The result is communicated via a result structure, a PGresult. Even when there is no data to return, PQexec will return a valid non-NULL pointer to a result structure that contains no data records.

---

**Note** On rare occasions, PQexec may return a NULL pointer if there is not enough memory to allocate a new result structure.

---

The string we pass to PQexec may contain any valid SQL statement, including queries, insertions, updates, and database-management commands. They are the equivalent of SQL statements run with the psql command-line tool, except that we do not need a trailing semicolon in the string to mark the end of the statement. The following are some examples we will use shortly:

```
PQexec(myconnection, "SELECT customer_id FROM customer");
PQexec(myconnection, "CREATE TABLE number (value INTEGER, name VARCHAR)");
PQexec(myconnection, "INSERT INTO number VALUES (42, 'The Answer')");
```

Note that any double quotes within the SQL statement will need to be escaped with backslashes, as is necessary with psql.

As with connection structures, result objects must also be freed when we are finished with them. We can do this with PQclear, which will also handle NULL pointers. Note that results are not cleared automatically, even when the connection is closed, so they can be kept indefinitely if required:

```
void PQclear(PGresult *result);
```

## Determining Query Status

We can determine the status of the SQL statement execution by probing the result with the PQresultStatus function, which returns one of a number of values that make up the enumerated type ExecStatusType:

```
ExecStatusType PQresultStatus(const PGresult *result);
```

The most common status types are listed in Table 13-2. Other status types indicate some unexpected problem with the server, such as it being backed up or taken offline.

**Table 13-2.** *Common PQresultStatus Status Types*

| Status Type | Description |
| --- | --- |
| PGRES_EMPTY_QUERY | Database access not required; usually, the result of an empty query string. This status often points to a problem with the client program, sending a query that requires the server to do no work at all. |
| PGRES_COMMAND_OK | Success; command does not return data. This status means that the SQL executed correctly, and the statement was of the type that does not return data, such as CREATE TABLE. |
| PGRES_TUPLES_OK | Success; query returned zero or more rows. This status means that the SQL executed correctly, and the statement was of the type that may return data, such as SELECT. It does not mean that there is, in this instance, data to return. Further inquiries are necessary to determine how much data is actually available. |
| PGRES_BAD_RESPONSE | Failure; server response not understood. This indicates that the SQL failed to execute. |
| PGRES_NONFATAL_ERROR | Failure; nonfatal, can be retried. This indicates that the SQL failed to execute. |
| PGRES_FATAL_ERROR | Failure; fatal, cannot be retried. This indicates that the SQL failed to execute. |

Here's an example of a code fragment that uses PQresultStatus to determine the precise results of a call to PQexec:

```
PGresult *result;
result  = PQexec(myconnection, "SELECT customer_id FROM customer");
switch(PQresultStatus(result)) {
case PGRES_TUPLES_OK:
    /* may have some data to process, find out */
    if(PQntuples(result)) {
        /* process data */
        break;
    }
    /* no data, drop through to no data case */
case PGRES_COMMAND_OK:
    /* all OK, no data to process */
    break;
case PGRES_EMPTY_QUERY:
    /* server had nothing to do, a bug maybe? */
    break;
case PGRES_NONFATAL_ERROR:
    /* can continue, possibly retry the command */
    break;
case PGRES_BAD_RESPONSE:
case PGRES_FATAL_ERROR:
default:
    /* fatal or unknown error, cannot continue */
}
```

We will cover PQntuples in more detail when we return to the PGRES_TUPLES_OK case for SELECT, in the "Extracting Data from Query Results" section later in the chapter.

One useful function that can aid with troubleshooting is PQresStatus. This function converts a result status code into a readable string:

```
const char *PQresStatus(ExecStatusType status);
```

When an error has occurred, we can retrieve a more detailed textual error message by calling PQresultErrorMessage, in much the same way as we did for connections:

```
const char *PQresultErrorMessage(const PGresult *result);
```

## Executing Queries with PQexec

Let's look at some simple examples of executing SQL statements. We will use a very small table in our database as a way of trying things out. Later, we will perform some operations on our sample customer table to return larger amounts of data.

We are going to create a database table called number. In it, we will store numbers and an English description of them. The table will have entries like this:

```
value |    name
-------+-------------
   42 | The Answer
   29 | My Age
   29 | Anniversary
   66 | Clickety-Click
```

To create the table and insert values into it, we just need to call PQexec with an appropriate string containing the SQL query we need to execute. Our program will contain calls like this:

```
PGconn *myconnection;
...
PQexec(myconnection,"CREATE TABLE number (value INTEGER, name VARCHAR)");
PQexec(myconnection,"INSERT INTO number VALUES (42, 'The Answer')");
```

We will need to take care of errors that arise. For example, if the table already exists, we will get an error when we try to create it. In the case of creating the number table when it already exists, PQresultErrorMessage will return a string that says this:

```
ERROR:  Relation 'number' already exists
```

To make things a little easier, we will develop a function of our own to execute SQL statements, check the results, and print errors. We will add more functionality to it as we go along. The initial version follows. With it, we can execute SQL queries almost as easily as we can enter commands to psql. Save this code in a file called create.c:

```
#include<stdlib.h>
#include<libpq-fe.h>

void doSQL(PGconn *conn, char *command)
{
  PGresult *result;

  printf("%s\n", command);

  result = PQexec(conn, command);
  printf("status is %s\n", PQresStatus(PQresultStatus(result)));
  printf("result message: %s\n", PQresultErrorMessage(result));
  PQclear(result);
}

int main()
{
  PGresult *result;
  PGconn *conn;

  conn = PQconnectdb("");

  if(PQstatus(conn) == CONNECTION_OK) {
    printf("connection made\n");

    /* doSQL(conn, "DROP TABLE number"); */
    doSQL(conn, "CREATE TABLE number ( \
                   value INTEGER,      \
                   name  VARCHAR       \
              )");
    doSQL(conn, "INSERT INTO number values(42, 'The Answer')");
    doSQL(conn, "INSERT INTO number values(29, 'My Age')");
    doSQL(conn, "INSERT INTO number values(29, 'Anniversary')");
    doSQL(conn, "INSERT INTO number values(66, 'Clickety-Click')");
  }
  else
    printf("connection failed %s\n", PQerrorMessage(conn));

  PQfinish(conn);
  return EXIT_SUCCESS;
}
```

Here, we create the number table and add some entries to it. If we rerun the program, we will see a fatal error reported, as we cannot create the table a second time. Uncomment the DROP TABLE command to change the program into one that destroys and re-creates the table each time it is run.

Of course, in production code, we would not be quite so cavalier in our approach to errors. Here we have omitted returning a result from doSQL to keep things brief, and we push on regardless of failures.

When compiled and run, the program should show some execution and status information:

```
$ make create
$ PGDATABASE=bpfinal ./create
connection made
...
INSERT INTO number VALUES(66, 'Clickety-Click')
status is PGRES_COMMAND_OK
result message:
$
```

## Creating a Variable Query

To include user-specified data into the SQL, we might create a string to pass to PQexec that contains the values we want. To add all single-digit integers, we might write this:

```
for(n = 0; n < 10; n++) {
    sprintf(buffer,"INSERT INTO number VALUES(%d, 'single digit')", n);
    PQexec(buffer);
}
```

## Updating and Deleting Rows

If we want to update or delete rows in a table, we can use the UPDATE and DELETE commands, respectively:

```
UPDATE number SET name = 'Zaphod' WHERE value = 42
DELETE FROM number WHERE value = 29
```

If we were to add suitable calls to PQexec (or doSQL) to our program, these commands would first change the descriptive text of the number 42 to Zaphod, and then delete both of the entries for 29. We can check the result of our changes using psql:

```
$ psql -d bpfinal
bpfinal=# SELECT * FROM number;
 value |       name
-------+-----------------
    66 | Clickety-Click
    42 | Zaphod
(2 rows)

bpfinal=#
```

DELETE and UPDATE may affect more than one row in the table (or *tuples* as PostgreSQL likes to call them); therefore, it is often useful to know how many rows have been changed. We can get this information by calling PQcmdTuples:

```
const char *PQcmdTuples(const PGresult *result);
```

Strangely perhaps, PQcmdTuples returns not an integer as you might expect, but a string containing the digits. We can modify the doSQL function to report the rows affected very simply:

```
printf("#rows affected %s\n", PQcmdTuples(result));
```

We will now see that PQcmdTuples returns an empty string for commands that do not have any effect on rows at all—like CREATE TABLE—and the strings "1" and "2" for those that do—like INSERT and DELETE.

We must be careful to distinguish commands that genuinely affect no rows, and those that fail and therefore affect no rows. We must always check the result status to determine errors, rather than just the number of rows affected.

## Extracting Data from Query Results

Up until now, we have been concerned only with SQL statements that have not returned any data. Now it is time to consider how to deal with data returned by calls to PQexec, the results of SELECT statements.

When we perform a SELECT with PQexec, the result set will contain information about the data the query has returned. Query results can seem a little tiresome to handle, as we do not always know exactly what to expect. If we execute a SELECT, we do not know in advance whether we will be returned zero, one, or several millions of rows. If we use a wildcard (*) in the SELECT query, we do not even know which columns will be returned or what their names are. In general, we will want to program our application so that it selects specified columns only. That way, if the database design changes, perhaps when new columns are added, a function that does not rely on the new column will still work as expected.

Sometimes (for example, if we are writing a general-purpose SQL program that is accepting statements from the user and displaying results), it would be better if we could program in a general way, and with libpq, we can. There are just a few more functions to learn:

- When PQexec executes a SELECT without an error, we expect to see a result status of PGRES_TUPLES_OK. The next step is to determine how many rows are present in the result set. We do this by calling PQntuples to get the total number of rows in our result (which may be zero):

  ```
  int PQntuples(const PGresult *result);
  ```

- We can retrieve the number of fields (attributes or columns) in our tuples by calling PQnfields:

  ```
  int PQnfields(const PGresult *result);
  ```

- The fields in the result are numbered starting from zero, and we can retrieve their names by calling PQfname:

  ```
  char *PQfname(const PGresult *result, int index);
  ```

- The size of the field is given by PQfsize:

  ```
  int PQfsize(const PGresult *result, int index);
  ```

- For fixed-sized fields, PQfsize returns the number of bytes that a value in that particular column would occupy. For variable-length fields, PQfsize returns –1.

- The index number for a column with a given name can be retrieved by calling PQfnumber:

  ```
  int PQfnumber(const PGresult *result, const char *field);
  ```

Let's modify our doSQL function to print out some information about the data returned from a SELECT query. Here's our next version:

```
void doSQL(PGconn *conn, char *command);
{
  PGresult *result;

  printf("%s\n", command);

  result = PQexec(conn, command);
  printf("status is %s\n", PQresStatus(PQresultStatus(result)));
  printf("#rows affected %s\n", PQcmdTuples(result));
  printf("result message: %s\n", PQresultErrorMessage(result));

  switch(PQresultStatus(result)) {
  case PGRES_TUPLES_OK:
    {
      int n = 0;
      int nrows = PQntuples(result);
      int nfields = PQnfields(result);
      printf("number of rows returned = %d\n", nrows);
      printf("number of fields returned = %d\n", nfields);
      /* Print the field names */
      for(n = 0; n < nfields; n++) {
          printf(" %s:%d",
                  PQfname(result, n), PQfsize(result, n));
      }
      printf("\n");
    }
  }
  PQclear(result);
}
```

Now when executing a SELECT, we can see the characteristics of the data being returned:

```
doSQL(conn, "SELECT * FROM number WHERE value = 29");
```

This call results in the following output:

```
status is PGRES_TUPLES_OK
#rows affected
result message:
number of rows returned = 2
number of fields returned = 2
 value:4 name:-1
```

Notice that an empty string is returned by PQcmdTuples for queries that cannot affect rows, and PQresultErrorMessage returns an empty string where there is no error. Now we are ready to extract the data from the fields returned in the rows of our result set. The rows are numbered, starting from zero.

Normally, all data is transferred from the server as strings. We can get at a character representation of the data by calling the PQgetvalue function:

```
char *PQgetvalue(const PGresult *result, int tuple, int field);
```

If we need to know in advance how long the string returned by PQgetvalue is going to be, we can call PQgetlength:

```
int PQgetlength(const PGresult *result, int tuple, int field);
```

As mentioned earlier, both the tuple (row) number and field (column) number start at zero.

Let's add some data display to our doSQL function:

```
void doSQL(PGconn *conn, char *command)
{
  PGresult *result;

  printf("%s\n", command);

  result = PQexec(conn, command);
  printf("status is %s\n", PQresStatus(PQresultStatus(result)));
  printf("#rows affected %s\n", PQcmdTuples(result));
  printf("result message: %s\n", PQresultErrorMessage(result));

  switch(PQresultStatus(result)) {
  case PGRES_TUPLES_OK:
    {
      int r, n;
      int nrows = PQntuples(result);
      int nfields = PQnfields(result);
      printf("number of rows returned = %d\n", nrows);
      printf("number of fields returned = %d\n", nfields);
      for(r = 0; r < nrows; r++) {
```

```
        for(n = 0; n < nfields; n++)
          printf(" %s = %s(%d),",
              PQfname(result, n),
              PQgetvalue(result, r, n),
              PQgetlength(result, r, n));
        printf("\n");
      }
    }
  }
  PQclear(result);
}
```

The complete result of the SELECT query is printed, including the lengths of the strings containing the data:

```
SELECT * FROM number WHERE value = 29
Status is PGRES_TUPLES_OK
#rows affected
result message:
number of rows returned = 2
number of fields returned = 2
 value = 29(2), name = My Age(6),
 value = 29(2), name = Anniversary(11),
```

Note that the length of the data string does not include a trailing null (the character '\0', not the SQL value NULL), which is present in the string returned by PQgetvalue.

---

■**Caution** String data, such as that used in columns defined as char(n), is padded with spaces. This can give unexpected results if you are checking for a particular string value or comparing values for a sort. If you insert the value Zaphod into a column defined as char(8), you will get back Zaphod<space><space>, which will not compare as equal to Zaphod if you use the C library function strcmp. This little problem has been known to plague even very experienced developers.

---

## Handling NULL Results

There is one small complication that we must resolve before we go any further. The fact that our query results are being returned to us encoded within character strings means that we cannot readily tell the difference between an empty string and an SQL NULL value.

Fortunately, the libpq library provides us with a function that we can call to determine whether a particular value of a field in a result set tuple is a NULL:

```
int PQgetisnull(const PGresult *result, int tuple, int field);
```

We should call PQgetisnull when retrieving any field that may possibly be NULL. It returns 1 if the field contains a NULL value; 0 otherwise. The inner loop of the previous sample program would then become as follows:

```
for(n = 0; n < nfields; n++) {
  if(PQgetisnull(result, r, n))
    printf(" %s is NULL,", PQfname(result, n));
  else
    printf(" %s = %s(%d),",
        PQfname(result, n),
        PQgetvalue(result, r, n),
        PQgetlength(result, r, n));
}
```

# Printing Query Results

The functions we have covered so far are sufficient to query and extract data from a PostgreSQL database. If all we want to do is print the results, we can consider taking advantage of a printing function supplied by libpq that outputs result sets in a fairly basic form. This is the PQprint function, which formats a result set in a tabular form, similar to that used by psql, and sends it to a specified output stream:

```
void PQprint(FILE *output, const PGresult *result, const PQprintOpt *options);
```

PQprint is no longer actively supported by the PostgreSQL maintainers, however, so you should not rely on it for production code. It is very useful during development and testing, perhaps before creating a more sophisticated way of displaying results in a client program.

The PQprint arguments are an open file handle (output) to print to, a result set (result), and a pointer to a structure that contains options that control the printing format (options). The structure follows:

```
struct {
    pqbool header;        /* print out names of columns in a header */
    pqbool align;         /* pad out the values to make them line up */
    pqbool html3;         /* format as an HTML table */
    pqbool expanded;      /* expand tables */
    pqbool pager;         /* use pager for output if needed */
    char *fieldSep;       /* field separator */
    char *tableOpt;       /* options for HTML table - place in <TABLE …> */
    char *caption;        /* HTML <caption> */
    char **fieldName;     /* Replacement set of field names */
} PQprintOpt;
```

The members of the PQprintOpt structure are fairly straightforward. The header member, if set to a nonzero value, causes the first row of the output table to consist of the field names, which can be overridden by setting the fieldName list of strings.

Each row in the output table consists of field values separated by the string fieldSep and padded to align with the other rows if align is nonzero. Here is an example of PQprintOpt output:

```
+-------------+-------+----------+--------------+----------+----------+
| customer_id | title | fname    | town         | zipcode  |   phone  |
+-------------+-------+----------+--------------+----------+----------+
|           1 | Miss  | Jenny    | Hightown     | NT2 1AQ  | 023 9876 |
+-------------+-------+----------+--------------+----------+----------+
|           3 | Miss  | Alex     | Nicetown     | NT2 2TX  | 010 4567 |
+-------------+-------+----------+--------------+----------+----------+
```

If the output is likely to be very long, we can set pager to a nonzero value to ask for the output to be paged; that is, passed through a filter that pauses the output every page or so. If expanded is set to a nonzero value, the output format is changed to list each field in each row on a line by itself.

We can produce HTML output suitable for inclusion in a web page by setting html3 nonzero. We can specify table options and a caption by setting the tableOpt and caption strings. Here is an example of a program (print.c) using PQprint to generate the HTML output:

```c
#include <stdlib.h>
#include <libpq-fe.h>

int main()
{
  PGresult *result;
  PGconn *conn;

  conn = PQconnectdb("");
  if(PQstatus(conn) == CONNECTION_OK) {
    printf("connection made\n");
    result = PQexec(conn, "SELECT * FROM customer WHERE town = 'Bingham'");
    {
      PQprintOpt pqp;
      pqp.header = 1;
      pqp.align = 1;
      pqp.html3 = 1;
      pqp.expanded = 0;
      pqp.pager = 0;
      pqp.fieldSep = "";
      pqp.tableOpt = "align=center";
      pqp.caption = "Bingham Customer List";
      pqp.fieldName = NULL;
      printf("<html><head><title>Customers</title></head><body>\n");
      PQprint(stdout, result, &pqp);
      printf("</body></html>\n");
    }

  }

  PQfinish(conn);
  return EXIT_SUCCESS;
}
```

The output of this program is HTML code, which is displayed on the screen (stdout). The output is as follows:

```
$ PGDATABASE=bpfinal  ./print

<html><head><title>Customers</title></head><body>
<table align=center><caption align=high>Bingham Customer List</caption>
<tr><th align=right>customer_id</th><th align=left>title</th><th align=left>fnam
e</th><th align=left>lname</th><th align=left>addressline</th><th align=left>tow
n</th><th align=left>zipcode</th><th align=right>phone</th></tr>
<tr><td align=right>7</td><td align=left>Mr  </td><td align=left>Richard</td><td
 align=left>Stones</td><td align=left>34 Holly Way</td><td align=left>Bingham</t
d><td align=left>BG4 2WE   </td><td align=right>342 5982</td></tr>
<tr><td align=right>8</td><td align=left>Mrs </td><td align=left>Ann</td><td ali
gn=left>Stones</td><td align=left>34 Holly Way</td><td align=left>Bingham</td><t
d align=left>BG4 2WE   </td><td align=right>342 5982</td></tr>
<tr><td align=right>11</td><td align=left>Mr  </td><td align=left>Dave</td><td a
lign=left>Jones</td><td align=left>54 Vale Rise</td><td align=left>Bingham</td><
td align=left>BG3 8GD   </td><td align=right>342 8264</td></tr>
</table>
</body></html>
```

To see this in a browser, all we need to do is to redirect the output of the program to a file (say list.html):

```
$ PGDATABASE=bpfinal ./print > list.html
```

Then we view the output. Figure 13-1 shows what the HTML page looks like when viewed in a browser.

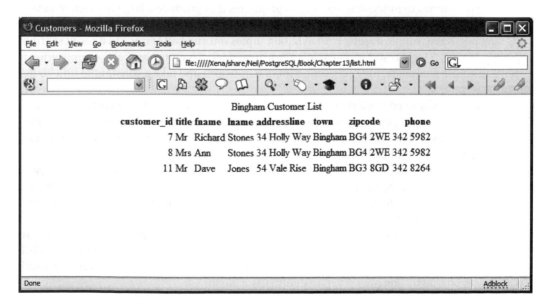

**Figure 13-1.** *Sample web page output*

# Managing Transactions

Sometimes, we will want to ensure that a group of SQL commands are executed as a group, so that the changes to the database are made either all together or none at all if an error occurs at some point. This form of query grouping, known as a *transaction*, was introduced in Chapter 9. As in standard SQL, we can manage this with libpq by using its transaction support.

Transaction behavior is implemented by calling PQexec with SQL statements that contain BEGIN, COMMIT, and ROLLBACK:

```
PQexec(conn, "BEGIN WORK");

/* Make changes */

if(we changed our minds) {
    PQexec(conn, "ROLLBACK WORK");
}
else {
    PQexec(conn, "COMMIT WORK");
}
```

All of the facilities described in Chapter 9 can be utilized by our libpq programs by passing the appropriate SQL query string to PQexec.

# Using Cursors

When writing real-world applications, it's likely we'll need to deal with large quantities of data. Thankfully, a PostgreSQL database is capable of storing tables with very large numbers of rows in them.

When it comes to processing the results of queries that produce a large amount of data however, we are at the mercy of the client application and its operating environment. A desktop PC may well have trouble dealing with a million tuples returned all at once in a result set from a single SELECT. A large result set can consume a great deal of memory and, if the application is running across a network, may consume a lot of bandwidth and take a substantial time to be transferred.

What we really need to do is perform the query and deal with the results bit by bit. For example, if in our application we want to show our complete customer list, we could retrieve all of them at once. However, it would be smarter to fetch them, say, a page of 25 at a time, and display them in our application page by page.

We can do this with libpq by employing *cursors*. Cursors are an excellent general-purpose way of accommodating the return of an unknown number of rows. If we search for a specific ZIP code, particularly one provided by users, it's not possible to know in advance if zero, one, or many rows will be returned.

In general, you should avoid writing code that assumes either a single row or no rows are returned from a SELECT statement, unless that statement is a simple aggregate, such as a SELECT count(*) FROM type query, or a SELECT on a primary key, where you can be guaranteed the result will always be exactly one row. When in doubt, use a cursor.

To demonstrate dealing with multiple rows being returned from a query, we will explore how to retrieve them one (or more) at a time using a FETCH, with the column values being received into a result set in the same way that we have seen for all-at-once SELECT statements. We'll walk through developing a sample program that queries and processes the customer list from the bpfinal database page by page using a cursor.

We will declare a cursor to be used to scroll through a collection of returned rows. The cursor will act as our bookmark, and we will fetch the rows until no more data is available. To use a cursor, we must declare it and specify the query that it relates to. We may use a cursor declaration only within a PostgreSQL transaction, so we must begin a transaction, too:

```
PQexec(conn, "BEGIN work");
PQexec(conn, "DECLARE mycursor CURSOR FOR SELECT ...");
```

Now we can start to retrieve the result rows. We do this by executing a FETCH to extract the data rows as many at a time as we wish (including all that remain):

```
result = PQexec(conn, "FETCH 1 IN mycursor");
result = PQexec(conn, "FETCH 4 IN mycursor");
result = PQexec(conn, "FETCH ALL IN mycursor");
```

The result set will indicate that it contains no rows when all of the rows from the query have been retrieved. When we have finished with the cursor, we close it and end the transaction:

```
PQexec(conn, "COMMIT work");
PQexec(conn, "CLOSE mycursor");
```

Let's take a moment to examine the general structure employed when using a cursor:

```
#include <libpq-fe.h>

main()
{
    /* Connect to a PostgreSQL database */

    /* Create cursor for SQL SELECT statement */
    DO
            /* Fetch batch of query results */
            /* Process query results */

        UNTIL no more results
        /* close cursor */

    /* Disconnect from database */
}
```

For each of the batches of query results we fetch, we will have access to a PGresult pointer that we can use in exactly the same way as before.

## Fetching All the Results at Once

First, let's see a cursor in use (in cursor.c) fetching all the results at once, to make sure that we have the correct SQL.

```c
#include <stdlib.h>
#include <libpq-fe.h>

void doSQL(PGconn *conn, char *command)
{
  PGresult *result;
  printf("%s\n", command);

  result = PQexec(conn, command);
  printf("status is %s\n", PQresStatus(PQresultStatus(result)));
  printf("#rows affected %s\n", PQcmdTuples(result));
  printf("result message: %s\n", PQresultErrorMessage(result));

  switch(PQresultStatus(result)) {
  case PGRES_TUPLES_OK:
    {
      int r, n;
      int nrows = PQntuples(result);
      int nfields = PQnfields(result);
      printf("number of rows returned = %d\n", nrows);
      printf("number of fields returned = %d\n", nfields);
      for(r = 0; r < nrows; r++) {
        for(n = 0; n < nfields; n++)
          printf(" %s = %s(%d),",
              PQfname(result, n),
              PQgetvalue(result, r, n),
              PQgetlength(result, r, n));
        printf("\n");
      }
    }
  }
  PQclear(result);
}

int main()
{
  PGresult *result;
  PGconn *conn;

  conn = PQconnectdb("");
```

```
  if(PQstatus(conn) == CONNECTION_OK) {
    printf("connection made\n");

    doSQL(conn, "BEGIN work");
    doSQL(conn, "DECLARE mycursor CURSOR FOR "
                        "SELECT fname, lname FROM customer");
    doSQL(conn, "FETCH ALL IN mycursor");

    doSQL(conn, "CLOSE mycursor");
    doSQL(conn, "COMMIT work");

  }
  else
    printf("connection failed: %s\n", PQerrorMessage(conn));

  PQfinish(conn);
  return EXIT_SUCCESS;
}
```

When we execute this program, we see the customers listed all at once:

```
connection made
BEGIN work
status is PGRES_COMMAND_OK
#rows affected
result message:
DECLARE mycursor CURSOR FOR SELECT fname, lname FROM customer
status is PGRES_COMMAND_OK
#rows affected

result message:
FETCH ALL IN mycursor
status is PGRES_TUPLES_OK
#rows affected
result message:
number of rows returned = 15
number of fields returned = 2
 fname = Jenny(5), lname = Stones(6),
 fname = Andrew(6), lname = Stones(6),
 fname = Adrian(6), lname = Matthew(7),
 fname = Simon(5), lname = Cozens(6),
 fname = Neil(4), lname = Matthew(7),
 fname = Richard(7), lname = Stones(6),
 fname = Ann(3), lname = Stones(6),
 fname = Christine(9), lname = Hickman(7),
```

```
     fname = Mike(4), lname = Howard(6),
     fname = Dave(4), lname = Jones(5),
     fname = Richard(7), lname = Neill(5),
     fname = Laura(5), lname = Hardy(5),
     fname = Bill(4), lname = O'Neill(7),
     fname = David(5), lname = Hudson(6),
     fname = Alex(4), lname = Matthew(7),
CLOSE mycursor
status is PGRES_COMMAND_OK
#rows affected
result message:
COMMIT work
status is PGRES_COMMAND_OK
#rows affected
result message:
```

## Fetching Results in Batches

To modify the program to deal with the results, say four at a time, we need to be able to tell when we have retrieved all of the results. This was easy when we were handling all of them at once, since PQntuples will tell us how many results there are in our set. If we fetch results four at a time, then PQntuples will return four for each batch of results, except the last, which will be less than four (possibly zero). This is the test we will use (in cursor2.c). As our doSQL function does not return a result, we will handle the batches directly with PQexec.

```c
#include <stdlib.h>
#include <libpq-fe.h>
void printTuples(PGresult *result)
{
     int r, n;
     int nrows = PQntuples(result);
     int nfields = PQnfields(result);
     printf("number of rows returned = %d\n", nrows);
     printf("number of fields returned = %d\n", nfields);
     for(r = 0; r < nrows; r++) {
     for(n = 0; n < nfields; n++)
       printf(" %s = %s(%d),",
             PQfname(result, n),
             PQgetvalue(result, r, n),
             PQgetlength(result, r, n));
     printf("\n");
     }
}

void doSQL(PGconn *conn, char *command)
{
  PGresult *result;
```

```
    printf("%s\n", command);

    result = PQexec(conn, command);
    printf("status is %s\n", PQresStatus(PQresultStatus(result)));
    printf("#rows affected %s\n", PQcmdTuples(result));
    printf("result message: %s\n", PQresultErrorMessage(result));

    switch(PQresultStatus(result)) {
    case PGRES_TUPLES_OK:
      printTuples(result);
      break;
    }
    PQclear(result);
}

int main()
{
    PGresult *result;
    PGconn *conn;
    int ntuples = 0;

    conn = PQconnectdb("");

    if(PQstatus(conn) == CONNECTION_OK) {
      printf("connection made\n");

      doSQL(conn, "BEGIN work");
      doSQL(conn, "DECLARE mycursor CURSOR FOR "
                  "SELECT fname, lname FROM customer");
      do {
        result = PQexec(conn, "FETCH 4 IN mycursor");
        if(PQresultStatus(result) == PGRES_TUPLES_OK) {
            ntuples = PQntuples(result);
            printTuples(result);
            PQclear(result);
        }
        else ntuples = 0;
      } while(ntuples);

      doSQL(conn, "CLOSE mycursor");
      doSQL(conn, "COMMIT work");

    }
```

```
    else
      printf("connection failed: %s\n", PQerrorMessage(conn));

    PQfinish(conn);
    return EXIT_SUCCESS;
}
```

With this version of the program, we can see several batches of four results processed at a time, followed by a short batch:

```
connection made
...
DECLARE mycursor CURSOR FOR SELECT fname, lname FROM customer
status is PGRES_COMMAND_OK
#rows affected
result message:
number of rows returned = 4
number of fields returned = 2
 fname = Jenny(5), lname = Stones(6),
 fname = Andrew(6), lname = Stones(6),
 fname = Adrian(6), lname = Matthew(7),
 fname = Simon(5), lname = Cozens(6),
number of rows returned = 4
number of fields returned = 2
 fname = Neil(4), lname = Matthew(7),
 fname = Richard(7), lname = Stones(6),
 fname = Ann(3), lname = Stones(6),
 fname = Christine(9), lname = Hickman(7),
number of rows returned = 4
number of fields returned = 2
 fname = Mike(4), lname = Howard(6),
 fname = Dave(4), lname = Jones(5),
 fname = Richard(7), lname = Neill(5),
 fname = Laura(5), lname = Hardy(5),
number of rows returned = 3
number of fields returned = 2
 fname = Bill(4), lname = O'Neill(7),
 fname = David(5), lname = Hudson(6),
 fname = Alex(4), lname = Matthew(7),
number of rows returned = 0
number of fields returned = 2
CLOSE mycursor
status is PGRES_COMMAND_OK
#rows affected
result message:
...
$
```

We can use all of the options of FETCH that we saw earlier to fetch results one at a time (with the NEXT option), a batch at a time (by specifying a number), or all at once (with ALL).

# Dealing with Binary Values

All of the data that we have dealt with in this chapter has been transferred in strings. We have created INSERT statements with values in strings and dealt with the results of a SELECT again in strings.

You might think that all this converting between formats is wasteful. Wouldn't it be better to have a binary interface? If you wanted to insert or select a floating-point value, such as average fuel consumption, wouldn't it be better to have it transferred directly from and to a C double?

The answer is both yes and no. PostgreSQL does have in libpq some ability to deal with binary values, but the benefits are probably fairly slim. Currently, we can retrieve binary values only if we use a cursor and include the BINARY option in its declaration:

```
DECLARE mycursor BINARY CURSOR FOR...
```

Then the PQbinaryTuples function will confirm that a result set returned from a FETCH of that cursor contains binary data:

```
int PQbinaryTuples(const PGresult *result);
```

Now, in the case where binary tuples are being used, PQgetvalue will return not a string pointer, but a pointer to a binary representation of the field, in the binary format native to the server.

Dealing with issues such as variable-length data and the byte-ordering of multibyte values (like currency data) can soon become decidedly messy. It is recommended that you stick with string representations when using libpq. As discussed in the next chapter, you can handle binary values a little more easily with embedded SQL.

# Working Asynchronously

All of the examples we have looked at so far are using the libpq functions in a *blocking mode*. This means that our programs call a libpq function and wait for it to return values. As we saw earlier, we might request a large amount of data that may take some time to be received. In a single-threaded (normal) application, if we're using PQexec, there is nothing we can do until PQexec returns. Users must wait. It's also tricky to cancel a query if the results are no longer needed. However, for most programs this will be sufficient, and short waits will not be a problem. Fetching results a few at a time with a cursor is probably sufficient. In this section, we will cover a more advanced technique that can give us precise control over the behavior of our application if we need it.

An alternative approach to blocking, typically used for applications with a graphical user interface, is to run in a *nonblocking* mode. In this type of program, we are sent messages when something has happened, and our application must respond to those messages. So, in a point-and-click application, we might be told when the user has pressed a mouse button, entered data in a field, moved a window, and so on.

The structure of a nonblocking program generally revolves around an event loop:

```
main()
{
    LOOP: {
        /* Wait for an event to occur */
        /* Find out what has event has occurred */
        switch(event type) {
            /* Process event */
        }
    }
}
```

We essentially do nothing until some event occurs. When we receive a notification that something has happened, we find out exactly what has occurred and perform an appropriate action.

Sometimes, the programming language we are writing in hides the event loop from us, and we just arrange for particular functions we have written to be called when a particular event occurs. These functions are often called *callbacks*, and the main loop that forms the heart of the application calls us back when it has something to say. This is the case for Visual Basic, for example.

In libpq, PostgreSQL has some support for this nonblocking way of programming. It is referred to as *working asynchronously*, because database actions performed on the server are not synchronized with the client application, which can be performing other tasks instead of simply waiting. Instead, we must ask PostgreSQL if anything has happened, and when it has, we resume processing.

## Executing a Query in Asynchronous Mode

Let's take a look at how we can execute a query in asynchronous mode. We will use a pair of functions that PQexec uses to do its work: PQsendQuery and PQgetResult.

The idea is that we call PQsendQuery to send our SQL to the server. Once it is on its way, we can get on with other things.

```
int PQsendQuery(PGconn *conn, const char *query);
```

PQsendQuery returns zero if the query is not dispatched, and sets an error condition we can retrieve with PQerrorMessage. Otherwise, it returns 1 to indicate successfully sending the query.

If the server responds immediately, the result set will be kept waiting for us until we are ready to retrieve it. When we are ready, we will call PQgetResult one or more times to retrieve the query results as they come in:

```
PGresult *PQgetResult(PGconn *conn);
```

PQgetResult will return a result set each time it's called, until all the results from the active query have been returned. The result set may contain no tuples if no further data was immediately available, but this does *not* mean that all the data has been received. At that point, PQgetResult returns a NULL pointer. Each of the result sets returned by PQgetResult must be cleared when we are finished with them by calling PQclear.

For this to work, we must make sure that neither PQsendQuery nor PQgetResult will block and leave our application waiting for them. To help with PQsendQuery, we can set the connection itself to a nonblocking state by calling PQsetnonblocking:

```
int PQsetnonblocking(PGconn *conn, int arg);
```

To prevent PQsendQuery from blocking, we make a call to PQsetnonblocking with a nonzero argument. Then PQsendQuery will return an error if it would have otherwise blocked, and the application may try again at a later point.

PQsetnonblocking returns zero if successful, and -1 if there is a problem in changing the mode of the connection. We can check the blocking mode of a connection by calling PQisnonblocking:

```
int PQisnonblocking(const PGconn *conn);
```

We get a nonzero value if the connection is in a nonblocking mode.

The programming we need to run this nonblocking operation is something like this (async1.c):

```
#include <stdlib.h>
#include <libpq-fe.h>

void printTuples(PGresult *result)
{
    int r, n;
    int nrows = PQntuples(result);
    int nfields = PQnfields(result);
    printf("number of rows returned = %d\n", nrows);
    printf("number of fields returned = %d\n", nfields);
    for(r = 0; r < nrows; r++) {
      for(n = 0; n < nfields; n++)
        printf(" %s = %s(%d),",
            PQfname(result, n),
            PQgetvalue(result, r, n),
            PQgetlength(result, r, n));
        printf("\n");
    }
}

int main()
{
  PGresult *result;
  PGconn *conn;

  conn = PQconnectdb("");

  if(PQstatus(conn) == CONNECTION_OK &&
     PQsetnonblocking(conn,1) == 0) {
    printf("connection made\n");
```

```
      PQsendQuery(conn, "SELECT * FROM customer");
      while(result = PQgetResult(conn)) {
        printTuples(result);
        PQclear(result);
      }
    }
    else
      printf("connection failed\n");

    PQfinish(conn);
    return EXIT_SUCCESS;
}
```

This program sends off a query, and then collects the results without blocking. As with the earlier example of using cursors, we now have no easy way of telling how many rows will be returned altogether, but this is rarely a problem in practice.

There are still some rare circumstances under which PQgetResult can block, one of them being while the back-end server is busy. There are ways around this, using some lower-level libpq functions. If you need to have very precise control over your connection, and you are executing very complex queries that will cause the server to be busy for significantly long periods, you can use the functions shown in Table 13-3.

**Table 13-3.** *libpq Functions for Controlling Blocking*

| Function | Description |
|---|---|
| int PQisBusy(PGconn *conn); | Returns 1 if the current query is busy, and PQgetResult would block if it were called. |
| int PQflush(PGconn *conn); | Tries to send any outstanding data that is waiting to go to the server. It returns zero if it successfully empties the queue, or it was already empty. |
| int PQconsumeInput(PGconn *conn); | Transfers data waiting to be read on the database connection into the internal libpq data structures. It is normally called by functions like PQexec, but you can make explicit calls to it when you need control over blocking behavior of your applications. |

Check out the PostgreSQL documentation that is included in the source code distribution or at http://www.postgresql.org for details on using the PQisBusy, PQconsumeInput, and PQflush functions.

If your application is using the select system call (not to be confused with the SQL SELECT statement) to react to read and write events on file descriptors or network sockets, you can include the PostgreSQL connection in the select, too. To do this, you must obtain the socket that is being used by the database connection. This can be obtained from PQsocket:

```
int PQsocket(const PGconn *conn);
```

The socket will signal activity when there is back-end data to be processed, but there are a couple of conditions that must be met for this to work:

- There must be no data outstanding to be sent to the server. We can ensure this by calling PQflush until it returns zero.

- Data must be read from the connection by PQconsumeInput before calling PQgetResult.

## Canceling an Asynchronous Query

If we need to cancel a query before we have read all of the results, we can do this by calling PQrequestCancel, which will send an indication to the server to stop processing the query:

```
int PQrequestCancel(PGconn *conn);
```

PQrequestCancel will return 1 if it was able to send the cancellation, or 0 if it was unable to, possibly because the query had already completed. A canceled query will manifest itself as a result set bearing an error. Regardless of the result of PQrequestCancel, we may still be too late to stop the results from appearing and may not see any error in a result set.

Although PQrequestCancel is useful when working in a nonblocking mode, it is also possible to call it from a signal handler to terminate a long-running query on a blocking connection.

## Making an Asynchronous Database Connection

It is also possible to establish the initial connection to the database in a nonblocking way by using PQconnectStart and PQconnectPoll:

```
PGconn *PQconnectStart(const char *conninfo);
PostgresPollingStatusType *PQconnectPoll(PGconn *conn);
```

PQconnectStart is similar to PQconnectdb, except that it returns immediately, before the connection requested in the conninfo string has been established. As long as the host name parameter does not result in a DNS lookup, PQconnectStart will not block.

Before using the new connection, we must be sure that it is ready. First, we must call PQstatus to make sure that the call to PQconnectStart did not fail and leave a connection with a status of CONNECTION_BAD. We can then check the connection's condition with PQconnectPoll, which will not block. The return results from PQconnectPoll include the following:

```
PGRES_POLLING_FAILED    /*the connection has failed*/
PGRES_POLLING_OK        /*the connection has been made*/
```

By polling while the result is not PGRES_POLLING_FAILED, and until it becomes PGRES_POLLING_OK, we can detect the end of the connection establishment process in a nonblocking fashion.

Here is a sample program (async2.c) that makes an asynchronous database connection:

```c
#include <stdlib.h>
#include <libpq-fe.h>

int main()
{
  PGresult *result;
  PGconn *conn;

  /* Start an asynchronous connection */
  conn = PQconnectStart("");

  if(PQstatus(conn) == CONNECTION_BAD) {
    printf(" cannot start connect: %s\n", PQerrorMessage(conn));
  }
  else {
    /* do some work, calling PQconnectPoll from time to time */
    PostgresPollingStatusType status;
    do {
      printf("polling\n");
      status = PQconnectPoll(conn);
    }
    while(status != PGRES_POLLING_FAILED &&
          status != PGRES_POLLING_OK);

    if(status == PGRES_POLLING_OK)
      printf("connection made!\n");
    else
      printf("connection failed: %s\n", PQerrorMessage(conn));
  }
  PQfinish(conn);
  return EXIT_SUCCESS;
}
```

When we run this program, we see many polling messages before the connection is reported as made or failed:

```
$ PGDATABASE=bpfinal ./async2
polling
polling
...
connection made!
$
```

---

**Note** If you run this program several times, you may see a different number of polling messages appear before the connection is made. The exact number will depend on how long it takes the server to respond to the connection request.

---

# Summary

In this chapter, we looked at creating PostgreSQL applications in C. We saw how the libpq library provides access to the low-level functions of PostgreSQL, allowing us to connect to a database on a local machine or on a server across the network. We have used sample programs to make and close connections, and execute SQL statements to query, insert, or update rows in our database tables.

We have considered problems of handling large volumes of data and looked at how to use cursors to marshal query results into manageable units. We have looked at the problem of blocking and considered ways of creating applications that continue to service the user while accessing a database server.

We can also access PostgreSQL from C using embedded SQL, which is the subject of the next chapter.

■ ■ ■

# CHAPTER 14

# Accessing PostgreSQL from C Using Embedded SQL

In the previous chapter, we introduced the libpq library, a collection of C functions specific to PostgreSQL that allow programs to connect to a database and select data from tables. We also saw how to effectively execute standard SQL queries and perform updates, insertions, and deletions on rows in the database tables using this library.

Although libpq does unleash the power of the PostgreSQL database system for our applications, it is in some ways unfortunate that the interface itself is unique to PostgreSQL, different from any other C API we might use for accessing other relational databases. Another drawback to using libpq is that it is not easy to see the SQL, as the supporting code tends to hide the all-important SQL statements, and that makes it more difficult to maintain the code.

Help is at hand however. Many database systems, particularly commercial ones, support the concept of *embedded SQL*. The SQL92 standard specified interfaces for embedding SQL in various languages, not only in C, but also in FORTRAN, ADA, and others. In December 1998, ANSI also ratified a standard for embedding SQL in Java, SQLJ, although that is not widely used.

Using embedded SQL in C code, following the SQL standards, enables us to create applications that are more portable to other databases. Furthermore, it makes writing code to access PostgreSQL easier, since it provides a higher-level, more intuitive way of writing an application. PostgreSQL supports this feature using a preprocessor known as ecpg, and an additional library to support the code that is generated from ecpg.

In this chapter, we will explore how to use SQL in C programs by embedding SQL statements directly in the source code. If you have used embedded SQL in another database system, you will be right at home in this chapter.

## Using ecpg

Using ecpg provides a method of writing SQL statements in a C program, rather than using libpq function calls directly. This translator, better known as a *preprocessor*, works in much the same way as the C preprocessor. It reads the program file and produces a C program file that the compiler can understand. The embedded SQL is replaced with calls to ecpg library routines, which, in turn, call the libpq library routines.

---

■**Note** Oracle and Informix also have such translators in the form of PRO*C and ESQL/C, respectively, as do many other commercial relational database systems. The PostgreSQL preprocessor for embedded SQL, ecpg, closely follows the ANSI standard.

---

For our examples in this chapter, we use a test database with a number table, created with psql as follows:

```
bpfinal=> CREATE database test;
CREATE DATABASE
bpfinal=> \c test
You are now connected to database "test".
test=> CREATE TABLE number (
test(> intval integer,
test(> name varchar
test(> );
CREATE TABLE
test=> INSERT INTO number(intval, name) VALUES(42, 'six times seven');
INSERT 19107 1
test=> INSERT INTO number(intval, name) VALUES(1, 'Numero Uno');
INSERT 19231 1
test=> INSERT INTO number(intval, name) VALUES(111, 'Nelson ');
INSERT 19253 1
test=>
```

## Writing an esqlc Program

Now let's look at a very simple example of an esqlc program titled update.pgc (we follow the PostgreSQL standard of using the extension .pgc for our esqlc programs):

```
int main()
{
  EXEC SQL CONNECT TO test;
  EXEC SQL UPDATE number
          SET name = 'The Answer to the Ultimate Question'
          WHERE intval = 42;
  EXEC SQL COMMIT;
  EXEC SQL DISCONNECT ALL;
  return 0;
}
```

This program connects to the database (assumed to be on the local machine and accessible using the same username as the current Linux login name without password) and updates one of the rows in the number table. By default, ecpg arranges for our statements to be executed within an open transaction, but it does not automatically end the transaction. At the end of our program, we need to explicitly end the transaction by executing a COMMIT if the database changes are correct. We will come back to more complex login requirements later in the chapter, in the section "Making Database Connections."

You can see that we have simply written some SQL inside the main program. The embedded SQL syntax is fairly simple, prefixing each SQL statement that needs to be translated with the string EXEC SQL and terminating it with a semicolon:

```
EXEC SQL <some SQL statement>;
```

The keywords in embedded SQL are case-insensitive, including EXEC SQL, so we may write them in either uppercase or lowercase. Variable names in embedded SQL are case-sensitive and must match the corresponding declarations.

---

■**Note**  Some developers like to use uppercase so that the SQL stands out from the surrounding C code; others regard that as ugly and use lowercase. You should pick one case style and stick to it. We will stick to our convention of putting structural SQL keywords in uppercase in the text of this book, which helps them to stand out from the surrounding C code.

---

The next step is to use the translator to create a C file that we can compile. We can translate our sample program by running ecpg, giving our program name as argument:

```
$ ecpg update.pgc
$
```

If you need to tell ecpg where to find additional include files, you can do so by adding a command-line argument: -I<include file directory>.

Now we also have a C program file, update.c, that includes the translated source code for our program. For the curious, let's take a peek and see what is going on. Here is update.c:

```c
/* Processed by ecpg (3.2.0) */
/* These include files are added by the preprocessor */
#include <ecpgtype.h>
#include <ecpglib.h>
#include <ecpgerrno.h>
#include <sqlca.h>
/* End of automatic include section */
#line 1 "update.pgc"

int main()
{
  { ECPGconnect(__LINE__, 0, "test" , NULL,NULL , NULL, 0); }
#line 5 "update.pgc"

  { ECPGdo(__LINE__, 0, 1, NULL, "UPDATE number SET name  =
'The Answer to the Ultimate Question'  WHERE
intval = 42", ECPGt_EOIT, ECPGt_EORT);}
#line 9 "update.pgc"
```

```
  { ECPGtrans(__LINE__, NULL, "COMMIT");}
#line 10 "update.pgc"

  { ECPGdisconnect(__LINE__, "ALL");}
#line 11 "update.pgc"

  return 0;
}
```

We can see that the SQL has been replaced by calls to functions. These ecpg functions all have names beginning with ecpg and are similar to the libpq ones we saw in the previous chapter. The ecpg functions are made available as a separate library, but they use the standard libpq library for their implementation.

To create an executable program, we need to compile update.c and link it with both the ecpg and libpq libraries:

```
$ cc -o update update.c -L/usr/local/pgsql/lib -lecpg -lpq
$
```

The exact location you need to specify with -L may be different on your system, depending on how PostgreSQL was installed. You may also need to add an -Idirectory command-line argument to specify the location of the ecpg include files, such as -I/usr/local/pgsql/include.

Now when we run the program, it connects to the database, updates the row, and disconnects:

```
$ ./update
$
```

If when you try to run the program you get an error that the shared library file libecpg.so.<some-numbers> does not exist, you may also need to set LD_LIBRARY_PATH to include the directory containing this file, as in this example:

```
$ LD_LIBRARY_PATH=$LD_LIBRARY_PATH:/usr/local/pgsql/lib
$ export LD_LIBRARY_PATH
$
```

There is nothing to see when the program runs, because it does not produce any output. We can check with psql to see whether the update has happened correctly:

```
$ psql -d test
test=> SELECT * FROM number;
  intval |                name
---------+-----------------------------------
       1 | Numero Uno
     111 | Nelson
      42 | The Answer to the Ultimate Question
(3 rows)
test=> \q
$
```

# Using a Makefile

To make the process of invoking the translator and building embedded SQL applications easier, we can use a makefile, similar to the one we used in the previous chapter. Here is a suitable makefile for ecpg programs:

```
# Makefile for sample programs
# In Beginning PostgreSQL

# Edit the base directories for your
# PostgreSQL installation

INC=/usr/local/pgsql/include
LIB=/usr/local/pgsql/lib

CFLAGS=-I$(INC)
LDLIBS=-L$(LIB) -lecpg -lpq
ECPGFLAGS= -I$(INC)

.SUFFIXES: .pgc
.pgc.c:
    ecpg $(ECPGFLAGS) $<

ALL= cursor insert insert2 select select2 select3 update update2
```

This makefile says that to create a .c file from a .pgc file, we need to run ecpg on the .pgc file. We set a variable ECPGFLAGS to pass any command-line arguments we need to the translator. The default rules take care of compiling and linking, so all we need to add is the ecpg library to the LDLIBS variable.

---

■**Note** The makefile provided in the code bundle (available from the Downloads section of the Apress web site, http://www.apress.com) has some additional options, notably an option to support the command make clean to ensure the directory is set back to a clean state ready to compile all the code. We suggest you do this, particularly if you change the version of PostgreSQL you are using, because if ecpg has changed, then it is important to restart the compilation from the original source files.

---

Using the makefile, we can see the steps taken in creating our program:

```
$ rm -f update.c update
$ make update
ecpg -I/usr/local/pgsql/include update.pgc
cc -I/usr/local/pgsql/include -c -o update.o update.c
cc update.o -L/usr/local/pgsql/lib -lecpg -lpq -o update
rm update.o update.c
$
```

Here, we have removed the intermediate file update.c and the executable update to force make to carry out all of the required steps in building our program. Also notice that (for the GNU version, at least) make deletes the intermediate file and object to keep things nice and tidy. We end up with just update.pgc, the source code of our embedded SQL program, and an executable binary, update.

## Using ecpg Arguments

We can use some command-line arguments to control the behavior of ecpg, in the following form:

```
ecpg [-v] [-t] [-I include-dir] [-o output-file] file1 [file2 ...]
```

Table 14-1 describes each of these arguments.

**Table 14-1.** *Principal Options for ecpg*

| Argument | Description |
| --- | --- |
| -v | Prints version and search path information to the standard error output (stderr) |
| --help | Prints some help, including some more esoteric options not listed here |
| -t | Turns on auto-commit mode, where each individual SQL statement is automatically committed to the database, unless it is inside a BEGIN/COMMIT block |
| -o | Specifies the name of the output file for the processed program code; defaults to the same name as the input filename, substituting .c for .pgc as the extension |
| -I | Adds the named directory to the list of directories searched to find header files included in the source file |

The -t option is the most important one. It controls the way that ecpg uses transactions. By default, no statements in the program will be committed to the database until we explicitly use the COMMIT statement. This makes us fully responsible for using BEGIN and COMMIT statements correctly. However, for simple programs, it's sometimes useful if the database automatically commits statements, one at a time, without requiring a COMMIT statement to be explicitly executed. If you specify the -t option to ecpg, any SQL statement not in an explicit BEGIN/COMMIT block will be automatically committed immediately after it is executed. (Note that this behavior has changed significantly from earlier versions of ecpg.) In the sample makefile, we have specified an explicit search path for include files (exactly as we did in the previous chapter for compiling libpq applications) and the option to control transactions ourselves.

---

■**Note** If you want to take full control of transactions within your program, which is normally a good idea, we recommend that you do not specify the −t argument to ecpg and use explicit BEGIN and COMMIT SQL statements. The remaining examples in the chapter will work correctly only if they are processed by ecpg without the -t argument.

---

# Logging SQL Execution

Many of the ecpg library functions call a logging function internally for debugging purposes. We can use this feature to generate a log of the SQL statements that our embedded SQL program executes. To do this, we enable the debug output with a call to ECPGdebug:

```
void ECPGdebug(int logging, FILE *logstream);
```

We pass any nonzero value as the logging parameter to enable the debug output, and a zero value to turn it off again. The information will be printed to the output stream given as the logstream parameter.

Add the following line to the start of main in update.pgc, and then rebuild it:

```
ECPGdebug(1,stderr);
```

We will now be able to see the progress of our program as it runs:

```
$ make update
$ ./update
[2684]: ECPGdebug: set to 1
[2684]: ECPGconnect: opening database test on <DEFAULT> port <DEFAULT>
[2684]: ECPGexecute line 10: QUERY: update number set name  =
'The Answer to the Ultimate Question'  where intval = 42 on connection test
[2684]: ECPGexecute line 10 Ok: UPDATE 1
[2684]: ECPGtrans line 13 action = commit connection = test
[2684]: ecpg_finish: Connection test closed.
```

The number given in brackets at the start of each debug line is the process identifier for the program, and it will be different for each run. This is useful for separating the output from several programs running at the same time.

As ECPGdebug (and the other ECPG functions, if you call them explicitly) is PostgreSQL-specific, if you use it in your applications, they will not be portable to other database implementations that support embedded SQL. You should probably confine calls to ECPGdebug to the test and debug phases of your application development, and either remove or include them only conditionally using the C preprocessor.

# Making Database Connections

The sample program update.pgc contains a very simple variant of the SQL statement to connect to the database, where almost all of the options we might have used in the equivalent libpq functions have been set to default values.

The following statement will attempt to connect to the database called test on the local machine, using the current user as the login account and offering no password:

```
EXEC SQL connect to test;
```

We can specify in more detail which server to connect to, which port the database server is listening on, and the user identity and password to use by employing the full version of the CONNECT statement:

```
EXEC SQL CONNECT database_url
    AS connection_name
    USER login_name
    USING password;
```

The connection parameters are as follows:

- The *database_url* specifies the location of the database and the method to be used to connect to it in much the same way as a URL on the Internet locates a file or a web page. An example of a common format would be bpfinal@docbox to specify a database bpfinal on the server docbox. This is only one of several formats that are acceptable; others are listed in Table 14-2.

- The *connection_name* is an identifier that can be used to identify the connection in subsequent SQL statements.

- The *login_name* is the user identity to use. The password may be added to the username, separated by a slash.

- The *password* is the user's password. The keyword IDENTIFIED BY may be used as a synonym for USING in a CONNECT statement when using passwords. The user details may be taken from a variable if required. See the "Using Host Variables" section later in this chapter for details on using variables in SQL statements.

**Table 14-2.** *Forms for database_url Connection*

| Form | Description |
|------|-------------|
| *database_name* | Database on the local machine |
| *database_name@server* | Database on a remote server |
| *database_name@server:port* | Remote database on a nonstandard port |
| tcp:postgresql://*server* | Default database on remote server connected via TCP socket |
| tcp:postgresql://*server:port* | Remote database on a nonstandard port |
| tcp:postgresql://*server/database_name* | Named remote database |
| Unix:postgresql://*server* | Database connected by UNIX domain socket |
| Default | Connect to the default database, unless the PGDATABASE environment variable is set, in which case the database specified in that is used |
| *:host_variable* | Connection details taken from a C string variable |

If you are writing a program that uses multiple connections, then assigning them names allows you to identify them as targets for SQL statements. To specify a particular database connection, we use an extended form of the EXEC SQL syntax:

```
EXEC SQL AT connection_name <sql statement>;
```

We can also change the connection that is used for SQL statements (the current connection) by using a SET statement:

```
EXEC SQL SET CONNECTION TO connection_name;
```

When we have finished with a database connection, we should close it to release the resources. A database connection is closed with the DISCONNECT statement:

```
EXEC SQL DISCONNECT connection;
```

Where the optional *connection* argument may be one of the following:

- Default, for the default connection

- Current, for the current connection

- ALL, for all connections

- *connection_name*, for a named connection

Using ALL is usually a safe choice.

One function included in the ecpg library that can sometimes come in handy is ECPGstatus, which returns a nonzero Boolean value (true) if a database connection is valid (that is, it is connected to a database), and false otherwise:

```
bool ECPGstatus(int lineno, char *connection_name);
```

The parameters to ECPGstatus follow the standard for ECPG functions. The first parameter is a line number (usually the C preprocessor macro __LINE__ is used). The second parameter is a string used to identify the connection of interest. You can use the same connection specifier or name as used in the embedded SQL CONNECT statement that established the connection.

To check that our sample program connected successfully, we could add this test to the code:

```
if(!ECPGstatus(__LINE__,"test")) {
    /* failed to connect */
}
```

Again, using ECPGstatus will make our program PostgreSQL-specific. The next section presents a more standard way of detecting whether the connection failed, but only immediately after the attempt to connect is made.

# Error Handling

Our sample program is rather cavalier in its approach. It carries on regardless of any errors that might occur in executing any of the embedded SQL. As such, it is possible that the program will hang if it fails to connect to a database and then attempts the update. As responsible developers, we will want to catch and attempt to recover from errors that may occur.

# Reporting Errors

The embedded SQL standard defines a mechanism for reporting errors in embedded SQL, and PostgreSQL supports this. A standard structure, the SQL control area, is defined and named sqlca. It has the following general layout, expressed as a C structure:

```
struct
{
    char        sqlcaid[8];
    long        sqlabc;
    long        sqlcode;
    struct
    {
        int         sqlerrml;
        char        sqlerrmc[70];
    } sqlerrm;
    char        sqlerrp[8];
    long        sqlerrd[6];
    char        sqlwarn[8];
    char        sqlext[8];
} sqlca;
```

The sqlca structure is used for communicating error messages and status values from embedded SQL statement execution. You can see the exact definition for your setup by looking in the sqlca.h include file installed with PostgreSQL. It is rather arcane, and the different codes can appear a little odd. Furthermore, PostgreSQL does not implement all of the possible information that can be communicated through sqlca fields, though it does implement all the generally useful ones.

The sqlca structure is reset after each embedded SQL statement, so you must retrieve any information you need from one statement before executing the next. The fields that are set in the structure will depend on precisely what has happened, and the key to that is the sqlcode field.

The variable sqlca.sqlcode will be set to a result code, which will be zero if all went well. For serious errors, a negative value will be returned. For example, if a database connection attempt fails, sqlca.sqlcode will be set to -402. Nonfatal errors return positive values. A very important positive result is the code 100, which is returned in the case where a SELECT returned no data—not in itself an error, but a condition we are frequently interested in trapping.

If an error occurs, the string sqlca.sqlerrm.sqlerrmc will contain a message that describes the error. The length of the error message string (which is null-terminated) is given in sqlca.sqlerrm.sqlerrml. With PostgreSQL, the error message might seem unhelpful, as it may contain text like error #-203 rather than anything truly meaningful. Several of the more common error codes and their meanings are listed in Table 14-3.

**Table 14-3.** *sqlca Error Codes*

| Error Code | Description |
|---|---|
| -12 | Out of memory. |
| -201 | Too many arguments. Generally caused by a mismatch between the number of host variables, which we will meet later in the chapter, and parameters in the SQL statement you are attempting to execute. |
| -202 | Too few arguments. Generally caused by a mismatch between the number of host variables and parameters in the SQL statement you are attempting to execute. |
| -203 | Too many matches. A query has returned multiple rows, but the variables receiving that data are only sufficient for a single row. |
| -208 | Empty query. This is equivalent to PGRES_EMPTY_QUERY being returned from libpq and probably indicates a program bug as the server was asked to do no work. |
| -220 | No such connection. The program tried to use a connection that does not exist. |
| -221 | Not connected. The program has attempted to access data without a valid connection being established. |
| -400 | PostgreSQL error. The message will contain details of the error from the server. |
| -401 | Transaction error. An error has occurred during a begin, commit, or rollback of a transaction. |
| -402 | Open failed. A connection to the database could not be established. |
| 100 | Not found. No data was returned by a query. |

After an INSERT, UPDATE, or DELETE has successfully executed, the number of rows that were affected is made available in sqlca.sqlerrd[2]. This field is also used when returning data with SELECT and using cursors. Implementing cursors in embedded SQL is discussed later in this chapter.

In some circumstances, a warning or other condition arises that, although not a fatal error, needs to be brought to the program's attention. When data is returned as a result of a SQL statement, such as a SELECT, we can arrange for C variables in our program to receive the data, as explained in the "Using Host Variables" section a little later in this chapter. If the data is too long for the variable, it is truncated and a warning is raised.

The sqlca.sqlwarn array is used to convey information about warnings:

- sqlca.sqlwarn[0] will be set to W if a warning has been issued.

- sqlca.sqlwarn[1] will be set to W if data has been truncated when received into a C variable.

- sqlca.sqlwarn[2] will be set to W when a nonfatal error has occurred.

To use the sqlca structure in our program, we need to instruct ecpg to include its definition for us. We do this by using an include directive, such as this:

```
EXEC SQL include sqlca;
```

Here is an example of an update program to check the number of rows affected by our update. This version (update2.pgc) alters the cost and sell price for an item in our main sample database, bpfinal:

```
#include <stdio.h>

EXEC SQL include sqlca;

main()
{
  ECPGdebug(1,stderr);

  EXEC SQL CONNECT TO bpfinal;

  EXEC SQL UPDATE item
          SET cost_price = 1.75, sell_price = 2.99
          WHERE description = 'Linux CD';

  if(sqlca.sqlcode == 0)
    printf("rows affected: %d\n", sqlca.sqlerrd[2]);

  EXEC SQL COMMIT;
  EXEC SQL DISCONNECT ALL;
}
```

When we run the program, we see quite a lot of output, because of the tracing:

```
$ ./update2
[2332]: ECPGdebug: set to 1
[2332]: ECPGconnect: opening database bpfinal on <DEFAULT> port <DEFAULT>
[2332]: ECPGexecute line 11: QUERY: update item set cost_price  = 1.75 ,
sell_price  = 2.99  where description = 'Linux CD' on connection bpfinal
[2332]: ECPGexecute line 11 Ok: UPDATE 1
rows affected: 1
[2332]: ECPGtrans line 18 action = commit connection = bpfinal
[2332]: ecpg_finish: Connection bpfinal closed.
$
```

The program extracts the number of rows affected by the UPDATE, if it completes successfully. A zero code in sqlca.sqlcode indicates a successful UPDATE, and sqlca.sqlerrd[2] contains the number of rows affected.

# Trapping Errors

We can arrange for our ecpg program to execute some code automatically whenever an error or warning occurs. We can also arrange for code to run whenever we encounter the no data pseudo-error code 100. For such tasks, the construct we use is the whenever statement:

```
EXEC SQL whenever condition action;
```

The *condition* can be one of the following options:

- sqlerror, for when an error has occurred

- sqlwarning, for when a warning was given

- not found, for when no data was returned

The *action* value can then be one of the following:

- sqlprint prints the error message to the standard error.

- goto *label* jumps to the specified label.

- continue is the default action of just continuing.

- do c_code executes a C function.

If it is acceptable just to print out messages for warnings, and to exit the program for fatal errors, we can include code such as this in our application to trap and handle errors:

```
EXEC SQL whenever sqlwarning sqlprint;
EXEC SQL whenever sqlerror do GiveUp();

void GiveUp()
{
    fprintf(stderr, "Fatal error\n");
    sqlprint();
    exit(1);
}
```

PostgreSQL implements the whenever statement in ecpg by generating code to check sqlca.sqlcode and sqlca.sqlwarn[0] after each embedded SQL statement and executing the specified action if the check fails. The keyword sqlprint is shorthand for do sqlprint(), which calls a library function to print out the associated error message.

These whenever functions to trap warnings and errors are PostgreSQL-specific, and not available in standard embedded SQL. For this reason, you shouldn't rely on them in your final program code if there is any possibility of needing to port your code to another database at a later date.

---

■**Tip** Unfettered use of whenever in embedded SQL can make your code impossible to follow, with some developers claiming that it's just as bad as using goto statements. Having said that, it may be worth experimenting with whenever in small doses and with simple action code, as it can make for applications that are easier to understand, and some programmers do prefer it. We generally err on the side of adding code to explicitly test error and warning codes in production code, as we did in the previous chapter. It is possible, and sometimes convenient, to mix the two approaches.

---

# Using Host Variables

So far, we have simply executed fixed SQL statements in our sample program, but you may be wondering how we can introduce some variable data. After all, using libpq, we could construct a SQL statement in a string using sprintf perhaps, and thereby arrange for it to contain data taken from variables.

Embedded SQL can also use variables in its statements, in a manner that is rather easier to use than the string-manipulation tasks we must follow with libpq. We can refer to variables in our embedded SQL by using their names prefixed by a colon. So, if we want to insert a new row in our item table, we can do it like this:

```
EXEC SQL INSERT INTO item(description, cost_price, sell_price)
    VALUES(:description, :cost_price, :sell_price);
```

Notice that we can omit a value for item_id, either by specifying the list of columns excluding item_id, as we do here, or by using the DEFAULT keyword in place of the host variable where item_id should be. We can do this because the value is generated automatically when a row is added to the item table. The variables found in this query (description, cost_price, and sell_price) are referred to as *host variables*, as they are variables contained in the client application, not within the server database.

Before we can use host variables in our program, we must let ecpg know about them. We do this by declaring the variables we want to use in SQL statements in special declaration sections:

```
EXEC SQL BEGIN declare section;
declare host variables here
. . . .
EXEC SQL END declare section;
```

Declaration sections must appear where it is legal to declare a C variable; in other words, at the start of a block or outside of functions. This is because they will be processed into normal C variable declarations, as well as being recorded by ecpg as host variables.

## Declaring Fixed-Length Variable Types

For simple values like integers and fixed-length strings, we can declare the host variables as we would in C. The following is an example of a program (insert.pgc) that will allow us to add new barcodes for an item in our database. We will accept the item identifier and barcode as command-line parameters.

```
#include <stdio.h>
#include <string.h>

EXEC SQL include sqlca;
EXEC SQL whenever sqlwarning sqlprint;
EXEC SQL whenever sqlerror do GiveUp();

void GiveUp()
{
    fprintf(stderr, "Fatal Error\n");
    sqlprint();
}

main(int argc, char *argv[])
{
  EXEC SQL BEGIN declare section;
  int item_id;
  char barcode[13];
  EXEC SQL END declare section;

// ECPGdebug(1, stderr); uncomment if you want to see some debug information

  if(argc != 3) {
    printf("usage: insert item barcode\n");
    exit(1);
  }

  item_id = atoi(argv[1]);
  strncpy(barcode, argv[2], sizeof(barcode));

  EXEC SQL CONNECT TO bpfinal;
  EXEC SQL BEGIN;
  EXEC SQL INSERT INTO barcode VALUES(:barcode, :item_id);
  EXEC SQL COMMIT;
  EXEC SQL DISCONNECT ALL;
}
```

Here, we declare two host variables, item_id and barcode, that correspond to the data types (integer and fixed-length character field) for columns in the item table. We can use them in our C code because they are normal C variables. We can use them in embedded SQL because we have declared them to ecpg within a declare section. We simply prefix their names with a colon when we use them in SQL.

When we compile and run the program, we can use it to add new barcodes to the database. If we try to add a duplicate barcode, a fatal error occurs, and it is handled by a sql whenever construction:

```
$ make insert
$ ./insert 2 1234567890123
$ ./insert 2 1234567890123

Fatal Error
sql error 'duplicate key violates unique constraint "barcode_pk"' in line 33.
$
```

If we want to deal with other data types for our attributes, we declare them accordingly. For floating-point numbers to handle prices that are stored in the database as numeric(7,2) we use the C double type. For dates, we can use a character type long enough to store the date as a string.

## Working with Variable-Length Data

We encounter a slight problem when we come to the varchar data type. This type contains a variable number of characters, and is not necessarily null-terminated, as with normal C character strings. We have no simple way of representing a varchar type in C, so we will need to resort to a structure with two members: a character array of maximum length and an integer count that records the number of valid characters in the array.

Fortunately, ecpg can take care of the declaration for us. We just need to use the pseudo-type varchar instead of char when declaring the variable. ecpg declares a structure with two members called arr and len, containing the characters and the length, respectively.

The next example, insert2.pgc, is a program for adding new products to the item table in our database. We take a product description (which is a varchar(64)) and two floating-point numbers representing cost and selling prices, and insert a new row in the table.

```c
#include <stdio.h>
#include <string.h>
#include <stdlib.h>

EXEC SQL include sqlca;
EXEC SQL whenever sqlwarning sqlprint;
EXEC SQL whenever sqlerror do GiveUp();

void GiveUp()
{
    fprintf(stderr, "Fatal Error\n");
    sqlprint();
}

main(int argc, char *argv[])
{
    EXEC SQL BEGIN declare section;
    char dbname[] = "bpfinal";
    double cost_price, sell_price;
    varchar description[64];
    EXEC SQL END declare section;
```

```
if(argc != 4) {
  printf("usage: insert description cost_price sell_price\n");
  exit(1);
}

strncpy(description.arr, argv[1], sizeof(description.arr));
description.len = strlen(description.arr);
cost_price = atof(argv[2]);
sell_price = atof(argv[3]);

EXEC SQL CONNECT TO :dbname as bpfinal;
EXEC SQL BEGIN;
EXEC SQL at bpfinal INSERT INTO
  item(description, cost_price, sell_price)
  VALUES(:description, :cost_price, :sell_price);
EXEC SQL COMMIT;
EXEC SQL DISCONNECT bpfinal;
}
```

We can insert a new item with a simple invocation:

```
$ ./insert2 "Widget" 1.87 2.93
$
```

Now check that the item table is updated with psql:

```
bpfinal=> SELECT * FROM item;
 item_id | description | cost_price | sell_price
---------+-------------+------------+------------
...
      12 | Widget      |       1.87 |       2.93

bpfinal=>
```

We declare our host variables in the declare section, and use both members of the description structure to create a host variable suitable to be used in the SQL statement for inserting a new row.

As the item table uses a serial item_id, we can (and should) omit an item_id when adding a new row to the table. We can do this by explicitly naming the columns we are going to supply data for in the INSERT.

---

**■Note** If you need to insert a NULL into a column of a table row, you can use the keyword NULL in the VALUES part of the INSERT statement.

---

In this program, by way of variation, we are also using a host variable to specify the database to connect to and demonstrate the use of a named connection.

# Retrieving Data with ecpg

Now that we have introduced host variables, it's time to consider extracting data from the database, since host variables can also provide the storage for tuples (rows) returned by SELECT. Here is a very simple example to get started. Let's count the number of customers we have:

```
EXEC SQL BEGIN declare section;
int count;
EXEC SQL END declare section;

EXEC SQL SELECT count(*) INTO :count FROM customer;
```

We extend SELECT with an INTO clause that specifies the host variables we want to use to retrieve information. In this example, an integer called count is declared, which after successful execution of this SQL statement will contain the number of customers in our database.

Similarly, we can extract a row of data into variables by giving a list of host variables in the INTO clause that matches the data we are selecting. To extract the details of a particular customer by customer_id, we could write:

```
EXEC SQL SELECT addressline, zipcode INTO :addr, :zip
        FROM customer
        WHERE customer_id = 15;
```

The selected columns should always be explicitly listed in SELECT statements, rather than using *. If there is a change to the database schema, your code will be much more resilient. If it does fail, for instance because a column you refer to has been removed, you will at least receive a helpful error message.

We can use host variables in the other clauses of SELECT statements, too. To take the customer_id from a host variable, we could write:

```
WHERE customer_id = :id;
```

The following program, select.pgc, finds the maximum customer_id and uses it to retrieve the ZIP code and first line of the address for that customer. Most of the code is very similar to our earlier examples. Notice that we don't need BEGIN or COMMIT statements, as no data in the database is being changed.

```
#include <stdio.h>
#include <string.h>
#include <stdlib.h>

EXEC SQL include sqlca;
EXEC SQL whenever sqlwarning sqlprint;
EXEC SQL whenever sqlerror do GiveUp();

void GiveUp()
{
    fprintf(stderr, "Fatal Error\n");
    sqlprint();
}
```

```
main(int argc, char *argv[])
{
  EXEC SQL BEGIN declare section;
  int id;
  char zip[10];
  VARCHAR address[64];
  int address_ind;
  EXEC SQL END declare section;

  EXEC SQL CONNECT TO bpfinal;
  EXEC SQL SELECT max(customer_id) into :id FROM customer;
  printf("we have %d customers\n", id);

  EXEC SQL SELECT addressline, zipcode INTO :address:address_ind, :zip
      FROM customer
          WHERE customer_id = :id;

  printf("address is%sNULL\n", address_ind? " ": " not ");
  printf("customer id: %d\n", id);
  printf("%.*s <%.*s>\n", sizeof(zip), zip, address.len, address.arr);

  EXEC SQL DISCONNECT ALL;
}
```

When we compile and run this program, we get the following output:

```
$ ./select
we have 15 customers
 address is not NULL
customer id: 15
MT2 6RT  <4 The Square>
```

The program extracts data returned by a SELECT into a number of host variables, handling both the possibility that the address is stored as a varchar, where we must retrieve the length of the string explicitly, and that the address could be NULL, rather than an actual string of characters.

The address host variable is specially declared, varchar address[64]; which results in a C structure containing both the length and the actual data; the possibility of NULL is handled using an indicator variable, address_ind. We will look at these issues in the next two sections.

## Dealing with Null-Terminated Strings

Ordinarily, C strings are terminated with a null character, and many library functions assume that one is present. For example, if you print a string, the printf function outputs characters until it reaches a null character in the string. Potentially worse is the case of copying character data, as strcpy will blindly copy until a null is encountered.

Character data in the database is not necessarily null-terminated, and therefore column data returned from a SELECT may cause a problem. When outputting data with printf, we may see garbage because printf outputs characters from memory locations beyond the limit of our data until it hits a C null character (\0). Copying with strcpy will continue until a null character is found, which may be at a location well beyond the end of the character data and, therefore, cause corruption when the target string is overwritten.

One way to deal with this is to be very careful when copying character data for use in our programs and make sure that we allow additional space for a null character and place one at the end of our string.

Our sample select.pgc program uses a feature of printf to limit the amount of character data that it will output. The precision field for the %s format allows us to state that we want a maximum of a certain amount of output for the character data.

The following line will print the 10 characters of the fixed-length ZIP code, without requiring a trailing null, and up to 64 characters of the first address line:

```
printf("%.10s %.64s\n", zip, address.arr);
```

In fact, for variable-length data, we will generally see a null terminator, except when the data is of maximum length.

We can be a little more general with the printing of character data by supplying the field precision in arguments to printf, so that if the database design changes, we can be a little more robust. Here's a version of the printf call that avoids explicit data lengths:

```
printf("%.*s %.*s\n", sizeof(zip), zip, address.len, address.arr);
```

## Dealing with NULL Database Values

The second subtlety that we need to address is NULL database values. For instance, it is possible that our customer has not given us an address and the column contains NULL.

We cannot readily distinguish between an empty string and a NULL value, or a zero integer value and NULL, when we retrieve data into host variables. The situation is similar to that we met in the previous chapter. In libpq, we have the function PQgetisnull to tell us whether a result we have retrieved represents a NULL. In embedded SQL, we need to use indicator variables if we want to be able to tell whether a returned value is NULL.

An *indicator variable* is an integer host variable that is used to show whether a retrieved column value is NULL. The indicator is specified with its associated host variable by appending the indicator to the variable, using a colon as a separator, as in this example:

```
SELECT addressline
      INTO :address:address_ind FROM customer
      WHERE ...
```

Here, we have used an indicator variable called address_ind, which will be set to a nonzero value if the value retrieved into host variable address represents a NULL. We should not rely on any particular value (empty string, zero, and so on) being transferred into a host variable that has a NULL value.

---

■**Tip** It is a good idea to name your indicator variables in a way that makes it clear which host variable it relates to. We suggest using a naming convention such as the one used here: adding a suffix _ind to mean indicator variable.

---

## Handling Empty Results

So far in our sample programs in this chapter, we have been careful to make sure that when we retrieve data, we obtain exactly one row. The column values are then extracted into host variables for our program to use.

By making a small change to our select program to look up customers according to ZIP code, we can demonstrate handling cases where no rows are returned. The following sample program (select2.pgc) detects the case where no data is returned from a SELECT:

```
#include <stdio.h>
#include <string.h>
#include <stdlib.h>

EXEC SQL include sqlca;
EXEC SQL whenever sqlwarning sqlprint;
EXEC SQL whenever sqlerror do GiveUp();

void GiveUp()
{
    fprintf(stderr, "Fatal Error\n");
    sqlprint();
    exit(1);
}

main(int argc, char *argv[])
{
  EXEC SQL BEGIN declare section;
  int id;
  char title[4];
  int title_ind;
  char zip[10];
  varchar lname[32];
  varchar town[64];
  int town_ind;
  EXEC SQL END declare section;

  if(argc != 2) {
    printf("Usage: select zipcode\n");
    exit(1);
  }

  strncpy(zip, argv[1], sizeof(zip));

  EXEC SQL CONNECT TO bpfinal;
```

```
        EXEC SQL SELECT customer_id, title, lname, town
                into :id, :title:title_ind, :lname, :town:town_ind
            FROM customer
                WHERE zipcode = :zip;

    if(sqlca.sqlerrd[2] == 0) {
       printf("no customer found\n");
    }
    else {
       printf("title is%sNULL\n", title_ind? " ": " not ");
       printf("town is%sNULL\n", town_ind? " ": " not ");
       printf("customer id: %d\n", id);
       printf("%.*s %.*s <%.*s>\n",
           sizeof(title), title,
           lname.len, lname.arr,
           town.len, town.arr);
    }
    EXEC SQL DISCONNECT ALL;
}
```

In this program, we use the fact the SQL control area will contain information about the number of rows returned in `sqlca.sqlerrd[2]`. If this is zero, then we found no rows. Let's use the program to query some data.

```
$ make select2
$ ./select2 "NT2 2TX"
title is not NULL
town is not NULL
customer id: 3
Miss Matthew <Nicetown>
$ ./select2 "BG4 2XE"
no customer found
$ ./select2 "BG4 2WE"
Fatal Error
sql error SQL error #-203 in line 37.
$
```

When we specify a `zipcode` search, where we find a customer with a `zipcode` that matches, we print out the details. Where there are no corresponding records, we get no records returned. The query detects this and prints a suitable message.

Unfortunately, the third run showed that our program is not yet sufficiently robust! We chose a `zipcode` that belonged to more than one customer, and this caused an error. In this case, two customers have the same `zipcode`. As we cannot store details about both customers in our host variables, the program aborted, displaying an error message. To solve the problem of multiple rows being returned, we need to use a cursor, much as we did in the previous chapter. This is the subject of the next section.

# Implementing Cursors in Embedded SQL

In general, if you cannot guarantee that your query will return a single row, the sensible approach is to use a cursor. We saw these in the previous chapter using libpq. Now let's see how to use cursors with ecpg.

In case you skipped the previous chapter, it is worth reiterating the advice given there. In general, you should avoid writing code that assumes a single row or no rows are returned from a SELECT statement, unless that statement is a simple aggregate, such as a SELECT count(*) FROM type query, or a SELECT on a primary key, where you can guarantee the result will always be exactly one row. When in doubt, use a cursor.

To deal with multiple rows being returned from a query, we retrieve them one at a time using a FETCH, with the column values being received into host variables in the same way as we have seen for single-row SELECT statements. As with the libpq library, we declare a cursor to be used to scroll through a collection of returned rows. The cursor acts as our bookmark, and we fetch the rows until no more data is available.

To use a cursor, we must declare it and specify the query that it relates to. We may use a cursor declaration only within a PostgreSQL transaction, even if the cursor does not update the database:

```
EXEC SQL BEGIN;
EXEC SQL declare mycursor cursor for SELECT ... ;
```

The SELECT statement that we use to define the cursor may contain host variables for conditions in WHERE clauses and so on, but it does not contain an INTO clause, as we are not extracting data into host variables at this stage.

The next step is to open the cursor, to make it ready for fetching the results:

```
EXEC SQL open mycursor;
```

Now we can start to retrieve the result rows. We do this by executing a FETCH with an INTO clause to extract the data values:

```
EXEC SQL fetch next from mycursor into :var1, :var2, ... ;
```

When there are no more result rows left to fetch, we will get a row count in sqlca.sqlerrd[2] of zero and an sqlca.sqlcode of 100.

When we have finished with the cursor, we close it and end the transaction:

```
EXEC SQL close mycursor;
EXEC SQL COMMIT;
```

The following is a sample program (cursor.pgc) that uses a cursor to retrieve the results, similar to a query we saw in Chapter 7. It extracts the dates on which the orders were placed by customers living in a specified town.

```
#include <stdio.h>
#include <string.h>
#include <stdlib.h>
```

```
EXEC SQL include sqlca;
EXEC SQL whenever sqlwarning sqlprint;
EXEC SQL whenever sqlerror do GiveUp();

void GiveUp()
{
    fprintf(stderr, "Fatal Error\n");
    sqlprint();
    exit(1);
}

main(int argc, char *argv[])
{
  EXEC SQL BEGIN declare section;
  varchar town[64];
  int town_ind;
  double shipping;
  char date[10];

  EXEC SQL END declare section;

  if(argc != 2) {
    printf("Usage: cursor town\n");
    exit(1);
  }

  town.len = strlen(argv[1]);
  strncpy(town.arr, argv[1], town.len);
  town.arr[town.len] = '\0';

// ECPGdebug(1, stderr);

  EXEC SQL CONNECT TO bpfinal;

  EXEC SQL declare mycursor cursor for
    SELECT oi.date_placed, oi.shipping FROM
        customer c, orderinfo oi WHERE
        c.customer_id = oi.customer_id and c.town = :town;

  EXEC SQL open mycursor;

  EXEC SQL whenever sqlwarning continue;
  EXEC SQL whenever sqlerror continue;

  while(sqlca.sqlcode == 0) {
```

```
    EXEC SQL fetch from mycursor into :date, :shipping;

    if (sqlca.sqlcode == 0) {
        printf("%.*s <%.2f>\n", sizeof(date), date, shipping);
    }
}

EXEC SQL whenever sqlwarning sqlprint;
EXEC SQL whenever sqlerror do GiveUp();

EXEC SQL close mycursor;
EXEC SQL DISCONNECT ALL;
}
```

This program now neatly takes care of the three cases we might have: finding no orders, finding exactly one order, and finding many orders.

```
$ make cursor
$ ./cursor Erewhon
$ ./cursor Milltown
2000-09-02 <3.99>
$ ./cursor Bingham
2000-06-23 <0.00>
2000-07-21 <0.00>
```

Notice we mix the use of EXEC SQL whenever and more conventional error checking, with the sqlca.sqlcode used to control the loop while data is successfully being retrieved from the database. To ensure the code behaves as we expect, we must reset the warning and error handing (EXEC SQL whenever sqlwarning continue and EXEC SQL whenever sqlerror continue) before we get to the code where we wish to check sqlca.sqlcode. Once we complete the section of code where we wish to handle errors by checking the sqlca.sqlcode explicitly, we return to our previous error-handling behavior.

# Debugging ecpg Code

Although ecpg does a good job of generating C code from pgc files, occasionally you will have a problem compiling the code. This is usually because of a mistake in your C code rather than anything ecpg has done, and you may want to look at the generated code from ecpg, using the real line numbers in the generated C code. To do this, you need to employ a little trick to remove the #line preprocessor directives ecpg inserts, which generally force compiler errors to refer to the original .pgc file, not the .c file that is actually being compiled. This involves the following steps:

- Manually run ecpg to generate a .c file from the .pgc file.

- Use grep to remove the #line directives, writing a new temporary file.

- Move the temporary file back to its rightful place.

- Allow compilation to continue, or invoke the C compiler manually.

Here is an example of how we might do this with `cursor.pgc`:

```
$ ecpg  -I/usr/local/pgsql/include cursor.pgc
$ grep -v '^#line' cursor.c > _1.c
```

At this point, we have a C file, `_1.c`, which contains the preprocessed version of `cursor.pgc`, but with all the compiler line control settings stripped out. We move this back to the original filename, `cursor.c`, and then call `make`, to allow it to perform the final step in the compilation process of generating an executable.

```
$ mv _1.c cursor.c
$ make
cc -I/usr/local/pgsql/include  -L/usr/local/pgsql/lib -lecpg -lpq
  cursor.c -o cursor
$ ./cursor Milltown
2000-09-02 <3.99>
$
```

When we run the code, we see exactly the same output as before. However, if we did get an error, the line numbers from `cursor.c` would be displayed, not those from `cursor.pgc`.

# Summary

This chapter explained how to use SQL in C programs by embedding SQL statements directly in the source code. The translator `ecpg` then generates C code that the compiler can understand to produce an executable.

We covered how to connect to a database and deal with errors that may occur. We demonstrated how to use host variables to provide values for `INSERT` and `UPDATE` statements.

Next, we saw how to implement simple `SELECT` statements and extract row data into host variables, and then use host variables to specify part of the `WHERE` clause. We also saw how to use indicator variables to detect null values in the data being retrieved. We then explored how to use a cursor to retrieve multiple rows returned as a result of a more complex query.

In this chapter, we have built on what we learned in the previous chapter and used a more portable way of interfacing PostgreSQL to C. In some ways, the `libpq` method allows slightly more control over result sets and status information. It also allows an asynchronous mode of operation. On the other hand, embedding SQL makes it easier to deal with binary values (as `ecpg` takes care of all of the conversions needed), is more portable, and generally makes it much easier to read the underlying SQL in the program. The method you choose depends on the requirements of your application.

In the next chapter, we move onto another programming language we can use with PostgreSQL: PHP.

■ ■ ■

# CHAPTER 15

# Accessing PostgreSQL from PHP

**W**ith the proliferation of web-based interfaces for everything from online banking to university course scheduling systems to online dating services, integrating database-driven back-ends with browser-based front-ends has become an incredibly important (and sensitive) aspect of online development. Web-based interfaces have achieved enormous success for the following reasons:

- Web browsers offer a common and familiar interface for browsing data.

- Web-based applications can easily be integrated into an existing web site.

- Web (HTML) interfaces are easily created and modified.

In this chapter, we will explore various methods for accessing PostgreSQL from PHP. PHP is a server-side, cross-platform scripting language for writing web-based applications. It allows programmers to embed program logic in HTML pages, and thus serve dynamic web pages. PHP allows us to create web-based user interfaces that interact with PostgreSQL. Here, we will focus on designing PHP scripts that make effective use of PHP's PostgreSQL interface.

---

■**Note**  In this chapter, we will assume at least a basic understanding of the PHP language and the use of PHP version 4 or 5 (most of the code examples and descriptions also apply to earlier versions of PHP, but there may be a few differences in functionality). If you are unfamiliar with PHP, you might want to explore the PHP web site, at http://www.php.net/. You can also refer to *Beginning PHP 5 and MySQL: From Novice to Professional*, by Jason Gilmore (Apress, 2004; ISBN 1-893115-51-8).

---

## Adding PostgreSQL Support to PHP

Before you can begin developing PHP scripts that interface with a PostgreSQL database, you will need to include PostgreSQL support in your PHP installation.

If you are unsure whether your existing PHP installation already has PostgreSQL support, create a simple script named phpinfo.php (which should be placed in your web server's document root), containing the following lines:

```
<?php
   phpinfo();
?>
```

Examine the output of this script in your web browser. If PostgreSQL support is available, the browser output will contain a section similar to that shown in Figure 15-1.

### pgsql

| PostgreSQL Support | enabled |
| --- | --- |
| PostgreSQL(libpq) Version | 7.3.9-RH |
| Multibyte character support | enabled |
| SSL support | enabled |
| Active Persistent Links | 0 |
| Active Links | 0 |

**Figure 15-1.** *Checking for PostgreSQL support in a PHP installation*

Alternatively, if you're running PHP version 4.3.0 or later, you can run php -m from the command line and look for pgsql in the list of modules.

If your PHP installation already has PostgreSQL support, you can skip to the next section in this chapter.

If you need to add PostgreSQL support and you are building PHP from source, this is fairly easy. Simply pass the --with-pgsql option to the configure script:

```
$ ./configure --with-pgsql
```

You can optionally specify the directory of your PostgreSQL installation if the configure script is unable to locate it by itself:

```
$ ./configure --with-pgsql=/var/lib/pgsql
```

Remember that you might need to pass additional options to the configure script depending on your build requirements. For example, to build PHP with support for PostgreSQL, IMAP, and LDAP, you would use the following command line:

```
$ ./configure --with-pgsql --with-imap --with-ldap
```

Refer to the PHP documentation (specifically, the INSTALL document included with the PHP distribution) for additional compilation options and installation instructions. You can also read these instructions online at http://www.php.net/manual/en/install.php.

# Using the PHP API for PostgreSQL

All of the interaction with the PostgreSQL database is performed through the PostgreSQL extension, which provides a comprehensive set of PHP functions. For a complete list of functions and further information about them, refer to http://www.php.net/pgsql.

A simple PHP script follows. It opens a connection to a PostgreSQL database named bpsimple, selects some rows, prints the number of rows in the result set, frees the memory consumed by the rows, and then closes the connection.

```php
<?php
    /* Connect to the PostgreSQL database and store the connection handle. */
    $db_handle = pg_connect('dbname=bpsimple user=jon password=secret');

    /* Define and execute our SQL query string. */
    $query = 'SELECT * FROM item';
    $result = pg_query($db_handle, $query);

    /* Print the number of rows in the result using pg_num_rows(). */
    echo 'Number of rows: ' . pg_num_rows($result);

    /* Free the memory used by the result set and close the connection handle. */
    pg_free_result($result);
    pg_close($db_handle);
?>
```

As you can see, interacting with the database from within PHP is fairly straightforward. We will now cover the various aspects of the PHP PostgreSQL extension in more depth.

# Making Database Connections

Before interacting with the database, a connection must first be opened. Each connection is represented by a single variable. We'll refer to this variable as the *connection handle*. PHP allows you to have multiple connections open at once, each with its own unique connection handle. This is useful in the case where a single PHP script needs to communicate with multiple database servers.

## Creating a New Database Connection

We open a database connection using the pg_connect() function. This function takes a connection string as its only argument and returns a database connection handle. Here's an example:

```php
$db_handle = pg_connect('dbname=bpsimple user=jon password=secret');
```

In this example, the connection string specifies the database name (dbname=bpsimple), a username (user=jon), and the user's password (password=secret).

You have the option of using single quotes to delimit the connection strings, as used in the previous example, but if you want to use PHP variables, remember to surround the connection string in double quotes:

```php
$dbname = 'bpsimple';
$user = 'jon';
$password = 'secret';

$db_handle = pg_connect("dbname=$dbname user=$user password=$password");
```

All of the standard PostgreSQL connection parameters are available in the connection string. The most commonly used parameters and their meanings are shown in Table 15-1.

**Table 15-1.** *Common Connection Parameters*

| Parameter | Meaning |
|---|---|
| dbname | The name of the database to which we want to connect |
| user | The username to use when connecting to the target database |
| password | The user's password, which authenticates the user's access to the database |
| host | The host name of the server on which PostgreSQL is running |
| hostaddr | The IP address of the server on which PostgreSQL is running |
| port | The TCP/IP port on which the PostgreSQL server is listening |

If the connection attempt fails, the pg_connect() function will return false. Failed connection attempts can thus be detected by testing the return value:

```php
<?php
    $db_handle = pg_connect('dbname=bpsimple user=jon password=secret');
    if ($db_handle) {
        echo 'Connection attempt succeeded.';
    } else {
        echo 'Connection attempt failed.';
    }
    pg_close($db_handle);
?>
```

As we mentioned, PHP supports multiple concurrent database connections. Each call to pg_connect() will return a new connection handle. Each connection attempt specifies its own connection string:

```php
$db_handle1 = pg_connect('dbname=billing user=dan');
$db_handle2 = pg_connect('dbname=inventory user=tom');
```

## Creating a Persistent Connection

PHP also supports *persistent* database connections. Persistent connections are held open beyond the lifetime of the page request, whereas normal connections are closed at the end of the page request. PHP maintains a list of currently open connections and, if a request is made for a new persistent database connection with the same connection parameters as one of the open connections in this list, a handle to the existing opened connection is returned instead. This has the advantage of saving the script the additional overhead of creating a new database connection when a suitable one already exists in the connection pool.

To open a persistent connection to PostgreSQL, use the pg_pconnect() function. This function behaves exactly like the pg_connect() function described in the previous section, except that it requests a persistent connection, if one is available.

The ideal use of a persistent connection is in those instances where multiple pages will always request the same kind of database connection (meaning one containing the same connection parameters). In such cases, persistent connections offer a substantial performance boost.

---

■**Caution** Use persistent connections with care. Overusing persistent connections could lead to a large number of idle database connections to your database, each of which contributes toward the total number of active connections. Once the maximum number of connections permitted by the database server is reached, new connection attempts will be denied.

---

## Closing Connections

When they're no longer needed, connection handles can be closed. This frees any client and server resources dedicated to maintaining the connection, thus making room for new connections.

PHP will automatically close any open nonpersistent database connections at the end of the script's execution. However, if necessary, such as when you need to close the connection immediately, you can explicitly close database connections using the pg_close() function:

pg_close($db_handle);

If the provided connection handle is invalid, pg_close() will return false. Otherwise, pg_close() will return true upon success.

---

■**Note** In the case of persistent connections, this function will not actually close the connection. Instead, the connection will just be returned to the database connection pool.

---

## Learning More About Connections

PHP provides a number of simple functions for retrieving information about a connection handle, as listed in Table 15-2.

**Table 15-2.** *Database Connection Information Functions*

| Function | Description |
| --- | --- |
| pg_dbname() | Returns the name of the current database |
| pg_host() | Returns the host name associated with the current connection |
| pg_options() | Returns the options associated with the current connection (except for the database name) |
| pg_port() | Returns the port number of the current connection |
| pg_tty() | Returns the TTY name associated with the current connection |

All of these functions require a connection handle as their sole argument and will return either a string or a number upon success. Otherwise, they will return `false`. Here is an example:

```php
<?php
    $db_handle = pg_connect('dbname=bpsimple user=jon password=secret');
    echo "<h1>Connection Information</h1>\n";
    echo 'Database name: ' . pg_dbname($db_handle) . "<br />\n";
    echo 'Hostname: ' . pg_host($db_handle) . "<br />\n";
    echo 'Options: ' . pg_options($db_handle) . "<br />\n";
    echo 'Port: ' . pg_port($db_handle) . "<br />\n";
    echo 'TTY name: ' . pg_tty($db_handle) . "<br />\n";
    pg_close($db_handle);
?>
```

# Building Queries

SQL queries are merely strings, so they can be built using any of PHP's string functions. Here is an example:

```php
$lastname = strtolower($lastname);
$query = "SELECT * FROM customer WHERE lname = '$lastname'";
```

This example converts `$lastname` to lowercase first. Then it builds the query string using PHP's standard string interpolation syntax.

Here is an alternative method for accomplishing the same task:

```php
$query = "SELECT * FROM customer WHERE lname = '" . strtolower($lastname) . "'";
```

This example uses an inline call to `strtolower()`. Functions cannot be called from inside string literals (in other words, between quotes), so we need to break our query string into two pieces and concatenate them (using the dot operator). Unlike with the previous example, the result of the `strtolower()` function will not affect the value of `$lastname` after this line is executed.

Here is another example that will build the same query:

```php
$query = sprintf("SELECT * FROM customer WHERE lname = '%s'",
                 strtolower($lastname));
```

This example uses the `sprintf()` function to generate the query string. The `sprintf()` function uses special character combinations (such as `%s`) to format strings. More information about the `sprintf()` function is available at `http://www.php.net/sprintf`.

Each of these approaches will produce exactly the same query string. The best method to use depends on the situation. For simple queries, a direct string assignment will probably work best, but when the situation calls for the interpolation or transformation of a large number of variables, you might want to explore different approaches. In some cases, you might encounter a trade-off between execution speed and code readability. This is true of most programming tasks, so you will need to apply your best judgment.

Here's an example of a complex query written as a long assignment string:

```php
$query = "UPDATE table $tablename SET " . strtolower($column) . " = '" .
         strtoupper($value) . "'";
```

This could be rewritten using the PHP sprintf() function as follows:

```
$query = sprintf("UPDATE table %s SET %s = '%s'", $tablename,
                strtolower($column), strtoupper($value));
```

The second expression is clearly more readable than the first, although benchmarking will show that this readability comes at a slight performance cost. In this case, the trade-off of readability over execution speed is probably worth it, unless you are executing many such string constructions per page request.

## Creating Complex Queries

In an ideal world, all of our queries would be as simple as those used in the previous examples, but we all know that is seldom true. Fortunately, PHP offers a number of convenient functions to aid us in building more complex queries.

For example, consider the case where we need to perform a large number of row deletions. In raw SQL, the query might look something like this:

```
DELETE FROM items WHERE item_id = 4 OR item_id = 6
```

Now, that query alone doesn't appear all that complicated, but what if this query needed to delete a dozen rows, specifying the item_id of each row in the WHERE clause? The query string gets pretty long at that point, and because the number of expressions in the WHERE clause will probably vary, we need to account for these details in our code.

We will probably receive our list of item IDs to be deleted from the user via some method of HTML form input, so we can assume they will be stored in some kind of array format (at least, that's the most convenient means of storing the list). We'll assume this array of item IDs is named $item_ids. Based on that assumption, the preceding query could be constructed as follows:

```
<?php
    $db_handle = pg_connect('dbname=bpsimple user=jon password=secret');
    $query = 'DELETE FROM item WHERE item_id = ';
    $query .= implode(' or item_id = ', $item_ids);
    $result = pg_query($db_handle, $query);
    echo pg_affected_rows($result) . ' rows were deleted.';
    pg_close($db_handle);
?>
```

This will produce an SQL query with an arbitrary number of item IDs. Based on this code, we can write a generic function to perform our deletions:

```
<?php
    function sqlDelete($tablename, $column, $ids)
    {
        $query = '';
        if (is_array($ids) && !empty($ids)) {
            $query = "DELETE FROM $tablename WHERE $column = ";
            $query .= implode(" or $column = ", $ids);
        }
        return $query;
    }
?>
```

## Executing Queries

Once the query string has been constructed, the next step is to execute it. Queries are executed using the pg_query() function, which is responsible for sending the query string to the PostgreSQL server and returning the result set.

Here's a simple example to illustrate the use of pg_query():

```php
<?php
    $db_handle = pg_connect('dbname=bpsimple user=jon password=secret');
    $query = 'SELECT * FROM customer';
    $result = pg_query($db_handle, $query);
    echo pg_num_rows($result) . ' rows were selected.';
    pg_close($db_handle);
?>
```

As you can see, pg_query() requires two parameters: an active connection handle and a query string. pg_query() will return a result set upon successful execution of the query. We will work with result sets in the next section.

If the query fails, or if the connection handle is invalid, pg_query() will return false. Therefore, it is prudent to test the return value of pg_query() so that we can detect such failures. The following example includes some result checking:

```php
<?php
    $db_handle = pg_connect('dbname=bpsimple user=jon password=secret');
    $query = 'SELECT * FROM customer';
    $result = pg_query($db_handle, $query);
    if ($result) {
        echo "The query executed successfully.<br />\n";
    } else {
        echo "The query failed with the following error:<br />\n";
        echo pg_last_error($db_handle);
    }
    pg_close($db_handle);
?>
```

In this example, we test the return value of pg_query(). If it is not false (in other words, it has a value), $result represents a result set. Otherwise, if $result is false, we know that an error has occurred. We can then use the pg_last_error() function to print a descriptive message for that error. We will cover error messages in more detail later in this chapter.

# Working with Result Sets

Upon successful execution of a query, pg_query() will return a result set identifier, through which we can access the result set. The result set stores the result of the query as returned by the database. For example, if a selection query were executed, the result set would contain the resulting rows.

PHP offers a number of useful functions for working with result sets. All of them take a result set identifier as an argument, so they can be used only after a query has been successfully executed. We learned how to test for successful execution in the previous section.

We'll start with the two simplest result functions: pg_num_rows() and pg_num_fields(). These two functions return the number of rows and the number of fields in the result set, respectively. Here is an example:

```php
<?php
    $db_handle = pg_connect('dbname=bpsimple user=jon password=secret');
    $query = 'SELECT * FROM customer';
    $result = pg_query($db_handle, $query);
    if ($result) {
        echo "The query executed successfully.<br />\n";
        echo "Number of rows in result: " . pg_num_rows($result) . "<br />\n";
        echo "Number of fields in result: " . pg_num_fields($result);
    } else {
        echo "The query failed with the following error:<br />\n";
        echo pg_errormessage($db_handle);
    }
    pg_close($db_handle);
?>
```

These functions will return -1 if they encounter an error.

There's also the pg_affected_rows() function, which will return the number of rows *affected* by the query. For example, if we were performing insertions or deletions with our query, we wouldn't actually be retrieving any rows from the database, so the number of rows or fields in the result set would not be indicative of the query's result. Instead, the changes take place inside the database. pg_affected_rows() will return the number of rows that were affected by these types of queries (in other words, the number of rows inserted, deleted, or updated):

```php
<?php
    $db_handle = pg_connect('dbname=bpsimple user=jon password=secret');
    $query = 'DELETE FROM item WHERE cost_price > 10.00';
    $result = pg_query($db_handle, $query);
    if ($result) {
        echo "The query executed successfully.<br />\n";
        echo "Number of rows deleted: " . pg_affected_rows($result);
    } else {
        echo "The query failed with the following error:<br />\n";
        echo pg_errormessage($db_handle);
    }
    pg_close($db_handle);
?>
```

The pg_affected_rows() function will return zero if no rows in the database were affected by the query, as in the case of a selection query.

## Extracting Values from Result Sets

There are a number of ways to extract values from result sets. We will start with the simplest: the pg_fetch_result() function, which retrieves a single value from a result set. In addition to a result identifier, we also specify the row and field that we want to retrieve from the result set.

The row is specified numerically, while the field may be specified either by name or by numeric index. Numbering always begins at zero. Here's an example using pg_fetch_result():

```php
<?php
    $db_handle = pg_connect('dbname=bpsimple user=jon password=secret');
    $query = 'SELECT title, fname, lname FROM customer';
    $result = pg_query($db_handle, $query);
    if ($result) {
        echo "The query executed successfully.<br />\n";
        for ($row = 0; $row < pg_num_rows($result); $row++) {
            $fullname = pg_fetch_result($result, $row, 'title') . " ";
            $fullname .= pg_fetch_result($result, $row, 'fname') . " ";
            $fullname .= pg_fetch_result($result, $row, 'lname');
            echo "Customer: $fullname<br />\n";
        }
    } else {
        echo "The query failed with the following error:<br />\n";
        echo pg_last_error($db_handle);
    }
    pg_close($db_handle);
?>
```

Using numeric indexes, this same block of code could also be written like this:

```php
<?php
    $db_handle = pg_connect('dbname=bpsimple user=jon password=secret');
    $query = 'SELECT title, fname, lname FROM customer';
    $result = pg_query($db_handle, $query);
    if ($result) {
        echo "The query executed successfully.<br />\n";
        for ($row = 0; $row < pg_num_rows($result); $row++) {
            $fullname = '';
            for ($col = 0; $col < pg_num_fields($result); $col++) {
                $fullname .= pg_fetch_result($result, $row, $col) . ' ';
            }
            echo "Customer: $fullname<br />\n";
        }
    } else {
        echo "The query failed with the following error:<br />\n";
        echo pg_errormessage($db_handle);
    }
    pg_close($db_handle);
?>
```

The first example is a bit more readable, however, and doesn't depend on the order of the fields in the result set.

PHP also offers more advanced ways of retrieving values from result sets, because iterating through rows of results isn't especially efficient. PHP provides two functions, pg_fetch_row() and pg_fetch_array(), that can return multiple result values at once. Each of these functions returns an array.

pg_fetch_row() returns an array that corresponds to a single row in the result set. The array is indexed numerically, starting from zero. Here is the previous example rewritten to use pg_fetch_row():

```php
<?php
    $db_handle = pg_connect('dbname=bpsimple user=jon password=secret');
    $query = 'SELECT title, fname, lname FROM customer';
    $result = pg_query($db_handle, $query);
    if ($result) {
        echo "The query executed successfully.<br />\n";
        for ($row = 0; $row < pg_num_rows($result); $row++) {
            $values = pg_fetch_row($result, $row);
            echo 'Customer: ' . implode(' ', $values) . "<br />\n";
        }
    } else {
        echo "The query failed with the following error:<br />\n";
        echo pg_last_error($db_handle);
    }
    pg_close($db_handle);
?>
```

As you can see, using pg_fetch_row() eliminates the multiple calls to pg_fetch_result(). It also places the result values in an array, which can be easily manipulated using PHP's native array functions.

In this example, however, we are still accessing the fields by their numeric indexes. Ideally, we should also be able to access each field by its associated name. To accomplish that, we can use the pg_fetch_array() function. This function also returns an array, but it allows us to specify whether we want that array indexed numerically or associatively (using the field names as keys). This preference is specified by passing one of the following as the third argument to pg_fetch_array():

- PGSQL_ASSOC, to index the resulting array by field name

- PGSQL_NUM, to index the resulting array numerically

- PGSQL_BOTH, to index the resulting array both numerically and by field name

If you don't specify one of these indexing methods, PGSQL_BOTH will be used by default. Note that this will double the size of your result set, so you're probably better off explicitly specifying one of the other options. Also note that the field names will always be returned in lowercase letters, regardless of how they're represented in the database itself.

Here's the example rewritten once more, now using pg_fetch_array():

```php
<?php
    $db_handle = pg_connect('dbname=bpsimple user=jon password=secret');
    $query = 'SELECT title, fname, lname FROM customer';
    $result = pg_query($db_handle, $query);
    if ($result) {
        echo "The query executed successfully.<br />\n";
        for ($row = 0; $row < pg_num_rows($result); $row++) {
            $values = pg_fetch_array($result, $row, PGSQL_ASSOC);
            $fullname = $values['title'] . ' ';
            $fullname .= $values['fname'] . ' ';
            $fullname .= $values['lname'];
            echo "Customer: $fullname<br />\n";
        }
    } else {
        echo "The query failed with the following error:</ br>\n";
        echo pg_last_error($db_handle);
    }
    pg_close($db_handle);
?>
```

PHP also allows us to fetch the result values with the pg_fetch_object() function. Each field name will be represented as a property of an object. Thus, fields cannot be accessed numerically. Written using pg_fetch_object(), our example looks like this:

```php
<?php
    $db_handle = pg_connect('dbname=bpsimple user=jon password=secret');
    $query = 'SELECT title, fname, lname FROM customer';
    $result = pg_query($db_handle, $query);
    if ($result) {
        echo "The query executed successfully.<br />\n";
        for ($row = 0; $row < pg_num_rows($result); $row++) {
            $values = pg_fetch_object($result, $row);
            $fullname = $values->title . ' ';
            $fullname .= $values->fname . ' ';
            $fullname .= $values->lname;
            echo "Customer: $fullname<br />\n";
        }
    } else {
        echo "The query failed with the following error:<br />\n";
        echo pg_last_error($db_handle);
    }
    pg_close($db_handle);
?>
```

## Getting Field Information

PostgreSQL supports a notion of NULL field values. PHP doesn't necessarily define NULL the same way PostgreSQL does, however. To account for this, PHP provides the pg_field_is_null() function so that we may determine whether a field value is NULL based on the PostgreSQL definition of NULL:

```
if (pg_field_is_null($result, $row, $field)) {
    echo "$field is NULL.";
}
```

The pg_field_name() and pg_field_num() functions return the name or number of a given field. The fields are indexed numerically, starting with zero:

```
<?php
    $db_handle = pg_connect('dbname=bpsimple user=jon password=secret');
    $query = 'SELECT title, fname, lname FROM customer';
    $result = pg_query($db_handle, $query);
    echo 'Field 1 is named: ' . pg_field_name($result, 1) . "<br />\n";
    echo 'Field item_id is number: ' . pg_field_num($result, 'fname');
    pg_close($db_handle);
?>
```

Note that pg_field_name() will return the field name as specified in the SELECT statement.

We can determine the (internal) size, printed (character) length, and type of fields using the functions pg_field_size(), pg_field_prtlen(), and pg_field_type(), respectively.

```
<?php
    $db_handle = pg_connect('dbname=bpsimple user=jon password=secret');
    $query = 'SELECT title, fname, lname FROM customer';
    $result = pg_query($db_handle, $query);
    echo 'Field fname is number: ' . pg_field_num($result, 'fname') . "<br />\n";
    echo 'Field 1 is named: ' . pg_field_name($result, 1) . "<br />\n";
    echo 'Type of field 1: ' . pg_field_type($result, 1) . "<br />\n";
    echo 'Size of field 1: ' . pg_field_size($result, 1) . "<br />\n";
    echo 'Length of field 1: ' . pg_field_prtlen($result, $row, 1);
    pg_close($db_handle);
?>
```

As usual, the numeric field indexes start at zero. Field indexes may also be specified as a string representing the field name.

Also, if the size of the field is variable, pg_field_size() will return a -1 or false on an error. pg_field_prtlen() will return -1 on an error.

## Freeing Result Sets

Query results will remain in memory until the script finishes execution. Typically, this won't present a problem, as the resources are released very quickly. However, in cases where several large datasets are required, you might want to consider releasing query resources as possible. One function, pg_free_result(), is available for this task.

```
pg_free_result($result);
```

Using this function is necessary only if you're especially worried about memory consumption in your script, and you know you won't be using this result set again later on in your script's execution.

## Type Conversion of Result Values

PHP does not offer the diverse data type support you might find in other languages, so values in result sets are sometimes converted from their original data type to a PHP-native data type. For the most part, this conversion will have very little or no effect on your application, but it is important to be aware that some type conversion may occur:

- All integer and OID types are converted to integer values.

- All forms of floating-point numbers are converted to double values.

- All other types (such as arrays) are represented as string values.

# Error Handling

Nearly all PostgreSQL-related functions return some sort of predictable value on an error (generally false or -1). This makes it fairly easy to detect error situations so that a script can fail gracefully. Here is an example:

```
$db_handle = pg_connect('dbname=bpsimple user=jon password=secret');
if (!$db_handle) {
    header("Location: http://www.example.com/error.php");
    exit;
}
```

In this example, the user would be redirected to an error page if the database connection attempt failed.

We can use pg_last_error() to retrieve the text of the actual error message as returned by the database server. pg_last_error() will always return the text of the *last* error message generated by the server. Be sure to take that into consideration when designing your error handling and display logic.

The pg_last_notice() function works exactly like pg_last_error(), except that it displays the last notice message (usually a nonfatal warning), instead of the last error message. pg_last_notice() is available only in PHP 4.3.0 and later.

You will find that, depending on your level of error reporting, PHP can be fairly verbose when an error occurs, often outputting several lines of errors and warnings. In a production environment, it is often undesirable to display this type of message to the end user. The most direct solution is to lower the level of error reporting in PHP (controlled via the error_reporting configuration variable in the php.ini). The second option is to suppress these error messages directly from PHP code on a per-function-call basis. The PHP language uses the @ symbol to request error suppression. For example, no errors will be output from the following code:

```
$db_handle = pg_connect('host=nonexistent_host');
$result = @pg_query($db_handle, 'SELECT * FROM item');
```

Without the @ symbol, the second line would generate an error complaining about the lack of a valid database connection (assuming your error reporting level was high enough to cause that error to be displayed). Note that this error could still be detected by testing the value of $result, though, so suppressing the error message output doesn't preclude our dealing with error situations programmatically. Furthermore, we could display the error message at our convenience using the pg_last_error() function.

## Getting and Setting Character Encoding

If character encoding support is enabled in PostgreSQL, PHP provides functions for getting and setting the current client encoding. The default encoding is based on whichever encoding was selected when the database was created, usually SQL_ASCII.

The supported character sets are SQL_ASCII, EUC_JP, EUC_CN, EUC_KR, EUC_TW, UNICODE, MULE_INTERNAL, LATIN[1-9], KOI8, WIN, ALT, SJIS, BIG5, and WIN1250.

The pg_client_encoding() function will return the current client encoding:

```
$encoding = pg_client_encoding($db_handle);
pg_set_client_encoding()
```

We can set the current client encoding using the pg_set_client_encoding() function:

```
pg_set_client_encoding($db_handle, 'UNICODE'
```

## Using PEAR

The PHP Extension and Application Repository (PEAR) is an attempt to replicate the functionality of Perl's CPAN in the PHP community. The following are the official goals of PEAR:

- To provide a consistent means for library code authors to share their code with other developers

- To give the PHP community an infrastructure for sharing code

- To define standards that help developers write portable and reusable code

- To provide tools for code maintenance and distribution

PEAR is primarily a large collection of PHP classes that make use of PHP's object-oriented programming capabilities.

---

■**Note** To use PEAR, you need to be familiar with PHP's syntax for working with classes. PHP 4's object-oriented extensions are documented at http://www.php.net/manual/en/language.oop.php. PHP 5's object-oriented extensions are documented at http://www.php.net/manual/en/language.oop5.php. More information on PEAR is available at http://pear.php.net/.

---

# Using PEAR's Database Abstraction Interface

PEAR includes a database (DB) abstraction interface. The advantage of using a database abstraction interface instead of calling the database's native functions directly is code independence. If you use a database abstraction interface, and you need to move your project to a different database, the task will be trivial.

PEAR's DB interface also adds some value-added features, such as convenient access to multiple result sets and integrated error handling. All of the database interaction is handled through the DB classes and objects. This is conceptually similar to Perl's DBI interface.

The main disadvantage to a database abstraction interface is the performance overhead it incurs on your application's execution. Once again, this is a situation where there is a trade-off between code flexibility and performance.

The following example illustrates the use of the DB interface. Note that this example assumes that the PEAR DB interface has already been installed and that it can be found via the current include_path setting.

```php
<?php
    /* Import the PEAR DB interface. */
    require_once "DB.php";

    /* Database connection parameters. */
    $username = "jon";
    $password = "secret";
    $hostname = "localhost";
    $dbname = "bpsimple";
    $protocol = "unix";

    /* Construct the DSN - Data Source Name. */
    $dsn = "pgsql://$username:$password@$hostname+$protocol/$dbname";

    /* Attempt to connect to the database. */
    $db = DB::connect($dsn);

    /* Check for any connection errors. */
    if (DB::isError($db)) {
        die ($db->getMessage());
    }

    /* Execute a selection query. */
    $query = 'SELECT title, fname, lname FROM customer';
    $result = $db->query($query);

    /* Check for any query execution errors. */
    if (DB::isError($result)) {
        die ($result->getMessage());
    }
```

```
    /* Fetch and display the query results. */
    while ($row = $result->fetchRow(DB_FETCHMODE_ASSOC)) {
        $fullname = $row['title'] . ' ';
        $fullname .= $row['fname'] . ' ';
        $fullname .= $row['lname'];
        echo "Customer: $fullname<br />\n";
    }

    /* Disconnect from the database. */
    $db->disconnect();
?>
```

As you can see, this code, while not using any PostgreSQL functions directly, still follows the same programmatic logic of our previous examples. It is also easy to see how this example could be adapted to use another type of database (Oracle or MySQL, for example) without much effort.

## Error Handling with PEAR

Using the PEAR DB interface offers developers a number of additional advantages. For example, PEAR includes an integrated error-handling system. Here is some code to demonstrate error handling:

```
<?php
    /* Import the PEAR DB interface. */
    require_once 'DB.php';

    /* Construct the DSN - Data Source Name. */
    $dsn = "pgsql://jon:secret@localhost+unix/bpsimple";

    /* Attempt to connect to the database. */
    $db = DB::connect($dsn);

    /* Check for any connection errors. */
    if (DB::isError($db)) {
        die ($db->getMessage());
    }
?>
```

Here, we see the first instance of PEAR's error-handling capabilities: DB::isError(). If the call to DB::connect() fails for some reason, it will return a PEAR_Error instance, instead of a database connection object. We can test for this case using the DB::isError() function, as shown in the example.

Knowing an error occurred is important, but finding out why that error occurred is even more important. We can retrieve the text of the error message (in this case, the connection error generated by PostgreSQL) using the getMessage() method of the PEAR_Error object. This is also demonstrated in the preceding example.

The error-handling system can be configured at runtime, as follows:

```
/* Make errors fatal. */
$db->setErrorHandling(PEAR_ERROR_DIE);
```

Note that we have changed PEAR's error-handling behavior with the call to the setErrorHandling() method. Setting the error-handling behavior to PEAR_ERROR_DIE will cause PHP to exit fatally if an error occurs.

Here's a list of the other error-handling behaviors:

- PEAR_ERROR_RETURN, to simply return an error object (default)

- PEAR_ERROR_PRINT, to print the error message and continue execution

- PEAR_ERROR_TRIGGER, to use PHP's trigger_error() function to raise an internal error

- PEAR_ERROR_DIE, to print the error message and abort execution

- PEAR_ERROR_CALLBACK, to use a callback function to handle the error before aborting execution

Additional information about the PEAR_Error class and PEAR error handling is available from http://pear.php.net/manual/en/core.pear.pear-error.php.

## Preparing and Executing Queries with PEAR

PEAR also includes a handy method of preparing and executing queries. Here's an abbreviated example demonstrating the prepare() and execute() methods of the DB interface. This example assumes we already have a valid database connection (from DB::connect()):

```
/* Set up the $items array. */
$items = array(
    '6241527836190' => 1,
    '7241427238373' => 2,
    '7093454306788' => 3
);

/* Prepare our template SQL statement. */
$statement = $db->prepare('INSERT INTO barcode VALUES(?,?)');

/* Execute the statement for each entry in the $items array. */
while (list($barcode, $item_id) = each($items)) {
    $db->execute($statement, array($barcode, $item_id));
}
```

The call to the prepare() method creates a SQL template that can be executed repeatedly. Note the two wildcard spots in the statement that are specified using question marks. These placeholders will be replaced with actual values later on when we call the execute() method.

Assuming we have an array of $items that contain barcodes and item IDs, we will want to perform one database insertion per item. To accomplish this, we construct a loop to iterate over each entry in the $items array, extract the barcode and item ID, and then execute the prepared SQL statement.

As we mentioned, the execute() method will replace the placeholder values in the prepared statement with those values passed to it in the second argument in array form. In this example, this would be the array($barcode, $item_id) argument. The placeholder values are replaced in the order that these new values are specified, so it's important to get them right.

# Summary

In this chapter, we examined the ways that a PostgreSQL database can be accessed from the PHP scripting language. We covered the various aspects of database connections, query building and execution, result set manipulation, and error handling. We also introduced the PEAR database abstraction interface.

In the next chapter, we'll explore how to access a PostgreSQL database from Perl.

# CHAPTER 16

■■■

# Accessing PostgreSQL from Perl

**A**s earlier chapters have shown, communicating with PostgreSQL generally involves a lot of string manipulation. One language that excels at string manipulation is Perl.

In Chapter 13, we demonstrated that the libpq interface is a powerful way to access a PostgreSQL database, but there are disadvantages. We need to use string manipulation to pass values to queries and to retrieve results, and for short programs, the C code dealing with strings can overshadow the database interactions. As Chapter 13 pointed out, although binary access is possible, its benefits are minimal. With Perl, strings are much more sophisticated, supporting functionality such as joining, splitting, pattern matching, and automatic conversion to and from other data types.

Perl has also historically been associated with web server processing (although more modern mechanisms such as PHP, described in the previous chapter, are taking over that role). Having interfaces to databases definitely adds benefits.

If you know even a little about Perl, you will be aware that one of the language's axioms is that there is always more than one way to tackle any given job. In fact, Perl enthusiasts would be disappointed if they had to limit their options to single figures. We do not propose to bombard you with numerous techniques for accessing PostgreSQL databases from Perl, however. Instead, we will present a single methodology.

There are essentially three ways to access PostgreSQL from Perl:

- Low-level access, which is essentially a Perl mapping of the libpq C interface (Module Pg)

- High-level access, using a database independent layer (DBI)

- Access by embedding the Perl interpreter (similar to the description in Chapter 14)

We will describe only the high-level DBI access mechanism, because it is the simplest to install and use. This method is database-independent, yet is still very flexible and powerful. If you are interested in a libpq-style of working, we suggest taking a look at Module Pg, which is part of the DBD::Pg database driver. PL/Perl requires a version of Perl to have been initially built as a shared library—libperl.so, as opposed to the more usual libperl.a (see the instructions for building Perl found in Perl source distributions).

---

■**Note** The code in this chapter will not make use of many Perl idioms, so it should be readable by most C programmers. However, we will assume a basic understanding of the Perl language. If you are unfamiliar with the language, some useful starting points are `http://www.perl.org` and `http://www.cpan.org`. You can also refer to *Beginning Perl, Second Edition*, by James Lee with Peter Wainwright and Simon Cozens (Apress, 2004; ISBN 1-59059-391-X) or *Learning Perl, Third Edition*, by Randal L. Schwartz and Tom Phoenix (O'Reilly, 2001: ISBN 0-59600-132-0).

---

# Installing Perl Modules

The Perl programming language supports the concept of modules—additional functions that can be integrated into a Perl installation to provide extra features. Many developers have developed modules to extend Perl, providing diverse functionality, including network protocols for file transfer or sending e-mail, parsing and manipulating XML documents, generating graphical images, and more. Much of Perl's standard functionality is provided by modules included with a basic Perl installation.

In this chapter, we will be using several modules that are not included in the base Perl installation. Because installing modules is a fairly common task, the Perl community has developed a standard process for finding and installing modules. This process has itself been encapsulated in a Perl module, the CPAN module, which we will meet in a moment.

Perl modules can be written in several languages, not just Perl. Modules written in a language other than Perl need to be compiled before they can be installed, but binaries are often available to download. On Linux systems, compiling from source rarely causes a problem, since programming language compilers are usually available in a Linux distribution. For Microsoft Windows users, compiling Perl modules from source will require a development environment (typically Visual C++ or Visual Studio .NET) to be installed. Precompiled modules for Windows users of ActiveState's version of Perl (`http://www.activestate.com`) are available and can be installed without a development environment by using the PPM (Perl Package Manager) utility provided with Perl.

We recommend that Windows users use ActiveState Perl and PPM to install the modules required for this chapter. Linux, UNIX, and Mac OS X users can use the CPAN module to build modules from source.

## Using CPAN

CPAN is the Comprehensive Perl Archive Network, at `http://www.cpan.org`, a central repository for virtually every Perl module in existence. It should be a familiar resource to just about any Perl programmer.

The source code for a module will typically be available as a compressed source tarball with a name that reflects the module name and version, for example `DBI-1.45.tar.gz`.

The build-and-install sequence is so uniform that there is a convenient shortcut. If you do not already have the CPAN module installed (you can check this by running `perldoc CPAN`), install that first (you *will* need to do this one installation manually). With the CPAN module installed, you can then download, build, and install any module from the CPAN archive with a single command.

**Note** The first time the CPAN module is used, it will prompt for configuration information, such as the locations of utilities it needs and the method needed to connect to the Internet. If you do not need to use a proxy and your Perl installation is a normal one, it is usually okay to allow the CPAN module to autoconfigure.

If you need to install a module manually, a standard command sequence for building and installing modules is used for all CPAN modules:

1. Configure any environment variables that might be needed in the compilation of the module. The details will be available in the documentation that accompanies each module.

2. Create a makefile by executing a Perl script that each module must provide:

   ```
   $ perl Makefile.PL
   ```

3. Use the makefile to build the module:

   ```
   $ make
   ```

4. Verifying that the build succeeded is optional, but usually a good idea. Modules will provide a test target in the makefile that will run tests to confirm that the module has been built correctly:

   ```
   $ make test
   ```

5. The final step copies the built files to their correct places within the local Perl installation. This installation step must be carried out by a user with permission to write files in the Perl installation. Usually, this will be the root user:

   ```
   # make install
   ```

**Note** CPAN modules adopt conventions beyond this build sequence, such as documentation, which can be viewed using the perldoc command after the module has been installed; for example: perldoc DBI.

## Using PPM

As mentioned earlier, users of ActiveState's Perl have a shortcut similar to the CPAN module in the ppm command. You can use ppm to download and install precompiled modules for Perl on Microsoft Windows.

```
C:\Documents and Settings\Neil>ppm
PPM - Programmer's Package Manager version 3.1.
Copyright (c) 2001 ActiveState Corp. All Rights Reserved.
ActiveState is a devision of Sophos.

Entering interactive shell. Using Term::ReadLine::Stub as readline library.

Type 'help' to get started.

ppm> install DBI
====================
Install 'DBI' version 1.45 in ActivePerl 5.8.4.810.
====================
```

# Installing the Perl DBI

If you have programmed databases in Windows, you will be familiar with the Open Database Connectivity (ODBC) API or more recent APIs, such as ADO or OLE DB. Similarly, if you have used Java with databases, you will have come across JDBC. These programming interfaces are an attempt to abstract from the details of the actual database in use and provide some higher-level, database-independent layer. The benefit to us is that we need to learn only one API, but can still use our applications with numerous different databases. DBI, the Database Interface, is Perl's implementation of this sort of scheme.

As with other database-independent APIs, DBI is structured as the client API module and one or more driver, or DBD (Database Driver), modules. You can have several different databases open at the same time and access them via essentially the same code in your Perl scripts, as illustrated in Figure 16-1.

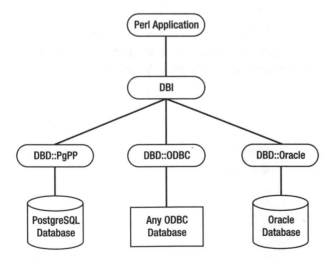

**Figure 16-1.** *Perl DBI architecture*

There are many DBD modules that provide DBI access to different data sources, including PostgreSQL and Oracle, as shown in Figure 16-1. In this chapter, we will be using DBD::PgPP, a Pure Perl module for accessing PostgreSQL databases specifically, and DBD::ODBC, a module for accessing ODBC data sources.

The DBI module is actually a collection of modules (called a *bundle*) that contains a few DBDs, but not one for PostgreSQL, so we will need to install a suitable DBD ourselves. You can find more information about DBI at its home page, http://dbi.perl.org/, or in *Programming the Perl DBI*, by Alligator Descartes and Tim Bunce (O'Reilly, 2000; ISBN 1-56592-699-4).

---

■**Tip** Another useful driver is DBD::CSV. This emulates database accesses using comma-separated value (CSV) text files, and it can be useful for quickly prototyping scripts without the need to set up a real database server.

---

## Installing DBI and the PostgreSQL DBD on Windows

The modules we need for this chapter are DBI, DBD::PgPP, and DBD::ODBC. All three of these are available via PPM and can be installed with the ppm command.

```
C:\Documents and Settings\Neil>ppm
PPM - Programmer's Package Manager version 3.1.
Copyright (c) 2001 ActiveState Corp. All Rights Reserved.
ActiveState is a devision of Sophos.

Entering interactive shell. Using Term::ReadLine::Stub as readline library.

Type 'help' to get started.

ppm>
```

---

■**Note** For the module installations to succeed, ppm requires an active Internet connection to download the module packages.

---

First, we install the DBI bundle:

```
ppm> install DBI
====================
Install 'DBI' version 1.45 in ActivePerl 5.8.4.810.
====================
Downloaded 537570 bytes.
Extracting 73/73: blib/arch/auto/DBI/Driver_xst.h
Installing C:\Perl\site\lib\auto\DBI\dbd_xsh.h
Installing C:\Perl\site\lib\auto\DBI\DBI.bs
Installing C:\Perl\site\lib\auto\DBI\DBI.dll
Installing C:\Perl\site\lib\auto\DBI\DBI.exp
Installing C:\Perl\site\lib\auto\DBI\DBI.lib
Installing C:\Perl\site\lib\auto\DBI\dbipport.h
Installing C:\Perl\site\lib\auto\DBI\dbivport.h

...

Installing C:\Perl\site\lib\Win32\DBIODBC.pm
Installing C:\Perl\bin\dbiprof
Installing C:\Perl\bin\dbiprof.bat
Installing C:\Perl\bin\dbiproxy
Installing C:\Perl\bin\dbiproxy.bat
Successfully installed DBI version 1.45 in ActivePerl 5.8.4.810.
ppm>
```

Next, we install the Pure Perl driver for PostgreSQL, DBD::PgPP:

```
ppm> install DBD::PgPP
====================
Install 'DBD-PgPP' version 0.04 in ActivePerl 5.8.4.810.
====================
Downloaded 10205 bytes.
Extracting 5/5: blib/arch/auto/DBD/PgPP/.exists
Installing C:\Perl\html\site\lib\DBD\PgPP.html
Installing C:\Perl\site\lib\DBD\PgPP.pm
Successfully installed DBD-PgPP version 0.04 in ActivePerl 5.8.4.810.
ppm>
```

Finally, we install the ODBC driver, DBD::ODBC:

```
ppm> install DBD::ODBC
====================
Install 'DBD-ODBC' version 1.11 in ActivePerl 5.8.4.810.
====================
Downloaded 76740 bytes.
Extracting 11/11: blib/arch/auto/DBD/ODBC/ODBC.lib
Installing C:\Perl\site\lib\auto\DBD\ODBC\ODBC.bs
Installing C:\Perl\site\lib\auto\DBD\ODBC\ODBC.dll
Installing C:\Perl\site\lib\auto\DBD\ODBC\ODBC.exp
Installing C:\Perl\site\lib\auto\DBD\ODBC\ODBC.lib
Installing C:\Perl\html\site\lib\DBD\ODBC.html
```

```
Installing C:\Perl\html\site\lib\DBD\ODBC\Changes.html
Files found in blib\arch: installing files in blib\lib into architecture depende
nt library tree
Installing C:\Perl\site\lib\DBD\ODBC.pm
Installing C:\Perl\site\lib\DBD\ODBC\Changes.pm
Successfully installed DBD-ODBC version 1.11 in ActivePerl 5.8.4.810.
ppm>
```

# Installing DBI and the PostgreSQL DBD from Source

On a Linux, UNIX, or Mac OS X system, we can install the Perl modules for DBI using the CPAN module described earlier.

---

■**Note** For these module installations to succeed, the CPAN module requires an active Internet connection to download the module source packages.

---

As noted earlier, it is possible to download, compile, and install a module in a single step if the installation is performed as a user with permission to write to the Perl installation. However, we recommend that you keep the use of superuser privileges to a minimum and install each module in two stages:

- The first stage is the downloading, compiling, and testing of each module. This can performed by a regular user.

- The second stage is the copying of the module files to the Perl installation, which is performed by an administration user (usually root).

For this chapter, we will install DBI and DBD::PgPP. The ODBC module DBD::OBDC can also be installed, but requires database-specific ODBC drivers to be installed first. As DBD::PgPP provides all of the functionality we need for accessing PostgreSQL, we will limit ourselves to that module.

---

■**Note** An alternative DBD module, DBD::Pg, is more commonly used on Linux and UNIX-based systems. The scripts used in this chapter should all work with DBD::Pg with little or no modification.

---

As a regular user, use the CPAN module to download, build, and test each module.

```
$ perl —MCPAN —e 'install DBI'
...
  /usr/bin/make install  -- NOT OK
    You may have to su to root to install the package
$
```

The CPAN module extracts the contents of the package in a subdirectory called .cpan. As you can see from the error message, the installation step will fail, as you do not have the correct permissions at this stage. To complete the installation, you must, as root, run make install in the appropriate package build directory:

```
$ su
password:
# cd ~neil/.cpan/build/DBI-1.45
# make install
...
#
```

The same procedure is used to build the PostgreSQL DBD driver:

```
$ perl -MCPAN -e 'install DBD::PgPP'
...
  /usr/bin/make install  -- NOT OK
    You may have to su to root to install the package
$
```

And then install it:

```
$ su
password:
# cd ~neil/.cpan/build/DBD-PgPP-0.05
# make install
...
#
```

# Using DBI

As you might expect, a database-independent layer does not have the same API as the PostgreSQL-specific API we met in Chapter 13. In fact, precisely because DBI aims to be totally database-independent, you may find that it cannot achieve the same level of conciseness and efficiency as a PostgreSQL-specific interface, such as libpq from C.

A Perl program using DBI generally takes the following form:

```
#!/usr/bin/perl -w

use DBI;
use strict;

# Connect to a PostgreSQL database
# Prepare reusable SQL statements
LOOP:
    # Execute a SQL statement
        # Read query results

# Disconnect from database
```

The first thing to notice is that *only* the DBI module is referenced:

```
use DBI;
```

You don't need to explicitly import the specific drivers for any particular databases you may be using.

When the database connection is made, DBI will locate and load the appropriate DBD if it is not already present, or fail with an error. This means that Perl database programs can be written in an entirely database-independent way, with the precise access mechanism being resolved at runtime.

In the following sections, we will look at DBI functions for each of the steps in this general Perl program.

## Making Database Connections

A Perl DBI client application may connect to one or more databases as it runs. We can connect to many databases managed by different servers at the same time if necessary. The DBI interface provides functions to create and use these connections.

We connect to a database using the DBI->connect function, which uses the name and location of the database, the method of connection (DBD driver), and user credentials to make the connection for us. It returns a handle to that database connection that we can then use to execute queries against the connected database.

As is traditional in Perl, there are several ways of passing the required information to DBI->connect, which can lead to some confusion. Here we will look at the most common mechanisms, starting with the full version of DBI->connect:

```
$dbh = DBI->connect($dsn, $uname, $pwd, \%attrs);
```

The first argument, $dsn, is a data source name (DSN). It specifies the database that we wish to connect to using a string of a particular form. The second and third arguments ($uname and $pwd) are the user ID and password with which to access the database, and the final, optional, argument (%attrs) is a hash containing attributes that are used to configure the behavior of this particular database connection.

---

■**Note** For those new to Perl, code that begins with a $ symbol represents scalar variables (numbers or strings—Perl converts between these data types as required). Lists (simple arrays) begin with an @ symbol, and hashes (associative arrays) with a % character. You use @ or % only when referring to the complete collection. For individual elements, you still use a $ symbol.

---

For example, to connect to our sample database over a network using a database username of neil with a password of password, we could use the following:

```
my $conn = DBI->connect("DBI:PgPP:dbname=bpfinal;host=192.168.0.111",
            "neil","password");
```

Of course, this does tie our program to connecting to a particular database, so it is usually better to use variable arguments derived from program arguments, defaults, and environment variables, as we will discuss shortly. First, let's look at the DSN specification and connection attributes you can configure.

## Specifying Data Source Names (DSNs)

The DSN string consists of three elements separated by colons:

- The first element is always dbi or DBI.

- The second element is the name of the DBD driver to use and is case-sensitive.

- The third element is driver-specific, but typically consists of a list of options to be passed to the driver.

For example, the following connects to a local database (running on the same machine as the Perl script using DBI) using the PgPP DBD driver:

```
dbi:PgPP:dbname=bpfinal
```

The following DSN uses the ODBC driver to connect to a data source called PostgreSQL:

```
DBI:ODBC:PostgreSQL
```

In Chapter 5, we created an ODBC data source for Windows that represented the sample database running on a remote server. This form of DSN can be used by a Perl DBI script to access that database.

Finally, here is an example that uses the PgPP DBD driver to connect to a database on a remote server:

```
DBI:PgPP:dbname=bpfinal;host=192.168.0.111;port=5432
```

Here, the IP address of the server is specified, but a DNS-resolvable host name could be used instead. If the PostgreSQL server is running on a nonstandard port number, this can be specified in the DSN as well, as shown here.

The most common driver options supported by PgPP are shown in Table 16-1. They are given in the DSN as a sequence of *option=value* pairs separated by semicolons, as shown in the preceding example. Other options supported by PgPP are described in the PgPP documentation.

**Table 16-1.** *Some PgPP Connection Options*

| PgPP Option | Meaning |
| --- | --- |
| dbname | Database names; defaults to the name of the current user |
| host | Host name or address; defaults to localhost |
| port | TCP port to connect to the database; defaults to PostgreSQL standard 5432 |

## Setting Connection Attributes

As noted earlier, you can optionally specify connection attributes in your connection statement. One important connection attribute is AutoCommit. Setting this to 1 causes DBI to treat each operation as a single transaction; setting it to 0 gives you explicit transaction processing:

```
$dbh = DBI->connect("DBI:PgPP:dbname=bpfinal",
                    "neil", "",
                    { AutoCommit => 0 });
```

This example disables automatic committing, so you must insert calls to $dbh->commit (or $dbh->rollback) as necessary to end transactions.

Table 16-2 lists some additional interesting attributes. There are a few other less common attributes; see the DBI and PostgreSQL DBD documentation for details.

**Table 16-2.** *Some DBI Connection Attributes*

| Attribute | Meaning |
|-----------|---------|
| PrintError | As well as filling in $DBI::errstr, this causes the error message to be sent to stderr. This can be useful for quick-and-dirty testing, but generally is not particularly friendly toward end users. |
| RaiseError | Errors will cause the program to die (unless you wrap the call in an eval block) instead of just returning an error status. Like PrintError, this is probably not something you will want end users to see. |
| Name | The name of the database, usually the same as the string passed into connect. |

You can access the attributes after connection and, in some cases, change them. For example, the following reads and sets the transaction state:

```
$oldState = $conn->{ AutoCommit };
$conn->{ AutoCommit } = 0;
```

---

■**Caution** Changing connection attributes after a connection is made is not recommended. This is because some DBDs do not support dynamic changing and, therefore, you would be limiting script portability.

---

## Using DBI Environment Variables

The DBI module takes note of some environment variables to set values for certain attributes and to configure some behavior. Table 16-3 shows some of the variables that are used by DBI->connect when making a connection to a database. We recommend that you do not use these environment variables, as it is better to be explicit about your intentions when calling DBI functions.

**Table 16-3.** *Some DBI Enviroment Variables*

| Variable | Usage |
|---|---|
| DBI_DSN | Used when a DSN is not specified, in DSN format dbi:*driver:options* |
| DBI_DRIVER | Used for a driver name if the DSN omits it, in the form dbi::*options* |
| DBI_USER | Used as the username if DBI->connect $uname parameter is undef (as distinct from an empty string) |
| DBI_PASS | Used as the user password if DBI->connect $pwd parameter is undef |

## Connecting to a Database

Here is a very simple program that we can use to try out various ways of connecting to a PostgreSQL database with Perl DBI (connect.pl).

```
#!/usr/bin/perl -w

use DBI;
use strict;

my $dsn = $ARGV[0] if defined $ARGV[0];
my $conn = DBI->connect($dsn,"neil","") || die "Error $DBI::err [$DBI::errstr]";
printf "Connected: State is %s\n", $conn -> state || "OK";
$conn -> disconnect;
```

In this code, we connect as user neil to a database given by a command-line argument. Processing is simply terminated on error, with the error number and error string printed out via Perl's die function.

If the DBI and DBD modules are installed correctly, we should be able to connect to our database using the DSN examples shown earlier:

```
S:\Chapter16>perl connect.pl DBI:ODBC:PostgreSQL
Connected: State is OK
S:\Chapter16>perl connect.pl DBI:PgPP:dbname=bpfinal;host=192.168.0.111
Connected: State is OK
```

If the DSN is incorrect, or a connection cannot be made, we will see an error message.

In some cases, particularly with the current PgPP driver, the error message is not as helpful as it might be, and Perl dies before we can print an error message (here, the server is not available):

```
S:\Chapter16>perl connect.pl DBI:PgPP:dbname=bpfinal;host=192.168.0.110
dbih_getcom given an undefined handle (perhaps returned from a previous call
which failed) at C:/Perl/site/lib/DBI.pm line 600.
```

■**Tip** To catch instances where Perl dies when loading a DBD driver, use Perl's eval to execute the connect.

The return value from DBI->connect is a handle to the database connection, or undef on error. If there has been an error, the variables $DBI::err and $DBI::errstr are set appropriately. Once a connection has been made and the variable $conn refers to a valid database connection handle, the variables $DBI::err and $DBI::errstr are also available as $conn->err and $conn->errstr, respectively.

At the end of processing, the database connection is closed with $conn->disconnect. Although the connection will be closed anyway when the application exits (possibly with a warning message appearing), it is recommended that you explicitly disconnect to avoid problems with uncommitted transactions.

## Executing SQL

When executing SQL against a database, DBI splits an operation into two or three steps: preparation then execution of a SQL statement and, if required, fetching the results of a query.

The preparation step is made explicit because it may be more efficient when executing the same operation several times. The database server may be able to optimize access by preparing a statement, saving the preparation results, and executing the prepared statement several times:

```perl
my $sth = $conn->prepare($command);
my $nrows = $sth->execute;
...
my $nrows = $sth->execute;
```

The result of the preparation step is a statement handle, which we use to process the operation, and the result value of the execution is the number of rows affected (or undef if there was an error, in which case $conn->err and $conn->errstr will be set).

In some cases, when we know we will want to execute the statement only once, the two steps can be combined into a single do function call:

```perl
my $nrows = $conn->do($command);
```

Notice the lack of a statement handle here. This means there is no way to extract the results of a query, so do is useful only for nonquery operations.

Here is an example Perl program that executes some SQL statements that do not return a set of results:

```perl
#!/usr/bin/perl -w

use DBI;
use strict;

# Function for nonquery commands
sub doSQL
{
    my ($conn, $command) = @_;

    print $command, "\n";
```

```perl
    my $sth = $conn->prepare($command);
    my $nrows = $sth->execute;
    print "status is ", $conn->err, "\n" if $conn->err;
    print "#rows affected is ", $nrows, "\n";
    print "error message: ", $conn->errstr, "\n" if $conn->err;
}

my $conn = DBI->connect("DBI:ODBC:PostgreSQL") or die $DBI::errstr;

doSQL($conn, "DROP TABLE number");
doSQL($conn, "CREATE TABLE number ( value INTEGER, name VARCHAR )");
doSQL($conn, "INSERT INTO number values(42, 'The Answer')");
doSQL($conn, "INSERT INTO number values(29, 'My Age')");
doSQL($conn, "INSERT INTO number values(29, 'Anniversary')");
doSQL($conn, "INSERT INTO number values(66, 'Clickety Click')");
doSQL($conn, "UPDATE number SET name = 'Zaphod' WHERE value = 42");
doSQL($conn, "DELETE FROM number WHERE value = 29");

$conn->disconnect;
```

Executing this program results in the SQL being executed as expected:

```
S:\Chapter16>perl select_dbi1.pl
DROP TABLE number
#rows affected is 0E0
CREATE TABLE number ( value INTEGER, name VARCHAR )
#rows affected is 0E0
INSERT INTO number values(42, 'The Answer')
#rows affected is 1
INSERT INTO number values(29, 'My Age')
#rows affected is 1
INSERT INTO number values(29, 'Anniversary')
#rows affected is 1
INSERT INTO number values(66, 'Clickety Click')
#rows affected is 1
UPDATE number SET name = 'Zaphod' WHERE value = 42
#rows affected is 1
DELETE FROM number WHERE value = 29
#rows affected is 2
```

When we execute a SQL query that returns results—a SELECT statement—we need to be able to examine the result set. DBI makes this very easy in Perl, as explained in the next section.

## Working with Result Sets

After a statement has been executed, the statement handle can be used to extract any results that have been returned. The return value of the execute call itself is intended to be the number of rows in the result set. However, some database systems do not actually report the number of rows returned by a query; they just return rows until none are left. Because DBI is database-independent and can be used with many different databases, strictly speaking, the return value of the execute function is deemed to be unreliable, but it does always appear to be correct for a PostgreSQL server.

## Fetching Results

The DBI->fetchrow_array function returns the next row of data from a query result set as a list of field values, with NULL values being represented by undef values. We can process a complete result set with the following Perl loop:

```
while(my @row = $sth->fetchrow_array) {
    # print out row fields
    print " ", join(" ", @row), "\n";
    # process the row as required ...
}
```

The join function simply concatenates all the elements in an array, regardless of its size, with the given separator string. If we do know how many columns there are, however, we can use another of Perl's tricks: an array of variables on the left side of an assignment.

```
($number, $value) = $result ->fetchrow_array
```

Here, $number and $value are a pair of variables to which the first and second column values will be assigned.

There are other variants of the fetchrow_array function, as listed in Table 16-4.

**Table 16-4.** *Some Functions for Fetching Rows*

| Function | Description |
|---|---|
| fetchrow_arrayref | Returns a reference to an internal array (which is reused when the next fetch occurs), thus avoiding the copy that fetchrow_array does, although the application must consume the data immediately. |
| fetchrow_hashref | Returns a reference to a hash with the column names as keys and the data as the corresponding values. |
| fetchall_arrayref | Returns all of the query results in a reference to a single array. This provides a portable and reliable way to determine the number of rows, but may lead to excessive memory use if there are a lot of them. |

We mentioned the do function for nonquery statements earlier. There is a similar shortcut, or to be more precise, a set of them, for queries that you know you will not want to reuse. selectrow_array and selectall_arrayref perform the prepare and execute operations followed by the corresponding fetch function in one call. Consult the documentation for further details on these and other variants of the query operations that DBI makes available.

## Using Statement Handle Attributes

The statement handle has a number of attributes that are useful for processing result sets. Typically, we would like to know the number of fields that are being returned in each row and the names of the fields. These usually correspond to the columns in the database table being queried. Some useful statement handle attributes are listed in Table 16-5.

**Table 16-5.** *Some Statement Handle Attributes*

| Attribute | Description |
|---|---|
| NUM_OF_FIELDS | Number of fields returned in a query |
| NUM_OF_PARAMS | Number of placeholders |
| NAME | Reference to an array containing the names of the columns |
| NAME_lc | Same as NAME, but always returns lowercase |
| NAME_uc | Same as NAME, but always returns uppercase |
| NULLABLE | Reference to an array containing flags indicating if each column can contain NULL values |
| Statement | The string used to create the statement |
| TYPE | Reference to an array indicating the type of each column |

■**Note** All of the statement attributes are read-only. Depending on the database, some may not be available until after execute has been called. It is best to examine them only after statement execution.

We can use the statement handle attributes to extend our sample program to display the results of a SELECT query. The following function will print a complete result set.

```perl
# Function specifically for queries
sub doSQLquery
{
    my ($conn, $command) = @_;

    print $command, "\n";

    my $sth = $conn->prepare($command);
    my $nrows = $sth->execute;
    print "status is ", $conn->err, "\n" if $conn->err;
    print "error message: ", $conn->errstr, "\n" if $conn->err;

    print "number of rows returned (unreliable) = ", $sth->rows, "\n";
    print "number of fields returned = ", $sth->{NUM_OF_FIELDS}, "\n";
    print "fields: ", join(" ", @{$sth->{NAME}}), "\n";

    while(my @row = $sth->fetchrow_array) {
        print " ", join(" ", @row), "\n";
    }
}
```

The following is an example of a call to doSQLquery:

```
doSQLquery($conn, "SELECT * FROM number WHERE value = 29");
```

When we run the sample program with this call included, we see the result set being printed:

```
S:\Chapter16>perl select_dbi2.pl
DROP TABLE number
#rows affected is 0E0
CREATE TABLE number ( value INTEGER, name VARCHAR )
#rows affected is 0E0
INSERT INTO number values(42, 'The Answer')
#rows affected is 1
INSERT INTO number values(29, 'My Age')
#rows affected is 1
INSERT INTO number values(29, 'Anniversary')
#rows affected is 1
INSERT INTO number values(66, 'Clickety-Click')
#rows affected is 1
SELECT * FROM number WHERE value = 29
number of rows returned (unreliable) = 2
number of fields returned = 2
fields: value name
 29 My Age
 29 Anniversary
UPDATE number SET name = 'Zaphod' WHERE value = 42
#rows affected is 1
DELETE FROM number WHERE value = 29
#rows affected is 2
```

When you have finished with a statement handle, you should release it by setting the variable to undef, or simply by leaving its scope. An alternative is to call the following:

```
$sth->finish;
```

You should also call this if you intend to reuse a query. It will flush the results buffer; otherwise, you run the risk of getting rows back from a previous query. Reusing queries is discussed in the next section.

## Binding Parameters

We said earlier that DBI splits operations into a preparation stage and an execution step, so that you could execute the same query multiple times. Why would you want to do that? Wouldn't you get the same result each time, assuming that some other process is not changing the database? This would be true, if not for one of the extra bits of functionality that DBI offers: the ability to bind parameters.

Instead of having a completely specified string as a SQL statement, we can insert question marks as *placeholders*, with which actual values are associated later. This is similar to ecpg's host variable syntax described in Chapter 14. We prepare the statement once and execute it with different values, with one argument for each placeholder. As an example, the following will return rows with value 14 and 15:

```
my $sth = $conn->prepare("SELECT * FROM number WHERE value = ?");
$sth->execute(14);
# Process rows...
$sth->execute(15);
# Process rows...
```

Each question mark placeholder in the SQL statement is replaced by the corresponding argument in execute. For example, $sth->execute(14) can be expressed as follows:

```
$sth->bind_param(1, 14);  # Note: parameters are numbered from 1
$sth->execute;
```

This hasn't bought us much; in fact, it's more typing. However, it can be useful when a statement has a large number of placeholders and we want to change only a few between executions. DBI also supports binding by reference, which, although intended for passing values in and out of shared procedures, can reduce the amount of typing a little:

```
my $num;
my $sth = $conn->prepare("SELECT * FROM number WHERE value = ?");
$sth->bind_param_inout(1,\$num, 10);
$num = 14;
$sth->execute;
# Process rows...
$num = 15;
$sth->execute;
# Process rows...
```

As this uses a reference, any changes in the value of the variable are immediately available to DBI without extra effort. Additionally, a third argument is necessary, to indicate the maximum size of a returned value, irrelevant in this particular instance, but required nonetheless.

Binding also works on the results of queries. The following is a replacement for doSQLquery's results processing:

```
sub doSQLquery
{
    my ($conn, $command) = @_;

    print $command, "\n";

    my $sth = $conn->prepare($command);
    my $nrows = $sth->execute;
    print "status is ", $DBI::err, "\n" if $DBI::err;

    print "number of rows returned (unreliable) = ", $sth->rows, "\n";

    my( $name, $value );
    $sth->bind_col(1, \$value); # 1st column mapped on to $value
    $sth->bind_col(2, \$name);  # 2nd column mapped on to $name
```

```
    while($sth->fetch) {
        print " name = ", $name, ", value = ", $value, "\n";
    }
}
```

Binding may offer some efficiency gains (this depends on the database in use), but it definitely can improve the clarity of the code.

## Using Other DBI Features

So far, we've mainly looked at PostgreSQL-specific use of DBI. Now let's briefly investigate some of the additional database-independent features.

We can enumerate the available drivers, and in some cases databases, quite easily, as shown in the following script:

```
#!/usr/bin/perl -w

use DBI;
use strict;

foreach my $driver (DBI->available_drivers())
{
    print "Driver ", $driver;

    eval { print "\n", join("\n ", DBI->data_sources($driver)), "\n\n" };
    print " - error ", $@, "\n\n" if ($@);
}
```

The DBI->available_drivers function returns a list of all the DBDs on the system, though it performs no tests that they are usable, or even loadable. For some DBDs, it is possible to determine which databases are available, via DBI->data_sources. This function does attempt to load the driver, which could fail for some reason, so we enclose it in an eval block. The return value of an eval is the expression inside the block, and any error status shows up in $@, hence the check for that being non-null. This script generates the following on one of our computers:

```
Driver ODBC
DBI:ODBC:MS Access Database
 DBI:ODBC:Excel Files
 DBI:ODBC:dBASE Files
 DBI:ODBC:PostgreSQL

Driver PgPP
dbi:PgPP:
```

We have only scratched the surface of DBI, there is much more information in the online documentation.

# Using DBIx::Easy

If you have been browsing the database sections of CPAN, you will have noticed a number of DBIx modules. These are miscellaneous modules enhancing various aspects of DBI programming. One of these modules is particularly interesting: DBIx::Easy (home page http://www.linuxia.de, though you should be able to find everything via CPAN), a simplified interface to DBI. DBIx::Easy supports only a limited subset of DBDs, but fortunately, PostgreSQL (via ODBC and Module Pg, but not PgPP at the time of writing) is one of them.

This module makes some database operations look, well, a little less "database-y." We'll leave it to you to decide whether this is a good thing. As an example, you can have the results of a query returned as a hash (strictly, a reference to a hash). One other useful feature is that you do not need to check the return value of every database operation. You can install a single error handler instead.

Here's our ubiquitous Perl script again, using DBIx::Easy, showing both of these features:

```perl
#!/usr/bin/perl -w

use DBIx::Easy;
use strict;
sub myErrorHandler
{
    my( $statement, $err, $msg ) = @_;
    die"Oops, \"$statement\" failed ($err) - $msg";
}

# Note: we have to specify the DB type and the dbname explicitly
my $conn = new DBIx::Easy("Pg", "bpfinal");

$conn->install_handler(\&myErrorHandler);

$conn->process("DROP TABLE number");
$conn->process("CREATE TABLE number ( value INTEGER, name  VARCHAR )");
$conn->insert("number", name => "The Answer",    value => 42);
$conn->insert("number", name => "My Age",        value => 29);
$conn->insert("number", name => "Anniversary",   value => 29);
$conn->insert("number", name => "Clickety-Click", value => 66);

my $numbers = $conn->makemap("number", "name", "value", "value = 29");
foreach my $name (keys(%$numbers)) {
    print $name, " has value ", $$numbers{$name}, "\n";
}

$conn->update("number", "value = 42", name => "Zaphod");
$conn->process("DELETE FROM number WHERE value = 29");
$conn->commit;
```

Now this looks quite a bit different from the earlier scripts. This is because DBIx::Easy provides separate process, insert, update, and makemap (query) operations, so it would be inappropriate to combine them all into the previous pair of doSQL functions.

Notice how the error handler is installed. Instead of testing each function for success or failure (which, admittedly, we have not been particularly rigorous about in earlier code samples), we can rely on the handler being called on any error. In this case, all it does is abort the script, but you may wish to provide something more sophisticated in your own programs.

The impact of process, insert, and update should be fairly obvious, but makemap deserves some explanation. This function takes the name of a table, two column names, and an optional WHERE clause:

```
$conn->makemap($table, $keycol, $valuecol, $where)
```

This effectively executes the following query:

```
SELECT $keycol, $valuecol FROM $table WHERE $where
```

The results are inserted into a hash, as if by the following code fragment:

```
while(my ($key, $value) = $sth->fetchrow_array) {
    $map{$key} = $value;
}
```

As a hash can map each key on to only one value, multiple mappings in the source table will be lost. For example, if the table contained two rows (A, B) and (A, C), only one of those will appear in the resultant hash, since the earlier one returned from the database is overwritten by the later one.

Another limitation is that only two columns can be processed at a time, unlike a general query that can return any specified number of columns. Note that this is not the same as the hash returned by fetchrow_hashref function in DBI. This function returns a single row, with the hash key attribute being the column name and the hash value the column data.

# Creating XML from DBI Queries

Now that we've broached the subject of DBIx modules, it's worth mentioning Matt Sergeant's DBIx::XML_RDB, for simplifying the creation of well-formed XML from the results of DBI queries.

Here is another version of the Perl script, this time producing XML as the query result (changes from the select_dbi.pl are highlighted):

```
#!/usr/bin/perl -w

use DBI;
use DBIx::XML_RDB;
use strict;

# Function for nonquery commands
sub doSQL
{
    my ($conn, $command) = @_;
```

```perl
    print $command, "\n";

    my $sth = $conn->prepare($command);
    my $nrows = $sth->execute;
    print "status is ", $DBI::err, "\n" if $DBI::err;
    print "#rows affected is ", $nrows, "\n";
    print "error message: ", $DBI::errstr, "\n" if $DBI::err;
}

# Function specifically for queries
sub doSQLquery
{
    my ($conn, $command) = @_;

    print $command, "\n";

    $conn->DoSql($command);

    print $conn->GetData;
}

my $connXml = DBIx::XML_RDB->new("bpfinal", "PgPP") or die $DBI::errstr;
my $conn = $connXml->{dbh};
doSQL($conn, "DROP TABLE number");
doSQL($conn, "CREATE TABLE number ( value INTEGER, name  VARCHAR )");
doSQL($conn, "INSERT INTO number values(42, 'The Answer')");
doSQL($conn, "INSERT INTO number values(29, 'My Age')");
doSQL($conn, "INSERT INTO number values(29, 'Anniversary')");
doSQL($conn, "INSERT INTO number values(66, 'Clickety-Click')");
doSQLquery($connXml, "SELECT * FROM number WHERE value = 29");
doSQL($conn, "UPDATE number SET name = 'Zaphod' WHERE value = 42");
doSQL($conn, "DELETE FROM number WHERE value = 29");
```

This time, the database is opened with the following:

```perl
my $connXml = DBIx::XML_RDB->new("", "PgPP") or die $DBI::errstr;
my $conn = $connXml->{dbh};
```

DBIx::XML_RDB->new returns an XML_RDB connection handle, which is not the same as a DBI handle. An examination of the module's source shows that it contains a DBI handle, however, which can be used for any nonquery operations (though, strictly, you should not rely on this, and it would be better not to mix XML_RDB operations with other database operations).

XML_RDB's query operation, DoSql, appends XML to an internal string, which can be extracted by GetData, as shown in the doSQLquery function. The results of our query are as follows:

```
<?xml version="1.0"?>
<DBI driver="dbname=bpfinal">
    <RESULTSET statement="SELECT * FROM number WHERE value = 29">
        <ROW>
            <value>29</value>
            <name>My Age</name>
        </ROW>
        <ROW>
            <value>29</value>
            <name>Anniversary</name>
        </ROW>
    </RESULTSET>
</DBI>
```

The DBIx::XML_RDB module itself is limited to producing XML from database queries, though the package includes a couple of scripts for converting a table to and from XML. sql2xml.pl uses the XML query facility to dump a complete table, and xml2sql.pl reads it back in again.

## SQL to XML

The sql2xml.pl script in the DBIx::XML_RDB package includes the options listed in Table 16-6.

**Table 16-6.** *Some Options for sql2xml.pl*

| Option | Description |
| --- | --- |
| -sn *servername* | Data source name |
| -driver *dbi_driver* | Driver that DBI uses; default is ODBC |
| -uid *username* | Username |
| -pwd *password* | Password (optional) |
| -table *tablename* | Table to extract |
| -output *outputfile* | File in which to place XML output |

If you dump the usage, for example, by executing the command with no parameters, it identifies itself as sql2xls.pl and mentions Excel files, so it looks like the documentation has not quite kept up with the code.

You can run the script on the table created by the earlier Perl programs with the following command (all one line):

```
$ /usr/lib/perl5/site_perl/5.6.0/DBIx/sql2xml.pl
        -sn dbname=bpfinal -driver PgPP
        -table number -output xml.txt -uid neil
```

It is more than likely that your path does not include the directory containing these scripts, so this example specifies the full path specification (you may need to alter this for your Perl installation's location). The output file, xml.txt, contains the following:

```xml
<?xml version="1.0"?>
<DBI driver="dbname=bpfinal">
    <RESULTSET statement="SELECT * FROM number ORDER BY 1">
        <ROW>
            <value>42</value>
            <name>Zaphod</name>
        </ROW>
        <ROW>
            <value>66</value>
            <name>Clickety-Click</name>
        </ROW>
    </RESULTSET>
</DBI>
```

As you can see, this looks almost identical in format to the earlier query example, showing that the script is a fairly thin wrapper on top of the DBIx::XML_RDB module's functionality.

## XML to SQL

The reverse script in the DBIx::XML_RDB package, xml2sql.pl, has similar options, as shown in Table 16-7.

**Table 16-7.** *Some Options for xml2sql.pl*

| Option | Description |
| --- | --- |
| -sn *servername* | Data source name |
| -driver *dbi_driver* | Driver that DBI uses; default is ODBC |
| -uid *username* | Username |
| -pwd *password* | Password (optional) |
| -table *tablename* | Table to create |
| -input *inputfile* | File to read XML input from |
| -x | Delete contents of table before inserting |

Before you can use the xml2sql.pl script, however, you need to install XML::Parser, again found via CPAN.

**Tip** Other packages, such as Ron Bourret's XML-DBMS, permit more complex interactions. See `http://www.rpbourret.com/xmldbms/` for more information.

# Summary

Although there are numerous ways to use databases with Perl, in this chapter, we concentrated on the most important as far as PostgreSQL programming is concerned: the database-independent layer, DBI.

Within the scope of DBI, we have the option of easily using other database back-ends with the same client code. There is also a lot of existing DBI extension code, in the form of `DBIx` modules, to make our programming job simpler.

In the next chapter, we'll explore how to access a PostgreSQL database from Java.

■ ■ ■

# CHAPTER 17

# Accessing PostgreSQL from Java

The Java Database Connectivity (JDBC) API is the de facto standard used by Java programs for accessing external resource managers, mainly relational databases, in a resource manager-independent manner. This means a Java application written with ANSI-compliant SQL can use standard JDBC classes and interfaces to be reasonably portable across databases from different relational database management system vendors. The JDBC API comprises the core JDBC API and the extension API. The core API mainly defines the standard interfaces for the following:

- Creating a connection to the database

- Creating statements

- Accessing result sets

- Querying database and result set meta data

The core classes and interfaces are defined in the java.sql package and are available with the Java 2 Platform, Standard Edition (J2SE).

The extension API defines more sophisticated interfaces for handling XA resources, distributed transactions, pooled connections, and connection factories. XA resources can be used to handle distributed transactions and two-phase commits, where a single transaction may need to span several multiple databases. These classes and interfaces belong to the javax.sql package and are available with the Java 2 Platform, Enterprise Edition (J2EE).

In this chapter, we will be concentrating on the JDBC core API, looking at how Java language programs can use JDBC for accessing data residing in PostgreSQL databases.

---

■**Note** In this chapter, we will assume that you have a basic understanding of Java, and also that you have a Java development environment installed.

---

## Using a PostgreSQL JDBC Driver

The JDBC API defines interfaces only for the objects used for performing various database-related tasks like opening and closing connections, executing SQL statements, and retrieving the results.

It doesn't provide the implementation classes for these interfaces. Nevertheless, portable Java language programs do not need to be aware of the implementation classes and should use only the standard interfaces.

As good object-oriented citizens, we all write our programs to interfaces and not implementations. Either the resource manager vendor or a third party provides the implementation classes for the standard JDBC interfaces. These software implementations are called *JDBC drivers*. JDBC drivers transform the standard JDBC calls to the external resource manager-specific API calls. Figure 17-1 depicts how a database client written in Java accesses an external resource manager using the JDBC API and the JDBC driver.

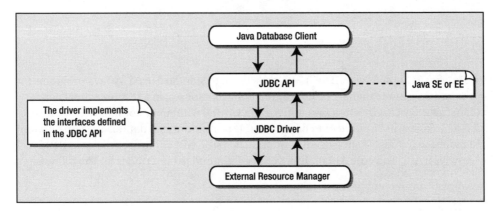

**Figure 17-1.** *JDBC API definition and implementation layers*

Depending on the mechanism of implementation, JDBC drivers are broadly classified into four types:

- Type 1 JDBC drivers implement the JDBC API on top of a lower-level API like ODBC. These drivers are not generally portable because of the dependency on native libraries. These drivers translate the JDBC calls to ODBC calls, and ODBC then sends the request to the external data source using native library calls. The JDBC-ODBC driver that comes with the software distribution for J2SE is an example of a type 1 driver.

- Type 2 drivers are written in a mixture of Java and native code. Type 2 drivers use vendor-specific native APIs for accessing the data source. These drivers transform the JDBC calls to vendor-specific calls using the vendor's native library. Like type 1 drivers, type 2 drivers are not portable, because they depend on native code. The advantage of type 2 JDBC drivers is that in some circumstances, particularly for local database access, they can be very efficient.

- Type 3 drivers use pure Java at the client, which then communicates with an intermediate middleware server for accessing the external data sources. The calls to the middleware server are database-independent. However, the middleware server makes vendor-specific native calls for accessing the data source.

- Type 4 drivers are written in pure Java and they implement the JDBC interfaces and translate the JDBC-specific calls to vendor-specific data-access calls. They implement the data transfer and network protocol for the target resource manager. Most of the leading database vendors provide type 4 drivers for accessing their database servers, and generally this is the best type of driver to choose. Type 4 drivers are available for PostgreSQL.

## Installing a PostgreSQL JDBC Driver

JDBC drivers for PostgreSQL can be downloaded from `http://jdbc.postgresql.org/`. There, you will find precompiled JDBC drivers for PostgreSQL. Be careful to select the appropriate combination of JDBC driver for your Java runtime and PostgreSQL version combination. You will normally be looking for a JDBC 3 driver for your release of PostgreSQL.

Once you have a driver file, which will probably be named something like `postgresql-8.0.309.jdbc3.jar`, you need to ensure it is in your `CLASSPATH`. You can do this by altering your environment, by copying the file to the `/lib/ext` subdirectory of your Java runtime environment, or by using the `-cp` option to the `java` command when you execute your program.

Additionally, the source for the driver is available from `http://jdbc.postgresql.org/` if you want to build it yourself (or just to have a look and see how it works). Instructions for building are contained in the download. Here are the general steps:

1. Download and install the latest version of the Ant build tool from `http://ant.apache.org/`. Since Ant is a Java-based build tool, these steps are applicable to all environments that support Java.

2. Unpack the PostgreSQL JDBC source file bundle to the local file system. The top-level directory contains a build definition for Ant, as well as a `Readme` file.

3. Make sure you have all the required class files for Ant in the `CLASSPATH`. The required files include the Ant classes available in the `lib` directory of the Ant installation and a JAXP-compliant XML parser.

---

**■Tip** JAXP stands for Java API for XML Processing. The Apache Xerces project is a JAXP-compliant XML parser that can be downloaded from `http://xml.apache.org`. This is split into two files: `xml-apis.jar`, for building, and `xercesImpl.jar`, which is required for both building and runtime.

---

4. Run the Ant build script.

## Using the Driver Interface and DriverManager Class

The `java.sql` package defines an interface called `java.sql.Driver`, which needs to be implemented by all the JDBC drivers, and a class called `java.sql.DriverManager`, which acts as the interface to the database. The primary task of the `DriverManager` class is to manage the various registered JDBC drivers. The DriverManager also provides methods for getting connections to databases, managing JDBC logs, and setting the login timeout. When a JDBC client requests the DriverManager to make a connection to an external resource manager, it delegates the task to an appropriate driver class implemented by the JDBC driver provided either by the resource manager vendor or a third party.

In this section, we will discuss the roles of java.sql.DriverManager and java.sql.Driver in the JDBC API. However, before we discuss the main JDBC functions, we need to briefly mention the way exceptions and warnings are handled.

## SQL Exceptions and Warnings

The core JDBC API provides four exception classes, which you may need to catch:

- BatchUpdateException: This exception is thrown when an error occurs during the execution of a SQL batch. The class gives a method to get the update counts of the SQL statements that were executed successfully in the batch as an array of integers.

- DataTruncation: This exception is thrown when the data is unexpectedly truncated during data reads or writes. The class provides methods to access the number of bytes that should have been transferred and those actually transferred, whether the truncation occurred for a column or a parameter, whether the truncation occurred on a read or a write, and the index of the column or the parameter.

- SQLException: This is the superclass of all the other SQL exceptions. This class provides access methods for the database error code and SQL state for the error that caused this exception. Most of the methods discussed in this chapter will throw an instance of SQLException if a database-access error occurs (as you'll notice from their signatures).

- SQLWarning: This subclass of SQLException is thrown to indicate warnings during database access.

## Managing Drivers

The DriverManager class provides the following methods for managing drivers:

- public static void registerDriver(Driver driver) throws SQLException: The registerDriver method is normally used by the implementation classes of the java.sql.Driver interface, provided by the JDBC drivers, to register themselves with the DriverManager. DriverManager uses registered drivers for delegating database connection requests.

- public static void deregisterDriver(Driver driver) throws SQLException: The deregisterDriver method is used for deregistering a driver that is already registered with the DriverManager.

- public static Enumeration getDrivers(): The getDrivers method returns an enumeration of all the drivers currently registered with the DriverManager. The signature shown here is for Java Development Kit (JDK) 1.4 and earlier versions. In JDK 1.5, the signature changes to public Enumeration<Driver> getDrivers().

- `public static Driver getDriver(String url) throws SQLException`: The getDriver method locates a driver corresponding to the passed JDBC URL.

## Specifying the Server and Database

JDBC URLs are used for uniquely identifying the resource manager type and resource manager location. This means that even though a JDBC driver can handle any number of connections identified by different JDBC URLs, the basic URL format, including the protocol and subprotocol, is specific to the driver used.

JDBC clients specify the JDBC URL when they request a connection. The DriverManager can find a driver that matches the requested URL from the list of registered drivers and delegate the connection request to that driver if it finds a match.

JDBC URLs take the following format:

*<protocol>*:*<subprotocol>*:*<resource>*

The *protocol* is always jdbc, but the *subprotocol* and *resource* depend on the type of resource manager you use. The URL for PostgreSQL has this format:

jdbc:postgresql://*<host>*:*<port>*/*<database>*

Here, *host* is the host address (either an IP address or a machine name) on which the PostgreSQL server process is accepting connections, and *database* is the name of the database to which the client wishes to connect. The *port* parameter is optional, and it is required only if your PostgreSQL service is listening on a port other than the default 5432.

As an example, if we wish to connect to the database bpfinal on the machine at IP address 192.168.0.3 using the default port, we would use the following URL in our Java code:

String url = "jdbc:postgresql://192.168.0.3/bpfinal";

## Managing Connections

The DriverManager class provides the getConnection method for managing connections to databases. This method has three alternative signatures:

- `public static Connection getConnection(String url) throws SQLException`: The getConnection method creates a connection to the database specified by the JDBC URL. The class java.sql.Connection is covered in detail in the "Making Database Connections" section later in this chapter.

- `public static Connection getConnection(String url, String user, String password) throws SQLException`: This form of the getConnection method gets a connection to the database specified by the JDBC URL using the specified username and password.

- `public static Connection getConnection(String url, Properties info) throws SQLException`: This form of the getConnection method gets a connection to the database specified by the JDBC URL, and the instance of the class java.util.Properties is used for specifying the security credentials. The user property is used for specifying the username, and the password property is used for specifying the password.

## Managing JDBC Logging

The DriverManager class provides the following methods for managing JDBC logs:

- public static PrintWriter getLogWriter(): The PrintWriter method gets a handle to an instance of the class java.io.PrintWriter to which the logging and tracing information are written.

- public static void setLogWriter(PrintWriter writer): The setLogWriter method sets the PrintWriter class to which all the log information is written by the DriverManager and all the registered drivers.

- public static void println(String message) throws SQLException: This println method writes the message to the current log stream.

## Managing Login Timeouts

Two methods are provided by the DriverManager class for managing logins:

- public static int getLoginTimeout(): The getLoginTimeout method gets the maximum time in seconds the DriverManager would wait for getting a connection.

- public static void setLoginTimeout(int seconds): The setLoginTimeout method sets the maximum time, in seconds, the DriverManager would wait for getting a connection.

## Implementing java.sql.Driver

The java.sql.Driver interface defines the methods that need to be implemented by all JDBC driver classes. The driver implementation classes are required to have static initialization code to register them with the current DriverManager. This is done so that the DriverManager has the driver in the list of registered drivers, and it delegates a connection request to an appropriate driver class depending on the JDBC URL specified. The curious can take a look at the source code for the org.postgresql.Driver class, which is the driver implementation for the PostgreSQL JDBC driver.

One obvious way of checking that you have a driver available is using the static forName() method on the class java.lang.Class:

```
try {
    Class.forName("org.postgresql.Driver");
} catch(ClassNotFoundException e) {
    // Handle exception
}
```

This will throw a ClassNotFoundException if the class org.postgresql.Driver is not found in the CLASSPATH. So, you need to make sure that the postgres.jar file that contains the required classes is available in the CLASSPATH, as we mentioned previously.

The sequence diagram shown in Figure 17-2 depicts a typical JDBC client getting a connection to a PostgreSQL database running locally, using the username meeraj and the password waheeda.

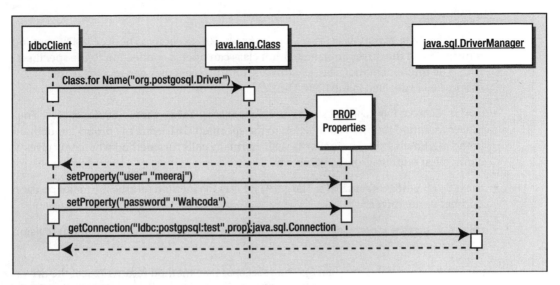

**Figure 17-2.** *Connection sequence*

The following code snippet corresponds to the sequence of events depicted in Figure 17-2, assuming a database named test on the local machine:

```
try {

    // Load the JDBC driver
    Class.forName("org.postgresql.Driver");

    // Create a properties object with username and password
    Properties prop = new Properties();
    prop.setProperty("user", "meeraj");
    prop.setProperty("password", "waheeda");

    // Set the JDBC URL
    String url = "jdbc:postgresql:test";

    // Get the connection
    Connection con = DriverManager.getConnection(url, prop);

} catch(ClassNotFoundException e) {
    // Handle exception
} catch(SQLException e) {
    // Handle exception
}
```

The following methods are defined for the `java.sql.Driver` interface:

- `public boolean acceptsURL(String url) throws SQLException`: The `acceptsURL` method returns `True` if the driver implementation class can open a connection to the specified URL. The implementation classes normally return `True` if they can recognize the subprotocol specified in the JDBC URL.

- `public Connection connect(String url,Properties info) throws SQLException`: The `connect` method returns a connection to the specified URL using the properties defined in the argument `info`. The `DriverManager` normally calls this method when it receives connection requests from JDBC clients.

- `public int getMajorVersion()`: The `getMajorVersion` method returns the major revision number of the driver.

- `public int getMinorVersion()`: The `getMinorVersion` method returns the minor revision number of the driver.

- `public boolean jdbcCompliant()`: The `jdbcCompliant` method returns `True` if the driver is JDBC-compliant. A fully compliant JDBC driver should conform strictly to the JDBC API and at least the SQL92 Entry Level specifications.

# Making Database Connections

The `java.sql.Connection` interface defines the methods required for a persistent connection to the database. The JDBC driver vendor implements this interface. A vendor-neutral database client will always use only the interface, not the implementation class.

JDBC clients use statements, prepared statements, and callable statements for issuing SQL statements to the database. Statements generally are used for the following tasks:

- Getting and setting auto-commit mode

- Getting meta information about the database

- Committing and rolling back transactions

In this section, we will cover the various methods defined in the `java.sql.Connection` interface. We will discuss statements in more detail in the "Using JDBC Statements" section later in this chapter.

## Creating Database Statements

Database statements are used for sending SQL statements to the database. The `java.sql.Connection` interface defines the following set of methods for creating database statements:

- `public Statement createStatement() throws SQLException`: The `createStatement` method is used for creating instances of the `java.sql.Statement` interface. This interface can be used for sending SQL statements to the database. The `java.sql.Statement` interface is normally used for sending SQL statements that don't take any arguments.

- `public Statement createStatement(int resType, int resConcurrency) throws SQLException`: This is the same as the previous method, but it lets the JDBC clients specify the result set type and result set concurrency. Result sets are used for retrieving the results back to the client from the database. Result sets are discussed in the "Working with JDBC Result Sets" section later in this chapter. The result set type identifies the direction in which the result set can be traversed. The concurrency defines how multiple threads can access the result set simultaneously.

- `public PreparedStatement prepareStatement(String sql) throws SQLException`: Prepared statements can precompile and store SQL statements. The `java.sql.PreparedStatement` interface is normally used for sending SQL statements that take arguments. To facilitate this process, this method is used to create instances of the `java.sql.PreparedStatement` interface. The SQL statements passed to prepared statements can use parameter place-holders using ? for sending IN parameters.

- `public Statement prepareStatement (String sql, int resType, int resConcurrency) throws SQLException`: This is the same as the previous method, but it lets the JDBC clients specify the result set type and result set concurrency.

- `public CallableStatement prepareCall(String sql) throws SQLException`: The prepareCall method is used to create instances of the interface `java.sql.CallableStatement`. The `java.sql.CallableStatement` interface is normally used for sending calls to the database's stored procedures that take IN and OUT parameters. The stored procedure calls, passed to prepared statements, can use parameter place-holders using ? for specifying both IN and OUT parameters.

- `public Statement prepareCall (String sql, int resType, int resConcurrency) throws SQLException`: This prepareCall method is the same as the previous method, but it lets the JDBC clients specify the result set type and result set concurrency.

## Handling Transactions

The `java.sql.Connection` interface defines the following methods for handling database transactions:

- `public boolean getAutoCommit() throws SQLException`: The getAutoCommit method gets the current auto-commit mode.

- `public void setAutoCommit(boolean autoCommit) throws SQLException`: The setAutoCommit method sets the auto-commit mode, which we discussed in Chapter 9. If it is set to True, SQL statements will be automatically committed; otherwise, the clients need to issue an explicit commit command.

- `public void commit() throws SQLException`: The commit method commits the current transaction associated with the connection.

- `public void rollback() throws SQLException`: The rollback method rolls back the current transaction associated with the connection.

- `public int getTransactionIsolation() throws SQLException:` The `getTransactionIsolation` method gets the current transaction isolation level. As explained in Chapter 9, the transaction isolation level dictates whether dirty reads, repeatable reads, or phantom reads can be performed.

- `public void setTransactionIsolation(int level) throws SQLException:` The `setTransactionIsolation` method sets the transaction isolation level.

## Retrieving Database Meta Data

The `java.sql.Connection` interface provides a method to get the database meta data:

`public DatabaseMetaData getMetaData() throws SQLException`

This method returns an instance of a class that implements `java.sql.DatabaseMetaData` interface, throwing an instance of `SQLException` if a database-access error occurs.

To demonstrate, the following is a simple example of using Java to retrieve and display some of the PostgreSQL meta data. The `PostgreSQLMetaData.java` class will first load the PostgreSQL JDBC driver and get a connection a database called `bpfinal`, running on the machine named `gw1`. Then it obtains a handle to the database meta data from the connection and prints the meta data to the screen.

```java
import java.sql.Connection;
import java.sql.DatabaseMetaData;
import java.sql.DriverManager;

public class PostgreSQLMetaData {

    public static void main(String args[]) throws Exception {

        Class.forName("org.postgresql.Driver");
        String url = "jdbc:postgresql://gw1/bpfinal";
        Connection con =
            DriverManager.getConnection(url,"rick","password");
        DatabaseMetaData dbmd = con.getMetaData();

        System.out.print("Database Product Name : ");
        System.out.println(dbmd.getDatabaseProductName());

        System.out.print("Database Product Version : ");
        System.out.println(dbmd.getDatabaseProductVersion());

        System.out.print("Driver Major Version : ");
        System.out.println(dbmd.getDriverMajorVersion());

        System.out.print("Driver Minor Version : ");
        System.out.println(dbmd.getDriverMinorVersion());
```

```
        System.out.print("Driver Name : ");
        System.out.println(dbmd.getDriverName());

        System.out.print("Driver Version : ");
        System.out.println(dbmd.getDriverVersion());

        System.out.print("JDBC URL : ");
        System.out.println(dbmd.getURL());

        System.out.print("Supports Transactions : ");
        System.out.println(dbmd.supportsTransactions());

        System.out.print("Default Transaction Isolation level : ");
        System.out.println(dbmd.getDefaultTransactionIsolation());

        System.out.print("Uses Local Files : ");
        System.out.println(dbmd.usesLocalFiles());

        con.close();

    }
}
```

You can compile the class with the following command:

```
$ javac PostgreSQLMetaData.java
```

Then invoke the Java interpreter on the class (assuming the JDBC driver .jar file is available in the CLASSPATH):

```
$ java PostgreSQLMetaData
```

If this fails with an error, such as Exception in thread "main" java.lang.ClassNotFoundException: org.postgresql.Driver, it indicates it cannot find the PostgreSQL JDBC .jar file. You should check that the .jar file is accessible in the CLASSPATH, or put it in the current directory and use the -cp option on the command line.

If everything is okay, running this code will produce something like the following output, depending on the version of PostgreSQL you are running:

```
Database Product Name : PostgreSQL
Database Product Version : 8.0.0
Driver Major Version : 8
Driver Minor Version : 0
Driver Name : PostgreSQL Native Driver
Driver Version : PostgreSQL 8.0devel JDBC3 with SSL (build 307)
JDBC URL : jdbc:postgresql://gw1/bpfinal
Supports Transactions : true
Default Transaction Isolation level : 2
Uses Local Files : false
```

The java.sql.DatabaseMetaData interface can be used to retrieve a lot more information, such as catalog names, table names, and SQL features supported. Refer to the Java documentation for more details.

# Working with JDBC Result Sets

A JDBC ResultSet object represents a two-dimensional array of data produced as a result of executing SQL SELECT statements against databases using JDBC statements. JDBC statements are covered in detail in the "Using JDBC Statements" section later in this chapter.

JDBC result sets are represented by the java.sql.ResultSet interface. The JDBC vendor provider supplies the implementation class for this interface.

## Getting the Result Set Type and Concurrency

Executing appropriate methods against JDBC Statement objects creates objects of type java.sql.ResultSet. As we have already seen in the section about using the java.sql.Connection interface, when we create Statement objects, we can specify the type and scroll sensitivity of the result sets that may be created by those Statement objects.

Result sets can be one of the following types:

- TYPE_FORWARD_ONLY: Forward-only result sets can be traversed only in the forward direction. This means once you move the current cursor pointer to the $n$th row, you can't move back to $(n-1)$th row. These are generally the most efficient types of result sets.

- TYPE_SCROLL_INSENSITIVE: This type of ResultSet object is scrollable and not sensitive to changes made by other threads.

- TYPE_SCROLL_SENSITIVE: This type of ResultSet object is scrollable and sensitive to changes made by other threads.

The ResultSet interface defines a method to get the result set type:

```
public int getType() throws SQLException
```

The type can be set only when the statements are created using Connection objects, as explained in the previous section.

Result sets also can have one of the two following concurrency types:

- CONCUR_READ_ONLY: These result sets are read-only and are not updatable.

- CONCUR _UPDATEABLE: These result sets are updatable.

The ResultSet interface defines a method to get the result set concurrency:

```
public int getConcurrency() throws SQLException
```

The concurrency can be set only when the statements are created using Connection objects, as explained in the previous section.

# Traversing Result Sets

The ResultSet interface defines various methods for traversing the result sets, manipulating the cursor position, and accessing fetch direction. In this section, we will look at these methods.

## Scrolling Result Sets

The following methods are available for scrolling result sets:

- `public boolean next() throws SQLException`: The next method moves the current cursor pointer to the next row and returns True if there are more rows.

- `public boolean first() throws SQLException`: The first method moves the current cursor pointer to the first row and returns True if the cursor is on the first row. This method cannot be executed against a forward-only cursor.

- `public boolean last() throws SQLException`: The last method moves the current cursor pointer to the last row and returns True if the cursor is on the last row. This method cannot be executed against a forward-only cursor.

- `public boolean absolute(int rows) throws SQLException`: The absolute method moves the current cursor pointer forward or backward from the start or end of the result set to the row specified by the argument. The cursor is moved forward from the start if the value of rows is positive, and it is moved backward from the end if the value of rows is negative.

- `public boolean relative(int row) throws SQLException`: The relative method moves the current cursor pointer forward or backward from the current position to the row specified by the argument. The cursor is moved forward if the value of rows is positive, and it is moved backward if the value of rows is negative.

- `public boolean previous() throws SQLException`: The previous method moves the current cursor pointer to the previous row. This method cannot be executed against a forward-only cursor.

## Querying the Cursor Position

The following methods are available for querying the cursor position:

- `public boolean isBeforeFirst() throws SQLException`: The isBeforeFirst method returns True if the cursor position is before the first row.

- `public boolean isAfterLast() throws SQLException`: The isAfterLast method returns True if the cursor position is after the last row.

- `public boolean isFirst() throws SQLException`: The isFirst method returns True if the cursor position is at the first row.

- `public boolean isLast() throws SQLException`: The isLast method returns True if the cursor position is at the last row.

- `public void beforeFirst() throws SQLException`: The `beforeFirst` method moves the cursor to the start of the result set, before the first row.

- `public void afterLast() throws SQLException`: The `afterLast` method moves the cursor to the end of the result set, after the last row.

### Manipulating Fetch Direction and Size

The `ResultSet` interface defines some methods that give a hint to the driver of the direction and the size in which the rows will be fetched, so that it can fetch records from the database accordingly. The following methods are available for manipulating the fetch direction and size:

- `public int getFetchDirection() throws SQLException`: The `getFetchDirection` method returns the current fetch direction. The JDBC API defines three fetch directions that might be returned, each declared as a `static final int` value of the `jdbcStatement` class: `FETCH_FORWARD`, `FETCH_REVERSE`, and `FETCH_UNKNOWN`.

- `public void setFetchDirection(int direction) throws SQLException`: The required direction is set using the `setFetchDirection` method. An instance of `SQLException` is thrown if a fetch direction other than `FETCH_FORWARD` to a forward-only result set occurs.

- `public int getFetchSize() throws SQLException`: The `getFetchSize` method gets the current fetch size.

## Accessing Result Set Data

The interface defines methods for retrieving data from the current row in the result set. The data can be retrieved as appropriate data types. These methods take the general format `getXXX(col)`, where XXX can be one of the different data types (such as `int`, `short`, `string`) and col is an integer giving the column number in the current row from which data is to be fetched. Column numbers start from 1. Alternatively, you can specify the column names instead, which is generally a safer approach because it protects you from schema changes. Regardless of the data type, all columns can be fetched as a string. All of these methods throw an instance of `SQLException` if a database error occurs.

Here are some of the main data-access methods for getting `boolean`, `int`, and `string` data (refer to the Java documentation for a complete list):

- `public boolean getBoolean(int i)`

- `public boolean getBoolean(String col)`

- `public int getInt(int i)`

- `public int getInt(String col)`

- `public String getString(int i)`

- `public String getString(String col)`

Table 17-1 lists the mapping of Java types to PostgreSQL data types and JDBC data types. The different JDBC types are defined in the class `java.sql.Types`.

**Table 17-1.** *Data Type Cross Reference*

| Java Type | JDBC Type | PostgreSQL Type |
|---|---|---|
| java.lang.Boolean | tinyint | int2 |
| java.lang.Byte | tinyint | int2 |
| java.lang.Short | smallint | int2 |
| java.lang.Integer | integer | int4 |
| java.lang.Long | bigint | int8 |
| java.lang.Float | float | float(7) |
| java.lang.Double | double | float(8) |
| java.lang.Character | char | char(1) |
| java.lang.String | varchar | text |
| java.sql.Date | date | date |
| java.sql.Time | time | time |
| java.sql.Timestamp | timestamp | timestamp |
| java.lang.Object | JAVA_OBJECT | oid |

# Working with Updatable Result Sets

We can create updatable result sets from statements that specified the result set concurrency as `CONCUR_UPDATEABLE`. We can modify the data in updatable result sets, as well as add and remove rows. In this section, we will look at the methods available for modifying the state of result sets.

## Deleting Data

The interface defines the following methods for deleting the current row and verifying the deletion:

- `public void deleteRow() throws SQLException`: This method deletes the current row from the result set and from the database. This method cannot be called when the cursor is on INSERT row (a special row in a result set for adding data to the underlying database).

- `public boolean rowDeleted() throws SQLException`: The `rowDeleted` method checks whether the current row has been deleted and returns `True` if it has been.

## Updating Data

The result set interface defines a set of update*XXX* methods for updating the data in the current row of the result set. However, these methods don't in themselves update the underlying data in the database; the updateRow method must be called to actually change the data in the database. The following lists a few of the more commonly used *updateXXX* methods (for a complete listing, see the Java documentation), and then the methods for processing updates:

- public void updateBoolean(int i, boolean x): Sets the data in the specified column to the specified boolean value.

- public void updateBoolean(String col, boolean x): Sets the data in the specified column to the specified boolean value.

- public void updateInt(int i, int x): Sets the data in the specified column to the specified int value.

- public void updateInt(String col, int x): Sets the data in the specified column to the specified int value.

- public void updateString(int i, String x): Sets the data in the specified column to the specified string value.

- public void updateString(String col, String x): Sets the data in the specified column to the specified string value.

- public void updateRow() throws SQLException: After updating the data in the result set, if you wish to write your change to the database, you must call the updateRow method. This method updates the underlying database with the data changed using the updateXXX methods.

- public void refreshRow() throws SQLException: The refreshRow method refreshes the current row the most recent data from the database.

- public void cancelRowUpdates() throws SQLException: This method cancels the updates made to the current row.

- public boolean rowUpdated() throws SQLException: The rowUpdated method checks whether the current row held in the working data set (not the one stored in the database) has been updated and returns True if it has been.

## Inserting Data

Result sets have a special row called the INSERT row for adding data to the underlying database. To move the cursor to the INSERT row, use the following method:

```
public boolean moveToInsertRow() throws SQLException
```

The cursor can then be returned to the previous row using this method:

```
public boolean moveToCurrentRow() throws SQLException
```

To actually insert the INSERT row into the database, use the following method:

```
public boolean insertRow() throws SQLException
```

An instance of SQLException is thrown if the cursor is not on INSERT row (or if a database-access error occurs).

## Using Other Relevant Methods

Two other relevant methods are available with the java.sql.ResultSet interface.

This close method releases the database and JDBC resources:

```
public void close() throws SQLException
```

The getMetaData method gets the result set meta data as an instance of a class that implements the java.sql.ResultSetMetaData interface:

```
public ResultSetMetaData getMetaData() throws SQLException
```

This interface defines a host of methods for accessing the result set meta data, including the following:

- Catalog name

- Column class name

- Column count

- Column display size

- Column label

- Column type

- Column type name

Refer to the Java documentation for a complete listing.

# Creating JDBC Statements

The JDBC API defines three types of statements for sending SQL statements to the database:

- **Statements:** Statements are generally used for sending SQL statements that don't take any arguments. The methods required for Statement objects are defined by the java.sql.Statement interface. The JDBC driver provider supplies the implementation class for this interface.

- **Prepared Statements:** Prepared statements are generally used for sending precompiled SQL statements that take IN arguments. The methods required for PreparedStatement objects are defined in the java.sql.PreparedStatement interface. This interface extends the java.sql.Statement interface.

- **Callable Statements:** Callable statements are generally used for making calls to database stored procedures and can take both IN and OUT arguments. The methods required for CallableStatement objects are defined in the java.sql.CallableStatement interface. This interface extends the java.sql.PreparedStatement interface.

---

**Note** Callable statements are supported in versions of the PostgreSQL JDBC driver from 7.4 onwards.

---

## Using Statements

The java.sql.Statement interface is normally used for sending SQL statements to the database that don't have IN or OUT parameters. The JDBC driver vendor provides the implementation class for this interface. The common methods required by the different JDBC statements are defined in this interface. The methods defined by java.sql.Statement allow you to perform the following tasks:

- Execute SQL statements

- Query results and result sets

- Handle SQL batches

- Get and set query time out

- Close the statement to release resources

- Get and set escape processing

- Get and clear SQL warnings

- Get and set cursor names

Here, we will cover the main tasks of executing statements, querying result sets, and handling SQL batches. See the Java documentation for information about the additional methods.

### Executing SQL Statements

The java.sql.Statement interface defines methods for executing SQL statements such as SELECT, UPDATE, INSERT, DELETE, and CREATE.

Use the executeQuery method to send a SELECT statement to the database and get back the result:

```
public ResultSet executeQuery(String sql) throws SQLException
```

Here is an example that simply returns a result set containing everything from the mytable table:

```
try {
    Connection con = DriverManager.getConnection(url, prop);
    Statement stmt = con.createStatement();
    ResultSet res = stmt.executeQuery("SELECT * FROM mytable");
} catch(SQLException e) {
    // Handle exception
}
```

You can use the execute method to send a SQL statement to the database that may fetch multiple result sets (like a stored procedure):

```
public boolean execute(String sql) throws SQLException
```

This returns True if the next result is a ResultSet object.

For SQL statements that don't return result sets—like INSERT, UPDATE, and DELETE statements, as well as data definition language statements—use executeUpdate:

```
public int executeUpdate(String sql) throws SQLException
```

This returns the number of rows affected by the SQL statement.

## Querying Results and Result Sets

The Statement interface defines various methods for retrieving information about the result of executing a SQL statement.

Although executing a SQL statement can create several result sets, a Statement object can have only one result set open at a time. The getResultSet method returns the current result set associated with the Statement object:

```
public ResultSet getResultSet() throws S.Exception
```

This method returns NULL if there is no more of the result set available or the next result is an update count generated by executing an UPDATE, INSERT, or DELETE statement.

The getUpdateCount method returns the update count for the last executed UPDATE, INSERT, or DELETE statement:

```
public int getUpdateCount() throws SQLException
```

This method returns -1 if there is no more update count available or the next result is a result set generated by executing a SELECT statement.

The getMoreResults method gets the Statement object's next result set:

```
public boolean getMoreResults() throws SQLException
```

This method returns False if there is no more of the result set available or the next result is an update count.

Methods are also provided for performing the following get or set tasks:

- The result set concurrency with which the statement was created

- The result set fetch direction

- The fetch size

## Handling SQL Batches

The Statement interface also provides methods for sending a batch of SQL statements to the database:

- `public void addBatch(String sql) throws SQLException`: The addBatch method adds the specified SQL to the current batch. Generally, the SQL statements are INSERT, UPDATE, or DELETE.

- `public void clearBatch() throws SQLException`: The clearBatch method clears the current batch.

- `public int[] executeBatch() throws SQLException`: The executeBatch method executes the current batch. This method returns an array of updated counts.

## Writing a JDBC Client Using Statements

It's time to try out the key elements we have learned so far. To demonstrate the use of JDBC, we will write a JDBC client, called StatementClient.java, that will perform the following tasks:

- Get a connection to the database.

- Create a Statement object.

- Insert two records into the customer table.

- Select those records back from the database.

- Delete those records.

- Close the connection.

Later, we will update this example to use prepared statements, which are generally more efficient.

First, we must import the relevant classes:

```
import java.sql.Connection;
import java.sql.Statement;
import java.sql.ResultSet;
import java.sql.ResultSetMetaData;
import java.sql.DriverManager;
```

Next, declare a main method:

```
public class StatementClient {

    public static void main(String args[]) throws Exception {
```

Load the driver, and connect to the database bpfinal on the server gw1:

```
        Class.forName("org.postgresql.Driver");
        String url = "jdbc:postgresql://gw1/bpfinal";
        Connection con =
            DriverManager.getConnection(url,"rick","password");
```

Create a statement, and add two INSERT statements using a batch:

```
Statement stmt = con.createStatement();
System.out.println("Inserting records");
stmt.addBatch("INSERT INTO customer(title,fname," +
    "lname,addressline,town,zipcode,phone) values " +
    "('Mr','Fred','Flintstone','31 Bramble Avenue'," +
    "'London','NT2 1AQ','023 9876')");
stmt.addBatch("INSERT INTO customer(title,fname," +
    "lname,addressline,town,zipcode,phone) values " +
    "('Mr','Barney','Rubble','22 Ramsons Avenue'," +
    "'London','PWD LS1','111 2313')");
```

Now execute the batch:

```
stmt.executeBatch();
System.out.println("Records Inserted");
System.out.println();
```

Select records from the table:

```
System.out.println("Selecting all records");
String selectSQL = "SELECT title, fname, lname, town" +
"FROM customer";
ResultSet res = stmt.executeQuery(selectSQL);
```

Retrieve the meta data for the result set, and use it to set the number of columns returned and display the column titles:

```
ResultSetMetaData rsmd = res.getMetaData();
int colCount = rsmd.getColumnCount();

for(int i = 1; i <= colCount; i++) {
    System.out.print(rsmd.getColumnLabel(i) + "\t");
}
System.out.println();
```

Loop through all the rows retrieved, displaying the data:

```
while(res.next()) {
    for(int i = 1;i <= colCount; i++) {
        System.out.print(res.getString(i) + "\t");
    }
    System.out.println();
}
System.out.println();
```

Delete the rows we just inserted, checking how many rows were deleted:

```
        System.out.println("Deleting records");
        String deleteSQL = "DELETE FROM customer" +
"WHERE (fname = 'Fred' AND lname = 'Flintstone')" +
"OR (fname = 'Barney' AND lname = 'Rubble')";
        System.out.println("Records deleted: "
+ stmt.executeUpdate(deleteSQL));
```

Finally, we must close the resources we have used:

```
        res.close();
        stmt.close();
        con.close();
    }
}
```

Compile the class:

```
$ javac StatementClient.java
```

The output will be similar to the following, truncated for brevity:

```
$ java StatementClient
Inserting records
Records Inserted

Selecting all records
title   fname   lname       town
Miss    Jenny   Stones      Hightown
Mr      Andrew  Stones      Lowtown
Miss    Alex    Matthew     Nicetown
Mr      Adrian  Matthew     Yuleville
...
Mr      David   Hudson      Milltown
Mr      Fred    Flintstone  London
Mr      Barney  Rubble      London

Deleting records
Records deleted: 2
```

## Using Prepared Statements

Prepared statements are used for executing precompiled SQL statements, and they are modeled in the JDBC API using the java.sql.PreparedStatement interface. This interface extends the java.sql.Statement interface, and the JDBC driver vendor must provide the implementation class for this interface.

Prepared statements are created using the Connection objects as we have already seen, but in addition, they can also be used for executing SQL statements with parameter placeholders for IN statements defined using the symbol ?.

Prepared statements are recommended for executing the same SQL statements more than once using different values for the IN parameters. This is because each time the database engine sees a SQL statement, it must parse it to determine its meaning, and also perform some processing to determine what it considers the most cost-efficient way of executing the statement. If the statement's execution doesn't involve much work, these preparatory steps can be a very significant part of the overall execution time of the command. Using a prepared statement allows the database to parse and generate an execution plan for the statement just once, which can significantly reduce the overhead.

## Executing Prepared SQL Statements

The java.sql.PreparedStatement interface defines methods for executing SQL statements, such as SELECT, UPDATE, INSERT, DELETE, and CREATE. Unlike the corresponding methods defined in the Statement interface, these methods don't take the SQL statements as arguments. The SQL statements are defined when the prepared statements are created using the Connection objects.

Use the executeQuery method to execute the SELECT statement associated with the prepared statement and get back the result:

```
public ResultSet executeQuery() throws SQLException
```

Here is an example:

```
try {
    String sql = "SELECT * FROM customer WHERE fname = ? ";
    Connection con = DriverManager.getConnection(url,prop);
    PreparedStatement stmt = con.prepareStatement(sql);
    stmt.setString(1, "Fred");
    ResultSet res = stmt.executeQuery();
} catch(SQLException e) {
    // Handle exception
}
```

The execute method executes SQL statements that return results associated with prepared statements:

```
public boolean execute() throws SQLException
```

This returns True if the next result is a ResultSet object.

The executeUpdate method executes SQL statements associated with prepared statements that don't return result sets, such as INSERT and UPDATE:

```
public int executeUpdate() throws SQLException
```

This returns the number of rows affected by the SQL statement.

## Updating Data

The prepared statement interface defines a set of set*XXX* methods for setting the values of the IN parameters for the precompiled SQL statements defined using the symbol ?. The parameter indexes start from 1. The set*XXX* method used should be compatible with the expected SQL type. The following are a few of the more common methods (see the Java documentation for others):

- `public void setBoolean(int index, boolean x)`: Sets the IN parameter specified by the argument index to the boolean value specified by x.

- `public void setInt(int index, int x)`: Sets the IN parameter specified by the argument index to the int value specified by x.

- `public void setString(int index, string x)`: Sets the IN parameter specified by the argument index to the string value specified by x.

The interface also defines a method for clearing the current values of all parameters immediately:

```
public void clearParameters() throws SQLException
```

## Writing a JDBC Client Using Prepared Statements

Now we will rewrite the previous StatementClient.java example using prepared statements and see how the same INSERT statement can be executed multiple times using different values.

The key changes are highlighted:

```
import java.sql.Connection;
import java.sql.PreparedStatement;
import java.sql.ResultSet;
import java.sql.ResultSetMetaData;
import java.sql.DriverManager;

public class PreparedStatementClient {

    public static void main(String args[]) throws Exception {

// Load the JDBC driver and get a connection.
// Create a prepared statement from the connection:

        Class.forName("org.postgresql.Driver");
        String url = "jdbc:postgresql://gw1/bpfinal";
        Connection con =
            DriverManager.getConnection(url,"rick","password");

        PreparedStatement stmt;

        String insertSQL = "INSERT INTO customer(title,fname," +
            "lname,addressline,town,zipcode,phone) VALUES " +
            "(?,?,?,?,?,?,?)";

        stmt = con.prepareStatement(insertSQL);

        System.out.println("Inserting records");
```

```java
        stmt.setString(1,"Mr");
        stmt.setString(2,"Fred");
        stmt.setString(3,"Flintstone");
        stmt.setString(4,"31 Bramble Avenue");
        stmt.setString(5,"London");
        stmt.setString(6,"NT2 1AQ");
        stmt.setString(7,"023 9876");
        stmt.executeUpdate();

        stmt.clearParameters();

        stmt.setString(1,"Mr");
        stmt.setString(2,"Barney");
        stmt.setString(3,"Rubble");
        stmt.setString(4,"22 Ramsons Avenue");
        stmt.setString(5,"London");
        stmt.setString(6,"PWD LS1");
        stmt.setString(7,"111 2313");
        stmt.executeUpdate();


// Select the records from the customer table and
// print the contents to the standard output:
        System.out.println("Selecting all records");
        String selectSQL = "SELECT title, fname, lname, town FROM customer";
        stmt = con.prepareStatement(selectSQL);
        ResultSet res = stmt.executeQuery();

// Retrieve the meta data from the result set
    ResultSetMetaData rsmd = res.getMetaData();
    int colCount = rsmd.getColumnCount();

// Display the column titles
    for(int i = 1;i <= colCount; i++) {
        System.out.print(rsmd.getColumnLabel(i) + "\t");
    }
    System.out.println();


        while(res.next()) {
            for(int i = 1;i <= colCount; i++) {
                System.out.print(res.getString(i) + "\t");
            }
            System.out.println();
        }
        System.out.println();
```

```
// Delete the records from the customer table and print the number of records
deleted:

        System.out.println("Deleting records");
        String deleteSQL = "DELETE FROM customer " +
"WHERE (fname = 'Fred' AND lname = 'Flintstone') " +
"OR (fname = 'Barney' AND lname = 'Rubble')";
        stmt = con.prepareStatement(deleteSQL);
        System.out.println("Records deleted: " + stmt.executeUpdate());


// Close the result set, statement and connection to free up resources:
        res.close();
        stmt.close();
        con.close();

    }
}
```

# Summary

In this chapter, we have seen how PostgreSQL databases can be accessed from Java language programs using JDBC.

The JDBC API continues to evolve. The JDBC 3 driver particularly saw significant changes, and the Java Development Kit (JDK) 1.5 platform also introduces some minor changes. Also starting to appear are persistence layers, such as Hibernate and Java Data Objects (JDO), which help to bridge the object world of the Java programmer to the relational world of the SQL-based database.

In the next chapter, we will look at how to access PostgreSQL databases from C#.

# CHAPTER 18

# Accessing PostgreSQL from C#

In the previous chapter, we explained how to access PostgreSQL databases from Java. In this chapter, we will look at how to access your PostgreSQL database from a similar language, C#. If you have Java experience, you'll be quite familiar with the similar C# syntax. However, the techniques for accessing PostgreSQL from C# are somewhat different from those used with Java.

In this chapter, we will look at three main ways to access PostgreSQL from C#:

- Using the ODBC .NET Data Provider on Windows

- Using the Npgsql library on Linux

- Using the Npgsql library on Windows

The first section of this chapter examines how to use the standard ODBC .NET Data Provider method with Windows systems. Then we will focus on using Npgsql. Other alternatives for C# access to PostgreSQL are starting to appear, such as PgOleDb (http://gborg.postgresql.org/project/oledb) and the Advanced Data Provider (http://advanced-ado.sourceforge.net/), but Npgsql has been around longer. Also, as of PostgreSQL release 8.0, Npgsql is an optional part of the Windows installation set.

## Using the ODBC .NET Data Provider on Windows

Users of Microsoft's Visual Studio will find that once the ODBC .NET foundation is working, ADO.NET (Microsoft's Database API for the .NET Framework) simply runs on top of the ODBC connection, exactly as it would for any other ODBC data source. This approach does not need any PostgreSQL-specific drivers, apart from the ODBC driver, which we assume you have already installed, as described in Chapter 3.

---

**Note** For more information about ADO.NET, see a book devoted to that topic, such as Mahesh Chand's *A Programmer's Guide to ADO.NET in C#* (Apress, 2002; ISBN 1-89311-539-9).

---

### Setting Up the ODBC .NET Data Provider

If you don't already have the ODBC data driver for ADO.NET, installing it is your first task. (This driver is not installed by default in the current release of Visual Studio 2003.) You can check by seeing if a resource called `Microsoft.Data.Odbc` is available to your projects. If not, you'll need to add it as an update.

To obtain the ODBC provider for .NET, go to the Microsoft MSDN site and look in the "SDKs, Redistributables & Service Packs" section for "ODBC .NET Data Provider." (Unfortunately, the exact location tends to move about, but it's usually fairly easy to find by searching.) This should take you to a page where you can download an installable file such as `odbc_netversion10.msi`. Go ahead and install this file.

Finally, add `Microsoft.Data.Odbc` as a reference, by right-clicking the References section of the Solution Explorer pane in your Visual Studio project before proceeding.

## Connecting to the Database

There are two ways to specify the database connection string, which determines how your program will connect to the database:

- Construct a connection string with the driver and details, such as database and user from within your program, much as you can for other databases, but using {PostgreSQL} as the driver choice.

- Create a predefined connection string through the Control Panel's Administrative Tools and add a new data source name (DSN). You can use either a User DSN, specific to the current user, or a System DSN, which will be available to all users. This will allow you to specify a name for the data source, plus the server, database name, username, and password (as well as many other options that you should leave as the default values). You can then use this DSN in your programs, without needing to specify any of the details again.

---

**■Note** Whether you should use a User DSN or System DSN depends on your circumstances. For example, if there are other users of the machine and they will also need access to the new DSN, you should use a Systems DSN. If you are the only user of the machine, a User DSN is probably more appropriate.

---

The following `vs-connect.cs` program demonstrates how to connect using both connection string styles. First, it specifies all the details in the connection string, and then it uses a preconfigured DSN, producing just enough output to demonstrate that both methods work correctly. The two key sections are highlighted.

```
// vs-connect.cs
using System;
using System.Data;
using Microsoft.Data.Odbc;

class PostgreSQL
{
    static void Main(string[] args) {

        // First all details in one version
        // The string is split and concatenated to fit the book layout
```

```
        const string CONNECTION_STRING =
          "DRIVER={PostgreSQL};SERVER=192.168.0.3;" +
          "UID=rick;PWD=password;DATABASE=bpfinal";
        OdbcConnection conn = new OdbcConnection();
        conn.ConnectionString = CONNECTION_STRING;
        conn.Open();
        Console.WriteLine("Version: {0}", conn.ServerVersion);
        conn.Close();
        Console.ReadLine();

        // And now using a preconfigured DSN
        conn.ConnectionString = "dsn=PostgreSQL-bpfinal";
        conn.Open();
        Console.WriteLine("Version: {0}", conn.ServerVersion);
        conn.Close();
        Console.ReadLine();
    }
}
```

Although specifying the complete list of connection variables is more long-winded, it does mean that you won't need to configure any DSNs on the machines where the code will execute, which may be a significant advantage.

## Retrieving Data into a Dataset

Once a connection has been established to a PostgreSQL database, you can use standard ADO.NET methods for accessing the data. The following vs-dataset.cs program demonstrates the basics, showing that once you have a connection to a PostgreSQL database, you really can treat it just like any other ODBC .NET data source. The key section is highlighted.

---

■**Note** Remember that you will need to add the Microsoft.Data.Odbc assembly to the project references.

---

```
// vs-dataset.cs
using System;
using System.Data;
using Microsoft.Data.Odbc;

class PostgreSQL
{
  static void Main(string[] args)
  {
```

```
    const string CONNECTION_STRING =
      "DRIVER={PostgreSQL};SERVER=192.168.0.3;" +
      "UID=rick;PWD=password;DATABASE=bpfinal";
  OdbcConnection conn = new OdbcConnection();
  conn.ConnectionString = CONNECTION_STRING;
  conn.Open();
  DataSet ds = new DataSet();
  OdbcDataAdapter da = new OdbcDataAdapter("SELECT * FROM customer", conn);
  da.Fill(ds, "customer");
  DataTable dt = ds.Tables["customer"];
  foreach(DataRow dr in dt.Rows)
  {
    Console.Write("Name: {0}, {1}, {2}\n", dr[1], dr["fname"], dr["lname"]);
  }
  conn.Close();
  Console.WriteLine();
  Console.ReadLine();
  }
}
```

This creates a new empty `DataSet` object, and then creates an `OdbcDataAdapter` using a selection of data from the `customer` table and the `OdbcConnection` object opened earlier in the code.

It then uses the data adapter to fill the dataset with the retrieved data, `da.Fill(ds, "customer")`, giving it the table name `customer`.

Next, the program instantiates a `DataTable` object from the `ds` table `customer`, `DataTable dt = ds.Tables["customer"]`. With a data table in hand, we are nearly finished, leaving only the step of iterating through the rows: `foreach(DataRow dr in dt.Rows)`. Each `DataRow` object then contains the columns for the current row, which we can access using either an index, `dr[1]`, or a column name, `dr["fname"]`.

As you can see, once you connect to PostgreSQL using a standard ADO.NET data adapter, you access PostgreSQL in basically the same way as you access other relational databases from C# using Visual Studio.

# Using Npgsql in Mono

In this section, we will look at Npgsql (http://gborg.postgresql.org/project/npgsql). This is a solution primarily for users of Mono (http://www.mono-project.com), the open-source implementation of the .NET Framework, based on the ECMA (http://www.ecma-international.org) standards for C# (ECMA 334) and its infrastructure (ECMA 335).

At the time of writing, Mono is the most practical way to use C# and its associated framework using exclusively open-source software. Npgsql is an open-source implementation of a .NET data provider for C#, roughly analogous to a Java class type 4 driver, as described in Chapter 17. It is implemented completely in C# and provides an interface directly to the network protocol that PostgreSQL uses. This makes it highly portable to any system supporting C# and its runtime, and enables access to PostgreSQL databases both locally and across the network. It can support all types of projects, from Console to Windows Forms.

Npgsql is available separately, but it is also bundled with the Mono distribution and the Windows distribution of PostgreSQL 8.0. (We also hope that, in the future, it will be available in any Mono package included by the main Linux distributions.)

At the time of writing, Npgsql is still evolving. Functionally, it is almost complete, but there may be some slight differences in the version you have from the one used here. In general, we will describe only the more important attributes that we need to get started. The Npgsql documentation is very detailed and contains the full list of classes, properties, and methods available.

# Connecting to the Database

The first thing we need to do is connect to our PostgreSQL database server. The Npgsql assembly (the Npgsql.dll file) provides an NpgsqlConnection class. This class provides the means of connecting to a PostgreSQL database, and then retains the connection information required to interact with the database.

## Creating an NpgsqlConnection Object

Most of the information required to connect to the database would normally be passed in the constructor to the NpgsqlConnection class. The Npgsql constructor accepts a connection string, which can pass in all the information required in a format very similar to an ODBC connection string. The options that may be included in the connection string are listed in Table 18-1.

**Table 18-1.** *Connection String Options*

| Option | Meaning |
|---|---|
| Server | The name or IP address of the server running PostgreSQL |
| Port | The port number to connect to; defaults to the standard port |
| Protocol | The protocol version number to use (2 or 3); if omitted, this will be chosen automatically |
| Database | The name of the database; defaults to the same value as the User Id |
| User Id | The username |
| Password | The password |
| SSL | Sets the connection security as true or false; defaults to false |
| Pooling | Sets connection pooling as true or false; defaults to true |
| MinPoolSize | Sets the lower bound of the connection pool size |
| MaxPoolSize | Sets the upper bound of the connection pool size |
| Timeout | Sets the time to wait for a connection before timing out |

Each option is set as an *option-name=value* string. Options are separated by semicolons. For example, to connect to our bpfinal database on the server 192.168.0.3 as user rick using the password password, we need to construct our connection object like this:

```
NpgsqlConnection(
    "Server=192.168.0.3;User Id=rick;Password=password;Database=bpfinal;"
);
```

The NpgsqlConnection class has a number of properties, as shown in Table 18-2. The State property can be retrieved at any time, to check if the object has a database connection. Connection options can be set using the ConnectionString property, but only before the object connects to the database. Once connected, you can get all of the properties listed in the table.

**Table 18-2.** *NpgsqlConnection Properties*

| Property | Meaning |
| --- | --- |
| ConnectionString | Gets or sets the connection string |
| Database | Gets the name of the current database |
| ServerVersion | Gets the version of the server currently connected to |
| State | Gets the current state of the connection |

Once the object is connected to a database, there are many methods you can call. Table 18-3 lists a few of the more important ones.

**Table 18-3.** *Common NpgsqlConnection Methods*

| Method | Meaning |
| --- | --- |
| BeginTransaction | Starts a transaction and optionally passes an isolation level to use |
| ChangeDatabase | Closes the connection and reconnects to a different database |
| Close | Closes the connection, or, if using connection pooling, releases the connection back to the pool |
| Open | Opens the connection |

To show how all this works, the following Connect.cs program makes a connection to the bpfinal database. We will stick to passing connection information in to the NpgsqlConnection object as it is created. To show that the connection actually works, we will get the database version string back from the connection object and display it.

```
// Connect.cs
// Connect to the bpfinal PostgreSQL database on the server 192.168.0.3 as
// the user rick, with a password of 'password'.

using System;
using Npgsql;

public class connect
{
  public static void Main(String[] args) {
    NpgsqlConnection conn = new NpgsqlConnection(
"Server=192.168.0.3;User Id=rick;Password=password;Database=bpfinal;");
    try {
      conn.Open();
      Console.Write(
"State: {0}, Server Version: {1}", conn.State, conn.ServerVersion);
      Console.WriteLine();
    }
    finally {
      conn.Close();
    }
  }
}
```

The two using statements give us access to the standard system features and the Npgsql assembly. We then create a new NpgsqlConnection object using a connection string constructor to define our database connection. Once the NpgsqlConnection object is instantiated, we use the Open method to connect to our database, and then retrieve the state and version information. Finally, we close the connection, which disconnects the program from the database. Although we wrap the connection attempt in a try block, we use the finally option only to ensure our connection is closed; we don't catch any exceptions thrown ourselves. In our trivial program, the finally block doesn't really have any benefit, but in more complex programs, it's necessary to keep careful track of resources and ensure they are properly released.

Now that we have our source code, we need to compile it. As we are using Npgsql, we are probably Linux users (although Mono and Npgsql are also available for Windows systems), so we can use either the command-line mcs compiler or the graphical MonoDevelop (http://www.monodevelop.com/) tool. Let's look at the command line first.

## Compiling with the Command-Line Compiler

We could copy the Npgsql.dll file to the Mono system library directory (probably something like /usr/lib/mono/1.0), but it would be somewhat untidy to copy additional libraries into the system library directory, so we will add an additional library path for the local additions. We will assume the Npgsql.dll file is stored in a directory ~/mono-local.

To compile the program, we need to set both the location for the additional assembly, using the -L option, and also tell the compiler the resources we need, using the -r flag:

```
mcs -L ~/mono-local -r:Npgsql.dll Connect.cs
```

This should result in a Connect.exe file, which can be executed using the mono command to interpret the intermediate language code generated.

---

■**Note** It's possible, depending on the way Npgsql and Mono are packaged at the time you are reading this, that you will also need to use Mono.Security.dll and possibly Mono.Security.Protocol.Tls.dll in addition to the main Npgsql.dll file.

---

Here it is in action:

```
$ mcs -L ~/mono-local -r:Npgsql.dll  Connect.cs
Compilation succeeded
$ mono Connect.exe
State: Open, Server Version: 8.0.0
$
```

## Compiling with MonoDevelop

Next, we will look at compiling the program with MonoDevelop. If you're not presently using MonoDevelop and would like to follow along with this section, you will need to download it from the web site: http://www.monodevelop.com/.

In order to build the project, you'll first need to add the Npgsql.dll resource to your project. To do this, start by creating a new solution containing a new empty Console project, then go to the References subsection of the solution, right-click it, and select Edit. This brings up a dialog box that allows you to add resources to the project. Click the .Net Assembly tab, browse to find the Npgsql.dll file, and then select Add. You can then go to the Global Assembly Cache tab and add Npgsql as a reference, as shown in Figure 18-1.

You will also need to add the System.Data resource, which should already be in the list of available references.

Once you have entered the code, you should be able to click the gear cog icon on the right side of the toolbar to compile and execute this simple C# program for attaching to a PostgreSQL database.

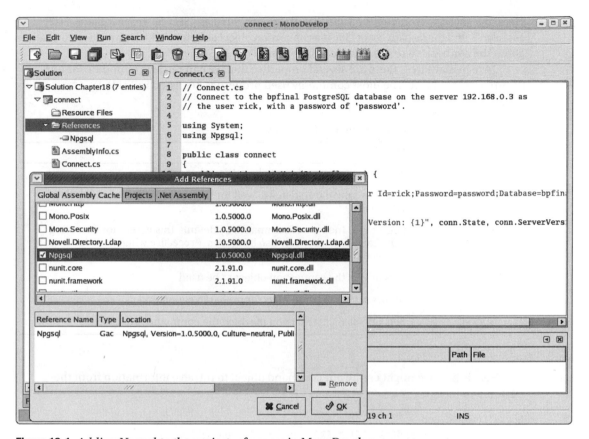

**Figure 18-1.** *Adding Npgsql to the project references in MonoDevelop*

# Retrieving Data from the Database

To retrieve data from the database, we need to use two additional Npgsql classes: the NpgsqlCommand class and the NpgsqlDataReader class. We will start by looking at the NpgsqlCommand class, which allows us to send commands, such as a SELECT statement, to the database.

## Sending Commands with NpgsqlCommand

The NpgsqlCommand class has a number of constructors. The most commonly used form is to pass the text of the command required and a connection object, as follows:

```
NpgsqlCommand(string SQLCommand, NpgsqlConnection connectionobject);
```

Here, the string parameter is a valid SQL statement, such as "SELECT fname, lname FROM customer", and the NpgsqlConnection is a connection object as before, which provides information about the connection to the PostgreSQL database.

Once instantiated, there are several properties that we can retrieve or update for our NpgsqlCommand object. The most commonly used properties are listed in Table 18-4.

**Table 18-4.** *Common NpgsqlCommand Properties*

| Method | Meaning |
| --- | --- |
| CommandText | Allows the command text to be retrieved or set |
| CommandTimeout | Sets how long the system will wait for the command to execute before terminating it |
| CommandType | Sets or gets the type of command; by default, this is Text for executing SQL statements, but can also be Stored Procedure when the command is to execute a stored procedure |
| Connection | Sets or gets the connection object to be used |
| Parameters | Allows access to parameters for prepared statements |
| Transaction | Sets or gets the transaction in which the command is to execute |

Here is how we might create our command object to retrieve information from the customer table:

```
NpgsqlCommand cmd =
    new NpgsqlCommand("SELECT * FROM customer", conn);
```

If we subsequently wanted to change the SQL statement, we just update the CommandText property, like this:

```
cmd.CommandText = "SELECT * from orderinfo";
```

Once we have a command object, we can use its methods to perform actions against the database. The main methods are shown in Table 18-5.

**Table 18-5.** *Common NpgsqlCommand Methods*

| Method | Meaning |
| --- | --- |
| Dispose | Releases all the resources in use |
| ExecuteNonQuery | Executes a SQL statement that doesn't retrieve data |
| ExecuteReader | Executes a SQL statement that will return data; returns an NpgsqlDataReader object |
| Prepare | Makes a prepared statement ready for execution |

The method we are most interested in is ExecuteReader, which returns an NpgsqlDataReader object. Here is an example:

```
NpgsqlDataReader datard = cmd.ExecuteReader();
```

The NpgsqlDataReader object is the next class we need to look at in the Npgsql assembly.

## Getting Data with the NpgsqlDataReader Class

The NpgsqlDataReader class is the one that actually allows us to get at the data (and meta data) when we retrieve data from the database. It's normally created by the execution of an ExecuteReader method on the NpgsqlCommand object. Since it has quite a bit of work to do, it's the most complex object we have yet encountered in the Npgsql assembly, but it's not hard to use. This class's most commonly used properties are listed in Table 18-6.

**Table 18-6.** *Common NpgsqlDataReader Properties*

| Property | Meaning |
|---|---|
| FieldCount | Provides the number of columns in the data row |
| HasRows | Set to true if there is one or more rows of data ready to be read |
| IsClosed | Set to true if the data reader has been closed |
| Item | Retrieves the column in its native format |
| RecordsAffected | Provides the number of rows affected by the SQL statement |

The Item property is quite clever. You simply use the name of the data reader object with an array accessor [ ], using either an index of the column offset or passing a string containing the name of the column. In either case, the data contents of the column are returned in its native format. We will see both of these types of array access in the next two code examples. This means that if we create an NpgsqlDataReader object datard, then once it is populated, we can access the value of the third column by writing datard[3], which leads to client code that is much easier to read. If we prefer, we can also access the data using the column name, by passing in a string as the array index: datard["lname"].

The data reader object also has quite a long list of methods. Table 18-7 lists the most commonly used methods.

**Table 18-7.** *Common NpgsqlDataReader Methods*

| Method | Meaning |
|---|---|
| Close | Closes the data reader object |
| Dispose | Releases all the resources in use |
| GetBoolean | Gets a column value as a Boolean value |
| GetDateTime | Gets a column value as a datetime value |

**Table 18-7.** *Common NpgsqlDataReader Methods (Continued)*

| Method | Meaning |
|--------|---------|
| GetDecimal | Gets a column value as a decimal number |
| GetDouble | Gets a column value as a double |
| GetFieldType | Returns the data type of the column at an index position |
| GetFloat | Gets a column value as a floating-point number |
| GetInt16 | Gets a column value as a 16-bit integer |
| GetInt32 | Gets a column value as a 32-bit integer |
| GetInt64 | Gets a column value as a 64-bit integer |
| GetName | Gets the column name of a column by index |
| GetString | Gets a column value as a string |
| IsDBNull | True if the value in a column is NULL |
| Read | Advances the data reader to the next row |

Remember that the easiest way to access the data value is via an array reference, using the Item property.

Retrieving data from the database is not difficult. In practice, you will often need only a small subset of the properties and methods available. Our next program, getdata1.cs, shows the basic properties and methods we need to retrieve some data. The key changes from our earlier program are highlighted.

```
// Getdata1.cs - a simple retrieve of data from the customer table

using System;
using Npgsql;

public class connect
{
  public static void Main(String[] args) {
    NpgsqlConnection conn = new
NpgsqlConnection("Server=192.168.0.3;Port=5432;
User Id=rick;Password=password;Database=bpfinal;");
    try {
      conn.Open();
      NpgsqlCommand cmd = new NpgsqlCommand("SELECT * FROM customer", conn);
      NpgsqlDataReader datard = cmd.ExecuteReader();
      while (datard.Read()) {
        for (int i=0; i<datard.FieldCount; i++) {
          Console.Write("{0}, ", datard[i]);
        }
```

```
      Console.WriteLine();
    }
  }
  finally {
    conn.Close();
  }
  }
}
```

When we run this in MonoDevelop, a console window opens and displays the retrieved data, as shown in the example in Figure 18-2.

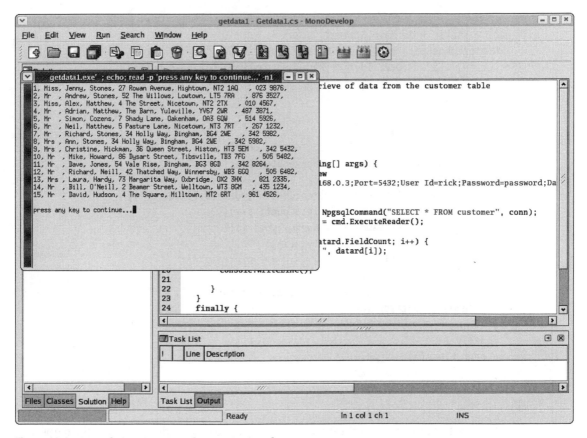

**Figure 18-2.** *C# code in MonoDevelop retrieving data*

The key changes are that we created a new NpgsqlCommand object, passing it a SQL statement to retrieve all the data from the customer table, as well as the NpgsqlConnection object we previously opened. We then call the ExecuteReader method, which returns a new NpgsqlDataReader object. By repeatedly calling the Read method, we iterate through the retrieved rows. We use the FieldCount property to determine how many columns there are in the row. Notice we access the data by using an index of the column number directly into the data reader object: datard[i]. This retrieves the actual data value, which we print to the console.

## Retrieving Meta Data

It's often very useful to be able to retrieve meta data, or data about the data, from a database. We can do this quite easily using the methods we have already seen. The following program, Getdata2.cs, builds on Getdata1.cs, adding code to retrieve the names and types of the columns being retrieved. The changed lines are highlighted.

```
// getdata2.cs - a simple retrieve of meta data from the customer table

using System;
using Npgsql;

public class connect
{
  public static void Main(String[] args) {
    NpgsqlConnection conn = new NpgsqlConnection(
"Server=192.168.0.3;User Id=rick;Password=password;Database=bpfinal;");

    try {
      conn.Open();
      NpgsqlCommand cmd =
new NpgsqlCommand("SELECT * FROM customer", conn);
      NpgsqlDataReader datard = cmd.ExecuteReader();
      datard.Read();
      Console.Write("There are {0} columns\n", datard.FieldCount);
      for (int i = 0; i < datard.FieldCount; i++) {
        Console.Write("Name: {0}, NpgsqlType: {1}",
datard.GetName(i), datard.GetFieldType(i));
        Console.WriteLine();
      }
      Console.Write("First row by named column: {0}, {1}",
datard["fname"], datard["lname"]);
    }
    finally {
      conn.Close();
    }
  }
}
```

We use the GetName and GetFieldType methods of the data reader to retrieve the name and column types. We also use a field name, rather than the column index as in the previous example, to retrieve data.

## Using Npgsql Event Logging

Before we move on, we will take a brief look at the event logging capabilities of Npgsql. We can debug programs using Npgsql in the same way that we debug any C# program: by adding statements to print out data or by stepping through the program in a debugger. However, for some types of error tracking, what we would like is an easy-to-use method of tracing what Npgsql is doing. The Npgsql assembly has a special event log for doing just that. It is very simple to use, with only the three properties listed in Table 18-8.

**Table 18-8.** *NpgsqlEventLog Properties*

| Property | Meaning |
| --- | --- |
| EchoMessages | Sets if message should be printed to the console: true or false |
| Level | Sets the level of messages required: None, Normal, or Debug |
| Logname | Sets the name of the file to write to, if required |

We can see this in action in a simple demonstration program, Debug.cs.

```
// Debug.cs

using System;
using Npgsql;

public class connect
{
  public static void Main(String[] args) {
    NpgsqlEventLog.Level = LogLevel.Debug;
    NpgsqlEventLog.LogName = "/tmp/Npgsqldebug.txt";
    NpgsqlEventLog.EchoMessages = true;

    NpgsqlConnection conn = new NpgsqlConnection(
"Server=192.168.0.3;User Id=rick;Password=password;Database=bpfinal;");

    try {
      conn.Open();
      NpgsqlCommand cmd = new NpgsqlCommand("SELECT * FROM customer", conn);
      NpgsqlDataReader datard = cmd.ExecuteReader();
      datard.Read();
      Console.Write("{0}, {1}, {2}",
datard[0], datard[1], datard[2]);
      Console.WriteLine();
    }
    finally {
      conn.Close();
    }
  }
}
```

When we run this program, a console window immediately opens, showing the logging text, as in the example in Figure 18-3.

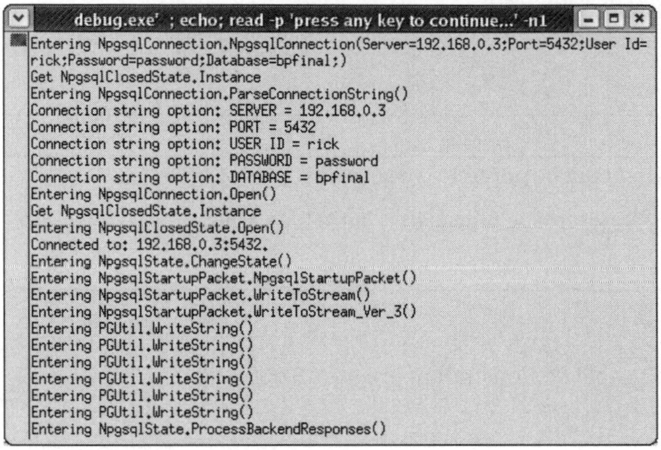

**Figure 18-3.** *Log tracing in progress*

The textual log file written is very similar, with the addition of timestamp information.

# Using Parameters and Prepared Statements with Npgsql

When PostgreSQL executes a SQL statement, a fair amount of work must be done to determine how the statement should be executed. When executing many very similar statements that differ only in the values used, such as in search criteria for SELECT statements, this can be very inefficient. This is because of the overhead PostgreSQL incurs each time it must parse and determine an execution plan from the SQL. Just as we can with host variables in embedded C (discussed in Chapter 14) and with prepared statements in Java (discussed in Chapter 17), we can also generate SQL statements with parameters using Npgsql.

First, we need to look at the NpgsqlParameter class, which lets us create parameters.

## Creating Parameters with the NpgsqlParameter Class

The NpgsqlParameter class is used to create parameter variables, which can be associated with a SQL statement in an NpgsqlCommand object. It's a relatively simple class; we really need to concern ourselves only with the parameter name and type, which are generally just passed in when the object is constructed. Table 18-9 lists the NpgsqlParameter properties.

**Table 18-9.** *NpgsqlParameter Properties*

| Property | Meaning |
|---|---|
| DbType | Gets or sets the parameter type |
| Direction | Indicates if the parameter is input-only, output-only, or bidirectional |
| IsNullable | Indicates if NULL values are allowed |
| NpgsqlDbType | Gets or sets the type of the parameter |
| ParameterName | Gets or sets the name of the parameter variable |
| Precision | Gets or sets the maximum number of digits |
| Scale | Gets or sets the number of decimal places |
| Size | Gets or sets the maximum in bytes of the column |
| Value | The actual data value to be used |

Generally, you will only need to use the constructor, which has many signatures, permitting most of the properties to be set as the object is constructed. The constructor format you are mostly likely to need is as follows:

```
NpgsqlParameter(string parametername, NpgsqlDbType ptype)
```

The NpgsqlDbType is simply an enumeration of the possible data types. The principal elements are Boolean, Date, Double, Integer, Numeric, Real, Smallint, Text, Time, and Timestamp.

## Creating Statements with Parameters

Parameters are sometimes useful even for statements that aren't executed many times, as they can simplify construction of the SQL statement. They are also an important step on the way to prepared statements. To create a SQL statement that has parameters, we replace the actual value in the SQL string with a variable name, which must start with a colon. Here is an example:

```
SELECT * FROM customer WHERE customer_id = :cid
```

We can then bind the variable name to an NpgsqlParameter object, which has the name of the variable and the data type. For example, where cmd is an NpgsqlCommand object, we could replace a parameter :cid with a 32-bit integer parameter like this:

```
cmd.Parameters.Add(new NpgsqlParameter("cid", DbType.Int32));
```

These steps need to be performed only once for each SQL string.

Last, but not least, we replace the parameter with an actual value, which can be done many times in a program:

```
cmd.Parameters[0].Value = 2;
```

We can see this in practice in the following program, Getdata3.cs. The key lines are highlighted.

```
// getdata3.cs - a retrieve of data from the customer table using parameters

using System;
using System.Data;
using Npgsql;

public class connect
{
  public static void Main(String[] args) {
    NpgsqlConnection conn = new NpgsqlConnection(
"Server=192.168.0.3;User Id=rick;Password=password;Database=bpfinal;");
    try {
      conn.Open();
      NpgsqlCommand cmd = new NpgsqlCommand(
"SELECT * FROM customer WHERE customer_id = :cid OR fname = :fn", conn);
      cmd.Parameters.Add(new NpgsqlParameter("cid", DbType.Int32));
      cmd.Parameters.Add(new NpgsqlParameter("fn", DbType.String));
      cmd.Parameters[0].Value = 2;
      cmd.Parameters[1].Value = "Jenny";
      NpgsqlDataReader datard = cmd.ExecuteReader();
      while (datard.Read()) {
        for (int i = 0; i < datard.FieldCount; i++) {
          Console.Write("{0}, ", datard[i]);
        }
        Console.WriteLine();

      }
    }
    finally {
      conn.Close();
    }
  }
}
```

Notice that we must be careful to get our parameters in the correct order as we move from replacing the variable names with parameter objects and then actual values.

## Creating Prepared Statements

Now that we understand how to replace variables in SQL statements with actual values, it's only a small step to see how we can then prepare the statement once, change the values, and reexecute it, without the database needing to reprocess the statement.

The Getdata4.cs script adds to the previous code, reusing a previously prepared statement with different values. Key lines are highlighted.

```
// getdata4.cs - a retrieve of data from the customer table using
// parameters and prepared statements

using System;
using System.Data;
using Npgsql;

public class connect
{
  public static void Main(String[] args) {
    NpgsqlConnection conn = new NpgsqlConnection(
"Server=192.168.0.3;User Id=rick;Password=password;Database=bpfinal;");
    try {
      conn.Open();
      NpgsqlCommand cmd = new NpgsqlCommand(
"SELECT * FROM customer WHERE customer_id = :cid OR fname = :fn", conn);
      cmd.Parameters.Add(new NpgsqlParameter("cid", DbType.Int32));
      cmd.Parameters.Add(new NpgsqlParameter("fn", DbType.String));
      cmd.Prepare();
      cmd.Parameters[0].Value = 2;
      cmd.Parameters[1].Value = "Jenny";
      NpgsqlDataReader datard = cmd.ExecuteReader();
      while (datard.Read()) {
        for (int i = 0; i < datard.FieldCount; i++) {
          Console.Write("{0}, ", datard[i]);
        }
        Console.WriteLine();
      }
      datard.Close();
      cmd.Parameters[0].Value = 3;
      cmd.Parameters[1].Value = "Adrian";
      datard = cmd.ExecuteReader();
      while (datard.Read()) {
        for (int i = 0; i < datard.FieldCount; i++) {
          Console.Write("{0}, ", datard[i]);
        }
        Console.WriteLine();
      }
    }
```

```
    finally {
      conn.Close();
    }
  }
}
```

We prepare the statement before executing it the first time, and we can then simply change the values of parameters, without needing to rebind them to NpgsqlParameter objects, and reexecute the statement.

# Changing Data in the Database

So far, all we have done is retrieve data from the database, which although very important, is really just covering the SQL SELECT statement. In this section, we will look at two ways we might make other changes to the database. First, we will look at executing statements that do not return data, such as INSERT, UPDATE, and DELETE statements. We will then look at a different way data might be inserted into the database, which involves using an ADO.NET data adapter.

## Using the NpgsqlCommand ExecuteNonQuery Method

We can very easily execute statements that don't return data by directly using the ExecuteNonQuery method of the NpgsqlCommand object. The Insert.cs script demonstrates how to add a new customer.

```
// insert.cs - insert data directly

using System;
using System.Data;
using Npgsql;

public class connect
{
  public static void Main(String[] args) {
    NpgsqlConnection conn = new NpgsqlConnection(
"Server=192.168.0.3;User Id=rick;Password=password;Database=bpfinal;");
    try {
      conn.Open();
      NpgsqlCommand cmd = new NpgsqlCommand("INSERT INTO customer(title, fname,
lname, addressline, town, zipcode, phone) VALUES('Mr.', 'Simon', 'Bennett',
'1 Victoria Street', 'Nicetown', 'NT4 2WS', '342 6352')", conn);
      int rowsaffected = cmd.ExecuteNonQuery();
      Console.Write("Rows affected {0}", rowsaffected);
    }
    finally {
      conn.Close();
    }
  }
}
```

In this example, we simply create a command object, as before, then execute it using the ExecuteNonQuery method. We can then use the return value to check that the correct numbers of rows were affected. The UPDATE and DELETE statements are carried out in the same fashion.

## Using a DataAdapter

Another way we might choose to alter data in the database is to use a DataAdapter object. This object logically sits on top of the connection object, and provides data to DataSet objects that manage the actual data. Figure 18-4 shows a very simplified representation.

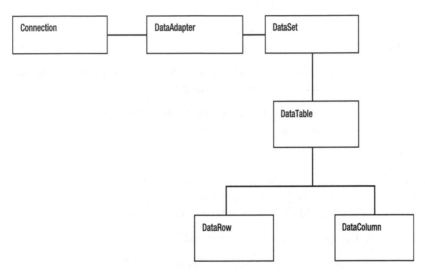

**Figure 18-4.** *Relationship of some of the ADO.NET objects*

The DataSet object contains many internals, but most important to us is the DataTable object (it actually can contain many table objects, but we will keep it simple here), which is itself composed of the DataRow and DataColumn objects that contain the actual data.

The insert-ds.cs script demonstrates how we can use DataAdapter and DataSet objects to insert rows into the bpfinal database. As a change, we add a new product to our catalog. Since it is quite long, and a somewhat different approach, we present the program in segments, with a brief comment preceding each section.

```
// insert-ds.cs - insert data via a database
```

This first part is the same code we have seen before.

```
using System;
using System.Data;
using Npgsql;

public class connect
{
  public static void Main(String[] args) {
```

```
NpgsqlConnection conn = new NpgsqlConnection(
"Server=192.168.0.3;User Id=rick;Password=password;Database=bpfinal;");
    try {
      conn.Open();
```

Next, we create a DataSet object ready for later use.

```
DataSet ds = new DataSet();
```

Now we create a DataAdapter object using a SQL command to retrieve data from the item table, and the connection object we created earlier.

```
NpgsqlDataAdapter da = new NpgsqlDataAdapter
("SELECT description, cost_price, sell_price FROM item", conn);
```

Next, we add an INSERT command in the DataAdapter, which we are going to use to add our new row. Notice we use a parameterized query for this example.

```
da.InsertCommand = new NpgsqlCommand("INSERT INTO item(description,
cost_price, sell_price) VALUES(:de, :cp, :sp)", conn);
```

Set the data type of the parameters.

```
da.InsertCommand.Parameters.Add(new NpgsqlParameter(":de", DbType.String));
da.InsertCommand.Parameters.Add(new NpgsqlParameter(":cp", DbType.Double));
da.InsertCommand.Parameters.Add(new NpgsqlParameter(":sp", DbType.Double));
```

Bind the parameters to the column names in the item table.

```
da.InsertCommand.Parameters[0].SourceColumn = "description";
da.InsertCommand.Parameters[1].SourceColumn = "cost_price";
da.InsertCommand.Parameters[2].SourceColumn = "sell_price";
```

Use our DataAdapter to populate the DataSet we created earlier.

```
da.Fill(ds);
```

Create a DataTable, as the first (and only) table in the DataSet.

```
DataTable dt = ds.Tables[0];
```

Create a new row and populate its columns.

```
DataRow dr = dt.NewRow();
dr["description"] = "Large Penguin";
dr["cost_price"] = 7.23;
dr["sell_price"] = 9.99;
```

Add the new row to our `DataTable`, and tell the `DataAdapter` to update, based on our `DataSet` with the new row.

```
dt.Rows.Add(dr);
da.Update(ds);
```

Last, we have the standard trailing elements of our program.

```
    }
    finally {
      conn.Close();
    }
  }
}
```

That is quite a lot more code than the previous example, but the use of `DataAdapter` and `DataSet` objects does give us a higher-level interface to the database, with access to more advanced features.

# Using Npgsql in Visual Studio

As Npgsql is implemented in pure C# code and accesses the PostgreSQL network protocol directly, we might reasonably hope that it will work unchanged on Windows inside Visual Studio, and indeed it does, once we set up our project to use it. This means that all of the techniques covered in the previous section also work when we are using Npgsql in Visual Studio.

First, we need to create a new location on our Windows system to store the `Npgsql.dll` file. At the time of writing, two other DLLs are also needed: `Mono.Security.dll` and `Mono.Security.Protocol.Tls.dll`. However, the packaging of Npgsql is currently under development, and they may no longer be required in the future. They can be found on the Npgsql site (`http://gborg.postgresql.org/project/npgsql`), along with the `Npgsql.dll` file.

Once we have a directory with the appropriate DLLs and we have created our project, we need to add the additional resources. Select the Add Reference option from the Project menu, browse to the directory containing the DLLs, and select Open.

We needed to make one very minor change to the source code. Namely, we added a final `Console.ReadLine();` near the end, because, by default, Visual Studio closes the console window when the program completes, but MonoDevelop (the graphical tool we used for the previous examples) does not. Apart from that minor tweak, the code is identical. Figure 18-5 shows our `getdata1.cs` project in Visual Studio.

Notice the References in the Solution Explorer window on the right side of Figure 18-5, showing the references we added to the project.

There is really nothing more involved in using Npgsql under Windows. Once the environment is set up correctly, it works identically on both platforms.

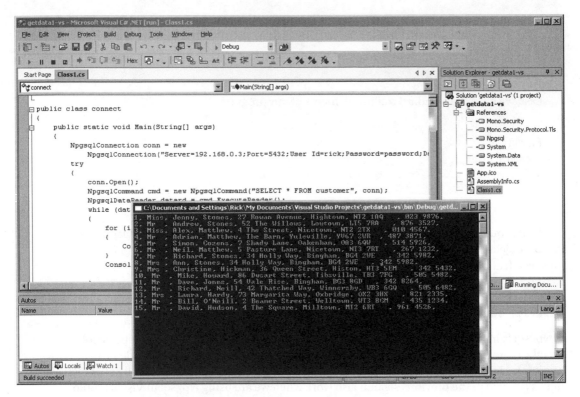

**Figure 18-5.** *Npgsql used in a Visual Studio project*

# Summary

This chapter has been a quick tour of three of the ways you might choose to access your PostgreSQL database from C#.

If your code is limited to Windows, and you have Microsoft's Visual Studio, you are most likely to use the PostgreSQL ODBC driver (although as we mentioned early in the chapter, it's not the only choice). We showed the two methods of using this driver to connect to your database: by specifying a driver string or a DSN. Finally, we demonstrated how, once you are connected to PostgreSQL, it behaves like any other ODBC data source, allowing you the full power of the Microsoft ADO.NET database technology.

If you are using Mono, you will probably choose to use the Npgsql data adapter, which (currently) ships with Mono. Npgsql provides a good range of data-access functions in a standard form. You could choose to use Npgsql on Windows systems, but this choice is more likely if you need code compatibility between Windows and other operating systems.

This chapter ends our journey from PostgreSQL novice to PostgreSQL professional. PostgreSQL has progressed enormously from its early research days, and matured into a very capable and stable product suitable for use in many production systems. Its support for standard SQL, already strong, continues to improve with each release, as does its impressive scalability. The new features in version 8, such as the native Windows port and tablespaces, make PostgreSQL an even more attractive choice as a database system. The Open Source license means that you can deploy PostgreSQL with no client or server license costs.

Coupled with the knowledge you have gained from this book, you should now be in a position to deploy a true database server in situations where license costs may have otherwise driven a less elegant solution. PostgreSQL already has a distinguished past, and as it continues to progress, we are sure it will be an ever more potent challenger to the commercial vendors with their huge development budgets, dedicated development teams, and expensive license fees.

We wish you, and the PostgreSQL developers, all the best with this outstanding open-source database.

# APPENDIX A

■■■

# PostgreSQL Database Limits

**W**hen we use a database to store information, we are tempted to ignore the fact that on no platform do we have the luxury of infinite storage. All database systems are limited in some way, and PostgreSQL is no exception. The amount of data that can be stored in a single column, the maximum number of columns allowed in a table, and the total size of any table all have limits, albeit quite large ones.

As a limit is approached, the performance of the database will degrade. If we are, for example, manipulating very large fields consuming a large fraction of available (virtual) memory, it is likely that performance will begin to be unacceptable. Finally, PostgreSQL will be physically unable to perform an update.

Recent releases of PostgreSQL have seen most database limits relaxed, and in many cases, effectively removed. In this appendix, we will mention some of the restrictions that remain as of PostgreSQL version 8.0. For updates on limits for later versions, check out the PostgreSQL web site at http://www.postgresql.org.

---

**Note** The information here is derived from the PostgreSQL FAQ and mailing list contributions made by PostgreSQL developers.

---

Where a size is given as "No Limit," this means that PostgreSQL alone imposes no limit. The maximum size will be determined by other factors, such as operating system limits and the amount of available disk space or virtual memory. The network transport may also impose limits. For example, there are typically limits on the size of a query that can be made via ODBC, depending on the driver. Memory limits may prevent very large columns, rows, or result sets from being created, transferred across a network (which in itself will be slow), or received by the client.

## Database Size: No Limit

PostgreSQL does not impose a limit on the total size of a database. Databases of 4 terabytes (TB) are reported to exist. A database of this size is more than sufficient for all but the most demanding applications.

Due to the way that PostgreSQL arranges its data storage, you may see some performance degradation associated with databases containing many tables. PostgreSQL may use a large number of files for storing the table data, and performance may suffer if the operating system does not cope well with many files in a single directory. The introduction of tablespaces in PostgreSQL 8.0 helps the database administrator to minimize these effects. Tablespaces are covered in Chapter 11.

### Table Size: 16TB–64TB

PostgreSQL normally stores its table data in chunks of 8KB. The number of these blocks is limited to a 32-bit signed integer (just over two billion), giving a maximum table size of 16TB. The basic block size can be increased when PostgreSQL is built, up to a maximum of 32KB, thereby giving a theoretical table size limit of 64TB.

Some operating systems impose a file size limit that prevent files of this size from being created, so PostgreSQL stores table data in multiple files, each 1GB in size. For large tables, this will result in many files and potential operating system performance degradation, as noted earlier.

### Rows in a Table: No Limit

PostgreSQL does not impose a limit on the number of rows in any table.

### Table Indexes: No Limit

There is no PostgreSQL-imposed limit on the number of indexes you can create on a table. Of course, performance may degrade if you choose to create more and more indexes on a table with more and more columns.

### Field Size: 1GB

PostgreSQL has a limit of 1GB for the size of any one field in a table. In practice, the limit comes from the amount of memory available for the server to manipulate the data and transfer it to the client.

### Columns in a Table: 250+

The maximum number of columns that can be accommodated in a PostgreSQL table depends on the configured block size and the type of the column. For the default block size of 8KB, at least 250 columns can be stored. This can rise to 1,600 columns if all of the columns are very simple fields, such as integer values. Increasing the block size increases these limits accordingly.

### Row Size: No Limit

There is no explicit maximum size of a row. But, of course, the size of columns and their number are limited as described in the preceding text.

# PostgreSQL Data Types

**P**ostgreSQL has a particularly rich set of data types, which are described in Chapter 11 of this book, as well as in Chapter 8 of the PostgreSQL documentation.

In this appendix, we list the more useful types, ignoring some of the very specialized types and those types used only internally by PostgreSQL. Use \dT (or \dT+ for even more detail) from psql for a definitive list of types.

In the tables in this appendix, the standard SQL name appears first, which PostgreSQL generally accepts, followed by any PostgreSQL-specific alternative names. Some types are specific to PostgreSQL and in such cases, no SQL standard name is given in the tables.

As long as it's practical, we suggest that you stick to the standard SQL types and names. Some of the official SQL names are almost invariably shortened in real use; for example int for integer, bool for boolean, and varchar for character varying. We have adhered to the common convention of using the shorter name in this book.

## Logical Types

Table B-1 shows the PostgreSQL logical data type: boolean. Note that boolean was not officially added to the SQL language until the SQL99 standard, although it was in common use long before that.

**Table B-1.** *PostgreSQL Logical Data Type*

| SQL Name | PostgreSQL Alternative Name | Notes |
|----------|------------------------------|-------|
| boolean  | bool | Holds a truth value. Will accept values such as TRUE, 't', 'true', 'y', 'yes', and '1' as true. Uses 1 byte of storage, and can store NULL, unlike a few proprietary databases. |

# Exact Number Types

Table B-2 shows the PostgreSQL exact number data types.

**Table B-2.** *postgresql Exact Number Types*

| SQL Name | PostgreSQL Alternative Name | Notes |
|---|---|---|
| smallint | int2 | A signed 2-byte integer that can store −32768 to +32767. |
| integer, int | int4 | A signed 4-byte integer that can store −2147483648 to +2147483647. |
| bigint | int8 | A signed 8-byte integer, giving approximately 18 digits of precision. |
| bit | bit | Stores a single bit, 0 or 1. To insert into a table, use syntax such as INSERT INTO … VALUES(B'1');. |
| bit varying | varbit(n) | Stores a string of bits. To insert into a table, use syntax such as INSERT INTO … VALUES(B'011101'); . |

# Approximate Number Types

Table B-3 shows the PostgreSQL approximate number data types. Note that the decimal type is just an alias for numeric, which is the term used by the SQL standard and generally preferred. Similarly, rather than float, use real or double precision.

**Table B-3.** *PostgreSQL Approximate Number Types*

| SQL Name | PostgreSQL Alternative Name | Notes |
|---|---|---|
| numeric (precision, scale) | | Stores an exact number to the precision specified. The user guide states there is no limit to the precision that may be specified. |
| real | float4 | A 4-byte, single-precision, floating-point number. |
| double precision | float8 | An 8-byte, double-precision, floating-point number. |
| money | | Equivalent to numeric(9,2), storing 4 bytes of data. Its use is discouraged, as it is deprecated and support may be dropped in the future. |

# Temporal Types

Table B-4 shows the PostgreSQL data types for date and time.

**Table B-4.** *PostgreSQL Types for Date and Time*

| SQL Name | PostgreSQL Alternative Name | Notes |
|---|---|---|
| timestamp | datetime | Stores dates and times from 4713 BC to 1465001 AD, with a resolution of 1 microsecond. You may also see timestamptz used sometimes in PostgreSQL, which is a shorthand for timestamp with time zone. |
| interval | interval | Stores an interval of approximately +/– 178,000,000 years, with a resolution of 1 microsecond. |
| date | date | Stores dates from 4713 BC to 32767 AD, with a resolution of 1 day. |
| time | time | Stores a time of day, from 0 to 23:59:59.99, with a resolution of 1 microsecond. |

# Character Types

Table B-5 shows the PostgreSQL character data types.

**Table B-5.** *PostgreSQL Character Types*

| SQL Name | PostgreSQL Alternative Name | Notes |
|---|---|---|
| char, character | bpchar | Stores a single character. |
| char(n) | bpchar(n) | Stores exactly *n* characters, which will be padded with blanks if fewer characters are actually stored. |
| character varying(n) | varchar(n) | Stores a variable number of characters, up to a maximum of *n* characters, which are not padded with blanks. This is the standard choice for character strings. |
| | text | A PostgreSQL-specific variant of varchar, which does not require you to specify an upper limit on the number of characters. |

# Geometric Types

Table B-6 shows the PostgreSQL geometric data types. These are specific to PostgreSQL, so there are no SQL names listed.

**Table B-6.** *PostgreSQL Geometric Types*

| PostgreSQL Name | Notes |
| --- | --- |
| point | An x,y value |
| line | A line (pt1, pt2) |
| lseg | A line segment (pt1, pt2) |
| box | A box specified by a pair of points |
| path | A sequence of points, which may be closed or open |
| polygon | A sequence of points, effectively a closed path |
| circle | A point and a length, which specify a circle |

# Miscellaneous PostgreSQL Types

As shown in Table B-7, PostgreSQL has some other data types, which do not fit into the previous categories. SQL names are not applicable to these types.

Note that PostgreSQL does not implement the serial type as a separate type, although it accepts the conventional SQL syntax. Internally PostgreSQL uses an integer to store the value and a sequence to manage the automatic incrementing of the value. When a table is created with a serial type, an implicit sequence (named using an underscore separated combination of the table name, the column name, and seq) is created to manage the serial data column. This implicit sequence will be dropped automatically if the table is dropped.

The cidr type refers to Classless Inter-Domain Routing (CIDR). This is a newer standard for IP addressing. This is in contrast to the original form of IP address assignment, which uses three classes—A, B, and C—that have a network part of 8, 16, and 24 bits, respectively, allowing 16.7 million, 65 thousand, and 254 hosts per network, respectively. CIDR allows network masks of any size, so you can better allocate IP addresses and route between them in a hierarchical fashion.

**Table B-7.** *Other PostgreSQL Types*

| PostgreSQL Name | Notes |
| --- | --- |
| serial | In conventional SQL usage, a serial (or auto-incrementing integer) is a numeric column in a table that increases each time a row is added. |
| oid | An object identifier. Internally, PostgreSQL adds, by default, a hidden oid to each row, and stores a 4-byte integer, giving a maximum value of approximately 4 billion. This type is also used as a reference when storing binary large objects. We recommend you do not use this type or rely on its existence. |
| cidr | Stores a network address of the form *x.x.x.x*/*y* where *y* is the netmask. |
| inet | Similar to cidr, except the host part can be 0. |
| macaddr | A MAC address of the form *XX:XX:XX:XX:XX:XX*. |

Table B-7. Other PostgreSQL Types

| PostgreSQL Name | Notes |
| --- | --- |
| serial | In conventional SQL usage, a serial (or auto-incrementing integer) a numeric column in a table that increases each time a row is added. |
| oid | An object identifier. Internally, PostgreSQL adds, by default, a hidden oid to each row, and stores a 4-byte integer, giving a maximum value of approximately 4 billion. This type is also used as a reference when manipulating large objects. We recommend you do not use this type or rely on its existence. |
| cidr | Stores a network address of the form x.x.x.x/y where y is the netmask. |
| inet | Like cidr, except that the netmask is... |
| macaddr | A MAC address of the form XX:XX:XX:XX:XX:XX. |

# PostgreSQL SQL Syntax Reference

**T**his appendix presents a list of the PostgreSQL commands, followed by the syntax for each of these commands. This set of commands is taken from the `psql` command-line tool. Using `psql`, you can generate the complete list of commands by using the `\help` command. For the syntax of a specific command, use `\help <command>`.

More detailed explanations are available in Part VI (Reference), Section I (SQL Commands) of the PostgreSQL manual.

## PostgreSQL SQL Commands

| | | |
|---|---|---|
| ABORT | CREATE INDEX | DROP TYPE |
| ALTER AGGREGATE | CREATE LANGUAGE | DROP USER |
| ALTER CONVERSION | CREATE OPERATOR CLASS | DROP VIEW |
| ALTER DATABASE | CREATE OPERATOR | END |
| ALTER DOMAIN | CREATE RULE | EXECUTE |
| ALTER FUNCTION | CREATE SCHEMA | EXPLAIN |
| ALTER GROUP | CREATE SEQUENCE | FETCH |
| ALTER INDEX | CREATE TABLE | GRANT |
| ALTER LANGUAGE | CREATE TABLE AS | INSERT |
| ALTER OPERATOR CLASS | CREATE TABLESPACE | LISTEN |
| ALTER OPERATOR | CREATE TRIGGER | LOAD |
| ALTER SCHEMA | CREATE TYPE | LOCK |
| ALTER SEQUENCE | CREATE USER | MOVE |
| ALTER TABLE | CREATE VIEW | NOTIFY |
| ALTER TABLESPACE | DEALLOCATE | PREPARE |
| ALTER TRIGGER | DECLARE | REINDEX |

| | | |
|---|---|---|
| ALTER TYPE | DELETE | RELEASE SAVEPOINT |
| ALTER USER | DROP AGGREGATE | RESET |
| ANALYZE | DROP CAST | REVOKE |
| BEGIN | DROP CONVERSION | ROLLBACK |
| CHECKPOINT | DROP DATABASE | ROLLBACK TO SAVEPOINT |
| CLOSE | DROP DOMAIN | SAVEPOINT |
| CLUSTER | DROP FUNCTION | SELECT |
| COMMENT | DROP GROUP | SELECT INTO |
| COMMIT | DROP INDEX | SET |
| COPY | DROP LANGUAGE | SET CONSTRAINTS |
| CREATE AGGREGATE | DROP OPERATOR | SET SESSION AUTHORIZATION |
| CREATE CAST | DROP OPERATOR CLASS | SET TRANSACTION |
| CREATE CONSTRAINT TRIGGER | DROP RULE | SHOW |
| CREATE CONVERSION | DROP SCHEMA | START TRANSACTION |
| CREATE DATABASE | DROP SEQUENCE | TRUNCATE |
| CREATE DOMAIN | DROP TABLE | UNLISTEN |
| CREATE FUNCTION | DROP TABLESPACE | UPDATE |
| CREATE GROUP | DROP TRIGGER | VACUUM |

# PostgreSQL SQL Syntax

### ABORT

Abort the current transaction.

```
ABORT [ WORK | TRANSACTION ]
```

### ALTER AGGREGATE

Change the definition of an aggregate function.

```
ALTER AGGREGATE name ( type ) RENAME TO new_name
ALTER AGGREGATE name ( type ) OWNER TO new_owner
```

### ALTER CONVERSION

Change the definition of a conversion.

```
ALTER CONVERSION name RENAME TO new_name
ALTER CONVERSION name OWNER TO new_owner
```

## ALTER DATABASE

Change a database.

```
ALTER DATABASE name SET parameter { TO | = } { value | DEFAULT }
ALTER DATABASE name RESET parameter
ALTER DATABASE name RENAME TO new_name
ALTER DATABASE name OWNER TO new_owner
```

## ALTER DOMAIN

Change the definition of a domain.

```
ALTER DOMAIN name
    { SET DEFAULT expression | DROP DEFAULT }
ALTER DOMAIN name
    { SET | DROP } NOT NULL
ALTER DOMAIN name
    ADD domain_constraint
ALTER DOMAIN name
    DROP CONSTRAINT constraint_name [ RESTRICT | CASCADE ]
ALTER DOMAIN name
    OWNER TO new_owner
```

## ALTER FUNCTION

Change the definition of a function.

```
ALTER FUNCTION name ( [ type [, ...] ] ) RENAME TO new_name
ALTER FUNCTION name ( [ type [, ...] ] ) OWNER TO new_owner
```

## ALTER GROUP

Change a user group.

```
ALTER GROUP groupname ADD USER username [, ... ]
ALTER GROUP groupname DROP USER username [, ... ]
ALTER GROUP groupname RENAME TO new_name
```

## ALTER INDEX

Change the definition of an index.

```
ALTER INDEX name
    action [, ... ]
ALTER INDEX name
    RENAME TO new_name
```

Where action is one of:

```
    OWNER TO new_owner
    SET TABLESPACE indexspace_name
```

## ALTER LANGUAGE

Change the definition of a procedural language.

```
ALTER LANGUAGE name RENAME TO new_name
```

## ALTER OPERATOR

Change the definition of an operator.

```
ALTER OPERATOR name ( { lefttype | NONE } , { righttype | NONE } )
    OWNER TO new_owner
```

## ALTER OPERATOR CLASS

Change the definition of an operator class.

```
ALTER OPERATOR CLASS name USING index_method RENAME TO new_name
ALTER OPERATOR CLASS name USING index_method OWNER TO new_owner
```

## ALTER SCHEMA

Change the definition of a schema.

```
ALTER SCHEMA name RENAME TO new_name
ALTER SCHEMA name OWNER TO new_owner
```

## ALTER SEQUENCE

Change the definition of a sequence generator.

```
ALTER SEQUENCE name [ INCREMENT [ BY ] increment ]
    [ MINVALUE minvalue | NO MINVALUE ]
    [ MAXVALUE maxvalue | NO MAXVALUE ]
    [ RESTART [ WITH ] start ] [ CACHE cache ] [ [ NO ] CYCLE ]
```

## ALTER TABLE

Change the definition of a table.

```
ALTER TABLE [ ONLY ] name [ * ]
    action [, ... ]
ALTER TABLE [ ONLY ] name [ * ]
    RENAME [ COLUMN ] column TO new_column
ALTER TABLE name
    RENAME TO new_name
```

Where action is one of:

```
ADD [ COLUMN ] column_type [ column_constraint [ ... ] ]
DROP [ COLUMN ] column [ RESTRICT | CASCADE ]
ALTER [ COLUMN ] column TYPE type [ USING expression ]
ALTER [ COLUMN ] column SET DEFAULT expression
ALTER [ COLUMN ] column DROP DEFAULT
ALTER [ COLUMN ] column { SET | DROP } NOT NULL
ALTER [ COLUMN ] column SET STATISTICS integer
ALTER [ COLUMN ] column SET STORAGE { PLAIN | EXTERNAL | EXTENDED | MAIN }
ADD table_constraint
DROP CONSTRAINT constraint_name [ RESTRICT | CASCADE ]
CLUSTER ON index_name
SET WITHOUT CLUSTER
SET WITHOUT OIDS
OWNER TO new_owner
SET TABLESPACE tablespace_name
```

## ALTER TABLESPACE

Change the definition of a tablespace.

```
ALTER TABLESPACE name RENAME TO new_name
ALTER TABLESPACE name OWNER TO new_owner
```

## ALTER TRIGGER

Change the definition of a trigger.

```
ALTER TRIGGER name ON table RENAME TO new_name
```

## ALTER TYPE

Change the definition of a type.

```
ALTER TYPE name OWNER TO new_owner
```

## ALTER USER

Change a database user account.

```
ALTER USER name [ [ WITH ] option [ ... ] ]
ALTER USER name RENAME TO new_name
ALTER USER name SET parameter { TO | = } { value | DEFAULT }
ALTER USER name RESET parameter
```

Where option can be:

```
[ ENCRYPTED | UNENCRYPTED ] PASSWORD 'password'
| CREATEDB | NOCREATEDB
| CREATEUSER | NOCREATEUSER
| VALID UNTIL 'abstime'
```

## ANALYZE

Collect statistics about a database.

```
ANALYZE [ VERBOSE ] [ table [ (column [, ...] ) ] ]
```

## BEGIN

Start a transaction block.

```
BEGIN [ WORK | TRANSACTION ] [ transaction_mode [, ...] ]
```

Where `transaction_mode` is one of:

```
    ISOLATION LEVEL { SERIALIZABLE | REPEATABLE READ | READ COMMITTED
                      | READ UNCOMMITTED }
    READ WRITE | READ ONLY
```

## CHECKPOINT

Force a transaction log checkpoint.

```
CHECKPOINT
```

## CLOSE

Close a cursor.

```
CLOSE name
```

## CLUSTER

Cluster a table according to an index.

```
CLUSTER index_name ON table_name
CLUSTER table_name
CLUSTER
```

## COMMENT

Define or change the comment of an object.

```
COMMENT ON
{
  TABLE object_name |
  COLUMN table_name.column_name |
  AGGREGATE agg_name (agg_type) |
  CAST (source_type AS target_type) |
  CONSTRAINT constraint_name ON table_name |
  CONVERSION object_name |
  DATABASE object_name |
  DOMAIN object_name |
  FUNCTION func_name (arg1_type, arg2_type, ...) |
```

```
    INDEX object_name |
    LARGE OBJECT large_object_oid |
    OPERATOR op (left_operand_type, right_operand_type) |
    OPERATOR CLASS object_name USING index_method |
    [ PROCEDURAL ] LANGUAGE object_name |
    RULE rule_name ON table_name |
    SCHEMA object_name |
    SEQUENCE object_name |
    TRIGGER trigger_name ON table_name |
    TYPE object_name |
    VIEW object_name
} IS 'text'
```

## COMMIT

Commit the current transaction.

```
COMMIT [ WORK | TRANSACTION ]
```

## COPY

Copy data between a file and a table.

```
COPY table_name [ ( column [, ...] ) ]
    FROM { 'filename' | STDIN }
    [ [ WITH ]
          [ BINARY ]
          [ OIDS ]
          [ DELIMITER [ AS ] 'delimiter' ]
          [ NULL [ AS ] 'null string' ]
          [ CSV [ QUOTE [ AS ] 'quote' ]
                [ ESCAPE [ AS ] 'escape' ]
                [ FORCE NOT NULL column [, ...] ] ]

COPY table_name [ ( column [, ...] ) ]
    TO { 'filename' | STDOUT }
    [ [ WITH ]
          [ BINARY ]
          [ OIDS ]
          [ DELIMITER [ AS ] 'delimiter' ]
          [ NULL [ AS ] 'null string' ]
          [ CSV [ QUOTE [ AS ] 'quote' ]
                [ ESCAPE [ AS ] 'escape' ]
                [ FORCE QUOTE column [, ...] ] ]
```

## CREATE AGGREGATE

Define a new aggregate function.

```
CREATE AGGREGATE name (
    BASETYPE = input_data_type,
    SFUNC = sfunc,
    STYPE = state_data_type
    [ , FINALFUNC = ffunc ]
    [ , INITCOND = initial_condition ]
)
```

## CREATE CAST

Define a new cast.

```
CREATE CAST (source_type AS target_type)
    WITH FUNCTION func_name (arg_types)
    [ AS ASSIGNMENT | AS IMPLICIT ]
```

```
CREATE CAST (source_type AS target_type)
    WITHOUT FUNCTION
    [ AS ASSIGNMENT | AS IMPLICIT ]
```

## CREATE CONSTRAINT TRIGGER

Define a new constraint trigger.

```
CREATE CONSTRAINT TRIGGER name
    AFTER events ON
    table_name constraint attributes
    FOR EACH ROW EXECUTE PROCEDURE func_name ( args )
```

## CREATE CONVERSION

Define a new conversion.

```
CREATE [DEFAULT] CONVERSION name
    FOR source_encoding TO dest_encoding FROM func_name
```

## CREATE DATABASE

Create a new database.

```
CREATE DATABASE name
    [ [ WITH ] [ OWNER [=] db_owner ]
           [ TEMPLATE [=] template ]
           [ ENCODING [=] encoding ]
           [ TABLESPACE [=] tablespace ] ]
```

## CREATE DOMAIN

Define a new domain.

```
CREATE DOMAIN name [AS] data_type
    [ DEFAULT expression ]
    [ constraint [ ... ] ]
```

Where constraint is:

```
[ CONSTRAINT constraint_name ]
{ NOT NULL | NULL | CHECK (expression) }
```

## CREATE FUNCTION

Define a new function.

```
CREATE [ OR REPLACE ] FUNCTION name ( [ [ arg_name ] arg_type [, ...] ] )
    RETURNS ret_type
  { LANGUAGE lang_name
    | IMMUTABLE | STABLE | VOLATILE
    | CALLED ON NULL INPUT | RETURNS NULL ON NULL INPUT | STRICT
    | [ EXTERNAL ] SECURITY INVOKER | [ EXTERNAL ] SECURITY DEFINER
    | AS 'definition'
    | AS 'obj_file', 'link_symbol'
  } ...
    [ WITH ( attribute [, ...] ) ]
```

## CREATE GROUP

Define a new user group.

```
CREATE GROUP name [ [ WITH ] option [ ... ] ]
```

Where option can be:

```
    SYSID gid
  | USER  username [, ...]
```

## CREATE INDEX

Define a new index.

```
CREATE [ UNIQUE ] INDEX name ON table [ USING method ]
    ( { column | ( expression ) } [ opclass ] [, ...] )
    [ TABLESPACE tablespace ]
    [ WHERE predicate ]
```

## CREATE LANGUAGE

Define a new procedural language.

```
CREATE [ TRUSTED ] [ PROCEDURAL ] LANGUAGE name
    HANDLER call_handler [ VALIDATOR val_function ]
```

## CREATE OPERATOR

Define a new operator.

```
CREATE OPERATOR name (
    PROCEDURE = func_name
    [, LEFTARG = left_type ] [, RIGHTARG = right_type ]
    [, COMMUTATOR = com_op ] [, NEGATOR = neg_op ]
    [, RESTRICT = res_proc ] [, JOIN = join_proc ]
    [, HASHES ] [, MERGES ]
    [, SORT1 = left_sort_op ] [, SORT2 = right_sort_op ]
    [, LTCMP = less_than_op ] [, GTCMP = greater_than_op ]
)
```

## CREATE OPERATOR CLASS

Define a new operator class.

```
CREATE OPERATOR CLASS name [ DEFAULT ] FOR TYPE data_type
  USING index_method AS
  {  OPERATOR strategy_number operator_name [ ( op_type, op_type ) ] [ RECHECK ]
   | FUNCTION support_number func_name ( argument_type [, ...] )
   | STORAGE storage_type
  } [, ... ]
```

## CREATE RULE

Define a new rewrite rule.

```
CREATE [ OR REPLACE ] RULE name AS ON event
    TO table [ WHERE condition ]
    DO [ ALSO | INSTEAD ] { NOTHING | command | ( command ; command ... ) }
```

## CREATE SCHEMA

Define a new schema.

```
CREATE SCHEMA schema_name
  [ AUTHORIZATION username ] [ schema_element [ ... ] ]
CREATE SCHEMA AUTHORIZATION username
  [ schema_element [ ... ] ]
```

## CREATE SEQUENCE

Define a new sequence generator.

```
CREATE [ TEMPORARY | TEMP ] SEQUENCE name
    [ INCREMENT [ BY ] increment ]
    [ MINVALUE minvalue | NO MINVALUE ]
    [ MAXVALUE maxvalue | NO MAXVALUE ]
    [ START [ WITH ] start ] [ CACHE cache ] [ [ NO ] CYCLE ]
```

## CREATE TABLE

Define a new table.

```
CREATE [ [ GLOBAL | LOCAL ] { TEMPORARY | TEMP } ] TABLE table_name (
  { column_name data_type [ DEFAULT default_expr ] [ column_constraint [ ... ] ]
    | table_constraint
    | LIKE parent_table [ { INCLUDING | EXCLUDING } DEFAULTS ] } [, ... ]
)
[ INHERITS ( parent_table [, ... ] ) ]
[ WITH OIDS | WITHOUT OIDS ]
[ ON COMMIT { PRESERVE ROWS | DELETE ROWS | DROP } ]
[ TABLESPACE tablespace ]
```

Where column_constraint is:

```
[ CONSTRAINT constraint_name ]
{ NOT NULL |
  NULL |
  UNIQUE [ USING INDEX TABLESPACE tablespace ] |
  PRIMARY KEY [ USING INDEX TABLESPACE tablespace ] |
  CHECK (expression) |
  REFERENCES ref_table [ ( ref_column ) ]
    [ MATCH FULL | MATCH PARTIAL | MATCH SIMPLE ]
    [ ON DELETE action ] [ ON UPDATE action ] }
[ DEFERRABLE | NOT DEFERRABLE ] [ INITIALLY DEFERRED | INITIALLY IMMEDIATE ]
```

And table_constraint is:

```
[ CONSTRAINT constraint_name ]
{ UNIQUE ( column_name [, ... ] ) [ USING INDEX TABLESPACE tablespace ] |
  PRIMARY KEY ( column_name [, ... ] ) [ USING INDEX TABLESPACE tablespace ] |
  CHECK ( expression ) |
  FOREIGN KEY ( column_name [, ... ] )
    REFERENCES ref_table [ ( ref_column [, ... ] ) ]
    [ MATCH FULL | MATCH PARTIAL | MATCH SIMPLE ]
    [ ON DELETE action ] [ ON UPDATE action ] }
[ DEFERRABLE | NOT DEFERRABLE ] [ INITIALLY DEFERRED | INITIALLY IMMEDIATE ]
```

## CREATE TABLE AS

Define a new table from the results of a query.

```
CREATE [ [ GLOBAL | LOCAL ] { TEMPORARY | TEMP } ] TABLE table_name
    [ (column_name [, ...] ) ] [ [ WITH | WITHOUT ] OIDS ]
        AS query
```

## CREATE TABLESPACE

Define a new tablespace.

```
CREATE TABLESPACE tablespace_name [ OWNER username ] LOCATION 'directory'
```

## CREATE TRIGGER

Define a new trigger.

```
CREATE TRIGGER name { BEFORE | AFTER } { event [ OR ... ] }
    ON table [ FOR [ EACH ] { ROW | STATEMENT } ]
    EXECUTE PROCEDURE func_name ( arguments )
```

## CREATE TYPE

Define a new data type.

```
CREATE TYPE name AS
    ( attribute_name data_type [, ... ] )

CREATE TYPE name (
    INPUT = input_function,
    OUTPUT = output_function
    [ , RECEIVE = receive_function ]
    [ , SEND = send_function ]
    [ , ANALYZE = analyze_function ]
    [ , INTERNALLENGTH = { internal_length | VARIABLE } ]
    [ , PASSEDBYVALUE ]
    [ , ALIGNMENT = alignment ]
    [ , STORAGE = storage ]
    [ , DEFAULT = default ]
    [ , ELEMENT = element ]
    [ , DELIMITER = delimiter ]
)
```

## CREATE USER

Define a new database user account.

```
CREATE USER name [ [ WITH ] option [ ... ] ]
```

Where option can be:

```
    SYSID uid
  | [ ENCRYPTED | UNENCRYPTED ] PASSWORD 'password'
  | CREATEDB | NOCREATEDB
  | CREATEUSER | NOCREATEUSER
  | IN GROUP group_name [, ...]
  | VALID UNTIL 'abs_time'
```

## CREATE VIEW

Define a new view.

```
CREATE [ OR REPLACE ] VIEW name [ ( column_name [, ...] ) ] AS query
```

## DEALLOCATE

Deallocate a prepared statement.

```
DEALLOCATE [ PREPARE ] plan_name
```

## DECLARE

Define a cursor.

```
DECLARE name [ BINARY ] [ INSENSITIVE ] [ [ NO ] SCROLL ]
    CURSOR [ { WITH | WITHOUT } HOLD ] FOR query
    [ FOR { READ ONLY | UPDATE [ OF column [, ...] ] } ]
```

## DELETE

Delete rows of a table.

```
DELETE FROM [ ONLY ] table [ WHERE condition ]
```

## DROP AGGREGATE

Remove an aggregate function.

```
DROP AGGREGATE name ( type ) [ CASCADE | RESTRICT ]
```

## DROP CAST

Remove a cast.

```
DROP CAST (source_type AS target_type) [ CASCADE | RESTRICT ]
```

## DROP CONVERSION

Remove a conversion.

```
DROP CONVERSION name [ CASCADE | RESTRICT ]
```

## DROP DATABASE

Remove a database.

```
DROP DATABASE name
```

## DROP DOMAIN

Remove a domain.

```
DROP DOMAIN name [, ...]  [ CASCADE | RESTRICT ]
```

## DROP FUNCTION

Remove a function.

```
DROP FUNCTION name ( [ type [, ...] ] ) [ CASCADE | RESTRICT ]
```

## DROP GROUP

Remove a user group.

```
DROP GROUP name
```

## DROP INDEX

Remove an index.

```
DROP INDEX name [, ...] [ CASCADE | RESTRICT ]
```

## DROP LANGUAGE

Remove a procedural language.

```
DROP [ PROCEDURAL ] LANGUAGE name [ CASCADE | RESTRICT ]
```

## DROP OPERATOR

Remove an operator.

```
DROP OPERATOR name ( { left_type | NONE } , { right_type | NONE } )
  [ CASCADE | RESTRICT ]
```

## DROP OPERATOR CLASS

Remove an operator class.

```
DROP OPERATOR CLASS name USING index_method [ CASCADE | RESTRICT ]
```

## DROP RULE

Remove a rewrite rule.

```
DROP RULE name ON relation [ CASCADE | RESTRICT ]
```

### DROP SCHEMA

Remove a schema.

```
DROP SCHEMA name [, ...] [ CASCADE | RESTRICT ]
```

### DROP SEQUENCE

Remove a sequence.

```
DROP SEQUENCE name [, ...] [ CASCADE | RESTRICT ]
```

### DROP TABLE

Remove a table.

```
DROP TABLE name [, ...] [ CASCADE | RESTRICT ]
```

### DROP TABLESPACE

Remove a tablespace.

```
DROP TABLESPACE tablespace_name
```

### DROP TRIGGER

Remove a trigger.

```
DROP TRIGGER name ON table [ CASCADE | RESTRICT ]
```

### DROP TYPE

Remove a data type.

```
DROP TYPE name [, ...] [ CASCADE | RESTRICT ]
```

### DROP USER

Remove a database user account.

```
DROP USER name
```

### DROP VIEW

Remove a view.

```
DROP VIEW name [, ...] [ CASCADE | RESTRICT ]
```

### END

Commit the current transaction.

```
END [ WORK | TRANSACTION ]
```

## EXECUTE

Execute a prepared statement.

```
EXECUTE plan_name [ (parameter [, ...] ) ]
```

## EXPLAIN

Show the execution plan of a statement.

```
EXPLAIN [ ANALYZE ] [ VERBOSE ] statement
```

## FETCH

Retrieve rows from a query using a cursor.

```
FETCH [ direction { FROM | IN } ] cursor_name
```

Where direction can be empty or one of:

```
NEXT
PRIOR
FIRST
LAST
ABSOLUTE count
RELATIVE count
count
ALL
FORWARD
FORWARD count
FORWARD ALL
BACKWARD
BACKWARD count
BACKWARD ALL
```

## GRANT

Define access privileges.

```
GRANT { { SELECT | INSERT | UPDATE | DELETE | RULE | REFERENCES | TRIGGER }
    [,...] | ALL [ PRIVILEGES ] }
    ON [ TABLE ] table_name [, ...]
    TO { username | GROUP group_name | PUBLIC } [, ...] [ WITH GRANT OPTION ]

GRANT { { CREATE | TEMPORARY | TEMP } [,...] | ALL [ PRIVILEGES ] }
    ON DATABASE db_name [, ...]
    TO { username | GROUP group_name | PUBLIC } [, ...] [ WITH GRANT OPTION ]

GRANT { CREATE | ALL [ PRIVILEGES ] }
    ON TABLESPACE tablespace_name [, ...]
    TO { username | GROUP group_name | PUBLIC } [, ...] [ WITH GRANT OPTION ]
```

```
GRANT { EXECUTE | ALL [ PRIVILEGES ] }
    ON FUNCTION func_name ([type, ...]) [, ...]
    TO { username | GROUP group_name | PUBLIC } [, ...] [ WITH GRANT OPTION ]

GRANT { USAGE | ALL [ PRIVILEGES ] }
    ON LANGUAGE lang_name [, ...]
    TO { username | GROUP group_name | PUBLIC } [, ...] [ WITH GRANT OPTION ]

GRANT { { CREATE | USAGE } [,...] | ALL [ PRIVILEGES ] }
    ON SCHEMA schema_name [, ...]
    TO { username | GROUP group_name | PUBLIC } [, ...] [ WITH GRANT OPTION ]
```

## INSERT

Create new rows in a table.

```
INSERT INTO table [ ( column [, ...] ) ]
    { DEFAULT VALUES | VALUES ( { expression | DEFAULT } [, ...] ) | query }
```

## LISTEN

Listen for a notification.

```
LISTEN name
```

## LOAD

Load or reload a shared library file.

```
LOAD 'filename'
```

## LOCK

Lock a table.

```
LOCK [ TABLE ] name [, ...] [ IN lock_mode MODE ] [ NOWAIT ]
```

Where lock_mode is one of:

```
    ACCESS SHARE | ROW SHARE | ROW EXCLUSIVE | SHARE UPDATE EXCLUSIVE
    | SHARE | SHARE ROW EXCLUSIVE | EXCLUSIVE | ACCESS EXCLUSIVE
```

## MOVE

Position a cursor.

```
MOVE [ direction { FROM | IN } ] cursor_name
```

## NOTIFY

Generate a notification.

```
NOTIFY name
```

## PREPARE

Prepare a statement for execution.

```
PREPARE plan_name [ (data_type [, ...] ) ] AS statement
```

## REINDEX

Rebuild indexes.

```
REINDEX { DATABASE | TABLE | INDEX } name [ FORCE ]
```

## RELEASE SAVEPOINT

Destroy a previously defined savepoint.

```
RELEASE [ SAVEPOINT ] savepoint_name
```

## RESET

Restore the value of a runtime parameter to the default value.

```
RESET name
RESET ALL
```

## REVOKE

Remove access privileges.

```
REVOKE [ GRANT OPTION FOR ]
    { { SELECT | INSERT | UPDATE | DELETE | RULE | REFERENCES | TRIGGER }
    [,...] | ALL [ PRIVILEGES ] }
    ON [ TABLE ] table_name [, ...]
    FROM { username | GROUP group_name | PUBLIC } [, ...]
    [ CASCADE | RESTRICT ]

REVOKE [ GRANT OPTION FOR ]
    { { CREATE | TEMPORARY | TEMP } [,...] | ALL [ PRIVILEGES ] }
    ON DATABASE db_name [, ...]
    FROM { username | GROUP group_name | PUBLIC } [, ...]
    [ CASCADE | RESTRICT ]
```

```
REVOKE [ GRANT OPTION FOR ]
    { CREATE | ALL [ PRIVILEGES ] }
    ON TABLESPACE tablespace_name [, ...]
    FROM { username | GROUP group_name | PUBLIC } [, ...]
    [ CASCADE | RESTRICT ]

REVOKE [ GRANT OPTION FOR ]
    { EXECUTE | ALL [ PRIVILEGES ] }
    ON FUNCTION func_name ([type, ...]) [, ...]
    FROM { username | GROUP group_name | PUBLIC } [, ...]
    [ CASCADE | RESTRICT ]

REVOKE [ GRANT OPTION FOR ]
    { USAGE | ALL [ PRIVILEGES ] }
    ON LANGUAGE lang_name [, ...]
    FROM { username | GROUP group_name | PUBLIC } [, ...]
    [ CASCADE | RESTRICT ]

REVOKE [ GRANT OPTION FOR ]
    { { CREATE | USAGE } [,...] | ALL [ PRIVILEGES ] }
    ON SCHEMA schema_name [, ...]
    FROM { username | GROUP group_name | PUBLIC } [, ...]
    [ CASCADE | RESTRICT ]
```

## ROLLBACK

Abort the current transaction.

```
ROLLBACK [ WORK | TRANSACTION ]
```

## ROLLBACK TO SAVEPOINT

Roll back to a savepoint.

```
ROLLBACK [ WORK | TRANSACTION ] TO [ SAVEPOINT ] savepoint_name
```

## SAVEPOINT

Define a new savepoint within the current transaction.

```
SAVEPOINT savepoint_name
```

## SELECT

Retrieve rows from a table or view.

```
SELECT [ ALL | DISTINCT [ ON ( expression [, ...] ) ] ]
    * | expression [ AS output_name ] [, ...]
    [ FROM from_item [, ...] ]
    [ WHERE condition ]
    [ GROUP BY expression [, ...] ]
    [ HAVING condition [, ...] ]
    [ { UNION | INTERSECT | EXCEPT } [ ALL ] select ]
    [ ORDER BY expression [ ASC | DESC | USING operator ] [, ...] ]
    [ LIMIT { count | ALL } ]
    [ OFFSET start ]
    [ FOR UPDATE [ OF table_name [, ...] ] ]
```

Where from_item can be one of:

```
    [ ONLY ] table_name [ * ] [ [ AS ] alias [ ( column_alias [, ...] ) ] ]
    ( select ) [ AS ] alias [ ( column_alias [, ...] ) ]
    function_name ( [ argument [, ...] ] )
        [ AS ] alias [ ( column_alias [, ...] | column_definition [, ...] ) ]
    function_name ( [ argument [, ...] ] ) AS ( column_definition [, ...] )
    from_item [ NATURAL ] join_type from_item
        [ ON join_condition | USING ( join_column [, ...] ) ]
```

## SELECT INTO

Define a new table from the results of a query.

```
SELECT [ ALL | DISTINCT [ ON ( expression [, ...] ) ] ]
    * | expression [ AS output_name ] [, ...]
    INTO [ TEMPORARY | TEMP ] [ TABLE ] new_table
    [ FROM from_item [, ...] ]
    [ WHERE condition ]
    [ GROUP BY expression [, ...] ]
    [ HAVING condition [, ...] ]
    [ { UNION | INTERSECT | EXCEPT } [ ALL ] select ]
    [ ORDER BY expression [ ASC | DESC | USING operator ] [, ...] ]
    [ LIMIT { count | ALL } ]
    [ OFFSET start ]
    [ FOR UPDATE [ OF table_name [, ...] ] ]
```

## SET

Change a runtime parameter.

```
SET [ SESSION | LOCAL ] name { TO | = } { value | 'value' | DEFAULT }
SET [ SESSION | LOCAL ] TIME ZONE { time_zone | LOCAL | DEFAULT }
```

## SET CONSTRAINTS

Set constraint checking modes for the current transaction.

```
SET CONSTRAINTS { ALL | name [, ...] } { DEFERRED | IMMEDIATE }
```

## SET SESSION AUTHORIZATION

Set the session user identifier and the current user identifier of the current session.

```
SET [ SESSION | LOCAL ] SESSION AUTHORIZATION username
SET [ SESSION | LOCAL ] SESSION AUTHORIZATION DEFAULT
RESET SESSION AUTHORIZATION
```

## SET TRANSACTION

Set the characteristics of the current transaction.

```
SET TRANSACTION transaction_mode [, ...]
SET SESSION CHARACTERISTICS AS TRANSACTION transaction_mode [, ...]
```

Where transaction_mode is one of:

```
ISOLATION LEVEL { SERIALIZABLE | REPEATABLE READ | READ COMMITTED
                  | READ UNCOMMITTED }
READ WRITE | READ ONLY
```

## SHOW

Show the value of a runtime parameter.

```
SHOW name
SHOW ALL
```

## START TRANSACTION

Start a transaction block.

```
START TRANSACTION [ transaction_mode [, ...] ]
```

Where transaction_mode is one of:

```
ISOLATION LEVEL { SERIALIZABLE | REPEATABLE READ | READ COMMITTED
                  | READ UNCOMMITTED }
READ WRITE | READ ONLY
```

## TRUNCATE

Empty a table.

```
TRUNCATE [ TABLE ] name
```

## UNLISTEN

Stop listening for a notification.

```
UNLISTEN { name | * }
```

## UPDATE

Update rows of a table.

```
UPDATE [ ONLY ] table SET column = { expression | DEFAULT } [, ...]
    [ FROM from_list ]
    [ WHERE condition ]
```

## VACUUM

Garbage-collect and optionally analyze a database.

```
VACUUM [ FULL ] [ FREEZE ] [ VERBOSE ] [ table ]
VACUUM [ FULL ] [ FREEZE ] [ VERBOSE ] ANALYZE [ table [ (column [, ...] ) ] ]
```

# APPENDIX D

■ ■ ■

# psql Reference

This appendix defines the psql command-line options and internal commands. This information is taken from the psql command-line tool's internal help.

## Command-Line Options

psql has the following command-line usage:

```
psql [options] [dbname [username]]
```

Table D-1 shows the command-line options.

*Table D-1. psql Command-Line Options*

| Option | Meaning |
|--------|---------|
| -?, --help | Show help, then exit |
| -a, --echo_all | Echo all input from script |
| -A, --no-align | Unaligned table output mode (-P format=unaligned) |
| -c, --command <command> | Run only single command (SQL or internal) and exit |
| -d, --dbname <dbname> | Specify database name to connect to (default: current username) |
| -e, --echo-queries | Echo commands sent to server |
| -E, --echo-hidden | Display queries that internal commands generate |
| -f, --file <filename> | Execute commands from file, then exit |
| -F, --field-separator <string> | Set field separator (default: "\|") (-P fieldsep=) |
| -h, --host <hostname> | Database server host or socket directory (default: "local socket") |
| -H, --html | HTML table output mode (-P format=html) |
| -l, --list | List available databases, then exit |
| -n | Disable enhanced command-line editing (readline) |
| -o, --output <filename> | Send query results to file (use -o \|program for a pipe) |
| -p, --port <port> | Database server port (default: 5432) |

*Table D-1. psql Command-Line Options (Continued)*

| Option | Meaning |
|---|---|
| `-P, --pset var[=arg]` | Set printing option var to arg (see \pset command) |
| `-q, --quiet` | Run quietly (no messages, only query output) |
| `-R, --record-separator <string>` | Set record separator (default: newline) (`-P recordsep=`) |
| `-s, --single-step` | Single-step mode (confirm each query) |
| `-S, --single-line` | Single-line mode (end of line terminates SQL command) |
| `-t, --tuples-only` | Print rows only (`-P tuples_only`) |
| `-T, --table-attr <text>` | Set HTML table tag attributes (width, border) (`-P tableattr=`) |
| `-U, --username <name>` | Database username (default: current username) |
| `-v, --set, --variable name=value` | Set psql variable name to value |
| `-V, --version` | Output version information, then exit |
| `-W, --password` | Prompt for password (should happen automatically) |
| `-x, --expanded` | Turn on expanded table output (`-P expanded`) |
| `-X, --no-psqlrc` | Do not read startup file (`~/.psqlrc`) |

# Internal Commands

Table D-2 lists the psql internal commands.

*Table D-2. psql Internal Commands*

| Command | Meaning |
|---|---|
| `\! <command>` | Execute command in shell or start interactive shell |
| `\a` | Toggle between unaligned and aligned output mode |
| `\c[onnect] [<dbname>|- [<user>]]` | Connect to new database |
| `\C <string>` | Set table title, or unset if none |
| `\cd <dir>` | Change the current working directory |
| `\copy` | Perform SQL COPY with data stream to the client host |
| `\copyright` | Show PostgreSQL usage and distribution terms |
| `\d, \d+ <name>` | Describe table, index, sequence, or view (with + gives expanded output) |
| `\d{t|i|s|v|S} <pattern>` | List tables/indexes/sequences/views/system tables |
| `\da <pattern>` | List aggregate functions |
| `\db, \db+ <pattern>` | List tablespaces (with + gives expanded output) |

*Table D-2. psql Internal Commands (Continued)*

| Command | Meaning |
|---|---|
| \dc <pattern> | List conversions |
| \dC | List casts |
| \dd <pattern> | Show comment for object |
| \dD <pattern> | List domains |
| \df, \df+ <pattern> | List functions (with + gives expanded output) |
| \dg <pattern> | List groups |
| \dn, \dn+ <pattern> | List schemas (with + gives expanded output) |
| \do <name> | List operators |
| \dl | List large objects, same as \lo_list |
| \dp <pattern> | List table, view, and sequence access privileges |
| \dT, \dT+ <pattern> | List data types (with + gives expanded output) |
| \du <pattern> | List users |
| \e[dit] [<file>] | Edit the query buffer (or file) with external editor |
| \echo <string> | Write string to standard output |
| \encoding [<encoding>] | Show or set client encoding |
| \f [<string>] | Show or set field separator for unaligned query output |
| \g <file> | Send query buffer to server (and results to file or \|program for a pipe) |
| \h[elp] [<name>] | Help on syntax of SQL commands; * for all commands |
| \H | Toggle HTML output mode |
| \i <file> | Execute commands from file |
| \l[ist], \l[ist]+ | List all databases (with + gives expanded output) |
| \lo_export <loboid> <file> | Export large objects |
| \lo_import <file> [<comment>] | Import large objects |
| \lo_list | List large objects |
| \lo_unlink <loboid> | Delete large objects |
| \o <file> | Send all query results to file or \|program for a pipe |
| \p | Show the contents of the query buffer |
| \pset name [value] | Set table output option (name := {format\|border\|expanded\|fieldsep\|footer\| null\|recordsep\|tuples_only\|title\|tableattr\|pager}) |
| \q | Quit psql |
| \qecho <string> | Write string to query output stream (see \o) |

*Table D-2. psql Internal Commands (Continued)*

| Command | Meaning |
| --- | --- |
| \r | Reset (clear) the query buffer |
| \s [<file>] | Display history or save it to file |
| \set [<name> [<value>]] | Set internal variable, or list all if no parameters |
| \t | Show only rows |
| \T [<string>] | Set HTML <table> tag attributes, or unset if none |
| \timing | Toggle timing of commands |
| \unset <name> | Unset (delete) internal variable |
| \w <file> | Write query buffer to file |
| \x | Toggle expanded output |
| \z <pattern> | List table, view, and sequence access privileges (same as \dp) |

# APPENDIX E

■ ■ ■

# Database Schema and Tables

The database schema used in the examples in this book is a simplified customer/orders/items database, as shown in Figure E-1.

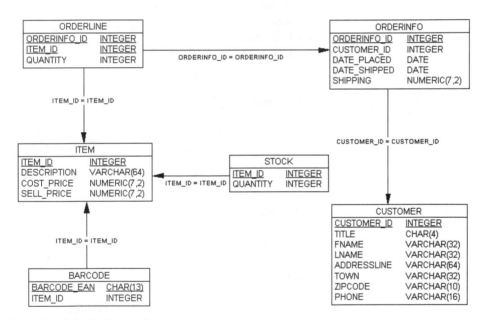

**Figure E-1.** *Final schema design*

The tables need to be created in an appropriate order so that dependent tables are created first, because of the foreign key constraints (see Chapter 8). This is the same order to be followed as data is inserted into the tables. The appropriate order is as follows:

- customer
- orderinfo
- item
- orderline
- stock
- barcode

The SQL to create the final version of this sample database, bpfinal, including the foreign key constraints follows. This code can be found in the download bundle available from the Downloads section of the Apress web site (http://www.apress.com) as create_tables-bpfinal.sql. The simplified version, bpsimple (see Chapter 3), excluding the foreign key constraints, can be found in create_tables-bpsimple.sql.

The download code bundle has the table-population commands, pop-all-tables.sql, in an appropriate order ready for populating either schema.

*Customer table*

```
create table customer
(
    customer_id                 serial,
    title                       char(4),
    fname                       varchar(32),
    lname                       varchar(32) not null,
    addressline                 varchar(64),
    town                        varchar(32),
    zipcode                     char(10) not null,
    phone                       varchar(16),
    CONSTRAINT                  customer_pk PRIMARY KEY(customer_id)
);
```

*Orderinfo table*

```
create table orderinfo
(
    orderinfo_id                serial,
    customer_id                 integer not null,
    date_placed                 date not null,
    date_shipped                date,
    shipping                    numeric(7,2) ,
    CONSTRAINT                  orderinfo_pk PRIMARY KEY(orderinfo_id),
    CONSTRAINT orderinfo_customer_id_fk FOREIGN KEY(customer_id) REFERENCES
customer(customer_id)
);
```

*Item table*

```
create table item
(
    item_id                     serial,
    description                 varchar(64) not null,
    cost_price                  numeric(7,2),
    sell_price                  numeric(7,2),
    CONSTRAINT                  item_pk PRIMARY KEY(item_id)
);
```

*Orderline table*

```
create table orderline
(
    orderinfo_id                integer not null,
    item_id                     integer not null,
    quantity                    integer not null,
    CONSTRAINT                  orderline_pk PRIMARY KEY(orderinfo_id,
item_id),
    CONSTRAINT orderline_orderinfo_id_fk FOREIGN KEY(orderinfo_id) REFERENCES
orderinfo(orderinfo_id),
    CONSTRAINT orderline_item_id_fk FOREIGN KEY(item_id) REFERENCES item(item_id)
);
```

*Stock table*

```
create table stock
(
    item_id                     integer not null,
    quantity                    integer  not null,
    CONSTRAINT                  stock_pk PRIMARY KEY(item_id),
    CONSTRAINT stock_item_id_fk FOREIGN KEY(item_id) REFERENCES item(item_id)
);
```

*Barcode table*

```
create table barcode
(
    barcode_ean                 char(13) not null,
    item_id                     integer not null,
    CONSTRAINT                  barcode_pk PRIMARY KEY(barcode_ean),
    CONSTRAINT barcode_item_id_fk FOREIGN KEY(item_id) REFERENCES item(item_id)
);
```

# APPENDIX F

■ ■ ■

# Large Objects Support in PostgreSQL

**T**raditionally, databases have been able to store data in a limited number of forms, usually as numeric values (integers, floating point, and fixed point) and text strings. Often, the size of the text data is limited. In the past, even PostgreSQL enforced a limit of a few thousand characters as the maximum length of a field.

It might be useful to be able to create a database application that can handle *arbitrary* unstructured data formats, such as images. As an example of how to handle large data items, we will consider how we might add photographs to a database. There are several ways we could do this:

- Use links into a file system or the Web

- Use encoded long text strings

- Use BLOBs

We will look at each of these approaches in this appendix, using the sample database we built in this book, bpfinal (see Chapter 8 and Appendix E for details on the bpfinal schema). We will see how we might add images of products, so that our web-based interface could provide an online catalog.

## Using Links

Our first option is to avoid storing images in the physical database at all. The idea is to place all of the images in the normal filing system of a server, which may be the database server, a file sharing server, or a web server. The database itself then only needs to contain a text link to the file. Any client application would follow the link to retrieve the image.

We need to create an additional table in the database to store the image links. It is very similar to the stock table in that we are providing additional information for each item we carry:

```
CREATE TABLE image
(
    item_id     integer NOT NULL,
    picture     varchar(512),
    CONSTRAINT  image_pk PRIMARY KEY(item_id),
    CONSTRAINT  image_item_id_fk FOREIGN KEY(item_id)
                REFERENCES item(item_id)
);
```

Here, we have added constraints to ensure that we can add images only for items that exist.

Now we can update the image table with links to product photographs:

```
INSERT INTO image VALUES (3, 'http://server/images/rubik.jpg');
INSERT INTO image VALUES (9, '//server/images/coin.bmp');
INSERT INTO image VALUES (5, '/mnt/server/images/frame.png');
```

This solution has both advantages and disadvantages. Storing links rather than pictures means that the database size is kept to a minimum and applications will be portable to other database systems, as we have not used any esoteric features to handle images. Furthermore, retrieving the actual images will also be very fast, as reading a file from the file system will typically be many times faster than querying a database. Also we have a wide choice of locations for storing the images. In this example, we have used the following:

- A URL to provide a link into a web server

- A UNC file reference for a Windows file server

- A reference to an NFS-mounted UNIX server

However, by using links we are unable to enforce referential integrity in the database. If the images that are stored elsewhere are changed or deleted, the database is not automatically updated. To back up our system, we will need to attend to image files on the file system (and elsewhere), as well as the database itself. We must also ensure that the links we use are in a form that all possible clients can use. For example, the NFS form requires that all clients access the shared files in the same way and have access rights on the server.

# Using Encoded Text Strings

In PostgreSQL 7.1, the limit on the size of a field was raised to 1GB. For all practical purposes, this is effectively unlimited. We could consider using the text type to store the images in the database directly. This is possible, if a little tricky.

Images are in general binary data, not well suited to a character type. So, we need to encode the image in some way, perhaps by using hexadecimal or MIME encoding. Handling the very long strings that result may also cause a problem with limits imposed by client applications, network transport mechanisms, or ODBC drivers. The storage space needed for encoded strings will also be up to double the size of the binary image file.

# Using BLOBs

One of the wide variety of data types PostgreSQL currently supports is the binary large object, or BLOB, which is suitable for storing large data items. This allows us to create a database application that can handle *arbitrary* unstructured data formats, such as images. Thus, we can store our image data, or any large or binary data object, in a PostgreSQL database by using BLOBs.

PostgreSQL supports a column type of oid, which is an object identifier, a reference to arbitrary data. These are used to manage the BLOBs and can be used to transfer the contents of any file into the database, and to extract an object from the database into a file. They can therefore be used to handle our product images, or any other data that we might wish to store.

We can modify the sample image table definition from earlier in this appendix to use BLOBs by specifying oid as the image data type:

```
CREATE TABLE image
(
    item_id      integer NOT NULL,
    picture      oid,
    CONSTRAINT   image_pk PRIMARY KEY(item_id),
    CONSTRAINT   image_item_id_fk FOREIGN KEY(item_id) REFERENCES item(item_id)
);
```

## Importing and Exporting Images

PostgreSQL provides a number of functions that can be used in SQL queries for inserting into, retrieving from, and deleting BLOB data in a table.

To add an image to the table, we can use the SQL function lo_import, like this:

```
INSERT INTO image VALUES (3, lo_import('/tmp/image.jpg'));
```

The contents of the specified file are read into a BLOB object and stored in the database. The image table will now have a non-NULL oid that references the BLOB:

```
bpfinal=# SELECT * FROM image;
 item_id | picture
---------+---------
       3 |  163055
(1 row)

bpfinal=#
```

We can see all of the large objects stored in the database by using a psql internal command, \lo_list, or \dl, to list them:

```
bpfinal=# \dl
    Large objects
   ID   | Description
--------+-------------
 163055 |
(1 row)

bpfinal=#
```

Large objects are retrieved from the database using `lo_export`, which writes a file containing the contents of the BLOB:

```
bpfinal=# SELECT lo_export(picture, '/tmp/image2.jpg')
bpfinal-# FROM image WHERE item_id = 3;
 lo_export
-----------
         1
(1 row)

bpfinal=#
```

We can delete a large object from the database with `lo_unlink`:

```
bpfinal=# SELECT lo_unlink(picture) FROM image WHERE item_id = 3;
 lo_unlink
-----------
         1
(1 row)

bpfinal=# \dl
  Large objects
 ID | Description
----+-------------
(0 rows)

bpfinal=#
```

We must be careful when we delete large objects, as any references to the BLOB will remain:

```
bpfinal=# SELECT * FROM image;
 item_id | picture
---------+---------
       3 |  163055
(1 row)

bpfinal=#
```

As operations on a large object and its object identifier are essentially decoupled, we must make sure to take care of both when manipulating BLOBs. So, when deleting a BLOB, we should set the object reference to NULL to prevent errors in our client applications:

```
bpfinal=# UPDATE image SET picture=NULL WHERE item_id = 3;
```

In the examples here, we have used `psql` to manipulate binary objects. It is important to understand that the import and export functions `lo_import` and `lo_export` are executed by the back-end database server, not by `psql`. Any client application using SQL statements can use these SQL functions to add and update BLOBs.

There are three caveats when importing and exporting BLOBs:

- As the import is performed by the server, the files read and written by the import and export must be specified using a path and filename that are accessible to the server, rather than the client. If in psql we had simply said this:

```
INSERT INTO image VALUES (3, lo_import('image.jpg'));
```

  and expected PostgreSQL to insert the contents of a file in the current directory, we would have received an error message. This is because the import fails to find the file. We need to arrange that files for import are (temporarily) placed in a location that the server can access. Similarly, we need to use full filenames for exporting binary objects.

- Exported files must be placed in a directory that the server user can write; that is, a location where the operating system user postgres has permission to create files.

- All large object manipulation must take place within a SQL transaction—between BEGIN and COMMIT or END statements. By default, psql executes each SQL statement in its own transaction, so this is not a problem, but client applications that perform imports and exports must be written with transactions.

## Remote Importing and Exporting

Because the SQL functions lo_import and lo_export use the server file system, using them can be inconvenient when creating BLOBs. However, psql contains internal commands that can be used to import and export binary objects from a remote client machine.

  We can add a BLOB to the database by using \lo_import and passing it a local filename. In this case, files in the current directory will work just fine, and we can see the object listed with \lo_list:

```
bpfinal=# \lo_import image.jpg
lo_import 163059
bpfinal=# \lo_list
    Large objects
   ID   | Description
--------+-------------
 163059 |
(1 row)

bpfinal=#
```

  Now we need to associate the BLOB with the image table by updating the appropriate row:

```
bpfinal=# UPDATE image SET picture=163059 WHERE item_id = 3;
UPDATE 1
bpfinal=# SELECT * FROM image;
 item_id | picture
---------+---------
       3 |  163059
(1 row)

bpfinal=#
```

We can extract a BLOB with \lo_export, specifying the required object identifier and a file to write. Again, a local filename is fine:

```
bpfinal=# \lo_export 163059 image2.jpg
lo_export

bpfinal=#
```

Finally, we can delete a large object with \lo_unlink:

```
bpfinal=# \lo_unlink 163059
lo_unlink 163059

bpfinal=#
```

## Programming BLOBs

As you might expect, it is possible to use BLOB import and export functions from the programming languages supported by PostgreSQL.

From C, using the libpq library (see Chapter 13), we can use the functions lo_import, lo_export, and lo_unlink in much the same way as described in the preceding sections:

```
Oid lo_import(PGconn *conn, const char *filename);
int lo_export(PGconn *conn, Oid lobjId, const char *filename);
int lo_unlink(PGconn *conn, Oid lobjId);
```

Here is a sample program that imports an image file into the database. Note that the large object functions must be called within a transaction:

```
#include <stdlib.h>
#include <libpq-fe.h>

int main()
{
  PGconn *myconnection = PQconnectdb("");
  PGresult *res;
  Oid blob;

  if(PQstatus(myconnection) == CONNECTION_OK)
    printf("connection made\n");
  else
    printf("connection failed\n");

  res = PQexec(myconnection, "begin");
  PQclear(res);

  blob = lo_import(myconnection, "image.jpg");
  printf("import returned oid %d\n", blob);
```

```
res = PQexec(myconnection, "end");
PQclear(res);

PQfinish(myconnection);
return EXIT_SUCCESS;
}
```

When we compile and run the program, we can see the new binary object identifier reported. (This program is included in the sample programs for Chapter 13.)

```
$ make import
cc -I/usr/local/pgsql/include  -L/usr/local/pgsql/lib -lpq  import.c   -o import
$ PGDATABASE=bpfinal ./import
connection made
import returned oid 163066
$
```

BLOBs can be imported and exported from other languages in similar ways.

For finer control over large object access, PostgreSQL provides a suite of low-level functions akin to open, read, write, and others for ordinary files:

```
int lo_open(PGconn *conn, Oid lobjId, int mode);
int lo_close(PGconn *conn, int fd);
int lo_read(PGconn *conn, int fd, char *buf, size_t len);
int lo_write(PGconn *conn, int fd, char *buf, size_t len);
int lo_lseek(PGconn *conn, int fd, int offset, int whence);
Oid lo_creat(PGconn *conn, int mode);
int lo_tell(PGconn *conn, int fd);
```

Refer to the online documentation for more details on these functions.

# INDEX

## ■H

# forums.apress.com

## FOR PROFESSIONALS BY PROFESSIONALS™

JOIN THE APRESS FORUMS AND BE PART OF OUR COMMUNITY. You'll find discussions that cover topics of interest to IT professionals, programmers, and enthusiasts just like you. If you post a query to one of our forums, you can expect that some of the best minds in the business—especially Apress authors, who all write with *The Expert's Voice*™—will chime in to help you. Why not aim to become one of our most valuable participants (MVPs) and win cool stuff? Here's a sampling of what you'll find:

### DATABASES
**Data drives everything.**

Share information, exchange ideas, and discuss any database programming or administration issues.

### INTERNET TECHNOLOGIES AND NETWORKING
**Try living without plumbing (and eventually IPv6).**

Talk about networking topics including protocols, design, administration, wireless, wired, storage, backup, certifications, trends, and new technologies.

### JAVA
**We've come a long way from the old Oak tree.**

Hang out and discuss Java in whatever flavor you choose: J2SE, J2EE, J2ME, Jakarta, and so on.

### MAC OS X
**All about the Zen of OS X.**

OS X is both the present and the future for Mac apps. Make suggestions, offer up ideas, or boast about your new hardware.

### OPEN SOURCE
**Source code is good; understanding (open) source is better.**

Discuss open source technologies and related topics such as PHP, MySQL, Linux, Perl, Apache, Python, and more.

### PROGRAMMING/BUSINESS
**Unfortunately, it is.**

Talk about the Apress line of books that cover software methodology, best practices, and how programmers interact with the "suits."

### WEB DEVELOPMENT/DESIGN
**Ugly doesn't cut it anymore, and CGI is absurd.**

Help is in sight for your site. Find design solutions for your projects and get ideas for building an interactive Web site.

### SECURITY
**Lots of bad guys out there—the good guys need help.**

Discuss computer and network security issues here. Just don't let anyone else know the answers!

### TECHNOLOGY IN ACTION
**Cool things. Fun things.**

It's after hours. It's time to play. Whether you're into LEGO® MINDSTORMS™ or turning an old PC into a DVR, this is where technology turns into fun.

### WINDOWS
**No defenestration here.**

Ask questions about all aspects of Windows programming, get help on Microsoft technologies covered in Apress books, or provide feedback on any Apress Windows book.

**HOW TO PARTICIPATE:**

Go to the Apress Forums site at **http://forums.apress.com/**.
Click the New User link.